Advance praise for *Reading Early M*

"This imaginatively conceived and brilliantly executed anthology with its ingeniously chosen texts, its illustrative images from the original books or manuscripts, and its impressive array of distinguished contributing editors shows that whatever their disadvantages and the injustices of their society early modern women did indeed have not just a room of their own but a whole house, a whole palace, and even (as Christine de Pisan insisted), a whole city. Ostovich and Sauer have produced an invaluable resource for anybody interested in Renaissance literature or women's studies."

—Anne Lake Prescott, Barnard College

"*Reading Early Modern Women* is an astonishing achievement. Bringing together nearly 150 manuscript and print texts—many published here for the first time—as well as commentaries by more than 80 scholars, this remarkable collection introduces us to a very broad spectrum of the literary achievements of women. It should quickly become the centerpiece of many undergraduate and graduate courses in early modern literature, history, and women's studies. Thanks to Ostovich and Sauer's extraordinary efforts, early modern women writers may finally get the Renaissance they so richly deserve."

—Douglas A. Brooks, Texas A&M University

'This book should certainly be recommended to students as an expert guide through a range of materials which will be new to them; it will also be of invaluable use to scholars in the field, as it makes available and discusses a fascinating number of texts otherwise available only in archives. One of the book's many strengths is the way in which each text and each genre is not only adeptly introduced, but is also cross-referenced with other works, primary and secondary, both in the anthology and beyond it. This serves not only to open up the expanding field of early modern women's writing to the newcomer, but also to indicate ways in which researchers can expand their studies across a number of interrelated literary areas."

—Hilary Hinds, Lancaster University, UK

"*Reading Early Modern Women* is an essential resource for teaching and research, providing as it does, a wide array of texts not easily accessed, from medical books, through prophecies and letters to poetry and music. Contextualized both critically and historically, this book allows contemporary readers to benefit from the dazzling array of early modern women's writing."

—Marion Wynne-Davies, University of Dundee

READING
EARLY
MODERN
WOMEN

READING EARLY MODERN WOMEN

An ANTHOLOGY *of* TEXTS *in*
MANUSCRIPT *and* PRINT,
1550–1700

Edited by HELEN OSTOVICH
and ELIZABETH SAUER

Assisted by Melissa Smith

ROUTLEDGE
NEW YORK & LONDON

Published in 2004 by
Routledge
29 West 35th Street
New York, NY 10001
www.routledge-ny.com

Published in Great Britain by
Routledge
11 New Fetter Lane
London EC4P 4EE
www.routledge.co.uk

Routledge is an imprint of the Taylor & Francis Group.

Printed in the United States of America on acid free paper.

Library of Congress Cataloguing-in-Publication Data

Reading early modern women : an anthology of texts in manuscript and print, 1550–1700 / edited by Helen Ostovich and Elizabeth Sauer ; assisted by Melissa Smith.
    p. cm.
Includes bibliographical references and index.
       ISBN 0–415–96645–0 (hardback : alk. paper) — ISBN 0–415–96646–9 (pbk. : alk. paper)
    1. English literature—Women authors. 2. English literature—Early Britain—History—17th century—Sources. 4. Women and literature—Great Britain—History—16th century—Sources.
I. Ostovich, Helen. II. Sauer, Elizabeth, 1964– III. Smith, Melissa.
    PR1110 .W6R43 2003
    820 .8'09287'09031—dc21
                                                                    2003007757

CONTENTS

CHAPTER 2
The Status of Women 55

A. *The Controversy about Women*

B. *Education and Philosophy*

Chapter 3
Mothers' Legacies and Medical Manuals 97

CHAPTER 4

Religion, Prophecy, and Persecution 131

CHAPTER 5

Letters 187

CHAPTER 6
Life-writing: Nonfiction and Fiction 241

A. Non-Fiction

CHAPTER 7

Translations / Alterations 317

CHAPTER 8

Poetry 359

CHAPTER 9
Plays 413

CHAPTER 10

Applied Arts and Music 465

ACKNOWLEDGMENTS

In a project of this magnitude it is almost impossible to keep track of all those who deserve thanks. We are grateful to all of our contributors for locating unusual entries for this collection and purchasing photographs, often without reimbursement. For that reason especially, we extend our thanks to those colleges and universities that awarded funds to support photographic expenses incurred by scholars who participated in *Reading Early Modern Women*. Significant funding has been supplied by Brock University (Office of the Vice-President of Research), McMaster University (Arts Research Board), and the Social Sciences and Humanities Research Council of Canada. In each case, we express our heartfelt thanks for that vital support.

Many libraries and institutions have been extraordinarily generous in waiving fees for permission to reproduce photographs in this volume. We are particularly grateful to the British Library for their agreement to waive permissions for forty-six photographs, approximately one-third of the project's illustrations, and are happy to acknowledge the assistance of Ms. S. Powlette in the Permissions Department for her efforts on our behalf.

Several other libraries also granted permission without fees. In Canada, they include Mills Memorial Library, McMaster University, whose Research Collections librarian, Dr. Carl Spadoni, assisted several contributors with their photographic orders, and (beyond the call of duty) delivered photographs by hand to the Department of English. The Fisher Rare Book Library, University of Toronto, declined fees, as did Queen's University Archives, Kingston, Ontario. In the United Kingdom, the Somerset Archive and Record Service's head of service Tom Mayberry negotiated on our behalf for permission from William Sanford, the owner of the Sandford papers, to use the Clarke letter reproduced in this volume. Stephen Freeth, the keeper of the manuscripts at the Guildhall Library, gave permission on behalf of the Corporation of the City of London. The London Metropolitan Archives (Rhys Griffith, principal archivist), the Society of Friends (Joanna Clark, librarian), the Nottinghamshire Archives, the York Minster Archives (Louise Hampson, collections manager, dean and chapter of York Minster), the Northamptonshire Libraries and Information Services (special thanks to Terry Bracher for rescanning material to suit our specifications), and the National Library of Scotland (Sheila Mackenzie, Manuscripts Division) all gave assistance in locating materials and waiving fees. In particular, we thank Thomas M. McCoog, S.J. of the Jesuit Archives, London, who took the extraordinary measure of taking photographs for us himself, to save us the charges of a professional photographer, and then waived fees as well. Finally, the Centre for Kentish Studies, Maidstone, Kent, helped obtain permission from Robert Sackville-West on behalf of the Knole Trustees. In France, the Archives départmentales de Lille granted permission without fee, as arranged by Mme Christine Paquet, archiviste. In the United States, Hamilton College Library, in Clinton, New York, waived fees, as did Yale's Beinecke Library; so too the William Andrews Clark Memorial Library, UCLA, whose staff, especially Suzanne Tatian, Reader Services, and Jennifer Schaffner facilitated our contributors' requests.

We acknowledge a special indebtedness to the Folger Shakespeare Library. The idea for this book project originated during the 1997 Folger Institute on "Habits of Reading in Early Modern England," directed by Steven Zwicker. The project is to some extent modeled on the pedagogical packet developed by the members of the Institute, although we moved in a different direction. Among the numerous contributors to *Reading Early Modern Women* are participants from the 1997 Folger Institute—Jennifer Andersen, Kathleen Lynch, and Elizabeth Sauer. Various other scholars associated with the Folger library, including Lena Orlin and Heather Wolfe, are among our contributors, and Georgiana Ziegler helped us with an inquiry. We are grateful to Richard Kuhta, chief librarian, and Michael Scott, who shepherded our request for reduced permissions fees for facsimiles from early printed books; manuscript permissions were allowed without fee.

We are grateful to all the holding institutions who negotiated with us for significantly reduced fees. The Bodleian Library, Oxford, generously coordinated our requests for reduced fees, and we extend particular thanks to two members of the Imaging Services Office, Susan Harris (researcher for the Printed Collections) and Patricia Buckingham (principal library assistant, Western Manuscripts Photographic Research) for their willingness to correspond and discuss details. We extend profuse thanks to the Public Record Office, now the National Archives, London, and Paul Johnson, Image Library manager, for assistance with complicated international orders. Steve Meckstroth, the special collections librarian at the Milner Library, Illinois State University, also facilitated our photographic and permissions request.

Finally, we want to acknowledge the extensive assistance of the staff at the Huntington Library, who processed at least twenty-five photographs and requests for permission to publish, on behalf of this publication; we thank Alan Jutzi and Donna Stromberg for their help. Cornell University Library Manuscript Collection, Kroch Library (Susan Szasz Palmer, then head of Public Services, Division of Rare & Manuscript Collections) and the Newberry Library, Chicago (John Powell, permissions librarian) also assisted scholars in this project.

To all who helped us coordinate this project, we express an enormous and unpayable debt. Among our own members, we of course thank everyone, but some went beyond our expectations in offering close readings of the introductions, scrutinizing entries as they appeared on our listserve during the first-round peer reviews, and helping generally with administrative and academic problems. Among those, Bob Evans was generous with much-needed advice and also helped to promote the project at Auburn, finding us new contributors. Elaine Hobby gave us a thorough final review of the introductions and was very kind about our shortcomings. Nely Keinanen also offered thoughtful critiques of entries and located colleagues at Helsinki for our Letters chapter. Liam Semler helped us deal with difficult attribution problems, and both James Daybell and Sarah Hutton advised us about the importance of including titles and maiden names of early modern women in our listings. Sarah Hutton undertook detective work to help us locate a missing participant in London, and Caroline Bowden assisted some of our members with library checks. Research assistants Bettina Stumm, MA (McMaster University, 2003) and Elizabeth D'Angelo, MA (Wilfrid Laurier University, 2003) both conducted research for some of the chapter introductions; Jennifer Dunford, MA (McMaster University, 2002) and Karen M. Oberer, MA (McMaster University, 2003) helped with copyediting and collation of materials. At Routledge, we have nothing but praise for Matthew Byrnie, who saw the great potential of our collection, and Emily Vail, who managed the complex process of corresponding with libraries about permission fees and making sure members of the project returned their publication agreements.

Our manuscript editor, Victoria Burke, spent many hours reviewing manuscript entries and rationalizing the transcriptions by our contributors. We thank her profusely for her good humor, her efficiency, and her evident pleasure in reading the manuscript pages and corresponding with participants about the details of secretary and italic hands.

Finally, our project manager and copyeditor, Melissa Smith, bore the burden of pulling the entire manuscript into a coherent format. The checking involved in this project had nightmarish proportions, especially after revisions and alterations began to appear in the last year of preparation. Those changes included editorial changes in the order or chapter assignment of various entries, the loss of two entries when one former participant disappeared, and the insertion of late entries to fill in gaps in the volume. Melissa also scanned backup copies of all the photographs for the collection and kept track of letters of permission and credit lines for all the institutions whose works were used in this publication. Without her, we would have been unable to complete this project.

The editors freely accept responsibility for any errors that may appear in this volume.

HELEN OSTOVICH   ELIZABETH SAUER
McMaster University   Brock University
                                    25 February 2003

A NOTE ON TRANSCRIPTIONS

The transcriptions from manuscript are standardized according to the following conventions. Original spelling, punctuation, and capitalization are preserved, but u/v and i/j are regularized (for example, "euer" to "ever", "enioy" to "enjoy"), and double "ff" at the beginning of a word is written "F". Superscripted letters and abbreviations are silently lowered and expanded (for example, "wᶜʰ" to "which", "yᵉ" to "the", "comon" with a tilde over the "m" to "common"). Deleted and erased words and scribal signs are for the most part ignored, and later insertions are silently incorporated into the text. Some punctuation has been modified. Editorial comments appear in square brackets. Manuscript titles appear in quotation marks, not in italics.

We chose this set of principles for various reasons. We wished to make these texts available to as wide an audience as possible, allowing people unfamiliar with manuscripts to read a "clean" transcribed copy for content. Those scholars interested in paleographical issues might have preferred a strictly diplomatic transcription; that is, one that noted expansions, insertions, and deletions in italics, parentheses, or other methods of notation. But diplomatic transcriptions are not easily comprehensible for those unfamiliar with the conventions, and comprehension was the primary purpose we wanted our transcriptions to serve. We decided that the difficulties of interpreting diplomatic transcriptions therefore outweighed the benefits of including them, and that readers interested primarily in manuscript studies could consult the facing facsimile for details modernized in the transcriptions. In this way, we believe we can best meet the needs of audiences with diverse interests and levels of expertise.

VICTORIA BURKE
MANUSCRIPT EDITOR

INTRODUCTION

Rereading Women's Literary History

This substantial collection of materials from original editions and manuscripts of sixteenth- and seventeenth-century English women's writings offers a research and pedagogical tool for investigating intersecting notions of authorship, gender, and literary and creative expression. Developed in collaboration with over 80 scholars, including some of the world's foremost scholars in English, history, and women's studies, *Reading Early Modern Women* encourages exploration into the material life of the manuscript and printed text, as well as into the women and the cultures that produced them. This book is designed as a resource to introduce and supplement course texts, while filling the gaps left in studies of major figures and events of the early modern period. Organized by genre ranging from legal documents to life-writing and applied arts, *Reading Early Modern Women* presents the literary and artistic achievements of women firsthand and is distinct from existing anthologies and editions in terms of the variety of manuscript and printed materials and amount of commentary it offers. This general introduction situates the volume theoretically and pedagogically. Chapter introductions synthesize the materials within the chapter, cross-reference the materials with other chapters, and suggest areas for further research and study. Equally valuable for preliminary or advanced studies, *Reading Early Modern Women* provides multiple points of entry into the expanding and vital field of women's literary history.

Scholarly understanding of what constitutes literature has gradually been expanding, challenging the primacy given to high culture over popular culture, printed writings over manuscripts, canonical literature over other kinds of writings, and male-authored texts over women's writings. The early modern era in particular is a pivotal period in feminist awareness.[1] Until as recently as two decades ago, however, the subject of women's social and literary history received minimal scholarly attention. Peter Burke in *Popular Culture in Early Modern Europe* admitted that he had "too little to say about women, for lack of evidence."[2] Such dismissals have come under scrutiny over the past two decades, particularly through social, political, and literary studies on women's history, but much work remains undone. In his introduction to *Trials of Authorship: Anterior Rooms and Poetic Reconstruction From Wyatt to Shakespeare* (1990), which maps out in an appropriately meta-critical fashion the poetics and practices of New Historicism, Jonathan Crewe examines the efforts made to "construct

authorial identity and appropriate the texts as an 'authorial' construction" in the
Renaissance.[3] The notion of authorship, he explains, "will always be on trial, subject to critical denial or self-erasure, yet that will precisely be its precarious and generally self-conscious condition" (15). Having acknowledged that his study runs the risk of "forgetting (yet
again) class as well as gender exclusion," not to mention "Foucault's critically enabling dissolution of the author" (14), he proceeds to tell a story of "privileged masculine authorship
during one phase of the English Renaissance" (20). Feminist critics have been wary of this
dissolution, claiming that it is in fact not "enabling" at all.

The tendency to privilege canonical male authors while disregarding women writers
and authors of the lower classes is commonly cited as one of the "discontents" with the
New Historicism. Moreover, the concept of the author as a product of historical and cultural forces that resist attempts at control has also been subject to much scrutiny.[4]
Scholarship on books and readerships in particular has demonstrated the contribution of
literary culture to shaping power relationships, building communities, and politicizing
writers and readers who developed a heightened sense of their contribution to culture and
politics. Writing, reading, and printing practices involve negotiations between individual
performances and social forms of agency, and are used "both for reinforcing conformity
and for improvising disruption," as Eve Sanders has recently demonstrated in a study on
Gender and Literacy.[5] Because the mass production and dissemination of printed texts in
England were unparalleled during the Civil War years and Interregnum, this period offers
an especially rich site for investigating the rise of literacy, manuscript and print culture,
interpretive practices, and emerging constructions of authorship. Women's contribution to
mid–seventeenth-century culture and their participation in print culture in manifold ways
heretofore underestimated or misunderstood is currently a subject of groundbreaking, vital
scholarly inquiry.

Research on women's cultural and literary contributions has also transformed our perceptions of history. The question "Did women have a Renaissance?" has haunted scholars
and students of sixteenth- and seventeenth-century English literature, history, cultural
studies, and women's studies ever since Joan Kelly raised the question.[6] In various ways
Kelly's study also anticipated the name change from "Renaissance" to "early modern,"
marking this period as one of tensions rather than triumphs.[7] Since the time the question
was posed, extensive research in the various disciplines has led to the conclusion that the
answer is no; that is, women's inferior social status and relegation to the domestic sphere
stifled their development at all levels. On another level, however, the answer may be yes,
since female experience was not transhistorical and was inevitably shaped by the very religious, political, social, cultural, and economic changes that gave rise to the early modern
man. The nature of women's "Renaissance" was nevertheless different from that of males,
and any examination of early modern culture that compares the achievements of the two
genders must attend to the complex network of social conditions that affected each differently. For that reason, feminists have recently rephrased the question by replacing the
idea of a "Renaissance" for women with the less celebratory concept of a "Reformation" to
remind us that social transformations occurred gradually and unpredictably for the different groups and individuals that made up early modern society.[8]

The site of our investigation in *Reading Early Modern Women* is the counter-canon of
early modern women's manuscripts and printed texts.[9] Our collection of materials from
early modern English writings does not propose to be comprehensive or exhaustive in any

terms; rather, it is intended to introduce scholars and students to the literary achievements of various women firsthand; to encourage further explorations into the emergence of the female writer and the fashioning of the female self; to demonstrate the ways manuscript and print culture enabled the construction of those identities; and to consider the full range of textual production. We have designed *Reading Early Modern Women* as an interdisciplinary research and pedagogical tool and as a resource text for courses on women's literature, history, and women's studies. The very broad spectrum of female writing we present is divided into chapters representing ten different genres, and many more subgenres, whose conventions frequently overlap, intersect, and condition the creation of new genres. Our decision to group the women's writings we have assembled in terms of manuscript and printed materials, as well as in terms of different genres enables us to present the history as well as the wide array of themes and styles of each genre. Featured in the edition are (1) legal documents and women's testimony; (2) the arguments about the status of women represented by the controversy about women and essays on and samples of female education, including philosophy produced by educated women; (3) mothers' legacies and medical manuals; (4) religious writings, including prophecy and persecution accounts and narratives; (5) letters; (6) life-writing, both nonfiction and fiction; (7) translations and alterations; (8) poetry; (9) plays; and (10) applied arts and music. The primary conventions of each genre are outlined in the chapter introductions, which serve as well to connect the individual entries in those genres. Certainly not all women who published thought of themselves as "writers" in a literary or even a broader sense, and that is why we have chosen to include entries on extraliterary writings, such as depositions, mothers' legacies, texts by female dissenters, and examples of artistic and musical performances.

We share with our contributors and other editors of women's writings the experiences, challenges, and rewards of undertaking this archival, bibliographic, and feminist work. In fact the "Renaissance" for women occurred in the late twentieth century, largely through the archival and editorial work of feminist scholars. Editor, author, and archivist, Betty S. Travitsky, whose groundbreaking editions include *The Paradise of Women: Writings by Englishwomen of the Renaissance* (1980) and *The Renaissance Englishwoman in Print: Counterbalancing the Canon*, edited with Anne M. Haselkorn (1990), was instrumental in bringing to light an early modern female literary tradition and enabling a renaissance of early modern women writers. The excavation and investigation continues at the hands of feminist scholars. Jeslyn Medoff recently described the role of Germaine Greer, Susan Hastings, Melinda Sansone, and herself in compiling the anthology *Kissing the Rod: An Anthology of Seventeenth Century Women's Verse* (1988, 1989), which introduced the use of manuscript writings in courses on women's poetry: "It took the four of us six years of trans-Atlantic travel and research to complete the anthology," explained Medoff, "but they were some of the best years of my life. It was a great privilege to ruminate among the rare books at Duke Humphrey's library at the Bodleian, bend my head beneath the sky-lit dome of the British Library's old reading room, unfurl parchment rolls at the old Public Records Office in Chancery Lane, and finger the Matchless Orinda's manuscripts at the National Library of Wales in Aberystwyth. I was conducting original research, following in the footsteps of people like Doris Stenton and Myra Reynolds; I was a woman with a cause."[10] As in the case of *Kissing the Rod*, many of the works we feature in *Reading Early Modern Women* were not printed in their own time, but comprised a rich manuscript culture, on which an impressive number of our contributors have shared their expertise.

The 1980s and 1990s have seen many more scholars and editors joining in the cause of excavating women's literary history.[11] *The Norton Anthology of Literature by Women: The Tradition in English*, edited by Sandra M. Gilbert and Susan Gubar (1985, 1996) contributed significantly to making the study of female-authored writings of various genres relevant for students of literature generally, though, as has often been observed, this anthology devotes, comparatively speaking, little attention to early modern women. In the first edition, women's literature produced between 1500 and 1700 is limited to 89 of 2,457 pages; the number of pages increases to 166 in the 2,452-page second edition. Resisting the notion of an evolutionary model of female authorship advanced by the editors of the *Norton Anthology*, we focus instead in *Reading Early Modern Women* on what the early modern period can teach us about women's literary history.[12] Yet, at the same time, we recognize, as Wendy Wall has recently observed, that early modern "conceptions of authorship and literary texts were undergoing changes that shaped modern ideas of literary history and intellectual culture."[13]

In North America, *The Norton Anthology* prepared the way for the production of many fine anthologies and editions, each of which must be credited for the increased pedagogical and critical engagement with early writings by and about women. In terms of its contents and aims, however, *Reading Early Modern Women* differs from the volumes and resources that have appeared thus far, and certainly we recommend using our edition to complement or supplement existing collections. *Renaissance Woman: A Sourcebook*, edited by Kate Aughterson (1995), which is more concerned with the representation of early women rather than female-authored writings, is arranged in nine sections, each of which focuses on a different subject or "discursive field," ranging from "theology" to "proto-feminisms." Writings by males make up much of the anthology, and in five of the sections (Theology, Physiology, Conduct, Politics and Law, and Education), male-authored texts represent at least 80 percent of the entries.[14] Randall Martin's 1997 edition, *Women Writers in Renaissance England*, begins with a section of epistles from women's writings and offers select prose works and poetry up to 1627. *Major Women Writers of Seventeenth-Century England*, edited by James Fitzmaurice, Josephine A. Roberts, Carol L. Barash, Eugene R. Cunnar, and Nancy A. Gutierrez (1997) includes writings by nine female authors.

A number of multigenre anthologies of prose writings have recently appeared. *Lay By Your Needles Ladies, Take the Pen: Writing Women in England, 1500–1700*, edited by Suzanne Trill, Kate Chedgzoy, and Melanie Osborne (1997), differs in various ways from Charlotte Otten's edition of *English Women's Voices, 1540–1700* (1992), particularly in terms of its inclusion of fictional prose writings and manuscripts. *Lay By Your Needles* juxtaposes female and male writings, a strategy also applied in *Female and Male Voices in Early Modern England* (2000), in which the editors, Betty S. Travitsky and Anne Lake Prescott, avoid the "ghettoization" of women's voices in rooms and canons of their own. Eleven female writers, nearly all poets, are represented in a recent edition of women's writings across fifty years, *Early Modern Women's Writings: An Anthology 1650–1700*, edited by Paul Salzman (2000). Besides publishing Salzman's anthology, Oxford University Press has also produced a series on individual female authors, titled "Women Writers in English, 1350–1850" (general editors Susanne Woods and Elizabeth H. Hageman).[15] On-line resources are also now available; the Brown University Women Writers Project developed a text base of writings by women titled *Women Writers Online*; and *Renaissance Women on Line*, a subtext of this text base, is in progress.[16]

Reading Early Modern Women is distinct from existing multigenre anthologies and editions in terms of its large number of manuscript and printed materials and the kind and amount of commentary it offers on each text. Its organization by genre and its concern with the materiality of texts also distinguishes it from other printed editions, as well as from databases.[17] Our project is accessible for those studying early modern women's literary history for the first time, and we provide multiple points of entry into this expanding field of inquiry. Moreover, our wide-ranging guide can be read without satiating the appetite for more. In fact this broad picture of female activity encourages readers to pursue further research into areas that they are interested in examining more intensively.

This collection, then, is intended to serve the following specific purposes: (1) to identify and present a substantial selection of materials from original editions of women's writings, which have traditionally been underrepresented in early modern literary studies, and thus to invite a reassessment of the literary canon and literary history; (2) to highlight what is unusual or compelling about specific women writers and their works; (3) to raise awareness of women's literary, cultural, and social history as represented by the texts they produced and circulated; (4) to offer a resource for teaching and learning about individual female authors, networks, and interpretive communities; (5) to invite investigations into the imprint of gender and the stigma of print; (6) to historicize early modern reading and writing practices; (7) to enrich students' understanding of manuscript and print cultures, and to stimulate interest in the production and consumption of early modern texts; (8) to enable examinations of what early modern readers were seeing on the page or, for that matter, how the reader and consumer were constructed through the prefatory materials and addresses to readerships in texts generally; (9) to document the life of ideas, their transmission through print, and the varying modes of exchange among female authors, publishers, and readers; and (10) to display the wide array of private and public genres in which women wrote.

The ten chapter introductions in this volume characterize the individual genres, the female and male contributions to those genres, and the social and historical issues engaged by the writers. The introductions also emphasize the interrelationships of the various writers featured in each chapter. The remainder of "Rereading Women's Literary History" addresses broader issues and outlines some of the many uses of this edition for scholars and students. In addition to serving as a resource for investigating individual women writers, *Reading Early Modern Women* offers insight into the representations of the female writer's identity, which might be studied by observing, among other things, the inclusion or omission of signatures across various genres. Or one might wish to investigate the ways in which the stigma of print or of public exposure affects women's writings. Research on the interaction of oral, visual, and literate cultures as well as of manuscript and print cultures—specific to women writers and even across gender divisions—might also begin here. The agents and forms of mediation for women writers—secretaries, translators, transcribers, publishers, or even different types of discourse—offer still another fascinating topic of inquiry, as does a study of the construction of female networks and of the interactions of female and male writers and editors.

Reading Women

On the basis of a study of signatures to depositions taken in ecclesiastical courts in southeast England, David Cressy, in his influential study of literacy, estimated that writing skills were limited to 30 percent of the total male population and 10 percent of the female population by 1640, reaching 45 percent and 25 percent, respectively, by the accession of George I. Cressy's figures have been emended by Keith Thomas, Margaret W. Ferguson, and Eve Rachele Sanders, among others, who have determined that levels of reading-literacy were vastly higher than those of signature-literacy.[18] Still, the large majority of women were illiterate or semiliterate. And while some illiterate women could manage household or estate affairs successfully by employing secretaries to produce their correspondence, most were handicapped by that lack.[19] To ensure that their stories are not wholly neglected, we have provided some accounts *about* illiterate women, particularly in chapter 1. Literacy itself is, as John Guillory reminds us, not "self evident or a homogenous phenomenon at all, but rather . . . a complex set of social facts" about "who reads [and] writes . . . in what languages and dialects . . . with what degrees of cultural prestige."[20] We need, then, to recognize the different kinds of literacies in the period and to conduct further research into the relationship between social status and literacy, as well as into the communication of ideas to the literate and illiterate alike.

Traditionally girls who received an education in the early modern period were taught to read in part that they might learn proper types of female conduct. Even then, the kinds of reading materials available to them were limited. Juan Luis Vives's *De institutione feminae Christianae* (1524), a conduct book translated and reprinted throughout the sixteenth century, discussed the dangers for women of reading the wrong kinds of texts and of failing to have even permissible texts mediated by male interpreters. Frances Dolan and Jacqueline Pearson have documented the "policing" of women's reading during the period, pointing to conduct books, educational treatises, and legal customs that circumscribed women's reading.[21] Richard Mulcaster's *Positions [concerning] the Training Up of Children* (1581) maintains that reading is intended to remind women of their religious beliefs and duties, without hindering their housewifery. Protestant religious works, marriage and conduct manuals, books on cooking or midwifery—most of which were male-authored—were, then, intended to keep women submissive and focused on domestic affairs.

Eighty-five percent of the 163 books in 500 editions addressed to women or largely concerned with women's behaviour or roles were published between 1570 and 1640. Suzanne Hull has described and analyzed these books, compiling a list of these "Books for Women."[22] Based primarily on prefatory definitions of intended readerships, Hull's list records what authors and publishers hoped women would read. But recently scholars have also demonstrated that women contested these constraints. Lady Bridgewater, for example, owned books addressed to "the vulgar sort" and to "young gentlemen."[23] In fact evidence of women's use of and engagement with texts addressed to male readers is extensive throughout this collection.

In examining different levels of literacy, we should also note the basic distinctions between silent reading, which frees readers from "the control of the group," and communal reading experiences.[24] Both types of reading practices enabled active exchanges with texts and ideas. *Reading Early Modern Women* is an excellent resource for investigating women's reading materials and women's habits of reading as conveyed in their writings. The extent and sophistication of women's engagement with existing works of literature depended in part on the availability of the relevant texts, as well as on the education and thus the social status of the reader/writer. To illustrate this point, one might wish to examine, among numerous other examples, Ester Sowernam's, Constantia Munda's, or

Rachel Speght's different responses to Joseph Swetnam's *The Araignment of . . . women* (1616) in the controversy about women. Among the numerous other examples of women writers' engagement with existing texts—female- or male-authored—are Lady Anne (Cooke) Bacon's translation of Bishop John Jewel's antipapal *An apologie or answere in defence of the Churche of Englande* (1564) and Elizabeth Russell's 1605 translation of John Ponet in *A Way of Reconciliation of a Good and Learned Man*. Lady Mary Wroth's *Urania* (1621) is modeled on *Arcadia* by her uncle, Sir Philip Sidney. The various readings of scripture provided by women across the genres present significant illustrations of literary engagement. Other notable examples of reading include Lady Margaret Wemyss's interpretation of music scripts by Thomas Morley and Thomas Campion (1640s); Eliza's reading of George Herbert's verses (1652); Philo-Philippa's indebtedness to Katherine Philips's verses (1667); Aphra Behn's feminist interpretation of Thomas Killigrew's *Thomaso* in *The Rover* (1677); Anne Finch's *The Spleen: A Pindarique Ode* (composed c.1694), which invites a rereading of Thomas Burton's *Anatomy of Melancholy*; Catherine Trotter's interpretation of John Locke's *Defence* in *A Defence of the Essay of Human Understanding, Written by Mr. Lock . . . in answer to some Remarks on that Essay* (1702); or any of the (other) translations and alterations in the collection, which reinterpret rather than just reproduce the source texts.

Writing Women

Despite the example set by Elizabeth I, who, as patroness-poet, inspired the works of aristocratic women, female literacy rates remained low. James's ascension to the throne saw a steady increase in literacy, though the education of elite Jacobean women declined in quality by comparison with the Humanist classical education enjoyed by some upper-class Tudor women (see chapter 2). Noting this distinction, Barbara Lewalski claims, nevertheless that, while Elizabethan women produced few original texts, Jacobean women wrote and sometimes published original poems, dramatic works, and prose writings, along with letters and memoirs. The emerging Protestant emphasis on individualism and responsibility to one's own conscience authorized women to resist their husbands' domination by claiming they were doing God's will. This is the case for many women writers in the edition, including Anne Locke, who deserted her husband for religious reasons in 1557 to join John Knox in Geneva; and Anne Wentworth, who circumvented secular authority, especially that of her husband, by dedicating herself in *A Vindication* (1677) to Christ in a "full communion between Christ and my soul, the love knot, the comely bands of marriage."[25] Some women also took oppositional support from other writings or performances. The entrance into the literary sphere or the production of original works might as well have been triggered by other examples of female resistance, like the acquisition of property, the rejection of male governance by will or defiance, or the performance by women of masculine roles.[26]

For contemporary readers, the primary marker of the success of early modern or present-day writers is usually determined by "the amount they *published*, with no mention of the amount they actually *wrote*," Margaret Ezell recently commented. In fact, however, print was not a marker of success in the early modern period. Though literary histories and anthologies have conditioned us to identify literary activity with print culture and to view literary history through the lens of printed documents, an investigation of the relationships between manuscript and print culture does greater justice to women's literary history and literary studies generally, and enables a reevaluation of both.[27]

A study of manuscript writings requires a consideration of the history of handwriting. While originating at the end of the medieval period, the secretary hand was not widely employed until the early modern period, by which time it had completely displaced the earlier court hands. The secretary hand eventually became the everyday hand of business, of correspondence, and of literary composition. This hand had many letters in common with the established hands, but several that were distinctive, like the long *h*, the *a*, the *e*, the *r*, the *c*, the *g*, and the final *s*. It was later replaced by a new hand from Italy—the italic or italian hand. Humanist scholars of early modern Italy became dissatisfied with the awkward hands they were taught and sought instead a form of clear writing. Turning to classical models, they developed the upright Roman hand and the sloping, cursive italic hand, both of which are still in use today. The italic hand was used by the learned, including Roger Ascham, and by writers of the secretary hand when they wished to highlight a quotation or passage and when they signed their names. It was also usually taught to women who were privileged enough to receive writing instruction.[28]

Many of the works featured in this edition did not appear in print in their own day but became part of the manuscript culture of the period. For women there were three forms of manuscript exchange: they could produce manuscript books, circulate writings in loose sheets, or engage in correspondence. Margaret Ezell, Arthur Marotti, and Harold Love have shown that women's poetry in particular was more regularly composed and circulated in manuscript than in print. Women also responded to manuscript poems in circulation. "The Lie" (1611), a popular poem by Sir Walter Ralegh, was, for example, emended by Anne Southwell in her commonplace book after an amanuensis transcribed it for her. Ann Bowyer's commonplace book also includes a transcribed version of Ralegh's poem. The commonplace books in turn provide evidence about the literary connections of the compilers, as well as about the family and social networks to which they belonged.

Selections from sixteenth- and early seventeenth-century manuscripts in this edition are wide ranging and intended not only to represent individual work but to provide insight into some of the "manuscript cultures" created by women.[29] The relevant entries include the collectively produced Devonshire Manuscript (c. 1530–45), Princess Elizabeth's manuscript translation of Marguerite d'Angouleme's *Le miroir de l'ame pécheresse* in the princess's awkward italic writing (1544); Frances Matthew's "The birthe of all my children," written between 1583 and 1629 in italic hand; Esther Inglis's calligraphic manuscript in the Huntington Library (c. 1600); a 1607 manuscript of Elizabeth Southwell's account of Elizabeth I's death, written in a clear secretary hand; Lady Mildmay's eighty-five–page manuscript "Autobiography," composed about 1617; the 1622 manuscript of Elizabeth Joscelin's "The Mothers Legacy to her Unborn Childe;" Lady Mary Wroth's two manuscripts of "Loves Victorie" (c. 1620), the complete Penshurst manuscript and an incomplete version from the Huntington Library that contains two types of handwriting—a formal italic hand and an informal cursive hand; Rachael Fane's manuscript notebooks in a secretary hand (1628); Sister Joan Seller's oath of obedience written in italic hand (1631); Joyce Jefferies's Financial Diary, completed between 1638 and 1649; and Lady Jane Cavendish and Lady Elizabeth Brackley's "The concealed Fansyes" (c. 1645).

We also feature a variety of manuscripts from the second half of the seventeenth century, among which are Lady Hester Pulter's folio bound manuscript of poetry and prose in the scribal hand (c. 1640–65); Sir Nicholas Le Strange's manuscript jestbook, "Merry Passages and Jeasts" (c. 1650), which includes jests supplied by Dame Alice L'Estrange; the notebook of Lucy Hutchinson's "The Memoirs of the Life of Colonel Hutchinson" (c. 1664); two related versions of Agnes Beaumont's autobiographical narrative, "Divine Appearances" (c. 1674); John Penington's transcription of the autobiographical manuscripts of his mother, Mary (Springett) Penington (c.1623–82); Mary More's "The Womans Right or Her Power in Greater Equality to Her Husband" (1680), found in Robert Whitehall's manuscript miscellany volume; and Elizabeth Freke's two 1684 manuscript autobiographical texts which exhibit different constructions of Freke's life.

The original manuscripts are located throughout Europe and the United States, including the University of Leeds Library; the British Library (multiple collections); the Library of the Religious Society of Friends; the Huntington Library; the Nottinghamshire County archives; the Centre for Kentish Studies, Maidstone, Kent University; the Folger Shakespeare Library; the Archives Départmentales du Nord, Lille; the Northampton Central Library; York Minster Archives; the Bodleian Library; and Stonyhurst College, Lancashire.

Authorship

"The poore woman is a little distracted, she could never bee soe rediculous else as to venture at writeing book's," Dorothy Osborne lamented.[30] Despite the fact that seventeenth-century women had increased access to the written word, their attitude toward their use of language was one of ambivalence and even suspicion.[31] Publication in particular defied early modern notions of female sexuality and authorship, and was linked to aggressive, provocative behavior: "to appear in print was to appear in public and hence also to seek male attention."[32] Public exposure and loquaciousness were "scandal[ous] to the modesty of [a woman's] sex," John Dryden insisted in reasserting the conventional attitude to the early modern female author.[33] Women thus frequently prefaced their texts with self-denigrating remarks and apologized for their poor literacy and spelling competence, thereby exposing their concerns about violating established gender codes. Some women even adopted pseudonyms, a matter that is somewhat more complicated in the case of Ester Sowernam and Constantia Munda, who may have been males (chapter 2).

Various entries in this collection feature marks of women's self-identification, signaling the authors' resistance to the stigma of public exposure and print. The inclusion of a signature, for example, is an act of self-assertion and ownership in this period, though anonymity must be recognized to be equally provocative at this time. Anne Southwell signed her name to her alteration of Sir Walter Ralegh's 1611 poem, thus laying claim to it. Elizabeth Cellier, who defended contemporary women medical practitioners, confronted her opponents in *To Dr., An Answer to his Queries*, to which she signed her name (1688). The title page of the printed version of *She Ventures and He Wins* (1696) identifies the playwright as "a Young Lady," though the preface is signed "Ariadne." The fact that Catherine Trotter signed her name to the Dedication to *Fatal Friendship* (1698) indicates that she was prepared to take a stand as a female writer. Susanna Centlivre was not so immediately assertive; it took nine years and nine plays between the time she wrote her first play, *A Perjur'd Husband* (1700), and the time her name began to appear regularly in the signatory position.

A portrait could serve both as a kind of signature and as a means of constructing alternative representations of the self. *The Worlds Olio* (1655), the third book published by Margaret Cavendish, duchess of Newcastle, contains a frontispiece of Cavendish drawn by Abraham van Diepenbeeck and engraved by Peter van Schuppen, which represents the playwright as one who seeks renown and public attention. Other copies of *Worlds Olio*, however, feature other frontispieces. The portraits framing the opening letter of *The case of Madam Mary Carleton, lately stiled the German Princess* (1663) demonstrate Mary Carleton's management of her image that she creates with the help of the public eye. Mary Beale's portrait of Aphra Behn (c. 1680) depicts a determined, ambitious woman who resembles in some ways Beale's own self-portraits, suggesting perhaps the painter's identification with her subject. The frontispiece portrait from Ephelia's *Female Poems on several Occasions* (1679, 1682) is more elusive than those of Cavendish, Carleton, and even Behn, since the historical identity of the woman who is pictured has until recently remained a matter of speculation (see chapters 8 and 10). The fictitious name "Ephelia" was likewise designed to complicate and ultimately frustrate the search for the poet's historical identity. Produced several years later, Anne Killigrew's engraved self-portrait, which prefaces her *Poems* (1686), reflects the poet's upper-class status, her mastery of contemporary artistic conventions, and her interest in notoriety.

Mediators, Collaborators, Publishers

While early modern writing in general needs to be reconceived as collective, collaborative, and occasional rather than just being identified with the production of completed, market-ready texts, this is especially true of women's writings, as many of our entries indicate.[34] Mary Sidney's "To the Angell spirit of the most excellent Sir Phillip Sidney," printed in Samuel Daniel's *The Whole Workes of Samuel Daniel Esquire in Poetrie* (1623), involved the combined efforts of sister and brother to translate the word of David, who in turn translated God's word. The manuscript of "The concealed Fansyes" (c. 1645), written by Elizabeth Brackley and Jane Cavendish, was a collaborative production, designed to appeal to a wider audience than might be assumed by its association with a period of royalist retreat. The two folio play collections (1662 and 1668) of their stepmother, Margaret Cavendish, constitute some of the earliest published evidence in English of literary collaboration between a wife and a husband.

Males often served as mediators or printers of women's writings, which appeared in print in conjunction with or in spite of the author's wishes. John Bale, whose texts were banned until Henry VIII's death in 1547, edited Anne Askew's *Examynacyon* for publication in Germany in 1546–47, and amended Elizabeth's translation of Marguerite d'Angouleme's *Miroir* (published in Marburg in 1548). The letters of Elizabeth produced during her reign are in themselves noteworthy of study, though the author's voice can barely be distinguished from the official style she developed in conjunction with her secretaries and ministers.[35]

Of the poetry by women that was actually published, most was handled by male printers. Richard Jones, for example, published all of Isabel Whitney's poetry.[36] In the seventeenth century, John Woodbridge, Anne Bradstreet's brother-in-law, arranged for the printing of *The Tenth Muse* (London, 1650). Bradstreet's denial of intent in response to the publication needs, like that of Katherine Philips, to be read in the context of the contemporary convention of trying the water through an "unofficial" edition before bringing out a "corrected" version if the former was well received. Richard Mariott's publication of Katherine Philips's octavo volume of verse, including her friendship poems to Anne Owen in 1664, provoked Philips's strongly worded response: "Tis impossible for Malice it self to have printed those Rhymes, which you tell me are got abroad so impudently, with so much Wrong and Abuse to them, as the very Publication of them at all, tho' never so correct, had been to me, who never writ a Line in my Life with the Intention to have it printed."[37] In terms of legal documents, male scribes compressed and sometimes distorted evidence while reconstructing narratives given in testimony (chapter 1). An examination of translations and alterations by women and of the circumstances in which they were produced also exposes the networks in which writers were involved at this time, and indicates how these interactions affected their writings and the interpretations thereof.

The politics of mediation is an important consideration in the context of women's religious writings in the period. The value accorded by Church of England members and by Puritans and dissenters to the chronicling of religious and spiritual experiences helps account for the large number of texts on this subject. Women became increasingly involved in the production and dissemination of religious writings from poems to prophetic treatises. In the case of the radical sects in particular, women also sometimes served as intermediaries. Hannah Allen and Elizabeth Calvert are known for this role; the former, a publisher and bookseller, issued at least fifty-four books and pamphlets on which her name is printed, while the latter likewise printed materials by dissenters during the Civil War through to the Restoration period.[38] More commonly, however, males served as mediators and printers of religious writings. A male recorded Anna Trapnel's prayers and verses in *The Cry of a Stone* (1654), claiming that he transcribed only as much as he could. During her 1654 trial, Trapnel denied authoring the text that was several times removed from her oral presentation. Between 1642 and 1685, the prophecies of Mother Shipton (reputedly born c. 1488) were reprinted and appropriated for political commentary by journal writers. Theodosia Pendarves intervened on the side of Elizabeth Poole, calling on those who were chastising her for her views on the execution of Charles I to stop maligning her, and asking her persecutors to leave a retraction at the Black Spread Eagle, the bookshop run by the Calverts. In 1662 Robert Wilson published Katharine Evans and Sarah Chevers's *Short Relation of Some of the Cruel Sufferings (For the Truths Sake) of Katharine Evans & Sarah Chevers*, which was edited by Daniel Baker, who mediated the narratives, letters, hymns, poems, and visions through editorial commentaries. This study of women's writings, then, has much to teach about how gender politics affected the production, editing, printing, and circulation of texts.

Reading texts of early modern women ultimately involves examinations of conflicting models of identity formation. Literature contributed to the making of identities that were available for public—largely male—scrutiny. Even texts designed for an audience of one become marked by "double-voicing" insofar as the recording of the private experience is determined by codes of conduct and hierarchical gender relations advanced by domestic manuals, political and religious tracts, conduct books, medical and obstetrical treatises, and legal documents. The woman's identity was also "packaged" by the physical presentation of her writing, often determined by the specifications of her printer and her sponsors, if she had them. The textual presentations of female writers reflect, for example, the status of purchaser and the purchaser's evaluation of the text so that even the choice of the paper for the printing of the text can make statements about the author and affect the reception of her work.

At the same time, *Reading Early Modern Women* encourages the study of how manuscript circulation and print helped shape power relationships and increased the awareness of writers and readers about their contribution to the production of culture. Building on theories of identity formation developed by Anthony Giddens, Pierre Bourdieu, and Louis Montrose, Eve Rachele Sanders maintains that individuals could, depending on their social position, ethnicity, and gender, practice certain self-fashioning techniques "for ends for which they were not originally intended." Reading and writing, for example, could be used "both for reinforcing conformity and for improvising disruption. The teaching of specific modes of expression and interpretation helped to create systemic differences between men and women but also created openings for inventive contestation" (Sanders 3). These possibilities for "inventive contestation" ultimately call for a reevaluation of early modern writings by males and females, as well as of the conventionally oppositional—and often gendered—relationship between private and public discourse,[39] and finally of the male construction of literary history.

Notes

1. Since the 1980s, historians and literary and cultural critics have replaced the term "renaissance" as a description of the period from 1400 to 1700 with "early modern" to identify the period as a precursor of "modernity." New historicism, cultural criticism, and cultural materialism, as well as feminist theory and scholarship on women's history, have contributed to this change.

2. Peter Burke, *Popular Culture in Early Modern Europe* (London: Temple Smith, 1978), 49.

3. Jonathan Crewe, *Trials of Authorship: Anterior Forms and Poetic Reconstruction From Wyatt to Shakespeare* (Berkeley: University of California Press, 1990), 14.

4. Edward Pechter, "The New Historicism and Its Discontents: Politicizing Renaissance Drama," *PMLA* 102 (1987): 292–302. Citing David Norbrook's 1984 *Poetry and Politics in the English Renaissance*, Robert Wilcher argues for the legitimacy of investigating "'authorial intention,' insofar as it can be reconstructed, since to ignore its 'substantial and underacknowledged political element' is 'effectively to depoliticize'" (Wilcher, *The Writing of Royalism 1628–1660* [Cambridge: Cambridge University Press, 2001], 3). See Patricia Fumerton's "Introduction: A New New Historicism" in *Renaissance Culture and the Everyday*, ed. Fumerton and Simon Hunt (Philadelphia: University of Pennsylvania Press, 1999), on the problematic foci of the New Historicism and its resultant blindspots; and on an emerging, "new" New Historicism.

5. Eve Rachele Sanders, *Gender and Literacy on Stage in Early Modern England* (Cambridge: Cambridge University Press, 1998), 3.

6. Joan Kelly, "Did Women Have a Renaissance?" *Women, History and Theory: The Essays of Joan Kelly* (Chicago: University of Chicago Press, 1984), 19–50.

7. "Renaissance" means "rebirth" and refers to the period of transition from the medieval to the modern world in Western Europe. In England, the Renaissance is identified with the years c. 1500–1660, when English authors felt the impact of humanism and classical learning generally. The period is marked by the Protestant Reformation, the introduction of the printing press, economic and political changes contributing to a nascent democracy and nationalist spirit, individualism, cosmological developments, and cultural revolutions.

8. Margaret W. Ferguson, "Moderation and its Discontents: Recent Work on Renaissance Women," *Feminist Studies* 20.2 (1994): 332. The time has come as well to ask whether women had a *revolution* in the seventeenth century. On this question, see Lois G. Schwoerer, "Women's public political voice in England: 1640–1740," *Women Writers and the Early Modern British Political Tradition*, ed. Hilda L. Smith (Cambridge: Cambridge University Press, 1998), 56–74; and Patricia Crawford, "The Challenges to Patriarchalism: How did the Revolution Affect Women?," *Revolution and Restoration: England in the 1650s*, ed. John Morrill (London: Collins and Brown, 1992), 112–28. Elissa A. Weaver concludes that Kelly's question can be answered with "a qualified 'yes'," but that "the Renaissance for women must be seen as open-ended, and as yet not fully realized" ("Gender," *A Companion to the Worlds of the Renaissance*, ed. Guido Ruggiero [Oxford: Blackwell, 2002], 204).

9. See Melinda Alliker Rabb, "The Work of Women in the Age of Electronic Reproduction: The Canon, Early Modern Women Writers and the Postmodern Reader," *A Companion to Early Modern Women's Writing*, ed. Anita Pacheco (Oxford: Blackwell, 2002), 339–60.

10. *Kissing the Rod: An Anthology of Seventeenth Century Women's Verse*, ed. Germaine Greer, Susan Hastings, Melinda Sansone, Jeslyn Medoff (London: Virago Press, 1988; New York: Farrar, Straus and Giroux, 1989); Jeslyn Medoff, "'This is joye, this is true pleasure:' Working on Early Modern Women Poets at the End of the 20th Century," National Women's Studies Association, Boston, June 2000.

11. On the construction of the self by early modern women writers, see, for example, Megan Matchinske, *Writing, Gender and State in Early Modern England: Identity Formation and the Female Subject* (Cambridge: Cambridge University Press, 1998); Hilary Hinds, *God's Englishwomen: Seventeenth-century Radical Sectarian Writing and Feminist Criticism* (Manchester: Manchester University Press, 1996); Elspeth Graham et al., "Introduction," *Her own Life: Autobiographical Writings by Seventeenth-Century Englishwomen*, ed. Elspeth Graham et al. (New York: Routledge, 1989). Sharon Cadman Seelig offers a survey of anthologies of early modern British literature and women's writings in "The Poets of the Renaissance: or The Illusions of My Youth," *Faultlines in the Field*, ed. Claude Summers and Ted-Larry Pebworth (Columbia: University of Missouri Press, 2002). Also see Suzanne W. Hull, "Traditional Studies of Early Women Writers," *Teaching Tudor and Stuart Women Writers*, ed. Susanne Woods and Margaret P. Hannay (New York: Modern Language Association, 2000), 348–56; Sara Jayne Steen, "'My Bookes and Pen I Wyll Apply': Recent Studies of Early Modern British Women Writers," *Teaching Tudor and Stuart Women Writers*, 357–72.

12. See Margaret J. M. Ezell's dismissal of an evolutionary model of female authorship, in *Writing Women's Literary History* (Baltimore: Johns Hopkins University Press, 1993), 21–24.

13. Wendy Wall, "Circulating Texts in Ealry Modern England," *Teaching Tudor and Stuart Women Writers*, 51.

14. *Renaissance Woman: A Sourcebook. Constructions of Femininity in England*, ed. Kate Aughterson (London: Routledge, 1995), 6.

15. Ashgate Press likewise has such a series of early women writers, titled "The Early Modern Englishwoman: A Facsimile Library of Essential Work: Printed Writings, 1500–1640" (general editors Betty S. Travitsky and Anne Lake Prescott).

16. For *Women Writers Online*, see www.wwp.brown.edu/wwp_home.html. The Perdita Project is producing a database guide to manuscripts compiled by women. Bibliographic records and links to bibliographical information about women writers can be accessed through *A Celebration of Women Writers* (digital.library.upenn.edu/women/), the *English Short Title Catalogue* (available through the Research Libraries Group and on microfilm), and *ITER* (http://iter.library.utoronto.ca/iter/index.htm).

17. On the book as material object, see Maureen Bell, "Introduction: The Material Text," *Reconstructing the Book: Literary Texts in Transmission*, ed. Maureen Bell et al. (Aldershot: Ashgate, 2001), 1–8, and the new series by the University of Pennsylvania Press, "Material Texts."

18. David Cressy, *Literacy and the Social Order: Reading and Writing in Tudor and Stuart England* (Cambridge: Cambridge University Press, 1980), tables 6.1–6.5. Keith Thomas, "The Meaning of Literacy in Early Modern England," *The Written Word: Literacy in Transition*, ed. Gerd Baumann (Oxford: Clarendon Press, 1986); Margaret W. Ferguson, "A Room Not Their Own: Renaissance Women as Readers and Writers," *The Comparative Perspective on Literature: Approaches to Theory and Practice*, ed. Clayton Koelb and Susan Noakes (Ithaca, N.Y.: Cornell University Press, 1988); and by Eve Rachele Sanders, *Gender and Literacy on Stage in Early Modern England* (Cambridge: Cambridge University Press, 1998).

19. Quoted in Margaret Ferguson, "Response: Attending to Literacy," *Attending to Women in Early Modern England*, ed. Betty Travitsky and Adele F. Seeff (Newark: University of Delaware Press, Associated University Presses, 1994), 273.

20. James Daybell, "Female Literacy and the Social Conventions of Women's Letter-Writing in England, 1540–1603," *Early Modern Women's Letter Writing, 1450–1700*, ed. James Daybell (Houndsmills: Palgrave, 2001): 72.

21. Frances Dolan, "Reading, Writing, and Other Crimes," *Feminist Readings of Early Modern Culture*, ed. Valerie Traub, M. Lindsay Kaplan, and Dympna Callaghan (Cambridge: Cambridge University Press, 1996); Jacqueline Pearson, "Women Reading, Reading Women," *Women and Literature in Britain, 1500–1700*, ed. Helen Wilcox (Cambridge: Cambridge University Press, 1996).

22. Suzanne W. Hull, *Chaste, Silent, and Obedient: English Books for Women, 1475–1640* (San Marino, Calif.: Huntington Library, 1988), 144–217.

23. See Heidi Brayman Hackel, "The Countess of Bridgewater's London Library," *Books and Readers in Early Modern England: Material Studies*, ed. Jennifer Andersen and Elizabeth Sauer (Philadelphia: University of Pennsylvania Press, 2002), 145. Brayman Hackel also observes: "Yet no marks of active readership survive in any of the Countess's books that I have located . . . It is not just Lady Bridgewater's seeming silence that puzzles me: in general, early modern women seem to have left very little marginalia—just one of the signs of active, engaged reading in the period."

24. Roger Chartier, "Reading Practices," *The Passions of the Renaissance*, ed. Roger Chartier (Cambridge, Mass.: Harvard University Press, 1989), 111–57. On women's reading groups, see Louise Schleiner, *Tudor and Stuart Women Writers* (Bloomington: Indiana University Press, 1994).

25. Anne Wentworth, *A Vindication of Anne Wentworth . . . preparing . . . all people for Her Larger Testimony* (1677), *Her own Life: Autobiographical Writings by Seventeenth-Century Englishwomen*, 193.

26. Barbara Kiefer Lewalski, "Writing Women and Reading the Renaissance," *Renaissance Quarterly* 44.4 (1991): 794–98.

27. Margaret J. M. Ezell, *Social Authorship and the Advent of Print* (Baltimore: Johns Hopkins University Press, 1999), 43–44; Ezell, *The Patriarch's Wife: Literary Evidence and the History of the Family* (Chapel Hill: University of

North Carolina Press, 1987); Harold Love, *Scribal Publication in Seventeenth-Century England* (Oxford: Clarendon Press, 1993); Arthur F. Marotti, *Manuscript, Print, and the English Renaissance Lyric* (Ithaca, N.Y.: Cornell University Press, 1995).

28. See Jean F. Preston and Laetitia Yeandle, *English Handwriting 1400–1650: An Introductory Manual* (Binghamton: Medieval & Renaissance Texts & Studies, 1992).

29. George Justice, "Introduction," *Women's Writing and the Circulation of Ideas: Manuscript Publication in England, 1550–1800*, ed. George L. Justice and Nathan Tinker (Cambridge: Cambridge University Press, 2002), 8. Of course, Margaret J. M. Ezell's scholarly contributions to this subject are unparalleled and invaluable. Her latest book, *Social Authorship and the Advent of Print*, demonstrates that practices of manuscript authorship coexisted with—and often dominated—literary culture in early modern England.

30. Dorothy Osborne, *The Letters of Dorothy Osborne to William Temple*, ed. G. C. Moore Smith (Oxford: Clarendon Press, 1928), 37.

31. Jacqueline Pearson, "Women Writers and Women Readers: The Case of Aemilia Lanier," *Voicing Women: Gender and Sexuality in Early Modern Writing*, ed. Kate Chedgzoy, Melanie Hansen, and Suzanne Trill (Pittsburgh, Pa.: Duquesne University Press, 1997): 45–54. For a study of female literary careers, particularly those of Anne Dowriche, Mary Sidney, Aemilia Lanyer, and Margaret Cavendish, see Susanne Woods, Margaret P. Hannay, Elaine Beilin, and Anne Shaver, "Renaissance Englishwomen and the Literary Career," *European Literary Careers: The Author from Antiquity to the Renaissance*, ed. Patrick Cheney and Frederick A. De Armas (Toronto: University of Toronto Press, 2003), 302–23.

32. Tina Krontiris, *Oppositional Voices: Women as Writers and Translators of Literature in the English Renaissance* (New York: Routledge, 1992), 17.

33. Dryden directed much of his criticism at contemporary female dramatists Aphra Behn and Margaret Cavendish. See John Dryden, *The Works of John Dryden*, ed. W. Scott, rev. G. Saintsbury, 18 vols. (Edinburgh, 1893), 18: 166.

34. On the communal nature of composition in the sixteenth century, see Wendy Wall, *The Imprint of Gender: Authorship and Publication in the English Renaissance* (Ithaca, N.Y.: Cornell University Press, 1993).

35. Leah S. Marcus, Janel Mueller, and Mary Beth Rose, "Preface," *Elizabeth I: Collected Works*, ed. Leah S. Marcus, Janel Mueller, and Mary Beth Rose (Chicago: University of Chicago Press, 2000).

36. On the collaboration between Isabella Whitney and her printer, Richard Johns, see Paul A. Marquis, "Oppositional Ideologies of Gender in Isabella Whitney's 'A Copy of a Letter,'" *Modern Language Review* 90 (1995): 314–24.

37. Quoted in Ezell, *Patriarch's Wife*, 86.

38. See Maureen Bell et al., "Women in the Book Trade," *A Bibliographical Dictionary of English Women Writers*, ed. Maureen Bell et al. (1990), 287–93.

39. David Norbrook recently discussed women's active participation in and intellectual contributions to the early modern public/political sphere in "Women, the Public Sphere, and the Republic of Letters in the Seventeenth Century," "When Is Public Sphere?" Modern Language Association Convention, New York, 2002.

CHAPTER 1

Legal Documents /
Women's Testimony

Records of secular and church court proceedings provide significant insights into the nature of social and political relationships, including the dynamics of the interpersonal conflicts and the communities created through participation in legal processes. The major role of the courts was to enforce consensus and maintain order through a system of communal discipline by publicly indicting and punishing those who violated the law. Ordinary people were involved in varying ways in litigation processes and in the administering of law. The place of women in the legal system has, however, only recently begun to receive attention.[1] With the notable exception of Elizabeth I, whose famous 1601 "Golden Speech" we feature here (also see chapter 5), women for the most part did not contribute to political policy and were excluded from public civil offices and barred from legal functions. Nevertheless, the involvement of single women in litigation and legal activities differed considerably from that of married women. While the former enjoyed property rights, the right to inherit legacies, and to conduct business affairs, married women under common law were required to leave legal affairs to their husbands. The English system of coverture, which identified husband and wife as one person for most civil matters and some criminal purposes, was responsible for many of the legal restrictions on women's agency.[2] Certainly women's participation as litigants or merely even as onlookers was restricted within the court system. Yet at the same time we can attempt to reconstruct the lives of early modern women by studying testimonies of and about women who made court appearances.[3]

A range of court systems enforced the different kinds of law in the nation. Law based on the king's conscience was administered by the Star Chamber in the Exchequer. Statute law was made in Parliament and administered by the court system. Among the different court systems, the Chancery was designed to make decisions case-by-case based on principles of equity rather than on a strict interpretation of common law. Canon law was established by the ecclesiastical courts, which in the seventeenth century became increasingly subsumed by the monarchical structures.[4] As ecclesiastical jurisdictions, the consistory courts handled cases dealing with private morality and complaints of sexual slander. Whereas civil courts usually litigated marriage suits in terms of remuneration for economic damages, consistory courts had wide authority concerning matrimonial matters, as the entries on the deposition of Margaret Christmas and the evidence against Joan Waters both illustrate.[5]

The printed history of the legal process is detailed in deposition books (*libri examinationum*). As records of the testimony of plaintiffs, defendants, and witnesses, deposition books offer rich sources of information about daily life in their accounts of matters at issue and inclusion of incidental information (see 1.5). Theoretically, depositions are verbatim transcriptions of responses by defendants and witnesses to questions asked and answered in private without the presence of the litigants or proctors. The accuracy of the printed records, however, remains indeterminable since it is impossible to discover whether witnesses in the suits were reliable or whether and how they altered the evidence. Characteristic of cases that came before the consistory courts, for example, witnesses who were present at the same time often gave very different testimonies. Legal accounts were shaped both by the questions put to the defendants and witnesses and by the scribe who translated their "narratives" for the court; testimonies were mediated by male clerks who inevitably altered them.[6] And women deponents participated in the art of testifying by censoring their words to conform with standards of female behavior. Nevertheless, evidence contained in the depositions could be presented with the expectation that it would be believed, and depositions do give us access to the representations of personal and social experiences of early modern lives, as entries throughout this chapter indicate.

The court system operated in terms of the politics of secrecy and revelation, that is, in accordance with the assumption that public—and often dramatized—exposures of deviant behavior could ultimately restore social order. Trials dealt in effect with the dangers of concealment.[7] The 1624 act to prevent the murdering of bastard children, for example, criminalized unmarried women even for hiding the birth of a stillborn child. This statute remained in place until 1803, the punishment for women convicted of infanticide being hanging. The examination of Anne Peace presents the trial of a single woman accused of infanticide in Billingley, Yorkshire, and examined by a justice of the peace for the North-Eastern Assizes circuit. The prosecution justified her conviction by citing her spinsterhood and her failure to publicize her pregnancy.

Women's legal status was interpreted in a variety of ways, depending on the type of law that was being applied. Among the various kinds of law in the early modern period was, first of all, natural law—that written by God on the conscience.[8] According to natural law, women were equal to men. However, the translation of this principle in the legal system often disadvantaged women, since both genders were then equally punished in matters of criminal law (though pregnant women and mothers of newborn children were often spared).[9] From a legal perspective, a person's identity was determined by position and property; and because women could for the most part only acquire either through their fathers or husbands, they were caught in a double bind. Under the common law, which was based on custom and precedent, marriage provided further opportunities for restricting women's legal rights. A married woman was not even considered to be a legal person but was instead her spouse's property. She was "of one flesh" with her husband (Gen. 2: 24), according to *Lawes resolutions of women's rights*, a celebrated first collection of English law affecting daughters, wives, and widows, which identified all women as "either married or to bee married."[10]

Early legal tracts, like theological, medical, and ethical treatises, reinforced the view of women's physical and mental inferiority.[11] Deviant and punishable behavior, labeled as "female" crime, included witchcraft and infanticide as well as scolding, suggesting that verbal violence committed by females was the equivalent to physical violence by males. Proper conduct was enforced in part through the documentation of women's crimes, and print thus served an increasingly significant role in regulating female activity. The account of the trial and execution of Elizabeth Abbot, as recorded in *The Apprehension, Arraignement, and execution of Elizabeth Abbot* (1608), is a case in point. Throughout the prevalently moralistic account, the author lists the various social ills, among them, Abbot's criminal act, that moved him to document the events of her trial and punishment. By contrast, William Dugdale's 1604 *A True Discourse Of the practises of Elizabeth Caldwell . . . on the parson of Master Thomas Caldwell* offers a rare example of a writer's ultimately unsuccessful defense of the personal and social character of a woman, who, like Elizabeth Abbot, is accused of murder. The murder of husbands by their wives appealed to the popular imagination. The anonymous play *Arden of Faversham* (c. 1591) is closely based on the trial of the conspirators, headed by Alice Arden, who murdered her husband almost fifty years beforehand. In another case involving a domestic murder, the indicted female, Leticia Wigington, allegedly presents her own defense. Yet *The Confession and Execution of Letitia Wigington of Ratclif . . . written by her own hand in the Goal of Newgate* (1681) was not authored by Wigington, but was "transcribed," "invented," "told to" an anonymous male writer who sold the pamphlet for profit as sensationalist prose, criminal histories being popular reading, especially if they seemed autobiographical.

The belief in the innate inferiority of the female sex ultimately prevented any great advances for early modern women, though it may be misleading to ignore some "evidence of a real improvement" in legal rights for women between 1400 and 1600 (Maclean 80). Laura Gowing demonstrates the ways in which women shaped both language and legal process to their own ends before tribunals where men's stories were accorded greater legitimacy and authority.[12] For example, the 1622 deposition featuring the defendant, William Windor, and his wife, Lady Elizabeth Vaux, presents the practical negotiations of a woman who resists patriarchal authority by reconstructing for the Star Chamber's audience the affray that led to their conviction.

Though gender became the determining factor in matters of title and property, Chancery developed the idea that a married woman could have separate property in addition to her dowry, and could act as the executor of another's will without the approval of her husband, something prohibited under the common law.[13] Certainly when women attempted to secure property rights in the courts, they were less successful than men. Still, generalizations based on common law practices and records are misleading, since girls were not universally disadvantaged by inheritance and wives did manage to retain property interests of their own, though the rights of the latter depended on their behavior in ways that the husbands' privileges did not. While, according to the common law, widows were to receive only one-third of their husband's property—which in most cases barely enabled their survival—Amy Erikson observes that the reality may have been different, that is, that widows enjoyed somewhat greater material well-being than historians have traditionally assumed.[14] Beginning in the reign of Henry VIII, women merely needed their husband's consent in order to write wills, and Mary Prior demonstrates that between 1558 and 1700, married women did make wills.[15] In this chapter we include an entry on Elizabeth Whipp who left a generous amount of money to relatives and friends in a will probated 17 February 1646. Except for male relatives and a godson, all of Whipp's beneficiaries were female.

While we continue to search public and private archives for the writings of women, we must also look for the stages and pages on which women appeared, and in turn reconstruct their stories insofar as that is possible. The legacies available to scholars of early modern literature and history in the form of legal sources produced by and about women provide revealing evidence of the nature of disciplinary jurisdiction and women's roles in the legal system, their positions within a patriarchal culture, their own sense of entitlement and struggle for rights, and even their personal histories. Such accounts also establish a broader and richer context for a range of writings featured in the following chapters of this book, writings including *The Lattre Examynacyon of Anne Askew* (1546), Ester Sowernam, *Ester hath hanged Haman* (1617), Mary Fane to Secretary of State Windebanke (6 May 1639), and Anna Trapnel, *The Cry of a Stone: Or a Revelation of Something Spoken in Whitehall* (1654). Moreover, legal writings by and about women's encounters with the law also illuminate a host of male-authored works like Shakespeare's *Measure for Measure*, *The Winter's Tale*, *A Midsummer Night's Dream*, *Much Ado About Nothing*, and *All's Well that Ends Well*. Ben Jonson also represented legalities, especially with contracts (*Epicoene*), the court of wards (*Bartholomew Fair*), and marriage contracts, which, when not carefully overseen by the bride's relatives, as in the case of *The Devil is an Ass*, fail to prevent a husband's misuse of his wife's dowry.

Notes

We gratefully acknowledge the assistance of Laura Gowing and Doreen Evenden.

1. Patricia Crawford, "'The Poorest She': Women and Citizenship in Early Modern England," *The Putney Debates of 1647: The Army, The Levellers, and the English State*, ed. Michael Mendle (Cambridge: Cambridge University Press, 2001), 197–218; C. B. Herrup, *The Common Peace: Participation and the Criminal Law in Seventeenth-Century England* (Cambridge: Cambridge University Press, 1987); *Women, Crime and the Courts in Early Modern England*, ed. Jenny Kermode and Garthine Walker (Chapel Hill: University of North Carolina Press, 1994); David Underdown, "The Taming of the Scold: The Enforcement of Patriarchal Authority in Early Modern England, *Order and Disorder in Early Modern England*, ed. Anthony Fletcher and John Stevenson (Cambridge: Cambridge University Press, 1985), 196–218.

2. Tim Stretton, *Women Waging Law in Elizabethan England* (Cambridge: Cambridge University Press, 1998), 129–35. This was also the subject of Patricia Crawford's "Women and Property: Women as Property," presented at "Women and Property in Early Modern England: An Interdisciplinary Colloquium," Australian National University, Canberra, Australia, 2000.

3. See, for example, Sara Heller Mendelson, "'To shift for a cloak': Disorderly Women in the Church Courts," *Women & History: Voices of Early Modern England*, ed. Valerie Frith (Concord, Ont.: Irwin, 1997).

4. Martin Ingram, *Church Courts, Sex, and Marriage in England, 1570–1640* (Cambridge: Cambridge University Press, 1987).

5. For catalogues on the range of early modern courts and the cases that came before each, see http://catalogue.pro.gov.uk.

6. Laura Gowing, *Domestic Dangers: Women, Words, and Sex in Early Modern London* (Oxford: Clarendon Press, 1996), 251. On legal narratives and the art of testifying in court as a form of storytelling, see Gowing, chap. 7, "Narratives of Litigation."

7. Allyson N. May, "'She at first denied it': Infanticide Trials at the Old Bailey," *Women & History: Voices of Early Modern England*, ed. Valerie Frith (Concord, Ont.: Irwin, 1997), 21.

8. Patricia Crawford and Sara Mendelson, *Women in Early Modern England 1550–1720* (Oxford: Clarendon Press, 1998), 36.

9. While women could "plead the belly," men could claim benefit of clergy.

10. T. E., *The Lawes Resolutions of Womens Rights* (London, 1632), 6. The original edition was titled [Sir John Dodderidge], *The Lavves Resolutions of Womens Rights; or, The Lavves Prouision for Women. A Methodicall Collection* (London, 1632). Editor's Note is signed "T.E." (Thomas Edgar?). The Preface, signed "I.L.", indicates that the material was "long since collected" and the author now deceased, suggesting Dodderidge as probable, posthumous author (ESTC R35396).

11. Ian Maclean, *The Renaissance Notion of Woman: A Study in the Fortunes of Scholasticism and Medical Science in European Intellectual Life* (Cambridge: Cambridge University Press, 1980), 68–81.

12. Laura Gowing, "Language, Power, and the Law: Women's Slander Litigation in Early Modern London," *Women, Crime and the Courts in Early Modern England*, ed. Jenny Kermode and Garthine Walker (Chapel Hill: University of North Carolina Press, 1994).

13. Maria Lynn Cioni, *Women and the Law in Elizabethan England with Particular Reference to the Court of Chancery* (New York: Garland, 1985).

14. Amy Louise Erickson, *Women and Property in Early Modern England* (London: Routledge, 1993).

15. Mary Prior, "Wives and Wills, 1558–1700," *English Rural Society, 1500–1800: Essays in Honour of Joan Thirsk*, ed. J. Chartres and D. Hey (Cambridge: Cambridge University Press, 1990), 201–25. Two sources that also cast some light on women as makers of wills are Susan Dwyer Amussen, *An Ordered Society* (Oxford: Basil Blackwell, 1988) and Philip Riden, ed., *Records and the Local Community* (Gloucester: Alan Sutton, 1985). Doreen Evenden, *The Midwives of Seventeenth-Century London* (Cambridge: Cambridge University Press, 2000) includes a number of seventeenth-century women's wills and inventories with appropriate commentary.

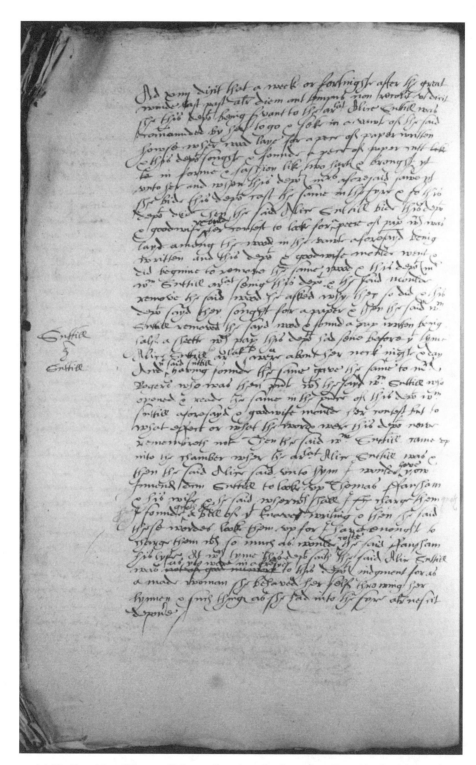

1.1: The Deposition of Margaret Christmas, Canterbury Consistory Court Deposition Book (1589-92).
By kind permission of the dean and chapter of Canterbury.

The Deposition of Margaret Christmas, "Suttill *contra* Suttill," Canterbury Consistory Court Deposition Book (1589–92)

Transcription

Ad xiiii [articulum] dicit that a week or fortnighte after the great winde last past aliter diem aut tempus non recolit ut dicit she this deponent being servant to the articulate Alice Suttill was commaunded by her to go & seke in a vawte of the said howse wher wood laye for a pece of paper written & this deponent soughte & founde a pece of paper cutt in forme & fashion like two hartes & brought yt unto her and when this deponentes mistress aforesaid sawe yt she bide [i.e., bid] this deponent cast the same in the fyre & so this deponent dide Then the said Alice Suttill bide this deponent & goodwife moulde her contestant to looke for a peece of paper which was layd among the wood in the vawte aforesayd being written and this deponent & goodwife moulde went & did beginne to remove the same wood & this deponentes master william Suttill articulate seing this deponent & the said moulde remove the said wood he asked why they so did & this deponent sayd they sought for a paper & then the said william Suttill removed the sayd wood & found a paper written being half a sheette which paper this deponent had sene before that tyme Alice Suttill articulate to weare about her neck night & day And the said suttill having founde the same gave the same to mistress Rogers who was then presente with the sayd william Suttill who opened & reade the same in the presence of this deponent william suttill aforesayd & goodwife moulde her contestant but to what effect or what the wordes were this deponent nowe remembreth not Then the said william Suttill came up into the chamber wher the articulate Alice Suttill was & then the said Alice said unto hym I woulde have yow Inuend dictum Suttill to looke up [i.e., lock up] Thomas Fansham & his wife & he said wherwith shall I charge them I founde quoth he a bill of that knave writing & then she said these wordes looke them up for I have enoughte to charge them with so much as woulde coste the said Fansham his lyfe At which tyme this deponent saith the said Alice Suttill was as yt were in a frensye to this deponentes judgment for as a made [i.e., mad] woman she behaved her self throwing her lynnen & such thinges as she had into the fyre aliter nescit deponere.

Commentary

In 1590 Alice Suttill's husband, William, sued for separation in the Consistory Court of Canterbury. Although William's formal charges are not recorded, Alice's oral responses are, and they reveal that she defended herself against accusations of committing adultery and practicing witchcraft. The principal witness in the case was the Suttills' former maidservant. Also testifying were a neighbor, the widow and doctor who cared for Alice during a period of emotional breakdown, and three agents of the High Commission of Canterbury (another court that came to be involved in the case).

One of William Suttill's first charges against his wife was that she took her mother and sister into their household against his wishes. Although Alice claims that her sister performed many of the chores of a maidservant, it may well have been that she sought female companionship and support. She seems otherwise to have been surrounded by abusive men—or so she deposes. She alleges that her husband "misused" her "both by words and by stripes," and, while she admits that she once locked him out of the house, she asserts that this was for "fear" of him. She depicts her stepfather, "Old Hopper," as encouraging the abuse. Her brother Henry Blackborne threatened to beat William for mistreating her, she says, but she displays fear even of this ally, whom she also describes as stealing a brass pot from her and boxing the ear of a maidservant. The advances of her purported lover were unwelcome, as Alice tells the story: Thomas Winterborne found her hanging up laundry in a cellar of the house, tried to kiss her, but was rebuffed when she protested, "Stand away, for my husband will see you." With respect to what appears to have been William's final charge, as with so many of the others, Alice admits to the circumstances that have been alleged but reinterprets her role in them. She confesses that she commissioned Thomas Fansham and his wife to make her a charm, but she calls that charm a token "to cause [her husband] to love her." When William concluded that the token had other, darker purposes, she declared that the Fanshams had "cozened" or deceived her, and she had them brought up before the High Commission on a charge of witchcraft.

Alice's maidservant Margaret Christmas, called to address William's allegations, spoke accordingly to Alice's behavior, which she depicts as shrewish, and not to William's conduct, even if it was abusive. Christmas tells how, when William threatened to take his goods and depart, rather than continue to board Alice's mother and sister, Alice "railed" that he spent twice as much on his whores as on her kinsmen's keep. (There is no evidence that this accusation had any substantive merit. Alice merely employed the inflammatory terms that were customary to express many sources of grievance in the period.) When Alice suspected Old Hopper of carrying "tales" about her, she rushed to strike him and was prevented only because William picked her up and carried her to another room. When William complained that Alice stayed out until nine or ten o'clock at night, Christmas recalls that Alice retorted "I will go when I list and come when I list." It was no use "to find fault with me," Christmas reports Alice saying to her husband, for "I am ordained to be a scourge and whip to plague and vex you withall." Christmas seems to have suspected that the accusations of adultery were true. She tells of a time when Alice sent her to Winterborne's house to procure twenty shillings, Winterborne referred her to a man named Ward, and, while Christmas was safely away at Ward's house, Winterborne came to Alice's. Christmas also has damaging things to say about the "love token." She recalls that Alice complained that William was still alive; Fansham had promised that he should be the next in the parish to die.

Neighbor Margaret Swift confirms that Alice referred to Fansham's promise in this manner, although she adds that Alice was very ill at the time. These were only a few of many "idle words." But both Swift and a later deponent, Jacob Fells, indicate that according to "common fame" in Canterbury (that is, general gossip), Alice's "love token" bore "crosses and invocations of Satan." John Hart heard Fansham say that Alice was so relentless in her demands for a charm against her husband's life that Fansham gave her a meaningless token merely to placate her. Fells further recalls a time when William Suttill asked Fansham directly if Alice "did desire any thing of you touching my life." Fansham refused to answer: "if I should say it did any way concern your life," he reportedly replied, "then it would also concern my life."

The page excerpted here from Margaret Christmas's testimony gives more details about her memories of the "token." Her deposition reveals the power of the recorded word even among—or especially among—illiterate men and women. William Suttill had to turn to the otherwise unidentified "Mistress Rogers" to read the words on the disputed charm, and elsewhere in the records Alice Suttill describes how she took a letter from her brother to a "Dr. Garret" to be read aloud. If John Hart's testimony is correct, then Fansham was little more than a petty con artist, exploiting Alice's illiteracy and credulity.

It is, unfortunately, impossible to know the truth of the story, as is characteristic of cases that came before the Consistory Court. Any two witnesses who were present at any one occasion often had two different tales to tell. Sometimes there was duplicity, sometimes contradiction, but sometimes it was simply a matter that each person remembered a different portion of an event or conversation. Alice's nurse, the widow Moulde, remembers—if Alice herself does not—that Alice told her husband that she had "defied" Fansham and "fell out into a rage" at his prediction of William's imminent death. A second way in which the Suttill case is representative of Consistory Court cases is that, although this is as close as documentary history allows us to get to the voices of Alice and Christmas and Moulde, the depositions are not direct transcriptions. The testimony is shaped both by the questions put to the deponents and by the scribes translating their narratives into legal form. Christmas, for example, probably did not call her former mistress "the articulate Alice Suttill"; this was a formula inserted to confirm identity legally. Third, as in so many such cases, there are hints of other persons and issues dimly seen at the fringes of the narrative that may have played larger roles than the record directly acknowledges. It is several times mentioned, for example, that Thomas Winterborne was the steward of the bishop of Dover, and it appears that Alice herself stayed at the bishop's house during her illness. Winterborne's connections open the story up to further networks of interested parties in what is otherwise depicted as a domestic dispute between two ill-matched people.

The Deposition Book in which these testimonies were recorded does not give the final disposition of the case. That survives in a companion volume known as the Instance Act Book. In a brief paragraph and in grammatically obscure Latin, it seems to be reported that William Suttill secured his separation. Neither William nor Alice would have been free to remarry, but they would no longer have been expected to cohabit. As an ecclesiastical court, the Consistory Court handled cases dealing with private morality, but complaints about broken betrothals were far more common than this rare instance of an authorized separation.

LENA COWEN ORLIN
UNIVERSITY OF MARYLAND BALTIMORE COUNTY

"Suttill *contra* Suttill," Canterbury Cathedral Archives and Library MS X.11.2, Consistory Court Deposition Book, 1589–92 and also 1591–92; MS Y.3.13, Instance Act Book, 1591–92.

HER MAIESTIES

moſt Princelie anſvvere,
deliuered by her ſelfe at the Court
at *VVhite-hall*, on the laſt day of Nouember 1601: When the Speaker of the Lower
Houſe of Parliament (aſſiſted with the greateſt part
of the Knights, and Burgeſſes) had preſented their
humble thanks for her free and gracious fauour,
in preuenting and reforming of ſundry grie-
uances, by abuſe of many Grants,
commonly called
Monopolies.

The ſame being taken verbatim *in writing*
by A.B. *as neere as he could poſſibly*
ſet it downe.

¶ Imprinted at London.

ANNO 1601.

1.2: Elizabeth I, "Her Majesties most Princelie answere" (30 November 1601).
By permission of the Folger Shakespeare Library.

Elizabeth I, "Her Majesties most Princelie answere" (1601)

Perhaps the most famous of Queen Elizabeth's speeches is the "Golden Speech," delivered at Whitehall to an assemblage of members of Parliament on 30 November 1601. Seen by some as the great summing up of Elizabeth's reign, this speech has often been republished.

One of the main items of business in the 1601 Parliament, convened on October 27, was the abuse of monopolies. There were several important constitutional issues at stake. The queen felt that any effort to regulate monopolies infringed on her royal prerogative, interfering with her right to award lucrative patents and monopolies to loyal subjects. Radical members of Parliament felt that if the queen failed to act, Parliament should pass a law banning such monopolies. A series of divisive committee meetings was held, and Parliament resorted to the tactic of withholding discussion on an all-important subsidy bill while the matter of monopolies was being debated. In a piece of clever timing, the queen then sent a message profusely thanking the deadlocked members for their "hasty and free. . . subsidy" (even though they had yet to read the subsidy bill) and announced that she would indeed reform the system of monopolies, for she had "never assented to grant anything that was *malum in se*." She issued a proclamation on 28 November ending certain monopolies, giving her subjects the right to seek compensation for unfair treatment under monopolies and forbidding her Privy Council from helping anyone gain a monopoly. Parliament was overjoyed and wished to thank her personally; the queen agreed to an audience. On 30 November, they crowded into the Council Chamber at Whitehall, where Elizabeth delivered a speech.

What she actually said is a matter of some conjecture, as four different versions of the speech survive. The title page reproduced here is from the official version, printed in December 1601, one of very few texts Elizabeth published in her lifetime. J. E. Neale argues that the text is "entirely the Queen's composition" and that it is unlikely that "A.B." (Anthony Blagrave, the only MP with those initials) or anyone else copied it down. Presumably the queen wanted to ensure an accurate text without seeming to engage in self-serving propaganda; this way of distancing herself from the published word reveals how Elizabeth tried to mold her public image without appearing to do so overtly.

There are significant differences between this official version and the so-called Parliamentary version, based on the diary of Hayward Townshed, a young lawyer and MP. Neale argues that the printed version "deservedly sank from memory under the leaden weight of its euphuistic artifice and obscurity." Frances Teague has helpfully outlined the differences as well as the similarities between these two versions. The official version is more concerned with the love Parliament and the people have shown her, whereas the Parliamentary version focuses more on Elizabeth's love for her subjects and Parliament. These multiple versions of the same speech offer us a rare chance to view the ways Elizabeth shaped her words for different audiences.

Nely Keinanen
University of Helsinki

Elizabeth I. *Golden Speech.* Folger Shakespeare Library STC 7578.

A
True Discourse
Of the practiſes of *Elizabeth Cald-*
well, Ma: *Ieffrey Bownd*, *Iſabell Hall* widdow,
and *George Fernely*, on the parſon of Ma: *Thomas*
Caldwell, in the County of Cheſter, to haue
murdered and poyſoned him, with
diuers others.

Together with her manner of godly life during her
impriſonment, her arrainement and execution, with
Iſabell Hall widdow; As alſo a briefe relation of Ma.
Ieffrey Bownd, who was the Aſſiſe before
preſt to death.

Laſtly, a moſt excellent exhortorie Letter, written by her own ſelfe
out of the priſon to her husband, to cauſe him to fall into conſidera-
tion of his ſinnes, &c. Seruing like wiſe for the vſe of euery
good Chriſtian. Beeing executed the
18. of Iune. 1603.

VVritten by one then preſent as witnes, their owne
Country-man, *Gilbert Dugdale.*
(⁞)

AT LONDON,
Printed by **Iames Roberts** for **Iohn Busbie**,
and are to be ſold at his ſhop vnder Saint Peters
Church in Cornewell. 1 6 o 4.

1.3: Elizabeth Caldwell, Letter from prison, *A True Discourse Of the practises of*
Elizabeth Caldwell (1604). Reproduced by permission of The Huntington Library,
San Marino, California.

Elizabeth Caldwell, Letter from prison, *A True Discourse Of the practises of Elizabeth Caldwell, master Jeffrey Bownd, Isabell Hall widdow, and George Fernely, on the parson of Master Thomas Caldwell, in the County of Chester, to have murdered and poysoned him, with divers others* (1604)

Elizabeth Caldwell's letter from prison is an unusual early modern document not only because Caldwell describes her actions in her own words, but because she defends herself as a victim of her husband's neglect, abuse, and "abominations." The letter's published context is also extraordinary: a popular crime pamphlet in which the author, Gilbert Dugdale, presents a sympathetic and partially exonerating account of a female murderer.

Murder pamphlets typically combined reports of shocking violence and illicit sex with outraged moral condemnation. To impose absolute closure on the varying personal circumstances of crimes, and to deflect impressions that writers were profiting from prurience and sensationalism, they also usually concluded with idealized accounts of the criminal's repentance and ghostwritten exhortations spoken from the scaffold. And indeed this is what the title page of *A True Discourse Of the Practises of Elizabeth Caldwell* would have led readers to expect. Its first section suggests that Caldwell's story will be a domestic murder conspiracy, reminiscent of infamous women such as Alice Arden and Anne Saunders, while its second and third sections anticipate Caldwell's becoming a public exemplum of piety. Together, these sections hint at a familiar pattern—the conversion narrative—in which the subject journeys from incremental sin and misconduct to disaster, followed by wonderful contrition. Conversion also becomes a main theme of the letter, but with a remarkable twist: Caldwell refashions herself as an agent of providential justice—"You see the judgements of God are already begun in your house"—who urges her reprobate husband "to turn unto the Lord."

Underpinning the crime pamphlet version of this commonplace genre were proverbial notions that one sin, unchecked, led inescapably to greater sins, and that "murder will out," that is, all-seeing providence will always uncover and revenge deadly crimes. Crime pamphlet writers normally sought to confirm an inescapable link between criminal justice and divine retribution. Such aims might have been expected in view of Dugdale's recent debut as a government apologist and patronage seeker in *The Time Triumphant* (1604), a flattering report of James's coronation pageants published immediately before *A True Discourse*.

Yet while Dugdale certainly condemns Caldwell's crimes and concludes his pamphlet with conventional speeches and prayers from her execution, his main account of Caldwell's attempted murder of her husband at the urging of her lover Jeffrey Bound and their accomplices, and of her new identity as spiritual counselor, is largely admiring and exculpatory. Acting as a kind of preliminary corroborating witness, he anticipates Caldwell's complaints in the letter of being an abandoned, sexually betrayed, and financially deprived wife victimized by Thomas Caldwell's dissolute behavior. The letter deploys a contrasting discourse of spiritual and social reform (e.g., sabbatarianism) to suggest alternative ethical and legal values that open up challenges to Caldwell's restricted rights as a married woman and to established jurisprudence. Such slippage hints at wider institutional and social conflicts between legal and moral equity that are an underlying theme in many early modern crime pamphlets.

Dugdale also refers twice on the title page to the fact that this was a provincial crime to which he is linked as both an eyewitness and a "countryman." Caldwell's case is complexly related to the local politics and legal culture of Caldwell's native Cheshire. Dugdale's dedicatory epistle is addressed to Lady Mary Cholmondeley (famously called the "bold lady of Cheshire" by King James) and twenty-seven other members of the county gentry—virtually the entire administrative and judicial elite of Cheshire. His dedication alludes to efforts made by Cholmondeley and others to obtain a royal pardon on Caldwell's behalf. Though they failed, Dugdale's published account validates their request and implicitly vindicates Caldwell from the official criminal charges.

Dugdale praises Caldwell's upbringing and status as a gentlewoman, attesting her to be a woman of excellent "credit" and personal character (traits echoed in a concluding dedication to Lady Mary Chandos by Robert Armin, Dugdale's kinsman and the volume's publisher). These factors were routinely given strong legal consideration by early modern courts in judging offenders; here they imply the attempted murder was an aberration (or as Caldwell puts it, "in his mercy [God] hath spared you") and that Elizabeth must have been extraordinarily abused by her disordered and socially inferior husband to have temporarily abandoned the social values of her class.

RANDALL MARTIN
UNIVERSITY OF NEW BRUNSWICK

Elizabeth Caldwell. Letter from prison. In Gilbert Dugdale, *A True Discourse Of the practises of Elizabeth Caldwell, Master Jeffrey Bownd, Isabell Hall widdow, and George Fernely, on the parson of Master Thomas Caldwell in the County of Chester, to have murdered and poysoned him, with divers others* (1604). Huntington Library 60571. Title page.

Woodcut of the execution of Elizabeth Abbott, *The Apprehension, Arraignment, and exe-*
cution of Elizabeth Abbot, alis Cebrooke, for a cruell amd horrible murther, committed on the
body of Mistris Killingworth in S. Creechurch parish neere Aldgate in London (1608)

Like many popular public events, executions were sometimes documented in ballads or
pamphlets. The anonymous *The Apprehension, Arraignement, and execution of Elizabeth*
Abbot, alias Cebrooke, for a cruell and horrible murther, committed on the body of Mistris
Killingworth in S. Creechurch Parish neere Aldgate in London (London, 1608) is in some
ways typical of such publications. The pamphlet provides a detailed account of Abbot's
victim, the thrice-widowed, alcoholic, inaptly named Mistress Killingworth, and of the
crime and its detection. The pamphlet stresses the "care and providence of our worthy
Justices" and employs a tone of moral superiority throughout. Even Abbot's gender is not
unusual: women's crimes were of particular interest as efforts to use print as a means to
control women's behavior intensified.

What sets Abbot's story apart from similar narratives is that she refused to admit her
guilt. Once convicted by the jury and sentenced to death by the judge, the accused was
expected to confess details of the crime. The official justification for this was the salvation
of the criminal's soul; a more practical reason was the need to salve the consciences of the
judge and jury in this preforensics age. Abbot was convicted on circumstantial evidence; it
was not even possible to produce a corpse. Bones were found in Mistress Killingworth's
fireplace that a surgeon determined were human; a neighbor found "a locke of
[Killingworth's] haire tide in her hairelace, and a stay which went under her chinne pinde
to it" behind some of the chimney bricks, and this was accepted as proof that the bones
belonged to Mistress Killingworth. But until Abbot's death, she "utterly denide to have
any knowledge with mistres Killingworth, or any acquaintance in the fault."

Shortly after Killingworth disappeared, Abbot was arrested for attempting to break
into a house near Nonesuch; the master of the house "pierst her in the arme" with a pitch-
fork. Abbot's husband escaped. Mistress Cox, "a substantiall woman, and of honest conversation" who lived in Killingworth's neighborhood, happened to be in a nearby inn, saw
Abbot, and thought she looked familiar. She had her brought to London, where other
neighbors of Mistress Killingworth identified Abbot as having performed various errands
for Killingworth shortly before her disappearance. One witness reported that Killingworth
claimed to have taken in a "stranger" whom she had "more reason to suspect than trust";
another heard Killingworth moaning the night of her disappearance but assumed she was,
as usual, drunk, and reported that Abbot had appeared at the window to confirm this.
Abbot was convicted on this evidence along with the report that, during Mistress Cox's
unofficial interrogation of her, she had replied "you goe about to entrap mee about the
woman that was burnt by Aldgate, but you are deceived in that in faith, as they that did it
were deceived of their expectation."

Abbot's steadfast denial of her guilt led to several unusual steps following her conviction. First, "she was called into the inner court, even to the barre where the foreman of the
jurie stood, that my lorde and the whole court might plainely heere what she could speake,
in her owne excuse, which was nothing but obstinacie the ground of all evil." Second, "they
sent into the prison unto her a reverend & grave doctor of divinitie, who with such strong
instances, beat against the dores of her harte, that had they not beene made of harder than
marble they had had power to have broke them open." Abbot still did not confess. Finally,

As also the Arraignment, Conuiction, and Execution of George
Larvis *Prieft after the order of Saint Benedils, both which*
suffered death on Munday the eleuenth
of April. 1 6 0 8.

Printed at London, for *Henry Goffon*, and are to be fold in
Paternofter-row, at the figne of the Sun. 1608.

1.4: Woodcut of the execution of Elizabeth Abbot, *The Apprehension, Arraignment, and execution of Elizabeth Abbot* (1608). By permission of The British Library.

she was brought to the scaffold, shown the "high erect gibbet," exhorted by the sheriffs "of their owne charitable disposition" to confess, and asked to look at Mistress Killingworth's house, which she could see from the scaffold, as "a remembrance to have her clense her soule." Yet Abbot "persisted in her deniall of being in any way guiltie of the fact, acquainted with the house, or knowne to Mistris Killingworth."

At this point, for reasons the pamphlet writer does not disclose, the lord mayor ordered Abbot to be removed from the scaffold and taken to a nearby church; "all those who gave evidence against her" were sent for and asked to "view her well" and repeat their testimony. All identified Abbot. Abbot was again warned to avoid going "with a charg'd soule, and smotherd sinnes to her grave," and asked not only to confess, but also to help the authorities locate her husband, who was still wanted in the Nonesuch robbery and who, they reasoned, might provide her with an alibi for the murder. Abbot again refused to confess, "by which it is evident," the pamphlet writer concludes, "the devill whom she served, had fully hardened her heart." It is perhaps not so evident to us whose heart was hardened; the pamphlet's final sentences reports, "So she was presently brought from the church againe, and there suffered Execution."

We do not have a first-person account for Abbot; as "a woman of loose life and base condition" she was probably illiterate. She is not the subject of a domestic tragedy, or even of a surviving ballad. But she clearly has a story to tell, one we must tease out from the moralizing of the pamphlet. The pamphlet writer begins with a long list of social ills that "hath made me find time to set pen to this discourse." Surely Abbot's own account of "The calamity of this age wherein we live, and the cruelty of us, who professe our selves Christians one to another" would be worth reading. While we continue to search public and private archives for the writing of early modern women, we must also look for places where illiterate women appear, and reconstruct their stories as best we can.

CATHERINE LOOMIS
UNIVERSITY OF NEW ORLEANS

Elizabeth Abbot. *The Apprehension, Arraignment, and execution of Elizabeth Abbot* (1608).
British Library 1471.R.20.

1.5: The Evidence against Joane Waters, London Consistory Court (1609/10). By permission of the London Metropolitan Archives and the Registrar, Consistory Court of London, Diocese of London.

The Evidence against Joane Waters, the Deposition of George Ireland, London Consistory Court (1609/10)

Transcription

were there, for that he was well acquainted with the said parties where he saith he sawe the said Joane Waters & John Newton together in verye loving & extraordinery kinde manner, making love & showing great kindenes ech to other by drincking one to another & kissing & embracing together very lovinglye [in so] and he verily beleeveth that the said Waters was then very much affected to him the said Newton in the way of marriage for that shee the said Waters did then with her lips sucke his the said Newtons necke in a manner of kindenes whereby shee made 3 red spottes arise wherupon the said Newton asking her what shee ment by it shee answering said that shee had marcked him for her owne. And after much kindenes & Confererence then & there passed betwixt them shee the said Waters requested him the said Newton to goe home with her saying that he shold be very welcome, which this deponent thincketh he did aliter nescit for that he this deponent then lefte their Company, then being present in their Company at the said taverne William duke, and the said Newtons sister besides the parties in sute and this deponent./

    Ad 3 articulum dicit quod nescit deponere./

    Ad 4 articulum deponit et dicit that upon the same day that the said meeting was at the signe of the Crowne and goat aforesaid ut supra deposuit & after that said meeting they the the said Newton & Waters about the evening of the said day mette againe together at the said taverne where the said Waters & Newton did showe great love & kindenes ech to other by kissing & kinde wordes ech to other, and saith that after sometime there spent they the said Newton & Waters together with this deponent & Gregory Saunders went to the said Waters house where they were kindely entertained especially the said Newton by the said

Commentary

The testimony of George Ireland, aged twenty-two, a gentleman from Gray's Inn, is part of the existing testimony from an early seventeenth-century lawsuit in which John Newton, a player and sharer of the duke of York's company, sued Joane Waters, a widow with a house and at least two servants of her own, for matrimonial enforcement in the early modern London Consistory Court. It is not unusual that Newton would sue Waters for the enforcement of a marital contract in this court. As an ecclesiastical court, it had wide jurisdiction concerning matrimonial matters, whereas civil courts usually litigated marriage suits in terms of remuneration for economic damages. Newton here tried to establish a valid marriage, which would force Waters to solemnize their vows and result in cohabitation.

    Ireland's testimony is from a deposition book (*Liber examinationum*) that records the testimony of plaintiffs, defendants, and witnesses and is a rich source of information about daily life, both for its full detail on matters at issue and for information in it given incidentally. Depositions are apparently verbatim transcriptions of responses by the witness to a series of questions, which were asked and answered in private without the presence of the litigants or proctors. It is impossible to discern whether witnesses in these suits are accurate, think they are accurate, or manipulate the evidence to affect the outcome of the case. Nonetheless, it is significant that the evidence contained in the depositions could be told in the expectation that it would be believed.

The affectionate behavior between Waters and Newton noted in the testimony served as contributing evidence of their consent to the contract. The manner in which, according to Ireland, Waters demonstrated her goodwill to Newton during their first meeting at the Crown and Goat is extraordinary in the depositions and in contemporary literary texts. That is, to give Newton "3 red spottes" or love bites in order to "marck him for her owne," she literally and symbolically marked his body as her territory, as her property. Peter Stallybrass comments on the long and widespread belief of considering the female body as property: "The conceptualization of woman as land or possession has, of course, a long history. . . . In early modern England, 'woman' was articulated as property not only in legal discourse . . . but also in economic and political discourse" (Stallybrass 127). Waters here reversed this ideology, since she put a boundary on Newton's body as her property, while she unenclosed her own. The accuracy of Ireland's account is impossible to determine; however, the unusual particularity with which he describes Waters's "marcking" strongly suggests that he gave an accurate account.

No sentence for the case remains in this series of records, but a parish register for St. James Clerkenwell indicates that "John Newton and Joan Walters wer maried by licence the 22 of August 1611" (London Metropolitan Archives, P76/JS1/2) While the register confirms the validity of the contract, the depositions from this case and others provide rich accounts of personal and social experiences of many early modern Londoners.

Loreen L. Giese
Ohio University

London Consistory Court Deposition. London Metropolitan Archives DL/C/219/418v.

The Star Chamber Deposition of Lady Elizabeth Vaux (1622)

Commentary

In January 1622 Elizabeth, Lady Vaux came to live in rooms rented by Robert Collins in the parish of St. Mary in the Strand in what is now London. Her "neare kinsman" Sir William Windsor and his wife, Marie, the Lady Nightingale, also lived in the same building, and Windsor being "desirous to have her to lodg neare unto him & his wife," arranged with Collins for Lady Vaux's "Lodging & beddings & furniture." Having been summoned to the lodgings after Vaux complained that arrangements were not as she had requested, Collins eventually arrived allegedly fresh from the tavern at 11:00 at night. The affray that ensued is colourfully but variably described, in a complaint lodged by Collins in the Star Chamber and in depositions provided by three of the seven defendants named in the complaint: Vaux, Windsor, and Thomas Gibbes (most likely a servant).

Vaux's deposition, from which this excerpt is taken, is of interest for a number of reasons. It is one of numerous documents—most of them legal—from which it is possible to reconstruct her life. Vaux, who would have been at least 59 in 1622, came from Sussex and Oxfordshire families with rescusant connections and first married William Wybarn (Shirley 296). Although there is no evidence that she herself ever had children, we know that her husband's orphaned nieces and nephew, William Windsor, lived with them at their home in Hawkswell, Sussex. The whole family (including a live-in priest) was cited for recusancy in 1592. Their home was searched and weapons were seized. William Wybarn was interrogated (Elizabeth was called but apparently did not testify), fined, and eventually excommunicated in 1600. Upon his death in the winter of 1612, Wybarn in his will made "liberal" provision for his "welbeloved wife," but Star Chamber and Chancery documents from later that year suggest that his widow was not to enjoy the lands and goods she inherited.

Most likely by August, Elizabeth had married Sir Ambrose Vaux, the third son of William, Lord Vaux of Harrowden, Northamptonshire. She thereby married into one of the most staunchly recusant families in England, a family that had been associated with the Gunpowder Plot in 1605. Her sister-in-law Elizabeth Roper Vaux was instrumental in maintaining and developing an underground Jesuit network in Jacobean England. Her new husband had been educated at the Jesuit college at Douay and knighted by the Franciscans in the Holy Land. However, copious extant materials, including legal documents and a satirical poem, also reveal that he was frequently in trouble with the law (imprisoned for debt and cited for destruction of private property and assault—including a bailiff) and not above the appropriation of a widow's inheritance, even when it was his own mother.

Apparently, when William Wybarn's executors (one of whom was Dudley Norton, former secretary to the earl of Salisbury and soon to be the chancellor of the exchequer for Ireland) learned of her marriage, they coerced her into signing over her inheritance to them and kept her away from her husband. When Ambrose Vaux learned that she was attending the Globe Theatre in their company on an August afternoon in 1612, he presented himself to them and demanded she come away with him. Supposedly because of "the great feare and perplexitie" Norton perceived she was in, Elizabeth was spirited off ("with force and in a ryotous manner," according to her husband) by Norton's servant. An

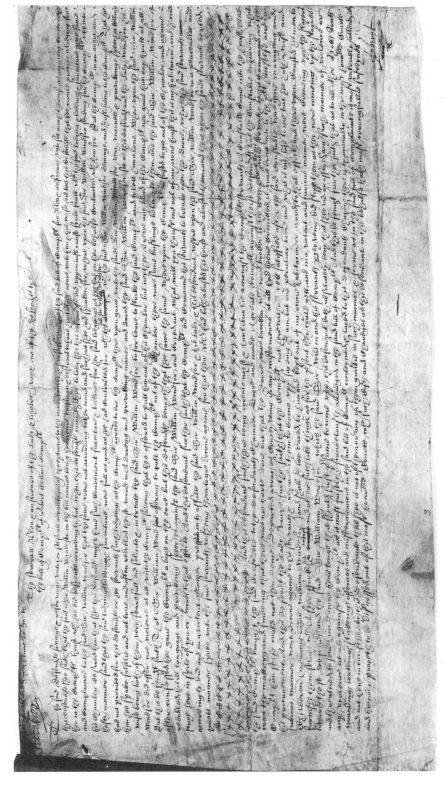

1.6: The Star Chamber Deposition of Lady Elizabeth Vaux (1622). The National Archives, London (formerly Public Record Office).

Transcription

The severall Plea & answeare of the Lady Elizabeth vaux one of the defendents to the bill of Complaint of Robert Collins Complainant

The said defendente savinge & reservinge unto her selfe all advantages of exceptions to the incertainty & insufficiency of the said bill of Complaint for Plea & answeare unto soe much thereof, as any way Concerneing this defendente shee saith that the said Sir William Windesor in the bill named being her neare kinsman & desirous to have her to lodg neare unto him & his wife, did tell this defendente that hee would provide a lodging for her in the Complainants house which hee did bespeake accordingly but when this defendente came thither to lodg shee this defendente did uppon just cause fynde fault with the said Lodging & beddings & furniture in the same and Complained to the said Sir William Windsor that the same were not according to her mind and such as shee had spoaken for, where upon the said Sir William Windsor sending for the Complainant upp into his Chamber desired him that shee this defendente might have such Convenient furniture & beddinge for her said lodgeings as hee had on her behalfe Contracted with him for. But the Complainante in an angry and hasty manner said that the said lodgings beddinges & furniture were full as good as hee had Contracted for with the said Sir William Wyndesor which the said Sir William Windsor deminge, and Justifieing to the Complainant That hee had not provided for this defendente or her servants such lodgeings as the Complainant agreed to doe the Complainant there upon gave unto the saide Sir William Windesor very uncivell & provokeinge speeches telling him hee spake falselie and not true, and often redobled theise words in A dareing and provokeing manner and dared the said Sir William Windsor soe as this defendent and the Lady Windsor his wife being both of them very fearefull did solicite & intreate the said Sir William Windsor to forbeare to strike the saide Complainant and to lett him alone. Where upon the said Sir William Windsor did offer noe violence at all unto the Complainant saveing that hee offered to putt him out of his Chamber but neyther drewe any blood of the Complainant nor gave him any hurte at all But this defendent saith That Sir William Windsor offering to putt the Complainant out of the Chamber there was some buslinge betwixte them and the said Sir William Windsor after confessed hee gave the Complainant a boxe on the eare but this defendente denyeth that shee sawe the same. Whereupon the Complainant refused to goe out of the Chamber, and againe redobled his ill language and provokeing speeches, against the said Sir William Windsor, and Cryed out what will you thrust me out of my owne house this is my habitacion, and I will staye here in spite of you or wordes to that effecte. And this defendant further saith that the Complainant did Comaund his servantes to breake open the doore, which the said servantes accordingly did and in a violent Manner pressed in to assalte the said Sir William Windsor & his Lady & this defendant where upon the said Sir William Windsor in a peaceable and quiett manner spoke unto the said servantes wisheing them to goe downe againe for that their Master had both abused his house and abused them and there upon the saide servantes departed xxx. . .xxx And this defendant saith there being a greate noyse & hurliburlie amongst the Complainantes servantes A Cunstable Came into the house, And the said Complainant brought the said Constable to the defendantes Chamber Doore and made A greate Complaint against theise Defendentes but the Constable enquiring what was the matter, and findeing that there was noe hurte done but that the doore was brooken which was broken by the Complainant & by his owne servantes & by his Comaund, as the Complainant him selfe could not then denye; departed away as Conceyveing if any mis-demeanor at all had beene Comitted it was done only by the plainant himselfe and by his procurement, And this defendent the Lady Vauxe furthe saith that the Complainant not herewithall yett satesfied after the said Constable was gone in a rageing and furious man-ner went downe againe to his servantes & required them to Come upp sayeing I am but one peculiar bodie and what is my life to me but hee hath a wife and Childeren (meaning Sir William Windesor) and shall I bee dared by him and kept out of my owne habitacion or wordes to that effect and there upon Caused his men to furnishe themselves with A fyer Forke spit & tongs and other such like thinges as for the present they could gett, and in a violent and furious manner were Comeing upp the stayers towardes these defendentes and the said Sir William Windesor which the said Sir William and his servantes perceyve-ing did stopp them as they were comeing up the stayres and threatned to send him downe headlonge that should first presume to come upp, this defendant doth absolutely deny that shee did or offered any such manner of violence or any vyolence at all against the Complainant as is most falsely & scandelously alleadged in the said bill of Complaint And this defendent further saith that as to all other Ryottes Routes woundinges beateinges strikeinges offences and misdeameanors in the said bill of Complaint conteyned & layed to this defendants Chardge there by examinably in this most honorable Courte and not therein confessed by this defendante that shee is not of them or any of them guiltie in such manner & forme as in the said bill of Complainte is most untruely alleadged and humbly prayeth to be dismissed out of this most honorable Courte with such Costs and Chardges as this defendant in this behalfe hath most wrongfullie susteyned

Amherst

---

affray ensued purportedly involving more than a dozen audience members "armed arraied and weaponed with Rapiars daggers Pystalls and other weapons as well defensive as offen-cive."

The affray in 1622, therefore, is the second such incident in which Lady Elizabeth Vaux played a central role. Although her agency makes her an instigating factor in both incidents, in 1612 she is virtually invisible and silent in her husband's complaint (mostly concerned with emphasizing the loss of her goods and leases) and the resulting deposi-tions. Despite the partially formulaic language of the deposition and the fact that we depend on a court official who would have recorded it, Vaux's 1622 statement appears to be her most direct opportunity to speak to us today in her own voice. She is clearly being asked to provide her own account of the events connected with the disturbance and to respond to Collins's charges of her participation in the "Ryottes Routes woundinges beat-einges strikeinges offences and misdeameanors." Taken within the context of the other 1622 Star Chamber documents, however, she provides a glimpse into the world of one woman whose voice we might not have otherwise heard if it had not been for her pro-clivity for litigious circumstances.

It is not possible to determine the truthfulness of her statement, although her denial of having seen the box on the ear to which Windsor had already confessed could be seen as placing her truthfulness in doubt. More important, however, is the sense of her voice that may be gained from her choice of descriptors (e.g., "buslinge," "hurliburlie") or the signs of independence and agency that qualify her self-characterization (consistent with that of Norton's 1612 deposition) as being "fearefull." Given her independence of mind in marrying Vaux in 1612, it is not surprising that she demonstrates an ability to insist on the domestic arrangements she had expected and to speak up in the midst of the affray. We are also left to wonder at her living arrangements with respect to her husband. Although Collins cites Ambrose Vaux as a defendant, none of the descriptions of the incident (including that of Collins) mention his involvement, and Windsor's deposition specifically indicates that only the two ladies and his servants were present. The depositions suggest that arrangements for accommodation were only for her and her servants.

More generally these 1622 documents provide a snapshot of an extended family arrangement and their domestic servants with dramatic characters worthy of theatrical parody: an allegedly drunken landlord marshaling his servants to break down a door in his own house; a knight dressed in his "pantables" and ready for bed, leaping onto his dining room table ready to draw in order to protect his "ladies"; a constable responding to the commotion only to find the landlord to be the chief perpetrator; and an undaunted land-lord organizing his maids to charge up the stairs with a fire fork and tongs.

MARY BLACKSTONE
UNIVERSITY OF REGINA

The Star Chamber Deposition of Lady Elizabeth Vaux. The National Archives, London (formerly Public Record Office) STAC 8/88/9.

1.7: The Information of Mary Hall, Westminster Sessions Roll (1626). By permission of London Metropolitan Archives.

The Information of Mary Hall, Westminster Sessions Roll (1626)

Transcription

Libertas Westmonasterii

The informacion of Mary Hall Spinster (against John Bankes and Jane his wife for keepinge a bawdie house) taken before Roger Bates Doctour in Divinitie &c 23°. Februarii 1625 [i.e. 1626 according to modern reckoning]. She saith, that Jane the wife of the said John Bankes is a bawde, in that she soulde this informantes maiden head twice vizt; First to one Master Freake whoe paid to the said Bankes his wife 10. peeces,[1] and gave her this informant xlvii shillings. The seacond tyme to one Master Waferer, whoe gave to Bankes his wife aforesaid vii peeces, and this Informant xxvii shillings she then lodginge in the said Bankes house. And further this informant saith that there is resorte of whores daylie to the said Bankes his house, and this daye there was in his house 7. whores whose names followe vizt [1. in margin] First Sara Waters livinge with her mother neere the 3. Tunnes at Ratcliffe (Jane Waters deceased sister of the said Sara lived in Bankes his house whose maidenhead was soulde 5. severall tymes by Bankes his wife, and this informant saith that the said Sara [sic, recte Jane] before her death meetinge with Bankes his daughter whose name was Fraunces (but nowe alsoe dead) said unto her hath your mother soulde your maiden heade, and she beinge a modest Civell maide tooke such greefe that she went home & shortlie after died; [2. in margin] The seaconde Elizabeth Ratcliffe lodginge at a brokerz[2] house neere Scroopes Court in Holborne. [3. in margin] The thirde Margaret Hammonde one Mistress Hammonds daughter dwellinge neere the White harte in the Stronde. [4. in margin] The 4th one Marye but where she lodgeth she knoweth not. [5. in margin] The 5th. Mary Etherington, whoe lodged latelie at the Windmill in the Stronde. [6. in margin] The 6. one Mistress Anne Edwardes a Ministers wife nowe lodginge at Bankes his house [7. in margin] The 7. one Elizabeth Hales whoe liveth with her mother in Cloth faire by Smithfeilde/

    <verso>

There is one Anne Cobbie a tawnie Moore that is often at the said Bankes his house and this informant saith she hath heard her and divers men report that they had rather give her a peece to lye with her then an other v shillings because of her softe skinne. And alsoe one Thomasine Greene hath frequented the said house much but nowe lies sicke of the pockes in Turne-ball streete and is almost consumed with them.

    [Signed] Roger Bates

Notes

    1. A "piece" was a gold coin worth at this time twenty-two shillings.

    2. The term "broker" had several meanings. Here it probably denotes someone who undertook to find places of employment for servants; such activities could easily double up with procurement to prostitution.

Commentary

Henry VIII closed down the licensed brothels known as the Southwark stews in 1546. But, of course, this by no means eliminated prostitution in and around London, which experienced phenomenal population growth in the later sixteenth and the seventeenth centuries. Ambassadors, courtiers, and merchants, with their servants and hangers-on, constituted an insistent market for sexual services, as also did a wide range of men of humbler status, including apprentices. While the authorities' efforts to stamp out sexual trade were doomed to failure, the records of policing activities provide a valuable supplement to references in contemporary drama and other literary accounts. The transcribed document is unusual in being an "information" brought by a woman against the keepers of a brothel or "bawdy house" in the parish of St. Clement Danes in Westminster, though the actual instigator of the prosecution appears to have been a Leicestershire clergyman, Clement Edwards, whose wife was "suspected to live incontinentlie" in the house. The statement was taken by a justice of the peace; it is sprinkled with legal phraseology, and its precise form was shaped to some extent by his questions and the words he chose to set down.

The account reflects a common means of organizing prostitution: the brothel keepers or "bawds"—in this case, a tailor and his wife—made available premises where sexual encounters could occur. The "whores" sometimes lodged there permanently, sometimes attended daily or as occasion warranted. Bawds took a substantial share of each woman's earnings. There were various means whereby young women were enticed or inveigled into the trade: the sexual services of newcomers commanded exceptionally high rates, and a bawd was not averse to selling a woman's "maidenhead" more than once, albeit at a diminishing price. Conventionally prostitutes—"common women" or "common whores," as they were called by contemporaries—were regarded as the antithesis of respectable or "civil" womanhood, for whom chastity was supposed to be so important that a woman who engaged in any form of sexual activity outside marriage, whether for money or not, was liable to be called "whore." The degree to which these values might be internalized by women is suggested by the account (whether true or not) of the girl who died of grief when it was implied that her maidenhead had been, or was about to be, sold by her mother. The attitude of the "tawny moor" appears to have been more robust. Yet the fate of Thomasine Greene reflects the dangers to which all women involved in this trade were subject from the sexually transmitted diseases that were rife in the metropolis.

Martin Ingram
Brasenose College, Oxford

London Metropolitan Archives, Westminster Sessions Roll, WJ/SR(NS) 15, no. 130; cf. nos. 24, 26, 71, 76, 104.

The Original Will of Elizabeth Whipp, Midwife (1645–46)

Commentary

Elizabeth Whipp, whose will was probated 17 February 1646 (new style), was a licensed midwife who resided in the parish of St. Ethelburga in London. Licensed midwives were a large and respected group of women whose important contribution to the lives of seventeenth-century London inhabitants has only recently been recognized. Elizabeth had been politically as well as professionally active in London, and her name appears on a petition to Parliament as one of two women (the other one was Hester Shaw) presenting a grievance against Peter Chamberlen, of the notorious Chamberlen family, who was attempting to gain control of the London midwives in 1633. Elizabeth was a widow who had borne nine children, but at the time of her death, only three daughters and one son survived.

Approximately the final third of Whipp's original will, written by a scribe on a large sheet of vellum, has been reproduced. After the customary proclamation of religious faith, she began listing her numerous bequests. Whipp left a number of small legacies amounting to more than £500—a substantial sum for the period—to relatives and friends. Aside from their cash bequests, she allocated to each of her sons-in-law and her son money for a new cloak for her funeral. Each of her three daughters and her daughter-in-law was to have a new mourning gown. Several friends and relatives were left sums of forty and twenty shillings for the purchase of mourning rings. While the practice of leaving a small sum of money for mourning rings was widespread, money designated for mourning garments was an indication of affluence and social prominence.

Whipp left each of her grandchildren small legacies, but she was particularly concerned about the well-being of the three orphaned children of her deceased daughter, Mrs. Jones. She stipulated that the two boys, James and John, and their sister, Elizabeth, were to live with the midwife's two married daughters and their legacies were to be administered by her sons-in law, Dr. George Shepheard and Waldegrave Sydey (Siday, Sidey, Syday), a prominent city merchant. It is significant that young Elizabeth's bequest was larger than her brothers' by one-third, indicating the midwife's sensitivity to the economic dependency experienced by young women of her time.

The section of the will that has been reproduced begins with a bequest regarding clothing. Elizabeth, like many female contemporaries, disposed of her colourful wardrobe by leaving cherished items to specific family members. To daughter Sara Sydey, she bequeathed a gown of watered taffeta (taffeta that had undergone a special process to give it a wavy look) with crimson satin petticoat trimmed with silver lace. Metallic laces containing gold and silver were sought after and costly trimmings, highly valued by those who could afford them in the early modern period. Earlier in the will, Whipp had left her damask gown and red petticoat with gold lace trim to daughter Anne Shepheard.

Whipp left small bequests to several of her own female servants, as well as to one female servant and two male servants at the home of her daughter Sara Sydey, with whom she was apparently living, possibly as a result of declining health.

Elizabeth carefully divided her ample supply of linen, leaving each of her three married children both everyday bed and table coverings, possibly made from unbleached flax or linen, and fine linens made of high-quality linen manufactured in the Netherlands. Her

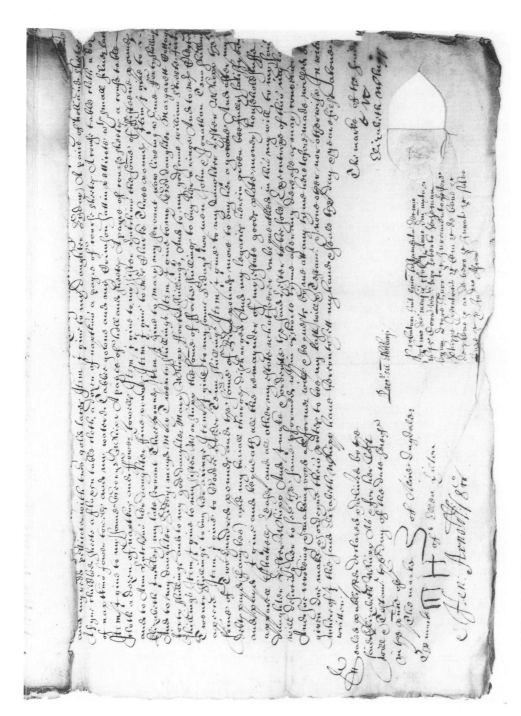

1.8: The Original Will of Elizabeth Whipp, Midwife (1645/6). By permission of the Corporation of the City of London Guildhall Library.

Transcription

and my redd petticote with two gold laces Item I give to my daughter Siday A paire of holland sheetes A fyne childbed sheete a flaxen table cloth, a dozen of naptkins a payre of course sheetes A course table cloth a dozen of naptkins fower towells and my waterd Tabbee gowne and my Crimson sattin petticote with small silver laces Item I give to my sonne George Whipp A payre of holland sheetes A payre of course sheetes a course table-cloth a dozen of naptkins and Fower Towells Item I give to my sister Hutchins the somme of Fifteene pounds and to Ann Hutchins her daughter Five pounds Item I give to mrs Clarke Three pounds Item I give to Elizabeth Inchley my late [former] servant Three pounds Item I give to Mary my servant now liveing with me Forty shillings And to My daughter Siday's mayd Mary Twenty shillings Item I give to my God daughter Margarett Cottage Forty shillings and to my god daughter Mary Whipp Fortie shillings, And to my godsonne william Streete Forty shillings Item I give to my sister Worshipp the somme of Fortie shillings to buy her a ringe and to mrs Cleyton Twenty shillings to buy her a ringe Item I give to my sonne [in-law] Sidays two men John & Jonathan Tenn shillings apeece Item I give to Goodee [goodwife] Holder Tenn shillings Item I give to my daughter Hester Whipp the some of Two hundred pounds and the some of six pounds more to buy her a gowne And after my debts payd (if any bee) and my buriall charges discharged And my legacies herein given bee fully satisfyed and payd I give and bequeath all the remaynder of my estate goods [silver] plate money household stuffe apparell Chattells Leases and all other my estate whatsoever unbequeathed in this my will, to my said daugh-ter Hester Whipp And I make & ordeyne the said Hester to bee sole Executrixe of this my last will desireing her to see the same performed within as shorte tyme after my decease as may convenien . . . And soe revokeing & makeing voyd all former wills & bequests by me att any tyme heretofore made willed or given doe make & ordeyne their presentes to bee my last will & Testament & none other nor otherwise In witness whereof I the said Elizabeth Whipp have hereunto sett my hand & seale the day & yeare first above written.

Sealed published declared & delivered by the said Elizabeth Whipp As & for her last will &

Testament the day of the date hereof in the presence of   The marke of the said
The marke of Alice Dugdale and Ellen Linton   Elizabeth Whipp
Henry Arnold Scrivener   (Mark where she placed her seal)
Parish of St. Ethelburga
[translation:] This will was probated 26 February 1645 in the presence of Robert Wyseman, Doctor of Laws, surrogate, by Hester Whipp, executrix, under oath.

two daughters were each given "a fyne childbed sheet." Traditionally, this "best" linen would be put on the bed after delivery to prepare the lying-in woman to receive relatives and friends. Although men's wills occasionally disposed of articles of furniture or the con-tents of a favorite room, women's wills frequently included bequests of linens, thereby demonstrating their awareness of the importance of a well-stocked linen cupboard to modest as well as more wealthy households.

Elizabeth's unmarried daughter, Hester, was the main beneficiary of her mother's estate. She received £200 in cash and, after the funeral charges, debts, and legacies were paid, she was to have the rest of the household contents and any other possessions (including leases). Despite the availability of several well-educated and prominent male family members, Hester was also to be the executor of her mother's estate. It is also noteworthy that, except for male relatives and a godson, all of Whipp's beneficiaries were female.

One of the most rewarding aspects of a will of this type is the connection it enables the historian to make. In this case, the name of Sara Sydey provided evidence of a matrilineal link in the training of midwives. Sara Sydey, Elizabeth Whipp's daughter, was also licensed as a midwife later in the century.

DOREEN EVENDEN
MOUNT SAINT VINCENT UNIVERSITY

The Original Will of Elizabeth Whipp. Guildhall Library, Corporation of London MS 9052/13.

The Examination of Anne Peace, Yorkshire Sessions (1659)

Commentary

Anne Peace was accused of infanticide in the Yorkshire town of Billingley in March 1659 (1600 by the modern calendar) and examined by a justice of the peace for the North-Eastern Assizes circuit. Under the infanticide statute of 1624, the facts of her spinsterhood and her failure to make public her pregnancy were damning evidence of an intent to murder her child.

Most women accused of infanticide were domestic servants; Anne Peace lived alone and made her own living. One of her neighbors, John Hill, informed that she had "for a long time last past lived a very suspicious and lewd life," and eventually his complaint to a justice of the peace provoked a search. Two married women, along with Hill, the constable, and other neighbors went to her house, where the searchers "drew" her breasts, and found fresh milk, certain evidence of recent childbirth. Under their questioning she admitted having given birth a month earlier; after a search, the child's body was eventually found in her house.

Anne Peace's examination echoes and rewrites her earlier confession to the searchers. After they drew her breasts, she cried and told them she had passed from her body a thing "like a gristle," but "what it was she could not tell." By the time she told the story again, the next day, to a magistrate, the "thing" had become a child that she knew she was carrying. What also emerges in the second telling is the significance of where, and how, the child's body got hidden. Originally Peace told the searchers she had left the body at the well where she had given birth; later, she told the magistrate that she had put the body into a bush, returning three days later to take it home, where she put it under a tub and covered it with earth. It was not an uncommon maneuver in her situation.

Both the words and the content of the examination are structured by legal norms. Phrases like "last past" and "the said" would be provided by the magistrate or clerk who recorded the examination; the admission of sex with only one man, once, initiated by him, is typical of illegitimacy confessions. But this text also departs from convention, notably in its description of birth and pregnancy. Few seventeenth-century women left any kind of testimony about such experiences; single women were especially likely to be excluded from public discussion of reproductive affairs. Anne Peace's description of "very much pain" is unusual for an infanticide examination; her shifting story of pregnancy, from an experience that she did not understand, to a knowledge that the child had not yet quickened, suggests a process of grasping, and learning to narrate, the experience of pregnancy and birth in an exceptionally traumatic context.

Although further documentation on Anne Peace's trial has not been traced, the relative leniency of seventeenth-century justice toward infanticide means she was likely to have escaped conviction. The man she named as father claimed to have had no dealings with her, and that he "did ever hate her company."

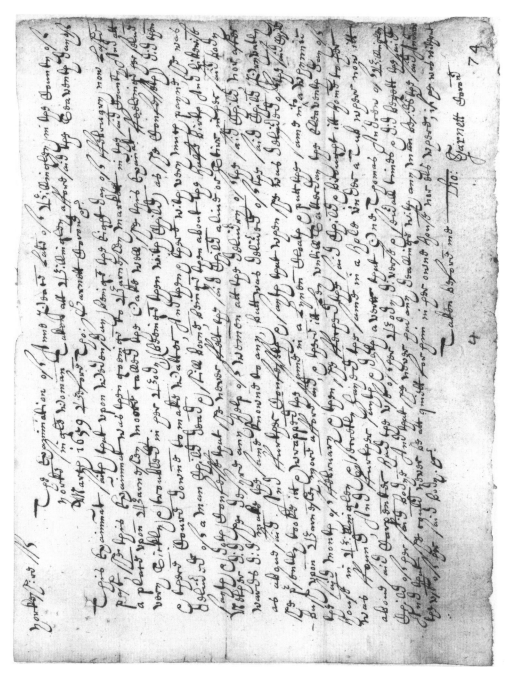

1.9: The Examination of Anne Peace, Yorkshire Sessions (1659). The National Archives, London (formerly Public Record Office)

Transcription

Yorkeshire sessions

The Examination of Anne Peace late of Billingley in the County of Yorke single woman Taken att Billingley afforesaid the Seaventh day of March 1659 Before Thomas Garnett Coroner &c.

This Examinate saith that upon Wedensday beinge the Eight day of February now Laste past, she this Examinate was then goeinge to Barnesley markett in the said County, And att a place upon Barnesley moore called the Oake well, she this Examinate Feelinge her selve very Sickly & troubled in her Body, (beeinge then with Child) as she Confesseth did then & there Coure downe to make Watter, And then & there with very much payne, she was delivered of a man Child dead & still borne, beinge then about the halfe birth And likewise sayth and doth Confesse that she never Felt the said Child alive or Stirr in her said body Nether did she desyre any help of wemmen att the delivery of the said Child, nor afterwards did make the same knowne to any, butt was delivered of her said Child Pryvatly as abovesaid. And further Confesseth & sayth that when she was delivered of the said Child she presently tooke itt & wrapped the same in a Lynen Cloath & put the same into a whynnie-bush upon Barnesley More afforesaid, & there itt Ley untill Satterday the Eleaventh day of the said month of February & then she Feched the said Child & brought itt home to her house in Billingley and secretly layed the same in a hole under a Tub, where now itt was Found, And Further sayth and doth averr that one Thomas Andrew of Billingley abovesaid Carpenter had the use of her Body diverse & severall times & did begett the said Child of her said bodye And that she never had any deallinge with any man besides the said Andrew And that she could never be att quiett for him in her owne house nor els where, if he was without the use of her said body &c.

    Taken before me Thomas Garnett Coroner

LAURA GOWING
KING'S COLLEGE, LONDON

The Examination of Anne Peace, Yorkshire Sessions (1659). The National Archives, London (formerly Public Record Office) ASSI 45 5/7/73.

CONFESSION and EXECUTION

OF

Leticia Wigington

Of Ratclif, who suffered at

TYBURN,

On *Fryday*, the 9 h. of this inftant *September*, 1681, written
by her own hand in the Goal of *Newgate*, two days before her death, being Condemned for whiping her
Apprentice Girl to Death.

We are fully fatisfied, that the following Paper was written by this unhappy womans own hand, a while before her Death, and though at her Tryal for this
horrid Fact, the Evidence againft her, was full, clear and undeniable, yea
which is more, though fhe was then fo ingenious to confefs her felf really guilty thereof, having lain fo many Months in *Newgate*, we have very great reafon
to judg fhe has been too well acquainted with that curfed crew of Popifh Priefts
and Jefuites, who it is to be feared have debauched her with their own damna-
ble Principles, whereby they have perfwaded her to deny what fhe before had
fo fully confeffed, which fhe does in the very words of thofe Jefuites who lately
defervedly fuffered for Treafon againft his Majefty, &c. who though they were
Tried and condemned (as well well as her felf) upon the cleareft Evidence
imaginable, yet *Atheiftically* even with their laft Breath affirmed, *That they were
as innocent as the Child unborn.*

   Micah the 7th Chap. and 8 v. Verfes.

Rejoyce not againft me, O mine Enemy: when I fall, I fhall arife; when
I fit in darknefs, the Lord fhall be a Light unto me.

   I will bear the Indignation of the Lord, becaufe I have finned againft
him, until he plead my caufe, and execute judgment for me: he will bring
me forth to the Light, and I fhall behold his Righteoufnefs.

THis place of Scripture I made choice of, as being fomewhat pertinent to
the bufinefs, and troubles and afflictions that are inflicted on me,
wherefore upon my bended Knees I humbly defire all you that have
been my loving Neighbours and Friends, and all other good Chriftians, that
have heard of this horrid and dreadful misfortune that hath befallen me, and
you that fhall read thefe doleful Lines, let pity move your hearts to read them,
and you that have had any hand in taking away my Life wrongfully, I pray
God forgive you all; but let me admonifh you not to abufe the dead by giving
out your cruel fpeeches by me, as you have done in my Life-time (that never did
you any harm) firft to Imprifon me wrongfully, and that not fatisfying, but to
prompt on one, that was my Apprentice, *Rebecka Clifford* by Name, who was not
full 12 years of age, to fwear againft me, fhe not being fenfible of the danger
of taking a falfe Oath, fo that you have ufed me at your pleafure. I fpeak to
you all, Rich and Poor, great and fmall, that have had any hand in my Death,
whoever you are, for you cannot be ignorant of the great evil you have done me,
(a poor friendlefs Creature) for you have made it your bufinefs to take away
my life, who am as innocent as concerning the Murder for which I fuffer as the
Child unborn: but why fhould I reflect upon my Innocence, and the abufes put up-

A   on

1.10: Leticia Wigington, *The Confession and Execution of Letitia Wigington of Ratclif* (1681).
Reproduced by permission of The Huntington Library, San Marino, California.

Leticia Wigington, *The Confession and Execution of Letitia Wigington of Ratclif, who suf-fered at Tyburn, on Fryday the 9th of this instant September, 1681, written by her own hand in the Gaol of Newgate two days be-fore her death, being Condemned for whiping her Apprentice Girl to Death* (1681)

On 9 September 1681, Leticia Wigington of Ratcliffe was hanged at Tyburn for her part in the beating-death of an unnamed thirteen-year-old apprentice the previous Christmas season and for which she was sentenced at trial in February 1680–81. Her alleged accom-plice, a household lodger named John Sadler, was convicted of the same crime on 26 February 1680/1, and it was largely his testimony combined with the eyewitness account (subsequently recanted) of another young apprentice named Rebecka Cliffard that led to the conviction of Wigington. The "Inhuman Barbarity" of the girl's murder made the case a public sensation in 1681, and Sadler's testimony was featured prominently in the titles and pages of two Tyburn news pamphlets (see *Tryal and Condemnation*; and *Last Dying Speeches*, which identifies the victim as Elizabeth Holton). Six months later, Wigington's execution prompted the publication of her lengthy *Confession*, a detailed account of the crime "written by her own hand in the Goal of Newgate two days before her death" (1), which contradicts much of Sadler's testimony and from which this excerpt is taken.

Deserted by her husband and with three small children to feed, Wigington was by all accounts forced by financial hardship to take in a lodger and two apprentices. When the older apprentice was caught pilfering linen from the house on Christmas Eve 1680, Sadler claims that he and Wigington set out to correct the girl by tying her up, stripping her, and whipping her with a cat-o'-nine-tails. Things got out of hand: the girl cried out, Wigington stopped her mouth with a cloth so as not to alert the neighbours, and the beat-ing continued for several hours—during which time the two rubbed salt into the girl's bleeding wounds. She died of her injuries three days later. In her account, Wigington denied participating in the torture of the girl, saying instead that she "came up when he was beating the Girl, and asked him, What he did?" (*Confession* p. 3). Wigington also claimed that she refused Sadler's offer of a "Crape Mourning Suit" and money to pay for a coffin in exchange for testimony that the mutilated girl had died of natural causes (p. 3). Even the local "Searchers" (i.e., female coroners), who were friends with Sadler, offered to confirm a falsified version of events, but Wigington cried out for neighbours to arrest Sadler. They delayed, allowing him to make a daring escape out a second-story window, so she was arrested and charged in his stead. Sadler was eventually arrested and confessed to the crime, but he implicated Wigington as "*the woman [who] had been a great Instrument to prompt him on to wickedness . . . the cause he had committed so foul a* Murther" (*Last Dying Speeches* p. 2). He was hanged 4 March 1680/1.

While in Newgate, Wigington learned that the prime witness against her (Cliffard) had recanted her testimony, so she falsely "pleaded the belly" in order to buy time and peti-tion for a retrial. This was a common strategy, as approximately 40 to 50 percent of women convicted of felonies during the period falsely claimed to be pregnant (Oldham 10–11). Unfortunately, Wigington's plan backfired. Her execution was stayed to wait for the birth, but during this time she claims that "Ballads and Books [were published] upon me after I was brought to Newgate; and raised great scandal and ignominy" (*Confession* p. 4), per-suading her remaining supporters that she and Sadler were lovers and that the unborn child was his: "people have been very cruel to us in giving out such gross Lies of me, as to say, that I lay with John Sadler, and that I was a Whore to others before; and upon no other grounds, but only by reason I did plead my Belly" (p. 3). The ensuing "scandal" jeopardized her chance to get a retrial; for example, when she wrote to her wayward husband for help, many of her letters were intercepted. When she did finally reach him, he was so angry at being made a cuckold that he refused any money to help with her reprieve, "so that [her] Life as to this World was lost through the Treachery of unkind Friends" (p. 4). When after eight months no baby appeared, she was duly hanged.

As Frances Dolan has demonstrated, postmortem printed confessions by women simultaneously constituted women as subjects and undermined this same subjectivity because of the fact that their words were often filtered and their voices mediated by men (158–61). The unnamed editors of Wigington's account insist that it "was written by this unhappy woman's own hand," and her choice of biblical references, in particular, reveals the subtle thinking and genuine frustration of a woman wrongly accused of adultery and murder. On the surface, the epigraph from Micah 7:7–9 seems an apt meditation for someone languishing in the squalor of Newgate prison because of its images of light and darkness, of judgment and release. Yet Wigington admonishes readers, "let pity move your hearts to read them [i.e., the words]," as if there were some hidden or additional meaning contained in the surrounding scriptures. And there is. Readers who looked up the context for Micah's lament would discover a moving portrait of a person falsely accused by a corrupt society. For instance, before the passage cited by Wigington, we find such lines as "Trust not in a friend, put ye not confidence in a guide . . . a man's enemies are the men of his own house" (7:5–6). And Micah concludes the passage with a bitter curse that seems particularly relevant to a woman who may have been as betrayed by women (e.g., her two apprentices, her neighbors, the local searchers) as she was victimized by men (her husband, her lodger, her judges and keepers): "Then she that is mine enemy shall see it, and shame shall cover her which said unto me, Where is the LORD thy God? mine eyes shall behold her: now shall she be trodden down as the mire of the streets" (Micah 7:10). Because the conventions of scaffold speeches and criminal confessions require explicit contrition and repentance, Wigington may have felt pressured to perform a kind of self-censorship, to couch her bitter indictment of personal betrayal and social injustice in more palatable Christian platitudes to slip it past her keepers and the watchful eyes of printers of true-crime ephemera. As Dolan points out, confessions tended to transform sinners into exemplars of virtue (169–70); but by refusing to play along and confess to the specific crime of murder, Wigington's *Confession* may voice her innocence precisely by using words left unsaid.

PHILIP D. COLLINGTON
NIAGARA UNIVERSITY

Wigington, Leticia. *The Confession and Execution of Leticia Wigington of Ratclif, who suffered at Tyburn, on Fryday the 9th of this instant September, 1681. written by her own hand in the Goal of Newgate, two days be-fore her death, being Condemned for whiping her Apprentice Girl to Death.* London [1681]. Early English Books, 1641–1700, microfilm reel 950:32; also available on-line at the Women Writers Resource Project, <http://chaucer.library.emory.edu/cgi- bin/sgml2html/wwrp.pl>. Huntington Library RB 133524 (WING 2110). Title page.

Bibliography

Adair, Richard. *Courtship, Illegitimacy and Marriage in Early Modern England.* Manchester: Manchester University Press, 1996.

Amussen, Susan Dwyer. *An Ordered Society: Gender and Class in early modern England.* Oxford: Basil Blackwell, 1988.

Archer, Ian W. *The Pursuit of Stability: Social Relations in Elizabethan London.* Cambridge: Cambridge University Press, 1991. ch. 6.

Bennett, Judith M., and Amy M. Froide. *Singlewomen in the European Past, 1250–1800.* Philadelphia: University of Pennsylvania Press, 1999.

Crawford, Patricia. "Sexual knowledge in England, 1500–1750. Ed. Roy Porter and Mikulas Teich. *Sexual Knowledge, Sexual Science. The History of Attitudes to Sexuality.* Cambridge: Cambridge University Press, 1994. 82–106.

Dolan, Frances E. "'Gentlemen, I have one more thing to say': Women on Scaffolds in England, 1563–1680." *Modern Philology* 92 (1994–95): 157–78.

Emmison, F. G. *Elizabethan Life: Morals and the Church Courts.* Chelmsford: Essex County Council, 1973.

Erickson, Amy. *Women and Property in Early Modern England.* London: Routledge, 1993.

Evenden, Doreen. *The Midwives of Seventeenth Century London.* New York and London: Cambridge University Press, 2000.

Faller, Lincoln B. *Turned to Account: The Forms and Functions of Criminal Biography in Late Seventeenth- and Early Eighteenth-Century England.* Cambridge: Cambridge University Press, 1987.

Fletcher, Anthony. *Gender, Sex and Subordination in England 1500–1800.* New Haven, Conn.: Yale University Press, 1995.

Giese, Loreen L. *London Consistory Court Depositions, 1586–1611: List and Indexes.* London: London Record Society, 1995.

Gowing, Laura. *Domestic Dangers: Women, Words, and Sex in Early Modern London.* Oxford: Clarendon Press, 1996.

———. "Secret births and infanticide in seventeenth-century England." *Past and Present* 156 (1997): 87–115.

Griffiths, Paul. "The Structure of Prostitution in Elizabethan London." *Continuity and Change* 8 (1993): 39–63.

———. *Youth and Authority: Formative Experiences in England 1560–1640.* Oxford: Clarendon Press, 1996.

Harding, Christopher, et al. *Imprisonment in England and Wales: A Concise History.* London: Croom Helm, 1985.

Houlbrooke, Ralph. *Church Courts and the People During the English Reformation, 1520–1570.* Oxford: Oxford University Press, 1979.

Ingram, Martin. *Church Courst, Sex and Marriage in England, 1570–1640.* Cambridge: Cambridge University Press, 1987.

Kane, Stuart. "Wives with Knives: Early Modern Murder Ballads and the Transgressive Commodity." *Criticism* 38 (1996): 219–37.

The Last Dying Speeches And Confessions of the Three Notorious Malefactors who were Executed at Tyburn, on the 4th. of this Instant March, 1681. London: Printed for T. B., 1681. [Wing L482A, on *Early English Books, 1641–1700*, microfilm reel 1339:29].

Neale, J. E. *Elizabeth and Her Parliaments: 1584–1601.* New York: St. Martin's Press, 1958.

O'Hara, Diana. *Courtship and Constraint: Rethinking the Making of Marriage in Tudor England.* Manchester: Manchester University Press, 2000.

Oldham, James C. "On Pleading the Belly: A History of the Jury of Matrons." *Criminal Justice History* 6 (1985): 1–64.

Riden, Philip, ed. *Probate Records and the Local Community.* Gloucester:Alan Sutton, 1985.

Sharpe, J. A. "Domestic Homicide in Early Modern England." *Historical Journal* 24 (1981): 29–48.

———. "'Last Dying Speeches': Religion, Ideology and Public Execution in Seventeenth-Century England." *Past and Present* 107 (May 1985): 144–67.

Shirley, Evelyn Philip. *Stemmata Shirleiana; or, The Annals of the Shirley Family.* 2nd ed. Westminster: Nichols, 1873.

Stallybrass, Peter. "Patriarchal Territories: The Body Enclosed." *Rewriting the Renaissance: The Discourses of Sexual Difference in Early Modern Europe.* Ed. Margaret W. Ferguson, Maureen Quilligan, and Nancy J. Vickers. Chicago: University of Chicago Press, 1986: 123–42.

Stavreva, Kirilka. "Scaffolds unto Prints: Executing the Insubordinate Wife in the Ballad Trade of Early Modern England." *Journal of Popular Culture* 31.1 (Summer 1997): 177–88.

Stretton, Tim. *Women Waging Law in Elizabethan England.* Cambridge: Cambridge University Press, 1998.

Teague, Frances. "Queen Elizabeth in Her Speeches." *Gloriana's Face: Women, Public and Private, in the English Renaissance.* Ed. S.P. Cerasano and Marion Wynne-Davies. New York: Harvestor, 1992. 63–78.

Thomas, J. E. *House of Care: Prisons and Prisoners in England 1500–1800.* Nottingham: University of Nottingham Department of Adult Education, 1988.

The Tryal and Condemnation of Several notorious Malefactors, at a Sessions of Oyer and Terminer which began at the Sessions House in the Old Baily, With the Names of those who received Sentence of Death, Burnt in the Hand, Transported, and to be Whipt. London: Printed for T. Davies, 1681. [Wing T2147A, on Early English Books, 1641–1700, microfilm reel 2046:38].

Todd, Barbara J. "The Remarrying Widow: A Stereotype Reconsidered." *Women in English Society 1500–1800.* Ed. Mary Prior. Cambridge: Cambridge University Press, 1985.

Wilson, Katharin M. *Women Writers of the Renaissance and Reformation.* Athens: University of Georgia Press, 1987.

Wrightson, Keith. "Infanticide in earlier seventeenth-century England." *Local Population Studies* 15 (1975): 10–22.

CHAPTER 2

The Status of Women

The status of "woman" at the beginning of the sixteenth century was determined by assumptions about women's inferior social status, domestic roles, and limited potential. Yet such factors as the rise in the number of court cases instigated by women and the Humanists' recommendations for educating women to be intelligent companions to men and helpers in the family business (as record-keepers, for example) suggest a concern about women's extra-domestic roles. An increasing amount of criticism of and even resistance to the gender hierarchy ignited the controversy about women, and informed emerging debates about women's education and participation in intellectual circles.

The Humanist program, which flourished in England in the first half of the sixteenth century and continued to influence English culture thereafter, was an educational and philosophical movement that emphasized classical learning and a civic education, and produced among the most important texts on women of the time. Informed by Christian values, the Northern Humanism associated with Juan Luis Vives, Thomas Elyot, and Thomas More connected traditional notions of female piety with biblical conceptions of the woman's role and encouraged women's learning. Influential works like Richard Hyrde's English translation of Vives's *De institutione feminae Christianae* (1524) called the *Instruction of a Christen Woman* (c. 1529)—the most popular conduct book for women in the Tudor period[1]; Vives's *De ratione studii puerilis* (*On a Plan of Study for Children* [1624]), in which Vives recommends, among other writings, those of Plato, More, and Erasmus; Elyot's *The Govenour* (1531) and *The Defence of Good Women* (1540); and Roger Ascham's *The Schoolmaster* (1570) acknowledged women's ability to learn and even recognized the value of an education for the female gender, but nevertheless maintained that education must be designed to remind women of their traditional, subservient roles. While submission to parental authority shaped educational practice even at boys' schools of the day, a much more restricted program was reserved for girls to ensure that they would conform to established modes of behavior.[2]

The Controversy about Women

The term "Renaissance" fails to account for the experiences of early modern women, whose status became an even more contested matter during the reign of James I, when strict measures were introduced to curtail female activities that challenged entrenched gender roles. Early modern English print culture reinforced assumptions about the immutability of identity and gender distinctions, and characterized self-transformation as illegitimate, monstrous, and threatening to hierarchical social and political order. Fears of male disempowerment, often represented as effeminacy and as female unruliness, led preachers, authors of conduct and advice books, and writers in general to create stereo-types that fixed gender categories and bolstered the ideology of female inferiority. Philosophical, political, medical, legal, and religious discourses represented women, including women writers, in terms of the weaker vessel, an image intended to essentialize gender distinctions. The hermaphrodite or "mannish woman" and the mother of monstrosity were among the labels affixed to females who violated their "natural roles" by transgressing the boundaries of the private sphere.[3]

Various explanations have been offered for the development of such portraits: a growing number of questions about the true differences between men and women, a backlash against female expression—including participation in print culture—as well as a defense against the threat of political, social, and economic changes. Reactions to unauthorized female activity included an increased surveillance of women, one focused on the three interconnected areas by which women were defined (and thus confined); Peter Stallybrass identifies these spaces as the womb, the mouth, and the home. The reading, inspection, and policing of these three spaces—through enforcement of laws and codes of behavior outlined in conduct books and through a "rigorous program of 'education'"—ensured that they would not become wild, unruly zones, and that women, though denied access to the political sphere, would be subject to the same scrutiny traditionally reserved for the public male figure.[4]

A specific group of early controversialist works contributed significantly to the arguments on the nature of women and their roles. Formal controversialist works were modeled on the defense, meaning that they were intended to generate and sustain debate and were addressed to an opponent—as often hypothetical as not—whose arguments were invoked and contested. The works relied on exempla from the classical and scriptural traditions in particular. Henry Cornelius Agrippa and Baldassare Castiglione enabled the genre's migration into England.

The genre known as the "controversy about women"—as the formalist controversy is more commonly called—usually took the form of written orations, dialogues, or structured responses, though in some cases, the counter-arguments presented in these works did not take issue with any particular text.[5] The polemical pamphlet *Jane Anger Her Protection for Women* (1589)—the first *likely* female-authored defense of women published in English[6]—answers an antiwoman text no longer extant, while I. G.'s *An Apologie for Women-Kinde* (1605) and Lodowick Lloyd's *The Choyce of Jewels* (1607) participate in the emerging formalist controversy without responding to any specific text. In the next decade, Barnabe Rich, William Goddard, Arthur Newman, and Christopher Newstead facilitated the development of the genre through their various treatises. Rich's *The*

Excellencie of good women (1613) offers an unconvincing defense of women that frequently lapses into misogyny. Goddard's *A Satirycall Dialogue Or a Sharplye invective conference, betweene Allexander the great, and that truelye woman-hater Diogynes* (1616) employs the conventional dialogue form but gives the upper hand to the attacker. Newman's *Pleasures Vision . . . A Short Dialogue of a Woman's Properties, betweene an old Man and a Young* (1619) dramatizes the debate over the nature of women, beginning with Eve; but this time the exchange, in which an aged misogynist and a youthful male defender of womankind participate, is more balanced. Newstead's 1620 *Apology for Women; or, Womens Defence* takes the side of women by attacking misogynistic jokes and exposing their malicious effects.

Questions about whether and how the attacks, defenses, and apologies that make up the formal controversy respond to other texts complicates the process of interpretation. Another debate arises about the tone of some of the texts, particularly those that take the form of a game or jest. Should they be read as serious attacks on women? Can antifeminist comments that are conveyed "in jest" actually affect social attitudes towards women? Christopher Newstead seemed to think so.

Any interpretation of Joseph Swetnam's *The Araignment of Lewde, idle, froward and unconstant women: Or the vanitie of them, choose you whether* (1616) must also bring such debates to the forefront. This work, originally published anonymously, ignited the early-seventeenth-century controversy about the nature and status of womankind (*Querelle des Femmes*).[7] By 1634, *The Araignment* had gone through ten editions. This misogynistic, highly derivative text announces its innocent intention to hurt no one; and yet Swetnam anticipates a counterattack: "Let them censure of me what they will, for I mean not to make them my Judges, and if they shoot their spite at me, they may hit themselves."[8]

Among the five responses generated by Swetnam's *Araignment* were three direct rebuttals, all printed in 1617: Rachel Speght's *A Mouzell for Melastomus* (A Muzzle for the Black-Mouth), Ester Sowernam's *Ester hath hang'd Haman*, and Constantia Munda's *The Worming of a madde Dogge*. Whereas Rachel Speght was an actual woman, as suggested in part by the hostile marginalia of a male contemporary who left his imprint on her work, Munda and Sowernam were likely men who responded to Swetnam for the sake of publicity and sales.[9] The recent revelation about the gender of these authors invites a reassessment of the defenses that Sowernam and Munda include in their pamphlets about the dangers of women venturing into print. A critical reading of *Ester hath hang'd Haman* and *The Worming of a madde Dogge* provides insights into the authors' efforts at self-representation and at resisting stereotypical gender roles. And yet contemporary readers should not ignore the possibility that these and other writings produced in the tradition of the controversy about women may have been male-authored rhetorical exercises or commissioned works designed to boost sales.[10]

The respondents to *The Araignment* engage not only Swetnam but also the received tradition of misogyny, and contemporary seventeenth-century cultural constructions of women as innately inferior, ignorant, or evil. To a certain degree, Humanism and the promotion of spiritual self-sufficiency by the Reformation movement and by Catholic women, who in the absence of priests and other advisers relied on their own resources, challenged the assumption that learning would derange "weaker female minds." Yet entrenched patriarchal attitudes and now print culture bestowed a long life on Swetnam's *Araignment* and its premises, while ultimately determining the demise of the early-seventeenth-century responses.[11] Though the rebuttals to Swetnam establish a "foundation[] for a women's critique of culture," conceptions of women's inferior status were not in fact effectively rebuked until the mid- and later seventeenth century by women like Margaret Cavendish, Duchess of Newcastle, and Mary Astell, who exhibited attributes traditionally associated with the "Renaissance man."[12]

Education and Philosophy

While contemporary male writings tended to emphasize the dominant role of the father or husband even in the domestic sphere, women nevertheless played an important part in the household as educators of their children and servants.[13] For example, Grace, Lady Mildmay—who makes a number of appearances in this book as the author of "The Autobiography of Grace Lady Mildmay" and as the mother of Mary Fane—lived for two years with her grandchildren during which time she contributed significantly to the education of Rachel Fane, as Fane's notebooks reveal. Mildmay's spiritual autobiography, which she bequeathed to her grandchildren in 1623, indicates her concern for her granddaughters' education. At the same time, it promotes the cultivation of feminine virtues of chastity, modesty, and silence, recommended to women by female and male writers alike.

Many girls who were taught literacy skills learned to read but not necessarily to write since handwriting seemed to present more difficulty.[14] At the same time, a male-dominated culture held fast to the assumption that while reading would expose women to the ideas of classical and Christian models of proper female conduct, writing might distract them from their duties or even offer a medium for independent thought. Richard Mulcaster, the first headmaster of the largest London grammar school, the Merchant Taylors, composed *Positions [concerning] the Training Up of Children* (1581), in which he states that reading is meant to remind women of their religious beliefs while not "hindering their housewifery."

Mulcaster objects to training women to write, even if such instruction be strictly regulated, unless the women's skills contributed to their husbands' material advantage.[15] Reservations about women writing find expression as well in the imaginative literature of the day, including city-comedies in which playwrights portray women who possessed such abilities as lewd and unchaste. In *Westward Ho!* by Thomas Dekker and John Webster, the citizens' wives' efforts at handling the pen become the basis for sexualized jokes. Their tutor remarks about Mistress Honeysuckle: "I trust ere few daies bee at an end to have her fal to her joyning: for she has her letters *ad unguem*: her A. her great B. and her great C. . . . hir double F. of a good length, but that it straddels a little to wyde . . . her O of a reasonable size."[16] Indeed, the women use their new writing skills to arrange amorous assignations but finally refuse to act upon the male expectation of fornication. Instead, they turn the tables and test their suspicious husbands' fidelity. The playwrights seem both to encourage and to repudiate assumptions about women and their ability to write, equivocating on the issue of women's right to education. Thus the "philosophical" meditations of sixteenth-century female poets like Isabella Whitney (also see chapter 8) or even the discovery of a work like "Verses made by a Maid under 14" is noteworthy because each offers, though in different ways, evidence of an education that extended beyond domestic prescriptions.

Yet the education and educational materials available to women tended to be restricted to books that reinforced their inferior social position: Protestant religious works, prayer-books, and marriage and conduct manuals, most of which were male-authored and intended to keep women "chaste, silent, and obedient."[17] Women sharing in the advantages of education was untenable not only because reading and writing would distract them from household duties but also because such an education might alter their view of their place in society. Still, even Anna Maria van Schurman, the best-educated woman of her day, denied that possibility: "the pursuit of letters does not involve any interference with public affairs."[18]

Van Schurman produced a treatise on women's education that grew out of her correspondence with contemporary theologians and scholars. In this Latin treatise, translated into English in 1659 as *The Learned Maid; or, Whether a Maid may be a Scholar?*, van Schurman explains why Lady Jane Grey's (1537–54) love of learning has particular resonance for her. Lady Jane Grey serves as a fitting example of the value of female education in the context of van Schurman's larger argument; by maintaining that the study of languages and scripture will increase women's love of God, Schurman develops creative strategies for avoiding the double binds of female authorship.

While even the advocates of women maintained that girls and boys should receive a different education, some reformers did argue for more intellectual and religious content in girls' schools. This is the basis for Bathsua Makin's *An Essay to Revive the Antient Education of Gentlewomen* (1673), appended to a prospectus for her school near London. Makin's *Essay* advanced arguments in van Schurman's *The Learned Maid*, and it catalogues classical and biblical women through to Makin's own time, including Elizabeth I and Margaret Cavendish, as well as those whom Makin had instructed: Charles I's daughter, the Princess Elizabeth, and Lucy Hastings, the Countess of Huntingdon.[19]

Shortly after the appearance of Makin's *Essay*, Mary More produced "The Womans Right, or Her Power in Greater Equality to Her Husband" (c. 1680), a manuscript treatise that anticipates later polemical writers such as Mary Astell, author of *A Serious Proposal to the Ladies* (1694, 1697), and Judith Drake, author of *An Essay in Defence of the Female Sex* (1696), by criticizing parents' neglect of their daughters' education. Were girls to be educated, More contends, "I doubt not but they would as much excel men in that as they do now in Virtue." Along the same lines, Mary Astell, who expresses her regret that convents were no longer an option for single women, strongly urges an education for women as a means to combat the moral and spiritual degeneration she perceived in her society. Margaret Cavendish, however, had already considered and repudiated that idea in her 1668 play, *The Convent of Pleasure* (chapter 9).

As well as containing writings that denounce and promote female education, this section includes various philosophical texts that exhibit the workings of the educated woman's mind. These comprise books by Margaret Cavendish, which exemplify the author's strategic use of the self-representation of natural genius to negotiate constraints against women's publication and to establish her legitimacy as a writer and thinker. Another playwright who, like Cavendish, also wrote and published philosophical commentaries—a highly unconventional undertaking for a woman in this period—was Catharine Trotter.[20] Trotter's printed letter addressed to John Locke, which prefaces her first published philosophical piece, *A Defence of the Essay of Human Understanding, Written by Mr. Lock . . . in answer to some Remarks on that Essay* (1702), concludes this section.

What constitutes a feminist critique in an early modern context, especially in the face of humanist and patriarchal Christian traditions and a male-dominated culture of print? A study of the formal controversy texts, educational writings, and philosophy invites us to ask such a question and to discover a host of intriguing responses. Finally, in addition to their own historical and cultural value, female-authored defenses and educational and philosophical writings merit close examination because their themes and arguments were transferred to other genres, including ballads, prose fiction, drama, and poetry.

Notes

We are grateful for the assistance of Nely Keinanen, Sarah Hutton, and Caroline Bowden. See Caroline Bowden, "Parental attitudes towards the education of girls in late sixteenth and early seventeenth-century England," *Education and Cultural Transmission*, ed. Richard Aldrich, Jeroen Dekker, Frank Simon, and Johan Sturm, *Paedagogica Historica*, Supplementary Series Vol. 2, Gent 1996. Also see Caroline Bowden, "Female education in the late sixteenth and early seventeenth centuries in England and Wales: a study of attitudes and practice," Institute of Education, London University, Ph.D., 1996.

1. On the popularity of *De institutione* in early modern Europe, see *Juan Luis Vives, The Education of a Christian Woman: A Sixteenth-Century Manual*, ed. and trans. Charles Fantazzi (Chicago: University of Chicago Press, 2000), 30–35.

2. Hilda L. Smith, "Humanist Education and the Renaissance Concept of Woman," *Women and Literature in Britain, 1500–1700*, ed. Helen Wilcox (Cambridge: Cambridge University Press, 1996), 9–29.

3. See Sandra Clark, "*Hic Mulier, Haec Vir*, and the Controversy over Masculine Women," *Studies in Philology* 82 (1985): 157–83.

4. Peter Stallybrass, "Patriarchal Territories: The Body Enclosed," *Rewriting the Renaissance: The Discourses of Sexual Difference in Early Modern Europe*, ed. Margaret W. Ferguson, Maureen Quilligan, and Nancy J. Vickers (Chicago: University of Chicago Press, 1986), 126.

5. See Linda Woodbridge's groundbreaking study on this subject in *Women of the English Renaissance: Literature and the Nature of Womankind, 1540–1640* (Chicago: University of Chicago Press, 1984).

6. See Danielle Clarke, *The Politics of Early Modern Women's Writing* (Harlow: Longman, 2001), 54; Barbara K. Lewalski, *Writing Women in Jacobean England* (Cambridge: Harvard University Press, 1993), 153–75.

7. See Elissa B. Weaver, "Gender," *A Companion to the Worlds of the Renaissance*, ed. Guido Ruggiero (Oxford: Blackwell, 2002), 197–201.

8. Joseph Swetnam's *The Araignment of Lewde, idle, froward, and unconstant women: Or the vanitie of them, choose you whether* (1616), *Half Humankind: Contexts and Texts of the Controversy about Women in England, 1540–1640*, ed. Katherine Usher Henderson and Barbara F. McManus (Urbana: University of Illinois Press, 1985), 193.

9. Barbara K. Lewalski, "Female Text, Male Reader Response: Contemporary Marginalia in Rachel Speght's *A Mouzell for Melastomus*," *Representing Women in Renaissance England*, ed. Claude J. Summers and Ted-Larry Pebworth (Columbia: University of Missouri Press, 1997), 136–62.

10. Diane Purkiss, "Material Girls: The Seventeenth-Century Woman Debate," *Women, Texts, and Histories, 1575–1760*, ed. Clare Brant and Diane Purkiss (London: Routledge, 1992), 69–101.

11. For a bibliography of works on the Renaissance debate about women, see Merry E. Wiesner, *Women and Gender in Early Modern Europe* (Cambridge: Cambridge University Press, 1993), 36–37. Aemilia Lanyer's poem, *Salve Deus Rex Judaeorum* (1611), is, according to Suzanne Trill, "an intervention in the controversy debate about the nature of 'women'" (Trill, "Religion and the Construction of Femininity," *Women and Literature in Britain, 1500–1700*, ed. Helen Wilcox [Cambridge: Cambridge University Press, 1996], 42).

12. Simon Shepherd, "Introduction," *The Women's Sharp Revenge*, ed. Simon Shepherd (London: Fourth Estate, 1985), 13.

13. See Kenneth Charlton, "Women and Education," *A Companion to Early Modern Women's Writing*, ed. Anita Pacheco (Oxford: Blackwell, 2002), 14–18.

14. This distinction complicates the attempt to establish literacy rates since the ability to sign one's name is the usual measure of literacy. On girls' formal schooling, see Josephine Kamm, *Hope Deferred: Girls' Education in English History* (London: Methuen, 1965). On the question of literacy and the methodology used to determine literacy rates, see "Reading Women's Literary History" in this book.

15. Richard Mulcaster, *Positions [concerning] the Training Up of Children* (1581), quoted in Nigel Wheale, *Writing and Society: Literacy, Print and Politics in Britain 1590–1660* (New York: Routledge, 1999), 52.

16. Thomas Dekker and John Webster, *Westward Ho!* (London, 1607), 2.1.

17. See Suzanne Hull, *Chaste, Silent and Obedient: English Books for Women 1475–1640* (San Marino: Huntington Library, 1982).

18. Anna Maria van Schurman, "Letter to Dr. Rivet," quoted in Una Birch, *Anna van Schurman: Artist, Scholar, Saint* (London: Longman, 1909), 70.

19. On female teachers, see Sara Mendelson and Patricia Crawford, *Women in Early Modern England 1550–1720* (Oxford: Clarendon Press, 1998), 321–26. In Lucy Hastings's Financial Papers are the payments to Mrs. Makins in 1662 for teaching Theophilus (Huntington Library, Hastings Financial Papers, Box 18, folder 32; with thanks to Caroline Bowden for this reference).

20. Cavendish's and Trotter's plays are featured in chapter 9.

for Women.

loue faith) that which is bꝛed in the bone, will not be bꝛought out of the fleſh. If we cloath our ſelues in ſackcloth, and truſſe vp our haire in diſhclouts, Venerians will neuertheles purſue their paſtime. If we hide our bꝛeaſtes, it muſt be with leather, foꝛ no cloath can kéep their long nailes out of our boſomes.

We haue rowling eies, and they railing tongues: our eies cauſe thē to lok laſciuiouſly, & why? becauſe they are geuen to lecherie. It is an eaſie matter to finde a ſtaffe to beate a Dog, and a burnt finger giueth ſound counſel. If men would as well imbꝛace counſel as they can giue it, Socrates rule wold be better follewed. But let Socrates, heauen and earth ſay what they wil, Mans face is worth a glaſſe of diſſembling water: and therfoꝛe to conclude with a pꝛouerbe, Write euer, and yet neuer write ynough of mans falſhoode, I meane thoſe that vſe it. I would that ancient wꝛiters would as well haue buſied their heades about diſciphering the deceites of their owne Sex, as they haue about ſetting downe our follies: and I wold ſome would call in queſtion that nowe, which hath euer bene queſtionleſſe: but ſithence all their wittes haue bene bent to wꝛite of the contrarie, I leaue them to a contrary vaine, and the ſurfaiting Louer, who returnes to his diſcourſe of loue.

Nowe while this gréedye grazer is about his intreatie of loue, which nothing belongeth to our matter: let vs ſecretlye our ſelues with our ſelues, conſider howe and in what, they that are our woꝛſt enemies, are both inferiour vnto vs, & moſt beholden vnto our kindenes.

The creation of man and woman at the firſt, hee being foꝛmed In principio of dꝛoſſe and filthy clay, did ſo remaine vntil God ſaw that in him his woꝛkmanſhip was good, and therfoꝛe by the transfoꝛmation of the duſt which was loathſome vnto fleſh, it became putrified. Then lacking a help foꝛ him, GOD making woman of mans fleſhe, that ſhe might bee purer then he, doth euidently ſhowe, how far we women are moꝛe excellent thē men. Our bodies are frutefull, wherby the woꝛld encreaſeth, and our care wonderful, by which man is pꝛeſerued. Frō woman ſpꝛāg mans ſaluation. A woman was the firſt that beléeued, & a woman likewiſe the firſt that repēted of ſin.

C				Iiɪ

2.1: Jane Anger, *Jane Anger Her Protection for Women* (1589). Reproduced by permission of The Huntington Library, San Marino, California.

Jane Anger, *Jane Anger Her Protection for Women* (1589)

Jane Anger Her Protection for Women. To defend them against the Scandalous Reportes of a late Surfeiting Lover, and all other like Venerians that complaine so to bee overcloyed with womens kindnesse, written by Ja: A. Gent (London, 1589), is the only work believed to have been written by the author known as Jane Anger. No biographical evidence exists to identify Anger as the author's true name or even to ensure that she was a woman, but records do show the existence of some women by that name in late-sixteenth-century England, one of whom may have been the author of this pamphlet. Anger identifies a misogynistic text entitled *Boke, His Surfiet in Love* (probably the so-named text entered in the Stationers' Register by Orwin in November 1588) as the source for the arguments against women that she must now refute. There is no extant copy of the *Surfeit,* and we have no evidence (outside of Anger's text) of its author. Early modern printing houses in England and Europe produced a considerable number of pamphlets and essays written against or in favor of women, the majority authored by men. Anger's *Protection for Women* lays claim to being the first female-authored defense of women published in English.

This excerpt from Anger's *Protection for Women* (Cr) displays many distinguishing features of this text and demonstrates the author's rhetorical and scholarly abilities. The direct references to "surfeiting lover," plays upon "anger," and analyses of specific terms (apparently those used by "Boke") create a style of specificity and sharpness to Anger's arguments characteristic of her "anger-y" discourse. Such forms of direct textual argumentation are evident in other female-authored polemics, such as those used by Rachel Speght in her early seventeenth-century pamplet. Anger's plain style is that favored by many early modern women authors, and appears in sharp contrast to the flowery "euphuistic" style of Lyly and other courtier prose writers of the period. Anger's scholarship mixes classical and biblical references with homey proverbs and lessons based upon personal experience: she can make oblique reference to "Socrates' rule," assuming that all her readers (both male and female) will understand her meaning; or she can offer her correction to Hesiod or Tibullus, as she does on the preceding pages; yet simultaneously she reminds her readers that "a burnt finger giveth sound counsel" and that "a man's face is worth a glass of dissembling water." Such features of Anger's writing, and those of other female polemicists after her, demonstrate the author's knowledge and inherent criticism of conventional authority.

Such a reevaluation of authority is nowhere more clearly displayed than in Anger's "feminist" reading of the book of Genesis. Following clear processes of logical reasoning, Anger argues "that women are more excellent than men." She explains that Adam was made from "filthy clay" which God "purified" by its transformation into flesh; therefore, when God subsequently made Eve from "man's flesh" He used a more refined and purified substance, so that logically woman is purer than man. Anger's revisionist approach to the Bible was to become a common feature of early modern women's religious and polemical writings (see Lanyer, Speght, and Sutcliffe).

Jane Anger's Protection for Women is a key text in England's involvement in the *querelle de femme* and a significant predecessor to later centuries' feminist writings.

LINDA VECCHI
MEMORIAL UNIVERSITY OF NEWFOUNDLAND

Jane Anger. *Jane Anger Her Protection for Women* (1589). Huntington Library RB 49047. Folio page Cr.

Eſter hath hang'd
Haman:
OR
AN ANSVVERE TO
a lewd Pamphlet, entituled,
The Arraignment of Women.

With the arraignment of lewd, idle,
froward, and vnconſtant men, and
Hvsbands.

Diuided into two Parts.

The firſt proueth the dignity and worthineſſe
of Women, out of diuine *Teſtimonies.*

The ſecond ſhewing the eſtimation of the Fœ-
minine Sexe, in ancient and Pagan times ; all which
is acknowledged by men themſelues in their
daily actions.

VVritten by *Eſter Sowernam,* neither Maide,
Wife nor Widdowe, yet really all, and therefore experienced to defend all.

Iohn 8. 7:
He that is without ſinne among you, let him firſt caſt a ſtone at her.

Neque enim lex inſticior vlla
———— *Quam necis Artificem arte perire ſua.*

LONDON,
Printed for *Nicholas Bourne,* and are to be ſold at his ſhop
at the entrance of the Royall Exchange. 1617.

2.2: Ester Sowernam, *Ester hath hang'd Haman* (1617). Reproduced by permission of The Huntington Library,
San Marino, California.

Ester Sowernam, *Ester hath hang'd Haman* (1617)

In 1615, a fencing master and writer named Joseph Swetnam published *The Araignment of Lewd, idle, froward and unconstant women,* a thick and repetitive book of antiwoman invective. He listed famous depraved women of history, anthologized proverbs against women, and concluded with a "bear-baiting of widows" in which he poured particular scorn upon them and their relative independence. Sowernam's work was part of a backlash against him that also included an anonymous but highly entertaining play, *Swetnam, the Woman Hater, Arraigned by Women* (1620), in which he was satirized on stage, and a pamphlet each by Rachel Speght and Constantia Munda.

The title page of Ester Sowernam's pamphlet poses an unsolved riddle about her identity. She claims to be "neither Maide, Wife, nor Widdowe, yet really all, and therefore experienced to defend all." The first part of the same riddle is posed by the betrothed but unmarried Mariana in *Measure for Measure* (5.1.177–80), causing the duke to ask: "Why, you are nothing then: neither maid, widow, or wife?" and leading onlookers to believe she may be a prostitute. But even these two proposed solutions to the first part of the riddle do not satisfy the extra condition added to it by Sowernam.

Sowernam's self-description may be a shrewd piece of reader mystification, perhaps even a strategy to titillate and intrigue potential buyers—after all, this is the title page of a pamphlet produced by a commercial publisher, and the equivalent of today's lurid back-cover blurb. But at the same time, it satirizes the inflexibility of society's categorizations of women and raises the alarmingly feminist prospect of a woman who is not defined by her relation to a man.

The title page also predicts what the main plank of Sowernam's response will be in the pamphlet that follows, namely, the Bible. She matches Swetnam's lists of sinful women with a list of virtuous women taken from the Old Testament; she points out that, although society blames Eve for the fall, she "was assaulted with a Serpent of the masculine gender" (7); she praises Rachel Speght's pamphlet; and she moves on to conduct an allegorical trial of Swetnam that inverts the idea of the *Araignment.* Another pseudonymous woman, "Joan Sharp," adds commendatory verses at the end of the pamphlet.

Ester Sowernam's name is clearly symbolic and polemical: her surname is the opposite of Swetnam's own, and her Christian name alludes to the Old Testament heroine of the book of Esther, thus denying Swetnam's implicit claim that there had never been any such thing as a heroic woman. Of course, there is no way of knowing whether the writer sheltering behind this pseudonym was "really" female, or male, and certainly one partial solution to Sowernam's teasing self-description could be to suppose her male. But then, this is part of the argument that the pamphlet poses, since, if gender is so easily and so impenetrably disguised in writing, it cannot really be the fundamental categorical boundary that Swetnam argues it to be.

MATTHEW STEGGLE
SHEFFIELD HALLAM UNIVERSITY

Ester Sowernam. *Ester hath hang'd Haman* (1617). Huntington Library RB 69499.

THE
WORMING OF
a madde Dogge.

HE itching defire of oppreſ-
sing the preſſe with many
fottiſh and illiterate Libels,
ſtuft with all manner of ri-
baldry, and ſordid inuenti-
ons, when euery foule-mou-
thed male-content may diſ-
gorge his *Licambæan* poyſon in the face of all
the world, hath broken out into ſuch a diſmall
contagion in theſe our dayes, that euery ſcanda-
lous tongue and opprobrious witte, like the Italian Mountebankes will aduance their pedling
wares of detracting virulence in the publique
Piatza of euery Stationers ſhoppe. And Printing that was inuented to be the ſtore-houſe of
famous wits, the treaſure of Diuine literature, the
pandect and maintainer of all Sciences, is become
the receptacle of euery diſſolute Pamphlet. The
nurſery and hoſpitall of euery ſpurious and pe-
nurious brat, which proceeds from baſe phrene-

*Tincta licam-
bæo ſanguine
tela dabit, Quid
in Ibin.*

B 2　　　　　　　　　　　ticall

2.3: Constantia Munda, *The Worming of a madde Dogge* (1617). Reproduced by permission of The Huntington
Library, San Marino, California.

Constantia Munda, *The Worming of a madde Dogge* (1617)

Like Ester Sowernam, Constantia Munda wrote her pamphlet in response to Joseph Swetnam's *The Araignment of Lewd, idle, froward and unconstant women,* and again like Sowernam, her name is clearly fictitious and polemical, being a Latin translation of the phrase "pure constancy." The surname suggests in particular sexual purity, while the Christian name addresses the assumption common in misogynist rhetoric and shared by Swetnam that women's bodies were naturally weaker than men's, and that this weakness determined and corresponded to a less firm sense of self and even of morality. Constantia Munda's name symbolically refutes this assumption, and also, in its Latinate form, the assumption that women know nothing of learning. However, nothing is known of the true identity or gender of the writer(s) of this pamphlet.

The Worming of a madde Dogge situates itself in the context of the preceding pamphlets of Speght and Sowernam but is far less measured and more gleeful than either of them in its assault upon Swetnam's factual errors, misunderstandings, and circular arguments. The extract chosen illustrates the rhetorical flourish with which she begins, typical of her technique. She uses a freewheeling style, learned marginal references, and dozens of quotations from learned authors in Italian, Latin, and ancient Greek to keep up a running fire against her adversary, whom she sets about mocking thoroughly on a personal level. This is not merely gratuitous insult, since she makes Swetnam serve as a living example of the inadequacy of men, and thus as a self-incriminating witness against his own argument for male superiority. In one passage, she uses university-style logical propositions to "prove" that Swetnam is himself a scold, and the gender-bending she inflicts upon Swetnam is made more piquant by the fact that she is using the methods of male-only university education to do it. (Swetnam himself had no university education.) Even the title of the pamphlet is polemical: Swetnam's pamphlet had reduced widows to the status of bears whom he sought to "bait," but here Swetnam himself is figured as a savage and stupid dog. Again, all this can be related to the strategies of the anonymous play *Swetnam The Woman-Hater,* in which all Swetnam's rhetoric is made laughable by being put in the mouth of a buffoon, and in which that character is frequently described as a snarling dog whose bark is worse than his bite.

All the same, it must not be overlooked that in commercial terms Swetnam's work was far more successful than that of his detractors. There are thirteen surviving seventeenth-century editions of the *Araignment,* and five from the eighteenth century, as well as Dutch translations. There is little evidence to indicate that the anonymous play was ever performed again, and no second edition ever appeared of the pamphlets of Munda, Sowernam, or Speght.

Matthew Steggle

Sheffield Hallam University

Constantia Munda. *The Worming of a madde Dogge: or, A soppe for Cerberus the jaylor of Hell. No confutation but a sharpe redargution of the bayter of women* (1617). Huntington Library RB 62679. B2.

To the Reader.

ALthough (curteous Reader) I am young in yeares, and more defectiue in knowledge, that little smattering in Learning which I haue obtained, being onely the fruit of such vacant houres, as I could spare from affaires befitting my Sex, yet am I not altogether ignorant of that Analogie which ought to be vsed in a literate Responsarie: But the Beare-bayting of Women, vnto which I haue framed my Apologeticall answere, beeing altogether without Grammaticall Concordance, and a promiscuous mingle methode, irregular, without Grammaticall mangle, it would admit no such order to bee obserued in the answering thereof, as a regular Responsarie requireth.

Wherfore (gentle Reader) fauorably consider, that a Painter is not to be held vnskilfull, which hauing a deformed Object, makes the like portriture; no more am I iustly to be blamed for my immethodicall Apologie, sith a-vy iudicious Reader may plainely see, that the Bayter of Women his pestiferous obtrectation is like a Taylers Cushion, that is botcht to-

F   gether

To the Reader.

gether of shreddes, so that, were it not to preuent future infection with that venome, which he hath, and daily doth sweate out, I would haue beene loath to haue spent time so idlely, as to answere it at all: but a crooked pot-lid well enough fits a wrie-neckt pot, an vnfashioned shooe a mis-shapen foote, and an illiterate answere an vnlearned irreligious prouocation. His absurdities therein contayned, are so many, that to answere them seuerally, were as friuolous a worke, as to make a Trappe for a Flea, and as tedious as the pursuite of an Arrow to an impotent man. Yet to preuent his hauing occasion to say, that I speake of many, but can instance none, I haue thought it meete to present a few of them to his view, as followeth, that if Follie haue taken roote in him, he may seeke to extirpate it, and to blush at the sight of that fruit, which he hath already brought foorth; a fruite I call it (not vnsitly I hope) because a Crabbe may so be termed, as well as a good Apple. Thus, not doubting of the fauour of well affected, and of their kinde acceptance of my indeuours, of which I desire not applaud, but approbation: I rest,

Your frien,

RACHEL SPEGHT.

2.4: Rachel Speght, "To the Reader," *A Mouzell for Melastomus* (1617). By permission of The British Library.

Rachel Speght, "To the Reader," *A Mouzell for Melastomus* (1617)

The daughter of a Calvinist minister, Rachel Speght was born in London about 1597 and raised in a bourgeois household in which her learning was apparently encouraged yet restricted by her gender. As its title indicates, this polemical tract was written in direct response to a misogynistic pamphlet, *The Araignment of Lewde, idle, froward and unconstant women: Or the vanitie of them, choose you whether*, published in 1616 under the pseudonym Thomas Tel-troth but really written by Joseph Swetnam, a London fencing master. Speght's text is significant because it marks the first time a real woman participated in the popular and long-standing genre of the controversy about the nature of women, which regularly generated both attacks and defenses (Woodbridge). Yet whether Speght's biological sex meant that she was more "sincere" than her male counterparts, or whether she was simply capitalizing on the commercial popularity of the debate genre, is still open to question.

Speght's defense was quickly followed by two others, by the clearly pseudonymous Ester Sowernam and Constantia Munda, who, whether or not they were actual women, adopted the tone of the shrew anticipated and mocked in advance by Swetnam (Purkiss). Unlike them, and probably to avoid being typecast in this way, Speght advances in the central part of her pamphlet a sober and carefully logical argument based on Scripture that ignores Swetnam's own tract, although she frames it with an ad hominem address to Swetnam himself on the one hand and a detailed refutation of individual points in his argument on the other ("Certaine Quaeres to the Bayter of Women"). The pages reproduced here ("To the Reader," F1r-F2v) introduce the latter section, and therefore follow the main argument.

Speght begins this preface with a standard humility topos, modestly claiming her own inadequacy for the task she has just accomplished. Significantly, however, she attributes her inadequacy not to her sex but to her gender and its attendant social constraints that do not allow her to acquire more than a "smattering in Learning." At the same time, she goes on to lay claim to knowledge that exceeds the requirements of her polemic: while she is "not altogether ignorant of that Analogie which ought to be used in a literate Responsarie," she has been forced to imitate the "promiscuous mingle mangle" of Swetnam's original in framing her response. Now readers who have worked their way through the careful logic of the tract know that this is not the case, but the reductive strategy works to increase the readers' estimation of Speght as author, who would have been capable of greater things given a worthier model. Speght also positions herself carefully in terms of class. If she associates Swetnam with artisans such as tailors (frequently mocked as emasculated servants to women), Speght is high-born enough to enjoy some "vacant houres," thus aligning herself with the "curteous" and "gentle" (genteel) reader. Aware, however, that these "vacant houres" come dangerously close to resembling the idleness in which Swetnam claims to have generated his tract (Henderson 190), Speght quickly adds that she "would have beene loath to have spent time so idlely, as to answere it at all." Thus, while Speght's address to the reader appears self-deprecatory, it is in fact a proud assertion of her own authorship.

Christina Luckyj

Dalhousie University

Rachel Speght. "To the Reader." *A Mouzell for Melastomus, the Cynicall Bayter of, and foule mouthed Barker against Evahs Sex. Or an Apologeticall Answere to that Irreligious and Illiterate Pamphlet made by Io. Sw. And by him Intituled, The Arraignement of Women* (1617). British Library 8415.e.24

12   *A Mouzell for Melastomus.*

be open according to her abilitie, in contribu-ting towards Gods seruice, and distressed ser-uants, like to that poore widdow, which cast two mites into the Treasurie; and as *Marie Magdalen, Susanna,* and *Ioanna* the wife of *Herods* Steward, with many other, which of their substance ministred vnto Christ. Herheart should be a receptacle for Gods Word, like *Mary* that treasured vp the sayings of Christ in her heart. Her feete should be swift in go-ing to seeke the Lord in his Sanctuarie, as *Marie Magdalen* made haste to seeke Christ at his Sepulchre. Finally, no power externall or internall ought woman to keep idle, but to im-ploy it in some seruice of God, to the glo-rie of her Creator, and comfort of her owne soule.

The other end for which woman was made, was to be a Companion and *helper* for man; and if she must be an *helper*, and but an *helper*, then are those husbands to be blamed, which lay the whole burthen of domesticall affaires and maintenance on the shoulders of their wiues. For, as yoake-fellowes they are to sustayne part of ech others cares, griefs, and calamities: But as if two Oxen be put in one yoke, the one being bigger then the other, the greater beares most weigh; so the Husband being the stronger vessell is to beare a greater burthen then his wife; And therefore the Lord said to *Adam, In the sweate of thy face shalt thou eate thy bread, till*

Luke 8.

Luke 1.51.

John 20.1.

Gen.3.19.

A Mouzell for Melastomus.   13

till thou returne to the dust. And Saint *Paul* saith, *That he that prouideth not for his houshold is worse then an Infidel.* Nature hath taught sense-lesse creatures to helpe one another; as the Male Pigeon, when his Hen is weary with sit-ting on her egges, and comes off from them, supplies her place, that in her absence they may receiue no harme, vntill such time as she is ful-ly refreshed. Of small Birds the Cocke alwaies helpes his Hen to build her nest; and while she sits vpon her egges, he flies abroad to get meat for her, who cannot then prouide any for her selfe. The crowing Cockrell helpes his Hen to defend her Chickens from perill, and will in-danger himselfe to saue her and them from harme. Seeing then that these vnreasonable creatures, by the instinct of nature, beare such affection each to other, that without any grudge, they willingly, according to their kind, helpe one another, I may reason *à minore ad maius*, that much more should man and wo-man, which are reasonable creatures, be helpers each to other in all things lawfull, they hating the Law of God to guide them, his Word to bee a Lanthorne vnto their feete, and a Light vnto their pathes, by which they are excited to a farre more mutuall participation of each others burthen, then other creatures. So that neither the wife may say to her husband, nor the husband vnto his wife, I haue no need of thee, no more then the members of the body may

1.Tim.5.8.

D 3   so

2.5: Rachel Speght, *A Mouzell for Melastomus* (1617). By permission of The British Library.

Rachel Speght, *A Mouzell for Melastomus* (1617)

In this central portion of the *Mouzell for Melastomus* (A Muzzle for a Black [or Foul] Mouth), we can see Speght drawing her exempla both from Scripture and from nature in her discussion of the "finall cause" of woman's creation: "to glorifie God, and to be a collateral companion for man to glorifie God" (11). This double agenda suggests woman's dual and somewhat contradictory role as theologically equal yet domestically subordinate to her husband. At the top of p. 12, Speght has just argued that a woman should offer her husband good counsel; here she moves to the more radical position that "her hands shold be open according to her abilitie," a suggestion that anticipates her more explicit defense of her own authorship at the opening of *Mortalities Memorandum*. As she continues, citing biblical women who "ministred unto Christ," she constructs woman increasingly as autonomous, defined primarily not by relation to her husband, but by her relation to God. This anticipates her argument later, that "women are enioyned to submit themselves unto their husbands no otherwaies then as to *the Lord*" (17), which carefully circumscribes a husband's authority while apparently elevating it by analogy with the divine.

In the second paragraph on p. 12, however, she returns explicitly to consider the relationship between husband and wife, and here Speght negotiates contemporary patriarchal ideology to advance a program of social reform and gender equality. Consistent with her earlier account of Adam as the "stronger vessel" (5) with consequently greater culpability for the Fall, here the husband "is to beare a greater burthen then his wife" (12). Speght thus clearly accepts and naturalizes the gender hierarchy, in which woman is the "weaker vessel" (1 Peter 3:7), but she interprets that hierarchy to argue that men must double their load, not only providing for the household but also taking on domestic responsibilities within it. This runs counter to the emergent early modern ideology of separate spheres: "for as the man is bound to make provision for his family and to bring it home, so is it the part of an honest and wise woman to provide that all things be safely kept," writes Thomas Becon (Aughterson 113). Speght is undoubtedly responding to Swetnam himself in the *Arraignment*, who writes: "But these men are to be laughed at who, having a wife and a sufficient wife to do all the work within doors which belongs for a woman to do, yet the husband will set hens abroad, season the pot, and dress the meat, or any the like work which belongeth not to the man. . . . For if they were employed abroad in matters belonging to men, they would be the more desirous, being come home, to take their ease than to trouble their wives and servants in meddling with their matters" (Henderson 213). By arguing for equal participation in domestic chores, Speght contests a gendered division of labour that was to become firmly entrenched and essentialized in early modern society. Otherwise, Speght's advocacy of marriage as a "mutuall participation of each others burthen" is perfectly orthodox, and frequently reiterated in Puritan conduct books; one might well argue (as does Purkiss) that Swetnam's misogyny is more culturally disruptive than Speght's defense because the former represents woman as unassimilable while the latter accommodates her to cultural norms. Speght's *Mouzell for Melastomus* accepts the traditional view that "the *Man is the Womans Head*" (16) but supplements it with a vision of mutual responsibility and practical equality.

CHRISTINA LUCKYJ
DALHOUSIE UNIVERSITY

Rachel Speght. *A Mouzell for Melastomus, the Cynicall Bayter of, and foule mouthed Barker against Evahs Sex. Or an Apologeticall Answere to that Irreligious and Illiterate Pamphlet made by Io. Sw. And by him Intituled, The Arraignement of Women* (1617). British Library 8415.e.24 pp 12–13.

The Auctors Testament,

In diuers places Players, that
   of wonders shall reporte.
Now London haue I (for thy sake)
   within thee, and without :
As coms into my memory,
   dispearsed round about
Such needfull thinges, as they should haue
   here left now vnto thee:
When I am gon, with consience
   let them dispearced bee.
And though I nothing named haue,
   to bury mee withall :
Consider that aboue the ground,
   annoyance bee I shall.
And let me haue a Shrowding Shéete
   to couer mee from shame:
And in obliuyon bury mee
   and neuer more mee name.
Ringings nor other Ceremonies,
   vse you not for cost:
Nor at my buriall, make no feast,
   your mony were but lost.
Reioyce in God that I am gon,
   out of this vale so vile,
And that of ech thing, left such store,
   as may your wants exile.
I make thee sole executor, because
   I lou'de thee best.
And thee I put in trust, to geue
   the goodes vnto the rest.

                                 Because

2.6: Isabella Whitney, *A Sweet Nosgay, or Pleasant Posye*, with "Wyll and Testament" (1573). By permission of The British Library.

Isabella Whitney, *A Sweet Nosgay, or Pleasant Posye,* **with "Wyll and Testament" (1573)**

Showing notable development in her skill as a writer, yet still maintaining a close relation to her personal experiences, Whitney's second publication, *A Sweet Nosgay, or Pleasant Posye: Contayning a Hundred and Ten Phylosophicall Flowers* (London, 1573) displays an even greater variety of subject matter and style than her *Copy of a letter.* It includes the 110 philosophical posies, 13 "Certain familiar Epistles and friendly Letters" (in verse and prose, most penned by Whitney, but also including replies from various male friends and relatives), and her "Wyll and Testament." The "Wyll" is Whitney's most sustained and original work, and is deserving of the attention it has so far received. The *Nosgay's* "Phylosophicall Flowers" are adapted directly from a contemporary work that Whitney cites, Hugh Platt's *The Floures of Philosophie* (1572), and are, as Betty Travitsky suggests, less "properly . . . described as philosophical," but are rather "a series of aphoristic reflections on the human condition" (81).

The biographical details given in the verse epistles printed in the *Nosgay* indicate that Whitney had been employed as a domestic servant in London, but that her employment had now been terminated. Whitney's personal anxiety and remorse provides a unifying mood of lamentation to her collection that is most clearly pronounced in the work's closing poem, "The Wyll and Testament." As Whitney states in the introduction to the poem, "The Authour (though loth to leave the Citie) upon her friends procurement, is constrained to departe: Wherefore (she fayneth as she would die) and maketh her WYLL and Testament" (E2). Following in the tradition of William Dunbar's "Testament of Mr. Andro Kennedy" (1508) and Robert Copland's *Jill of Breyntford's Testament* (c. 1563) and perhaps influencing George Gascoigne's "Last Will and Testament of Dan Bartholomew of Bath," Whitney constructs a fictionalized will by which she bequeaths to the city of London all of its variety of riches. In the course of the poem's approximately 375 lines, she envisions the city's "Brave buildyngs" (E3v), bustling streets, merchandise-laden shops, and diverse citizens. She scans the cityscape from Paul's Cross to London's numerous prisons, on which she dwells with particular poignancy and sympathy. This is clearly *her* town; she knows its denizens and activities personally, reveling in its joys and bemoaning its sorrows.

Yet Whitney's focus is not solely on London's earthly pleasures. One of the most notable features of her "Wyll and Testament" is its balanced presentation of humor and lament, abundance and want. Having remembered herself to all its people (including Richard Jones, "my Printer" [E6v]), Whitney closes her poem (as indicated by the excerpt shown on the facing page, E7v) by requesting nothing for herself. In the Protestant *ars moriendi* (art of dying) tradition that Whitney's poem clearly addresses itself to, the dying Christian was instructed to settle his or her earthly affairs (often by producing wills and testaments), unburden his or her mind from the woes of this world, and prepare his or her soul for the glories of the next. Here Whitney asks only for "a shrowding Sheete" (line 15) so that she may be buried "in oblivyon" (17). No costly ceremonies or celebrations are to be made in her memory. Rather she prays that London will quietly acknowledge her passing and "Rejoyce" in her reunion with God (23), and that it will then go about its business since that is why she "lov'de" it "best" (28). Whitney's "Wyll and Testament" is a fitting end to her literary endeavors. Through it, as with all her writings, she has bequeathed to future generations of readers a treasury of poetic skill and expression that will no longer allow her to be lost to "oblivyon."

LINDA VECCHI
MEMORIAL UNIVERSITY OF NEWFOUNDLAND

Isabella Whitney. *A Sweet Nosgay, or Pleasant Posye* (1573). British Library C.39.b.45.

2.7: Rachael Fane, Page of her school notebook (c.1628). Reproduced with permission of Robert Sackville-West on behalf of the Knole Trustees, and the Centre for Kentish Studies, Maidstone, Kent.

Rachael Fane (1613? –1680), Page of her school notebook (c. 1628)

Transcription

But both to use in modesty
Are signes of good sivillity
Sleape only nature to suffise
But sleapes for pleasures cause despise
Doe not thou rashly plight thy troth
But justly swearing keepe thy othe
In drinking wine be modarate
Drinke not to much in any rate
for gaine ore mallice doe not fight
But for thy kinge and countries right
Beleve not rashly any thing
Which to thine eares reporte shall bring
Of dangrous counsayle be thou ware
To counsaile safely have a caire
In private staite to self best knowne
Thy safest counsell make thine owne
from whores and lust fly and abstaine
for after plasur folloues paine
furnish thy mind with learned skill
When goods doe faile learning bids still
from falchood and from lies abstaine
In every thing be just and plaine
Doe well to all to good men most
To bade men, what thou dost is lost
Thy nighbours life doe not defame
Nor speake noe ill to hurt his name
Thy craditt and thy good report
Retaine and keepe in any sortt
In judgment equity regard
Judge not for favour ore rewarde
Subdue with patients parents wroth
Allthough they stray from reasons path
Thare weakenesse labour thou to hide
If errer make them swarve aside
Be mindfull of a benifitt
That good thou givest thou maigt forgett
Resorte to place where justise sitts
Whare thou maiest know what thee befitts

Note on transcription

Rachael has used a single minuscule *f* rather than the double used more conventionally to indicate the capital *F*.

Commentary

Rachael Fane was the granddaughter of Grace, Lady Mildmay. Aged five, she arrived from Kent with her parents, Sir Francis and Lady Mary Fane and (eventually) thirteen siblings to live with her grandmother at Apethorpe, Northamptonshire. Rachael thus grew up in a household in which she was part of the third generation of educated women. Grace, Lady Mildmay lived on for only two years with her grandchildren, but she had a significant impact on Rachael's education. Grace explained in her writings that she wanted her granddaughters to be educated and at the same time to conform to conventional feminine characteristics of chastity, modesty, and silence. Her lengthy Meditations and spiritual autobiography were bequeathed to her grandchildren.

Some of Rachael's notebooks illustrating her schooling have survived. The main part of the collection consists of some twelve notebooks dating mainly from 1623–33. They fall into two main categories: religious and moral studies and translations from and into French based on selections from Seneca, Isocrates, and Amadis de Gaul. This undated notebook starts as "Meditations upon the 50 Psalm" but after three pages changes into what Rachael describes as "Sentances translated out of Catto into Inglish newe." Three editions of Cato appeared in English between 1623 and 1636. The preface to the 1624 edition of *Cato in English Verse* indicates that it was published for use in school or at home by those who had not learned Latin either to learn to read or for copying. The verses in all these editions contain sentiments very similar to those copied by Rachael, emphasizing reverence for parents, leading a moral life, and the importance of learning:

> Thy parents favour let thy patience gaine,
> Lie not, read bookes, and beare them in thy braine. (*Cato in English Verse*, 1624,
>   p. 23)
> Loosing thy riches, doe not fall aweeping,
> But rather joy, thou hadst them to let fly. (*Cato Variegatus* 1636, p. 97)

In this page Rachael is copying moral distichs, an exercise extensively performed by both boys and girls to learn virtuous behavior while improving writing skills. The verses stress that moderation in all things, including eating, drinking, personal behavior, and chastity, is at the heart of morality. Obedience to parental authority permeated sound educational practice even at the great boys' schools of the day.

For girls, parental fears of raising daughters who would not conform to conventional behavioral norms and be difficult to marry led to a restricted program of learning to read and write based on a careful choice of texts.

The breadth of Rachael Fane's studies as seen in her notebooks is unusual. She translated fluently, if inaccurately, from French; she learned to write in both cursive script and secretary hand, and she also appears to have learned some Spanish and Latin. Rachael here practices secretary hand, a hand rarely used by women of the period in their letters.

Rachael has had lines drawn for her in pencil to keep the lines straight in her notebook, which, like the others in the collection, has been made for her by stitching the pages together at home. Hers is a neat, well-practiced hand with few mistakes and crossings out and few blots.

CAROLINE BOWDEN
ST. MARY'S COLLEGE, MIDDLESEX

Rachel Fane. Notebook. Centre for Kentish Studies Maidstone, Kent U269 F38/1
No 14, opening f7v-8r.

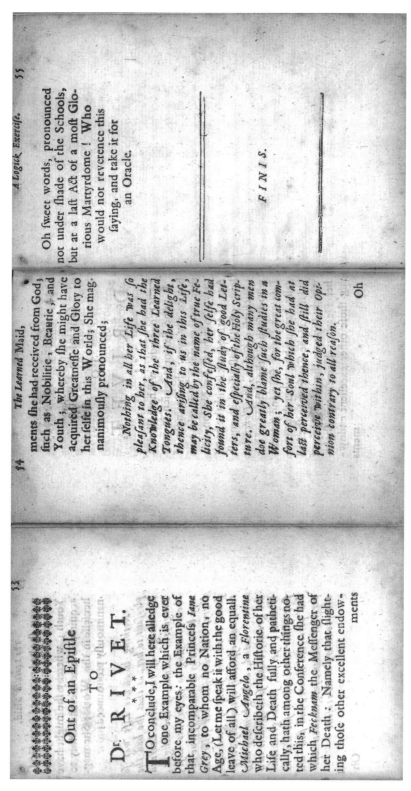

2.8: Anna Maria van Schurman, *The Learned Maid; or, Whether a Maid may be a Scholar?* (Latin, 1638 and 1641; English translation, 1659). Reproduced by permission of The Huntington Library, San Marino, California.

Anna Maria van Schurman, *The Learned Maid; or, Whether a Maid may be a Scholar?*
(Latin treatise, Paris, 1638; Leiden, 1641; English translation, London, 1659)

Anna Maria van Schurman (1607–78) was widely regarded in her own century as the best-educated woman of the time; by sitting in a cubicle that opened into a lecture hall, Anna Maria managed to become the first female student at a Dutch university. This excerpt comes from her treatise on women's education, which grew out of her correspondence with contemporary theologians and scholars. This correspondence documents her acquaintance with continental works concerning the debate about women and learning. Schurman found inspiration for her ideas not only from the humanist-inspired manifestoes of continental women, but also from supportive Dutch reformed theologians such as Gisbertus Voetius and Jan van Beverwyck, who publicized her accomplishments and supported her printed works in complimentary prefaces. While Schurman carried on a lively and rich correspondence with many contemporaries, it seems that she published her treatise on women's education only reluctantly to correct a pirated edition. When Schurman learned that an unauthorized version of the text, full of errors, was circulating in Paris in 1639, she decided to publish her authoritative version, which appeared in Leiden in 1641. Schurman uses her learned correspondence to buttress the authority for her treatise by situating it within a circle of accredited scholarly discourse.

The pages reproduced here exemplify such correspondence in a letter to her friend and teacher André Rivet. In the excerpted pages Schurman explains why the English Lady Jane Grey's (1537–54) love of learning has particular resonance for her. Lady Jane Grey serves as a fitting example of the value of female education in the context of Schurman's larger argument, which holds that the study of languages and scripture will increase women's love of God. Jane Grey finds consolation in learning, which helps her withstand the temptation to recant her religion. Yet this example also raises some of the ambiguities in Schurman's defense of learning for women that would surface in her later life and work. If women do not participate in public life, what practical application will their learning have? Jane Grey's example brings out these paradoxes because through self-negation and martyrdom, her learning finds its test and practical application. Later in life Schurman left the Dutch Reformed state church to join the religious movement of Jean de Labadie and rejected her earlier intellectual pursuits in favor of a life of practical piety guided by Scripture reading. She explains this change in a later autobiographical work, *Eukleria, seu melioris partis electio* (1673), which frames her choice in the traditional dichotomy of the contemplative and active lives, represented by the biblical Mary and Martha.

Schurman's Latin treatise on the education of women was translated into English in 1659 as *The Learned Maid; or, Whether a Maid may be a Scholar?*. Bathsua Makin, who had admired and corresponded with Schurman, published *An Essay to Revive the Antient Education of Gentlewomen, in Religion, Manners, Arts and Tongues* in 1673. Like Schurman, Makin develops creative strategies for avoiding the double binds of female authorship.

Jennifer L. Andersen
California State University

Anna Maria van Schurman. *The Learned Maid; or, Whether a Maid may be a Scholar?*
(London, 1659). Huntington Library RB 58117. Pages 53–55.

Margaret Cavendish, Marchioness of Newcastle, *Philosophical and Physical Opinions* (1655). Reproduced by permission of The Huntington Library, San Marino, California.

2.9: Margaret Cavendish, Marchioness of Newcastle, *The Worlds Olio* (1655). Bodleian Library, University of Oxford.

Margaret Cavendish, Marchioness of Newcastle, *The Worlds Olio* **(1655) and** *Philosophical and Physical Opinions* **(1655)**

These two portraits of Margaret Cavendish (1623–73) represent two key moments in early modern women's struggle to gain the freedom to do and be recognized for intellectual work. The frontispiece to Cavendish's *Philosophical and Physical Opinions* depicts the author in her study, spontaneously generating fresh thoughts. The portrait registers the agency, space, and process of a woman's free thinking. The solitary figure is at her desk with a clock, paper, and pen poised for use; only the bell (to summon the servants, perhaps) differentiates her from any other working writer. Although it is her "library," she is not oppressed by old books or musty philosophical legacies; she is entertained, and also crowned with laurels, by her own lively thoughts. Cavendish often refers to her ideas self-deprecatingly as "fancies," but here the cherubs circling her head are labeled "thoughts" and "philosophical and physical opinions." The inscription beneath the figure reiterates the point: "Studious She is and all Alone/ Most visitants when She has none,/ Her Library on which She looks/ It is her Head her Thoughts her Books/ Scorning dead Ashes without fire/ For her owne Flames doe her Inspire." Richard Flecknoe no doubt had this particular engraving in mind when he wrote "On the Dutchess of Newcastle's Closset," which begins by puzzling over the rare depiction of a female figure inhabiting her own space for study: "she / Makes each place where she comes a Librairie" (Flecknoe 46–47).

The frontispiece to *The Worlds Olio* reiterates a typical Cavendish motif: her desire to obtain an illustrious name in history. It is the most frequently reproduced Cavendish portrait (Fitzmaurice 203). The august figure of Cavendish is depicted in a rich ermine-lined robe, raised in a niche, flanked by the two columns of Minerva and Apollo, the classical gods of judgment and imagination. In a short "Epistle to the Reader," we learn that *Worlds Olio* was one of her earliest works, written around 1650 while she was living in Rubens's house in Antwerp. The statues of Apollo and Minerva (still standing in Rubens's garden) may have inspired the columns here, although Van Diepenbeeck used similar framing devices in other portraits (Steadman 38). The poem beneath offers the expected compliments to Cavendish's beauty, judgment, wit, and above all, originality: "read those Lines which Shee hath writt,/ By Phancy's Pencill drawne alone/ Which Peece but Shee, Can justly owne." *Worlds Olio* is about the risky and elusive nature of fame. The incongruity of the elements in this frontispiece—Cavendish's elevated placement in relationship to classical powers, the looseness of her hair and clothing, along with the rakish angle of her cornet—add "a touch of insouciance to the proud pose" (Grant 142). The amused ambiguity of Cavendish's bearing here may suggest the irony, the novelty, and the insecurity of her desired positioning. Taken together, these two portraits signal Cavendish's strategic use of self-representation to establish her legitimacy as a writer, to confront the constraints against women's publication, and to negotiate new space for women's intellectual work.

Sylvia Bowerbank

McMaster University

(3)

Verſes made by a Maid under 14.

With God the Lord would I could walk,
    Then ſhould I not tormented be;
But I ſhould live in quietneſſe,
And he ſhould be glorifi'd by me.
In Chriſt is reſt as I ſhall find,
If I upon him ſet my mind,
For he ſhews mercy unto all,
Therefore upon him will I call.
O mercy Lord, mercy to me,
That Chriſt my dwelling place may be:
Then ſhall my ſoul raviſhed be,
And ſing Hallelujahs unto thee·
Chriſt is a pattern of patience pure,
And thoſe that truſt in him are ſure;
Though Satan ſeeks ſouls to devour,
Yet Chriſt is of Almighty power,
Then let us all on him depend,
That we may make a Godly end:
That then our ſouls to heaven may flie,
Where we ſhall live, and never die.
In this world is but filthy droſſe,
Which at the laſt will prove a croſſe;
If we in it do live in ſin,
It had better we had never bin.
Come quickly, Lord, and do not ſtay,
That I from ſin may turn away;
For ſin is loathſome unto thee,
Lord grant it may be the ſame to me.
Lord, teach us all to put on Chriſt,
Who hath bought us at ſo dear a price;
For where thou putteſt that garment on,
It makes them glorious like the Sun.
          A 3   Out

2.10: Anonymous, "Verses made by a Maid under 14" (c.1657-8). By permission of The British Library.

Anonymous, "Verses made by a Maid under 14" (c. 1657–58)

"Verses made by a Maid under 14" appeared with two other poems in a booklet "Printed for Richard Woodnothe . . . 1658." However, a handwritten note in the British Library's copy suggests that it was in print during the year we would call 1657. Dates are especially important in the present case, since a fairly precise dating might help identify the poem's author. Her "Verses" are sandwiched between two other poems ("Religious Principles" and "Of Christ Crucified"), presumably written by adult males. It seems unlikely that she wrote all three, not only because it would presumably have been to the publisher's advantage to advertise such a claim, but also because of differences in the style and quality of the three works. The maid's verses, in fact, seem clearly the best of the lot.

Whoever the "Maid" was, she had a good ear, a precocious command of syntax, and an impressive familiarity with Scripture, especially for a thirteen-year-old girl. She writes mainly in lines of eight syllables, and, when she does vary her line lengths, good arguments can be made for the effectiveness of the variations. Generally she has firm control of her basically iambic lines, and she makes effective use of such devices as alliteration, repetition, anaphora, balanced syntax, ironic juxtaposition, and four-line syntactical units. The poem alternates between what might be called the private and the social "modes" (ll. 1–16: private; ll. 17–24: social; ll. 25–28: private; ll. 29–32: social; ll. 33–48: private; ll. 49–76: social), and this skillful alternation not only gives the lyric an interesting balance but also makes it far more engaging than the blandly impersonal poems on either side of it. The young poetess works biblical allusions smoothly into her own generally clear diction, and her sentence structure rarely if ever falters. No rhymes seem forced and no phrasing seems labored and, even if the poem says nothing surprising, it still seems more full of personal conviction than either of the surrounding efforts. In short, the thirteen-year-old girl who composed this lyric seems to have had the makings of a talented writer of verse.

Who was she? At this point her identity is unknown, and perhaps it will never be discovered. She seems to have been well educated, but the only present clue to her identity is the one provided by her poem's title, and even that clue is more ambiguous than it first appears. If we assume that the title refers to a maid who was just shy of fourteen years in 1657 or 1658 (when the poem was first printed), then her year of birth would presumably have been 1644 or 1645. However, it is possible that the poem was written years—perhaps many years—before being printed, in which case the poet may have been born considerably earlier than 1644. Assuming that she *was* born in 1644 or 1645, we still are not much helped, because the exact years of birth of many early modern women writers are unknown.

Only careful stylometric comparison and contrast of the poem by the "Maid" with the poems of other female writers from the same period may help us trace her. Or perhaps newer, better evidence (such as a signed manuscript) may yet turn up. In any case, her poetic skill suggests much about the education to which one young girl had been exposed during a time when education for women was becoming an increasingly debated topic. Someone seems to have felt, correctly, that this girl had a mind worth nurturing.

Robert C. Evans
Auburn University Montgomery

Anonymous. "Verses Made by a Maid Under 14." *Religious Principles in Verse* (1657/8). British Library E.936.(8.). Page A3.

(10)

publick Lectures in that Language. She was also reputed to be well skilled in Divinity.

The Lady *Jane Grey* excelled *Musæa* in this, the underftood the *Hebrew* alfo. There is a large Difcourfe of her Learning (in which fhe took great delight) and Piety, in the Book of Martyrs.

The prefent Dutchefs of *New-Caftle*, by her own Genius, rather than any timely Inftruction, over-tops many grave Gown-Men.

I am forbidden to mention the Counteſs Dowager of *Huntington* (inftructed fometimes by Mrs. *Makin*) how well fhe underftands *Latin, Greek, Hebrew, French* and *Spanifh*; or what a proficient fhe is in Arts, fubfervient to Divinity, in which (if I durft I would tell you) fhe excels.

The Princefs *Elizabeth*, daughter to King *Charles* the firft, to whom Mrs. *Makin* was Tutrefs, at nine Years old could write, read, and in fome meafure underftand, *Latin, Greek, Hebrew, French* and *Italick*. Had fhe lived, what a Miracle would fhe have been of her Sex!

The Princefs *Elizabeth*, eldeft Daughter to the Queen of *Bohemia*, yet living, is verfed in all forts of choice Literature.

Mrs. *Thornold*, Daughter of the Lady *Car* in *Lincolnfhire*, was excellent in Philofophy, and all forts of Learning.

I cannot without Injury forget the Lady *Mildmay*, and Dr. *Love's* Daughters; Their Worth and Excellency in Learning is yet frefh in the Memory of many Men.

Cornelia read publick Philofophy-Lectures at *Rome*; fhe brought up her Sons, the *Gracchi*, fo, that they were the only Men famous in their Dayes. She was admired by *Cicero* for diverfe of her Works.

The Papal Chair could not defend it felf, but was invaded by a Woman, for her Excellency in Learning above the men of her Times; As *Volaterian, Sigebertus, Platina* and others, that have writ the Lives of the Roman Bifhops, do declare. She is remembred likewife to this purpofe by *Boccafius* in his Book *de Claris Mulieribus*.

Rofvida, a Saxon by Nation, She lived under *Lotharius the firft*; She was Eloquent in the *Greek* and *Roman* Tongues, and practifed in all good Arts. She compofed many Works, not without great commendation from the Readers. One to exhort to Chaftity, Virtue, and Divine Worfhip. She published fix Comedies; befides a noble Poem in *Hexameter verfe*, of the Heroick Acts done by the *Otho Cæfars*; with divers others.

Elizabeth of *Schonaugia*, zealoufly inftructed the Study and Practice of this *Rofvida*. She writ many things in the *Latin* Tongue; namely, a Book

(11)

Book intituled, *A Path to direct us the way to God*; as alfo a Volumn of Learned Epiftles; with many other Books.

I cannot omit *Conftantia* the Wife of *Alexander Sforza*; She was fo Learned, that upon the fuddain and without any premeditation She was able fufficiently to difcourfe upon any Argument, either Theological, or Philofophical; Befides, She was very frequent in the works of St. *Hierome, Ambrofe, Gregory, Cicero*, and *Lactantius*. She was much admired for her Extempory vaine in Verfe. Her Daughter *Baptifta* was equal to Her in Fame and Merit, and was reckoned among the beft Learned, and moft Illuftrious Women.

Chriftina late Queen of *Sweden* underftood feveral Languages, and was well verfed in Politicks, and acquainted with moft Arts and Sciences.

I thought of Queen *Elizabeth* firft, but purpofely mention Her laft;as the Crown of all. How learned She was, the World can teftifie. It was ufual for her to difcourfe with Forraign Agents in their own Languages. Mr. *Afcam*, her Tutor, ufed to fay, She read more *Greek* in a day then many of the Doctors of her time did *Latin* in a week. You fee fome Women have been good Proficients in moft kinds of Learning. I fhall now fhew you how they have been excellent in fome particular parts of it, as the *Tongues, Oratory, Philofophy, Divinity*, and laftly *Poefry*.

Women have been good Linguifts.

It is objected againft Women, as a reproach,that they have too much Tongue: but it's no crime they have many Tongues; if it be, many Men would be glad to be guilty of that fault. The Tongue's the only Weapon Women have to defend themfelves with, and they had need to ufeit dextroufly. Many fay one tongue is enough for a Woman: it is but a quibble upon the word. Several Languages underftood by a Woman, will do our Gentlemen little hurt, who have little more than their Mother-Wit, and underftand only their Mother-Tongue: thefe moft ufually make this Objection, to hide their own Ignorance. Tongues are learnt in order to Things. As things were, and yet are in the World, its requifite we learn Tongues to underftand Arts: It's therefore a Commendation to thefe Women after mentioned, that they were Miftreffes of Tongues.

There is an antient Copy of the *Septuagint*, fent from the Patriarch of *Alexandria* to King *James*, written by a Woman called *Tecla*, fo accurate and excellent, that the Authors of the Polyglot-Bible chofe it

B 2

2.11: Bathsua Makin, *An Essay to Revive the Antient Education of Gentlewomen* (1673). Reproduced by permission of the Huntington Library, San Marino, California.

Bathsua Makin, *An Essay to Revive the Antient Education of Gentlewomen* (1673)

Pages ten and eleven of Bathsua Makin's *An Essay to Revive the Antient Education of Gentlewomen, in Religion, Manners, Arts & Tongues* (1673) show part of her honor roll of famous (and famously learned) women, ranging, like much seventeenth-century polemic, from classical and biblical examples through to famous English and European women of Makin's own time. This page praises writers found elsewhere in this volume (Margaret Cavendish, Elizabeth I), as well as those whom Makin had herself taught: Charles I's daughter, Princess Elizabeth, and Lucy Hastings, Countess of Huntingdon. Makin taught the first from 1640 to 1644; in the late 1640s she was employed by the Hastings family. She wrote elegies for Lucy Hastings' son, Henry Hastings (who died of smallpox in 1649), and for the countess herself. These are preserved in the Hastings family papers in the Huntington Library, San Marino, California.

Makin was herself prodigiously learned. The daughter of a schoolmaster, she was fluent in Greek, Latin, French, Spanish, and Italian, and had some knowledge of Hebrew and Syriac. Her polyglot skills are well displayed in *Musa Virginea Graeco-Latino-Gallica* (1616). Though not a great collection of poetry, stylistically speaking, the volume certainly demonstrates a high level of accomplishment.

The honor roll in the open pages of the *Essay* forms a key part of Makin's argument in favor of women's education. Here she draws on a convention of compiling lists of learned women to advance the argument for educating them more rigorously. It anticipates the (now canonical) arguments made by Virginia Woolf in her classic *A Room of One's Own* (1929) where, unable to discover women writers before Aphra Behn, she invents the imaginary woman writer Judith Shakespeare. Ironically Woolf lacked the scholarly education that would have enabled her to discover in the British Library works by Makin and the other "real" female authors Makin recommends.

The *Essay* uses the mode of a satirical debate, a standard format in seventeenth-century polemic. Makin adopts the mask of a concerned male, but references to her own achievements and the epilogue plugging her school on Tottenham Court road in the north of London on "the Road to Ware" suggest that Makin was the real author of the *Essay*.

During the 1640s and 1650s many proposals for the reform of education were put forward. Makin was influenced in particular by the curriculum suggested by the Czech educational theorist and reformer Jan Comenius, who had many English followers. Makin, who had considerable experience as a tutor, gives Comenius's ideas a feminist spin. She offered, in her Tottenham School, to induct her pupils in a range of traditionally female skills as well as in more "masculine" fields of scholarship. Pupils would spend half their time on dancing, music, singing, writing, and keeping accounts, "the other half to be imployed in gaining the *Latin* and *French* Tongues." Those who could afford the considerable fee of twenty pounds a year would thus find their daughters both accomplished and learned. In brief they would aspire to the arts of their instructor for "in all" these arts, the *Essay* modestly comments "this Gentlewoman [Makin] hath a competent knowledge."

MARK HOULAHAN
UNIVERSITY OF WAIKATO

Bathsua Makin. *An Essay to Revive the Antient Education of Gentlewomen* (1673). Wing M309. Huntington Library RB 312803. Pages 10–11.

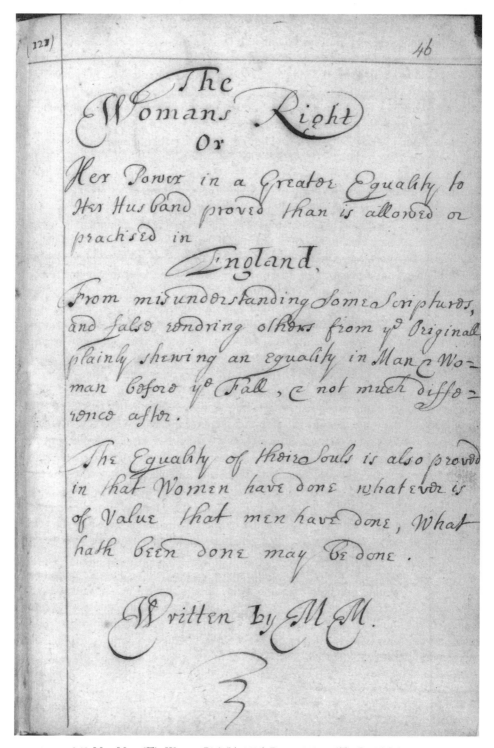

(123)

46

The
Womans Right
Or

Her Power in a Greater Equality to Her Husband proved than is allowed or practised in

England,

From misunderstanding some Scriptures, and false rendring others from y[e] Originall, plainly shewing an equality in Man & Woman before y[e] Fall, & not much difference after.

The Equality of their Souls is also proved in that Women have done whatever is of Value that men have done, What hath been done may be done.

Written by M M.

2.12: Mary More, "The Womans Right" (c.1680). By permission of The British Library.

Mary More, "The Womans Right" (c. 1680)

Transcription

The
Womans Right
Or
Her Power in a Greater Equality to
Her Husband proved than is allowed or
practised in
England,
From misunderstanding some scriptures,
and false rendring others from the Originall,
plainly shewing an equality in Man & Wo=
man before the Fall, & not much diffe=
rence after.

The Equality of their souls is also proved
in that Women have done what ever is
of Value that men have done, What
hath been done may be done.

Written by M. M.

Commentary

Mary More (d. c. 1714), artist and writer, remains a mystery on many levels. Nothing is known of her parentage, or of her marriages to Mr. Waller and to Mr. More. What we know about her life comes through traces found in her children's lives, her one known surviving painting, this essay, and a set of verses. In the correspondence of her son, Richard Waller, the secretary for the Royal Society of London (1687–1709), we catch glimpses of her London life in the early years of the eighteenth century, residing near Gresham College in Crosby Square; she numbered among her well-wishers other members of the Royal Society, including Hans Sloane and the eminent scientist Robert Hooke. Her earliest reputation was not as a commentator on Englishwomen's rights but as a portrait painter. In 1674 she presented the Bodleian Library with a copy of a Holbein portrait of Thomas Cromwell (mistakenly identified at that time as being of Sir Thomas More). This occasion is her first known link to the Oxford academic Robert Whitehall, in whose manuscript miscellany volume her essay, "The Woman's Right," is preserved, along with his rebuttal, "The Womans Right Proved False" (British Library Harley MS 3918). The contents of the volume suggest it was compiled between 1674 and Whitehall's death in 1685. More dedicates her essay to her daughter, Elizabeth Waller, noting in the preface that given the happy situation of More's marriages, Elizabeth might find it strange that her mother had given thought to this subject. Her reason for writing, More states, is "from a trouble in me observing ye sad consequences & events that have fallen on men and their Wives, through this mistake of mens pretending a Power over their Wives, that neither

God nor nature doe allow." As the title page sets forth, More argues that it is through custom alone, "by a long practising of Power towards Wives, (impowered to it by laws of their
own making)," that Englishmen and women accept the notion of the inequality of the
sexes, "which I do not find allowed neither by the Laws of God nor Nature." More's principle line of argument is that male translators of the King James Bible have translated the
same Greek verb differently when it is applied to men and to women: "Our modern
Writers," More declares, "will have ye Geneva translation read with ye Spectacles of their
Marginal notes, where they make yt which they render subject, to be obedient, & this
onely to wives." Foreshadowing later polemical writers such as Judith Drake and Mary
Astell, More concludes that "it is ye want of learning, & ye same education in women, yt
men have, which makes them loose their right. Men always held ye Parliament & have
enacted their own wills . . . .Were this Errour in Parents amended in their not bringing up
their Daughter[s] learned, then I doubt not but they would as much excel men in that as
they do now in Virtue."

Margaret Ezell
Texas A&M University

Mary More, "The Womans Right or her Power in a Greater Equality to Her Husband Proved than is
Allowed or Practised in England" (c. 1680) British Library MS Harley 3918. f. 46.

A Serious

PROPOSAL

To the

Ladies,

For the Advancement of
their true and greatest
Interest.

By a Lover of Her **SEX**.

L O N D O N,
Printed for **R. Wilkin** at
the *King's Head* in St. *Paul's*
Church-Yard. 1694.

2.13: Mary Astell, *A Serious Proposal to the Ladies* (1694). Reproduced by kind permission of
The Newberry Library, Chicago, Illinois.

(64)

You are therefore Ladies, invited into a place, where you shall suffer no other confinement, but to be kept out of the road of sin : You shall not be depriv'd of your grandeur, but only exchange the vain Pomps and Pageantry of the world, empty Titles and Forms of State, for the true and solid Greatnefs of being able to difpife *them*. You will only quit the Chat of infignificant people, for an ingenious Converfation; the froth of flafhy wit for real wifdom; idle tales for inftructive difcourfes. The deceitful Flatteries of thofe who under pretence of loving and admiring you, really ferved their

[65]

their *own* bafe ends, for the feafonable Reproofs and wholfom Counfels of your hearty well-wifhers and affectionate Friends ; which will procure you thofe perfections your feigned lovers pretended you had, and kept you from obtaining. No uneafy task will be enjoyn'd you , all your labour being only to prepare for the higheft degrees of that Glory, the very loweft of which, is more than at prefent you are able to conceive, and the profpect of it fufficient to out-weigh all the Pains of Religion, were there any in it, as really there is none. All that is requir'd of you

2.13: Mary Astell, *A Serious Proposal to the Ladies* (1694). Reproduced by kind permission of The Newberry Library, Chicago, Illinois.

Mary Astell, *A Serious Proposal to the Ladies* (1694)

Mary Astell (1666–1731) was a prolific and energetic polemicist, philosopher, and poet. Born into the increasingly powerful and educated middle class, she studied with an uncle from a young age and published her first book of poetry by the time she was twenty. She wrote with verve and rhetorical sophistication on a wide range of issues and has been credited with being one of the earliest recognizably feminist voices.

In *A Serious Proposal to the Ladies* Astell argues energetically for the education of women as a means to combat the moral and spiritual degeneration she perceived in her social sphere. In the pages illustrated here she calls on her young female readership to embrace learning by entering the religious college for women, which is the central proposition in the pamphlet, in which scholarship was to be supported and framed by proper devotional exercises and instruction. In a carefully constructed combination of zeugma and antithesis, she sets the spiritual benefit of retirement in a place of learning against the tawdry pleasures of the world and, most radically for this time, the value of female community and friendship against the empty flattery of men.

The pamphlet is directed to an audience of the young women whom Astell wishes to influence, and she is uncompromising in her position that instead of paying attention only to their appearance and possessions, women need to develop their minds and souls: "your Glass," she admonishes with typically acerbic wit, "will not do you half so much service as a serious reflection on your own Minds." Like Bathsua Makin, Astell is firm in her emphasis on women's scholarly ability and potential, pointing out that men would hardly be as wise as they claim if they were denied education, and that the frivolous conduct they despise in women is itself the direct result of this denial.

A Serious Proposal was very well received and widely read during the last decade of the century, although the college itself never came into being. The title page reproduced here is from the first edition (1694), published anonymously "By a lover of Her Sex," and shows a relatively plain and undecorated text in the small duodecimo size intended for carrying on the person, and therefore for frequent reading. Astell herself was irritated and disappointed in the lack of active response from her women readers, and she included a preface in the second and subsequent editions expressing her disappointment. Still, *A Serious Proposal* went through four editions in five years, suggesting a very substantial readership; in addition, one of the copies in the British Library is inscribed "Mary Turner, from her Mother, 1724," attesting to its continuing presence well into the eighteenth century.

HEATHER CAMPBELL
YORK UNIVERSITY

Mary Astell. *A Serious Proposal to the Ladies* (1694). Newberry Library, Chicago, Ill., HQ1201.A8. Title page, and pages 64–65.

To the Excellent Mr. Lock.

SIR,

I Do not prefume to addrefs thefe Papers to you as a Champion in your Caufe, but as an Offender, to make the beft Apology I can for a Bold unlicenc'd Undertaking; that Excellence of the Effay of *Human Underftanding*, which gave me Courage in encountring a Caviller againft it, ftrikes me with Shame and Awe, when I think of coming before you; like a Rafh Lover, that fights in Defence of a Lady's Honour, the jufter his Caufe is, the more Reafon he has to fear her Refentment, for not leaving it to affert it felf by its own Evidence, and the more it fecures him of Succefs againft his Adverfary, the lefs Pretence he has to her Forgivenefs : But, Sir, The Effay of *Human Underftanding* is a Publick Concern, which every one has a Right and Intereft to defend ; It came too late into the World to be receiv'd without Oppofition, as it might have been in the firft Ages of Philofophy, before Mens Heads were prepoffeft with imaginary Science; at leaft, no doubt, if fo Perfect a Work cou'd have been produc'd fo Early, it wou'd have prevented a great deal of that unintelligible Jargon, and vain Pretence to Knowledge of things out of the reach of Human Underftanding, which make a great part of the School-Learning, and difufe the Mind to Plain and folid Truth.

But

2.14: Catharine Trotter (Cockburn), "To the Excellent Mr. Lock" (1702).
By permission of The British Library.

Catharine Trotter (Cockburn), "To the Excellent Mr. Lock," *A Defence of the Essay of Human Understanding* (1702)

"To the Excellent Mr. Lock" is a printed letter dedicatory addressed to John Locke that prefaces Catharine Trotter's *A Defence of the Essay of Human Understanding, Written by Mr. Lock. Wherein Its Principles, with reference to Morality, Revealed Religion, and the Immortality of the Soul, are consider'd and justify'd: in answer to some Remarks on that Essay* (London, 1702).

Catharine Trotter (1674– or 1679–1749) was a playwright who also wrote and published philosophical commentaries, achievements extremely unusual for a woman in this period. Her first published philosophical piece was her *A Defence of the Essay of Human Understanding written by Mr. Lock.* Although it later became known that this was her work, the piece was published anonymously, because Trotter was worried that attaching the name of a female author would prejudice readers against it. In a letter of December 9, 1701, to her friend Thomas Burnet of Kemnay, she wrote, "A woman's name would give a prejudice against a work of this nature." The body of the work was prefaced by an address to Mr. Locke, the first page of which is reproduced here. Locke's *Essay*, published originally in 1690, had caused something of a stir among churchmen, as many of them interpreted it as undermining some of the fundamental tenets of the Christian religion, for example, the doctrine of the Trinity and the immortality of the soul. As a consequence, many people regarded him as a dangerous thinker. It was therefore a brave and radical act for a woman to put her intellect on the line in defending such a controversial theorist. Trotter refers in lines 6–7 to a "Caviller against it," the "Caviller" being Thomas Burnet of the Charterhouse (a different Burnet from her correspondent mentioned above), to whose *Remarks* on Locke's work her *Defence* was addressed.

Hers was in fact the only published reply to Burnet's *Remarks.* Her prefatory letter is very deferential, referring to herself as "a rash lover" in defending a work of so much merit that it needs no defense, but claiming nonetheless that Locke's work is so relevant to the public good that it justifies her action. Significantly, she makes a point of praising his writing by positioning it in opposition to "the unintelligible jargon, and vain pretence to knowledge of things" that she links to "School-Learning." The term "school learning" refers to the old philosophical scholastic method, often referred to as the learning of the schools or schoolmen, which relied heavily on set piece formulas and unintelligible jargon in arcane language or medieval Latin. The point she is making about philosophical method is a particularly significant one for women in this period, because the old scholastic approach had made philosophical discourse accessible only to those coming out of the traditional university education in the classics. As women were excluded from higher education, they were also excluded from participating in intellectual debate of this kind. Locke was working from a completely different basis, using an inductive epistemological approach, with an emphasis on the rational faculty of each individual. He eschewed jargon and archaic debating methods, opening up a more broadly based debate, which gave women the chance to participate. A number of women corresponded regularly with Locke on philosophical questions, among them Lady Damaris Masham and Mrs. Elizabeth Burnet.

Trotter's concern in her *Defence* of Locke is predominantly to support his ideas on the origins of ethics, an area in which she displayed great interest in all her writings, both philosophical and literary. She continued to write in defense of Locke's theories until her death in 1749.

ANNE KELLEY
INDEPENDENT

Catharine Trotter. "To the Excellent Mr. Lock." *A Defence of the Essay of Human Understanding, written by Mr Lock* (1702). British Library 117.a.31. First page.

Bibliography

Astell, Mary. *A Serious Proposal to the Ladies, Parts I and II.* Ed. Patricia Springbourg. London: Pickering and Chatto, 1997.

Aughterson, Kate, ed. *Renaissance Woman: Constructions of Femininity in England: A Sourcebook.* London: Routledge, 1995.

Beilin, Elaine V. *Redeeming Eve: Women Writers of the English Renaissance.* Princeton, N.J.: Princeton University Press, 1987, 97–8.

Bolton, Martha Brandt. "Some Aspects of the Philosophical Work of Catharine Trotter." *Journal of the History of Philosophy* 31 (1993): 565–88. Repr. in *Hypatia's Daughters: Fifteen Hundred Years of Women Philosophers.* Ed. Linda Lopez McAlister, Bloomington: Indiana University Press, 1996. 139–64.

Bowden, Caroline. "Parental attitudes towards the education of girls in late sixteenth and early seventeenth-century England." *Education and Cultural Transmission.* Ed. R. Aldrich, J. Dekker, F. Simon and J. Sturm *Paedagogica Historica*, Supplementary Series Vol. 2, Gent, 1996. 607–11.

———. "'For the Glory of God': a study of the education of English Catholic women in convents in Flanders and France in the first half of the seventeenth century." *Paedagogica Historica*, Supplementary Series Vol. 5, Gent, 1999. 56–77.

Brink, Jean R. "Bathsua Makin: Educator and Linguist (1608?-1675?)." In *Female Scholars; A Tradition of Learned Women Before 1800.* Ed. J. R. Brink. Montréal: Eden Press, 1980. 86–100.

———. "Bathsua Makin: "Most Learned Matron." *Huntington Library Quarterly* 54 (1991): 313–26.

Butler, Charles, ed. *Female replies to Swetnam the Woman-Hater.* Bristol: Thoemmes Press, 1995.

Clark, Sandra. "*Hic Mulier, Haec Vir*, and the Controversy over Masculine Women." *Studies in Philology* 82 (1985): 157–83.

Crandall, Coryl, ed. *Swetnam, the Woman-hater: The Controversy and the Play.* Indiana: Purdue University Press, 1969.

Davis, Natalie Zemon. "Women on Top." *Society and Culture in Early Modern France.* Stanford, Calif.: Stanford University Press, 1975. 124–51.

de Baar, Mirjam et al., eds. *Choosing the Better Part: Anna Maria van Schurman (1607–1678).* Boston: Kluwer Academic Publishers, 1996.

Evans, Robert C. "'New' Poems by Early Modern Women: 'A Maid Under 14,' Elizabeth With, Elizabeth Collett, and 'A Lady of Honour,'" *Ben Jonson Journal* 7 (2000): 447–515.

———. *Renaissance Texts in Context: Studies of Unusual Early Modern Documents.* (forthcoming).

Ezell, Margaret J.M. *The Patriarch's Wife: Literary Evidence and the History of the Family.* Chapel Hill: University of North Carolina Press, 1987. Appendix of More's essay, 191–203.

Fitzmaurice, James. "Fancy and the Family: Self-Characterizations of Margaret Cavendish." *Huntington Library Quarterly* 53.3 (Summer 1990): 198–209.

Flecknoe, Richard. "On the Dutchess of Newcastle's Closset." *Epigrams of all Sorts, Made at Several Times, on Several Occasions.* London, 1671. New York: Garland Facsimile, 1975.

Grant, Douglas. *Margaret the First: A Biography of Margaret Cavendish, Duchess of Newcastle 1623–1673.* Toronto: University of Toronto Press, 1957.

Gubar, Susan. "'The Blank Page' and the Issues of Female Creativity." *Writing and Sexual Difference.* Ed. Elizabeth Abel. Chicago: University of Chicago Press, 1982. 73–93.

Helm, J.L. "Bathsua Makin's An Essay to Revive the Antient Education of Gentlewomen in the Canon of Seventeenth-Century Educational Reform Tracts." *Cahiers Élisabéthains* 44 (1993): 45–51.

Henderson, Katherine Usher, and Barbara F. McManus. *Half Humankind: Contexts and Texts of the Controversy about Women in England, 1540–1640.* Urbana and Chicago: University of Illinois Press, 1985.

Howard, Jean E. "Renaissance Antitheatricality and the Politics of Gender and Rank in *Much Ado about Nothing.*" *Shakespeare Reproduced: The Text in History and Ideology.* Ed. Jean E. Howard and Marion F. O'Connor. New York: Methuen, 1987. 163–87.

Hutton, Sarah. "Cockburn, Catharine (Trotter)." *The Cambridge Dictionary Of Philosophy.* Gen. ed. Robert Audi. Cambridge: Cambridge University Press, 1995. 127.

Irwin, Joyce. "Anna Maria Van Schurman: From Feminism to Pietism." *Church History* 46.1 (1977): 48–62.

———. "Anna Maria van Schurman. The Star of Utrecht (1607–1678)," in *Female Scholars: A Tradition of Learned Women before 1800.* Ed. J.R. Brink. Montreal: Eden Press Women's Publications, 1980. 68–85.

Jones, Ann Rosalind. "Maidservants of London: Sisterhoods of Kinship and Labor." *Maids and Mistresses, Cousins and Queens: Woman's Alliances in Early Modern England.* Ed. Susan Frye and Karen Robertson. Oxford: Oxford University Press, 1999. 21–32.

Kelley, Anne. *Catharine Trotter: An Early Modern Writer in the Vanguard of Feminism.* Aldershot: Ashgate, 2002.

Magnusson, A. Lynne. "'His Pen With My Hande': Jane Anger's Revisionary Rhetoric." *English Studies in Canada* 17 (1991): 269–81.

Matchinske, Megan. "Legislating 'Middle-Class' Morality in the Marriage Market: Ester Sowernam's *Ester hath hang'd Haman.*" *English Literary Renaissance* 24 (1994): 154–83.

O'Neill, Eileen. "Disappearing Ink: Early Modern Women Philosophers and Their Fate in History." Janet Kourany, ed., *Philosophy in a Feminist Voice: Critiques and Reconstructions.* Princeton, N.J.: Princeton University Press, 1998, 17–62.

Perry, Ruth. *The Celebrated Mary Astell: An Early English Feminist.* Chicago: University of Chicago Press, 1986.

Phillippy, Patricia. "The Maid's Lawful Liberty: Service, the Household, and "Mother B" in Isabella Whitney's *A Sweet Nosegay.*" *Modern Philology* 95.4 (1998): 439–62.

Pollock, Linda. *With Faith and Physic: The Life of a Tudor Gentlewoman, Lady Grace Mildmay 1552–1620.* London: Collins and Brown, 1993.

Purkiss, Diane. "Material Girls: The Seventeenth-Century Woman Debate." *Women, Texts and Histories 1575–1760.* Ed. Clare Brant and Diane Purkiss. London: Routledge, 1992. 69–101.

Sharrock, Catherine. "De-ciphering Women and De-Scribing Authority: The Writings of Mary Astell." *Women, Writing, History 1640–1740.* Ed. Isobel Grundy and Susan Wisemen. Athens: University of Georgia Press, 1992. 109–24.

Shepherd, Simon, ed. *The Women's Sharp Revenge: Five Women's Pamphlets from the Renaissance.* London: Fourth Estate, 1985.

Speght, Rachel. *The Polemics and Poems of Rachel Speght.* Ed. Barbara Kiefer Lewalski. Oxford: Oxford University Press, 1996.

Steadman, David W. *Abraham van Diepenbeeck: Seventeenth-Century Flemish Painter.* Ann Arbor, Mich.: UMI Research Press, 1982.

Swetnam, Joseph. *The Araignment of Lewd, Idle, Froward and Unconstant Women.* Ed. F.W. Van Heertum. Nijmegen: Cicero Press, 1989.

Teague, Frances. *Bathsua Makin, Woman of Learning.* Lewisburg: Bucknell University Press, 1998.

Travitsky, Betty. "The 'Wyll and Testament' of Isabella Whitney." *English Literary Renaissance* 10 (1980): 76–94.

———. *The Paradise of Women: Writings by Englishwomen of the Renaissance.* Conn.: Greenwood Press, 1981.

———. "'The Lady Doth Protest': Protest in the Popular Writings of Renaissance Englishwomen." *English Literary Renaissance* 14 (1984): 255–84.

van Schurman, Anna Maria. *Eukleria seu melioris: Whether a Christian Woman Should be Educated and Other Writings From her Intellectual Circle.* Ed. and trans. Joyce L. Irwin. Chicago: University of Chicago Press, 1998.

Woodbridge, Linda. *Women and the English Renaissance: Literature and the Nature of Womankind, 1540–1620.* Urbana and Chicago: University of Illinois Press, 1984. 74–113.

CHAPTER 3

Mothers' Legacies and Medical Manuals

Advice Books and Mothers' Legacies

The Autobiography of Mrs. Alice Thornton is a history of deliverances that relies on a self-generated, clinical, biblical vocabulary to convey a woman's experience of coming into being. In one representative episode, Alice Thornton (b. 1626) describes the horrendous ordeal of her three-day labor, which ends with the breech birth of her fifth child:

> I fell into exceeding sharpe travaill in great extreamity, so that the midwife did believe I should be delivered soone. But loe! it fell out contrary for the child staied in the birth, and came crosse with his feete first . . . att which time I was upon the racke in bearing my childe with such equisitt torment, as if each lime weare divided from other, for the space of two houers; when at length, beeing speechlesse and breathlesse, I was, by the infinitt providence of God, in great mercy delivered.[1]

Confusion marks this painful account until the bodily and spiritual deliverance of mother restores order: "Tho' my body was torne in pieces, my soule was miraculously delivered from death" (Thornton 95n). Speechless and breathless, Thornton denies her agency to become a fit instrument of God. Though the child dies shortly after birth, the mother's ordeal is justified in the context of the providential narrative in which the writer locates the numerous tragic episodes of the history she develops. By juxtaposing maternity with infancy, birth with death, and self-assertion with self-denial, the mother's account of her ordeal establishes an important context for examining the language of birth and of female expression in the early modern literature.

Thornton's *Autobiography* is neither a mother's advice book nor a medical handbook—the two genres featured in this chapter. But it is nevertheless one of a number of valuable autobiographical writings that apply the discourses of gynecology, obstetrics, miscarriages, labour, and birth (including breech births). Thus its purpose is similar to that of the mothers' advice books or mothers' legacies—a subcategory of the conduct manual or genre of advice. Males in the early modern period actually produced the vast majority of women's household advice books, not to mention medical and midwifery manuals, and

even though mothers' legacies constitute a distinctly female genre, they too may have originated with a male author.[2]

An early entry we feature here, Isabella Whitney's "A Modeste Meane for Maides"
(1573), is not the work of a mother, though the poet assumes a related role as mentor in
advising her younger sisters of the duties attendant upon Christian maidservants. Elder sisters in fact served in a quasi-maternal capacity for their younger sisters, especially when their
domestic jobs put them at risk with gentlemen of the house. In addition to spiritual advice,
Whitney's warnings reflect concerns about gossip, sexuality, and the mere appearance of mis-
behavior, which might compromise the "freedom" of single young working women.

More typical was the advice book produced by mothers who offered spiritual guidance
to children—the intended readers and primary recipients of the genre. Publication of some of
these works in the early seventeenth century increased their popularity and thus established
the advice book as "a recognizable literary form."[3] Elizabeth Grymeston's posthumously published, composite text, *Miscelanea. prayers. meditations. memoratives* (1604) and Elizabeth
Joscelin's "The Mothers Legacy to her Unborn Childe" (1622) are examples of early advice
books. The former was intended to provide religious (Catholic) instruction for Grymeston's
son; the latter, a devotional work in the Protestant plain style, was directed at an unborn child.[4]
Dorothy Leigh's Puritan text, *The Mothers Blessing* (1616; 5th ed., 1618), which Joscelin's
"Mothers Legacy" occasionally echoes, is a mother's legacy originally designed for publication
to ensure its preservation for the author's children.

Leigh, who cites her impending death, shares with Grymeston and Joscelin a concern
to justify her act of writing.[5] Paradoxically, the "rhetoric of the deathbed legacy" offered
women a medium through which they could express themselves and challenge "cultural
demands for their silence."[6] M. R. used a different strategy; by preserving her anonymity,
she enjoyed more freedom than her sister writers, thus accounting for the greater sense of
assurance she exhibits in producing *The Mothers Counsell or, Live within Compasse. Being
the Last Will and Testament to her dearest Daughter* (c.1630).

Like M. R., whose goal is to reach an audience that includes but extends beyond her
daughter, Elizabeth Knyvet Clinton's *The Countesse of Lincolnes Nurserie* (1622) also has a
private and public function. Moreover, *The Countesse of Lincolnes Nurserie* straddles the two
genres represented in this chapter—the more personal mother's legacy and the public
medical manual—in being dedicated to the author's daughter-in-law and yet directed to
a wider audience. Clinton focuses on a particular social practice in need of reform: the tendency by upper-class women to assign the role of breast-feeding their infants to wet
nurses. She strengthens her case for the advantages of mothers nursing their own children
by invoking biblical precedents, a common practice among authors of advice books.
Likewise directed to mature female readers, Elizabeth Richardson's *A Ladies Legacie to Her
Daughters* (1645) was intended to build a sense of community among women: Richardson
proposed to create both an implied and an actual society of prayerful women who would
achieve a sense of autonomy through devotional practices.

Thematically linking the two main sections of this chapter is Hannah Wolley's
Supplement to the Queen-like Closet; or, a little of Every Thing (1674–75), which serves as an
instructional manual and household advice book for subjects as diverse yet interrelated as
food preparation, interior decoration, and needlework. One of the most widely published
female writers of the seventeenth century, Wolley also prided herself on her abilities as a
medical practitioner, the main focus of *The Supplement*.

Medical Manuals

Since at least the fifteenth century, men attempted to prevent women's entry into the healing professions. Male physicians in 1421 petitioned parliament to have the uneducated, including women, barred from practicing medicine. In 1518 Thomas Linacre established the College of Physicians to distinguish men who possessed medical degrees from unauthorized practitioners and women who presumed to have any knowledge of medicine.[7]

Male writers had their own stories to tell about the womb and in turn of the act of gestation and the art of (self-)generation. "Ironically, while massive practical ignorance and nascent professional avarice made motherhood appallingly perilous, the development of new life in women's wombs was the focus of lively philosophical debate and theoretical disputation," John Rumrich observes.[8] Though identified as base, women's reproductive functions were a source of much curiosity; even the physician William Harvey, whose dissection of a female body enabled him to see the reproductive organs with his own eyes, attributes to males privileged access to the otherwise impenetrable mystery of the womb and, by extension, generative entitlement in reference to intellectual labor.

In describing the mysterious processes of pregnancy and labor, philosophers and physicians used female inferiority to interpret an internal structure that otherwise resisted examination. The treatises of Vesalius (1543; English translations from 1545), Thomas Willis, Thomas Sydenham, and Nicholas Culpeper, which addressed such subjects as gynecology, women's diseases, and medical cures, exposed the authors' underlying assumption about the chaotic state of the womb and of the woman. Nicholas Fontanus in *The Womans Doctour* explains that the Matrix "hath a Sympathy with all the parts of the body," and thus is responsible for the many diseases—physical, spiritual, and moral—experienced by women.[9] The conclusions of the primitive gynecologists were shaped by a belief in woman's essential inferiority and in the necessity of restricting women to "Household employments" that would prevent the disruption both of the bodily cycle and of the hierarchical social order.

The failure to recognize the influence that entrenched views on women's defective nature had on shaping ideas about gynecology and obstetrics accounts for the lack of critical responses to these crude readings of the womb and interior female spaces. The government of a woman with child had, moreover, been a male prerogative and was handled by male writers. In Jacques Guillimeau's *Child-birth, or the Happy Delivery of Women*, the translator's preface indicates that the text is directed at "chuirurgions and midwives"; "as for women (whom I am most afraid to offend) they must bee content to have their infirmities detected, if they will have helpe for them."[10] The publication in English of writings by Guillimeau, Culpeper, Harvey, and Jacob Rueff facilitated the learning about midwifery, but, as Elizabeth D. Harvey observes, "the appropriation of the midwives' voices in the obstetrical books of the early seventeenth century" is another means by which medical control was exerted over the female body.[11]

Between 1658 and 1664, the London astrologer Sarah Jinner published a series of almanacs for women that provided medical advice, including cures for complaints of the Mother or Matrix (womb or uterus). In turn she asserted women's rights in addressing issues on women's health in a period when women's control of the birth process was being threatened. Not until 1671, however, would an English female writer and midwife, Jane Sharp, produce a medical handbook for her "sister" midwives in England. Apologizing her way into print and defending the necessity of anglicizing the language of sexuality, she announces at the end of book I in *The Midwives Book*:

> Thus I have as briefly and as plainly as I could, laid down a description of the parts of generation of both sexes, purposely omitting hard names, that I might have no cause to enlarge my work, by giving you the meaning of them where there is no need, unless it be for such persons who desire rather to know Words than Things."[12]

Sharp defended the rightful place of women in the profession and, having judged difficult words as impediments, she reproduced the medical discourses in the mother's and mother tongue.[13] Her criticism about an elite vocabulary (in the passage quoted above) is largely directed at Culpeper's very popular manual, *The Dictionary For Midwives* (1651), from which she distinguishes her own approach. Sharp was also familiar with some continental sources on midwifery, including Eucharius Roesslin's *The byrth of mankynde, otherwyse named the womansbooke* (London, 1545), an early guide to childbirth, with sections on, for example, "Of the wombe and his partes" and "Howe a woman with chylde shall bee her selfe, and what remedies be for them that have hard labour." Concerned about the hardships women experienced at the hands of unskilled midwives, Sharp was determined to educate her readers—a goal shared by Mary Trye and Elizabeth Cellier.[14] While mother's legacies like Richardson's negotiate between the individual author and her community, the authors of medical manuals direct attention to more public collective anxieties.

Mary Trye, the daughter of Thomas O'Dowde, a member of the Society of Chemical Physicians created alongside and in defiance of the College of Physicians, published her defence of the chemical physicians, called *Medicatrix, or The Woman-Physician*, in 1675. It recommends her father's approach to medicine—specifically, his use of herbal remedies and drugs—over that of the college members who advocated bleeding as a cure. Moreover, since Trye continued to apply the medical skills passed on to her by Thomas O'Dowde, her treatise is designed in part to dismiss the assumption that an elite education required by the college is necessary for practitioners.

Elizabeth Cellier takes up a similar argument: around 1680, she prepared a proposal directed at James II for establishing a hospital that would train midwives and care for the poor. The Cellier entry in this chapter focuses on the second pamphlet she produced on this subject, which addresses an unidentified doctor, *To Dr.——, an Answer to his Queries* (1688). Setting out to defend contemporary women practitioners, Cellier cites biblical and classical precedents of males who ultimately recognized women's rights as midwives or healers. She also campaigns for the replacement of ecclesiastical licensing of midwives by a system that would provide proper training and introduce professional standards, having provided a (somewhat misguided) history of changes to licensing procedures since the mid-seventeenth century. The proposal is compromised by her rhetoric of self-justification as she seeks to establish control of midwives' training herself. As a Roman Catholic (who would eventually be tried, pilloried, and imprisoned for her faith), she was unable to obtain the license afforded well-trained midwives of London, though most midwives practiced without a license. Like Sharp and Trye, Cellier maintains that a formal, classical education is no substitute for the practical experience enjoyed by midwives, experience that needs to be supplemented by the kind of instruction that her proposed college would provide. The college was never built, however; as the discourse and practice of medicine were increasingly subsumed by males, represented by the College of Physicians, women struggled to pass on their learning and their legacies to each other and their children.

Despite the constraints to which their authors were subject, the mothers' legacies and medical manuals left their impressions. These works provided women with a means of articulating their knowledge, their faith, and their influence upon the lives of others. The influence was felt directly by the children for whom the works were most often written; but also indirectly—and more significantly for the development of women's writing in the period—by the other readers of the legacies and manuals, especially after they appeared in print.

Notes

We acknowledge most gratefully the invaluable assistance of Doreen Evenden, Elaine Hobby, and Marjorie Rubright.

1. Alice Thornton, *The Autobiography of Mrs. Alice Thornton, of East Newton, County York*, ed. C. Jackson (Durham: Published for the Surtees Society by Andrews and Co., 1875), 95. "As if each lime weare divided from other" probably refers to the common belief that the pelvis itself opens during birth (correspondence with Elaine Hobby, 01.2003).

2. See Suzanne W. Hull, *Chaste, Silent, and Obedient: English Books for Women, 1475–1640* (San Marino: Huntington Library, 1988); Doreen Evenden suggests that the "mother's manual" genre may have originated with Nicholas Breton's 1601 advice book, *The Mothers Blessing*. Breton wrote the manual to a young man named Thomas Rowe and assumed the voice of Mr. Rowe's mother, Lady Bartley, and styled his text as maternal advice (Evenden, chapter 1, *The Midwives of Seventeenth-Century London* [Cambridge: Cambridge University Press, 2000]). On the ideological construction of motherhood by men as it informed the genre of advice, see Valerie Wayne, "Advice for Women from Mothers and Patriarchs," *Women and Literature in Britain, 1500–1700*, ed. Helen Wilcox (Cambridge: Cambridge University Press, 1996), 56–79.

3. See Elaine V. Beilin, *Redeeming Eve: Women Writers of the English Renaissance* (Princeton, N.J.: Princeton University Press, 1987), 266–67; Mary Beth Rose, "Where Are All the Mothers in Shakespeare? Options for Gender Representation in the English Renaissance," *Shakespeare Quarterly* 42 (1991): 311; and *The Mothers Legacy to her unborn Childe: Elizabeth Joscelin*, ed. Jean LeDrew Metcalfe (Toronto: University of Toronto Press, 2000), 6. Joscelin's title (ms. 1622, pub. 1624) influenced that of Susanna Bell's *The Legacy of a Dying Mother* (1673).

4. Megan Matchinski, "Gendering Catholic Conformity: The Politics of Equivocation in Elizabeth Grymeston's Miscelanea," *Journal of English and Germanic Philology* 101.3 (2002): 329–57.

5. On the relationship of the texts of these three authors, see *Women's Writing in Stuart England: The Mothers' Legacies of Dorothy Leigh, Elizabeth Joscelin, and Elizabeth Richardson*, ed. Sylvia Brown (Littlehampton, West Sussex: Sutton, 1999).

6. Wendy Wall, *The Imprint of Gender: Authorship and Publication in the English Renaissance* (Ithaca, N.Y.: Cornell University Press, 1993), 289, 296.

7. Elaine Hobby, "Skills Books—Housewifery, Medicine, Midwifery," *Virtue of Necessity: English Women's Writing, 1649–88* (Ann Arbor: University of Michigan Press, 1989), 177.

8. Rumrich analyzes the poetics of generation in seventeenth-century England in *Milton Unbound: Controversy and Reinterpretation* (Cambridge: Cambridge University Press, 1996), 102.

9. Nicholas Fontanus, *The Womans Doctour: or, an exact and distinct Explanation of all such Diseases as are peculiar to that Sex* (London, 1651), 2; also see Hilda Smith, "Gynecology and Ideology in Seventeenth-Century England," *Liberating Women's History*, ed. Berenice A. Carroll (Urbana: University of Illinois Press, 1976).

10. Jacques Guillimeau, *Child-birth, or the Happy Delivery of Women* (London, 1635). For a historical, socioeconomic study of midwifery, see Doreen Evenden, *The Midwives of Seventeenth-Century London* (Cambridge: Cambridge University Press, 2000). On the contributions of women from a cross section of society to health care, see Doreen Evenden Nagy, *Popular Medicine in Seventeenth-Century England* (Bowling Green: Bowling Green State University Popular Press, 1988).

11. Elizabeth D. Harvey, *Ventriloquized Voices: Feminist Theory and English Renaissance Texts* (New York: Routledge, 1992), 92.

12. Jane Sharp, *The Midwives Book* (1671) (New York: Garland, 1985), 80.

13. Elaine Hobby explains that though Sharp borrowed heavily from male-authored medical books, her rewordings present a different perspective on the female body and sexual practices ("Recovering Early-Modern Women's Writing," *Women Writing 1550–1750*, ed. Jo Wallwork and Paul Salzman, *Meridian, The La Trobe University English Review* 18.1 (2001): 18–19. Also see Hobby's edition of *The Midwives Book* (Oxford: Oxford University Press, 1999).

14. See Hobby's *Virtue of Necessity*, 178–89.

by the Auctor : with Replies .

2. ¶ Then iustly do such deedes,
    as are to you assynde :
All wanton toyes, good sisters now
    exile out of your minde,
I hope you geue no cause,
    wherby I should suspect:
But this I know too many liue,
    that would you soone infect .
yf God do not preuent,
    or with his grace expell:
I cannot speake, or wryte to much,
    because I loue you well.

3. ¶ Your busines soone dispatch,
    and listen to no lyes:
Nor credit euery fayned tale,
    that many wyll deuise.
For words they are but winde,
    yet words may hurt you so:
As you shall neuer brook the same,
    yf that you haue a foe.
God shyld you from all such,
    as would by word or Byll.
Procure your shame, or neuer cease
    tyll they haue wrought you yll.
                         ¶ See

3.1: Isabella Whitney, "A Modest Meane for Maides" (1573). By permission of The British Library.

Isabella Whitney, "A Modest Meane for Maides" (1573)

Included among the thirteen "familiar Epistles and friendly Letters by the Auctor: with Replies" appended to Whitney's poetical *Nosgay*, "A Modest meane for Maides" is a verse letter of practical advice directed to "two of her yonger Sisters servinge in London" (C7v). Whitney, like her sisters (and at least one of her brothers), had been employed as a domestic servant in a London household. The occasion of her writing *A Nosgay*, based upon the details given in the attached epistles, seems to have been the termination of this employment. With her time "unfettered" by household duties, Whitney turned her energies to her writing; but conscious of the dangers that attended her new-found freedom, she filled her verses with admonitions and gentle "rules," the observance of which "shal you wealth posses, and quietnesse of mynde" (C7v). These two traits seem most to have escaped Whitney herself in her experiences in London, for *A Nosgay* resonates with complaints of the author's poverty and expressions of anxiety over what her future might hold.

"A Modeste meane for Maides" is framed by the daily duties of the obedient Christian maidservant whose first and final act is to pray to God for protection and guidance. As older sister and experienced worker, Whitney appropriates this divine role and offers her readers guidance on the personal conduct, habits, and household duties pertinent to a member of the serving class. Of particular concern to Whitney, as shown by the excerpt given here (C8), is that women in service should avoid any activities that might "infect" their lives or ruin their reputations. Here Whitney draws our attention (and that of her sisters) to the double bind in which many London maidservants found themselves during their years of service: their freedom as unattached, single women bound them to the suspicious threats of a society that perceived such freedom as the breeding ground of sin and licentiousness (for more on this topic see Patricia Phillippy).

Drawing upon her model (both literary and personal), Whitney encourages her readers to take responsibility for the management of their own lives. To "exile" all "wanton toyes" by rejecting any romantic invitations and to avoid the "lyes" and "fayned tale(s)" of the gossip. Whitney's writings display a certain degree of familiarity with both these potential dangers. Her earlier "The Copy of a Letter" voices the lamentations of a maiden whose betrothed has forsaken her for the affections of another, and a significant number of the *Nosgay*'s 110 "posyes" warn its readers of the miseries attendant upon "A hasty tonge" (C4v). Whitney's admonishing verses, such as "A Modest Meane for Maids," articulate many of the concerns of the sixteenth-century London maiden. As such, they not only provided pleasing and informative instruction to readers of her own age, but now also convey much worthwhile instruction about the lives of early modern women to ours.

Linda Vecchi
Memorial University of Newfoundland

Isabella Whitney. *A Sweet Nosgay, or Pleasant Posye* (1573). British Library C.39.b.45, C8.

Tota vita dies vnus.

Elf: t bnt as me Eye

CHAP. I.
A short line how to leuell your life.

Hen thou rifeſt, let thy thoughts aſcend, that grace may deſcend: and if thou canſt not weepe for thy ſinnes, then weepe, becauſe thou canſt not weepe.

Remember that Prayer is the wing wherewith thy ſoule flieth to heauen; and Meditation the eye wherewith we ſee God; and Repentance the *Superſedeas* that diſchargeth all bond of ſinne.

Let thy ſacrifice be an innocent heart: offer it dayly at ſet houres, with that deuotion that well it may ſhew, thou both knoweſt and acknowledgeſt his greatneſſe before whom thou art. So carrie thy ſelfe as woorthie of his preſence.

Where thou oweſt, pay duetie: where thou findeſt, returne curteſie: where thou art knowen, deſerue loue. Deſire the beſt: diſdaine none, but euill companie. Grieue, but be not angrie at diſcourteſies. Redreſſe, but reuenge no wrongs. Yet ſo remember pitie, as you forget not decencie.

Let your attire be ſuch, as may ſatisfie a curious eye; and yet beare witneſſe of a ſober minde.

Arme your ſelfe with that modeſtie, that may ſilence that vntemperate tongue, and controll that vnchaſte eye, that ſhall aime at paſſion.

Be mindfull of things paſt; Carefull of things preſent; Prouident of things to come.

Goe as you would be met.

Sit as you would be found.

Speake as you would be heard: And when you goe to bed, read ouer the carriage of your ſelfe that day. Reforme that is amiſſe; and giue God thanks for that which is orderly: and ſo commit thy ſelfe to him that keepes thee.

3.2: Elizabeth Grymeston, *Miscelanea. prayers. meditations. memoratives* (1604). W.D.
Jordan Special Collections & Music Library, Queen's University at Kingston, Canada.

Elizabeth Grymeston, *Miscelanea. prayers. meditations. memoratives* (1604)

Because her book was published posthumously, Elizabeth Grymeston had no part in its printed versions, and according to her dedicatory epistle to her son, she had no intention of her writing being seen beyond the eyes of her husband and son, most often posited as the possible editor(s) of both editions. The lack of editorial imposition is clear in the short title, which describes the contents and forgoes the apology, justification, or pathos found in the titles of other legacy books. Grymeston characterizes her work as "the true portraiture" of her mind, and her *Miscelanea* stand as evidence of her wide intellectual pursuits. These sections include both borrowed and original work: poems from Richard Rowlands and Robert Southwell, an imaginative and powerful prose soliloquy spoken by Dives, essays of moral instruction, and essays on political and judicial authority. These latter are the "Other hir meditations" used to expand the second edition of 1610 and may well have been left out of the first edition because they stray from the domestic into the civil arena. Their inclusion attests to the continued popularity of Grymeston's work and suggests editorial intent to present her writing as she left it. The *Memoratives,* a series of maxims and precepts intended to guide her son's conduct in his religious and secular life, frame her work in both editions and are the most didactic of her chapters.

Chapter 1, "A short line how to levell your life," is the first of Grymeston's Memoratives and shows clearly her assumption of the empowered voice of the religious instructor. It is preceded by Grymeston's epistle to her son, in which she points out her responsibility to write to him, in order to instruct him in the Catholic faith. However, Grymeston closes the epistle with rhetorical maneuvers in which she distances herself from her text as she moves past religion to add worldly advice to a young man. She then begins weaving together religious and secular instruction in the first chapter, which is her prescription for Bernye's daily life and is written completely in the imperative. These Memoratives instruct in the leveling of one's life and advocate the kind of controlled moderation that M. R. proscribes for her daughter in *The Mothers Counsell.* The distant, third-person narrative voice outlines the actions for every day. Of primary importance is prayer, "the wing wherewith thy soule flieth to heaven," to be said morning, evening and at set times during the day. Next, Grymeston points out the need for constant attention to the heart, the seat of the conscience that she positions as the motherly voice, which must be worthy and free of sin. She continues with maxims about conduct in secular life, with advice as sound, but far more succinct, than that of Polonius. Her maxims are overbearingly Christian and subtly nongendered, as they include mandates about the young man's chastity and modesty. Grymeston closes the chapter with an insistence on evening reflection and prayer, but she includes a daily thanksgiving, thereby confirming her assurance that these Christian mandates will be followed, and her son will have reason to thank God every night, as he includes his mother's prayer among his own. Grymeston's success as mother and legacy writer is resounding as she negotiates religion into a vehicle of expression, and motherhood into a means of empowerment.

ROXANNE HARDE
QUEEN'S UNIVERSITY

Elizabeth Grymeston. *Miscelanea. prayers. meditations. memoratives* (1604). W. D. Jordan Special Collections & Music Library, Queen's University at Kingston Dated 1604.G8. Chapter 1, pages B2–B3.

M.H.Park.

THE
MOTHERS
BLESSING:
Or,

The godly Counsaile of a
Gentle-woman, not long since
deceased, left behind her for her
CHILDREN:

Contayning many good exhortations, and godly admonitions, pro-
*fitable for all Parents, to leaue as
a Legacy to their Children.*

By Mris. DOROTHY LEIGH.

The fift Edition.

Prouerbs 1. 8. *My sonne, heare the instruction
of thy father, and forsake not the lawe of
thy mother.*

Printed at *London* for *Iohn Budge*,
and are to be sold at his shop, at the
Greene Dragon in Pauls
Churchyard. 1618.

3.3: Dorothy Leigh, *The Mothers Blessing* (1618). Reproduced by permission of The Huntington
Library, San Marino, California.

Dorothy Leigh, *The Mothers Blessing* (1618)

Dorothy's Leigh's very popular legacy book was first published in 1616, the year of her death, and was reprinted into the eighteenth century. As she explains in her dedicatory epistles to her sons and to Princess Elizabeth, Leigh wrote her mother's legacy book specifically for publication, sending it "abroad" to preserve it for her children. Like Elizabeth Grymeston and Elizabeth Jocelin, Leigh justifies the public act of writing *The Mothers Blessing* by invoking her impending death, but where they write only for the private audience of husband and/or child, Leigh writes for both private and public audiences in a manner well suited to the pulpit. There is evidence of her editorial control throughout the book, in the consistency of speaking voice and reliance on favorite biblical passages for support and expansion of argument.

Leigh's title page is indicative of these, and the titles, authorship statement, and quotation are an apt synthesis of both her aims and her accomplishments. As a woman, Leigh is meant to be chaste and silent, but as a mother she writes from the patriarchally sanctioned enterprise of the religious instruction of her children. Empowerment in mother's legacy writing comes chiefly through the author's placement of herself firmly within her roles as wife, Christian, and mother. By signing herself as "Mris. Dorothy Leigh" Leigh humbles herself before the private authority of her husband as she assumes the public authority of publishing author. By indicating in the title and alternate title her fulfillment of her role as Christian mother, Leigh humbles herself before the church as she assumes empowerment as a Christian parent, an empowerment that becomes far more like autonomy as she sets for herself, in the subtitle, the role of preacher before a public ministry. The whole of the compound title indicates an intention to operate within the widest paradigms of her culturally inscribed roles.

Similarly, the quotation on the title page indicates Leigh's concern that her book move from private instruction of her own sons to public instruction of the Christian community. Leigh's wide knowledge and graceful use of the Bible, in quotation and paraphrase, supports her rhetoric throughout her book, and this quotation invokes the multiplicity of meaning upon which she relies. The quotation is first a personal instruction to her own sons, but its situation in the laws of Solomon and in the laws of the Pentateuch indicates patriarchal endorsement of Leigh's authority; as set out in the Fifth Commandment, the one subscribed subjection of male to female in early modern England is that of son to mother. With this quotation, Leigh positions herself as every Christian mother, whose instruction and law every Christian son must wear as "an ornament of grace" (Proverbs I:9).

In the sum of its parts, Leigh's title page first introduces the rhetorical strategies she employs as she assumes, without apology and as a chaste, responsible Christian mother, the public role of publishing author, then indicates her move into the far more transgressive role of spiritual leader to a wider audience.

ROXANNE HARDE
QUEEN'S UNIVERSITY

Leigh, Dorothy. *The Mothers Blessing. Or. The godly counsaile of a Gentle-woman not long since deceased, left behind her for her Children: Containing many good exhortations, and godly admonitions, profitable for all Parents to leave as a Legacy to their Children.* 5th ed. (1618). EEB 1455. Huntington Library RB 20955. Title page.

(19)

at the care to hire others to doe your *owne worke* : bee not so *vnnaturall* to thrust away your owne children: be not so *hardy* as to venter a *tender Babe* to a *lesse tender heart* : bee not *acceffary* to that diforder of caufing a *poorer woman to banifh her owne infant,* for the entertaining of a *richer womans child,* as it were, bidding her *vnloue her owne to loue yours.* Wee haue followed *Eue* in tranfgreffion, let vs follow her in obedience. VVhen God laid the forrowes of conception, of breeding, of bringing forth, and of bringing vp her children vpon her, & fo vpon vs in her loynes, did fhee reply any word againft ? Not a word ; fo I pray you all mine owne *Daughters,* and others that are ftill child-bearing reply not againft the duty of fuckling them, when God hath fent you them.

    Indeed I fee fome, if the wether be wet, or cold; if the way be fowle; if the Church be far off, I fee they are fo coy, fo nice, fo luke-warme, they will not take paines for their *own foules.* alas, no maruell if thefe will not bee at trouble, and paine to nourifh their *childrens bodies,* but feare God, bee diligent to ferue him;

D 2

ap-

3.4: Elizabeth (Knyvet) Clinton, Countess of Lincoln, *The Countesse of Lincolnes Nurserie* (1622). By permission of The British Library.

Elizabeth (Knyvet) Clinton, Countess of Lincoln, *The Countesse of Lincolnes Nurserie* (1622)

The Countesse of Lincolnes Nurserie, published in 1622, is a markedly public document that combines autobiographical experience with scriptural precedent to exhort "the duty of nursing due by mothers to their own children"(1). A mother of eighteen children and widowed for three years, Elizabeth Knyvet Clinton dedicates her treatise in the opening epistle to her daughter-in-law Briget, Countess of Lincoln, who, against the aristocratic fashion of her times, nursed her own children. Clinton's prose is spare, and her penchant for autobiographical detail reveals an author who values the authority born of what she "know[s] in [her] owne experience"(12).

Often anthologized as an "advice book," Clinton's treatise stands apart from the works of her contemporaries, Grymeston, Jocelin, Leigh, and M.R., in an important way: Clinton's audience is not her children; rather she explicitly addresses other upper-class women who, she avers, "deny Gods will," by "refus[ing] to nurse their owne children"(10). As the reader progresses through the treatise, she discovers herself part of an ever-broadening, public audience. What begins as Clinton's praise of her daughter-in-law in the opening epistle dilates to include her own daughters and the aristocratic women who might read her treatise. Elaine Beilin has argued that by reaching beyond the private discourses between mother and child into the public domain, Elizabeth Clinton "participates in the woman writer's traditional identification and explication of women's concerns for other women"(282).

Aware that her imperative has implications for women of both the highest and lowest social orders, Clinton charges her aristocratic peers with culpability: "this is one hurt which the better ranke doe by their ill example, egge, and imbolden the lower ones to follow them to their losse"(11). While humanists and writers of domestic conduct books in the seventeenth century routinely called for women to nurse their own children and rooted their case in natural and biblical law, Clinton boldly ventures to address the class-based distinctions that perpetuated an "unnatural" divide between the role of mother and that of nurse. Her treatise, therefore, should be read as a radical protest against a practice that made aristocratic women an "accessory" to an industry that would have less affluent mothers neglect and "banish" their own infants (19). In the facing passage, Clinton strikes a hortatory tone as she appeals to aristocratic women not to "disorder" the natural "duty"(19) of all women to breast-feed their own children.

Clinton advances her critique of the wet-nurse industry by marshaling evidence of biblical exemplars of the nursing mother, Eve, Sarah, Hannah, and Mary, and by asserting the tradition of natural law that a woman's body dictates her duties. Early in the treatise, Clinton questions why young and healthy women should not breast-feed when Sarah "put her selfe to this worke when shee was very old, and so might the better have excused her selfe, then we younger women can"(4). As her treatise unfolds, Clinton alters her rhetorical strategy as she posits that by granting mothers the ability to nurse, God "doth plainly tell them that he requires it"(10). Those whose "vaine lusts"(5) lead them to deny God's ordinance and to ignore scriptural precedent are denounced by this author as "monstrous unnaturalnesse"(10).

Having rooted her case in biblical exemplars and traditional assertions of natural law, Clinton sets into relief a striking personal confession. Late in the treatise, Clinton announces her regret that she did not nurse her own eighteen children; moreover, she fears that "the death of one or two of my little Babes came by the defalt of their nurses"(18). Clinton's final rhetorical strategy weaves personal experience into the more familiar warp of received authority, thus creating a sophisticated public appeal for all mothers to nurse their own children.

Marjorie Rubright
University of Michigan–Ann Arbor

Elizabeth Clinton, Countess of Lincoln. *The Countesse of Lincolnes nurserie* (Oxford, 1622). STC 5432, reel 984. British Library C.40.d.30. Page 19 (D2).

Elizabeth Joscelin, "The Mothers Legacy to her Unborn Childe" (1622)

Commentary

The manuscript of Elizabeth Joscelin's "The Mothers Legacy to her Unborn Childe" was written in 1622. Joscelin was pregnant at the time of writing, and the work, she explains, was motivated by her fear that she might not survive childbirth. Following the example of earlier writers of the mother's advice book (Elizabeth Grymeston and Dorothy Leigh), Joscelin composed a devotional work intended to ensure the salvation of her child. Unlike her predecessors, however, Joscelin addresses her work to an "unborn" child. On October 22, 1622, Joscelin gave birth to a daughter, Theodora. The fears she expressed in writing proved prophetic, when she died nine days later of a fever. The manuscript of "The Mothers Legacy" was discovered posthumously in her writing desk. Under the supervision of the Anglican clergyman Thomas Goad, the work was printed in 1624. Goad's "Approbation," praising the work and its author, precedes Joscelin's text in the first and all subsequent editions. Goad is also responsible for assigning to the work its title. The published version was printed eight times in the seventeenth century. A Dutch translation appeared in 1699 and 1784. During the Victorian period, it saw a renewed popularity with the issuing of several editions, including an American one in 1871.

Joscelin's manuscript opens with a letter to her husband, Taurell. The affectionate tone of her salutation continues throughout the letter and attests to her close relationship with her husband and her sincere desire for a child. As a loving wife and conscientious mother, Joscelin legitimates the potentially transgressive act of writing, explaining to her husband, "I send it ["The Mothers Legacy"] only to the eys of a most loving housband and a childe exceedingely beloved to whom I hope it will not be all together unprofitable." Consistent with humanist constructions of motherhood, Joscelin defines her maternal duty as "the religious trayninge" of her child. Thus, her responsibility for the spiritual education of her son or daughter inspires the writing of the work. Her text, which she refers to as "my little legacy," will compensate for her absence, allowing her to educate her child after her own death. Her letter also provides her husband with practical directions concerning their child; she advises him on the choice of a nurse, the education of the child, the need for strict discipline, and the importance of modest dress for children. Finally, Joscelin's letter explains the secrecy surrounding her composition of "The Mothers Legacy," when she reminds her husband of his displeasure at hearing her speak of the possibility of her death.

Having explained the purpose of the work and justified her writing of it in the letter, Joscelin goes on to address her child in "The Mothers Legacy." She frames her advice as a series of instructions, teaching her reader how to serve God and warning against the temptations of vice. Joscelin's method is to describe a model Christian day, setting out times for prayer, meditation, study, and recreation. She also encourages the proper observation of the Sabbath, and concludes with a discussion of the Ten Commandments and the Golden Rule.

To my truly louinge and
most Dearly loued husband
Taurell Jocelin

Myne own deare loue I no
sooner conceyued a hope that I
should bee made a mother by thee
but wth it entered the considera=
tion of a mothers duty, and shorth
after followed the apprehension of
danger that might preuent me
for executinge that care, I so ex=
ceedingly desired. I mean in reli
gious trayninge our childe, and
intruthe deathe appearinge in
this shape was doubly terrible
vnto mee first in respect of the
payntfullnes of that kinde of death
an next the losse my littell one
should haue in wantinge mee
but I thanke god theas fears were
cured wth the remembrance that
all things worke together for the
best to those that loue god.

3.5: Elizabeth Joscelin, "The Mothers Legacy to her Unborn Childe" (1622).
By permission of The British Library.

Transcription

To my truly lovinge / and most Dearly loved husband / Taurell Jocelin

Myne own deare love I no / sooner conceyved a hope that I / should bee made a mother by thee / but with it entered the considerat / ion of a mothers duty, and shortly / after followed the apprehension of / danger that might prevent me / for executinge that care, I so ex / ceedingly desired. I mean in reli / gious trayninge Our childe, and / in truthe deathe appearinge in / this shape was doubly terrible / unto mee first in respect of the / paynfullnes of that kinde of death / an next the losse my littell one / should have in wantinge mee / but I thanke god theas fears wear / cured with the remembrance that / all things worke together for the / best to those that love god.

JEAN LeDREW METCALFE
WILFRID LAURIER UNIVERSITY

Elizabeth Joscelin. "The Mothers Legacy to her Unborn Childe" [1622]. British Library, Additional MS 27,467. First page.

3.6: M.R., *The Mothers Counsell or, Live within Compasse* (c.1630). By permission of The British Library.

M. R., *The Mothers Counsell or, Live within Compasse. Being the Last Will and Testament to her dearest Daughter* (c. 1630)

Perhaps because of her anonymity, M. R. is the least self-conscious of the mother's legacy writers. In her *Mothers Counsell* (entered in the printers' register in 1623, but not printed until 1630 or so), she neither apologizes nor justifies as she instructs her daughter in the authoritative and empowered voice of a Christian mother. M. R. also shows herself to be a Puritan evangelist, and one with literary inclinations. Betty Travitsky points out that M. R.'s "remarks assume both mature sense and a prior acquaintance with and understanding of Christian doctrine on the part of her daughter" ("New" 37). This shared understanding of religious doctrine between women forms the basis of M. R.'s rhetorical strategies, which set forth modesty and virtue as attributes young women may achieve and sustain, for the sake of their souls, rather than as something imposed upon them. The title page illustrates the theme: chastity, temperance, beauty and humility are goals toward which women must actively strive, not silent roles to which they passively submit.

The compass emblem and titles make clear M. R.'s first purpose in writing: to fulfill her role as a Christian mother teaching her daughter. At the page's center, a mother hands a Bible to the equally restrained and modestly dressed figure of her daughter; together they make clear the active role they have taken in living by and personifying the "Modesty" that hangs over their heads. The concentric circles around them name the standards, "Chastity," "Temperance," "Beauty," and "Humility," by which modesty is judged, governed, and maintained. Outside the circles, the four corners name the sins that occur when virtues are violated: "Wantonesse, "Madness," "Odiousness," and "Pride." The book is divided into four sections, one for each desired standard, and each discusses its opposition. The title page thus serves as a table of contents. Her subtitle is couched in the nongendered imperative that M. R. uses for the series of aphorisms that follow the title page, and together they make clear that her rhetoric is meant for an audience larger than one "dearest Daughter." The maxims in the outer circle describe each standard, are also couched in the genderless imperative, and indicate the governing principles behind *The Mothers Counsell*. "Chastity of body is the key to Relig." and "Temperance is the mother of [Virtue]" are central to M. R.'s socially accepted position as Christian mother and teacher. However, these hint at the active roles of chastity and virtue in a woman's secular and religious life, enhanced by "Beauty is a womans golden Crowne" and "Humilitie is a womans best Armor."

While her text shows her to be a Puritan, M. R. does not abide by exhortations from the Puritan pulpit that women remain silent. Speaking in the voice of the Calvinist who has undergone conversion and is exhorted to evangelicalism, she makes clear both her awareness of her own transgression of patriarchal impositions and her belief that there are worse things than public speech, when she later claims "Forbearance of speech is most dangerous when necessitie requireth to speake." Although her book shows thoroughgoing cultural inscriptions, as she exhorts her daughter to virtue, M. R.'s rhetorical strategies turn each patriarchal reference point into a place of potential empowerment for women.

Roxanne Harde
Queen's University

M. R. *The Mothers Counsell or, Live within Compasse. Being the Last Will and Testament to her dearest Daughter.* 163[0?] EEB 1033. British Library Huth128. Title page.

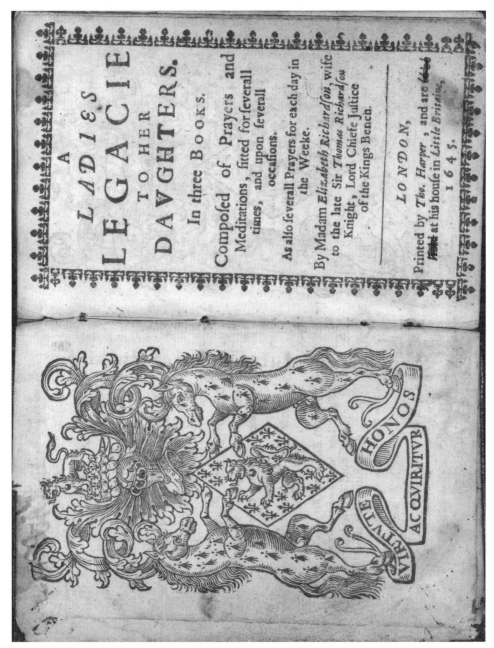

3.7: Elizabeth Richardson, Baroness Cramond, *A Ladies Legacie to Her Daughters* (1645). By permission of the Houghton Library, Harvard University.

Elizabeth Richardson, Baroness Cramond, *A Ladies Legacie to Her Daughters* (1645)

Elizabeth Richardson was born *circa* 1580, the daughter of Sir Thomas Beaumont and his wife, Lady Stoughton. Her first husband, John Ashburnham, died in 1620, after wasting his estate. Richardson worked with her eldest son, John, to repair the family fortunes. She drew on family connections, particularly her cousin, Lady Villiers, mother of the Duke of Buckingham, to place John in the court of Charles I. Her second son, William, became a government official. The fortunes of both men waxed and waned with the Caroline and Restoration courts but both did very well eventually. Richardson's second husband, Thomas Richardson, an MP, lawyer, and innovative justice, died in 1634. Before his death, and because of his political service to the crown, in 1651 his wife was made Baroness of Cramond for life, but the title's patent was for "heirs male of the body," meaning that Richardson's stepsons, not her sons, would receive the title after her death. The event of her elevation is noted with a good deal of astonishment in the contemporary peerages.

The Baroness chose the arms that appear in the frontispiece upon the creation of her title, and like her many epistles and the text of her book, they indicate her awareness of women's roles and means of empowerment. The arms are dominated by the two large unicorns, as noted by peerages and arms books, which point out that the Cramond arms always had unicorns, and that rampant stallions were never used on family arms. Horns were added when Richardson's stepson assumed the title, and the arms continued to be modified to suit later male heirs. While Richardson's unicorns are priapically male, unicorns themselves are an emblem of chastity, and their ermine denotes purity. Richardson thus sets her chastity in the most prominent position on her arms. The two very small lions are also unusual, in that two lions rarely appear together on a coat of arms. The two here assume different positions and meanings: the standing lion is the emblem for guardianship and vigilance, the rampant lion for courage and power. In addition, lions are the symbol for Saint Mark the Evangelist, and both of these are positioned on symbols of the holy Trinity. The helmet, an emblem for salvation and the ability to resist, also indicates Richardson's ambition, as helmets of the baronetcy were to be open; a five-barred helmet was the emblem of the viscountcy. Her motto, "Honour is acquired by virtue," with the prominence of the emblems that set forth her chastity, faith, and courage. These virtues are the bedrock of Richardson's rhetoric as in her motherly and evangelical move to instruct her female heirs in the faith by which she has acquired honor.

Richardson's title page is evidence of her hand in the editing of her book, and indicates her concerns, strategies, and contents. It juxtaposes Richardson's religious and motherly concerns with her continuing focus on worldly power. By signing her book with her married name, Richardson delineates her solid social position as wife to a famous Chief Justice and Knight. By choosing "Ladies," rather than "Mothers" for the finished book's title, Richardson indicates her status and its importance to her and to her children. However, the title also makes clear that this book is for her daughters, a point supported by the warm dedications and the detailed religious instruction that follow.

ROXANNE HARDE
QUEEN'S UNIVERSITY

Elizabeth (Beaumont) Ashburnham Richardson, Baroness Cramond. *A Ladies Legacie to Her Daughters. In three Books. Composed of Prayers and Meditations, fitted for severall times, and upon severall occasions. As also severall Prayers for each day in the Weeke* (1645). Thomason Tracts 251. Houghton Library, Harvard University. Frontispiece and title page.

for this present year, 1659.

A Pessary for the Whites in Women.

Take some whites of eggs, and beat them well in red rose-water, and make it into a Pessary, with some cotten or linen cloaths wet in it, and so put it up into the Matrix, always remembring to tie a string to it, to pull it out again when you please. If the Whites flow from abundance of superfluous humor, it will not be unnecessary to endeavour to evacuate the same through the skin, by using often frictions, or rubbing of the whole body, first gently, and then more hard, by which means the humors may be purged through the skin.

Of the Fits of the Mother, or suffocation, or drawing up of the Matrix.

This happens to women through several causes. Oftentimes when there is an obstruction, or stoppage of the Terms, which do burthen the Brain and Matrix with bad humors. Sometimes by reason of the retention of their natural Seed, as in Widows, and old Maids; for this retention causeth wind to ascend, and ill vapours from the Matrix.

But to proceed to remedies when this Disease cometh suddenly, speedily cast cold water on her face, and give her cold water to drink.

A Powder to be used in the nature of a Pessary, against the suffocation of the Matrix, or fits of the Mother.

Take red Storax, Lignum Aloes, Cloves, of each a Dram: Musk, Amber, of each half a Dram: make them altogether into a powder, and then bind it up in a cloth, in the form of a Pessary, and put it up into the Matrix.

A Fumigation for this Disease.

Take Gallia Moscata, Cassia wood, Cynamon, Time, of each a like quantity: mix these together, and make a perfume thereof, and let the smoke be received up into the Matrix, through a tunnel for that purpose.

If the Patient be a Maid, a husband is the best medicine, if she can get one: but in case that cannot be, then
let

Sarah Jinner, *An Almanack and Prognostication for the year of our Lord 1659* (1659)

Sarah Jinner was a London astrologer who published a series of almanacs for women from 1658 to 1664 containing political prophecies and popular medical advice. She championed the rights of women to speak on matters of women's health and political events. Some of her cures are derived from Alessandro Massario's *The Woman's Counsellour* (translated 1657), who in turn based his medicine on Galen and Hippocrates, the two standard medical authorities of both classical and early modern times. Women were prevented from receiving professional training in medicine in England in the sixteenth and seventeenth centuries, although they could legally practice medicine with a license from the local bishop. Although the London College of Physicians attempted to regulate medical practice for the benefit of its wealthy, university-trained male members by suppressing lower-class and female healers, women nevertheless practiced surgery, apothecary, and physick [medicine] frequently among the lower and middle classes, particularly in areas outside of London. In addition, female midwives could be highly trained by informal female apprenticeship and could in turn offer medical services to other women.

Drawing on the precedent of the medieval women medical authorities Trotula of Salerno and Hildegard of Bingen, several seventeenth-century women also published medical works, including Elizabeth Grey's *The Choice Manual* (1653), Jane Sharp's *Midwives Book* (1671), Queen Henrietta Maria's *The Queen's Closet Opened* (1655), Alethea Talbot's *Natura Exenterata* (1655), and a series of books by Hannah Wolley.

Jinner realized that she would be accused of pandering to pornographic tastes by discussing female sexuality and gynecological matters in her almanacs, but, as she explained in the preface to her 1659 almanac: "It is not fit the world should be deprived of such helps to Nature; for want of which, many by their Modesty, suffer much." A spurious *Womans Almanack* by a "Sarah Ginnor" satirizing female sexuality did in fact appear in 1659, realizing Jinner's fears.

Jinner's cures reproduced here refer to complaints of the Mother or Matrix (womb or uterus), which in classical and early modern medicine was believed to account for most female diseases. As Jinner explains, it was believed that bad humors or vapors ascended to the brain from the diseased womb, causing the fits or mental imbalance called Hysteria, or "suffocation of the mother." Also, the hysterical womb supposedly wandered in the body, and the placing of sweet or stinking odors from burnt herbs (fumigations) at the nose and vagina would coax the wandering womb back into its proper position. The pathology of this "disease" was influenced by the general belief in the irrationality of women, and their primary definition as sexual beings and bearers of children.

Jinner may have also been secretly supplying advice on abortifacient drugs by recommending emmenagogic herbs (which cause menstruation) for curing "obstruction of the terms" or the ceasing of the menstrual flow. Herbs such as mugwort (*Artemisia vulgaris*) recommended by Jinner had been listed since classical times as abortion-causing drugs, although she does not reveal their use as such.

ALAN S. WEBER
CORNELL UNIVERSITY

Sarah Jinner. *An Almanack and Prognostication for the year of our Lord 1659* (1659). Wing 1845; UMI Film 1084. Huntington Library 353427. B7r.

THE
MID-WIVES BOOK.

BOOK I.

The Introduction.

*Of the necessity, and Usefulness of the
Art of Midwifry.*

THe Art of *Midwifry* is doubtless one of the most useful and necessary of all Arts, for the being and well-being of *Mankind*, and therefore it is extremely requisite that a *Midwife*, be both fearing God, faithful, and exceeding well experienced in that profession. Her fidelity shall find not only a reward here from man, but God hath given a special example of it, *Exod.* 1. in the Midwives of *Israel*, who were so faithful to their trust, that the Command of a King could not make them depart from it, viz. *But the Mid-*
wives

---

2   *The Midwives Book.*   Book I.

wives feared God, and did not as the King of Egypt commanded them, but saved the men children alive. Therefore God deals well with the Midwives; and because they feared God, he made them Houses.

As for their knowledge it must be two-fold, *Speculative*, and *Practical*, she that wants the knowledge of Speculation, is like to one that is blind or wants her sight: she that wants the Practice, is like one that is lame and wants her legs, the lame may see but they cannot walk, the blind may walk but they cannot see. Such is the condition of those Midwives that are not well versed in both these. Some perhaps may think, that then it is not proper for women to be of this profession, because they cannot attain so rarely to the knowledge of things as men may, who are bred up in Universities, *Schools* of learning, or serve their Apprenticeships for that end and purpose, where Anatomy Lectures being frequently read, the situation of the parts both of men and women, and other things of great consequence are often made plain to them. But that *Objection* is easily answered, by the former example of the Midwives amongst the *Israelites*, for though we women cannot deny, that men in some things may come to a greater perfection

3.9: Jane Sharp. *The Midwives Book.* (1671) By permission of The British Library.

Jane Sharp, *The Midwives Book* (1671)

Jane Sharpe's *The Midwives Book*, published in 1671, is one of the first textbooks written by a British midwife and addressed specifically to her colleagues. The obtaining of an official license for practicing midwifery was regulated beginning in 1662 by the Church of England, but was increasingly governed by the professional midwives themselves. In turn, any infrastructural and didactic contributions to the field were especially welcome, and Jane Sharp's book was a major contribution to the study of this subject. There was already a tradition of such texts in Europe, especially in France, where the example of Louise Bourgeois's *Observations* had established high standards for the subject; but this was a more detailed text than those published before it. In the book converged two different traditions. One was the tradition of scholarly medical books on midwifery, modeled on Louise Bourgeois's *Observations*, which Sharp had been able to read in translation. The other tradition is the store of oral culture related to midwifery. Because of the inclusion of these popular, and often superstitious elements, Jane Sharp's volume has been compared disadvantageously to previous works on midwifery (she includes, to quote only one example, a definition of hermaphrodites being "only women who have their clitorises greater"). Still, the quantity of scientific knowledge that she incorporates, and that she explicitly addresses to women midwives, exceeds that of any other female English author before her. The book includes detailed examinations of the female genitalia (richly illustrated in one fold-out picture), and a painstaking analysis, also of the various positions that the fetus may adopt before birth, accompanied by a series of graphics.

The facsimile from the introduction (pp. 1–2) showcases Jane Sharp's unambiguous vindication of the need to combine scientific knowledge with direct practice. Midwifery is a twofold form of knowledge, both "speculative and practical"; to have access to only one of these aspects might leave the practitioner, figuratively speaking, blind or lame (p. 2). Here Sharp has to justify the acquisition of specialized scientific knowledge by women: "some may think that it is not proper for women to be in this profession," yet these misogynistic objections are quickly turned on their head by a biblical reference to the Israelite midwives from Exodus I, 36–37 (a classic argument in the defense of this subject, also used by Elizabeth Cellier in her 1681 pamphlet). Sharp strategically acknowledges the authority of the College of Physicians ("I cannot deny the honour due to able Physicians and Chirurgians," p. 3), a necessary move in the face of the continued opposition of the college to any institutions for midwives. But she immediately goes on to vindicate their practice as one developed among women, and advanced by them: "the women are sufficient to perform this duty." For Sharp, midwifery is a form of knowledge that has belonged to female popular culture, developed outside of elite circles; it is because of this that country women "are . . . as safe and as well delivered, if not much more fruitful, and better commonly in Childbed than the greatest Ladies of the Land" (p. 3). Thus, despite its display of scientific knowledge, Sharp's *The Midwives Book* takes its place alongside the defense of the popular culture of midwifery that would be voiced seven years later, in other circumstances, by Elizabeth Cellier.

JOAN CURBET
UNIVERSITAT AUTÒNOMA DE BARCELONA

Jane Sharp. *The Midwives Book, or the whole art of midwifery discovered* (1671).
British Library 1177–619. Pages 1–2.

The TABLE.

3.10: Hannah Wolley, *A Supplement to the Queen-Like Closet* (1674-75).
By permission of The British Library.

Hannah Wolley, *A Supplement to the Queen-Like Closet* (1674–75)

Between 1661, when *The Ladies Directory* was printed, and 1670, which saw the appearance of *The Queen-like Closet*, Hannah Wolley (sometimes Woolley) published a series of books on cookery, conserve-making, and medical remedies. In 1674–75, with the issuing of *A Supplement to the Queen-like Closet; or, a little of Every Thing*, she expanded her repertoire still further. As this facsimile indicates, in *A Supplement* she additionally presented instructions on interior decoration, cleaning, dyeing, and needlework. The matter indicated under "L," for instance, reads: "To make clean *gold* and *Silver Lace*," "To make *Lip salve*," "For the *Leprosie*, or other venemous Humor," "*Lozenges*." Even such a list does not do justice to the book's scope, however. Wolley offers advice on making waxwork and on relations with servants and wetnurses, and provides model letters, indicating how her reader might communicate with absent family members, would-be patrons, or unwanted suitors. *A Supplement* is, then, a firsthand account of the activities and expertise expected of a middling-sort Restoration woman when running her household. Interspersed throughout this small-format (duodecimo), two-hundred-page guide are brief autobiographical narratives. These variously explain how, first as a servant to a "great lady," and then as the wife of schoolmaster Jeremy Wolley, she acquired and exercised her skills in household management; and express her fury that the bookseller Dorman Newman had profited from her burgeoning reputation by publishing under her name a book that, though based in part on her works, also included "scandalous, ridiculous and impertinent" matter (p. 132). Ironically, in our own time, this repudiated work, *The Gentlewomans Companion*, is the "Wolley" title most often cited (see Hobby, "A woman's best").

The table of contents of *A Supplement* was probably the work of the printer employed by Wolley's publisher, Richard Lowndes. Accurately indicating much of the scope of Wolley's book (though omitting all reference to its autobiographical segments), it is a useful point of entry. Listed here are eleven cookery recipes, ranging from meat and fish to common vegetables, and various jellies and marmalades. The instructions for potting fowl, dressing mutton, and boiling pork were reproduced, verbatim and unacknowledged, in the oft-reprinted, anonymous *Compleat Servant-Maid*, sometimes attributed to Wolley in its entirety. Wolley's concerns here are far less showy than those of some of her famous male contemporaries, such as William Rabisha and Robert May, who gave little space to such ordinary and inexpensive foods. Another recipe, "*Jelly* of Fruits," ends with reflections on its medical applications, and in this it intersects with the major preoccupation of *A Supplement*, which is with medical remedies. Thirty-three of the headings on this page list instructions for making medicines, including not only Wolley's preferred treatments for plague, uterine prolapse ("Falling down of the *Mother*") and "sore *Nipples*," remedies for which appear in a huge variety of early modern medical and cookery guides, but also the somewhat unusual advice on how "To cure a *Horse* of a Cold." Finally, and most strikingly, are instructions on washing, cleaning, needlework, and such matters as "*Puff-work*" (the making of artificial flower decorations). Wolley's sense of the variety of a woman's household tasks is catholic indeed, and her eye is always on the practical; she constantly assures her reader that by following her instructions, fine results can be achieved "with less cost" (in "*Petticoats, Bodice* or *Belts* embroidered," p. 81), offering for a fee of "four shillings the day" to teach her skills.

Elaine Hobby
Loughborough University

Hannah Wolley. *A Supplement to the Queen-like Closet* (1674–75). British Library 1037. a. 38. sig. A4v.

4 *Medicatrix*, or the *Woman Physician.*

nell, and such Phanatick Brains allow; and more then such soring Clouds, and Tempestuous Scriblers will ever attain too; In sum, his rude, idle Papers, blotted with Folly, and uncivilly reflecting on this deceased Physician I have mentioned, together, with some other bold and intollerable errors, imposed on the World by Mr. *Stubbe,* provokes; And therefore I proceed thus to Defend and Challenge.

SECT. I.

Stubbe in nomination with *Cicero.*

ALthough I dare not pretend to be so much a Linguist, or capable of such great Studies, Readings, and verbal Acquirements, as the *Medicus* of *Warwick* owns; whose business it is to be famous in those Accomplishments: and who hath need enough of them to maintain and carry on the most prodigious and impossible Aims he drives at

Medicatrix, or the *Woman Physician.* 5

at; (though I do not see that all his noise of Languages and Schollarship he so much boasts of, hath furnisht him with that perfection Learning ought to produce, or what is commonly expected from it.) Yet I hope I may retain so much confidence in Mr. *Stubb's* ingenuity; That if I presume to use sometimes, only an Author English'd, as *Plutarch,*&c. or it may be *Esop,* or the like; this Age being pretty kind to us Females in such assistance; and give him likewise a reasonable measure of sense, which I believe is as much, and more, then he expects from a Woman; he will be so kind as to excuse me for the vacancy of those Masculine Capacities he himself glories in: And the rather, because he well understands, that such fine things, as are prettily term'd Philosophical in him, will scarce be thought rational in me.

This being an Age so subject to Division and Subtlety, and so full of contention, between Interest and Truth, Ignorance and Ingenuity, Purity and Impurity; and last of all Loyalty and

B 3   Re-

3.11: Mary Trye, *Medicatrix* (1675). By permission of The British Library.

Mary Trye, *Medicatrix, or The Woman-Physician* (1675)

Mary Trye published *Medicatrix, or The Woman-Physician* (1675) to defend the memory of her father, Thomas O'Dowde, and the reputation of his fellow chemical physicians against the university-educated Henry Stubbe and other members of the Royal College of Physicians. Although *Medicatrix* is not the first medical treatise by an Englishwoman, it is the first tract of medical controversy so authored. Hobby situates Trye's text in the context of female-authored "skills books," which include works on housewifery and nursing (178–80), but unlike these books Trye's 126–page treatise includes no recipes to cure various ailments. Instead, *Medicatrix* mixes controversy, autobiography, and hagiography, connecting the saintly life of O'Dowde (who died nursing the poor during the 1665 plague) with his royalism and his anti-Galenical, anti-venesectionist medical theories; the attacks on the new chemical physicians with the College's desire to maintain an oppressive monopoly over medical services, one driven by class prejudice and grasping materialism; and Trye's own apprenticeship as her father's assistant with a validation of experience over learning as the true path to medical expertise. This championing of experience underpins Trye's claim that women have the right to be physicians, both in the areas of practice and of controversy. She fashions a new model for medical professionals, balanced between the ideal Christian healer and the doctor who "makes a living" at medicine.

Trye's comment in her dedication to Jane Lead that "it is of little Novelty to see a Woman in print" (A2ʳ) is characteristic of her ironic tone. Here, she ridicules Henry Stubbe, "the Medicus of Warwick," by mocking the basis of his claims to medical superiority: his classically focused university education. She archly admits that, unlike Stubbe, she is no "Linguist" nor "capable of such great Studies, readings, and verbal Acquirements." Since Stubbe's "business is . . . to be famous in those Accomplishments," clearly his true intent is not the cure of the sick but self-aggrandizement. Indeed, later she scornfully labels Stubbe a "verbalist," while she is a "medicinalist": Stubbe talks, while she heals. Thus, she champions the medical pragmatism of the experientially trained chemical physician over the medical intellectualism of the university-educated doctor. Stubbe's education leaves him without the "perfection Learning ought to produce"—the development of moral and ethical understanding. Trye's attack on Stubbe's empty intellectualism and moral degeneracy underpins her attack on his contemptuous assessment of women. Since universities were upper-class male bastions, Stubbe's criteria mean that only men of a certain class can be physicians. Trye notes, however, that knowledge of the classics is no sure mark of class and gender privilege, thus ridiculing the classical education that the college required for its exclusive coterie. She has access to English translations of important classical authors, like Plutarch and Aesop, "this Age being pretty kind to us Females in such assistance." Given that she later applies the life of Cicero to that of Stubbe with devastatingly satirical results, her apology for intruding into the masculine world of medicine and controversy implies that Stubbe's education has not granted him even that "reasonable measure of sense" that he expects from a female opponent, and that the world holds Stubbe and herself to different standards in the arena of controversy, since "such fine things, as are prettily termed Philosophical in him, will scarce be thought rational in me."

MARIE LOUGHLIN
OKANAGAN UNIVERSITY COLLEGE

Trye, Mary. *Medicatrix, or The Woman-Physician* (1675). Wing T3174, R1296. British Library 780 a.40. Pages 4–5.

...tries, *Germany*, and most of the Northern Parts of the World.

And here in London were Colledges of Women about the Temple of Diana, who was Goddess of Midwives here, as well as at Ephesus. From whence the Grecians say, she was ableast at *Olympia's* Labour, who was that Night deliver'd of *Alexander the Great*; where she was so fully employed, that she could not defend her Stately Temple, which was burned down by *Herostratus* the Shoemaker, to perpetuate his Name.

Nor did the Bishops pretend to Licence Midwives till Bp. *Bonner's* time, who drew up the Form of the first Licence, which continued in full force till 1642, and then the Physicians and Chirurgions contending about it, it was adjudged a Chyrurgical Operation, and the Midwives were Licensed at *Chirurgions-Hall, but not till they had passed three Examinations, before six skilful Midwives, and as many Chirurgions experts in the Art of Midwifery.* Thus it continued until the Act of Uniformity passed, which sent the Midwives back to *Doctors Commons, where they pay their Money, (take an Oath which is impossible for them to keep)* and return home as skilful as they went thither.

I make no Reflections on those learned Gentlemen the Licensers, but refer the curious for their further satisfaction, to the Yearly Bills of Mortality, from 42 to 62: Collections of which they may find at *Clerks-Hall:* Which if they please to compare with these of late Years, they will find there did not then happen the eight part of the Casualties, either to Women or Children, as do now.

I hope, Doctor, these Considerations will deter any of you from pretending to teach us Midwifery, especially such as confess they never delivered Women in their Lives, and being asked *What they would do in such a Case?* reply they know not perswaded it, but will when occasion serves; *This is something to the purpose I must confess, Doctor:* But I doubt it will not satisfy the Women

(7)

Women of this Age, who are so sensible and impatient of their Pain, that few of them will be prevailed with to bear it, in Complement to the Doctor, *while he fetches his Book, studies the Case, and teaches the Midwife to perform her work,* which she hopes may be done before he comes.

I protest, Doctor, I have not Power enough with the Women to hope to prevail with them to be patient in this case, and I think if the Learned'st of you all should propose it *whilst the Pains are on,* he would come off with the same Applause which *Phormio* had, who having never seen a Battel in his Life, read a Military Lecture to *Hannibal the Great.*

But let this pass, Doctor, as I do the Discourses you have often made to me on this Subject, and I will tell you something worthy of your most serious Consideration: Which is,

That in *September* last, our Gracious Soveraign was pleased to promise to unite the Midwives into a Corporation, by His Royal Charter, and also to found a *Cradle-Hospital,* to breed up exposed Children, to prevent the many *Murders, and the Executions which attend them;* which pious Design will never want a suitable Return from God, who no doubt will fully reward his Care for preserving so many *Innocents* as would otherwise be lost.

And I doubt not but one way will be by giving him a Prince by his Royal Consort, who like another *Moses* may become a Mighty Captain for the Nation; and lead to Battel the Soldiers which the Hospital will preserve for him.

And now, Doctor, let me put you in mind, that tho you have often Laughed at me, and some Doctors have accounted me a Mad Woman these last four Years, for saying Her Majesty was full of Children, and that the *Bath* would allift her Breeding: 'Tis now proved so true, that I have cause to hope my self may live to praise God, not only for a *Prince of Wales, and a Duke of York,* but for many other Royal Babes by Her; and if the over Officious will but be pleased to let them live, *I hope im-*

3.12: Elizabeth Cellier, *To Dr.—, an Answer to his Queries* (1688). By permission of the British Library.

Elizabeth Cellier, *To Dr.—, an Answer to his Queries, concerning the Colledg of Midwives* (1688)

The institution of a corporation for midwives in the seventeenth century was prevented by the College of Physicians since the early Stuart period; the Church of England licensed practitioners in that field since 1662. In this context Mrs. Elizabeth Cellier undertook, beginning about 1680, the project of a college for midwives; her pamphlet to an unidentified doctor, *To Dr.—, In Answer to his Queries,* is a response to the opposition of the College to an improvement in the legislation and teaching of midwifery. All the evidence we have seems to indicate that Cellier's position in this matter was motivated by her own intended profit; yet her pamphlet remains a shrewd piece of polemical prose.

Cellier's defense of midwives and of their authority follows a rigorous humanistic pattern, joining biblical scholarship and classical *auctoritas* in support of her argument; it is only in the final part of the pamphlet (pp. 6 and 7, presented in this facsimile) that the vindication of her own college is explicitly addresssed. The pamphlet is carefully structured in three parts, starting from biblical precedent, following with an array of classical quotations, and finally arriving at the polemics that had been affecting the practice of midwifery since the early seventeenth century. She starts by citing and commenting on verses 15 to 21 of the first chapter of the book of *Exodus,* where there is an explicit defense of the obedience to God shown by the Hebrew midwives during the escape from Egypt; she establishes a close parallel between the Hebrew "Magi"'s support of the midwives and the institutional support Cellier needs for her own college. Her next step is to collect several examples from the classical tradition (references to the goddess Agnodicea and to Phanarota, Socrates' mother, in pp. 3–5), but it includes a more heterodox moment, which breaks the traditional humanistic combination of biblical and classical precedent: Cellier comments on the tradition of "Women practicing Physick" in pre-Roman Britain, going so far as to invoke the precedent of "old British Songs" composed "in the time of the Druids" in support of her argument (p. 5).

But it is in the final part of the pamphlet that Cellier subverts the rhetoric of humanistic learned discourse and turns to a documented discussion of her present circumstances. In defense of her college, Cellier even makes an intelligent use of the yearly Bills of Mortality, which showed a significant descent of the death rate at childbirth (both for women and for children) between 1642 and 1662 (p. 6). The culminating moment, however, comes when she directly addresses, with a biting irony, her critics in the College of Physicians: "I hope, Doctor, these Considerations will deter any of you from pretending to teach us Midwivery, especially such as confess *they never delivered Women.*" The doctors who theorize on the matter are compared to Formio (who had "never seen a Battel in his Life" p. 7) delivering a lecture to Hannibal: direct expertise and practice are taken here as the main source of the midwives' authority, against the censorship of learned but inexpert scholars. Cellier's project did not materialize at last; yet, the confidence with which she invoked here the very support of the king ("our Gracious Soveraign was pleased to promise to unite the Midwives into a Corporation") authorized her signing her own name, as she had confronted her adversaries in a very public debate.

JOAN CURBET
UNIVERSITAT AUTÒNOMA DE BARCELONA

Elizabeth Cellier. *To Dr.—, an Answer to his Queries, concerning the Colledg of Midwives* (1688). British Library 1178.h 2(2). Pages 6–7.

Bibliography

Aughterson, Kate, ed. *Renaissance Women: A Sourcebook*. London and New York: Routledge, 1995.

Beilin, Elaine V. *Redeeming Eve: Women Writers of the English Renaissance*. Princeton, N.J.: Princeton University Press, 1987.

Bradstreet, Anne. *The Works of Anne Bradstreet*. 1867. Ed. John Harvard Ellis. Gloucester: Peter Smith, 1962.

Brown, Sylvia. "Over her Dead Body: Feminism, Post-structuralism, and the Mother's Legacy." *Discontinuities: New Essays on Renaissance Literature and Criticism*. Ed. Viviana Comensoli and Paul Stevens. Toronto: University of Toronto Press, 1998. 3–26.

Calloway, Stephen, ed. *The Elements of Style: An Encyclopedia of Domestic Architectural Detail*. New Edition. London: Reed International, 1996.

Capp, Bernard. "English Almanacs 1500–1800: Astrology and the Popular Press." *Women, Science and Medicine 1500–1700: Mothers and Sisters of the Royal Society*. Ed. Lynette Hunter and Sarah Hutton. Phoenix Mill, Gloucestershire: Sutton, 1997.

Cooke, Harold. "The Society of Chemical Physicians, the New Philosophy, and the Restoration Court." *Bulletin of the History of Medicine* 61 (1987): 61–77.

Eccles, Audrey. *Obstetrics and Gynaecology in Tudor and Stuart England*. London: Croom Helm, 1982.

Evenden, Doreen. *Popular Medicine in Seventeenth Century England*. Bowling Green, Ohio: Bowling Green State University Popular Press, 1988.

———. *The Midwives of Seventeenth-Century London*. Cambridge: Cambridge University Press, 2000.

Feroli, Teresa. "'In felix Simulacrum': The Rewriting of Loss in Elizabeth Jocelin's *The Mothers Legacie*." *ELH* (1994): 89–102.

Fildes, Valerie A. *Breasts, Bottles and Babies*. Edinburgh: Edinburgh University Press, 1986.

———. *Wet Nursing: A History from Antiquity to the Present*. Oxford: Basil Blackwell, 1988. 68–100.

Green, Monica Helen, ed. *The Trotula: A Medieval Compendium of Women's Medicine*. Philadelphia: University of Pennsylvania Press, 2001.

Hannay, Margaret P. "'O Daughter Heare': Reconstructing the Live of Aristocratic Englishwomen." *Attending to Women in Early Modern England*. Ed. Betty S. Travitsky and Adele F. Seeff. Newark: University of Delaware Press, 1994. 35–63.

Hobby, Elaine. *Virtue of Necessity: English Women's Writing 1649–1688*. London: Virago, 1988.

———. "'A woman's best setting out is silence': the writings of Hannah Wolley." *Culture and Society in the Stuart Restoration: Literature, Drama, History*. Ed. Gerald Maclean. Cambridge: Cambridge University. Press, 1995. 179–200.

Hunter, Lynette, and Sarah Hutton. "Women, Science and Medicine: Introduction." *Women, Science and Medicine, 1500–1700*. Ed. Lynette Hunter and Sarah Hutton. Phoenix Mill, Gloucestershire: Sutton, 1997. 1–6.

Jorden, Edward. *A Briefe Discourse of a Disease Called the Suffocation of the Mother*. London, 1603.

Joscelin, Elizabeth. *The Mothers Legacy to her Vnborn Childe*. Ed. Jean LeDrew Metcalfe. Toronto: University of Toronto Press, 2000.

Kusunoki, Akiko. "'Their Testament at Their Apron-strings': The Representation of Puritan Women in Early-Seventeenth-Century England." *Gloriana's Face: Women, Public & Private in the English Renaissance*. Ed. Marion Wynne-Davies and Susan Cerasano. New York: Harvester Wheatsheaf, 1992. 185–204.

Linden, Stanton J. "Mrs Mary Trye, Medicatrix: Chemistry and Controversy in Restoration England." *Women's Writing* 1.3 (1994): 341–53.

Mahl, Mary R., and Helene Koon, eds. *The Female Spectator*. Bloomington: Indiana University Press, 1997.

Markham, Gervase. *The English Housewife*. Ed. Michael R. Best. Montreal: McGill-Queen's University Press, 1986.

Marland, Hilary, ed. *The Art of Midwifery*. London: Routledge, 1993.

Martensen, Robert. "The Transformation of Eve: Women's Bodies, Medicine and Culture in Early Modern England." *Sexual Knowledge, Sexual Science: The History of Attitudes to Sexuality*. Ed. Roy Porter and Mikulas Teich. Cambridge: Cambridge University Press, 1994. 107–133.

Martin, Randall, ed. *Women Writers in Renaissance England*. London: Longman, 1997.

May, Robert. *The Accomplist Cook: or, the Art and Mystery of Cookery*. Facsimile of 1685 ed. Introd. Alan Davidson, Marcus Bell, and Tom Jaine. Totnes, Devon: Prospect Books, 1994.

Mendelson, Sara, and Patricia Crawford. "Medical practitioners: midwives, surgeons, physicians, healers." *Women in Early Modern England*. Oxford: Oxford University Press, 1998. 314–21.

O'Dowde, Thomas. *The Poor Man's Physician, Or the True Art of Medicine, as it is Chymically prepared and administred, for healing the several Diseases incident to Mankind*. 3 ed. London: F. Smith, 1665.

Otten, Charlotte F., ed. *English Women's Voices 1540–1700*. Miami: Florida International University Press, 1992.

Paston-Williams, Sara. *The Art of Dining: A History of Cooking and Eating*. London: National Trust, 1993.

Pearson, Jacqueline. "Women Reading, Reading Women." *Women and Literature in Britain 1500–1700*. Ed. Helen Wilcox. Cambridge: Cambridge University Press, 1996. 80–99.

Phillippy, Patricia. "The Maid's Lawful Liberty: Service, the Household, and 'Mother B' in Isabella Whitney's *A Sweet Nosegay*." *Modern Philology* 95.4 (1998): 439–62.

Poole, Kristen. "'The fittest closet for all goodness': Authorial Strategies of Jacobean Mothers' Manuals." *SEL* 35 (1995): 69–88.

Rabisha, William. *The Whole Body of Cookery Dissected*. London: E. C. for Francis Smith, 1675.

Schoonover, David E., ed. *Ladie Borlase's Receiptes Book*. Iowa City: Iowa University Press, 1998.

Sharp, Jane. *The midwives book, or, The whole art of midwifry discovered.* Ed. Elaine Hobby. New York: Oxford University Press, 1999.

Sizemore, Christine W. "Early Seventeenth-Century Advice Books: The Female Viewpoint." *South Atlantic Bulletin* 41 (1976): 41–48.

Smith, Hilda. "Gynecology and Ideology in Seventeenth-Century England." *Liberating Women's History: Theoretical and Critical Essays*. Ed. B. A. Carroll. Urbana: University of Illinois Press, 1976. 97–114.

Sommerville, Margaret R. *Sex and Subjection: Attitudes to Women in Early-Modern Society*. London: Arnold, 1995.

Theophano, Janet. *Eat My Words: Reading Women's Lives Through the Cookbooks They Wrote*. New York and Basingstoke: Palgrave, 2002.

Thornton, Peter. *Authentic Decor: The Domestic Interior 1620–1920*. London: Weidenfeld and Nicolson, 1984.

Travitsky, Betty S. "The New Mother of the English Renaissance: Her Writings on Motherhood." *The Lost Tradition: Mothers and Daughters in Literature*. Ed. Cathy N. Davidson and E. M. Broner. New York: Frederick Ungar, 1980. 33–43.

———. *The Paradise of Women: Writings by Englishwomen of the Renaissance*. Westport, Conn.: Greenwood, 1981.

Trill, Suzanne, Kate Chedgzoy, and Melanie Osborne, eds. *Lay By Your Needles Ladies, Take the Pen: Writing Women in England, 1500–1700*. London: Arnold Press, 1997.

Veith, Ilza. *Hysteria: The History of a Disease*. Chicago: University of Chicago Press, 1965.

Walker, Kim. *Women Writers of the English Renaissance*. New York: Twayne, 1996.

Wall, Wendy. *The Imprint of Gender: Authorship and Publication in the English Renaissance*. Ithaca, N.Y.: Cornell University Press, 1993.

Wayne, Valerie. "Advice for Women from Mothers and Patriarchs." *Women and Literature in Britain 1500–1700*. Ed. Helen Wilcox. Cambridge: Cambridge University Press, 1996. 56–79.

Weber, A.S. ed. *Almanacs* . The Early Modern Englishwoman: A Facsimile Library of Essential Works - Printed Writings 1641–1700: Series 2, Part One, Vol. 6. Gen. Eds. Betty S. Travitsky and Patrick Cullen. Aldershot: Ashgate, 2003.

Webster, Charles, ed. *Health, Medicine and Mortality in the Sixteenth Century.* Cambridge: Cambridge University Press, 1979.

Wilcox, Helen. "'My Soule in Silence?': Devotional Representations of Renaissance Englishwomen." *Representing Women in Renaissance England*. Ed. Claude J. Summers and Ted-Larry Pebworth. Columbia: University of Missouri Press, 1997. 9–23.

Wolley, Hannah. *The Cooks Guide*. London: for Peter Dring, 1664.

———. *The Ladies Delight*. London: T. Milbourn for N. Crouch, 1672.

———. *The Ladies Directory*. London: T. M. for Peter Dring, 1661, 1662.

———. *The Queen-like Closet* . London: for R. Lowndes, 1670.

———. (false attrib.). *The Accomplisht Ladies Delight*. London: B. Harris, 1675.

———. (false attrib.). *The Gentlewomans Companion*. Introd. Caterina Albano. Totnes, Devon: Prospect Books, 2001.

———. (false attrib.). *The Compleat Servant-Maid; Or, The Young Maidens Tutor*. London: T. Passinger, 1677.

CHAPTER 4

Religion, Prophecy,
and Persecution

The majority of English people were suspicious at best and contemptuous at worst about religious toleration in the early modern period. The Church of England, with the monarchy as its head, enforced both religious and political conformity. Catholicism was denounced and discredited for its doctrines and alleged association with foreign powers which, according to English Protestants, conspired to destroy their nation. The Church of England dominated not only religious but also state affairs; but as people became increasingly literate and able to make their own judgments about doctrines, worship practices, and church government, some sought to distinguish themselves from the dominant religious institution. Religious dissenters deemphasized ceremony and rites (associated with the Book of Common Prayer), while placing greater importance on individual conscience and expression. This departure in matters of belief and religious practice from the traditions of the national religion soon posed a threat to the episcopacy, which sought to maintain the status quo. The one concession made by James to the Puritans in the early seventeenth century was the translation of the bible in 1611. Dedicated to the king, the King James Bible replaced the Bishops' Bible and the Geneva Bible and made scripture more readily accessible and available for the people.

Escalating political and religious tensions in the 1630s and 1640s and strong resistance to the English court's censorship laws weakened the authority of the Church of England. Numerous independent sects that developed exhibited a zeal for advancing the reformation, with each group redefining the terms for salvation. Levellers, who were led by John Lilburne, Richard Overton, and William Walwyn, envisioned social democracy and promoted the universal toleration of religious beliefs. As supporters of a seventeenth-century form of communism, Diggers urged that the common people assume control of the land for the benefit of all. Most Baptists maintained that the one true way could be found only after adult baptism; Ranters undermined Calvinist notions of the sinful individual, as did Antinomians; Brownists and Muggletonians were separatist groups whose members adhered to the doctrines of their individual leaders. Familists denied Christ's divinity and identified heaven and hell as states of mind. Many of the dissenters, but in particular the Fifth Monarchists, advanced millenarian beliefs. Quakers, one of the most prominent of the radical sects, were known for their political activism and opposition to secular authority, as well their numerous literary contributions produced by males and females of their group. With notable exceptions like the Quakers, the life of these sects was, however, severely limited. The brief promise for toleration in the Restoration for dissenters and Catholics abruptly ended when the king and parliament imposed the Act of Uniformity in 1662, reintroduced High Church liturgy, and persecuted nonconformists.[1]

During the early modern period, religious beliefs and biblical accounts were, along with biological and intellectual arguments, often invoked to justify the maintenance of the gender hierarchy. The postlapsarian relationship between Adam and Eve, which required Eve to submit to her husband as her sentence for beguiling him, served as a model for gender relations generally (I Tim. 2:11–12). Women thus were denied the right to speak, teach, and preach in public, and required to heed male authority. In the Civil War and Interregnum years, many of the sects that emerged, however, advanced a position of greater equality between the genders, based on the assumption that all are equal before God; thus during this brief period, an increased number of men and women had the opportunity to choose their religious affiliation. Moreover, female members of dissenting groups enjoyed an unprecedented amount of freedom to express their views, though toleration often did not extend beyond the limits of their community. Nevertheless, the greater visibility of female nonconformists in the public sphere explains the concentration of mid-seventeenth-century female-authored texts about religion and dissent in this chapter.

Religious Texts

The texts featured here are of a religious or spiritual nature and include meditations and poems, prophecies, and persecution narratives. As observed in this book so far, much of the literature produced by women (and men) during the time engaged religious issues and spirituality, topics that women writers in particular could discuss without having to devote considerable effort to justifying their entry into the literary sphere. In the initial image of this chapter, the title-page woodcut from *The Lattre Examynacyon of Anne Askew* (1546), Anne Askew seizes the role of a martyr of the primitive church as she triumphs over the Roman Catholic Church. As John Bale, her first editor, claims, after 1546 Anne Askew's execution encouraged others to convert, and her text may have inspired further conversions. *The Examynacyon* combines spiritual autobiography with dramatic dialogue and offers a history of political and religious life in mid–sixteenth-century London. In the tradition of dissenters before and after her, Askew contributed to the development of a literature of suffering, for which the Quakers would become best known in the seventeenth century. Askew's manuscript was apparently smuggled out of England by Dutch merchants, and Bale printed it in the Duchy of Cleves in 1546–47. After Edward VI's ascension in 1547, numerous editions of *The Lattre Examynacyon* were published in England. The text, which enjoyed a remarkable life in print as a martyr story, was read not only in her own era, but consulted by historians, biographers, religious writers, and novelists for generations after.[2]

The Welsh-born Sister Joan Seller took other measures to practice her religion, though of a very different tradition. The document associated with her, a manuscript in italic hand from the Benedictine Convent at Cambrai, features an oath of obedience (1631) she took after joining the English Benedictine convent in Flanders in May 1628, where Elizabeth Cary had also sent her daughters. This record of Seller's vows provides insight into the life of her community, which, though austere, offered an intellectually vigorous setting. Seller is one of a number of Catholic women writers featured in this book. Others include Elizabeth Grymeston and Elizabeth Cellier (chapter 3), Elizabeth Cary (chapters 5 and 9), and possibly Margaret Tyler (chapter 7).[3]

Along with Catholics and other recusants, we include the writings by several moderate Protestant women, Elizabeth Russell, Alice Sutcliffe, the anonymous author of *Eliza's Babes*, and Elizabeth Warren. Anne Conway (chapters 5, 7), who was a convert to Quakerism, might also have been included in this list; her example demonstrates that Quakerism accommodated a range of politics and beliefs and that not all Quaker followers were necessarily radical. The religious writings of the women represent a range of genres: prose translations, meditations, poetry, and pamphlets. Trained in the classical languages, Elizabeth Russell, the earliest of these writers, produced a number of elegies and translated *A Way of Reconciliation of a good and learned man* (1605) from Latin to English. The original Latin text was authored by John Ponet, a Protestant intellectual who was made Bishop of Winchester under Henry VIII and who fled England during Mary's reign, having actively denounced governmental corruption and tyranny. Elizabeth Russell's translation of the polemical, religious text of this Marian exile reveals her participation in the dissemination of important policy, while also complementing the work of her sister, Anne Bacon, whose translation is discussed in chapter 7. The work of both sisters demonstrates that learning was second nature for these "vigorous, indomitable women [who] energetically pursu[ed] their affairs in a world not always sympathetic to their needs."[4]

Like Russell's dedication, "To the Right Honourable my most entirely beloved and onely daughter, the Lady Anne Herbert," which emphasizes Russell's maternal care for her daughter's spiritual well-being, Sutcliffe's *Meditations of man's mortalitie* (1634), and the anonymously written *Eliza's Babes* (1652) all possess both an instructive and a meditative quality. In the early modern period, the term "meditation" referred to works as diverse as poetry and sermons. Sutcliffe's *Meditations* and *Eliza's Babes* each include prose and verse and thus are featured in two chapters (4 and 8). Sutcliffe's six prose meditations are followed by a long poem of 88 stanzas and a passage from the poem, "Of our losse by Adam" (see chapter 8). The dedications and encomia in the *Meditations* are partly self-promotional and are directed at an upper-class readership.[5] The poet of *Eliza's Babes*, by contrast, preserves her anonymity, while still justifying her incursion into the literary sphere by declaring her compulsion to publicize her relationship with God for the benefit of others. Her poems and meditations bear comparison with the devotional works of George Wither and Francis Quarles, but hypotheses identifying "Eliza" with Elizabeth Major or Wither's wife, Elizabeth Emerson, remain tentative.[6]

The Puritan Elizabeth Warren, who, like Elizabeth Russell, enjoyed the benefits of classical training, commented on church politics in the pamphlets she produced between 1645 and 1649. At a time when radical sects were emerging, Warren opposed changes in the ministry, though she argued for better-educated preachers. In conjunction with the view that women should be barred from the public functions of teaching, preaching, and prophesying, Warren sought no advances for women in the church.

134

Prophecy

Women's authority to speak and preach finds justification particularly in the prophetic texts of the period, which became more numerous when mid–seventeenth-century millenarianists proclaimed the imminent establishment of God's kingdom and the destruction of competing worldly powers. Female and male prophets of the time relied heavily on biblical allusion and citation, which were part of a mnemonic culture, "a range of symbols and stories derived from the Old and New Testaments whose meanings would be universally understood and whose power, they hoped, would be universally acknowledged."[7] Channeling male power through the vessel of the repressed woman's body, the prophet developed a language that eschewed traditional forms of representation and interpretation. Visionaries including Eleanor Davies, Elinor Channel, Anna Trapnel, Mary Cary, and Elizabeth Poole assimilated prophetic utterances and metaphors of reproduction in their visions, casting themselves as handmaids of God whose Word they bore and communicated.[8]

In the process of constructing and articulating an identity through the act of writing, self-other relations are constantly renegotiated. The prophet moves between self-affirmation and self-annihilation, and through the act of ventriloquism or the projection of another's voice—that of God—she brings forth the Word. The concept of ventriloquism, "literally the act of appearing to speak from the abdomen or belly," establishes a link between prophecy and maternity, as well as between voice and female physiology: "Voice or language appears to emerge from her body in a process analogous to birth; the woman is impregnated or filled with voice (as, in Christian tradition, Mary becomes the receptacle of the Word); she produces what issues from the belly."[9] The prophet's own voice—as opposed to the voices of God speaking through her—is thus "silenced," a condition under which her public speaking could be vindicated and thus tolerated.

The connection between paternity and licensing in many of the prophetic tracts further emphasizes the need for the speaker/author's words to be legitimized by male authority. But not all female prophets were prepared to submit to patriarchal commands and codes of conduct; in *The Restitution of Prophecy; that Buried Talent to be revived*, for example, Lady Eleanor Davies—the first Englishwoman "to appropriate the printing press for the public expression of her vision of herself in her world"[10]—usurps male power to become a producer of meaning and a conscious fashioner of an elusive, cross-gendered identity. She achieves this authority by complicating the question of agency, by introducing multiple subject-positions, intertextual references, and biblical and contemporary allusions in her texts, and by manipulating tropes of the virgin female body. Curiously, her work is still misjudged in our own day as it was in the seventeenth century; consequently, Davies's writings, Megan Matchinske maintains, "have been relegated to the margins, to the margins of history and of sanity."[11]

Imaginative and reproductive activities outside of paternal control, which "much unbeseemed [the female] Sex," were performed by prophets of various radical sects.[12] Through visionary writings, prophetic utterances, and in the case of the Quakers, through physical deprivation and the shaking and quaking of the body, which served as a theatrical signifier, women developed a collective identity and a language of intellectual renunciation. But neither the words nor the body was left unpoliced: adversaries diagnosed the prophets' delirium as psychological and moral instability and stereotyped them as devils, witches, monsters, and madwomen. This was the case for the prophets in this chapter, including Mary Cary, Anna Trapnel, and Mother Shipton, who were accused of sedition, witchcraft, and madness. The Fifth Monarchists, Cary and Trapnel, were intent on polit-ical engagement, with Cary's publications forming the basis for the Fifth Monarchist pro-gram in later years.[13] Trapnel's dramatic entry into the political arena the following year saw the publication of four texts after the Barebones Parliament was dissolved by conser-vatives in Cromwell's assembly. Once the army seized control, Cromwell was made Lord Protector, a treacherous act according to Fifth Monarchists like Trapnel, who represents him as the Antichrist in *The Cry of a Stone*. This autobiographical, prophetic treatise—a transcription of the verses and prayers she spoke while in a trance at Whitehall—was recorded by a male "relator," who acknowledges that he transcribed only as much as he could.[14] Though at several removes from the speaker and from the speech community that received the prophecy firsthand, *The Cry of a Stone* was at the centre of controversy at Trapnel's 1654 trial, recorded in *Anna Trapnel's Report and Plea*, which recounts her prophetic mission to the southwest and her imprisonment.

An ambiguous quality also lent currency to the prophecies of the legendary Mother Shipton (b. 1488? [if she existed at all]); the various seventeenth-century writers, includ-ing Mercurius Propheticus, who (re)printed the prophecies between 1642 and 1685, con-temporized, politicized, and reinterpreted them. Prophecy lent itself to conflicting inter-pretations as confirmation of inspiration or possession. The female prophet, moreover, could appear either self-effacing or self-aggrandizing. Further, she could on the one hand gain a privileged status in the society by way of the anxious respect she aroused; or her example might, on the other hand, merely reinforce the stereotype of women as irrational, even hysterical creatures, or as passive instruments of external powers. Often, however, passivity and empowerment went hand in hand. The prophet Hester Biddle, for instance, ventriloquizes God's voice while, like Davies and Trapnel, situating herself in the tradition of male prophets, such as St. John and Daniel, to authorize her attack on social, religious, and political establishments.

Other intermediaries of the same period who also had connections to the radicals were Hannah Allen and Elizabeth Calvert. Within the first five years after her first hus-band's death, Allen, a publisher and bookseller who inherited her husband's book trade, issued at least 54 books and pamphlets on which her name is printed. Elizabeth Calvert likewise printed materials by dissenters during the Civil War and Interregnum. By per-sisting with her work even after the Licensing Act (1662), she helped ensure the contin-uation of Puritan and oppositional publishing in the increasingly hostile climate of the Restoration years.[15]

Persecution Narratives

Along with fellow followers, authors of religious texts were concerned to record their spir-itual progress (as pilgrims) and thus confirm their election—a condition for membership in the church. Protestants, particularly Puritans and dissenters, modeled their autobiogra-phies on the popular form of the conversion narrative to map out their route to salvation. In a broader context, sectarians like the Quakers relied heavily on the printed word not only to spread dissenting opinions, as Margaret Spufford demonstrated in *Contrasting Communities*, but also to document their trials and produce a literature of suffering as part of their communal identity.[16] The compilation of narratives, letters, and editorial commentaries that constitute Katharine Evans and Sarah Chevers's *Short Relation of Some of the Cruel Sufferings* (1662), for example, is reminiscent of John Foxe's *Acts and Monuments*, and locates the trials of these two women preachers in a historical and providential context, as well as in relation to Quaker publishing practices.[17] This text invites comparison with accounts by other religious women, like the Quaker Barbara Blaugdone, who situates her travel experiences in the context of a spiritual narrative in which she expresses the divine favor she receives during her time of trial.

The authority of the writer to engage religious or spiritual matters conventionally depended on her affiliation with godly communities (Smith 51); and indeed during the midcentury, prophets (with the notable exception of Eleanor Davies) generally belonged to particular religious congregations and often even female communities.[18] But what shape does the narrative or spiritual autobiography of one deprived of authority in the gathered church or one dismissed by the community assume? The prophetic, autobiographical treatises written in the Restoration period by the Baptist and millenarian Anne Wentworth provide a partial answer. Accused by her fellow Baptists of being "*a proud, passionate, revengeful, discontented,* and *mad* woman . . . that has unduly published things to the prejudice and scandal of my husband, and that hath wickedly left him,"Wentworth was intent on setting the record straight.[19] Like Katherine Sutton, Wentworth uses her narrative to assure herself of God's grace during a period of affliction, including marital conflict.

For Hannah Allen—to be distinguished from the publisher of the same name (see 4.7)—writing served as a personal outlet and outreach to a community whose assistance she sought; her autobiographical text, *A Narrative of God's Gracious Dealings* (1683), records the deep melancholic state from which she eventually recovered through her friends' support. The publication of her narrative, Allen maintained, was intended to *justify the ways of God* to herself and her readers, a statement echoed by many writers who engaged religious issues during this period.

Notes

We are grateful for the assistance of Elaine Hobby, Caroline Bowden, Catherine Loomis, Doreen Evenden, and Liam Semler.

1. Nigel Smith, *Perfection Proclaimed: Language and Literature in English Radical Religion 1640–1660* (Oxford: Clarendon Press, 1989). Also see *Radical Religion in the English Revolution*, ed. J.F. McGregor and B. Reay (Oxford: Oxford University Press, 1984). On female radicals specifically, see Hilary Hinds, *God's Englishwomen: Seventeenth-century Radical Sectarian Writing and Feminist Criticism* (Manchester: Manchester University Press, 1996).

2. Elaine V. Beilin, *The Examinations of Anne Askew. Women Writers in English 1350–1850* (New York: Oxford University Press, 1996), lx.

3. On Catholic women writers, see John N. King, Frances E. Dolan, and Elaine Hobby, "Writing Religion," *Teaching Tudor and Stuart Women Writers*, ed. Susanne Woods and Margaret P. Hannay (New York: The Modern Language Association, 2000), esp. 90–99.

4. Mary Ellen Lamb, "The Cooke Sisters: Attitudes toward Learned Women in the Renaissance," *Silent But for the Word: Tudor Women as Patrons, Translators, and Writers of Religious Works*, ed. Margaret Patterson Hannay (Kent, Ohio: Kent State University Press, 1985), 121.

5. Patrick Cullen, "Introduction," *Alice Sutcliffe*, vol. 7 of *The Early Modern Englishwoman, Part 1*, ed. Betty Travitsky and Patrick Cullen (Brookfield: Scolar Press, 1996), x.

6. Liam Semler, "Who is the Mother of *Eliza's Babes* (1652): 'Eliza,' George Wither, and Elizabeth Emerson," *JEGP* 99.4 (2000), 513–36. "My personal opinion is that the question of the authorship of *Eliza's Babes* is NOT closed; and I have not changed my opinion that the text is best regarded officially as 'anonymous'" (email correspondence with Liam Semler, Dec. 2002).

7. Phyllis Mack, "Gender and Spirituality in Early English Quakerism 1650–1665," *Witnesses for Change: Quaker Women over Three Centuries*, ed. Elisabeth Potts Brown and Susan Mosher Stuard (New Brunswick, N.J.: Rutgers

University Press, 1989), 137. Also see Mack, *Visionary Women: Ecstatic Prophecy in Seventeenth-Century England* (Berkeley: University of California Press, 1992), and *Hidden in Plain Sight: Quaker Women's Writings 1650–1700*, ed. Mary Garman, et al. (Wallingford, Pa.: Pendle Hill, 1996).

8. See Elaine Hobby's excellent overview of the prophetic mode: "Prophecy," *A Companion to Early Modern Women's Writing*, ed. by Anita Pacheco (Oxford: Blackwell, 2002), 264–81.

9. Elizabeth D. Harvey, *Ventriloquized Voices: Feminist Theory and English Renaissance Texts* (New York: Routledge, 1992), 93–94.

10. Beth Nelson, "Lady Elinor Davies: The Prophet as Publisher," *Women's Studies International Forum* 8 (1985): 403.

11. Megan Matchinske, *Writing, Gender and State in Early Modern England: Identity Formation and the Female Subject* (Cambridge: Cambridge University Press, 1998), 128.

12. Eleanor Davies, *The Blasphemous charge against her* ([London], 1649), 9.

13. Jane Baston, "History, Prophecy, and Interpretation: Mary Cary and Fifth Monarchism," *Prose Studies* 21.3 (1998): 2.

14. Hilary Hinds observes that "the genres of prophecy and spiritual autobiography are not sharply separable: *The Cry of a Stone* is itself primarily prophetic, but also has an initial section which follows the conventions and structures of the spiritual autobiography" (Hilary Hinds, ed. and intro., *"The Cry of a Stone" by Anna Trapnel* [Tempe: Arizona Center for Medieval and Renaissance Studies, 2000], xlii–xlv).

15. Maureen Bell, "'Her Usual Practices': The Later Career of Elizabeth Calvert, 1664–75," *Publishing History* 35.4 (1994): 44.

16. Margaret Spufford, *Contrasting Communities: English Villagers in the Sixteenth and Seventeenth Centuries* (New York: Cambridge University Press, 1974).

17. Rosemary Kegl, "Women's Preaching, Absolute Property, and the *Cruel Sufferings (For the Truths sake) of Katharine Evans & Sarah Chevers*," *Women's Studies: An Interdisciplinary Journal* 24 (1994): 51–83.

18. On female communities in particular, see Elaine Hobby, "'Come to live a preaching life': Female Community in Seventeenth-century Radical Sects," *Female Communities 1600–1800: Literary Visions and Cultural Realities*, ed. Rebecca D'Monté and Nicole Pohl (London: Macmillan; New York: St. Martin's Press, 2000), 76–92; Margaret Benefiel, "'Weaving the Web of Community:' Letters and Epistles," *Hidden in Plain Sight: Quaker Women's Writings 1650 -1700*, ed. Mary Garman et al. (Wallingford, Pa.: Pendle Hill, 1996), 443–52.

19. Anne Wentworth, *A Vindication of Anne Wentworth . . . preparing . . . all people for Her Larger Testimony* (1677), *Her own Life: Autobiographical Writings by Seventeenth-Century Englishwomen*, ed. Elspeth Graham et al. (New York: Routledge, 1989), 185.

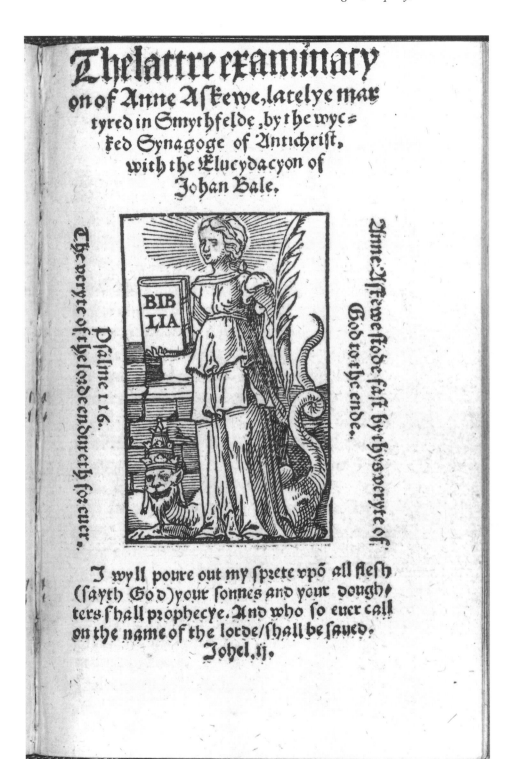

4.1: *The Lattre Examynacyon of Anne Askew* (1546). By permission of the Folger Shakespeare Library.

Anne Askew, *The Lattre Examynacyon of Anne Askew* (1546)

Although Anne Askew (ca. 1521–46) associated with the Reformers who surrounded Katherine Parr and there were many similarities between the two women's religious experience and beliefs, Parr escaped persecution while Askew was condemned as a heretic. Askew's independence, temerity, and vulnerability perhaps account for her harsh treatment. A gentlewoman from an established Lincolnshire family, Askew was cut off from paternal and marital protection, her father having died in 1541, and her husband (whose surname she refused to take) having cast her out for her religious beliefs. She bore witness to her faith in public speaking and disputation pertly and brashly, defying Catholic churchmen who accused her of heresy, and showing her education by quoting extensively from Scripture to defend her views.

The *Lattre Examynacyon* documents the stages in Askew's journey to Smithfield. Beginning with an exposition of Askew's belief about the Lord's Supper, the text continues with "The summe of my examynacyon afore the kynges counsell at Grenewyche," 18 and 19 June 1546, where she refuses to sign a document recanting her beliefs and is sent sick to Newgate. There follows a "confessyon" of faith from prison; prayers and meditations; a summary of her condemnation for heresy at the Guildhall on June 28; a letter to Lord Chancellor Wriostheley requesting that he bring her suit to the attention of the king; a letter to the king; and an account of her torture on the rack and her refusal to incriminate others of her "sect." The last items are the "confession of her fayth" and her "balade," which she purportedly wrote and sang in Newgate. Refusing to recant, Askew was burned 16 July 1546 at the age of twenty-five.

The title-page woodcut reproduced here shows how John Bale, her first editor, worked to shape a text that supported his polemical evangelical agenda. The woodcut represents a woman clothed as an early Christian martyr, holding the Bible and a martyr's palm, and trampling a beast wearing the tiara of the Roman papacy. These images draw on a visual vocabulary developed in German Reformation propaganda, and this edition was published in Wesel in the Protestant Duchy of Cleves, since it could not legally be published in England. The symbolism subsumes Anne's trials into the larger historical struggle of the "true" church, linking her to the primitive church and strict scripturalism. The image of the early martyr may even pick up a textual identification that Bale makes between Anne Askew and Blandina, a second-century martyr described by the early church historian Eusebius. The writing surrounding the picture ("Anne Askewe stode fast by thys veryte of God to the ende" and "Psalme 116. The veryte of the lorde endureth for ever") reinforces the stress on Askew's defiant verbal confession of faith that occupies so much of the narrative of both her examinations. Such a stress on the confession of faith, rather than on bodily suffering, as defining Askew's sanctity, casts her as a distinctly Protestant saint.

Jennifer L. Andersen
California State University

Anne Askew. *The Lattre Examynacyon of Anne Askew* (1546). Folger Shakespeare Library STC 850
Bdw. STC 848. Title Page.

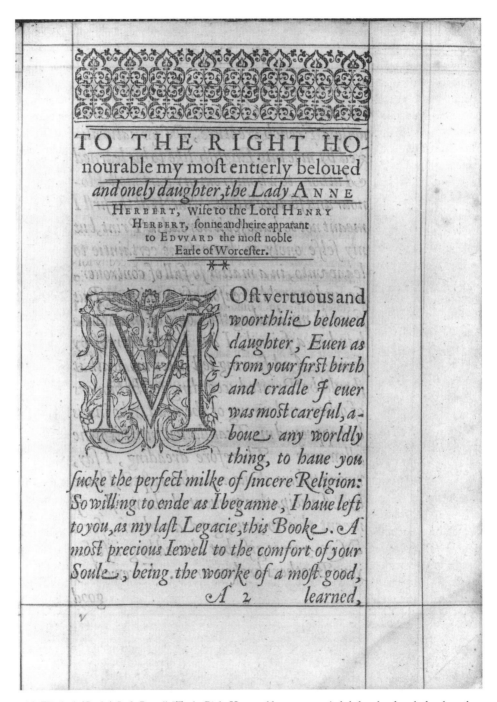

TO THE RIGHT HO-
nourable my moſt entierly beloued
and onely daughter, the Lady ANNE
HERBERT, Wiſe to the Lord HENRY
HERBERT, ſonne and heire apparant
to EDVVARD the moſt noble
Earle of Worceſter.
✶✶

Oſt vertuous and
woorthilie beloued
daughter, Euen as
from your firſt birth
and cradle I euer
was moſt careful, a-
boue any worldly
thing, to haue you
ſucke the perfect milke of ſincere Religion:
So willing to ende as I beganne, I haue left
to you, as my laſt Legacie, this Booke. A
moſt precious Iewell to the comfort of your
Soule, being the woorke of a moſt good,
        A 2   learned,

4.2: Elizabeth (Cooke), Lady Russell, "To the Right Honourable my most entierly beloved and onely daughter, the Lady Anne Herbert" (1605). By permission of the Folger Shakespeare Library.

Elizabeth (Cooke), Lady Russell, "To the Right Honourable my most entierly beloved and onely daughter, the Lady Anne Herbert," *A Way of Reconcilitation of a good and learned man, touching the Trueth, Nature, and Substance of the Body and Blood of Christ in the Sacrament* **(1605)**

Classically educated like her learned sisters, Mildred, Katherine, and Anne, Elizabeth Cooke grew up at Gidea Hall, Essex, under the tutelage of her parents, Sir Anthony Cooke and Lady Anne (Fitzwilliam) Cooke. We know something of her life from her correspondence, from her funerary verse, and from her one printed translation. In 1558, she married Sir Thomas Hoby, the diplomat, scholar, and translator. To commemorate Hoby's death in 1566, Russell wrote elegies for his tomb at Bisham, Berkshire, composing over eighty lines in English and Latin to Sir Thomas and his half-brother, Sir Philip. When her two young daughters, Elizabeth and Anne, died in 1571, she wrote elegies for their tomb, as she did for her sister, Katherine. As a tender mother, she mourns Elizabeth as "virgo tenella," a delicate maiden, and Anne as "aurea virgo," a golden maiden; as a loving sister, she mourns Katherine's piety, learning, and modest life (Schleiner 209–10). In 1574, she married John, Lord Russell, but he died ten years later, occasioning her Greek and Latin elegiac verses for his tomb in Westminster Abbey. She also commissioned her own monument at Bisham.

Russell's translation of Bishop John Ponet's Latin *Diallacticon viri boni et literati, de veritate, natura, atque substantia corporis et sanguinis Christi in eucharistia* was published in 1605 as *A Way of Reconciliation of a good and learned man, touching the Trueth, Nature, and Substance of the Body and Blood of Christ in the Sacrament.* Ponet wrote the treatise in Germany at least fifty years earlier, and Sir Anthony Cooke, Russell's father, published the first edition in 1557 in Strasbourg. At an unknown date, but most likely before Ponet's death in 1556, Russell "naturalized" it into English. In the dedication to her sole surviving daughter, Lady Anne Herbert, Russell implies that her translation had been approved by Ponet "with his owne allowance," thus impelling her to publish an accurate version of his work before she dies. In the dedication to her daughter, she emphasizes her role as a religious guide, offering the book as a last legacy to her "good sweet Nanne"; she concludes with four lines of Latin verse blessing Anne's husband and children, and praying for her daughter's serene life.

Ponet's treatise attempts to reconcile diverse Protestant positions on the Eucharist and to mediate "a controversie full of thornes" by demonstrating that Scripture and the "ancient opinion of the true beleeving Fathers," both Greek and Latin, are in doctrinal agreement about the nature of the sacrament as "a signe or figure." Like his friend John Bale and other Reformed scholars, Ponet views the English church in a historical context, claiming that it returns to the teachings of the primitive church. While Russell's translation dates from the early days of the English Reformation, its publication in 1605 may suggest her awareness of growing religious controversy between the new king, James I, and the Puritan wing of the church over issues of conformity. Like her sister, Anne Cooke Bacon, who translated *An apologie or answere in defence of the Churche of Englande* (1564), Russell made an important theological text accessible to English readers at a time of national religious debate.

ELAINE BEILIN
FRAMINHAM STATE COLLEGE

Elizabeth (Cooke), Lady Russell. "To the Right Honourable my most entierly beloved and onely daughter, the Lady Anne Herbert. " *A Way of Reconcilitation of a good and learned man, touching the Trueth, Nature, and Substance of the Body and Blood of Christ in the Sacrament* (1605). Folger Shakespeare Library STC 21456. sig. A2r

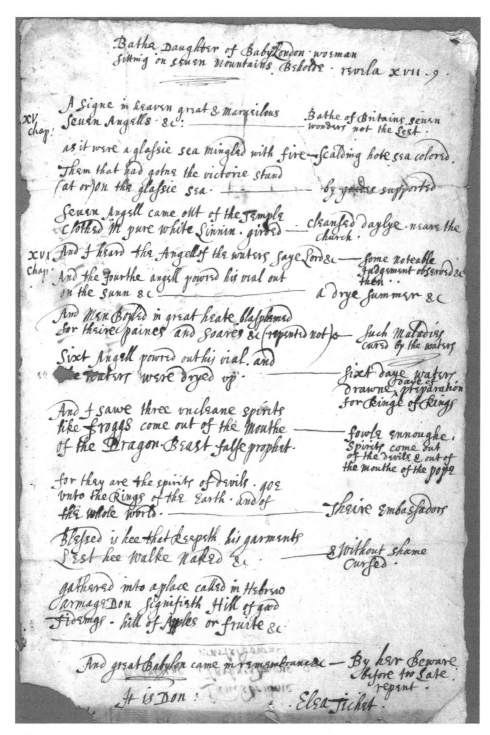

4.3: Eleanor Davies (Lady Douglas), "Bathe Daughter of BabyLondon" (c.1630). Reproduced by permission of The Hungtington Library, San Marino, California.

Eleanor Davies (Lady Douglas), "Bathe Daughter of BabyLondon" (c. 1630)

Transcription

Bathe Daughter of BabyLondon woeman
Sitting on seven mountains Beholde revela XVII.9

XV   A signe in heaven great & marveilous
   chap: Seven Angells &c:

   Bathe of Britains seven
   wonders not the Lest

   as it were a glassie sea mingled with fire

   scalding hote seacolored

   Them that had gotne the victorie stand
   (at or) on the glassie sea

   by guides supported

   Seven Angell came out of the Temple
   Clothed in pure white Linnin girded

   cleansed daylye neare the
   church

XVI And I heard the Angell of the waters saye Lord &
chap
   And the fourthe angell powred his vial out
   on the sunn &

   some noteable
   Judgement observed &c
   then
   a drye summer &c

And Men Boyled in great heate blasphemed
for theire paines and soares &c (repented not)

   such maladies

   cured by the waters

Sixt Angell powred out his vial and
The Waters were dryed up

   sixt daye waters
   drawne daye of preparation
   for Kinge of Kings

And I sawe three uncleane spirits
like froggs come out of the Mouthe
Of the Dragon Beast false prophet

   fowle ennoughe
   Spirits come out
   of the devils & out of
   the mouthe of the pope

for they are the spirits of devils goe
unto the Kings of the Earth and of
the whole world

   Theire Embassadors

Blessed is hee that keepeth his garments
Lest hee walke naked &c

   & Without shame
   Cursed

gathered into a place called in Hebrew
armageDon signifieth Hill of good
Tideings hill of Apples or fruite &c

And great Babylon came in remembranc &c

   By her Beware
   before too Late
   repent

   It is Don:
   Elea Tichet

Commentary

Eleanor Davies's draft prophecy "Bathe Daughter of BabyLondon," which survives in a unique manuscript in the Hastings papers in the Huntington Library, is a rare example of prophetic work in progress. The left column shows a series of quotations from the book of Revelation; the right shows brief notes by Davies working out the analogies between the first century New Testament prophecy (written around 90 A.D.) and seventeenth-century England. The notes show Davies's prophetic method, worked out in full in her published prophecies.

Here she signs herself "Elea Tichet," meaning Tuchet or Touchet, which was her family name. She puns frequently also on the other surnames that she claimed: Audley (her father's barony), Davies (her first husband, the jurist and poet Sir John Davies); and Douglas (her second husband, Sir Archibald Douglas). The vigor of this signature suggests the relish with which Davies claimed authorship. This is evoked also by the matching claim in the lefthand column: "It is Don." Her declaration seems to apply to the encroachments of Babylon, emphasized also by the swirls of the quill pen under "great Babylon"; and to Davies's own achievement in conceiving the prophecy.

The prophecy is keyed to the Book of Revelation and is best decoded using the King James (AV) translation, open at chapters fifteen through to seventeen. The left column of this page is a series of quotations from those chapters. Horizontal lines link each verse with Davies's world. What she produces is then an exegetical commentary on Revelation, demonstrating its pertinence to her own times. She does not claim directly to prophesy the future, but here she is clear that the end times are at hand. The pouring out of the vial of the sixth angel (Rev. 16:12) is a sign of a "daye of preparation for King of Kings." She does not name the exact hour of the Lord's return, but choosing this sequence from late in the Revelation shows she believes the time is very near. Thus she remarks at the bottom of this page, just above her signature, "Beware before too Late repent."

As throughout her writings, Davies anticipates an English apocalypse. The striking title refers to Revelation 17:5, where Babylon the Great is described as "THE MOTHER OF HARLOTS AND ABOMINATIONS OF THE EARTH." Davies' coinage "BabyLondon" assigns that role to the London of Charles I and his wife, Henrietta Maria, a city (and a royal couple) she came to despise. In Revelation Babylon sits on seven hills. In Davies's English terms the Hills around "Bathe" take on this role; the verso of this page mentions three mountains (Landsdowne, Clarknesdowne, and Warlesdowne) near Bath. These hills support the daughter of London (or Babylon), containing small versions of the abominations visible to Davies in the capital city. The weather around Bath is folded into this scenario: "And the fourthe angell powred his vial out on the sunn" (Rev 16:8) is equated to "a drye summer &c." The summer heat suggests that the final fires purging evil, transforming the good, are at hand.

MARK HOULAHAN
UNIVERSITY OF WAIKATO

Eleanor (Davies), Lady Douglas. "Bathe Daughter of BabyLondon" (c.1630). Huntington Library, HA Religious Box 1 (28).

Sister Joan Seller, English nun's oath of obedience (1631)

Commentary

Sister Joan Seller, born in Orcop, Monmouthshire, on the Welsh borders in 1603, joined the English Benedictine convent known as Our Lady of Consolation in Cambrai, Flanders, in May 1628. Her name appears in the convent records as Jane Cellar. The convent had been founded in 1623 under the jurisdiction of the English Benedictine congregation. From the beginning of the seventeenth century a substantial number of new convents had opened in Flanders to which devout English Catholic families could send their daughters either for their education or to become nuns. Many of the convents were small, but taken together, by the 1620s, several hundred English women were involved.

In this document Joan Seller made her solemn profession as a lay sister, and this single statement defines the parameters of her life for the next fifty years. According to the constitutions formally adopted a year later, Sister Joan had to bring with her an assured pension of ten pounds a year for life. The evidence suggests that in the Benedictine houses of the seventeenth century the lay sisters were not left to do all the menial work, although this cannot be proved. The constitutions said that converse or lay sisters were no less religious than the choir nuns. There were a number of reasons why girls might choose to become converse sisters, although the most likely reason was the lack of a dowry. The families of choir sisters at Cambrai had to find the considerable sum of £400.

Nothing is known of Joan Seller's parentage from the convent records or of the detail of her life in the convent. Her date of death was noted as 11 April 1683. Joan Seller's profession is significant for what it represents about a group of women, lay sisters, in a contemplative English convent in the seventeenth century, rather than illustrating an individual. From the information given in the profession and contextual evidence we have an insight into her life in the convent. Like the choir nuns, lay sisters in Benedictine houses promised to keep perpetual enclosure and took four vows of poverty, chastity, obedience, and the reform of manners. Joan Seller made her profession in English; in another profession from the same year at Cambrai a choir nun, Bridget More, in September 1630 made her vows in Latin, writing out the document in her own hand. Catherine Gascoigne became Abbess in 1629 and remained so until her death in 1673, being reelected every four years. The president of the English Benedictine Congregation, Sebert Bagshow, was present at both professions in 1630–31.

Joan Seller was joining a contemplative order with a strong intellectual tradition that the nuns continued. One major preoccupation after their foundation was the lack of a library, which was partially solved by extensive copying carried out in the convent. The nuns at Cambrai had a reputation among contemporaries for beautiful calligraphy and careful style. This can be seen in this copy of the profession. Many of their number were able to make translations of French books, some of which were published, and their library held books in at least three languages including Latin. Although Joan Seller was a lay sister and unlikely to have had the same level of education as a choir nun, circumstantial evidence suggests that she was able to read and probably able to write. The choice of English for the language of her profession was a deliberate attempt to involve her in the words of the promise.

In the name of our Lord Jesus Christe Amen.

J Sister Joan Seller de Sancto Michaele, of the Parish of Orcoppe in the Countie of Monmouth, Promise before God and his Saints, Pouertie, Chastitie and Obedience, and Conuersion of my maners, according to the Rule of our most holie Father Saint Benett, and perpetuall inclosure in this Conuent of the Blessed Virgin Marie of the Order of the same Saint Benett at Cambray. In the presence of the Reuerende Mother the Ladie Catherine Gascoigne Abbesse of the said Conuent, and vnder the Obedience of the Verie Reuerend Father, Father Scholie Bagshaw President of the whole English Congregation of the same Order.

In the yeare of our Lord 1631. the 20 day of March.

Sister Joan Seller

✝

4.4: Sister Joan Seller, English nun's oath of obedience (1631). Courtesy of the Archives départmentales du Nord, Lille. Photo: Jean-Luc Thierry.

Transcription

In the name of our Lord Jesus Christe. Amen.

I Sister Joan Seller de Sancto Michaele, of the Parish of Orcoppe in the Countie
of Monmouth; Promise before God and his Saints, Povertie, Chastitie and Obedience,
and Conversion of my maners, according to the Rule of our most holie Father
Saint Bennett, and perpetuall inclosure in thies Convent of the Blessed Virgin
Marie of the Order of the same Saint Benett at Cambray. In the presence of
the Reverende Mother the Ladie Catherine Gascoigne Abbesse of the said Convent,
and under the Obedience of the Verie Reverend Father, Father Seberte Bagshaw
President of the whole Inglish Congregation of the same Order.

In the yeare of our Lord 1631. the 20 day of March.

Sister Joan Seller

CAROLINE BOWDEN
ST. MARY'S COLLEGE, TWICKENHAM

Sister Joan Seller. English nun's oath of obedience (1631). Archives départementales du Nord, Lille,
France. MS archives 20 H 1 1.

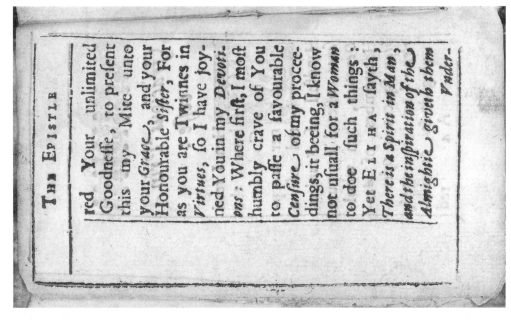

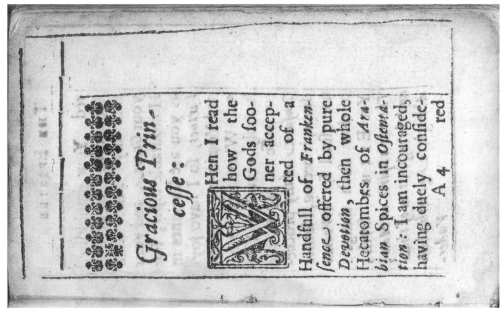

THE EPISTLE

red Your unlimited Goodnesse, to present this my Mite unto your *Grace*, and your Honourable *sister*, For as you are Twinnes in *Virtues*, so I have joyned You in my *Devotions*: Where first, I most humbly crave of You to passe a favourable *Censure* of my proceedings, it beeing, I know not usuall for a *Woman* to doe such things: Yet Eliha sayth, *There is a Spirit in Man, and the inspiration of the Almightie giveth them* Under-

THE EPISTLE

Gracious Prin-cesse:

Hen I read how the Gods sooner accepted of a Handfull of *Franken-sence* offered by pure *Devotion*, then whole Hecatombes of *Ara-bian* Spices in *Oscurda-tion*: I am incouraged, having duely confide-

A 4   red

4.5: Alice Sutcliffe, "Epistle Dedicatory," *Meditations of man's mortalitie, or, A way to true blessednesse* (1634). By permission of the Folger Shakespeare Library.

Alice Sutcliffe, "Epistle Dedicatory," *Meditations of man's mortalitie, or, A way to true blessednesse* (1634)

Alice Sutcliffe's *Meditations of man's mortalitie, or, A way to true blessednesse*, published in 1634, is a relatively unknown religious tract containing six prose meditations preceded by a long poem of eighty-eight sestets (ababcc). It first received modern scholarly attention from Ruth Hughey (1934), who identified much of what is currently known about Sutcliffe. There are only four extant copies of *Meditations*, a duodecimo volume, housed in the Folger Shakespeare Library, British Library, Huntington Library, and Peterborough Cathedral (Cullen xii). The title page specifies that it is the "Second Edition, enlarged." Since no copy of the first edition survives, what constitutes the enlargement can only be speculated. It may refer to the addition of the commendatory poems to the author in the preface, or it may refer to the appendage of the poem, as it is not mentioned in the table of contents. No other work by Sutcliffe has been identified, and no modern edition of her work has been published.

Little is known about the life of Alice Sutcliffe, not even the dates of her birth and death. She was the daughter of Luke Woodhouse of Kimberly, Norfolk, belonging to the family of Sir Thomas Woodhouse, attendant to Prince Henry in the Jacobean court (Greer 90). Sutcliffe was married, sometime before 1624, to John Sutcliffe, "Esquire to the Body of James I," who received confirmation of his arms in that year. His most notable relative was his uncle, Matthew Sutcliffe, the dean of Exeter and well-known anti-Catholic polemicist (Hughey 160–61) (see "Sutcliffe, Matthew" DNB). John eventually became, as the title page of *Meditations* conveys, "Groome of his Majesties [Charles I (1625–49)] most Honorable Privie Chamber."

The preface to *Meditations* includes a dedicatory epistle addressed to Catherine Villiers, the Duchess of Buckingham, and Catherine's sister-in-law, Susan Villiers (wife of William Fielding, Earl of Denbigh and Master of the Great Wardrobe). It also includes an acrostic encomium to each of the joint dedicatees and to Philip, Earl of Pembroke and Montgomery, Lord Chamberlain of the Household and joint dedicatee of Shakespeare's First Folio. The acrostics are proceded commendatory verses to the author by such notables as Ben Jonson, Thomas May, George Wither, and Francis Lenton. The dedicatory epistle and acrostics create the sense of an elite social milieu enjoyed by Sutcliffe and her husband, and along with the commendatory verses were likely intended to promote the author and her husband at court.

Like other women writers of her day, Sutcliffe may have felt compelled to defend her sex when presenting her work in a public forum. In the dedicatory epistle, she implores Catherine and Susan "to passe a favourable *Censure* of my proceedings, it beeing, I know, not usuall for a *Woman* to doe such things." Sutcliffe seeks protection from the Duchess against the "mocking Ishmaels" who may criticize her work, and also from the Earl of Pembroke and Montgomery, whom she asks in an acrostic to "guerdon my weake pen, / If this doth show my imbecilitie, / Like a good patron shroud it from bad men." She suggests that with Pembroke's encouragement of her "*Minervae's* infant Muse" and with the assistance of her "Coelique Muse" ("celic," heavenly, OED) she may write a "vertuous tract," and perhaps even follow in the acclaimed path of the biblical Deborah, whose song is given in Judges 5. Sutcliffe cites the Song of Deborah to prove that women could and did produce acclaimed literary works, at least, as she suggests, when the loftiness of their subject allowed for it.

Darcy Maynard
Memorial University of Newfoundland

Alice Sutcliffe. *Meditations of man's mortalitie, or, A way to true blessednesse* (1634). Folger Shakespeare Library STC 23447. FILM fo. 4071.2. Epistle Dedicatory.

(14)

De Verbo dici-
mus, ô lucernâ
dignè super can-
delabrum Eccle-
siæ posita. Amb.
Sit discretio vir-
gæ quæ feriat, sit
consolatio quæ
sustentat baculi.

Architects, or Master-builders, expressing their skilfulnesse and divine dexterity, which justly reproves three sorts of men: First, those who in their senslesse stupiditie account this calling more easie than any other, and will take no knowledge by respective reverence of the painfull labours of their faithfull Ministers, which grosse mistake might be soone removed, did they but consider those sacred re-quisites, which in the discharge of this weighty calling, imposeth such duty on godly Pastours.

2 Tim. 4 1,2.
Quemadmodum
medicus qui bili
vult mederi, ama-
ris utitur Phar-
macis, ita obdu-
rati, præfracti, &
contumaces ho-
mines, duris ver-
bis arguendi sunt.
Exod. 5. 2.
Exod. 5. 17.
Contra injurias
vitæ, beneficium
mortis habeo.
Justè judicat Deus
& rependit im-
probis,

These are required to preach the Word, to be instant in season and out of season, to reprove, rebuke, and exhort, with all long-suffering and doctrinall purity, and this imposed with a solemne charge, and in the presence of God and Jesus Christ; whereunto watching and endu-ring afflictions are added, to make full proofe of their Mi-nistery, *2 Tim. 4.* Yet such is the stability of Atheisticall spirits, who resembling *Pharaoh,* the Arch-type of obdu-racy, that not only secretly and mentally they murmur, *Who is the Lord, that we should heare his voyce?* but speak a-loud in his reproachfull dialect, saying to his Messengers, Yee are idle, yee are idle; and therefore as he (in his rigo-rous tyranny) doubled the burthens of the oppressed Israe-lites, so these in stead of supporting their Ministers, detract from their honour and deserved maintenance.

Pastorale magi-
sterium est ars
artium, & regi-
men animarum.
Greg.
Hab. 2 1.
In custodia mea
stanti & consi-
stentimihi in mi-
nutione, ac specu-
lanti ad videndū
quid eloquereur
mihi.

Ier. 13. 17.

Is then the work of a godly Minister, who vigilantly careth for the weale of his flock, so light and easie as these suppose, who under-value their precious labours? No surely, if wee view them, it will plainly appeare, that such must be waking when others sleep, to procure our safety, and prevent our danger, standing like *Habbakuk* upon the Tower, and sounding the Trumpet with *Ezechiels* watch-man, mourning in secret with holy *Jeremy,* and powring forth teares for the pride of stubborne sinners, not only la-bouring to find out wholsome food, fit for the nourish-ment of severall persons; but to feed on those truths by divine meditation and holy practice, before hee present

4.6: Elizabeth Warren, *The Old and Good Way Vindicated* (1646). Courtesy of William Andrews Clark Memorial Library, University of California, Los Angeles.

Elizabeth Warren, *The Old and Good Way Vindicated in a Treatise Wherein Divers Errours (both in judgement and practice, incident to these declining Times) are unmasked, for the Caution of humble Christians* (1646)

Elizabeth Warren, a gentlewoman of Woodbridge, Suffolk, was a Moderate Puritan who supported traditional preaching and opposed radical changes in the ministry. Her pamphlets, advising men to be mindful of their social place and women to follow their husbands, appeared from 1645 to 1649. In addition to criticizing poorly trained ministers, she condemned the Civil War. In contrast to self-educated radicals such as Anna Trapnel, Warren was a Latin scholar well read in Plato, Aristotle, Cicero, Plutarch, and Augustine. Her writings include references to classical myths, and the margins are filled with Latin quotations.

Warren criticizes preachers who do not value university learning and who have not received the traditional education in preparation for the ministry. She argues in *The Old and Good Way* that some preachers not only lack formal training in the ministry, but also deliver God's word in a mechanical and unenthusiastic manner. Husbandmen keep their bodies strong to do God's work in the field; laborers in the ministry need to keep themselves healthy in mind and body to do their work. Servants of God's word should labor with a creative energy and limitless love for their work.

On page 14 of this treatise, Warren describes preachers as "Architects, or Masterbuilders" who should possess "skilfulnesse and divine dexterity." She sets up her clearly defined argument by disapproving of three types of men. First, she discusses "those [preachers] who in their senslesse stupiditie account this calling more easie than any other." They make the mistake of refusing to learn from the "painfull labours of their faithfull Ministers." New preachers would more easily correct their mistakes if they would put their own egos aside and follow the example of successful, experienced pastors.

The other two types she discusses on the following pages are first, the type who enters the ministry without calling or ability, thus causing him to be mechanical in his duties. The third type is the one who becomes arrogant and refuses to learn because he thinks men are qualified by "immediate inspiration" (16).

One would think that Warren's writings would be more easily understood than those of the less educated female radicals, but that is not the case. Her extensive learning instead results in convoluted sentences consisting of classical allusions and unending topic strings sprinkled generously with Latinate words. For example, the following sentence is typical of her style: "Yet such is the stability of Atheisticall spirits, who resembling Pharaoh, the Arch-type of obduracy, that not only secretly and mentally they murmur . . . but speak aloud in his reproach full dialect, saying to his Messengers, Yee are idle, yee are idle; and therefore as he (in his rigorous tyranny) doubled the burthens of the oppressed Israelites, so these in stead of supporting their Ministers, detract from their honour and deserved maintenance." Warren claimed that she did not write for publication because of her gender and her deficiencies, yet her material is clearly a product of a very educated person directed at other educated readers and thinkers.

LINDA C. MITCHELL
SAN JOSE STATE UNIVERSITY

Elizabeth Warren. *The Old and Good Way Vindicated in a Treatise Wherein Divers Errours (both in judgement and practice, incident to these declining Times) are unmasked, for the Caution of humble Christians* (1646). University of California, Los Angeles, William Andrews Clark Library Pam. Coll. Page 14.

Many visiters of her in despaire.   9

vous horrour day and night; concluding shee was
a Cast-away, a Reprobate, walking daily in the
midst of fire and brimstone, as one in Hell already. Till the Lord (who had loved her with an
everlasting love, and in loving kindnesse prevented
her ruine,) at last *restored comforts to her, and to
those that had prayed and mourned for her.*

. And since her much prayed-and hoped-for-*deliverance*, amongst many that have visited her,
were these *Ministers*; Mr *Palmer*, Mr *Sprigge*, and
Mr *Simpson* beforesaid, Mr *Peters*, Mr *Charnock* of
London, Mr *Atberley* of the Charterhouse(with his
wife,) Mr *Hide* of Wighton in *Yorkshire*, and the
Relator. Also the Lady *Willoughby*, the Lady *Renu-
la*, and the Lady *Clotworthy*, the Lady *Vermuiden*,
with her daughters M^ris *Sarah*, and M^ris *Katharine*,
Sir *Ric: Philips*, and his Lady, dau: to Dr *Oxenbridg*,
Sir *Richard Saltonstall*, with his Lady; Dr *Coxe*, D
Debote, Dr *Worsley*, Dr *Paget*, Physicians; M^ris *Pal-
mer*, wife to Mr *Palmer*. Also M^ris *Fines*, wife to my
Lord *Says* eldest Son, and M^ris *Harrison*, wife to the
Chamberlain of *London*, M^ris *Sarah Jones*, wife to M^r
Tho. Jones Esquire of Tower-hill, Col. *Langhams*
wife, daughter to the Lady *Roberts*; M^r and M^ris
Liggon, Capt. *Price*, and his wife, M^ris *Wilson* at
Nags-head; M^ris *Lane*, Mr *P. Barbon*, and his wife;
M^ris *Owen*, and M^ris *Hannah Allen*, Bookseller, M^ris
Manning of Tower-street, M^ris *Elizabeth Waldo*,
sister to Mr *John Pocock*; Mr *Ellis* and M^ris *Ellis*, M^ris
Hawkins, M^ris *Flood*, and M^ris *Thare*, all neer Lon-
don-

4.7: Hannah Allen, publisher of *The Exceeding Riches of Grace Advanced by the Spirit of Grace*
(1647). By permission of The British Library.

Hannah Allen, publisher of *The Exceeding Riches of Grace Advanced by the Spirit of Grace, in an Empty Nothing Creature, Viz. Mris Sarah Wight* (1647)

Hannah Allen enjoyed a brief career as a bookseller between the death of her first husband, Benjamin Allen, in 1646 and her marriage to their erstwhile apprentice, Livewell Chapman, in 1651. Allen, who likely came from a family established in the book trade, ran her husband's bookshop at the sign of the Crown in Pope's Head Alley after his death. The evidence for her involvement in bookselling between 1646 and 1651 lies in the Stationers' Register and in the 54 books and pamphlets that survive with her name in the imprint. Allen benefited from the liberal policies of the Stationers' Company, which ceded husbands' businesses and their part in the company stock to wives. She may also have benefited from the drop in membership in the Stationers' Company during the Civil War, when opportunities for enlisting as a soldier or going off to Ireland—or even farther west—tempted apprentices from seeing their service through.

The years of Allen's publishing career coincide with the disruptions of the second Civil War, the defeat of the Levellers, Pride's Purge, and the execution of the king; works sold by and printed for Hannah Allen engage in debates about relations of church and state then in progress. Allen's shop was located in a parish notable for its Independency and anti-Royalism, and Allen's business connections reveal a network of associations with people committed to radical change. The core of Hannah Allen's output has been characterized as representing Independent, New England Congregationalist, and pro-Parliament opinion—all at the radical end of the spectrum.

The selection presented here is from a very popular work that was frequently reissued. The narrative is derived from a journal kept by the author, Henry Jessey, leader of the first Independent congregation. Jessey recorded the experience of Sarah Wight, then fifteen years old, who fasted for seventy-six days and underwent a profound religious conversion. For Puritans there was a particular interest in accounts of conversions and spiritual experiences of this kind because in such narratives the mind and body become the battleground for the contest between God and the devil, and the person experiencing the battle becomes a living example of divine intervention. The page reproduced here is intended to show Hannah Allen's personal involvement in the sectarian world, beyond her trade interest as a publisher of the account. Allen is listed by Jessey "amongst many that have visited" Sarah Wight "since her much prayed- and hoped-for-deliverance," thus placing Allen in a particular religious community testifying to the "experimental" religion of a coreligionist. The catalogue of reputable witnesses in which Allen's name appears lends credibility to the marvelous event and, in theory, gives contemporary readers the opportunity to check the story with a firsthand witness. This rhetorical strategy for legitimation was also employed by prominent Presbyterian controversialists such as Thomas Edwards, whose 1646 publication, *Gangraena*, spread sensational reports and atrocity tales about the practices of Independent congregations like the ones with whom Allen was associated.

Jennifer L. Andersen
California State University

Henry Jessey. *The Exceeding Riches of Grace Advanced by the Spirit of Grace, in an Empty Nothing Creature, Viz. Mris Sarah Wight.* Hannah Allen, publisher (1647). British Library 1418.i.52, Page 9.

Foureteene ſtrange

PROPHESIES: 7

Beſides Mother *Shiptons*, and Mr. *Saltmarſh*, predicting
wonderfull events to betide theſe yeares of calamity, in
this Climate, whereof divers are already come to
paſſe, worthy of obſervation.   *Prophecies*

1. A Propheſie of K. *Richard* the 3.   5. *Ignatius* Propheſie.   K
2. Mother *Shiptons* Propheſie.   6. *Merlins* Propheſie.
3. Mr. *Truſwels*, Recorder of Lincolne.   7. *Otwel Bins* Propheſies.
4. *Sibyllaes* Propheſies.   8. Mr. *Brightmans* Propheſies
                   6. Ancient Propheſies in Meeter.

Whereto is added the Predictions of Mr. *John Saltmarch*, to his Excellency, and the
Counſell of his Army. And the manner of his Death.

Printed by an exact true copy, with new marginall Notes
on Mother *Shiptons* Propheſies.

Wolſey.

Mother Shipton.

Printed for *Richard Harper*, at the Bible and Harpe in Smithfeld. 1648.

4.8: Woodcut of Mother Shipton, *Foureteene Strange Prophesies* (1648).
By permission of The British Library.

Woodcut of Mother Shipton, *Foureteene strange Prophesies* (1648)

The various surviving portraits of the secular prophet Mother Shipton of Knaresborough, Yorkshire, reveal the ambivalent attitudes toward women prophets in the sixteenth and seventeenth centuries. The woodcut reproduced here, from *Foureteene strange Prophesies* (1648), reveals the stereotypical image of the witch, with wart, bedraggled hair, and crooked nose and chin. An earlier portrait from Richard Lownd's printing of *The Prophesie of Mother Shipton in the Raigne of King Henry the Eighth* (1641) depicts a respectable-looking, well-dressed woman. A woodcut in Richard Head's *The Life and Death of Mother Shipton* (1687) shows a pious old woman kneeling in prayer. In spite of Shipton's reputation as a witch, Head defended her prophetical gifts: "and though she was generally believed to be a Witch, yet all persons what ever, that either saw, or heard of her, had her in great esteem" (30).

Women who foretold future events in the sixteenth and seventeenth centuries can be categorized as (1) middle-class cunning or wise women (sometimes dispensing medical services), (2) fortune tellers (who used the face, lines of the palm, or other signs to predict events and character), (3) religious visionary prophets such as Eleanor Davies who predicted the future based on biblical passages, (4) Quaker Prophets (much of the surviving women's prophetic writing of this period is Quaker in origin), and (5) women astrologers, such as Mary Holden and Sarah Jinner—also included in this volume—who foretold the future by calculating the positions of the planets. Members of all these groups were open to the charges of witchcraft or specifically of practicing evil deeds (*maleficia*), which carried the death penalty. The connection of these women to both supernatural phenomena (either the word of God or devils) and the unknown (future events) provoked an uneasy mixture of respect, awe, and fear. Women were generally discouraged from expressing opinions on politics, medicine, and religion during the period, and female prophets therefore presented serious threats to the existing political and religious institutions of early modern Europe.

Shipton was reputedly born in 1488, although no evidence of her exists before 1641. The events recorded by Shipton took place during the reign of Henry VIII (reigned 1509–47). Shipton's prophecies are political in nature, foretelling Cardinal Wolsey's journey and death, and Thomas Cromwell's beheading, although their exact purpose is difficult to determine. It was precisely this ambiguity that gave the prophecies their power, because the various writers who reprinted the prophecies from 1642 to 1685 could project their own meanings onto the text. For example, the author of *Mercurius Propheticus* (1643) interpreted Shipton's lines "the first coming in of the king of Scots shall be at Holgate Towne, but he shall not come through the bar" to mean: "This was fulfilled in K. James his coming in, for such a multitude of people stood at Holgate Bar to behold him, as that to avoid the prease [crowd] he was forced to ride by another way" (3).

ALAN S. WEBER

CORNELL UNIVERSITY

Mother Ursula Shipton. *Foureteene strange Prophesies: Besides Mother Shiptons, and Mr. Saltmarsh, predicting wonderfull events to betide these yeares of calamity, in this Climate, whereof divers are already come to passe, worthy of observation* (1648). Wing 3444: British Library Thomason Tracts E. 527 (7). Title page.

THE LITTLE HORNS DOOM & DOWNFALL:

OR A Scripture-Prophesie OF

King James, and King Charles, and of this present Parliament, unfolded.

Wherein it appeares, that the late Tragedies that have bin acted upon the Scene of these three Nations; and particularly, the late Kings doom and death, was so long ago, as by *Daniel* predeclared.

AND

What the issue of all will be, is also discovered; which followes in the second Part.

By M. Cary, a servant of Jesus Christ.

AMOS 3. 7, 8.

Surely the Lord God will do nothing but he revealeth his secrets unto his servants the Prophets: The Lion hath roared, who will not feare? the Lord God hath spoken, who can but Prophesie?

London, Printed for the Author, and are to be sold at the sign of the *Black-spread Eagle*, at the West end of *Pauls*, 1651.

582

A new AND MORE EXACT MAPPE OR, DESCRIPTION OF

New *Ierusalems* GLORY when Jesus Christ and his Saints with him shall reign on earth a Thousand yeares, and possess all Kingdoms.

WHEREIN

Is discovered the glorious estate into which the Church shall be then put both in respect of externall and internall glory, and the time when.

And also,

What hath been done these eight yeares last past, and what is now a doing, and what shall be done within a few years now following in order to this great work.

Wherein also

That great Question, whether it be lawfull for Saints to make use of the materiall Sword in the ruining at the enemies of Christ, and whether it be the mind of Christ to have it so, is at large debated and resolved in the Affirmative from clear Scriptures, and all others answered,

By M. Cary a servant of Jesus Christ.

Rev. 22 6, 7.

And he said unto me, These sayings are faithfull and true, and the Lord God of the holy Prophets sent his Angell to shew unto his Servants the thing which must shortly be done. Behold, I come quickly.

LONDON, *April 17.*

Printed by W. H. and are to be sold at the sign of the *Black-spread Eagle* at the West end of *Pauls*. 1651.

4.9: Mary Cary (Rande), *Little Horns Doom and Downfall* and *A New and More Exact Mappe of the New Jerusalems Glory* (1651). By permission of The British Library.

Mary Cary (Rande), *Little Horns Doom and Downfall* and *A New and More Exact Mappe of the New Jerusalems Glory* (1651)

Little is known about Mary Cary's life, and her published writings do not offer much insight. She began printing her prophecies in the tumultuous years immediately prior to the execution of Charles I and continued into the early days of the Interregnum. The quotation from Amos (on the title page for *Little Horns Doom*) suggests that, having heard the "Lion's roar," she is compelled to prophesy regardless of limitations imposed on her sex.

This single volume, the third of her four published volumes, contains two lengthy visionary tracts: *The Little Horns Doom and Downfall*, apparently written seven years prior to publication, and the much longer *New and More Exact Mappe of the New Jerusalems Glory*. On its title page, the first book identifies Charles I as the little horn of *Daniel* and relates Daniel's visions to the English Civil War. The second book weaves together *Isaiah*, *Daniel*, and *Revelation* to detail the thousand-year earthly reign of Christ that Fifth Monarchists such as Cary believed was imminent. Far from being a fringe movement, millenarianism was widespread in the seventeenth century, and its proponents included to varying degrees intellectuals and politicians such as Cromwell, John Milton, and Sir Isaac Newton. In addition, Fifth Monarchists were a strong presence in the army, a powerful political force in the early years of the Civil War. Later in the revolutionary years, Cromwell turned his back on the radical sects; millenarianism, which had earlier seemed a necessary and urgent response to acute political crisis, fell out of political favor.

New Jerusalems Glory debates the use of force—the "materiall Sword" (title page)—to bring about Christ's return. In one lengthy section, Cary defends the use of violence (122–38). She was one of the few sectarian writers to endorse the regicide. Not only does she assert the justness of the King's execution in *Little Horns*, but also insists that it could have been achieved only with God's help (31, 32). Cary's optimism about achieving the godly commonwealth under Cromwell's reign can be gauged in part by the tract's dedication, addressed to Cromwell's wife Elizabeth and daughter Bridget Ireton (married to a prominent army general Henry Ireton). Cary explains that she has selected these women because they will be sympathetic to her millennial vision. "I have therefore chosen, (because of your own sex) to dedicate these Treatises to your Ladyships," she writes, "being assured both, First, of your ingenuous, and gracious acceptation hereof; . . . And also secondly, of your owning, and defending, and maintaining all the truths, which are therein laid down." These dedications to women also construct a community of female readers for Cary's visions.

Although Cary's beliefs are completely in line with the Fifth Monarchy canon, she offers an apology at the end of *Little Horns*. After calculating the date for Christ's return as 1701, Cary absolves herself of any inaccuracies in her prediction since only God can know the exact date of Christ's return to this world. Her views were questioned even within Fifth Monarchist and millennial circles. The three prominent radicals who offer prefatory letters to this volume either reduce Cary's tract to a lesson to women not to be idle or cast doubt on the authorship of the texts. Puritan minister and regicide Hugh Peters conveys ambiguous praise, finding in Cary's text "Scriptures cleerly opened, and properly applied; yea, so well, that you might easily think she plow'd with anothers Heifer." Peters casts doubt on Cary's authorship and, simultaneously, brands her as an adulteress for daring both to interpret scripture and to *publish* her interpretations.

RACHEL WARBURTON, LAKEHEAD UNIVERSITY

Mary Cary (Rande). *Little Horns Doom and Downfall* (1651). British Library E. 1274. Title pages.

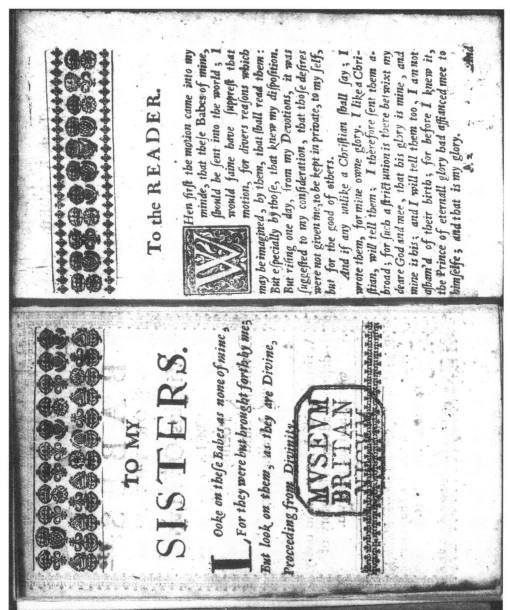

4.10: Anonymous, "To my Sisters" and "To the Reader," *Eliza's Babes* (1652). By permission of The British Library.

Anonymous, "To My Sisters" and "To the Reader," *Eliza's Babes* **(1652)**

Only one complete copy of the 103–page octavo volume, *Eliza's Babes; Or, The Virgin's Offering* (1652), is known to remain extant. The book was published anonymously, its title page bearing this inscription: "Written by a LADY, who onely desires to advance the glory of GOD, and not her own." Convention has christened its female author "Eliza" and, as no other book or manuscript is yet known to have been written by her, any determination of her political or religious contexts relies entirely on evidence internal to the text itself. From this evidence we may conclude that her fundamental theological position aligns with mainstream reformed Protestantism, particularly as codified in the Westminster Confession (1646). She believes in the Trinity, a traditional heaven and hell, and the complete justification and ongoing sanctification of believers who are saved by faith in Christ. While Eliza believes in her own foreordained salvation—*before I knew it, the Prince of eternall glory had affianced mee to himselfe*" (A2r)—her most significant departure from the Confession is her failure to endorse the tenet of the predestination of the reprobate. The ardent zeal of her faith suggests possible contact with the Independents or even the Particular (that is, Calvinistic) Baptists. Her political position is basically reformist. In the poem, "To the King. writ, 1644," she advises Charles I to submit to parliamentarian proposals for reform, and in "To Generall Cromwell" she castigates Oliver Cromwell for not adequately reforming the laws following the regicide.

The book is divided between Eliza's poems (pp. 1–59, 103) and prose meditations (pp. 59–102), which she refers to as her "Babes." The dedicatory poem "To my Sisters" and the preface "To the Reader" indicate that these literary children are the offspring of her heavenly marriage of salvation to Jesus Christ. The babes proceed from God and through Eliza (A1v) in emulation of the "proceeding" of the Holy Spirit in the Thirty-Nine Articles (Article 5). Their existence, characterized by thanks and praise, testifies to the fruitfulness of her spiritual marriage. In other words, the existence of the book *Eliza's Babes* serves as evidence of its author's salvation, assuring both herself and her religious mentors that her faith is genuine and her estate elect.

A great many early modern writers, male and female, employ the literary childbirth conceit—for example, Aemilia Lanyer, Francis Quarles, George Wither, An Collins, Margaret Cavendish, Rachel Speght, Elizabeth Warren, and Elizabeth Major—yet Eliza surpasses them all. She takes what is usually a tired old conceit normally found in the frame of a literary work and elaborates it into an overarching aesthetic design that is both original and personally efficacious.

Major, for example, introduces her *Sin and Mercy Briefly Discovered*—the collection of poems annexed to *Honey on the Rod* (1656)—with this: "I was not ambitious of a beautiful babe, yet I confess I would gladly have had it appear comely." She hopes "that in it you may finde truth and plainness" (sig. h3v). Major may have been inspired by the preface to *Eliza's Babes* preface. Unlike other users of the trope, Eliza saturates her book with it: it demonstrates and guarantees her salvation as surely as it justifies her decision to publish. She drives home the point by comparing her literary babes with another woman's real babes: "Thine doth delight in nought but sin, / My Babes work is, to praise heav'ns King" (p. 55).

Liam E. Semler
University of Sydney

Anonymous. *Eliza's Babes, Or, the Virgin's Offering* (1652). British Library E 1289 (1). A1v and A2r.

(160)

morrow be incompassed with tenn thousand enemies, though not to me in particular, yet to those among whom I am now in safety: But if thou art pleas'd I shall be so inclos'd, then let not me be afraid of them, for thou canst preserve me, either by destroying those that would harme me, or by letting me finde favour in the fight of mine enemies, or by their hands canst thou send me to thy blessed Tabernacle of security, where I shall never need any more to send up prayers for deliverance, but shall alwayes sing praises to thee, for thaleaving so many wayes to deliver me.

And so all fear I now may bid adieu,
Goe enemies, I'me secur'd from you.

The Royall Priest-hood.

PEace! Present now no more to me (to take my spirit from the height of felicity) that I am a creature of a weaker sex, a woman. For my God! If I must live after the example of thy blessed Apostle, I must live by faith, and faith makes things to come, as present; and thou hast laid by thy servant, that we shall be like thy blessed Son: then thou wilt make all thy people as Kings and Priests, Kings are men, and men are Kings; And Souls have no sex; the hidden man of the heart, makes us capable of being Kings; for I have heard it is that within makes the man; then are we by election capable of as great a dignity as any mortall man; But thoughts of mortals! I will close the eyes of my Soul, to mortality, and will not open them but to eternity; seeing that by thy grace and faith in thee, thou hast made us partaker of thy divine nature, by thy assistance I will live by faith; I will no more

now

(161)

now see my self as mortall, but as an immortall King will I begin to live, that hidden man never dies, but when mine immortall King, that plac'st me in this Kingdome of felicity with him; shall see it fit time; he will raise me on a triumphant Chariot, compos'd of the wings of bright Angel, to his immortall Kingdome of Glory, where I shall raigne with him for all eternity, and never more desire to change. And as a Royall Priest must I be to thee; ever offering up the sweet incense of my praises to thy divine Majesty, for thy infinite mercies to me, thy unworthy servant.

The secure Pavillion.

MY God, Thy children need not now pray that those lips may be put to silence that speak grievous things against them; they have long since had a freind, and thou a servant, that sent up his petitions to thee for that, and as if he had been ravisht with a present answer from thee, he cryes out; O how great is thy goodnesse, that thou hast laid up in store for them that fear thee, before the Sons of men, that would dishonour thy servants. And now he hath brought us so pleasing a message from thee, that it is no wonder if we with disregard flight those unsavory words which we hear. And now look here all you who shall any way flight or annoy his children, by your odd speeches; they are plac'd above your reach, for God will hide them in the secret of his presence, from the pride of men, he will keep them secretly in his Pavilion, from the strife of tongues, you may shoot, but your aime must be above your head, if you think to hit them; and when you have shot, your arrows cannot reach them, but they may light where you would not have them, on your own heads.

A.

4.11: Anonymous, "The Royal Priest-hood," *Eliza's Babes* (1652). By permission of The British Library.

Anonymous, "The Royal Priest-hood," *Eliza's Babes* **(1652)**

"The Royal Priest-hood" (pp. 100–101) comes very near the end of Eliza's text, and its opening lines imply the author is responding to prolonged criticism of her attitudes and behavior. Elsewhere, her text reflects the attacks on her by critics who view her outspokenness and religious confidence as proud, unwomanly, and ambitious. Independent, Baptist, and Quaker women frequently endure this sort of attack from conservative male polemicists with the Church of England or Presbyterianism. Her self-defense (which amounts also to a defense of Christian women) in this meditation progresses logically through a patchwork of biblical texts and commonplaces, aphorisms, and assertions. Her intention, as always, is to demonstrate that her strident religious practice is "lawful," that is, in accordance with the Scriptures. Saint Paul has urged (Galatians 2:20, 3:28; 2 Corinthians 5:7) that we live now by faith according to our justified and glorified estate in Christ, which will find complete fulfillment in the future. The Bible promises that at the end we will be "like" Jesus and will be "as" kings and priests.

Although sons, priests, and kings are all definitively male, Eliza takes the latter as her specific example. She may adopt this male role according to at least three rationales. First, she repeats the apothegm that souls have no sex. Second, she liberates Saint Peter's idea of "the hidden man of the heart" from his discussion of women's subordination in 1 Peter 3:4 and literalizes the idea so that it supports the notion that women are "capable" of being "Kings" according to an inner masculinity. Third, she refers to God's "election," which brings the preceding privileges equally to women as to men and does not recognize gender distinction (Galatians 3:28). Furthermore, with rising enthusiasm, she leaves logic behind to affirm instead her position, by faith, in Christ as a "partaker of thy divine nature" (2 Peter 1:4). This being so, she has every right to live now "as an immortall King."

This combination of brash confidence in her saintly justification and rather freestyle logical progression of argument is a characteristic feature of *Eliza's Babes*. It also indicates how her reformed theology is enhanced by a zeal that makes gender distinctions irrelevant. She is even brave enough in the meditation, "Ambition," to proclaim her desire to "reach unto thy [God's] Throne; Nothing will now satisfie me, but to be inthron'd with thee in glory" (p. 85). Such enthusiasm suggests Eliza is not just relying on conservative models but perhaps, for example, on the sermons of Independent Calvinist John Simpson—published in *The Perfection of Justification* (1648)—which urge believers to live as kings now. It was under Simpson that Anna Trapnel was converted, and there are ideas in her texts that Eliza would share. Both women acknowledge that God has compelled them into the public arena, where they have become, because they are women who speak and publish boldly, "wonders" in the world's eyes.

Liam E. Semler
University of Sydney

Anonymous. "The Royal Priest-hood." *Eliza's Babes, Or, the Virgin's Offering* (1652). British Library E 1289 (1). Pages 100–101.

(8)

should certainly come to pass: but I remained in grievous bitterness, being hurried by *Sathan*, and he prevailing over me in a very high nature, moving me to blaspheme; but the Lord kept me from uttering any such thing, though I was tortured in my body, as if he had the full possession thereof, and being perswaded that he had power over my body, and natural life to make an end of it, though I believed from the seal that I had had eight years before, that I should be saved through the fire: This temptation remained with me from the first of the twelfth moneth, 1653. till the latter end of the second moneth, called *April*, lying in the Mineries seven days, in which time I had two Godly men, and a Godly woman watched with me every night; temptations of all sorts were so violent upon me: And at the end of those seven days, my body was freed from that torture caused by *Sathan*, and I repaired home to *Hackney*, to my Kinsmans house, Mr. *Wythe*, and there I remained till the latter end of *April* under very bitter storms, being forced by *Sathan* to walk up and down the fields, attempting to throw my self into a Well, saying, God shall not be dishonored; For it shall be thought, said *Sathan*, some put thee in, and so thou shalt be in happiness presently; For what can pluck thee out of thy Fathers hand, he hath made an everlasting Covenant with thee, Ordered in all things, and sure, and this is all thy desire, and all thy Salvation, which thou hast made mention of to many; and I was forced to lye in ditches frequently, till it was dark night, that some found me, and led me home; And again frequently I took Knives to bed with me, to destroy my self, and still they were snached out of my hand, I know not how, nor by any Creature: I durst not eat nor drink for four days together, because it was said to me, If thou doest, thou worshippest the Devil; For in every thing give thanks, whether thou eatest or drinkest, do it all to the glory of God: but thou canst do nothing to the glory of God, therefore thou gratifiest *Sathan*; And do not add sin to sin by so doing; In this time still *Sathan* came as an Angel of light, though I was so full of terror, he still affrighted me in every thing; If I did so and so, I should sin, that I durst not speak to any that feared the Lord, nor I durst not have any prayer, because he said, I sinned if I prayed, or suffered any to pray for me; and I was exceeding affraid to sin, though he drew me abundantly by his false pretences to vow against coming ever among the Saints, or into institutions more; and said to me also, That if I did, I were the most notorious lyer that ever spake; and that made me affraid, because of that

dreadful

4.12: Anna Trapnel, *The Cry of a Stone* (1654). Courtesy of William Andrews Clark Memorial Library, University of California, Los Angeles.

Anna Trapnel, *The Cry of a Stone: Or a Revelation of Something Spoken in Whitehall* (1654)

Anna Trapnel first had visions at age nine, but, because of her Anglican upbringing, she still subscribed to the doctrine of works, a doctrine she later found false. In *The Cry of a Stone: Or a Revelation of Something Spoken in Whitehall* (1654), she recounts how she came to have trances, how she struggled with Satan, and how she had an epiphany that freed her from the devil. She also denounces Cromwell for betraying the revolutionary cause and for letting poor people starve. This treatise illustrates her role as a visionary. Visionaries were passionate and ardent in their trances, casting themselves in states of emotional catharsis and psychic instability, while identifying themselves as empty vessels who preached from their sickbeds.

Trapnel (a Baptist Fifth Monarchist from London) describes in *Cry of a Stone* how during her teen years she struggled with Satan but kept her faith. Even though the Lord allowed Satan to test her, she never questioned the truth of her "Visions and Revelations." If she "shall be thrown into hell," she accepts it as the truth of the Lord. She admits, however, that she remains in "grievous bitterness" because Satan moved her "to blaspheme." Her body is "tortured," and she believes the devil has full possession of it. During the last seven days of her fight with Satan, "two Godly men" and "a Godly woman" watch over her at night, and she is finally freed from the torture.

When Trapnel goes to stay at her kinsman's house in Hackney, she discovers that her struggle with Satan is not finished. There she feels that Satan forces her to walk in the fields during storms, and, in her misery, she attempts to throw herself into a well so that "God shall not be dishonored." She claims she was "forced to lye in ditches frequently, till it was dark night," until someone found her and took her home. She takes knives to bed "to destroy" herself, but they are "snached out of" her hands. She does not eat for four days because she is told she would be worshipping the devil by adding "sin to sin." At this time Satan then comes to her as an Angel of light. Satan tells her that if she speaks to anyone who fears the Lord, or if she prays, or has anyone pray for her, she will be sinning. She fears she is among the damned.

Finally, in desperation, Trapnel throws herself on the ground and tells the Lord he cannot save her from Satan's clutches. Then a light comes and she hears the following saying: "Arise, why lyest thou upon thy face, pray and eat, this is Salvation come to thy house." She asks the Lord to give her a "a humble, broke, melting frame of Spirit" and pour upon her "a Spirit of prayer and supplication." She becomes ill with a high fever because of the exposure to cold weather and lack of nourishment, but just as God cured her spirit, he also restores her body and makes her well. She asks God to reassure her that she will not again be tempted to believe Satan when he tells her she will not be among saints. She opens the Bible to the quote about Job when he is returned from iniquity. The Lord tells her she is to go out and help the tempted.

Trapnel's significance lies in her public prophecies, delivered in a trance state, that combined biblical themes with images of women's fluidity in order to validate her own authority to prophesy.

Linda C. Mitchell
San Jose State University

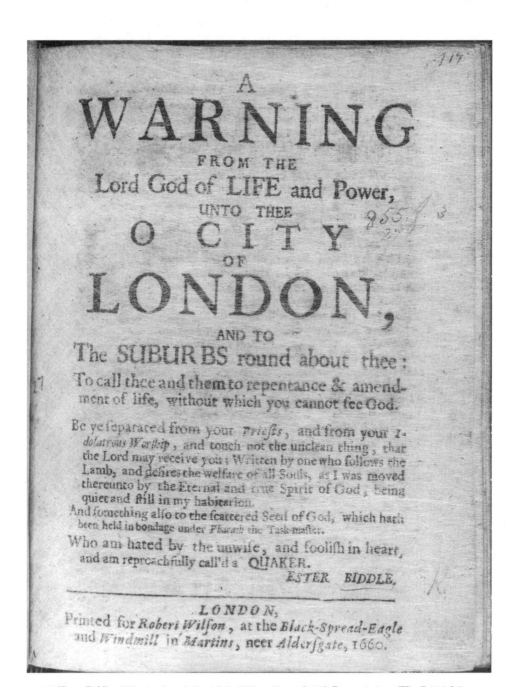

4.13: Hester Biddle, *A Warning from the Lord God of Life and Power* (1660). By permission of The British Library.

Hester Biddle, *A Warning from the Lord God of Life and Power* (1660)

Originally from Oxford, Hester Biddle was raised in the national church. After her convincement (conversion to the Society of Friends) in 1654, Biddle began a career of public preaching and prophesying that included the publication of several tracts between 1655 and 1662. The title page outlines the Quaker understanding of "convincement" when it describes Biddle as being "moved . . . by the Eternal and true Spirit of God." Like many women in seventeenth-century dissenting sects, large numbers of Quaker women took up the work of preaching and writing sermons during the Civil War years (1642–60). Her career and those of other Quaker women ministers were supported by the Friends' belief that both the Light and the ability to preach were equally available to women and men.

Written on the eve of the Restoration, Biddle's *Warning* powerfully records some of the persecutions of Quakers in a chaotic climate increasingly intolerant of religious dissent. In impassioned prose, Biddle urges her oppressors and all the inhabitants of London to abandon their ungodly ways and to embrace the Light within: the Quaker belief that the spirit of Christ resides within the individual and is equally available to all. Here, on the title page, Biddle entreats her audience to ignore their priests and abandon what she now understands to be "Idolatrous Worship." Biddle also uses her pamphlet, an exhortation to conversion, to launch a critique of social inequalities.

A Warning was published in the midst of the political upheaval between Cromwell's death in 1658 and the restoration of the monarchy in 1660. It was in a context of increasing political instability and religious intolerance that she wrote this pamphlet. Persecution of Quakers intensified in the years immediately following the Restoration, and some legislative measures, including the Quaker Act of 1662, the Act of Uniformity of 1662, and the Conventicle Act of 1664, were aimed directly at the Society of Friends. Indeed, this title page refers to Biddle as one "hated by the unwise" and "reproachfully call'd a Quaker." The term "Quaker" was one of general derision. Thousands of Quakers were imprisoned during these tumultuous years, including Biddle herself, who went to jail on a number of occasions. She may well have given birth in prison and probably wrote a later tract, *The Trumpet of the Lord Sounded Forth* (1662), from her cell in Newgate.

Her earlier broadsides, *Wo to the city of Oxford* (1655) and the almost identical *Wo to the towne of Cambridge* (1655), weave together numerous biblical references and predict that grief and torment will be inflicted upon the two university towns for their sinfulness. In the manner of biblical prophets, Biddle prophesies the destruction of a city that has forsaken God. In so doing, she inserts herself into a tradition of prophetic writings.

One of the most significant differences between Biddle's earlier broadsides and the first section of her *Warning* to London is that the latter insists on its own historical moment and upon the earthly sufferings of fellow Friends. Biddle denounces the inhabitants of London for their treatment of Quakers, who, "for clearing their consciences, and being obedient unto the Commands of the Lord" (2), have suffered at the hands of magistrates and lawyers. Directing her plain speech against her tormentors and the tormentors of her sect, Biddle catalogues a litany of abuses endured by Quakers: "some of them hast thou stoned, and some imprisoned, and cruelly beat, and unmercifully used them" (2). She levels her critique against lawyers in particular, who, "having no Law, are a Law unto themselves" (2). In a world that privileges worldly laws over God's Law, she suggests, Quakers like herself who speak their consciences are prosecuted. "[I]n this our day, which

(1)

A *Warning unto the City of* London, *and the Suburbs round about, &c.*

O The day and hour of thy Visitation is now, O City of *London!* with all thy Suburbs, and likewise the day, hour, and time of Gods righteous Judgements is at hand, and will be executed upon thee in flames of fire from heaven: O my soul mourneth for thee, and my bowels is troubled, and my heart is pained within me, to see thy desolation, my eyes runneth down as a Fountain for the misery that is overtaking thee: O the fury of the Lord! it is terrible, and who may stand, when it waxeth hot, and burneth as a flaming fire: O repent, repent, repent! for thy wickedness surmounteth the wickedness of *Sodom* and *Gomorrah*, thy pride and ambition far exceedeth *Jerusalems*: *Jerusalem* had one Temple to worship in, and it was commanded of the Lord to be built, and the Lord commanded them to worship in it; but according to your imaginations, so is your worship, and as your streets are, so are your Idols Temples, and thy Idolatrous Worship; the abomination of desolation, sitteth where it ought not, and the Seed that belongeth to Immortal Life, is buried in thee! O *London*, *London!* how art thou fallen? and from whom art thou gone astray? even from the righteous Judge, and pure God of heaven, and of earth, O thou art dead, and dying from the true worship and service of the Lord, which is in Spirit & in truth; thou art groaping at noon-day, and thy light is not risen out of obscurity, that should give thee the knowledge of the Glory of God in the Face of Jesus Christ, although the measure of Gods grace hath called thee to repentance, and doth strive with thee against thy pride, cruelty, hard-heartedness, and oppression, but thou wilt not lend

thine

A 2

4.13: Hester Biddle, *A Warning from the Lord God of Life and Power* (1660). By permission of The British Library.

is the Lords," she laments, "if any in the Spirit of the Lord come amongst you, and be moved to speak in his power, thou beatest, and bruisest, and hallest before thy Magistrates, and castest into prisons" (4).

Unafraid of temporal authority, Biddle extends her warning of pending judgment to all those in positions of earthly power. "Howl ye Lawyers, weep bitterly ye Rulers, and Judges, lament ye Priests, for the day of Gods account is coming on, and it hasteneth" (5). In a later passage, she insists that "Kings and Princes, Dukes and Earls, Lords and Ladies, Governours and Magistrates, Priests and Jesuites" (17) will be subject to God's judgment, irrespective of social standing. This was precisely the sort of "leveling" sentiment that had earned Quakers both the mistrust of Cromwell and a reputation for rebelliousness. While Cromwell had been a supporter of dissenting sects earlier in the revolutionary years, he later could not countenance such radicalism for fear of alienating his supporters among the propertied classes.

Throughout her *Warning*, Biddle extends her predictions of impending destruction to include more detailed depictions of social inequities. *A Warning* uses the language and imagery of *Isaiah* to draw a poignant portrait of urban poverty. The "old and young, blind and lame, lieth in thy streets, and at thy Masse-houses doors crying for bread, who are almost naked for want of cloathing, and fainting for want of bread" (11). But the "proud and haughty," Biddle exclaims, "canst passe by them in thy gaudy apparel, and out-stretched neck" (11, *Isaiah* 3:16).

Biddle's writings are at once religious and political. There is no clear line between the two in the seventeenth century. Accordingly, she uses religious discourse as the basis for her sociopolitical analysis, while simultaneously viewing social ills as always also evidence of moral and religious corruption. Her tracts are "responsive to events or circumstances of the time" as Lois Schwoerer describes early modern women's political and religious writings (64). But in keeping with her rejection of the things of the world, those writings are also deeply invested in issues that transcend the moment.

RACHEL WARBURTON
LAKEHEAD UNIVERSITY

Hester Biddle. *A Warning from the Lord God of Life and Power unto thee, O city of London, and to the suburbs round about thee* (1660). British Library 855.f.3.(27.). Title page and Page 1.

our hands too late to accompany these which we have now
published. We shall therefore reserve them together with
what of the like kind may for the future from good hands be
communicated to us (wherein we beg the utmost assistance
from all the Lords People in the several Countries) to an-
ther season, which if the Lord vouchsafe, they shall see the
Light also. In the mean while, we cannot but recommend
to the Readers most serious perusal, an excellent Discourse
of D*r.* Martin Luther (that Faithful Servant of Jesus
Christ against Antichrist) upon Luke 21. vers. 25, 26.
&c. being very lately by an able and faithful hand, with
great exactness Translated out of his Enarrations on the
Gospels and Writings of the Apostles and other places of
Scripture, Printed at Busil, Anno. 1546. Which Sermon as we judge, doth most lively open and apply the foregoing History of the great and marvelous Works of the Lord
which cannot indeed be rightly known or understood but by
his Word. And what this Famous and Eminent Light of
the Church did Declare and Teach so long agoe, is exactly
calculated for this Year of Prodigies and Wonders. We
read in Rev. 4. vers. 5. That out of the Throne of
God, proceeded Lightnings, and Thundrings, and
Voices, &c. By Lightnings and Thundrings, we may
well understand the Terrible and Dreadful Works and Dis-
pensations of God, which being alone, make but a very uncertain sound, but Voices (which signifie the Preaching
of the Word) being joyned with them, they may the more
clearly be understood, and the better improved by all those
that take pleasure therein. Now as Face answers Face
in a Glass so truly and fully doth the foregoing Narrative in
all things comport with the forementioned Sermon, upon wch
account we do the more affectionately at this time recommend
it to the Sober and Judicious Reader, praying unto the
Lord, that all those who shall have Hearts and Opportuni-
tie to look seriously into it, may thereby through Divine
Blessing, be fully instructed in the Mind and Meaning of
God, in these late eminent and Signal Works and Wonders
of his Providence amongst us.

FINIS.

** This is not that
Sermon of Luthers,
upon the same Text
which was hereto-
fore translated into
English, and Printed
at London, Anno.1570.
though that also be a
Discourse well wor-
thy the Readers most
diligent perusal,*

55393

4.14: Elizabeth Calvert, publisher of *Mirabilis annus, Or, the Year of Prodigies and Wonders* (1661). Reproduced by
permission of The Huntington Library, San Marino, California.

Elizabeth Calvert, publisher of *Mirabilis annus, Or, the Year of Prodigies and Wonders* (1661)

Elizabeth Calvert's husband, Giles Calvert, the notorious radical publisher, was in prison when she published *Mirabilis annus* in 1661, and after he died in 1663 she continued her husband's shop at the Black Spread Eagle at the west end of St. Paul's until 1675. Elizabeth was the sole executrix of her husband's will, and according to the custom of the city of London she was to receive a third of the estate. Despite regular harassment by the authorities and numerous imprisonments, she continued to publish material unwelcome to the government for another ten years. Elizabeth Calvert's association with a company of ex-Quakers and religious radicals in 1671 suggests that she sustained friendships with members of radical sects established during her husband's lifetime.

Mirabilis annus was the first in a series of three prodigy pamphlets that consist, for the most part, of recitations of strange events and wonders happening at particular times and places. Prodigy pamphlets had been among the staples of cheap pamphlet literature since Elizabethan times; in these pamphlets, as in Renaissance drama, supernatural portents symbolized God's anger at human misdeeds. The concluding passage, reproduced here, reveals something about the way in which such accounts were compiled and printed in that it refers to material from which sequel pamphlets will be printed, but which reached the author too late to be published in the current text: "We shall therefore reserve them together with what of the like kind may for the future from good hands be communicated to us (wherein we beg the utmost assistance from all the Lords People in the several Countries)." The passage goes on to urge the reader to seek the right understanding of such signs and wonders in the context of preaching. *Mirabilis annus*, published in the first year of Charles II's reign, implied indirectly that God disapproved of the restoration. Such pamphlets were considered seditious under the definition of Roger L'Estrange, Charles II's Surveyor of the Press, and probably inspired L'Estrange's Licensing Act of 1662 "for preventing the frequent abuses in printing seditious, treasonable, and unlicensed Books and Pamphlets, and for regulating of Printing and Printing Presses." Maureen Bell suggests that Elizabeth Calvert probably escaped prosecution for publishing the *Mirabilis annus* pamphlets owing to the legal principle of coverture, which protected a wife even when her husband was absent. The essence of coverture was the legal view that a married woman, a "feme covert," was under civil subjection to the husband, and therefore was not responsible for a crime committed by her in her husband's presence or in concert with him. Women in the book trade such as Elizabeth Calvert could turn the law's view of them to their own advantage by playing up to the role of simple-minded incompetents. Enforcement of the Licensing Act failed for the most part and thus enabled Elizabeth Calvert to continue operating as an oppositional publisher producing an output almost totally of illegal books. In the long run, the Restoration government responded to such oppositional publications more effectively through official propaganda than through censorship. John Dryden's poem "Annus Mirabilis," for example, pointedly sends up the providentialist assumptions of prodigy pamphlets on the *mirabilis annus*.

JENNIFER L. ANDERSEN
CALIFORNIA STATE UNIVERSITY

Anonymous. *Mirabilis annus, or, The year of prodigies and wonders, being a faithful and impartial collection of several signs that have been seen in the heavens, in the earth, and in the waters, etc.* (1661). Huntington Library RB 55393. Page 88.

821

(11)

and the Lord said unto me, *Herod will seek the yong childes life to destroy it yet again*; and great was my affliction; so that my dear fellow and labourer in the Work of God, did look every hour when I should depart the body for many days together, and we did look every hour when we should be brought to the stake day and night, for several weeks, and *Isaac was freely offered up.* But the Lord said, he had provided a Ram in the Bush. Afterwards the Fryer came again with his Physician; I told him, that I could not take any thing, unless I was moved of the Lord. He said, *we must never come forth of that Room while we lived, and we might thank God and him it was no worse, for it was like to be worse.* We said, if we had died, we had died as innocent as ever did servants of the Lord. He said, it was well we were innocent. They did (also) look still when I would dye.

The Fryer bid my friend *take notice what torment I would be in at the houre of Death, thousands of Devils* he said) *would fetch my soule to Hell.* She said, she did not fear any such thing.

And he asked *if I did not think it expedient for the Elders of the Church to pray over the sick?* I said, yea, such as were eternally moved of the Spirit of the Lord. He fell down of his knees and did howle, and wish bitter wishes upon himself if he had not the true faith; but we denied him. The Physitian was in a great rage at *Sarah*, because she could not bow to him, but to God onely.

The last day of my fast I began to be a hungry, but was afraid to eat, the enemy was so strong; but the Lord said unto me, *If thine enemy hunger, feed him; if he thirst, give him drink. In so doing thou shalt heap coales of fire upon his head; be not overcome of evil, but overcome evil with good.* I did eat, and was refreshed, and glorified God; and in the midst of our extremity the Lord sent his holy Angels to comfort us, so that we rejoiced and magnified God; and in the time of our great trial, the Sun and Earth did mourn visibly three dayes, and the horror of death and pains of Hell was upon me; the Sun was darkned, the Moon was turned into Blood, and the Stars did fall from Heaven, and there was great tribulation ten dayes, such as never was from the beginning of the world;

C 2   and

4.15: Katharine Evans and Sarah Chevers, *A short Relation of some of the Cruel Sufferings (For the Truths Sake) of Katharine Evans & Sarah Chevers* (1662). Reproduced by permission of The Huntington Library, San Marino, California.

Katharine Evans and Sarah Chevers, A *short Relation of some of the Cruel Sufferings (For the Truths Sake) of Katharine Evans & Sarah Chevers, To the Inquisition in the Isle of Malta* (1662)

In 1658, Katharine Evans (d. 1692) and Sarah Chevers (d. 1664) began a journey to Alexandria to preach. They traveled as far as Malta, where the two members of the Society of Friends were detained by the Inquisition. Imprisoned for three years, they were finally freed, thanks to the efforts of their fellow Friend Daniel Baker, and returned to England by 1663. *This is a Short Relation* was published in quarto by Robert Wilson in 1662, edited and presented by Baker; it appears to have been part of Baker's campaign for the women's release. Wilson brought out two further versions of the story in 1663: *A True Account of the Great Tryals and Cruel Sufferings,* a revised and expanded octavo version of *Short Relation*; and the quarto *A Briefe Discovery of God's Eternal Truth,* Evans's revised account of her experiences. All three versions are very rare. Five exemplars of *Short Relation* survive, two of *True Account,* and four of *Briefe Discovery*. *Short Relation* is not a single, unified narrative. Instead, it is a collection of narratives, letters, hymns, other poems, accounts of visions, and Baker's editorial commentaries. Its multiple voices engage multiple audiences: the readers of the book, the addressees of the letters, and, in the case of the hymns, both readers and God.

The selection, page 11 (sig. C2r), comes from a portion titled by Baker "*Here followeth a Copy of some more words which they had written before the former [narrative] was given forth.*" The typography indicates four speakers: Evans and Chevers in roman, the Friar in italics, and God in black letter. Readers may therefore immediately see that the women's experience exists on several different levels. There is Evans's description of and concern about her failing health, brought about by fasting; the dispute between the women and the Friar; and the immanent presence of God. The alternating roman and italic type emphasizes the dialogue within the narrative, while the black letter, archaic by the mid–seventeenth century, appears as the voice of God speaking directly to Evans. The page thus echoes visually the effect of the entire book: multiple voices convey the story, providing many layers of meaning through a variety of perspectives. Evans and Chevers relate their experiences through narrative and dialogue, and then recast them through letters to their families and other Friends. Their hymns and descriptions of visions testify to their ever-present spirituality. Baker's commentaries connect their captivity to the larger struggle of the Friends to bring their beliefs to often hostile audiences, whether abroad or in England. Evans and Chevers's experiences are simultaneously personal and exemplary.

The dialogue with the Friar, and the description of the Physician's reaction to Chevers, together with the account of the imprisonment itself, are evocative of the accounts of the suffering of Protestant martyrs in such famous works as John Foxe's *Acts and Monuments.* Both Foxe and *Short Relation* present both the narrative (the acts) and supporting documents—letters, commentary, and testimonials—(the monuments) to put events in a larger historical and providential context. *Short Relation* differs from Foxe by depicting God's speech: a representation of the Friends' belief in the inner light, the speaking of God within. As she does on this page, Evans always depicts God as speaking directly to her, not to any other person or persons in her company. The apocalyptic imagery at the bottom of the page echoes the language of the visions presented elsewhere in the book. As the women saw them, the visions were testimonials of their closeness to the spirit of God. The narrative here is also testimonial to the companionship of the two women, and to the empowerment they experienced (traveling away from their homes and families and speaking publicly) as they testified to what they believed to be the truth of their convictions.

ELIZABETH SKERPAN-WHEELER

TEXAS STATE UNIVERSITY-SAN MARCOS

This is a short Relation of some of the Cruel Sufferings (For the Truths sake) of Katharine Evans & Sarah Chevers, In the Inquisition in the Isle of Malta (1662). Huntington Library RB 94144. Page 11 (sig. C2).

Katherine Sutton, *A Christian Womans experiences of the glorious working of Gods free grace* (1663)

The epigram on the title page of Katherine Sutton's book, *A Christian Womans experiences*, is a quotation from Luke 24:24: *"And they found it even so, as the VVomen had said."* Sutton's narrative strives to validate women's speech and spirituality. In this short book (forty-four pages), Sutton describes a series of physical and emotional trials as a means of presenting herself as a woman specially favored by God with the gifts of singing and prophecy. While the narrative and examples of hymns and prophecy are striking, the reader also notices the acknowledgment and recognition Sutton received from others, evident in the book itself. While most religious tracts of this kind are cheaply printed, *A Christian Womans experiences* is beautifully produced. Published in Rotterdam, and exceedingly rare (it survives in only three exemplars), it bears a printer's device on the title page, and both an ornamental header and initial on the first page of Sutton's text. It also carries a list of errata and, most notably, a preface by the Baptist minister Hanserd Knollys, who was evidently traveling in the Netherlands at the time of publication. In his preface, Knollys takes great pains to introduce Sutton as an example to other Christians, a woman whose singing reveals the direct inspiration of God. He cites her style as particularly noteworthy, cautioning the reader, "In the reading of her Book, thou wilt meet with some suddain and unexpected Transition from one thing to another, (and thou mayest think it to be some what abruptly) yet Censure not too Rashly, but rather consider, that even this also may, yea doth hold some proportion unto the course of Heaven and Heavenly communications" (sig. *2).

Sutton herself tells a story of alternating trials and moments of great elevation. In her youth, she periodically suffered from depression, to the point of deciding at one time to starve herself to death to prevent herself from sinning further. Her marriage brought additional challenges, as she and her husband frequently disagreed. Sutton, however, chooses to interpret these arguments as vehicles for bringing her closer to God, as she sees the marriage as part of God's will; as proof, she dates her "dreames and visions of the night" (p. 3, sig. A2) as well as her eventual "gift of singing" (p. 13, sig. B3) to giving her trust completely to the Lord. Ultimately, she concludes that these gifts are meant to be shared so that she might bring others to salvation.

The selection (p. 16, sig. B4v) offers some samples of Sutton's prophecies and her determination to make them public: "I looked upon it as my duty to make this known." The linking narrative shows a variety of responses to her utterances, responses that Sutton places in a providential context. God eventually punished those who rejected Sutton's "councel," and thus readers should take warning and amend their own lives. The bracketed comment in the middle of the page about the lost book is a reference to additional confirmation of Sutton's mission. She explains later in the narrative that she initially hesitated to publish her experiences, hymns, and prophecies, and subsequently lost all her papers and, temporarily, her gift of singing, during a storm at sea while she and her husband were crossing to the Netherlands. While the losses were a punishment for recalcitrance, her ability to reconstruct her story for publication is a sign of God's returning favor.

Sutton concludes her narrative with several of her hymns and an affirmation of the significance of her experiences. Her book is a testament of faith, "and let this not be dispised, because it is the spirits working in the weakest vessel; for Christ did not reject

Then I looked upon it as my duty to make this known, that people might be warned to depart from ſin, that ſo they might not partake of the great wrath and ſore diſpleaſure of God, which I much feared, was coming.

Then ſoon after I had an oppertunity to declare this to ſome that then were in high places, and in the very entring I had this added, which I alſo declared.

> *Didſt thou not hear a voyce from on high,*
> *Deny your ſelves (take up the croſſe) or verily you ſhall die?*

And this was approved on by ſome, and received as a very ſuitable and ſeaſonable word; but pour ſoules, for not hearkening unto councel in departing from ſin they were ſoon brought down, and laid low, yet there is mercy with the Lord that he may be feared, and he will manifeſt his love to all them that truely repent, and we may all make a good uſe of this experience; therefore let others harms become our warnings. Alſo about the year 1658. to the beſt of my remembrance *[for having loſt my book, in which I had ſet them down in order, I now wait onely upon the Lord, and as he by his Spirit helps mee, ſo I give an account of theſe things)* It was given in with aboundance of power upon my ſpirit, theſe few words following.

> *Awake therefore to righteouſneſs,*
> *The Lord is near at hand:*   } This was again brought to
> *And will afflict now very ſore*   } mind in January 1662.
> *By ſea and like by land.*

And this ſeemes to agree with, and is a further addition to what was given mee in before in the Year 1657. which is as followeth.

> *There is a time approaching near at hand,*
> *That men ſhall be in fear by ſea and land:*
> *There is a time, there will be alteration;*
> *And this ſame time doth haſten to this nation;*
> *Let now my children hearken to my will,*
> *And they ſhall ſee I will be with them ſtill.*

Theſe with many more ſuch things came upon my ſpirit, and then after ſeeking the Lord he was pleaſed to ſhew mee by degrees what was the work of the day (for I am a ſtranger and a Pilgrim, therefore I ſeek for a Kingdom

4.16: Katherine Sutton, *A Christian Womans experiences of the glorious working of Gods free grace* (1663). By permission of Cambridge University Library.

the woman though weak, ignorant, and sinful" (p. 40, sig. E4v). Sutton's faith tells her that the Holy Spirit has chosen to communicate through her in a powerful and moving manner. In publishing her book, Sutton both serves the Lord and creates a monument to the value of her own life.

ELIZABETH SKERPAN-WHEELER
TEXAS STATE UNIVERSITY-SAN MARCOS

Katherine Sutton. *A Christian Womans experiences of the glorious working of Gods free grace* (Rotterdam, 1663). Cambridge University Library R. 11. 89 (3). Page 16 (sig. B4v).

[7]

And I do further declare, that the things I have published and written, and which are such an offence to my Husband, and indeed the cause of all the Persecutions I have suffered from others, were written sorely against my own natural *mind* and *will*; That I often beg'd of God I might rather die, then do it. That I was commanded of God to record them. That my own natural temper was so greatly averse to it, that for eleven months together I withstood the Lord, till by an Angel from Heaven he threatned to *kill me*, and took away my sleep from me: And then the *terrors of the Lord* forced me to obey the command. And indeed, the writings that man was so displeased with, were in themselves very warrantable, if I had not had any such command of God, for I only wrote the *way* he lead me in a wilderness of affliction for 18 years, to do me good; and declared my *experiences*, my *great* and *wonderful deliverances*, my many *answers* of Prayers in difficult cases from time to time: but most true it is, I did not speak of these things, nor set Pen to paper (for several reasons) till the Lord *commanded* and by his word and Spirit constrained me so to do at 18 years end, after I was consumed with grief, sorrow, oppression of heart, and long travail in the wilderness, and brought even to the gates of Death, and when past the Cure of all men, was raised up by the immediate and mighty hand of God. And being thus *healed*, I was commanded to write, and give glory to him who had so miraculously raised me up from the grave. And I do further declare, the things I have written are *true*, and *no lye*: and that what is so distasteful in them to man, are such things as I could not leave out, without *prejudice* to the Truth, and *disobedience* to God. And what ever censures I now undergo from *mans day* and *judgment* for this plain dealing in matters which concern so near a Relation in the flesh, I am well assured my faithfulness to God herein, will be owned in the *day* of his *impartial* and *righteous judgment*. And yet I must declare, it would have been much more agreeable to my Spirit, to have concealed the miscarriages of my Husband, then to have exposed them, if I had not been under a *command* herein not to be *disputed*: and it was not without great *resistings* that I was at length made *obedient*, *having tasted of that love, which both covers, and teaches us to cover a multitude of sinnes*: And yet I am fully perswaded, that my duty

4.17: Anne Wentworth. *A Vindication of Anne Wentworth, Tending to the Better Preparing of All People for Her Larger Testimony, which is Making Ready for Publick View* (1677). By permission of The British Library.

Anne Wentworth, *A Vindication of Anne Wentworth, Tending to the Better Preparing of All People for Her Larger Testimony, which is Making Ready for Publick View* (1677)

By her own account, Anne Wentworth (fl. 1650s-1677) suffered for years in a difficult marriage until she left her husband and made her case public. Her first published work, *A True Account of Anne Wentworths Being Cruelly, Unjustly, and Unchristianly Dealt with by Some of those People Called Anabaptists* (1676), supports her action with arguments from the Scriptures and describes the reaction of her religious community to her radical decision. The second, *A Vindication of Anne Wentworth, Tending to the Better Preparing of All People for Her Larger Testimony, which is Making Ready for Publick View* (1677), includes an anonymous but supportive letter testifying to her sincerity, and two poems—the first called a "Song of Tryumph"—that Wentworth claims were taught to her by God during the night. Both are exceedingly rare works, each existing in only two exemplars. Both are also cheaply printed quartos, with no printer or place of publication identified. Wentworth later wrote two religious works, and several of her letters appear in the *Calendar of State Papers, Domestic*.

This selection, page 7 (sig. A4r) of *A Vindication* shows Wentworth's characteristic way of arguing and of justifying both herself and her writings. Wentworth overtly disclaims any responsibility for her actions. Both leaving her husband and publishing her writings were commands of God. Her own desire was to remain silent, but she submitted to God's will, out of obedience and also out of gratitude for God's having healed her after years of suffering poor health. Nevertheless, Wentworth asserts that, even without God's command, she would have been right to do what she did. Earlier in the tract, she explains that "it would be very easie for me, from the great Law of *self-preservation* to justifie my present absence from my Earthly Husband" (p. 4, sig. A2v). Here, she says that publication of her experiences was "very warrantable" because she was merely illustrating the ways God preserved and saved her. Thus, Wentworth claims her own agency by justifying it in terms likely to be acceptable to her audience.

Especially noteworthy is Wentworth's rhetorical strategy for transforming her actions from something shocking to something praiseworthy. As everyone in the seventeenth century knew, a good wife was to be chaste, silent, and—most particularly—obedient. Wentworth declares that her true husband is God: "my heavenly Bridegroom" (p. 9, sig. B). Hence, by following God's command to publish her experiences, she is abandoning her own will and submitting to God's. Her perseverance in the face of condemnation is a tribute to her perfect obedience to God. The appended poems are further evidence of her submission: they are not her own creations, but words God taught her to speak. Wentworth thereby claims her own instrumentality by presenting herself an instrument. It is a perfect, trumping argument. As the supporting letter asks, "Can you prove that God hath not spoken to her and by her?" (p. 15, sig. B4r).

Puritan writers of the period frequently disclaimed responsibility for their thoughts and feelings by attributing them to interventions by the Holy Spirit. Such explanations are common features of the conversion narratives required by many sects for membership in their congregations. Wentworth's narratives are unusual not only because they justify two actions ordinarily considered defiance of God's will (disobedience to one's husband and public speaking), but because they rebuke a religious community for their inability to accept God's mysterious ways.

ELIZABETH SKERPAN-WHEELER
TEXAS STATE UNIVERSITY-SAN MARCOS

Wentworth, Anne. *A Vindication of A. W., Tending to the Better Preparing of All People for Her Larger Testimony* (1677). Wing W. 1356. British Library T. 370 (2). Page 7 (sig. A4).

Hannah Allen, *A Narrative of God's gracious dealings* (1683)

Early in 1663, Hannah Allen (c.1638–before 1683) descended into a condition all too common among seventeenth-century puritans: she became profoundly depressed, "perswaded I had sinned the Unpardonable Sin" (p. 4, sig. D8v). Her account of her struggle with depression, which she called "Satan's Methods and Malice baffled," appeared in 1683, some time after her death. The book, titled *A Narrative of God's gracious dealings With that choice Christian Mrs. Hannah Allen*, was printed by John Wallis. This rare book exists in only seven exemplars, all apparently missing pages 75–78. Allen's narrative is framed by a preface addressed "To the Reader," which suggests that her story might serve as a comfort and encouragement to those similarly afflicted, asking, "How knowest thou but it may be thine own Case?" (p. v, sig. D3). Certainly, Allen would have been a candidate for depression whatever her religious convictions. Her father died when she was very young, she suffered from poor health, and, from the time she was in her early teens, she became convinced that Satan was provoking "horrible blasphemous thoughts and injections into my mind" (p. 3, sig. D8r). Moreover, in 1662, after about eight years of marriage, Allen lost her husband, who died while traveling abroad. His death precipitated her crisis. Allen's narrative recounts not only her own reflections on her psychological and spiritual state, represented by some entries from a diary she kept during the period, but the efforts of relatives and friends to help her as she and they endured her suicidal urges, self-starvation, and at least one violent outburst. Through their care, Allen gradually emerged from her depression and remarried. She closes her story expressing the hope that its publication might help others.

The page selected (p. 25, sig. E3r) is a remarkably self-reflective example of Allen's process of thought during her depression. The page begins in the middle of a paragraph that explains how Allen terrified herself as she read the Bible. Instead of searching the Scriptures for comfort, she concentrated on passages condemning the reprobate. The paragraph begins with a quotation from Jeremiah 6:29 and 30, which concludes "*Reprobate silver shall men call them, because the Lord hath rejected them*" (p. 24, sig. E2v). The following quotation, concluded at the top of the reproduced page, comes from Ezekiel 24:13, and begins, "*In thy filthiness is lewdness, because I have purged thee and thou wast not purged.*" Allen understands how her judgment was clouded, seeing her spiritual confusion as a result of Satan's interference. The page ends with the beginning of her relatives' intervention and Allen's tacit acknowledgment that they were perceiving her more accurately than she was seeing herself.

Allen's account thus presents a view of herself from both inside and out. Although she herself casts her depression as a result of temptation by Satan, her relatives see it in psychological terms. Her aunt, for example, remarks, "*Cousin, would you but believe you were melancholy it might be a great means to bring you out of this Condition*" (p. 60, sig. G3v), and observes that Allen had suffered such mental "Afflictions, from . . . Child-hood" (p. 63, sig. G6r). When Allen describes her cure, she makes little mention of Bible reading or other spiritual consolation. Instead, her relatives and minister emphasize medical treatment for her physical frailty, walks in the country, and visits with friends. The book concludes with Allen's evidence of her spiritual and mental health: passages from the *and Malicice Baffled.*   25

I have purged thee and thou waſt not purged; thou ſhalt not be purged from thy filthineſs any more, till I have cauſed my fury to reſt upon thee : Luke xiii. 24. Strive to enter in at the ſtrait gate, for many I ſay unto you, will ſeek to enter in and ſhall not be able : This laſt Scripture I would expreſs with much paſſionate weeping, ſaying, *This is a dreadful Scripture, I ſought, but not in a right way; for the Devil blinded mine eyes, I ſought to enter but was not able.*

When both my inward and outward diſtempers grew to ſuch a height, my Aunt acquainted my Friends at *London* with my condition, for at *London* I had formerly had four loving Un-

E 3   cles,

4.18: Hannah Allen, *A Narrative of God's gracious dealings* (1683). By permission of The British Library.

Scriptures that offer consolation and the promise of salvation, and that were "great supports and refreshments to me in the time of my various Temptations and Afflictions" (p. 74, sig. H3v). Her cure is manifest in her restored ability to read rightly.

ELIZABETH SKERPAN-WHEELER
TEXAS STATE UNIVERSITY-SAN MARCOS

Hannah Allen. [*Satan his methods and Malice baffled.*] *A Narrative of God's gracious dealings, with that choice Christian Mrs. Hannah Allen, afterwards married to Mr. Hatt.* (1683). Wing A 1025. British Library 1415. a. 10. Page 25 (sig. E3).

(11)

place and Steeple-houfe, where I
had pretty much Service, where
they put me in Prifon for fix
Weeks, where I Fafted fix Days
and fix Nights, and neither eat
Bread nor drank Water, nor no
earthly thing; then I came to
a feeding upon the Word, and
had experience that man doth
not live by Bread alone, but by
every Word that proceedeth out
of the Mouth of the Lord. And
when I was releafed, I went to
Ifaac Burges, the man that committed me, and difcourfed with
him; and he was really Convinced of the Truth, but could
not take up the Crofs; but was
afterwards very loving to Friends,
and ftood by them upon all oc-
cafions, and never Perfecuted a
Friend any more: and when he
came unto this City, he came
unto my Houfe to fee me, and
confeft, That he could not take
                                          up

4.19: Barbara Blaugdone, *An Account of the Travels, Sufferings & Persecutions of Barbara Blaugdone* (1691). Courtesy of
the Library Committee of Britain Yearly Meeting, Library of the Religious Society of Friends, London.

Barbara Blaugdone, *An Account of the Travels, Sufferings & Persecutions of Barbara Blaugdone* (1691)

Barbara Blaugdone lived from 1609 to 1704. She spent most of her incredibly long adult life traveling through England and Ireland, preaching the faith of the Society of Friends. Her monument to her work is the short book, *An Account of the Travels, Sufferings & Persecutions of Barbara Blaugdone*, published in octavo by the Quaker printer Tace Sowle. Only four exemplars survive of this testament to Blaugdone's persistence in her convictions in the face of considerable opposition. As she presents it, her narrative, and therefore her life, begins with her joining the Friends and willingly adopting their outward signs: "plainness of Speech and in my Habit" (p. 6, sig. A5v [for A4v]). This plainness of speech included determined public speaking, an act that repeatedly resulted in imprisonment. As Blaugdone saw it, her endurance of prison was an indication of inner strength: "For whosoever shuns the Cross, and goes out of the Power, they lose their way, and dishonour God; but whosoever keep in the Faith, and abide in the Power, they are in Safety: I have had living Experience of it" (p. 7, sig. A4). Taking up the cross involved far more than prison, however. In thirty-eight small pages, Blaugdone also describes such physical hardships as encountering violent storms at sea, being stabbed, being whipped until she bled, facing an accusation of witchcraft, and anticipating attack by a "great Wolf-Dog," which the "Power of the Lord smote . . . so that he whined, and ran in crying, and very Lame" (p. 12, sig. A6v). Her outward struggles are confirmation of inner strength, and she testifies to the truth of both by providing specific names of both persons and places, so that it is possible for a reader to map her journeys.

    The page selected (p. 11, sig. A6r) describes an incident in Marlborough, where Blaugdone "was moved to go" (p. 10, sig. A5v) after the stabbing. In Marlborough, she follows her usual practice in going to speak at the "Market-place and Steeple-house," that is, the local church: two of the most public places imaginable. During the imprisonment that follows, she contrasts the outward suffering imposed upon her (prison) to her inward, self-imposed suffering (her undertaking a complete fast). She thus transforms her hardship into an opportunity for her own spiritual growth, as she lives the meaning of the scriptural text "that man doth not live by Bread alone" by "feeding upon the Word." Her deep immersion in the Word gives strength and power to her own words, as, upon her release, she speaks with the man responsible for her prison sentence and converts him. Her account of the conversion shows the larger repercussions of her action: the Friends now have a supporter in place of a persecutor. Moreover, the narrative testifies to her faith. When she says her convert "could not take up the Cross," readers recall that Blaugdone's entire story is an example of her taking up the Cross, and the episode becomes an illustration of what the Lord can accomplish when He finds a willing agent.

    While it echoes the spiritual autobiographies of other Quaker writers, *An Account of the Travels* diverges from them in presenting very little debate. We see no careful recounting of spiritual conflict, either with opponents or her own, inner voice. Instead, Blaugdone emphasizes her actions as witnesses to her faith: the deeds she performs and the suffering she endures are the embodiment of the spirit of God moving within her. The book is yet another act. She writes "that Friends may be encouraged, and go on in the Faith" (p. 38, sig. C4v), reproducing her words so that others may reproduce her commitment to their shared beliefs.

ELIZABETH SKERPAN-WHEELER
TEXAS STATE UNIVERSITY-SAN MARCOS

Barbara Blaugdone. *An Account of the Travels, Sufferings & Persecutions of Barbara Blaugdone.* (1691). Wing A 410. Library of the Religious Society of Friends, London, Box 11. Page 11 (sig. A6).

Bibliography

Baston, Jane. "History, Prophecy, and Interpretation: Mary Cary and Fifth Monarchism." *Prose Studies* 21.3 (1998): 1–18.

Beilin, Elaine V. "A Challenge to Authority: Anne Askew." *Redeeming Eve: Women Writers of the English Renaissance*. Princeton: Princeton University Press, 1987. 29–47.

———. "Anne Askew's Dialogue with Authority." In *Contending Kingdoms: Historical, Psychological, and Feminist Approaches to the Literature of Sixteenth-Century England and France*. Ed. Marie-Rose Logan and Peter Rudnytsky. Detroit: Wayne State University Press, 1991. 313–22.

———, ed. *The Examinations of Anne Askew*. New York: Oxford University Press, 1996.

Bell, Maureen. "Hannah Allen and the Development of a Puritan Publishing Business, 1646–1651." *Publishing History* 26 (1989): 5–66.

———. "Elizabeth Calvert and the 'Confederates'." *Publishing History* 32 (1992): 5–49.

———. "'Her Usual Practices': The Later Career of Elizabeth Calvert, 1664–75." *Publishing History* 35 (1994): 5–64.

Blagden, Cyprian "The Stationers' Company in the Civil War Period." *The Library* 13.1 (1958): 1–17.

Crawford, Patricia. *Women and Religion in England 1500–1720*. London: Routledge, 1993.

Cope, Esther. *Handmaid of the Holy Spirit: Dame Eleanor Davies Never Soe Mad a Ladie*. Ann Arbor: University of Michigan Press, 1992.

Cullen, Patrick. "Introduction." *Dictionary of National Biography*. Ed. Leslie Stephen and Sidney Lee, 22 vols. Oxford: Oxford University Press, 1933. 1.ix–xiv.

Dailey, Barbara Ritter. "The Visitation of Sarah Wight: Holy Carnival and the Revolution of the Saints in Civil War London." *Church History* 55 (1986): 438–55.

Davies, Eleanor. *The Prophetic Writings of Lady Eleanor Davies*, New York: Oxford University Press, 1995.

Easton, Jon, ed. *Mother Shipton, The Prophecies of Ursula Sontheil*. Chester: Fenris Press, 1998.

Garman, Mary, et al, eds. *Hidden in Plain Sight: Quaker Women's Writings 1650–1700*. Wallingford, Pa: Pendle Hill, 1996.

Greaves, Richard L., and Robert Zaller. *Biographical Dictionary of British Radicals in the Seventeenth Century*. Brighton, Sussex: Harvester Press, 1984.

Greer, Germaine, Susan Hastings, Jeslyn Medoff, and Melinda Sansone, eds. *Kissing the Rod: An Anthology of Seventeenth-Century Women's Verse*. London: Virago 1988; New York: Farrar Straus & Girous, 1989.

Head, Richard. *The Life and Death of Mother Shipton*. London: W. Harris, 1687 (Wing H1259; UMI Film 789).

Hinds, Hilary. *God's Englishwomen: Seventeenth-century Radical Sectarian Writing and Feminist Criticism*. Manchester: Manchester University Press, 1996.

———, ed. *Anna Trapnel: The Cry of a Stone*. Tempe, AZ: Arizona Center for Medieval and Renaissance Studies, 2000.

Hobby, Elaine. *Virtue of Necessity: English Women's Writing 1649–88*. London: Virago, 1988.

———. "'Oh Oxford Thou Art Full of Filth': The Prophetical Writings of Hester Biddle 1629[?]-1696." *Feminist Criticism: Theory and Practice*. Susan Sellers, ed. Toronto: University of Toronto Press, 1991. 157–69.

———. "Handmaids of the Lord and Mothers in Israel: Early Vindications of Quaker Women's Prophecy." *The Emergence of Quaker Writing*. Ed. T. Corns and D. Loewenstein. London: Frank Cass. 1995, 88–98.

Hughey, Ruth. *Meditations of Man's Mortalitie or, A Way to True Blessedness*, 2d ed. London: Alsop and Fawcett, 1634. Facsim. ed. Betty S. Travitsky and Patrick Cullen, eds. *The Early Modern Englishwoman: A Facsimile Library of Essential Works, Part 1: Printed Writings, 1500–1640*. Vol. 7. Aldershot: Scholar, 1996.

Johns, Adrian. *The Nature of the Book: Print and Knowledge in the Making*. Chicago: University of Chicago Press, 1998.

Kegl, Rosemary. "Women's Preaching, Absolute Property, and the Cruel Sufferings (For the Truths sake) of Katharine Evans & Sarah Chevers." *Women's Studies: An Interdisciplinary Journal* 24 (1994): 51–83.

King, John N., Frances E. Dolan, and Elaine Hobby. "Writing Religion." *Teaching Tudor and Stuart Women Writers*. Ed. Susanne Woods and Margaret P. Hannay. New York: Modern Language Association, 2000. 84–103.

Lamb, Mary Ellen. "The Cooke Sisters: Attitudes toward Learned Women in the Renaissance." *Silent But for the Word: Tudor Women as Patrons, Translators, and Writers of Religious Works*. Ed. Margaret Hannay. Kent, Ohio: Kent State University Press, 1985. 107–125.

The Life and Prophecies of Ursula Sontheil, Better Known as Mother Shipton. Compiled for Dropping Well Estate, Yorkshire. Leeds: Waverly Press, 1967.

Lilley, Kate. "Blazing Worlds: Seventeenth-Century Women's Utopian Writing." *Women, Texts, and Histories: 1575–1760*. Ed. Clare Brant and Diane Purkiss. London: Routledge, 1992. 102–33.

Mack, Phyllis. *Visionary Women: Ecstatic Prophecy in Seventeenth-century England*. Berkeley: University of California Press, 1992.

Matchinske, Megan. "Holy Hatred: Formations of the Gendered Subject in English Apocalyptic Writing, 1625–1651." *English Literary History* 60 (1993): 349–77.

———. *Writing, Gender and State in Early Modern England: Identity Formation and the Female Subject*. Cambridge: Cambridge University Press, 1998.

McDonald, Michael. *Mystical Bedlam: Madness, Anxiety and Healing in Seventeenth Century England*. Cambridge: Cambridge University Press, 1981.

McIntosh, Marjorie Keniston. "Sir Anthony Cooke: Tudor Humanist, Educator, and Religious Reformer." *Proceedings of the American Philosophical Society* 119 (1975): 233–50.

"Mother Shipton." *Dictionary of National Biography*. Ed. Leslie Stephen and Sidney Lee.

Nelson, Beth. "Lady Elinor Davies: the Prophet as Publisher." *Women's Studies International Forum* 8.5 (1985): 403–9.

Prineas, Matthew. "The Discourse of Love and the Rhetoric of Apocalyse in Anna Trapnel's Folio Songs." *Comitatus* 28 (1997): 90–110.

Protestant Translators: Anne Lock Prowse and Elizabeth Russell. The Early Modern Englishwoman: A Facsimile Library of Essential Works. Series I, Part 2. Aldershot, Hants: Ashgate, 2001. Volume 12.

Purkiss, Diane. "Producing the voice, consuming the body: Women prophets of the seventeenth century." In *Women, Writing, History: 1640–1740*. Ed. Isobel Grundy and Susan Wiseman. Athens: University of Georgia Press, 1992. 139–58.

Raymond, Joad. "The Newspaper, Public Opinion, and the Public Sphere in the Seventeenth Century." *News, Newspapers, and Society in Early Modern Britain*. Ed. Joad Raymond. London: Frank Cass, 1999. 109–40.

Richey, Esther Gilman. *The Politics of Revelation in the English Renaissance*. Columbia: University of Missouri Press, 1998.

Sauer, Elizabeth. "Maternity, Prophecy, and the Cultivation of the Private Sphere in Seventeenth-Century England." *Explorations in Renaissance Culture* 24 (1998): 119–48.

Schleiner, Louise. *Tudor and Stuart Women Writers*. Indianapolis: Indiana University Press, 1994.

Schwoerer, Lois. "Women's Public Political Voice in England: 1640–1740." *Women Writers and the Early Modern British Political Tradition*. Cambridge: Cambridge University Press, 1998. 56–74.

Semler, L. E. *Eliza's Babes or The Virgin's Offering (1652): A Critical Edition*. New Jersey: Fairleigh Dickinson University Press, 2001.

Shipton, Mother Ursula. *The Prophesie of Mother Shipton in the Raigne of King Henrie the Eighth. Fortelling the death of Cardinall Wolsey, the Lord Percy and others, as also what should happen in insuing times*. London: Richard Lownds, 1641. (Wing 3445; UMI film Thomason Tracts E.181 [15]).

Smith, Hilda L. *Reasons Disciples: Seventeenth-Century English Feminists*. Urbana: University of Illinois Press, 1982.

"Sutcliffe, Matthew." *Dictionary of National Biography*. Ed. Leslie Stephen and Sidney Lee.

Thomas, Keith. *Religion and the Decline of Magic: Studies in Popular Beliefs in Sixteenth and Seventeenth Century England*. Oxford: Oxford University Press, 1971.

Walker, Kim. *Women Writers of the English Renaissance*. Twayne's English Authors' Series 521. New York: Twayne-Simon Macmillan, 1996.

Warburton, Rachel. "Contextual Materials for 'A Warning from the Lord God' by Hester Biddle" *Renaissance Women Online*. Brown Women Writers Project. <http://www.brown.edu/texts/rwoentry.html> September, 1999.

Watt, Diane. *Secretaries of God: Women Prophets in Late Medieval and Early Modern England*. Cambridge: D.S. Brewer, 1992.

Wilson, Violet. *Society Women of Shakespeare's Time*. London: John Lane, 1924. Rpt. Port Washington, N.Y.: Kennikat Press, 1970.

Wiseman, Sue. "Unsilent intruments and the devil's cushions: authority in seventeenth-century women's prophetic discourse." *New Feminist Discourses*. Ed. Isobel Armstrong. London: Routledge, 1992. 176–196.

CHAPTER 5

Letters

Letter writing was a formal art and performance in the Humanist tradition. The earliest and most influential letter-writing manual was Erasmus's *De Conscribendis Epistolis* (1522), a Latin schoolbook for boys. The epistolary maintenance of friendship between equals (usually exchanges between learned men) was Erasmus's chief model. Later manuals, notably Angel Day's *The English Secretary* (1586, 1592, 1595, etc.), which, like *De Conscribendis* ran to many editions, was produced in the vernacular and offered detailed models of letters for those seeking social advancement. Day's book contains examples of model letters for women, as do manuals like William Fulwood's the *Enemie of Idlenesse* (1568, 1578, 1582, 1586, 1593, etc.).

With notable exceptions like formal letters of petition or suitors' letters, modeled on the kinds of rhetorical examples outlined in Erasmus (see Mary Fane's letters to government officials), women's correspondence offers little evidence of the letter writers' engagement with the manuals, particularly in the sixteenth and early seventeenth centuries.[1] Instead, women tended to derive their models from ordinary contact with letters available to them. The genre itself was a very popular one, and while the number of extant letters by women is considerably smaller than the quantity by men, scholars have identified about 10,000 examples of women's correspondence dating up to 1642. Though epistolary frames also served as vehicles through which women could negotiate social relations, letter-writing tended to be a chiefly private exercise for women. In fact the genre of the letter anticipates that of life writing (chapter 6) in terms of its traditional identification as one of the most personal forms of expression. More often than not, correspondence—one of the three kinds of manuscript exchange for women in the period—was unintended for public view or publication.[2] Nevertheless, the wider range of private, introspective, and flexible uses for employing letters distinguished the late medieval from the early modern epistolary form.[3]

An examination of women's letters, while frequently confirming the perception of the unpolished, unsophisticated nature of the texts, also reveals the richness of the genre and the complex construction of the female authorial self. Moreover, though most letters produced by women were directed to an audience of one, many were written with a broader readership in mind. Some even display a rhetorical dexterity and a formal observance of laws of politeness, as seen in Elizabeth I's letters or in Grace O'Malley's deployment of a courtly administrative language and a discourse of civility. In general these letters reflect, though in different ways, the writers' concern with conscious self-fashioning, as well as with familial relations and social status in the domestic or public sphere.[4]

Besides the practical purpose of enabling communication, correspondence allowed writers to compose autograph letters or personal histories (Lettice Gawdy, Katherine Oxinden) and legacies to children (Mary Fane, Eleanor Davies, Elizabeth Richardson). The epistolary form also enabled women's participation in self-analysis or devotional exercises, and even offered access to the public or political spheres (Grace O'Malley, Elizabeth I, Elizabeth Cary, Mary Fane). Dorothy Osborne's love letters arose from her need to maintain a connection with William Temple despite—or because of—the opposition of their families and, of course, civil war. At the same time, they exhibit a delight in the art of writing by displaying the writer's reflections on that process (also see Elizabeth I's letter to Frances, Countess of Hertford [1595]).[5]

The letters women composed range from ones concerned with domestic affairs to epistles or essays in letter form that addressed social, philosophical, or, in the case of Elizabeth I, political matters. Less attention has been devoted to the latter kind of correspondence, Margaret Ezell observes (73). Letters with a public purpose featured in this chapter include ones by Elizabeth I, who was most prolific as a letter writer; her extant letters produced between 1544 and the year of her death (1603) total about 1000. The Queen's correspondence consisted of "business" letters, which dealt with everything from land grants to lessons in statecraft—directed in particular to her successor, James VI of Scotland—to appointments and disciplinary actions. Elizabeth's letter to the Lord Mayor of London (August 1586), one of the Queen's few texts to be printed during her life, has not only a political objective but also indicates Elizabeth's concern with self-representation, though it is often difficult to distinguish the Queen's "authentic" voice from the official style she developed in conjunction with her secretaries and ministers.[6] The letter to Sir Richard Bingham (1593), who abused his position as English governor of Connaught, illustrates that the Queen's reproof of her own officials was part of her mandate in managing state affairs at home and abroad. Lady Elizabeth Cavendish's correspondence with her bailiff, Francis Whitfield (1552), is provoked by a related set of circumstances, though Cavendish was of course concerned with domestic, not international, affairs: having entrusted Whitfield to run her estate in her absence, Cavendish chides him in her letter for mistreating her sister, who was charged with managing the household.

One specific type of public letter produced by women was the letter of petition or suitor's letter, interchangeably known as "letters of request" by Erasmus, which addressed government officials or monarchs on matters of patronage, land, legal suits, titles, wardships, and offices.[7] Angel Day defines an "epistle petitorie" thus: "these Epistles are so named for the earnest Petition or request in euery of them conteined, and that the varietie of things are such to be demaunded, and mens conditions so diuers, at whose hands or from whome the same are to be receaued, required or obtained, it falleth out by consequence that according thereunto, the manner of Epistle muste needes also be diuers and variable."[8] An example of a letter of petition is Mary Fane's letter to Secretary of State Windebanke, 6 May 1639. Exercising her authority and responsibilities as the remaining parent in her family and a spokesperson for women and children who would suffer the consequences of politically disastrous decision-making, the widowed Fane condemns Charles I's incursion into Scotland. Importantly, such epistles as Fane's are different from legal petitions—a formal application made in writing to a court—and parliamentary petitions (by which the Houses of Parliament presented a measure for the monarch's granting), as well as petitions written in the third person and presented to the monarch for signing. The last mentioned, of which numerous examples by women are extant, were drawn up after a provisional promise of royal favor had been secured. They represent a carefully negotiated agreement over terms between the suitor and royal advisers, usually in the face of competing claims. Petitions of this sort are formal documents and generally conform to a three-part structure: the heading, the suit or problem, and the proposed solution.[9]

The typical letter comprised a quarto sheet with the inscription on the recto side. Poor literacy skills accounted for the phonetic spelling and reliance on speech conventions that characterize the style of so many letters by women. Illiteracy itself did not prevent them from contributing to household management.[10] Women of the lower classes would have had access to scriveners, an alternative to Day's *Secretary*, while secretaries were available for members of the nobility and gentry. Letters produced by scriveners or secretaries, however, rarely survive and tend to be cited only in court records or in the diaries and accounts of scriveners.

As a number of the letters included in this chapter indicate, the private-public dichotomy could be reconceived even within the confines of the domestic. As the head domesticity of her family and as a mother concerned for her sons' rights and future, Mary Fane, daughter of Grace, Lady Mildmay, comments in her letter on national affairs and questions Charles I's decision to compel the Scots to adopt the Book of Common Prayer (1639). Another widow, Eleanor Davies, inscribes her roles as political prophet, mother, and even grandmother in her letters to her daughter, Lucy Hastings (1629). Glimpses into Eleanor Davies's private world afforded by her correspondence to Lucy present a largely unfamiliar representation of this political visionary as a compassionate parent.

Examples of more conventional letters of upper-class women include those by Lettice Gawdy (c. 1620), Katherine Oxinden (1636), and Elizabeth Richardson (1645), whose dedicatory epistle to her grandson, Sir Edward Dering, is featured in this chapter. These letters tend to focus on news about the authors themselves, as well as on local issues and the welfare of the writers' children, friends, and relatives. Typically, female authors also commented on domestic and social duties, including financial or business affairs, which present statements "about what women considered an appropriate text act."[11] Domestic relations represent the bulk of Dorothy Osborne's letters to her future husband, William Temple (1652–54), though Osborne's style differs from that of Gawdy and Oxinden in terms of her wit and command of language. Her letters demonstrate, through their content and form, Osborne's appreciation of a wide range of literary texts, including theological works and verse by notable poets like Katherine Philips (see chapter 8), thereby offering information about reading practices in the early modern period.

Intellectual and philosophical concerns are woven into the correspondence of Mary Clarke with her husband, Edward Clarke (6 January 1695/6) and the philosopher John Locke. As a talented writer, Clarke wrote insightfully on a range of topics, from domestic economy to politics. The letters she composed during the 1680s evolved into a three-way discussion among the Clarkes and their friend, John Locke, on procedures for educating children. Although Mary's letters to Locke have been printed, and answered in part by Locke in *Some Thoughts Concerning Education* (1693), her letters to her husband have never been published. A 1696 manuscript letter to Edward Clarke is featured here.

Besides Clarke, John Locke had a number of other female correspondents, including Damaris, Lady Masham (the daughter of the Cambridge Platonist Ralph Cudworth), Lady Elizabeth Guise, and Elizabeth Burnet. A similar kind of relationship developed between Anne Finch, Viscountess Conway, and the Cambridge Platonist Dr. Henry More (1696). As printed treatises of the early modern period sometimes evolved from letter exchanges, the correspondence of Conway and More inspired various of More's treatises. Conway's own philosophical treatise, *The Principles of the most Ancient and Modern Philosophy*, was published anonymously in a Latin translation in Amsterdam (*Principia philosophiae antiquissimae et recentissimae*, 1690) (see chapter 7). It invites comparison with Conway's letters, which examine a range of topics from medical issues to family concerns, political events, and religious and philosophical movements of the time. Both genres offer valuable insights into the personal and intellectual life of this early modern woman. It is therefore unfortunate, maintained an early-twentieth-century editor of *The Conway Letters*, that the work of letter writers like Anne Finch had "lain neglected" for centuries and that Finch herself had been confused with another remarkable woman of the period, the poet Anne (Kingsmill) Finch, Countess of Winchilsea (see chapter 10).[12]

A study of early modern women's letter writing demonstrates the inherently interactionist, social, and dramatic nature of the language of letters within the culture at large, and at the same time offers a window into the construction of inwardness and the formation of the female identity as shaped by women's marital relations, friendships, intellectual milieu, and writing of the self. As social documents, letters lend themselves to a wide range of analyses and are an important source for historians and social historians as well as for cultural and literary critics interested in material culture. The malleability of the genre is evident throughout this volume, as epistolary conventions are translated into such genres of the early modern period as autobiographies, prose fiction, memoirs, sonnets, prefaces and prologues to dramas, character dialogues (see Magnusson, *Shakespeare*), and eventually novels.

Notes

We are most grateful for the assistance of James Daybell and Heather Wolfe.

1. Hannah Wolley's *Supplement to the Queen-like Closet; or, a little of Every Thing* (1674–75), however, does include model letters, indicating how her reader might communicate with absent family members, patrons, or suitors; see chapter 3.

2. The production of manuscript books and the circulation of writings in loose sheets are the other forms of manuscript circulation. See Margaret J. M. Ezell, *The Patriarch's Wife: Literary Evidence and the History of the Family* (Chapel Hill: University of North Carolina Press, 1987), 65.

3. James Daybell, "Introduction," *Early Modern Women's Letter Writing, 1450–1700*, ed. James Daybell (Houndsmills: Palgrave, 2001), 2. Also see James Daybell, "Recent Studies in Renaissance Letters," forthcoming in *English Literary Renaissance*; and Heather Wolfe, *Elizabeth Cary: The Lady Falkland: Her Life and Letters* (Binghamton: Medieval & Renaissance Texts & Studies, 2001), 25–28.

4. See Lynne Magnusson, *Shakespeare and Social Dialogue: Dramatic Language and Elizabethan Letters* (Cambridge: Cambridge University Press, 1999).

5. Helen Wilcox, "Private Writing and Public Function: Autobiographical Texts by Renaissance Englishwomen," *Gloriana's Face: Women, Public and Private, in the English Renaissance*, ed. S. P. Cerasano and Marion Wynne-Davies (Detroit: Wayne State University Press, 1992), 49.

6. Leah S. Marcus, Janel Mueller and Mary Beth Rose, "Preface," *Elizabeth I: Collected Works*, ed. Leah S. Marcus, Janel Mueller and Mary Beth Rose (Chicago: University of Chicago Press, 2000), xiii. Also see Susan Doran, "Elizabeth I's Religion: Clues from her letters," *Journal of Ecclesiastical History* 51.4 (2000): 699–720.

7. Frank Whigham, "The Rhetoric of Elizabethan Suitors' Letters," *PMLA* 96 (1981): 864; and also see Lynne Magnusson, "A Rhetoric of Requests: Genre and Linguistic Scripts in Elizabethan Women's Suitors' Letters," James Daybell, ed. *Women and Politics in Early Modern England, 1450–1700* (Ashgate, forthcoming 2004); and Wolfe, 25–45.

8. Angel Day, *The English Secretary* (1595), 91.

9. See James Daybell's forthcoming book *Pricy and Powerful Communications: Women Letter Writers in Tudor England* (Oxford University Press).

10. James Daybell, "Female Literacy and the Social Conventions of Women's Letter-Writing in England, 1540–1603," *Early Modern Women's Letter Writing*, 72.

11. Carol L. Winkelmann "A Case Study of Women's Literacy in the Early Seventeenth Century: The Oxinden Family Letters," *Women and Language* 19.2 (1996): 17. On domestic relations, see Alison Wall, "Elizabethan Practice and Feminine Precept: The Thynne Family of Longleat," *History* 75 (1990): 23–38.

12. Anne Conway, *The Conway Letters: The Correspondence of Anne, Viscountess Conway, Henry More, and Their Friends 1642–1684*, ed. Marjorie Hope Nicolson (New Haven, Conn.: Yale University Press, 1930), rev. ed. by Sarah Hutton (Oxford: Clarendon Press, 1992), 1.

ffrancys I haue spoken to your mayster
for the clythes or houses that you
wrote to me of and he ys contente
that you shall take fourre for
your nyecyte by the apoyntemente
of newsame so that you take
sertie as I well do tyme no
saruese aboute hus byldynge at
chattysworthe. I pray you loke
well to alltynges at chattysworthe
tyll my auntes comynge whome
whyche I hope shalbe shortely
and yn the meane tyme cause
brownhaue to loke to the pryntes
and all other tynges at pentryge
lete the brewar make bere for me
fourtene for my owne drynkyng
and your mayster and se that I
haue good store of yet for yf I lacke
eyther good bere or chaycole or woode
I well blame nobody so muche
as I well do you cause the
flore yn my bede chaunbe to be

29

Lady Elizabeth Cavendish (Bess of Hardwick) to Francis Whitfield (14 November 1552)

Transcription

francys I have spoken with your mayste[r][1] for the clyltes [cleats] or bordes that you wrete to me of and he ys contente that you shall take some for your nesecyte by the apounte-mente of neusante.[2] so that you take seche as wyll do hyme no sarvese aboute hys byldynge at chattysworthe.[3] I pray you loke well to all thynges at chattysworthe tyll my auntes[4] comynge whome whyche I hope shalbe shortely and yn the meane tyme cause bronshawe to loke to the smethes and all other thynges at penteryge[5] lete the brewar make bere for me fourthewith for my owne drynkyng and your mayster and se that I have good store of yet for yf I lacke ether good bere, or charcole or wode I wyll blame nobody so meche as I wyll do you. cause the flore yn my bede chambe[r] to be [fol. 1ᵛ] made even ether with plaster claye or lyme and al the wyndoyes were the glase ys broken to be mendod and al the chambers to be made as close and warme as you cane. I here that my syster jane[6] cane not have thynges that ys nedefoulle for hare to have amoungste you yf yet be trewe you lacke agreat of honyste as well as dyscrescyon to deny hare any thynge that she hathe a mynde to beynge yn case as she hathe bene. I wolde be lothe to have any stranger so yoused yn my howse and then assure your selfe I cane not lyke yet to have my syster so yousede. lyke as I wolde not have any superfleuete or waste of any thynge so lyke wysse wolde I have hare to have that whyche ys nedefoulle and nesesary. at my comynge whome I shal knowe more. and then I wyll thy[n]k as I shall have cause. I wolde haue you to geve to my mydwyffe frome me and frome my boye wylle.[7] and to [fol. 2ʳ] my syster norse frome me and my boye as hereafter folowyet[h] fyrste to the mydwyfe frome me tene shyllynges. and frome wylle fyve shyllynges to the norse frome me fyve shyllynges. and frome my boye iii fore pence. so that yn the wolle you mouste geve to them twenty thre shyllynges and fore pence make my syster jane prevye of yet and then paye yet to them fourth with yf you have no other money take so metche of the rente at penteryge tyll my syster jane that I wyll geve my dowter[8] somethynge at my comyng whome and prayinge you not to fayle to se all thynges done accordyngely I bede you fare well frome london the xiiii of novemeber your mystrys Elyzabethe Cavendysh tyll james crompe[9] that I have resavyed the fyve ponde and ix shillings that he sente me by heue alsope.[10]

[address leaf] to my sar[vant] francys wytfelde [delive]r thys at chattysw[orth]e

[*notes in another hand*] for the mylle for tak[in]g shepe for tak[in]g C ll woode for capons to be fatt for swyne / for the hard cornefelde for a pynder[11]

[*notes in modern hand*] Elizabeth Wife of Sir William Cavendish of Chatsworth, afterwards Countess of Shrewsbury

Notes

1. Her husband, Sir William Cavendish.
2. Neusante, a master carpenter, was paid 8 pence a day and his assistant 5 pence: Williams, *Bess of Hardwick*, p. 90.
3. Chatsworth House, Derbyshire.
4. Marcella Linacre, her maternal aunt, the widow of a Derbyshire gentleman, appears to have lived with Lady Cavendish.
5. Pentrich Woods, Derbyshire.

6. Jane Hardwick, wife of Godfrey Boswell (gent.) of Gunthorpe, Yorkshire, afterward wife of Thomas Kniveton of Mercaston.

7. William Cavendish (1551–1626), Bess of Hardwick's second son, created Baron Cavendish in 1605 and Earl of Devon in 1618.

8. Her first daughter, Frances, who was born in 1548 and married Sir Henry Pierrepont in the 1560s, rather than her second daughter, Temperance, who was born in 1549 and died in her first year.

9. Crompe was steward of Chatsworth.

10. Hugh Alsope, a carrier.

11. Pinder, *OED*: "An officer of a manor, having the duty of impounding stray beasts."

Commentary

Elizabeth Cavendish (c.1527–1608), perhaps better known as "Bess of Hardwick," was the fourth daughter and coheiress of John Hardwick (1495–1528) of Hardwick, Derbyshire, by his wife, Elizabeth, daughter of Thomas Leake of Halsland. She first married Robert Barlow (or Barley; d.1544) circa 1543. Her second husband was Sir William Cavendish (c.1505–57), a member of the Privy Council; she married him as his third wife on 20 August 1547. By Cavendish she had six children (her sole issue): Frances, Temperance, Henry, William, Charles, and Elizabeth. In 1559, Elizabeth married Sir William St. Loe (d.1565), captain of the guards, as her third husband. She finally married her fourth husband, George Talbot, sixth earl of Shrewsbury (c.1528–90) in 1567, as his second wife; the couple later separated. In marrying well, Bess achieved a higher level of social status and sphere of influence than that to which she was born. She inherited handsomely from all her husbands and is well known as a builder. In addition to the Elizabethan mansion at Chatsworth, she built the seats of Oldcotes, Worksop, and Bolsover, and, after the death of Shrewsbury in 1590, she set to work on building a new Hardwick Hall.

Over 100 of Bess of Hardwick's letters survive, written to various correspondents: family, servants, friends, neighbors, and government officials. The example reproduced here is the earliest known extent letter written by her. This letter is printed in Joseph Hunter (107) and in Maud Stepney Rawson (9–10), but both Hunter's and Rawson's transcripts contain numerous inaccuracies. Extracts of the letter are also printed in Basil Stallybrass (351–52), and E. Carleton Williams (23–24). It elicits further interest in that it was addressed to a male servant, Francis Whitfield, her bailiff. Her letter (one of two written by Bess to Whitfield, the other being Folger X.d. 428 (84), October 20, [1560]) was penned probably in 1552, while she was married to Sir William Cavendish. During this period, Chatsworth, which had been purchased in June 1549, underwent major rebuilding, and Bess and Sir William divided their time between there and London. In her absence from Chatsworth, Bess placed her sister Jane in charge of running the household, with Francis Whitfield responsible for running the estate. The letter instructs Whitfield to look well to all things at Chatsworth until her aunt Marcella Linacre arrives; to cause Bronshawe to manage things at Pentrich Wood; to stock up with charcoal, wood, and beer; to ensure that the floor in her bedchamber is made even and to mend the glass in the windows; to provide for her sister Jane's needs; to pay her midwife and her sister's nurse; and to inform James Crompe that she received the five pounds he sent her. On the address leaf, there is a list of things to do written in another hand. The authoritarian manner with which Bess delivered these orders is characteristic of other letters from aristocratic women to servants, though its severity is heightened by her displeasure at the poor way in which her sister Jane was treated at Chatsworth. She charges Whitfield with a lack of honesty and discretion in his dealings with her sister, adding that she would not wish a stranger in her house to be used in such a manner. Perhaps Whitfield's behavior reflects a jurisdictional conflict within the household between Jane and himself, yet clearly Bess expected her sister to be treated with the respect due a woman of her gentle status.

In 1560 a new phase of building work began at Chatsworth, during a time when Bess was interested in contemporary architectural developments. She was in touch with Sir John Thynne, for example, during his overseeing of the first rebuilding of Longleat. (Longleat House, Thynne MS 13 no. 3: Lady Elizabeth St. Loe to Sir John Thynne, April 25, 1560). Her keen interest in Chatsworth is reflected in the way in which her husband, William St. Loe, addressed her as "my honest swete chatesworth," a reference to the considerable time she spent there (Folger X.d. 428 f. 77: Sir William St. Loe to Lady Elizabeth St. Loe, 24 Oct. [1560]). In rebuilding the property, a task that required lavish expenditure, Bess was constructing a house of magnificence suitable to the dynasty that she was founding.

James Daybell
Central Michigan University

A letter from Lady Elizabeth Cavendish to Francis Whitfield, 14 November [1552], Folger Shakespeare Library (Cavendish/Talbot MS) X.d. 428 (82); *holograph*

BY THE QVEENE.

To our right truſtie and welbe-
loued, the Lord Maior of our Citie of London, and
his brethren the Aldermen of the ſame.

Ight truſtie and welbeloued, wee
greete you well. Being giuen to vn-
derſtand how greatly our good and
moſt louing Subiects of that Citie
did reioyce at the apprehēſiō of certaine deuiliſh and wicked minded
ſubiects of ours, that through the
great and ſingular goodnes of God
haue bene detected, to haue moſt wickedly and vnnaturally
conſpired, not onely the taking away of our owne life, but alſo to haue ſtirred vp (as much as in them lay) a generall rebellion throughout our whole Realme : we coulde not but
by our owne letters witneſſe vnto you the great and ſingular contentment we receiued vpon the knowledge thereof,
aſſuring you, that we did not ſo much reioyce at the eſcape
of the intended attempt againſt our owne perſon, as to ſee
the great ioy our moſt louing Subiects tooke at the appre-
henſion of the contriuers thereof, which, to make their loue
more apparant, they haue (as we are to our great comfort
informed) omitted no outwarde ſhewe, that by any externall acte might witneſſe to the world the inwarde loue and
duetifull affection they beare toward vs. And as we haue
as great cauſe with all thankfulneſſe to acknowledge Gods
great goodneſſe toward vs, through the infinite bleſſings
he layeth vpon vs, as many as euer Prince had, yea rather,
as euer Creature had : yet doe we not for any worldly bleſſing receiued from his diuine Maieſtie, ſo greatly acknow-

A.ij.

ledge

5.2: Elizabeth I, "The true copie of a letter from the Queenes Majestie, to the Lord Mayor of London, and his brethren" (22 August 1586). By permission of the Folger Shakespeare Library.

Elizabeth I, "The true copie of a letter from the Queenes Majestie, to the Lord Mayor of London, and his brethren: conteyning a most gracious acceptation of the great ioy which her Subjectes tooke upon the apprehension of divers persons, detected of a most wicked conspiracie, read openly in a great assemblie of the Commons in the Guildhall of that Citie" (22 August 1586)

Queen Elizabeth's letter to the Lord Mayor and aldermen of London, thanking them for their support during the Babington plot, is a rare example of Elizabeth's using the press to construct her public persona. In May 1586 it became clear that a group of Catholic supporters of Mary, Queen of Scots, were planning to assassinate Elizabeth, but the plot was revealed and the main conspirators were apprehended on August 4. The citizens of London greeted their arrests with an outpouring of joy that apparently moved Elizabeth very much. On August 18, she wrote this letter in Windsor Castle, asking that it be read out to the citizens of London. This was done on August 22, prefaced by a speech by James Dalton. The letter and preface must have been published soon after, for they were printed in 1586. That Elizabeth would address her subjects through the medium of print was highly unusual; this is one of only a handful of her texts published in her lifetime.

Visually, this page resembles a proclamation, probably the most public and visible means the Queen had of communicating with her subjects. Although it is unlikely that Elizabeth herself wrote the 377 proclamations issued in her reign, they were issued with her approval and in her name, and were posted and read out in public places, such as the marketplace or church. At the top in prominent letters is the phrase "By the Queene," followed by an elaborately carved opening letter. This "R" begins the phrase "Right trustie and welbeloved, wee greete you well," the opening formula used in official royal letters beginning with the first such letters written in English under Lancastrian rule.

Thematically, the letter echoes ideas found in many of Elizabeth's writings: her faith in God and Divine Providence, her love of her subjects, her joy at their displays of affection for her, her wish to be an even better ruler. Even as she deliberates what to do with Mary, Queen of Scots, Elizabeth is also characteristically vague about the specifics of the plot against her, or the conflict between the Church of England and Catholicism, a reticence all the more noticeable given Dalton's direct references to the "immoderate affectors of the Romish religion and superstitions" in his preface to the Queen's speech. In another typical display of self-effacement, Elizabeth says that she rejoices not so much "at the escape of the intended attempt against our owne person," but "to see the great ioy our most loving Subjects tooke at the apprehension" of the criminals. Her joy thus grew out of their joy, not out of self-preservation, and she links both to "Gods great goodnesse towards us."

Elizabeth was well aware of the power of her own written word, as she acknowledges here in her wish "by our owne letters" to thank her people publicly. Compare this public letter with her private letter to Frances, Countess of Hertford, where Elizabeth similarly draws attention to the significance of a letter in her "own handwriting."

NELY KEINANEN
UNIVERSITY OF HELSINKI

Elizabeth I. "The true copie of a letter from the Queenes Majestie, to the Lord Mayor of London, and his brethren . . . (22 August 1586)" Folger Shakespeare Library STC 7577. Sig. Aii.

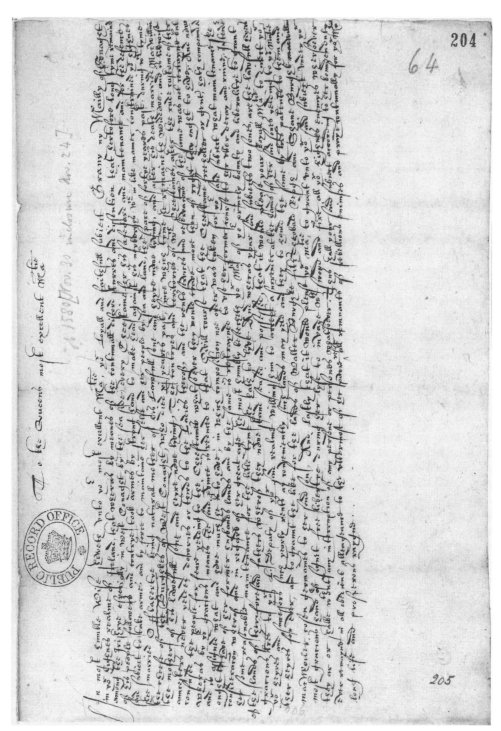

5.3: Grace O'Malley to Elizabeth I (1593). The National Archives, London (formerly Public Record Office).

Grace O'Malley to Elizabeth I (1593)

Transcription

To the Queen's most excellent Majestie

In most humble Wise sheweth unto your most excellent Majestie your Loyall and faithfull subject Grany ny Mailly of Conaght in your highnes realme of Ireland, that wheras by meanes of the continnuall discord sturres and dissention that hertofore long tyme remained among the Irishrye (especially in west Conaght by the sea side), every Cheeftaine for his safegard and maintenance and for the defence of his people followers and contrye took armes, by strong hand to make head against his neyborghs: which in like manner constrained your highnes said subject to take armes: and by force to maintaine her selfe and her people by Sea and land, the space of fortye yeares past, during which tyme shee married Offlahertye being naturall mother of his lawfull sone and heyre nowe lyving, and after his death married Mac William the cheefe of the Burghkes of West Conaght, who died xi yeares past, since which tyme she remaineth widdowe, and is likewise the mother of his lawefull sone and heyre nowe lyving, The contryes and teritories of which Cheeftaines, after the rude custome of ther auncesters never yelded dowries or thirds to the Ladies therof, and the rents services and reservacions of the same was not certayne but confused the people for feare yelding to the Cheeftaines whatsoever they would crave more then of ryght they ought to have. And nowe wheras by your gracious meanes the said province is reduced to that Civill course that the Cheeftaine freeholder or gent, hath compounded and is assigned what and howe much he is to have, in which composition noe order was taken for your said subject what maintenance she ought to have of her former husbands lands and by the same is restrayned to use her former course to her utter decay and ruine; In tender consideracion wherof and in regard of her great age she most humbly beseecheth your Majestie of your princly bounty and liberalitye to grant her some reasonable maintenance for the litle tyme she hath to lyve. And wheras your said subjects two sones, are the lawfull heyres of the lands of there foresaid fathers wherof they nowe stand seased and possessed, that it would please your Royall Majestie to direct your gracious letters to your L. Deputy of your said realme willing him to accept a surrender at her hands of her said sones yelding to your Majestie your heyres and successors such yearly rents as conveniently such lands may yeld and they to hould the same by letters patents to them and ther heyres for ever, and to graunt the like for the lands of Walter Burghke Fitztheobald Reogh and Shane Burghk MacMoiler cosen germaines to her said son. And lastly that it would please your Majestie to grant unto your said subject under your most gracious hand of signet free libertye during her lyfe to invade with sword and fire all your highnes enemyes whersoever they ar or shalbe without any interruption of any persone or persones whatsoever. Thus shall your said subject according to her bounden duty ever remayne in all obedient alleageance to the uttermost of her powre resist all remnants of rebellious enimies and praye continually for your Majesties long life and prosperous raygne.

Commentary

Gráinne Uí Mháille (or Grace O'Malley, as she was known to the English), was an Irish leader on the west coast of Ireland during the late 1500s whose notoriety won her a place in literary works such as Edmund Spenser's *Faerie Queene* and Philip Sidney's *Arcadia*. Like many Irish leaders of the period, she played a canny political game in the face of English colonial expansion, sometimes siding with the English colonial governors against local Irish enemies, at other times fiercely resisting English encroachment by forming alliances with other clan leaders of the region. By continually playing both sides to her advantage, Grace managed to accrue a considerable amount of power and authority, securing for herself and her children political and economic dominance over a significant portion of the western coastline. Her fame grew, her influence grew, and so grew the English determination to curb the "woman that hath impudently passed the part of womanhood and been a great spoiler and chief commander and director of thieves and murderers at sea" (S.P.I. 63.19.56). O'Malley's letter of 1593 is, among other things, indicative of the ways in which gender expectations and rhetorical finesse could be employed to shape the course of politics.

In 1584, Richard Bingham was given the English governorship of Connaught and immediately began a fierce attempt at suppressing all who had until then resisted English rule. O'Malley and her fleet proved to be especially irksome to Bingham, and she became the focus of several campaigns to smother political and economic resistance on the west coast. In spite of twice being captured, having to attack one of her own sons for colluding with the English, and repeatedly defending her person from other Irish leaders eager to please the colonial government or hoping to protect local shipping trade, O'Malley's success at running her own network of ports and castles in the service of piracy by sea and cattle raids by land made the attempt at suppression difficult. However, by 1593 Bingham had managed to hem O'Malley's fleet so tightly that she was virtually bound. Cannily taking advantage of a significant level of inconsistency in the apportionment of jurisdiction between the London and Dublin seats of colonial government, Grace bypassed Bingham and the submission he was attempting to enforce and instead appealed directly to the Queen of England, Elizabeth Tudor.

Grace's letter to Elizabeth, written in English, demonstrates a keen sense of rhetorical judgment. Although O'Malley's biographer, Anne Chambers, points out that the letter may not be in Grace's own hand (she appears to have employed a scribe), the letter's content certainly matches the tone and manner of a wealth of previous social encounters with English governors in which the Irish woman's deft handling of rhetorical nuance in social situations earned her a certain degree of popularity with the colonial elite. Henry Sidney, for instance, was still sharing stories about Grace long after his stay in Ireland was over. Moreover, historical examples of social and political discourse in which O'Malley figures suggest that she preferred mix-strategy advances against her rivals (sometimes pointedly agreeable, at other times proudly bellicose), another clearly discernible trait in her letter to Elizabeth. Indeed, the letter demonstrates the degree to which O'Malley's political success was in part a self-conscious braiding of personal charisma, a canny sense of immanent advantage, and the will to gamble—a leadership stance not unlike Elizabeth Tudor's.

Like Elizabeth, Grace knew how to rework discursively the political moment to her own advantage. Framed in the conventional language of courtly administrative discourse, what Lynne Magnusson terms the "politeness" of repair and maintenance, O'Malley's letter is chiefly a masterpiece of euphemism and judicious hyperbole. Grace knew that the English queen was aware of the exploits that had earned O'Malley the title of "great spoiler" among the English colonial governors in Ireland. Interestingly, Grace avoids the language of flamboyant self-debasement popular among English politicos petitioning Elizabeth; her tone is less like that found in the correspondence of men such as Henry Sidney to Elizabeth, and more like that of foreign kings and princes who politely proffered various services to the English queen while courteously petitioning for a political favor. Grace's euphemistic recapitulation of past events is, therefore, less an attempt to obscure her resistance to Elizabeth's rule and more a nod of acknowledgment, one ruler to another, of the current success and eminence of her sometime opponent.

Moreover, by recasting her past exploits as *necessary* given the "continnuall discord sturres and dissention that hertofore long tyme remained among the Irishrye," O'Malley proffers the possible grounds for her own pardon: she claims to have been forced to fight against a general Irish chaos during the course of her career, and should therefore be seen as an ally of sorts. To this end, O'Malley's piracy and coastline raids are euphemistically recapitulated as maintenance "by sea and land," and Bingham's harsh success in Connaught becomes a failure of English law to protect Elizabeth's much embattled "subject." More pointedly, the same Grace who in the past had threatened one of Elizabeth's tax collectors with physical harm now explains that the current situation (her inability to continue in her former occupation of sea and land raids) is such that it is impossible for her and her sons to "conveniently" yield the "yearly rents" to Elizabeth. O'Malley carefully construes the success of the colonial government on the west coast of Ireland as an obstacle to the proper disbursement of revenues requisite for Elizabeth's successful rule.

Given the trouble Elizabeth had in controlling her colonial governors, as well as the continued threat of Spanish invasion and the likelihood of an alliance between the Spanish and the followers of Hugh O'Neill, O'Malley's timing and tone are well considered. The poetic hyperbole of offering to invade "with sword and fire all your highnes enemyes" concludes the letter with the Bellona-like image of a warrior queen that must have mirrored gratifyingly Elizabeth's own self image. This final boast and pledge also gives the lie to the plea that O'Malley was in need of special consideration "in regard of her great age" and due to the "litle tyme she hath to lyve" (after all, while there is some truth to both points, the intent of the letter is to make possible O'Malley's former buccaneering activities). In short, these hyperbolic gestures serve to politely cloak—while frankly asserting—a pragmatic point: Elizabeth can use O'Malley's unusual gifts to openly reprimand English governors in Connaught, and to shore up local power against the likelihood of trouble with the Spanish. Both promises bolster the positive rhetorical effect of the euphemistic recounting of O'Malley's situation.

Shortly after sending her letter to London, O'Malley was faced with a further complication. Bingham arrested her son, Tibbet-ne-Long, for supposedly colluding with the supporters of O'Neill. Her brother was also still in Bingham's custody, and both family members were in danger of being executed. Determined to best Bingham, and in spite of unfavorable odds (she was, after all, also known as Grace of the Gamblers), O'Malley followed her letter to London, where she obtained an audience with Elizabeth. Although Bingham attempted to sway the London government against O'Malley with letters of his own, Grace's powers of persuasion stood her in good stead. The subsequent letter from Elizabeth to Bingham was a bitter pill to swallow for the English governor in Connaught (demonstrated by his letters of complaint to other officials at court), for the queen commands him to set free O'Malley's son and brother, and further commands him to protect O'Malley and family in the pursuit of their livelihood. In short, what O'Malley failed to obtain by *sword* from one enemy, the English governor Bingham, she successfully secured by *word* from an enemy-made-ally, Elizabeth Tudor.

Brandie Siegfried
Brigham Young University

Grace O'Malley. "To the Queen's most excellent Majestie" (July 1593). *Calendar of State Papers Relating to Ireland*. National Archives (Public Record Office) SP 63/170, fol. 204, item 64.

5.4: Elizabeth I to Sir Richard Bingham (6 September 1593). By permission of Lord Salisbury for the Marquess of Salisbury's Library.

Elizabeth I to Sir Richard Bingham (6 September 1593)

Transcription

where our treasuror of england, by his letters in July last, did inform you of the beyng here of thre several persons of that our provynce of Connaugh under your chardg, that is of Sir Morogh oflaharty, knight, Grany ne maly and roobuck french, requiryng to understand your opinion of every of them concerning ther sutes, we perceave by your late letters of answer what your opinion is of them and ther causes of Complaynt or of sutes wherof you have gyven them no Just cause. but wher Grany ne Maly hath made humble sute to us, for our favor towards hir sons Morogh oflaharty and Tibbott burk, and to hir brother Donnell opiper, that they might be at liberty, we perceave by your letters that hir eldest son, Morogh oflaharty, is in no trouble, but is a principall man of his Country and as a dutifull subject hath served us whan his mother beyng than accompanyed with a numbre of disordred persons, did with her Gallyes spoyle hym; and therfor by yow favored and so we wish yow to contynew. but the second son, Tibbott burk, one that hath bene brought up civilly with your brother and can speak english, is by yow Justly deteyned because he hath bene accused to have wrytten a letter to bryan orork, the late traytor's son, though it cannot be fully proved, but is by hym utterly denyed; and for hir brother Donald he hath bene ymprisoned 7 months past beyng charged to have bene in Company of certen that killed some soldiers in a ward, but for these twoo, you thynk they may be both desmissed uppon bonds for their good behavor, wherwith we ar content, so as the old woman may understand that we yeld therto in regard of hir humble sute; and so she is hereof informed and departeth with great thankfullnes, and with many most ernest promises, that she will as long as she lyve contynew a dutifull subject, yea, and will employe all hir power, to offend and prosequut any offender ageynst us. and further, for the pite [pity] to be had of this aged woman, havyng not by the Custom of the Irish, any title to any lyvehood or portion of hir ii husbands lands, now beyng a wydow, and yet hir sons enjoyeng ther fathers lands, we require yow to deale with hir sons in our name to yeld to hir some mayntenance for hir lyvyng the rest of hir old yers, which yow may with persuasion assure them that we shall therin allow of them; and yow also shall with your favor in all ther good causes protect them to lyve in peace to enjoy their lyvehoods. and this we do wryt in hir favor, as she now sheweth hirself dutefull, although she hath in former tymes lyved out of ordre, as beyng charged by our Tresuror with the evill usadg to hir son that served us dutifully, she hath Confessed the same, with assured promises by oth, to contynew most dutifull, with offer, after hir foresaid Manner that she will fight in our quarrell with all the world.

Commentary

The letter of Elizabeth Tudor to Richard Bingham provides an intimate view of Anglo-Irish politics at the end of the sixteenth century and sketches the Queen's encounter with Gráinne Uí Mháille (or Grany Ne Maly, as the letter names her), an Irish leader from the west coast of Ireland whose exploits on sea and land had frustrated the English colonial government for several decades. Elizabeth's colonial policy in Ireland consisted in continuing the strategy begun by her father, an inconsistent implementation of surrender and regrant, by which Gaelic chieftans were harried by the English military and then invited to submit to the English monarch; in return, the English monarch promised to uphold their local authority (as liege subjects) against local rivals. Gaelic lords granted such status were expected to facilitate the extension of English law and the expansion of English colonization on the island.

In reality, Old English settlers (the English had by now been in Ireland for over four hundred years) often allied themselves with the Gaelic chieftans against acquisitive New English colonials; on other occasions, Gaelic leaders teamed up with New English adventurers to pry Old English leaders from coveted positions of influence. Not surprisingly, efforts at conquest were sporadic, often ineffectual, and fraught with a perplexing number of economic and social complications. Grace O'Malley was a Gaelic leader whose growing influence in Connaught had become just such a complication.

Richard Bingham, who was given the English governorship of Connaught in 1584, was one of many holding positions in the provinces to use authority to engage in widespread freebooting. His purpose was to acquire as much property as possible during his tenure, and to inspire insurrection among the local Irish so that he could then rationalize to the London government his frequent military onslaughts. However, the actions of such as Bingham had not gone unnoticed by Elizabeth, who on several occasions intervened on behalf of the Irish, blaming many of the sporadic rebellions on poor governorship. Although Elizabeth acknowledges having considered Bingham's concerns, she dismisses them by turning the governor's own words against him. Indeed, the reminder that Bingham favors one of O'Malley's sons—the one whom O'Malley had despoiled with her galleys for colluding with the English—is a purposefully backhanded gesture of conciliation since it pointedly reminds Bingham of O'Malley's past successes. Bingham's correction is made complete when he is ordered to give aid to his former enemy and her family.

Perhaps more interesting than her treatment of Bingham is Elizabeth's handling of O'Malley. While the Queen willingly proffers the very grounds for pardon that O'Malley had blandly advanced in her own letter (see O'Malley's letter, 5.3), including old age and a reformed character, Elizabeth seems most taken with the notion that O'Malley will "fight in our quarrell with all the world," for she mentions it twice and chooses to end her letter on that note. At the very least, Elizabeth is taken with the idea of adding a female captain to her already infamous flock of unofficially sanctioned privateers. Thus, in addition to exhibiting the Queen's usual flair for creative strategies in affairs of state, the letter suggests some identification with the influential figure of the Irish "pirate queen."

BRANDIE SIEGFRIED
BRIGHAM YOUNG UNIVERSITY

Elizabeth Tudor. "The Queen to Sir Richard Bingham, 6 September 1593." Original no longer extant. Published copy in *Calendar of the Manuscripts of the Marquis of Salisbury, Part IV*. London: Historical Manuscripts Commission, 1892, 368–369.

Elizabeth I to Frances (Howard) Seymour, Countess of Hertford (November 1595)

Commentary

The following document is a secretary's copy of the letter Queen Elizabeth I wrote in November 1595 to Frances, Countess of Hertford, the wife of Edward Seymour, Earl of Hertford, transcribed here with original spelling and punctuation. It is an extraordinary declaration of the queen's loyalty to Frances despite the fact that her husband was engaged in activities Elizabeth considered treasonous. Frances and Elizabeth were related on her mother's side: Frances was the daughter of William Howard, Lord Howard of Effingham, Anne Boleyn's uncle, so Frances was Elizabeth's mother's cousin. Frances's mother, Margaret, had been appointed a Gentlewoman of the Privy Chamber at the beginning of Elizabeth's reign, and Frances herself became a Gentlewoman in 1568, when she was only 14. She received wages for this post until her death in 1598. Frances's older brother, Charles, Baron Howard of Effingham, was Elizabeth's Lord Admiral, most famous for having defended against the Spanish Armada. He is no doubt the brother Elizabeth "would have used" to deliver her message had he been available.

Edward Seymour was the eldest son of Edward Seymour, Duke of Somerset and Lord Protector during the reign of Edward VI. In 1560 Edward had secretly married Catherine Grey, who under the terms of Henry VIII's will was next in succession after Elizabeth herself (Catherine was descended from Henry VIII's younger sister Mary). By law, they needed Elizabeth's permission to marry, but fearing her refusal, they arranged a clandestine marriage. When Elizabeth found out about it, she had the marriage declared void and threw both parties into prison when they failed to produce the clergyman who had married them. In prison, Catherine gave birth first to a son named Edward, and then later to a second son, Thomas, apparently to Elizabeth's exceeding disgust. When Catherine died in 1568, both children were still officially illegitimate. Edward was released from prison in 1571 and married Frances in 1586; they had no children. Both Edward and Frances seem to have gone out of their way to court Elizabeth's favor. Most famously, in 1591 they invited the queen to Elvetham, where they lavishly entertained her. A contemporary observer described Elizabeth's entrance to the house, where "accompanied with divers honourable Ladies and Gentlewomen, [Frances] moste humbly on hir knees welcomed hir Highnesse to that place: who most graciously imbracing hir, tooke hir up, and kissed hir, using manie comfortable and princely Speeches, as wel to hir, as to the Earl of Hertford standing hard by, to the great rejoysing of manie beholders."

In 1595 Edward again stirred up trouble, petitioning to have his first marriage declared valid, thus legitimizing his sons and making them possible heirs to the throne. By this point, Elizabeth was already growing old, and, disturbingly for her, there was some public support for putting a Grey heir on the throne. When Elizabeth heard about Edward's latest efforts, she was furious and had him thrown into the Tower again. Learning how distressed Frances was, she wrote this letter, assuring her that no matter what her husband did, Frances would always retain Elizabeth's favor. Notice especially the familiar term of address, "Good Francke," repeated twice in the letter. This letter is all the more significant given Elizabeth's supposed comment on her deathbed, when asked whether the young Edward Seymour should be her successor. Apparently she replied, "I will have no raskalls son in my seat but one worthy to be a king" (but see chapter 6,

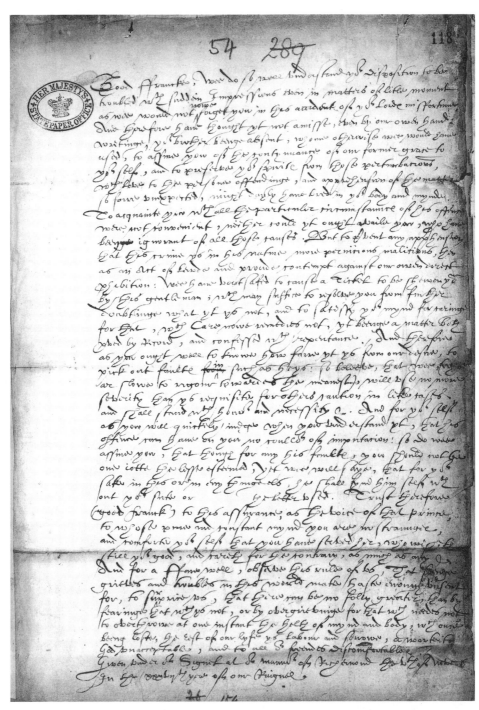

5.5: Elizabeth I to Frances (Howard) Seymour, Countess of Hertford (November 1595). The National Archives, London (formerly Public Record Office).

Elizabeth Southwell's "A True Relation of what succeeded at the sickness and death of Queen Elizabeth.") Edward's sons were eventually legitimized in 1606, three years after Elizabeth's death, when the clergyman who had married Edward and Catherine mysteriously reappeared fifty years after performing the ceremony. Legends about Elizabeth usually emphasize her jealousy of her women; letters like this remind us that she could also be a warm and supportive friend.

Transcription

Good Francke, Wee do so well understand your disposition to be troubled with sudden Impressions even in matters of litle moment as wee would not nowe forget yow in this accident of your Lords misfortune. And therefore have thought yt not amisse, even by owr owen hand writinge, your brother beinge absent, whome otherwise wee would have used, to assure yow of the contynuance of our former grace to yourself, and to preserve your spirites from those perturbacions, which love to the persone offendinge, and apprehension of the matter so farre unexpected, might dayly have bred in your body and mynde. To acquainte yow with all the particuler circumstaunces of his offence were not convenient, neither could yt ought availe yow, who have ben ignorant of all those causes. But to prevent any apprehension that this crime ys in his nature more pernicious, malicious than as an Act of lewde and proude contempt against owr owen direct prohibition: Wee have voutsafed to cause a Ticket to be shewen you by this gentleman; which may suffice to resolve you from further doubtinge what yt is not, and to satesfy your mynd for caring for that, which Care nowe remedies not, yt beinge a matter both proved by record, and confessed with repentance. And therefore as you ought well to knowe how farre yt ys from owr desire, to pick out faultes in such as Heys: so beleeve, that wee, (who ar slowe to rigour towardes the meanest), will use no more severity than ys requisite for others caution in like cases, and shall stand with honour and necessity. And for yourself as yow will quickely judge when yow understand yt, that his offence can have on you no coullour of imputacion: so do wee assure yow, that though for any [of] his faultes, yow should not be one jotte the lesse esteemed, Yet wee will saye, that for your sake in this or in any thinge els, he shall fynd him self with out your sute or [blank space] the better used. Trust therefore (good franck) to this assurance, as the voice of that prince, to whose pure and constant mynd you are no straunger, and comforte yourself that you have served her, who wisheth still your good, and careth for the contrary, as much as [indecipherable.] And for a Fare well, observe this rule of us, That seeing grieves and troubles in this world make haste enough unsent for, to surprise us, that there can be no folly greater than by fearinge that which ys not, or by overgrievinge for that which needes not, to overthrowe at one instant the helth of mynd and body, which once being loste, the rest of owr lyfe ys labour and sorrowe, a woork to God unacceptable, and to all our freendes discomfortable. Gyven under our Signet at our mannour of Richemond the vth of november In the xxxviith yere of owr Raigne.

NELY KEINANEN
UNIVERSITY OF HELSINKI

Elizabeth I, letter to Frances, Countess of Hertford (November 1595). The National Archives, London (formerly Public Record Office) S.P. 12/254.

Deare father I doo hear that you ar going in to
Oxford shear I ully besech you to remember my
vmbull seryice to my lord and my lady and
that you will speak to my lady to send me
som cloutes and shall think my self much
bound to hur for she pomest me sum whem I
was with child of my furst but I was so well
prouided, that I thoucht to rescavce them till
I had sum ned of them which is nou for I haue
had somany that thay haue wouren vu my all
thinges, therfor I must try my frindes a
gaine for I truf that you haue sum ould
shurtes in a cornot for me or som old thinges
and I do hear giue you many vmbull thank
es for the stouelef you sent me by my
husbond and I besech you to send me the
yala tafaty quilt that if to the blak velua
bead if you do not youesit which I do think
you haue no caues to youes it being the bed
if gon thus with my vmbull sarues to yr
your self crauing your blesiig I rene
your duty full dauter
I to command Lettis Gaudy

Child bed lennen

chillderic

and

wrought stuols

yellow tafaty quilt

5.6: Lettice Gawdy to her father Sir Robert Knollys (c. 1620). By permission of The British Library.

Lettice Gawdy to her father Sir Robert Knollys (c. 1620)

Transcription

	Deare father I doo hear that you ar going into
	Oxfordshear I umbully besech you to remember my
	umbull seryice to my lord and my lady and
	that you will speak to my lady to send me
	som cloutes and I shall think my self much
Child bed	bound to hur for she pomest me sum whem I
linnen	was with child of my furst but I was so well
	provided, that I thouht to researve them till
	I had som ned of them which is nou for I have
	had so many chilldric that thay have wouren pu all my

had so many chilldric that thay have wouren pu all my
thinges and therfor I must try my frindes a
gaine for I trus that you have sum ould
shurtes in a cornor for me or som old thinges
and I do hear give you many umbull thank
wrought =es for the to rout stoueles you sent me by my
Stools husbond and I besech you to send me the
yellow yala tafaty quilt that is to the blak velvat
taffaty Quilt bead if you do not youes it which I do think
you have no caues to youes it being the bed
is gon Thus with my umbull sarves to
your self craving your blesing I [unclear]ene
your duty full dauter
to command Lettis Gaudy

Commentary

The Gawdy family of Norfolk, England, rose to distinction in the Tudor period, when the fortunes of the family were founded by three half-brothers who achieved positions of eminence as lawyers. The eldest was Thomas Gawdy, sergeant-at-law, who became recorder of Norwich and Lynn; the second, Sir Thomas Gawdy, became justice of the Queen's Bench; the third brother, Sir Francis Gawdy, was chief justice of the Common Pleas. The influence of these three lawyers eventually brought the Gawdys into very close contact with prominent persons and state affairs, a situation that lasted throughout the sixteenth and seventeenth centuries.

In 1608, Framlingham Gawdy, the great-grandson of Thomas Gawdy Sr., married Lettice, daughter of Sir Robert Knollys (Knowles) of Berkshire, in London. The wedding took place in Sir Robert's private house, which later (after Lettice's death) caused a member of the Gawdys of Claxton, George Gawdy, to attempt to prove that their marriage was invalid because it had not been registered in the church. By claiming that Framlingham and Lettice had not in fact been lawfully married, George Gawdy hoped to have their children disentitled to any inheritance on their father's part. Fortunately, the case was tried and the marriage declared valid.

The marriage seems to have been a happy one. Framlingham was generally considered a kindly, affectionate person, which, among other things, can be seen by his role as the kind of head of the family to whom friends and relatives wrote about the troubles and joys in their lives. Unfortunately, there are not many facts told about Lettice herself in the Gawdy pedigree, except that after giving birth to ten children, she died in 1630.

Lettice's letters are full of everyday gossip and greetings from relatives and friends, as well as news about the health of her children and herself. It also seems that she greatly misses the fashion scene in London, since she frequently asks for clothes that are better than those in Norfolk. Her postscripts are filled with requests for diverse things, and she does not seem to let her addressees forget their duty to her at any time.

The letter presented here was written to her father as a request for clothes for herself and her children. She uses clear italic hand, and her spelling is typical of women in the seventeenth century. The spelling variants in the letter also reflect her pronunciation and, what has become evident after a further study of her letters, her dyslexia. The endorsement reading "To my uery louing father Sr Robt Knollys knight in the newe buyldnigs at St Martyrs lane in Westminster. theis be del" is written on the reverse side of the folio.

MINNA NEVALA
UNIVERSITY OF HELSINKI

Lettice Gawdy. Letter to her father Sir Robert Knollys. British Library MS Additional 27,395, f. 125.

Elizabeth (Tansfield) Cary, Viscountess Falkland, to Susan (Villiers) Fielding, Countess of Denbigh (c. December 1626)

Commentary

Elizabeth Cary, Viscountess Falkland (1585/6–1639) addresses this holograph letter: "To my noble frend the lady Countesse of Denbigh." Although undated, it was written soon after her conversion to Roman Catholicism in November 1626. Of the fifteen letters in her hand known to be extant, this is the only one addressed to a woman. As sister to the duke of Buckingham, Lady Falkland's kinswoman Susan (Villiers) Fielding, Countess of Denbigh, was one of the "three Buckingham ladyes," as Lady Falkland referred to them, along with Katherine (Manners) Villiers, Duchess of Buckingham, who had been Catholic prior to her marriage to the king's favorite, George Villiers, Duke of Buckingham, and the duke's mother, Mary (Beaumont), Countess of Buckingham, who converted c. 1622.

In the year leading up to this letter, Lady Denbigh and Lady Falkland frequented the London residence of Richard Neile, Bishop of Durham, where they were introduced to the tenets of English Arminianism, a more "Catholic" and anti-Calvinistic version of the Church of England, by its two chief proponents, Richard Montague and John Cosin. In August 1626, Montague reported to Cosin that at a dinner with the duke and duchess of Buckingham, the countess of Buckingham, and Lady Denbigh, he had "mett, and had much good talke with, that worshipfull Lady Faulkland" (Durham Univ., Mickleton MS 26, fol. 20). However, Lady Falkland was not swayed by the proselytizing of Montague and Cosin and began spending time at the residence of the Catholic earl of Ormond, where she "mett and grew acquainted with some catholikes and Priests," and where "she was soone convinced" that her conscience could be clear only as a member of the Church of Rome (*Lady Falkland: Her Life*, fol. 13ʳ).

Despite her resolution, Lady Falkland delayed her conversion for nearly half a year because Lady Denbigh repeatedly promised to convert with her "after hearing one more dispute . . . which having heard, she desired another . . . and after that another" (*Life*, fol. 13ʳ). When Lady Falkland finally went to court to issue an ultimatum to her friend, Lady Denbigh responded, "Well, I have you now in the court, and heere I will keepe you, you shall lye in my chamber and shall not goe forth" (*Life*, fol. 13ʳ). However, Lady Falkland managed to escape to Lord Ormond's house, where she was reconciled in a stable by an English Benedictine priest. Lady Denbigh promptly reported her friend's conversion to her brother, who then informed Charles I.

A newsletter dated 17 November 1626, notes that "the Lady Falkland is newly banished the Court, for lately going to Masse with the Queene: in whose conversion the Romane Church will reape no great credit, because she was called home out of Ireland for hir greivious extortions" (BL, Harleian MS 390, fols 161–62). Two weeks later, Alexander Cook reported to James Ussher, Archbishop of Armagh, that Lady Falkland "hath declared her self to be a Papist," and that when she was berated by Montague and Cosin for damaging the reputation of English Arminians, she "protested, that if ever she turned again, she will turn puritan, not moderate protestant, as she phraseth it, for moderate protestants, viz. Mr Coosens &c. are further from the catholics than puritans" (Parr, 1686, pp. 372–73). According to *Lady Falkland: Her Life*, when Cosin learned of Lady Falkland's

5.7: Elizabeth (Tanfield) Cary, Viscountess Falkland, to Susan (Villiers) Fielding, Countess of Denbigh (c. December 1626). The National Archives, London (formerly Public Record Office).

Transcription

Madam

I am much perplexed with many worldly accidents, as you know I have cause. I intend within this two dayes for ought I yet know, to goe downe to Aldnam, where though there bee no stuffe for my children, there is a bed for my selfe. I beseech you let mee know whither togither with your frendship to mee, you have cast of all your care of what belongs to mee. I have heere sent you the gentlewoman, mrs Waterhouse, I meane, that is to attend your daughter. if please you to talke with hir, you shall see, shee is able to give you con-tentment. I desire to know whither Victoria may waite upon you, or no, for shee greeves so, heere, as I know not what to doe, with hir. I beseech you have a care of hir. shee comes as of your beliefe, and free from any thoughts of the contrary, and so doth their attendant. I humbly thanke you and my lord your brother, for your care of mee, though I wish it had bene in another kinde, but I must thinke my selfe bound to mr cosens, while I live, for the paines hee takes, though, I wish any man else, had bene imployde rather. secretary cooke was with mee even now, and brought mee a most gracious message, from the kinge, and showed a greate deale of care to persuade mee himselfe, but to whom shall I goe, to learne, which of the two to beleeve, for mr cosens taught mee one doctrine, and hee another, but madam if the question were betweene those two, I coulde well tell, what to resolve. for hee ses, I must onely bee guided by illumination, and not beleeve the church of england, as it is the church of england, but as I am instructed, out of the scripture. I humbly rest your ladyships servant E Falkland

conversion, he "fell into so great and violent a trowble, that casting himself on the ground he would not rise nor eate from morning till night, weeping even to roaring; using for arguments (to make her returne) the disgrace of their company, and that she would hurt others making them afraid of them, and that every one would say this was the end of those that received their opinions" (*Life*, fols. 13ᵛ-14ʳ).

Lady Falkland opens her letter by expressing her sadness at Lady Denbigh's apparent betrayal of their pact to convert together and her subsequent reporting of Lady Falkland's conversion to the duke of Buckingham. As a result, Charles I (whose wife, Henrietta Maria, was Catholic) confined Lady Falkland to her house on Drury Lane for six weeks and her husband, living in Dublin as Lord Deputy of Ireland, cut off all support. While Lady Falkland intended to take refuge at her manor house at Aldenham, Hertfordshire, she needed to find places for the rest of her household, particularly her daughter Victoria, who "greeves so, heere." Lord Falkland was equally concerned about Victoria's welfare, asking the king to vouchsafe that he would take "my Innocent child hir Daughter" into the royal household, to "deliver the Innocent soule from the certaine and imminent perill of utter perdition; and not to impute the sinns of the Mother onto the Daughter" (Ezekiel 18:20) (PRO, SP 63/243/503).

While the letter initially sounds heartfelt, the tone rapidly shifts from genuine despair to disappointment and cynicism. Lady Falkland perhaps hints at Lady Denbigh's hypocrisy in remaining with the Church of England when she writes that Victoria "comes as of your beliefe." With no small irony, she thanks Lady Denbigh and her brother, the duke, for their "care" of her though she wishes "it had bene in another kinde," and expresses gratitude to John Cosin for the "paines" he took in trying to persuade her to return to the Church of England, but wished that "any man else, had bene imployde rather." She refers to the opposing doctrines of Cosin and Sir John Coke, her mortal enemy, and seemingly enjoys that she had been told that she must be guided by "illumination" and Scripture. Roman Catholics believed that the continuous visibility of their church and its traditions indicated that it was the true church, while Protestants argued that their church, always visible to the elect, followed the pure doctrine of Scripture and had not fallen into the corruption of the Church of Rome.

The rift between Lady Falkland and Lady Denbigh was short-lived. Within months of this letter, the "three Buckingham ladyes" were again supporting Lady Falkland's cause at court, as well as loaning her money (for two letters from the duchess of Buckingham on her behalf, see PRO, SP 16/58/17 and SP 16/71/55). By 1636, six of Lady Falkland's nine surviving children converted to Catholicism. The duchess of Buckingham returned to the Church of Rome in 1635, shortly after marrying her second husband, Randal Macdonnell, Earl of Antrim. Lady Denbigh finally converted in Paris in 1651.

HEATHER WOLFE
FOLGER SHAKESPEARE LIBRARY

Elizabeth Cary, Viscountess Falkland. Letter to Susan (Villiers) Fielding, Countess of Denbigh (c. December 1626). The National Archives, London (formerly Public Record Office) SP 16/522/117.

Eleanor Davies (Lady Douglas) to her daughter Lucy Hastings (7 December 1629)

Commentary

A letter from Eleanor Davies to her daughter Lucy Hastings (HA 2334), dated 7 December 1629, is part of a cache of twelve letters from Davies to her daughter which survive in the Correspondence Folders in the Hastings papers in the Huntington Library. These mingle prophetic commentary (like those found in her published prophecies); discussion of Davies's own complex lawsuits (the Hastings papers record the litigation Davies resorted to, in order to control her estates after the death of her first husband, Sir John Davies); and, as here, discussion of more personal matters. This letter is a rare example of a grandmother from this period expressing concern for her grandchildren. Davies was notorious for being an eccentric (perhaps even lunatic) prophet. In these Huntington letters we see rather Davies with a strong grasp of the quotidian: "keepe your little one warme, this winter with wollen Cotes." The "little one" is evidently the Lady Elizabeth Langham, Lucy Hastings's daughter, who lived until 1664, and who was herself commemorated in an elegy by Bathsua Makin.

The relationship between Davies and her daughter was clearly very close. Davies herself had three children, but only one, Lucy, survived childhood. She and her husband, Ferdinando, Lord Hastings, supported Davies during her litigious period in the 1620 and 1630s. Their petitions were crucial in having Davies released from Bedlam in 1640. Davies had been incarcerated for despoiling Lichfield Cathedral in 1636. Lucy's epitaph for her mother praised her as "erudita super sexum" (more learned than her sex); the Hastings papers contain notebooks and reflections that suggest Lucy inherited her mother's religious obsessions; and finally the Folger Library holds the largest surviving collection of Davies prophecies, some forty in all, bound together by her daughter.

This is a very typical seventeenth-century letter. It is comprised of a single quarto sheet, with the message written on the recto side. The letter would then be folded, sealed, and delivered. The physical manuscript of these letters still show the folds; often part of the wax seals survives also. Until 1635 there was no government postal service, but many private agents transported the mail by horse and on foot.

Seventeenth-century scribes were trained in secretary hand to be regular and anonymous. More private communications, such as this letter, show a great deal of individuality. The power of Davies's personality resonates through all these letters. The force of the downstrokes here is striking. The signature shows a vigor evident whenever Davies signs her own name (see, for example, "Bathe daughter of BabyLondon" in chapter 4). The "Douglas" here is for Davies's second husband, Sir Archibald Douglas, whom she married in 1628. The initial letters "E" and "D" are especially forceful. These alphabetical letters formed part of Davies's prophetic repertoire, available also through the name of her first husband, Sir John Davies. The swirls beneath "uppon" and "Eleanor Douglas" show the pugnacious élan that was Davies's characteristic address to her world.

Daughter Hastings, J am indebted
Vnto you for many letters. it is not
forgetfullnefs that puts mee fo much
Vpon the feore. J pray remember
My blefeing to your little Daughter
J hope J shall not fayle in My prayers
to god for you bothe. J thanke you
for puting mee m Minde, fo often
thereof. and this charge J laye
Vpon you. to fieepe your little one
Warme, this winter with wollen
Cotes / Children perish as foone
through pride as pouertye, the lords
blefeing. bee vppon you bothe

your very louing
mother
Eleanor Douglas

St James December y 7
. 1629 .

your Aunts my la Amy.
& my la elizabeth commend
their affections vnto you.

5.8: Eleanor Davies (Lady Douglas) to her daughter Lucy Hastings (7 December 1629). Reproduced by permission of The Huntington Library, San Marino, California.

Transcription

Daughter Hastings, I am indebted unto you for Many letters. it is not forgetfullness that puts Mee so Much upon the score. I pray remember My bleseing to your little Daughter I hope I shall not fayle in My prayers to god for you bothe. I thanke you for puting mee in Minde so offten thereof. and this charge I laye upon you. to keepe your little one warme, this winter with wollen Cotes / Children perish as soone throughe pride as povertye, the lords bleseing. bee uppon you bothe

your very loving
Mother
Eleanor Douglas

St James December the 7
          1629

[written sideways]
your aunts my lady Amy & my my lady Elizabeth commend Their affections unto you.

MARK HOULAHAN
UNIVERSITY OF WAIKATO

Eleanor Davies, Lady Douglas. Letter to her daughter, Lucy Hastings (7 December 1629). Hastings MS, Huntington Library HA 2334.

Sonn

i reseaued your letter and kniely thanke
you and my Dester for your pie
i did not know ma Swan was gon doune
i had though to haue sent a letter by him
i did mariel i did not heare from you
before at last i gessed you weare not com
home from keepeing your crismus i am
sorri you haue struch a greate cold
i haue been ueri ill with a cofe sence
which is not yet gon i had a lamenes in
my wrist which cassed a great paine in
my hann that i cold not doo ani thinke
with it pray send to the wuddow fakele
for my rent an if Sir tomines Derten
com up this tearme intreate hem
to bring it up James is not yet gon
out of London what his case of sta
is i know not heare is a gread dele
of nues but i am not at this time
well a noufe to relate it unto you
my cossen esday has a nague
my sonn Barrow an his wife with
your sister Bess remembers theare
loues to you an theare sester
thus in hast i rest your touenig
mother Katherin Oxinden
                January 14 1635

5.9: Katherine (Sprakeling) Oxinden to her son Henry Oxinden (14 January 1636). By permission of The British Library.

Katherine (Sprakeling) Oxinden to her son Henry Oxinden (14 January 1636)

Transcription

Sonn

i reseived your letter and kinely thanke you and my Dafter for your Pie i did not know Msa Swan was gon doune i had though to have sent a letter by him i did marvel i did not heare from you before at last i gessed you weare not com home from keepeing your Crismus i am sorri you have shuch a greate cold i have binn veri ill with a coffe sence which is not yet gon i had a lamenes in my wrist which cassed a great paine in my hann that i cold not doo ani thinke with it pray send to the widdow fakele for my rent an if Sir Tommis Payten com up this tearme intreate hem to bring it up James is not yet gon out of London what his case of stay is i know not heare is a great dele of nwes but i am not at this time well a noufe to relate it unto you my Cossen esday has a nague My son Barrow an his wife with your sister Bess rememberes theare loves to you an theare Sister thus in hast i rest

your loveing mother

Kathrin Oxinden

Januari 14 1636

Commentary

Katherine Oxinden's (1587–1642) extant letters reveal something of the everyday life in the seventeenth-century Kent, England. The autograph letters now preserved in the British Library were written in the 1630s, when Katherine was in her forties and already a widow. The recipients of these letters were Katherine's close relatives, namely, her eldest son, Henry, and her son-in-law Thomas Barrow, whose house was periodically her home too, and her landlord, Sir Peter Heyman. Common topics include thanking for the previous letter or a particular favor, money, local events, and news about friends and relatives; particularly their health is frequently commented on. In this letter Katherine writes to Henry, a married man in his late twenties, and thanks him and his wife for a pie they have probably sent her, tells them about her poor health, and asks Henry to deal with the rent.

Katherine was born into the large family of Sir Adam Sprakeling, of St. Paul's Parish and of Ellington in the Isle of Thanet, and Lady Sprakeling. She married Richard Oxinden (1588–1629) in 1607, when she had just come of age. Her nineteen-year-old husband was the younger son of Sir Henry Oxinden, of Deane near Canterbury. Their first son, Henry, was born the following year, and a couple of years later in 1610, Richard was settled on the property once belonging to his maternal grandfather. A busy period must have followed, as the couple started developing the estate, planting hedges, and enlarging the houses. Two more sons and two daughters were yet to come.

Katherine's italic hand, typical of the women of the period, reveals a fairly poor level of literacy. The lack of proper education is reflected in her idiosyncratic phonetic spelling—she writes as she speaks—and in the absence of punctuation marks. For example, she spells "daughter" (meaning daughter-in-law) as "dafter" (indicating the pronunciation). Literacy in general was rare in the early seventeenth century and started to improve only towards the end of the century. Approximately 90 percent of the women and 70 percent of the men of the time were illiterate. However, the number of those who could not read or write varied according to region and social rank. For instance, Londoners were more literate than the inhabitants of the provincial areas, and the male members of the gentry, the clergy, and the professionals were more literate than the lower social ranks. Irrespective of social status, women's literacy lagged far behind. Most women simply did not need writing skills in their daily household and child-rearing routines, and even higher up in the social hierarchy educating women was seldom considered necessary. Reading and writing were, moreover, taught separately in this order, so that writing was clearly a more advanced skill that required both time and money to acquire. It is possible that in Katherine's childhood family money was spent on the education of her several brothers and the girls had to manage with far less formal education.

Minna Palander-Collin
University of Helsinki

Katherine Oxinden to her son Henry Oxinden, 14 January 1636. British Library MS Additional 27,999 f. 277.

Mary (Mildmay) Fane, Countess of Westmorland, to Secretary of State Windebanke (6 May 1639)

Commentary

Mary Fane, Countess of Westmorland, was born in 1582, the only child of Sir Anthony and Grace Sherrington Mildmay. Little information about her childhood is available; even the celebrated autobiography of her mother, Grace Mildmay, (see chapter 6) makes scant mention of her only daughter. However, given her mother's own impressive education, including her knowledge of domestic matters and religion, as well as her own later writings, we can conclude that Mary was encouraged from an early age to study both the traditional skills of a sixteenth-century gentlewoman and the more learned subjects of languages and religion.

In 1599, Mary Mildmay married Sir Francis Fane of Mereworth in Kent. Francis Fane was named Knight of the Bath at the 1603 coronation of James I and then first Earl of Westmorland in 1624. When Mary's father, Sir Anthony Mildmay, died in 1617, she and Sir Francis moved to the Mildmay estate at Apethorpe in Northamptonshire, which became the primary residence and financial holding for the Westmorland family. Sir Francis died in 1628, passing his title to their eldest son, Mildmay Fane, then age twenty-five. In many ways, however, Mary Fane assumed the role of family patriarch after the death of her husband and continued in that role until her own death in 1640. Her letters of advice to her children, contained in collections in the Northamptonshire Records Office and the Folger Library, but not released at this time for publication, show her to be a strong-willed and capable woman. The same qualities appear in the letters she wrote to Charles I's secretaries of state, especially the one transcribed here, written to Windebanke in May, 1639.

Of all the extant letters of Mary Fane, the one transcribed here in its entirety is the most engaging. In it she critiques one of Charles I's most significant and ultimately disastrous military and political decisions, that of sending an army into Scotland to enforce the adoption of his revised Book of Common Prayer. That she is aware she has entered into a dangerous arena is clear from her opening sentence. What is not clear is whether her reference to "things above us" is an acknowledgment of her stepping out of a woman's role by engaging in political discussion of such weighty matters or whether she is suggesting that any of the king's subjects would be "meddling" by writing a letter taking exception to such a decision as that of warring against the Scots. At the very least, the content, if not the tone, of this letter affirms Margaret Ezell's contention in *The Patriarch's Wife*, that "the early demise of the patriarchal figure and transference of his authority to his widow, even if his place was later taken by a stepfather, sharply undercuts the image of the seventeenth-century patriarchalism as an unbroken right of male dominance passed from father to husband" (34). What is clearly gender-based, however, is her justifying her need to speak through the maternal concern for unborn children who will be affected by the events unfolding and by alluding to the influence of women in Scotland on the actions of the husbands and sons. Her reference to personal interest is maternal as well; both her eldest sons, Sir Mildmay and Sir Francis, accompanied the king on his expedition. Even this gender-based, maternal concern affirms Margaret P. Hannay's contention that "the public nature of many of these duties (recorded in diaries) warns us against taking too much for

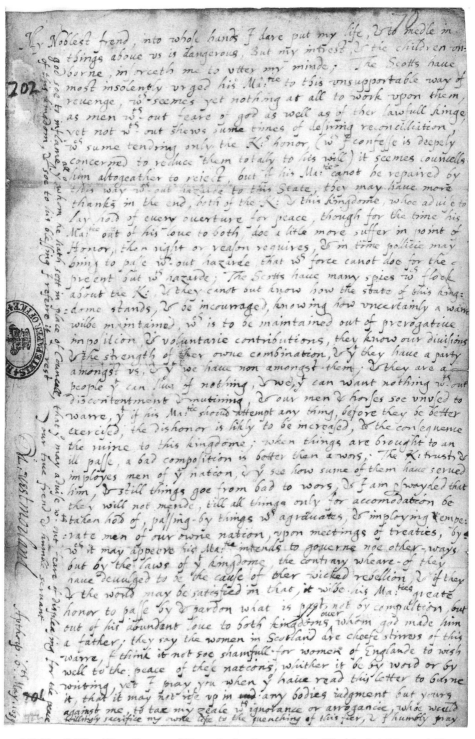

5.10: Mary (Mildmay) Fane, Countess of Westmorland, to Secretary of State Windebanke (6 May 1639). The National Archives, London (formerly Public Record Office).

Transcription

My noblest frend, into whose hands I dare put my life, & to medle in things above us is dangerous, But my intrest, & the children unborne, inforceth me to utter my minde; The Scotts have most insolently urged his Majestie to this unsupportable way of revenge, which seemes yet nothing at all to work upon them, as men without feare of god as well as of ther lawfull kinge, yet not without shews sumetimes of desiring reconcilliation, which sume tendring only the King's honor (which I confesse is deepely concerned to reduce them totally to his will) it seemes councells him altogeather to reject, but if his Majestie canot be repaired by this way without hazarde to this State, they may have more thanks in the end, both of the King & this kingdome, whoe advise to lay hold of every overture for peace, though for the time his Majestie, out of his love to both, doe a litle more suffer in point of Honor, then right or reason requires, & in time pollicie may bring to passe without hazarde that which force canot doe for the present but with hazarde; The Scotts have many spies which flock about the King & they canot but know how the state of this kingdome stands, & be incourraged, knowing how uncertainly a war wilbe maintained which is to be maintained out of prerogative, imposition, & voluntarie contributions, they know our divisions, & the strength of ther owne combination, & that they have a party amongst us, & that we have non amongst them; & they are a people that can live of nothing, & we that can want nothing without discontentment & mutining, & our men & horses so unused to warre, that if his Majestie should attempt any thing, before they be better exercised, the dishonor is likly to be increased, & the consequence the ruine to this kingdome; when things are brought to an ill passe, a bad composition is better then a wors. The King trusts & imployes men of that nation, & you see how sume of them have served him, & still things goe from bad to wors, & I am perswayded that they will not mende, till all things only for accomodation be taken hold of, passing-by things which agravates, & imploying temperate men of our owne nation, upon meetings of treaties, by which it may appeere his Majestie intends to governe noe other-ways but by the laws of that kingdome, the contrary wheare-of they have devulged to be the cause of ther wicked rebellion, & if they & the world may be satisfied in that, it wilbe his Majesties greate honor to passe by & pardon what is past, not by compultion, but out of his abundant love to both kingdoms over whom god made him a father; they say the women in Scotland are cheefe stirrers of this warre, I think it not soe shamfull for women of Englande to wish well to the peace of these nations, whither it be by word or by writing; that I pray you when you have read this letter, to burn it, that it may not rise up in any bodies judgment but yours against me, to tax my zeal with ignorance or arrogance, who would willingly sacrifice my owne life for the quenching of this fier, & I humbly pray [written sideways in left margin] god soe to inflame all you whom he has sett in place of Councell that you may advise without feare of displeasing for the peace of this kingdom, & soe to his blessing I referre it & rest your true frend & humble servant,

      M. Westmorland Apthorp 6th May, 1639

granted the new truism that women were increasingly relegated to the private sphere in the Renaissance. This may well be true in a general sense, but historical documents establish that it is not true of these aristocratic women, for responsibilities to their families provided an entry into the public world" (48). Clearly, Mary Fane saw her dual responsibility as "head" of the family and concerned mother as sufficient justification to comment on what she considered a serious miscalculation on the part of the king, a conclusion that history bears out as being valid.

Also interesting about this letter is Mary Fane's judgment that the king has not been well served by those who offer advice; historians have concluded the same about Charles I's reign for the past three and a half centuries. By offering words that suggest a desire to advise the king, and in that advice rejecting the words of men who she felt misled him, Mary Fane clearly felt no constraint based on gender, except in the fact that she asked Windebanke to destroy her letter, indicating her knowledge that were the missive to fall into other hands, it would serve her ill. Yet, in these times when Charles I was faced with such adversity, any writer attacking his policies might well have wished for the same consideration, be that writer male or female.

GERALD W. MORTON
AUBURN UNIVERSITY MONTGOMERY

Mary (Mildmay) Fane, Countess of Westmorland, to Secretary of State Windebanke (6 May 1639). The National Archives, London (formerly Public Record Office) SP16/420 f. 202.

Elizabeth Richardson, Baroness Cramond, Autograph dedicatory epistle to Sir Edward Dering, *A Ladies Legacie to Her Daughters* (1645)

Commentary

In *A Ladies Legacie to Her Daughters*, Elizabeth Richardson heads the first printed dedicatory epistle with the engraving of an ornately carved chest, rather than the typical flourish or abstract ornamentation. Like the other overt and implied juxtapositions of her private and public obligations, the chest suggests, as do her many references to legacies, that Richardson was aware that this book was the extent of material wealth she could bequeath her children. On the blank page preceding this dedication, Richardson inscribed a copy of her legacy book with this autograph letter to her grandson, son of her daughter Anne, wife of Sir Edward Deering, Knight and Baronet. In this gift copy, held by the Houghton Library, Richardson amends the title to *A Mothers Legacie to Her Six Daughters*, and her awareness of her duties as mother and grandmother seems foremost on her mind as she inscribes this text. At the same time, Richardson's preoccupation with social status, power, and autonomy is evident in her use of both filial and baronetcy titles for her grandson in the salutation, "This, for my deerly beloved & worthy Grandson, Sr. Ed: Dering Kt. Baronet," and for herself in her closure, "Your most affectionate Granmother. Elizabeth Cramond."

The issue of title and the rhetoric of this epistle indicate Richardson's vexed relationship with her male heirs in general. Her notation of family and peerage titles in the letter makes clear not just her connection to this boy, but her elevation over him, as grandmother and baroness over grandson and knight baronet. She apologizes to Edward for the unworthiness of the book and notes that she has corrected this copy for him, but she also asserts that because he is one of hers, she does not doubt his "loving acceptance of it." Richardson's motives for this epistle become apparent in the book's second printed epistle, "A letter to my four daughters," in which she discusses her vexed relationship with her sons. Richardson makes it quite clear that these problems are due wholly to their maleness; the fault is theirs, not hers:

> I know you may have many better instructers then my self, yet can you have no true mother but me, who not only with great paine brought you into the world, but do now still travell in care for the new birth of your soules. . . . And howsoever this my endeavour may be contemptible to many, (because a womans) which makes me not to joyne my sons with you, left being men, they misconstrue my well-meaning; yet I presume that you my daughters will not refuse your Mothers teaching.

In an apology set between the two printed epistolary dedications, Richardson describes her book as written wholly for women; it is "devotions or prayers, which surely concernes and belongs to women as well as to the best learned men." But if Richardson embraces the opportunity to instruct her daughters, she is also aware of her obligation to instruct her male progeny, at least in their religious lives. The dichotomy of Richardson's difficulties with her sons and her duty seems to prompt both her apologies to her grandson and her insistence that he "will gently censure, & beare with all." She draws empowerment and

5.11: Elizabeth Richardson, Baroness Cramond, Autograph dedicatory epistle to Sir Edward Dering, *A Ladies Legacie to Her Daughters* (1645). By permission of the Houghton Library, Harvard University.

autonomy from religious endorsement that she instruct all her children in the ways of "Godes servis & glory," and from her elevated position in the peerage in order to insist that he, like her female children "make daily use" of her teaching.

Transcription

This, for my deerly beloved & worthy Grandson, Sir Edward Dering Knight Baronet.

My love-worthy, & first Grand-Child, I present (as due) this poore Booke unto you, which I at first Intended, only for all my Children & Grand-children; for their Instruction in their youth, & for their use, & remembrance of me afterwardes; now you being one of mine, & this coming from me, I nothing doubt of your loving acceptance of it, for my sake, though in it selfe, unworthy to have a roome in your Liberary, or to come into the veiw of any Judicious eye, that may soone spye more faultes, than leaves; yet I know you would in your owne goodnes, pardon & excuse, all defectes therein, that comes from me, a weake unlearned woman, who being so neare unto you, you will gently censure, & beare with all. But indeed it is so falsly Printed, as without it be corrected, you will meet with many adsurdities, which by some may be imputed unto me, though not by you; therefore I have a little helped the most faulty places, desiring you to do the like by this, in the other 2. bookes. Now I hope of one Comfort, which you will vouchsafe me, at my ernest request, that you will not faile, to make daily use thereof, to Godes servis & glory; which I beleeve will turne to your owne happines, in drawing downe all blessinges from God upon you, as is desired by,

   Your most affectionate
   Granmother. Elizabeth Cramond.

Roxanne Harde
Queen's University

Elizabeth (Beaumont) Ashburnham Richardson, Baroness Cramond. *A Ladies Legacie to Her Daughters. In three Books. Composed of Prayers and Meditations, fitted for severall times, and upon severall occasions. As also severall Prayers for each day in the Weeke* (1645). Houghton Library, Harvard University. Thomason Tracts 251. Autograph letter.

5.12: Dorothy Osborne to William Temple (1652-4). By permission of The British Library.

Dorothy Osborne to William Temple (1652–4)

Transcription

[fol. 60v]

how few there are that Ever heard of such a thing, and Fewer that understand it, besyd's
it tis not to bee taught or Learn'd it must come Naturaly to those that have it and they
must have it before they can know it, but I admire since she has is not how she can bee
sattisfyed with her condition, nothing Else sure can recompence the Alteration you say is
made in her fortune, what was it took her, her husbands good face, what could invite her
where there was neither fortune witt nor good usage and a husband to whome she was but
indifferent which is all one to mee if not worse then an Aversion and I should sooner hope
to gaine upon one that Hated mee then upon one that did not consider mee Enough
Either to Love or hate mee; ile swere she is much Easyer to please then I should bee, there
are a great many ingredients must goe to the makeing mee happy in a husband, first as my
Cousin Fr: say's our humors must agree and to doe that hee must have that kinde of breeding that I have had and used that kinde of company that is hee must not bee soe much a
Country Gentleman as to understand Nothing but hawks and dog's and bee fonder of
Either then of his wife, nor of the next sort of them whose aime reaches noe farther then
to bee Justice of peace and once in his life high Sheriff, who read noe book but statut's and
study's nothing but how to make a speech enterlarded with Latin that may amaze his dis-
agreeing poore Neighbours and fright them rather then perswade them into quietnesse;
hee must not bee a thing that began the world in a free scoole was sent from thence to the
university and is at his farthest when hee reaches the Inns of Court has noe acquaintance
but those of his forme in these places speaks the french hee has pickt out of old Law's and
admires nothing but the storry's hee has hear[d] of the Revells that were kept there before
his Time; hee may not bee a Towne Gallant neither that lives in a Tavern and an ordinary
that cannot imagin how an hower should bee spent without company unlesse it bee in
sleeping that makes court to all the

[fol. 61r]

the women hee sees thinks they beleeve him and Laughs and is Laught at Equaly; nor a
Traveld Mounsieur whose head is all feather inside and outside that can talk of nothing
but dances and Duetts and has Courage Enough to were slashes when Every body Else
dy's with cold to see him; hee must not bee a foole of noe sort, nor peevish nor ill Natur'd
nor proude nor Coveteous, and to all this must bee added that hee must Love mee and I
him as much as wee are capable of Loveing without all this his fortune though never soe
great would not sattisfye mee and with it a very moderat one would keep mee from Ever
repenting my disposall; I have bin as Large and as perticuler in my discriptions as my
Cousen Molle in his of Moore Park, but that you know the place soe well I would send it
you, nothing can come neer his Patience in writeing it but my reading ont; but would you
had sent mee your fathers letter it would not have bin lesse welcome to mee then to you,
and you may safely beleeve that I am Equaly concern'd with you in any thing, I should bee
pleased too to see somthing of my Lady Carlisles writeing because she is soe
Extreordinary a Person; I have bin thinking of sending you my Picture till I could come
my self but a Picture is but dull company and that you need not, besyd's I cannot tell

whither it bee very like mee or not though tis the best I have Ever had drawne for mee
and Mr Lilly will have it that hee never took more pain's to make a good one in his life
and that was it I think that spoiled it hee was condemned for makeing the first hee drew
for mee a litle worse then I and in makeing this better hee has made it as unlike as tother;
hee is now I think at my Lord Pagetts at Marloe where I am promised hee shall draw a
Picture of my Lady for mee, she giv's it mee she say's as the greatest testimony of

---

Commentary

Dorothy Osborne is known for seventy-seven letters she wrote to her future husband
William Temple from 1652–1654. The letters are an important source for the study of
women's lives in the early modern period and for historians of the family. Preserved by the
Osborne family in their manuscript form, the letters were first published in their entirety
in 1888.

The letters were written in Osborne's early twenties as she kept up a clandestine correspondence with Temple. Both their families opposed the marriage, seeking more financially advantageous unions. Osborne, a gentlewoman who valued her good reputation, was
severely challenged to find a balance between her wish to marry Temple and her family's
desire that she marry purely for status and money. Osborne's letters to Temple describe the
ideal marriage as rooted in both love and practical considerations. Osborne's remarks on
marriage unions around her and her hopes for her own marriage add to our understanding of a woman's marital expectations in the mid–seventeenth century, and are an excellent source for historians of private life. The couple was finally allowed to marry in
December 1654, and the letters cease at that point. After the marriage, Osborne wrote
only a few letters, most of which are intensely practical and businesslike in nature.

In addition to what they show us about a midcentury gentlewoman's ideas about marriage and courtship, Osborne's letters are a treasure trove of information about daily life in
the 1650s. Her avid consumption of a variety of literary and theological works adds to our
knowledge of reading in the early modern period and her description of her illnesses, particularly melancholy, demonstrate the intersection of physical suffering and identity for an
early modern woman. Virginia Woolf, who mentioned Osborne as a capable writer in *A
Room of One's Own*, praised Osborne's vibrant subjectivity in *The Second Common Reader*.
Her letters "make us feel that we have our seat in the depth of Dorothy's mind, at the heart
of the pageant which unfolds itself page by page as we read" (Woolf 53).

The letter reproduced here is Osborne's description of her ideal husband. It is typical
of her writing in that she does not hesitate to heap scorn on unsuitable men, from the
oblivious country gentleman to the dissolute town gallant. She also displays a balance of
romantic and practical considerations. As she remarks that her prospective mate must have
"that kinde of breeding that I have had," she acknowledges that socioeconomic compati-
bility plays an important role in the success of a marriage. Yet she ends the segment by
rapturously concluding: "he must Love mee and I him as much as wee are capable of
Loveing." Osborne eliminates all other possibilities until only Temple is left; the shift in
tone from high-spirited disdain to tenderness is clearly meant for him. This segment,
somewhat more crafted than Osborne's other letters, comes across like a premeditated set
piece (as opposed to her other missives, which often seem to arise from an impromptu
stream of consciousness). This segment is particularly remarkable for its use of types (such

as the pedantic Sheriff) who later surfaced in Restoration drama, and even in the satirical "characters" written by authors such as Samuel Butler. With this passage, Osborne appears as a real-life precursor to the sparkling, outspoken women of Restoration comedy, such as Millimant in *The Way of the World*.

CARRIE HINTZ
QUEENS COLLEGE/CUNY

Dorothy (Osborne) Temple. Correspondence with William Temple (1652–54).
British Library 33, 975.

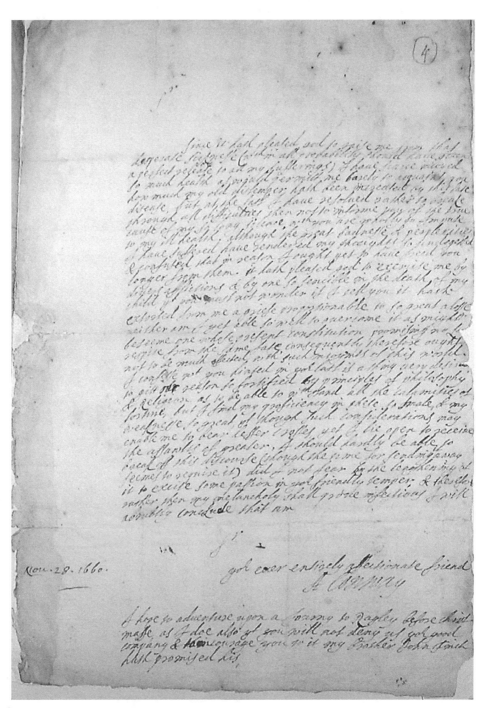

5.13: Anne (Finch), Viscountess Conway, to Henry More (28 November 1660). Reproduced by permission of the Master and Fellows of Christ's College, Cambridge.

Anne (Finch) Conway, Viscountess Conway, to Henry More (28 November 1660)

Transcription

Sir,

Since it hath pleased god to raise me from that desperate sicknesse (which in all probability should have given a perfect release to all my sufferings), I have scarce injoyed so much health as would permitt me barely to acquaint you how much my old distemper hath been increased by this late disease, but at the last I have resolved rather to breake through all difficulties then not to informe you of the true cause of my so long silence, which you are wholly to Impute to my ill health, although the great sadnesse of perplexities I have suffered have rendered my thoughts so undegested & confused, that in reason I ought yet to have freed you longer from them. it hath pleased god to exercise me by divers afflictions & by one so sencible in the death of my child, that you must not wonder if I tell you it hath extorted from me a griefe proportionable to so great a losse. neither am I yet able so well to overcome it as might beseeme one whose present constitution promising no later respite from the same fate consequently therefore ought not to be so much affected with such injoyments of this world. I confesse what you hinted in your last is a thing very desirous, to gitt our reason so fortified by principles of philosophy & Religion as to be able to with stand all the calamities of fortune, but I find my proficiency in these so smale, & my weaknesse so great, that though such considerations may enable me to bear lesser crosses, yet I lie open to receive the assawlts of greater. I should hardly be able to break off this discourse (though the time for sending it away seemes to require it) did I not fear by the lengthening of it to excite some passion in your friendly temper; & therefore rather then my melancholy shall prove infectious I will abrubtly conclude, that am

    Sir

        your ever entirely affectionate friend,

           A Conway

Nov. 28, 1660.

I hope to adventure upon a Journy to Ragley before christmasse, as I doe also that you will not deny us your good company, & to encourage you to it my brother John Finch hath promised his.

Commentary

Anne Conway (1631–79) was the posthumous daughter of Heneage Finch and his second wife, Elizabeth Cradock. In 1651 she married Edward Conway, the eldest son of the second Viscount Conway and Kilultagh, who owned estates at Ragley Hall, Warwickshire, and Portmore in Ulster. Her only child, Heneage, named after Anne Conway's half-brother, Heneage Finch, was born on 6 February 1658, but died of smallpox two and a half years later. Unusually for a woman of her time, Anne Conway was able to study philosophy, thanks to the Cambridge Platonist Henry More (1614–87), who agreed to give her tuition by letter. This was the beginning of a friendship that lasted until Lady Conway died in 1679. Her philosophical treatise *Principia philosophiae antiquissimae et recentissimae* was published anonymously in a Latin translation in Amsterdam in 1690.

For most of her life Anne Conway suffered chronic pain from an incurable illness, from which she sought a cure in vain, from such leading medical practitioners of her time, as Sir Theodore Turquet de Mayerne, William Harvey, and Thomas Willis. Her search for a cure brought her into contact with Francis Mercury van Helmont, who inspired her to study of the Jewish kabalah, and introduced her to Quakerism, to which she converted just before her death.

As a philosophically minded woman denied the possibility of a university education, Anne Conway valued Henry More as a means of access to the intellectual world. His correspondence with her, preserved in *Conway Letters,* is invaluable for the insights it gives us into the personal and intellectual life of a seventeenth-century woman. More was a loyal friend in times of both joy and trouble, visiting her as often as his duties as a Cambridge don would permit. He shared her joy in the birth of her son, whom he endearingly calls "your little son, my pupil." This letter is a reply to one he wrote after what was probably the worst crisis in Anne Conway's life, the death of her child. However, the best comfort he could offer Anne Conway was philosophical and religious. He urged her "by all the power of Reason, Philosophy and Religion" not to give way to grief least she endanger her life. Her reply is the most personal of her surviving letters and a rare admission, on her part, of the pain she suffered. The letter highlights the limitations of formal comforting and bespeaks the reaches of experience that social categories and rational discourse do not penetrate—an inarticulate realm of immediate emotion ("thoughts so undegested & confused") that cannot be easily tidied into a rational moral order— the reactions of a mother which a childless bachelor don, for all his good intentions, cannot share. "That desperate sicknesse" refers to the smallpox she contracted while nursing her sick son. The "old distemper" is the chronic illness from which she had suffered since her late teens. She also mentions her brother, John Finch, who had recently returned from travels in Europe.

SARAH HUTTON
MIDDLESEX UNIVERSITY

Lady Anne Conway to Henry More. Cambridge, Christ's College MS 21, no. 4. Also printed in Nicolson, *Conway Letters.* Pages 180–81.

Mary (Jepp) Clarke to her husband Edward (6 January 1695/6)

Commentary

Mary Clarke, the daughter of Elizabeth and Samuel Jepp of Sutton Court, Somerset, was born in the mid- or late 1650s. The Jepp family were cousins and neighbors of the philosopher John Locke, and despite the difference in their ages (Locke was born in 1632), he and Mary Jepp became lifelong friends. In 1674, Locke tried to arrange an aristocratic match for Mary, but instead she married Locke's friend Edward Clarke in 1675. Their first child was born the following spring, and a succession of daughters and sons followed during the 1670s and 1680s. The marriage was an extremely happy one; Mary's first surviving letter to her husband claimed she could not possibly live any longer "without the sight of him that is most dear to me" (see Crawford and Gowing, p. 177). The couple continued to write affectionately to each other until Mary's death in 1705.

The Clarke family settled at Edward's estate in Somerset, where he was elected MP for Chipley. Clarke's political office entailed lengthy sojourns in London whenever Parliament was sitting. During his absences, Mary managed the farm and estate and supervised a growing household of children and servants. Whenever they were separated from each other, the Clarkes wrote lengthy letters at frequent intervals. A large number of these have survived in manuscript, now preserved at the Somerset Archive in Taunton (DD/SF 4515, Clarke Letters). Although Mary's letters to John Locke have been printed in *The Correspondence of John Locke and Edward Clarke*, edited by B. Rand (1927), and *The Correspondence of John Locke,* edited by E. S. de Beer (8 vols., 1976), her letters to her husband have never been published.

Like her contemporary Dorothy Osborne, Mary Clarke displayed the natural gifts of a writer in her everyday correspondence. Her letters cover an immense variety of subjects, ranging from intimate family concerns, farming, and estate management to an engaged and perceptive commentary on the political and social issues of the day. The letter reproduced here, although comparatively brief (most of Mary's letters to her husband run to three pages or more), hints at the breadth of her interests, and the wit and ironic humour with which she described everything that came within her purview.

Childrearing and education were constant preoccupations, alluded to here in Mary's reference to a letter written to the children's tutor, "Monsieur." Previous letters during the 1680s had evolved into a three-way epistolary discussion among the Clarkes and their friend John Locke on the best way of educating their eldest son and daughter, Edward and Elizabeth (whom Locke always referred to jokingly as "my wife"). Locke later published a revised version of his replies to the Clarkes as the influential treatise, *Some Thoughts Concerning Education* (1693).

Mary took a lively interest in politics, revealed here in her thanks to Edward for sending a report on the Parliamentary "votes," including the new and unpopular Window Tax. Mary employs one of her frequent tropes to ridicule the nation's legislators, a comparison of public and private, the male world of politics with the female domain of the household. Here she questions the justice of a tax on windows which do not even keep out the winter rains. In a postscript Mary shows her interest in another topic of political and social concern, the distressing economic effects of recent currency and coinage reform (enacted under the direction of the Clarkes' friend John Locke and Isaac Newton) on the general

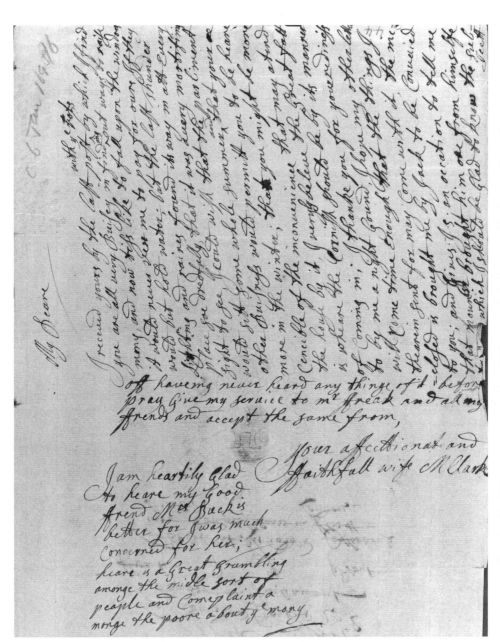

5.14: Mary (Jepp) Clarke to her husband Edward (6 January 1695–96). Courtesy of the Somerset Archive, Taunton. Reproduced by permission of William Sanford.

Transcription

6 January 1695/6[1]

My Deare,

I receved yours by the last post with the votes by which I find you[2] are all very Buisey in finding out ways to raise mony, and now tiss like to fall upon the windoes[3] it would never vex me to pay for ours If they would but hold water; but the last Thunder Lightning and raines found its way in att Every place soe dredfully, that it was a very mortifiing sight to see. I could wish that the Parliment would sitt some whole summer and that your other Buisness would permitt you to be heare more in the winter; that you might be more sensible of the inconvenience that may atend the house by it,[4] I veryly beleve the Great falt is wheare the Cornish [cornice] should be by its manner of Coming in. I thanke you for your rediness to by me a night Gound.[5] I hope my other letters will Come time Enough that the things I thearein sent for may Come with it. the inclosed is brought me by Jack[6] to be Convaied to you; and Gives J.S. an occation to tell me that mounsieur[7] brought him one from himselfe to which I should be Glad to know the subjectt off, haveing never heard any thinge of it before. Pray Give my service to Master Freak and all my Frends and accept the same from,

Your affecttionate and faithfull wife M Clarke

I am heartily Glad to heare my Good Frend Mistress Buck is better, for I was much Concerned for her. here is a Great Grumbling amonge the midle sort of people and Comeplaint amonge the poore about the mony.[8]

Notes

1. Until the calendar was reformed in 1752, the English calendar year officially began on March 25. Hence some 17th and early 18th century correspondents recorded "double" years for dates falling between January 1 and March 25.

2. Parliament, of which Mary Clarke's husband, Edward, was currently sitting as a member.

3. Parliament at this time was about to levy a tax on house windows, first imposed in 1696, repeatedly increased, and not repealed until 1851.

4. I.e., by the leaks through the windows.

5. A loose gown often worn in daytime or out-of-doors.

6. One of their sons.

7. The older childrens' tutor.

8. English currency was in such poor condition and short supply at this time that Parliament (with the advice of Isaac Newton and Mary Clarke's friend John Locke) instituted a scheme for complete recoinage, carried out in 1695–97.

populace, especially on the poorer inhabitants. There are also hints of London's important economic role as the great emporium for clothing and other material goods, as Mary commissions Edward to buy her a "nightgown," a fashionable garment meant for day wear. Even in this brief sample of Mary Clarke's writing, we can reconstruct some of the most significant themes in the private and public worlds of late seventeenth-century England.

SARA MENDELSON
McMASTER UNIVERSITY

Mary Clarke. Letter to her husband, Edward, 6 January 1695/6. Somerset Archive, Clarke Papers, DD/SF 4515/44

Bibliography

Beilin, Elaine V. *Redeeming Eve: Women Writers of the English Renaissance.* Princeton, N. J.: Princeton University Press, 1987.

Bradshaw, Brendan. Andrew Hadfield, and Willy Maley, eds. *Representing Ireland: Literature and the Origins of Conflict, 1534–1660.* Cambridge: Cambridge University Press, 1993.

Bradstreet, Anne. *The Works of Anne Bradstreet. 1867.* Ed. John Harvard Ellis. Gloucester: Peter Smith, 1962.

Cecil, David. *Two Quiet Lives.* London: Constable, 1948.

Chambers, Anne. *Granuaile: The Life and Times of Grace O'Malley, c. 1530–1603.* Dublin: Wolfhound Press, 1983.

Clancy, Thomas H. "Papist-Protestant-Puritan: English Religious Taxonomy 1565–1665." *Recusant History* 13 (1975–76): 227–53.

Cockayne, G.E. *The Complete Peerage.* Ed. V. Gibbs. 14 vols. London: St Catherine Press, 1910.

Conway, Anne. *The Principles of the Most Ancient and Modern Philosophy.* Ed. P. Loptson. Delmar, N.Y.: Scholars Facsimiles and Reprints, 1998.

Cope, Esther. *Handmaid of the Holy Spirit: Dame Eleanor Davies Never Soe Mad a Ladie.* Ann Arbor: University of Michigan Press, 1992.

Crawford, Patricia. "Public Duty, Conscience, and Women in Early Modern England." *Public Duty and Private Conscience in Seventeenth Century England: Essays Presented to G.E. Aylmer.* Ed. John Morrill, Paul Slack, and Daniel Woolf. Oxford: Clarendon Press, 1993. 57–76.

———, and Laura Gowing, eds. *Women's Worlds in Seventeenth-century England.* London and New York: Routledge, 2000.

Cressy, David. *Literacy and Social Order. Reading and Writing in Tudor and Stuart England.* Cambridge: Cambridge University Press, 1980.

Daybell, James, ed. *Early Modern Women's Letter Writing, 1450–1700.* Houndsmills: Palgrave, 2001.

Durant, David N. *Bess of Hardwick: Portrait of an Elizabethan Dynast.* London: Weidenfeld and Nicolson, 1977; Rev. ed. London: Owen, 1999.

Ezell, Margaret J. M. *The Patriarch's Wife: Literary Evidence and the History of the Family.* Chapel Hill, N.C.: University of North Carolina Press, 1987.

Fitzmaurice, James, and Martine Rey. "Letters by Women in England, the French Romance, and Dorothy Osborne." *The Politics of Gender in Early Modern Europe.* Ed. Jean R. Brink, Allison P. Coudert, and Maryanne C. Horowitz. Kirksville, Mo.: Sixteenth Century Journal Publishers, 1989. 149–160.

Gardiner, Dorothy. *The Oxinden Letters 1607–1642, Being the Correspondence of Henry Oxinden of Barham and His Circle.* London: Constable, 1933.

———. *The Oxinden and Peyton Letters 1642–1670, Being the Correspondence of Henry Oxinden of Barham, Sir Thomas Peyton of Knowlton and Their Circle.* London: Sheldon Press, 1937.

Hannay, Margaret P. "'O Daughter Heare': Reconstructing the Live of Aristocratic Englishwomen." *Attending to Women in Early Modern England.* Ed. Betty S. Travitsky and Adele F. Seeff. Newark: University of Delaware Press, 1994. 35–63.

Harrison, G. B., ed. *The Letters of Queen Elizabeth I.* Westport, Conn.: Greenwood Press [1935], 1968.

Hintz, Carrie. "Desire and Renunciation: The Letters of Dorothy Osborne." Ph.D. diss. University of Toronto, 1998.

———. "All People Seen and Known: Dorothy Osborne, Privacy, and Seventeenth-Century Courtship." *Dalhousie Review* 78.3 (1998): 365–83.

———. *An Audience of One: Dorothy Osborne's Letters to William Temple.* Toronto: University of Toronto Press, forthcoming.

Historical Manuscripts Commission *A Calendar of the Shrewsbury and Talbot Papers in Lambeth Palace Library and the College of Arms, Volume 1: Shrewsbury MSS. in Lambeth Palace Library (MSS. 694–710).* Ed. Catherine Jamison. Revised and indexed by E. G. W Bill. London: Her Majesty's Stationery Office, 1966.

———. *A Calendar of the Shrewsbury and Talbot Papers in Lambeth Palace Library and the College of Arms, Volume 2: Talbot Papers in the College of Arms.* Ed. G.R. Batho, London: Her Majesty's Stationery Office, 1971.

———. *Calendar of the Manuscripts of the Marquis of Bath, Preserved at Longleat, Wiltshire, Volume 5: Talbot, Dudley and Devereux Papers, 1533–1659.* Ed. G. Dyfnallt Owen. London: Her Majesty's Stationery Office, 1980.

Hobby, Elaine. *Virtue of Necessity: English Women's Writing 1649–1688.* London: Virago, 1988.

Hunter, Joseph. *Hallamshire, The History and Topography of the Parish of Sheffield.* London: Virtue and Co., 1869.

Hutton, Sarah. "Of Physic and Philosophy. Anne Conway Francis Mercury van Helmont and Seventeenth-Century Medicine." *Religio Medici.* Ed. A. Cunningham and P. Grell. London: Scolar Press, 1997. 228–46.

———. "Anne Conway, Margaret Cavendish and Seventeenth-Century Scientific Thought." *Women, Science and Medicine, 1500–1700.* Ed. L. Hunter and S. Hutton. Stroud: Alan Sutton, 1997.

Kusunoki, Akiko. "'Their Testament at Their Apron-strings': The Representation of Puritan Women in Early-Seventeenth-Century England." *Gloriana's Face: Women, Public & Private, in the English Renaissance.* Ed. Marion Wynne-Davies and Susan Cerasano. New York: Harvester Wheatsheaf, 1992. 185–204.

Lerch-Davis, Genie. "Rebellion Against Public Prose: The Letters of Dorothy Osborne to William Temple (1652–54)." *Texas Studies in Literature and Language* 20 (Fall 1978): 386–415.

MacCurtain, Margaret, and Mary O'Down, eds. *Women in Early Modern Ireland.* New York: Columbia University Press, 1991.

Magnusson, Lynne. *Shakespeare and Social Dialogue: Dramatic Language and Elizabethan Letters*. Cambridge: Cambridge University Press, 1999.

Martin, Randall, ed. *Women Writers in Renaissance England*. London: Longman, 1997.

McLeod, Bruce. *The Geography of Empire in English Literature, 1580–1745*. New York: Cambridge University Press, 1999.

Milligan, Percy. "The Gawdys of Norfolk and Suffolk." *Norfolk Archaeology*, vol. 26. Norwich: Goose and Son, 1974.

Milton, Anthony. *Catholic and Reformed*. Cambridge: Cambridge University Press, 1995.

Moore Smith, G. C., ed. *The Letters of Dorothy Osborne to Sir William Temple*. Oxford: Clarendon Press, 1929.

Murphy, Andrew. *But the Irish Sea Betwixt Us: Ireland, Colonialism, and Renaissance Literature*. Lexington: University Press of Kentucky, 1999.

Myers, James P., ed. *Elizabethan Ireland: A Selection of Writings by Elizabethan Writers on Ireland*. Hamden, Conn.: Archon Books, 1983.

Neale, J. E. *Queen Elizabeth*. London: Jonathan Cape, 1934.

Nevala, Minna. "'With out any pregyduce or hindranc': Editing women's letters from 17th-century Norfolk." *Neuphilologische Mitteilungen* 102.2 (2001): 151–71.

Nicolson, Marjorie H., ed. *The Conway Letters*. Revised by Sarah Hutton. Oxford: Clarendon Press, 1992.

Ó Céirín, Kit, and Cyril Ó Céirín. *Women of Ireland: A Biographic Dictionary*. Kinvara: TírEolas, 1996.

Otten, Charlotte F., ed. *English Women's Voices 1540–1700*. Miami: Florida International University Press, 1992.

Parker, Kenneth, ed. *Dorothy Osborne : Letters to Sir William Temple, 1652–54: Observations on Love, Literature, Politics, and Religion*. Rev. ed. Aldershot: Ashgate, 2002. Previously published as *Letters to Sir William Temple*. London: Penguin Books, 1987.

Parry, Edward Abbott, ed. *Letters from Dorothy Osborne to Sir William Temple, 1652–54*. London: Griffith, Farren, Okeden & Welsh, 1888.

Pearson, Jacqueline. "Women Reading, Reading Women." *Women and Literature in Britain 1500–1700*. Ed. Helen Wilcox. Cambridge: Cambridge University Press, 1996. 80–99.

Questier, Michael. *Conversion, Politics and Religion in England 1580–1625*. Cambridge: Cambridge University Press, 1996.

Rawson, Maud Stepney. *Bess of Hardwick and Her Circle*. London: Hutchinson, 1910.

Sommerville, Margaret R. *Sex and Subjection: Attitudes to Women in Early-Modern Society*. London: Arnold, 1995.

Stallybrass, Basil. "Bess of Hardwick's Buildings and Building Accounts." *Archaeologia* 64 (1913): 347–98.

Travitsky, Betty S. "The New Mother of the English Renaissance: Her Writings on Motherhood." *The Lost Tradition: Mothers and Daughters in Literature*. Ed. Cathy N. Davidson and E. M. Broner, New York: Frederick Ungar, 1980. 33–43.

———. *The Paradise of Women: Writings by Englishwomen of the Renaissance*. Westport, Conn.: Greenwood, 1981.

Walker, Kim. *Women Writers of the English Renaissance*. New York: Twayne, 1996.

Wall, Alison. "Elizabethan Practice and Feminine Precept: The Thynne Family of Longleat." *History* 75 (1990): 23–38.

Wall, Wendy. *The Imprint of Gender: Authorship and Publication in the English Renaissance*. Ithaca, N.Y.: Cornell University Press, 1993.

Ward, Richard. *The Life of Henry More, Parts 1 and 2*. Ed. S. Hutton et al. Dordrecht: Kluwer Academic Publishers, 2000.

Watt, Diane, *Secretaries of God:Women Prophets in Late Medieval and Early Modern England*. Cambridge: D.S.Brewer, 1992.

Wayne, Valerie. "Advice for Women from Mothers and Patriarchs." *Women and Literature in Britain 1500–1700*. Ed. Helen Wilcox. Cambridge: Cambridge University Press, 1996. 56–79.

Wilcox, Helen. "'My Soule in Silence?': Devotional Representations of Renaissance Englishwomen." *Representing Women in Renaissance England*. Claude J. Summers and Ted-Larry Pebworth. Columbia: University of Missouri Press, 1997. 9–23.

Williams, E. Carleton. *Bess of Hardwick*. London: Longmans, Green, 1959.

Winkelmann, Carol L. "A Case Study of Women's Literacy in the Early Seventeenth Century: The Oxinden Family Letters." *Women and Language* 19.2 (1996): 14–20.

Wolfe, Heather, ed. *Elizabeth Cary, Lady Falkland: Life and Letters*. Tempe, AZ: and Cambridge, UK: MRTS and RTM, 2001.

Woolf, Virginia. *The Second Common Reader* (1932). New York: Harcourt, Brace, 1960.

CHAPTER 6

Life-writing:
Nonfiction and Fiction

Nonfiction

The study of biography and autobiography has become central to textual analysis in our own time. Biographical and autobiographical studies are, moreover, the place where the disciplines of literature and history, now compartmentalized, were established in the universities. Scholars working in the area of life-writings can conduct their research "unfettered" by disciplinary constraints, though the task of analyzing this genre is demanding, for as Lisa Jardine recently reminded us, scholars must attend to the critical methodologies and specific intellectual milieu that influenced individual authors in the production of their works. Furthermore, as Elaine Beilin observed, biographies in particular are subject to rewritings over the course of their reception histories, and the cultural work involved in recovering the history of representation offers additional challenges for scholars.[1]

The theories and practices of self-representation have varied from period to period and culture to culture.[2] History, culture, categories of class, and political structure, as well as narratives of self-fashioning, establish the conditions for the construction of identities through a dialectic between social relations and autonomy.[3] The fashioning of identities is, moreover, determined by official requirements for gendered conduct and the discourses in which those requirements become inscribed.

Autobiographical writing in the early modern period evolved in response to the Reformation emphasis on self-governance and self-examination. It accompanied the emergence of bourgeois individualism, an increase in literacy, changes in print culture, and, in the mid–seventeenth century, the relaxing of state regulations over the press. In accordance with the etymological significance of the word, "autobiography" is the life of a self who is writing. In his classic study, Paul Delany defines autobiography as an analytical and introspective record intended to provide a coherent account of the author's life, or of an extensive period or series of events in his life. Autobiographical texts, he continues, are composed after a period of reflection and form a unified narrative.[4]

In a more recent investigation of the genre of autobiography, Estelle Jelineck distinguishes between female and male secular autobiographies, noting that while the latter were primarily military, travel, and political memoirs with little reference to domestic affairs or the kind of introspection found in poetry and philosophy of the period, women's autobiographical writings revealed their emotional lives, their personal experiences, and their engagement in self-analysis.[5] But interdependence, collectivity, and community are also key elements in the formation of the female identity. As the products of the small minority of literate women in the early modern period, women's autobiographical texts are few, and most remained in manuscript form. While early modern autobiographies written by women represent a diverse range of social, religious, and political positions, the majority of authors like Lady Anne Clifford, Grace, Lady Mildmay, and Elizabeth Freke, were from the upper classes. Exceptions include writers like Martha Moulsworth and certain members of dissenting groups.

Life-writing assumed a variety of forms: diaries, meditations, memoirs, character sketches, hagiographies, conversion narratives charting a person's spiritual experiences, chronicles, prayers, instructions for children, journals, poems, and letters (see chapter 5). By no means does "life-writing" constitute a genre unto itself; the designation is fluid though nevertheless informative.[6] Many life-writings featured conventions of different genres, and some served as the basis for the creation of the novel at the end of the seventeenth century, as noted in the next section, Fiction.

In the end, however, we cannot determine whether the extant autobiographical writings are wholly representative of all the writings of the self produced at this time. In his introduction to *Trials of Authorship*, Jonathan Crewe explains that the notion of authorship "will always be on trial, subject to critical denial or self-erasure, yet that will precisely be its precarious and generally self-conscious condition."[7] Indeed we can never be assured of hearing the authentic voice of the author in her work. Extant writings of women often contain testimonies of the author's piety, a reminder of the influence of religious and moral codes of conduct that defined the lives and life stories of early modern women. Effie Botonaki observes that "the spiritual diary was probably the only form of writing that early modern women could pursue without ever having to excuse themselves for doing so."[8] The devotional content undoubtedly helped ensure the survival of these texts, whereas secular writings and even secular insertions in devotional texts were less likely to be passed on. Still examinations of extant autobiographical writings are valuable for the perspectives they offer on women "from the female point of view."[9]

The autobiographies tend to reflect the female author's identification with her husband, children, and household. At the same time, many were actually intended for circulation or publication and thus are directed toward a social purpose. Grace, Lady Mildmay's manuscript "Autobiography" (1617–20) offers her readers moral and spiritual advice, outlining her position in an inheritance dispute with her sister. While frequently challenging the private-public dichotomy, autobiographical writings also display some other common features. These include the presentation of a female perspective on experience and self-expression. Female writers define themselves in relation to overpowering expectations and socially constructed conceptions of womanhood; most experience some kind of oppression: marital strife, depression, and even, as in the case of Leticia Wigington in 1681, imprisonment (see 1.10). A second characteristic is a consciousness of the writing process, both the opportunities and obstacles it presents. A third element is an avowed concern with the truth, often provoked by a "legalistic desire for self-defence."[10]

The writing of the self was not always spontaneous, as some women appeared to have deliberately altered the narratives of their lives, on occasion even supplying front and end matter for their accounts. Frances Matthew's manuscript, "The birthe of all my children," included in this chapter, was revised and appears to have been composed in at least two stages, between 1583 and her death. Reports of the deaths of three of Matthew's children are located in the remaining spaces on the manuscript and produced in a different ink. Another example of the reshaping of the autobiographical text is found in the diary of Lady Anne Clifford (1590–1676), who created a coherent narrative of her life from the perspective of old age. Elizabeth Freke (c. 1641–1714) did the same in her domestic memoirs, which deal with the rather untraditional matter of the female autobiographer's secular materialism. A comparison of Freke's later memoir with her manuscript diary accounts exhibits "the refashioning [of selfhood] inherent in each stage of writing and rewriting."[11]

Radical sects were most likely to question gender inequality and in turn even encourage women to produce autobiographical texts, especially on their spiritual development. Despite the lack of a printed version, two related manuscript versions of Agnes Beaumont's narrative provide evidence of the work's circulation. Another female-authored sectarian autobiography, the manuscript writings of Mary Penington (c. 1625–82), illuminates the obstacles facing women who sought a spiritual life outside of the established church. Like Agnes Beaumont, Mary Penington suggests in her spiritual autobiography that the autobiographer's double bind and the silences it produces are a function of female authorship.[12]

The self fashioned in the majority of life-writing is characteristically multidimensional, fragmented, and in need of authentication. The corresponding style of these works is episodic and anecdotal, nonchronological, and unpolished. The nature of articulating selfhood is a complex undertaking for female authors, who sought to comply with conventional gender politics. Life-writings thus invite a variety of questions: What is the relationship between the self who writes and the self represented in the front matter of a text? Is there even a self prior to the act of writing? Certainly writing always involves interpretation, thus undermining the notion of a truthful account of selfhood on which most of the autobiographers insist. How do symbolic systems of culture and language contribute or impede self-representation? Ultimately, we discover, even texts designed for an audience of one are marked by "double-voicing" insofar as the recording of the private experience involves an engagement with codes of conduct and hierarchical gender relations.[13]

The early modern period witnessed the production of numerous biographical writings. Biographies represented the subject in terms of a standard, structured narrative, conventionally derived from classical and early modern sources, including Thomas Wilson's *The Arte of Rhetorique* (1553), which relied heavily on the prescriptions outlined by Quintilian and Cicero. Typical biographies thus described the subject's parentage, family history, education, virtues, friends, and also her/his exemplary art of dying. As Heather Wolfe observes, readers would have recognized and expected differences between the represented and the actual life of the biographical subject.[14] We feature only a few though nevertheless significant examples: a 1607 manuscript entry on Elizabeth Southwell's account of Elizabeth I; Elizabeth Cary's 1627–28 history of Edward II; and in turn a manuscript biography of Elizabeth Cary's life, titled "Lady Falkland: Her Life" (c. 1645). Lucy Apsley Hutchinson, a poet and translator (chapter 7), who also produced biographical and autobiographical works, is featured here as the author of "The Memoirs of the Life of Colonel Hutchinson" (c. 1664). The memoirs, which romanticize the Hutchinson marriage, invite comparison with a fragment of her autobiography, "Life of Mrs. Lucy Hutchinson, Written by Herself," and possibly with Mary Carleton's

The case of Madam Mary Carleton (1663), in which the romance tradition is used for a different end.

Fiction

Prose fiction emerged as one of the most popular genres of the early modern period through its appeal to people across the social classes. In an attempt to satisfy the ever-increasing number of readers, authors of fiction frequently recycled their texts, pouring fresh ideas in old molds. The most engaging kind of fiction was "simultaneously representational and referential, revealing both observation and tradition."[15] The result was a marketable commodity, which served primarily as a popular form of entertainment, though promises of moral instruction were included to defend its value in the period.

Courtly and popular prose fiction commonly dealt with relations between the sexes and with love in marriage and society—the primary subject of romances. The early modern period witnessed the flowering of romance, of which Sir Philip Sidney's *The Countesse of Pembroke's Arcadia* and Edmund Spenser's *Faerie Queene* are the most famous examples. When referred to pejoratively, romance designated imaginary, flighty stories of extraordinary adventures presented episodically and involving lower-class, stereotypical characters; when used favorably, romance was identified with what John Milton described as "those lofty fables and Romances, which recount in solemne canto's the deeds of Knighthood founded by our victorious Kings; & from hence had in renowne over all Christendome."[16] Following the death of Elizabeth, the romance tradition—which was hybrid and experimental from the start—underwent various metamorphoses in response to the growing disenchantment with courtly life and the escalation of civil war, which inevitably affected cultural expression and literary tastes.[17] The Restoration witnessed the revival of the romance tradition.

In the early modern period, romance fiction was associated with female readers when courtship rather than chivalric adventure became the focus of the texts.[18] Traditionally literary scholars have devoted considerably more attention to women readers of romance fiction than female writers because so few works of romance fiction by women exist. Aside from *The Mirror of Knighthood*, translated from the Spanish by Margaret Tyler (1578), Lady Mary Wroth's *The Countesse of Mountgomeries Urania* (1621) is the only example of a female-authored romance at this time. Since the romance genre thrived largely in a courtly tradition, little fiction was produced again until the Restoration, thus partly accounting in this chapter for the gap between Wroth and Lady Hester Pulter.[19] In Restoration fiction, the nature of female-authored fiction, moreover, changed when the distinctions among the roles of female readers, writers, and heroines of romance increasingly broke down, as the final entries in this chapter demonstrate.[20]

The framing folio pages of Wroth's *The Countesse of Mountgomeries Urania* present an important narrative in themselves. Representative of the story of *Urania* at large, the first and last pages of the folio are marked by a tension between continuity and rupture. Consisting of four books totaling about 600 pages of prose and poetry, *Urania* locates its origin in Sir Philip Sidney's *The Countesse of Pembroke's Arcadia*. However, while her uncle's romance commences with Urania's departure from Arcadia, Wroth's begins with Urania's search for her parents, anticipating her own quest for an identity.[21] As for Wroth herself, her apologetic letter to the Duke of Buckingham for the publication of her book serves as a reminder of the challenge she faced in resisting the stigma against female authorship.

Moreover, the intricate title page of her romance reveals the deliberation that went into preparation of the book. Wroth constructs a genealogy of upper-class relatives with well-known connections to the literary world in order to defend her own act of literary composition. Her volume ends with an appended sonnet sequence, *Pamphilia to Amphilanthus*, which reworks the Petrarchan sonnet tradition from a female perspective. The continuation of the narrative of Urania is to be found in "The Second Part of the Countesse of Mountgomeries Urania," which stops midsentence, like the earlier volume and like Sidney's *Arcadia*. A manuscript in Wroth's hand extends the story, which nevertheless remains incomplete.

In conjunction with the restoration of the Stuart monarchy and royalist literary tastes, the romance genre again resurfaced toward the end of the Interregnum. Women contributed to the production of romances as well as of comedies that would make their way into the Restoration theaters (see chapter 9). One of the lesser-known female-authored romances was Lady Hester Pulter's "The Unfortunate Florinda," a two-part manuscript prose work from the late 1650s or early 1660s that presents conflicting portraits of the female romantic hero. In the second part of Pulter's romance, Fidelia—who is, ironically, also the main character of part one—succumbs to the same fate as Florinda in the first part. Curiously, part two, which is unfinished, stops in mid-sentence like Wroth's *Urania*.

Mary Carleton's *The case of Madam Mary Carleton* (1663) serves as a pivotal text between the life-writing and the fiction sections in this chapter. The pamphlet attributed to Mary (Moders) Carleton, a notorious impostor, defends her against charges of bigamy, of which she is acquitted. Ten years later, Carleton would, however, be hanged for larceny. Part of the work of *The case of Madam Mary Carleton* is to convince its readers of the noble (German) lineage she invents for herself. The two portraits that frame the opening letter of *The case* illustrate Carleton's development of an alternative identity, a task enabled by the viewers/readers of *The case* who interpret them. The elusiveness of the portraits anticipates the narrative at large in its adaptation of romance conventions as Carleton assumes the masculine role of the rogue characteristic of romances. The text serves as an example of how women's writing could redefine concepts of self and gender rather than just reproduce them.[22]

Front matter from two of Aphra Behn's works of romance fiction is featured in the final entries of this chapter. The title page from *Love-Letters Between a Nobleman and His Sister* (1684) and the epistle dedicatory to Richard Lord Maitland in *Oroonoko* (1688) direct the reader's attention to such concerns as the hybrid nature of the emerging novel form, the relationship between history and romance, and the authority of the female author. Both of these early novels—a form Mikhail Bakhtin would characterize as "ever questing, ever examining itself and subjecting its established forms to review"[23]—reveal their reliance on other genres, including the romance, letters, diary entries, and confessions. They also challenge the distinctions between romance and history; the narrative Behn composed through the correspondence between "Silvia" and "Philander" in *Love-Letters Between a Nobleman and His Sister* runs alongside and even counter to the political and romantic scandal involving Henrietta Berkeley, the daughter of a prominent Tory, and the Whig rebel Lord Grey, the seductive rake of Behn's novel. In *Oroonoko* the last two pages of the dedication to Maitland emphasize the verity of the subsequent story, labeled a "True History." Behn's negotiation of her self-effacing yet authoritative stance and her multiple roles as narrator, character, and author in *Oroonoko* are notable examples of the acts of self-fashioning that accompanied the female author's entry into print.

Notes

We gratefully acknowledge the assistance of Heather Wolfe, Margaret Ferguson, Katherine Acheson, and Kathleen Lynch.

1. Lisa Jardine, "Introduction: Lives and Letter"; Elaine Beilin, "The After-Life of Anne Askew," "Early Modern Lives: Biography and Autobiography in the Renaissance and Seventeenth Century," organized by Sarah Hutton (London, 2002). The Centre for Editing Lives and Letters (CELL) is a vital research centre for studies of biography and autobiography (www.english.qmw.ac.uk/Cell).

2. Linda Gregerson, *The Reformation of the Subject: Spenser, Milton, and the English Protestant Epic* (Cambridge: Cambridge University Press, 1995), 150. In shifting the focus of the debate to the study of "inwardness," Katherine Eisaman Maus has argued that subjectivity is constructed and reconstructed by different speakers in terms of the situations in which they are cast, and in terms of the historical moment and cultural contexts in which they are situated (*Inwardness and Theater in the English Renaissance* [Chicago: University of Chicago Press, 1995]).

3. Theodore Leinwand, "Negotiation and New Historicism," *PMLA* 105 (1990): 480.

4. Paul Delany, *British Autobiography in the Seventeenth Century* (London: Routledge & K. Paul, 1969), 1.

5. Estelle Jelineck, *The Tradition of Women's Autobiography: From Antiquity to the Present* (Boston: Twayne, 1986), 24.

6. See Debora Shuger's study of male life-writing: "Life-writing in Seventeenth-century England" in *Representations of the Self from the Renaissance to Romanticism*, ed. Patrick Coleman, Jayne Lewis, and Jill Kowalik (Cambridge: Cambridge University Press, 2000), 63–78.

7. Jonathan Crewe, *Trials of Authorship: Anterior Forms and Poetic Reconstruction From Wyatt to Shakespeare* (Berkeley: University of California Press, 1990), 15.

8. Effie Botonaki, "Seventeenth-Century Englishwomen's Spiritual Diaries: Self-Examination, Covenanting, and Account Keeping," *Sixteenth Century Journal* 30.1 (1999): 4.

9. Sara Heller Mendelson, "Stuart women's diaries and occasional memoirs," *Women in English Society 1500–1800*, ed. Mary Prior (New York: Methuen, 1985), 181.

10. Elspeth Graham et al., "Introduction," *Her Own Life: Autobiographical Writings by Seventeenth-Century Englishwomen*, ed. Elspeth Graham et al. (New York: Routledge, 1989), 24.

11. *The Remembrances of Elizabeth Freke 1671–1714*, ed. Raymond A. Anselment, Camden Fifth Series, 18 (London: Cambridge University Press, 2001), 3.

12. See Kathleen Lynch's forthcoming book, tentatively titled "'A Pattern or More for the Age He Lived in': The Uses of Religious Experience in Seventeenth-Century Britain."

13. On theories of autobiography and self-formation, see Shari Bestock, "Authorizing the Autobiographical," *The Private Self: Theory and Practice of Women's Autobiographical Writings*, ed. Shari Benstock (Chapel Hill: University of North Carolina Press, 1988). On the creative concealments operating in autobiography and negotiations between effacement and empowerment, see Elspeth Graham, Hilary Hinds, Elaine Hobby, and Helen Wilcox, "Pondering All These Things in Her Heart: Aspects of Secrecy in the Autobiographical Writings of Seventeenth-century Englishwomen," *Women's Lives/Women's Times: New Essays on Auto/Biography*, ed. Linda Anderson (Albany: SUNY Press, 1997).

14. Heather Wolfe, "Introduction," *Elizabeth Cary, Lady Falkland: Her Life and Letters*, ed. Heather Wolfe (Binghampton, N.Y.: 2001), 65. Hundreds of lives/obituaries written by English nuns also appeared in the seventeenth century (see Wolfe 457–9; 579–92 for two examples).

15. Donald Beecher, "Introduction," *Critical Approaches to English Prose Fiction 1520–1640*, ed. Donald Beecher (Ottawa: Dovehouse Editions, 1998), 13.

16. John Milton, *Apology for Smectymnuus, Complete Prose Works of John Milton*, ed. Don Wolfe et al., 8 vols. (New Haven, Conn.: Yale University Press, 1953–82), 1:891.

17. See Elizabeth Sauer, "Emasculating Romance: Historical Fiction in the Protectorate," *Prose Fiction and Early Modern Sexualities*, ed. Constance Relihan and Goran Stanivukovic (New York: Palgrave, forthcoming).

18. See Helen Hackett, *Women and Romance Fiction in the English Renaissance* (Cambridge: Cambridge University Press, 2000).

19. Anna Weamys's *Continuation of Sir Philip Sidney's Arcadia* (1651) is an exception.

20. See Caroline Lucas, *Writing for Women: The Example of Woman as Reader in Elizabethan Romance* (Philadelphia: Open University Press, 1989), 4–6; and Jane Spencer, *The Rise of the Woman Novelist from Aphra Behn to Jane Austen* (Oxford: Blackwell, 1986), 23, 41.

21. Carolyn Ruth Swift, "Feminine Identity in Lady Mary Wroth's Romance *Urania*," *Women in the Renaissance: Selections from English Literary Renaissance*, ed. Kirby Farrell, Elizabeth H. Hageman, and Arthur F. Kinney (Amherst: University of Massachusetts Press, 1971–1988), 154–74.

22. See Hero Chalmers, "'The Person I am, or what they made me to be': The Construction of the Feminine Subject in the Autobiographies of Mary Carleton," *Women, Texts and Histories, 1575–1760*, ed. Clare Brant and Diane Purkiss (New York: Routledge, 1992), 164–94.

23. M.M. Bakhtin, *The Dialogic Imagination: Four Essays*, trans. Caryl Emerson and Michael Holquist, ed. Michael Holquist (Austin: University of Texas Press, 1981), 39.

Frances Matthew, "The birthe of all my children" (1583–1629)

Commentary

This previously unpublished manuscript is written on paper in italic in Frances Matthew's own hand. An italic hand suggests education and may well indicate that she knew Latin, particularly since the only book she is known to have owned personally is a Latin work on botany now in York Minster Library.

A passionate Puritan, Frances Matthew was probably born in 1551 and died in 1629. She was the daughter of William Barlow, Bishop of Chichester, and was a member of a family of bishops. This manuscript lists her children by her first marriage to Matthew Parker, son of Matthew Parker, Archbishop of Canterbury, and by her second marriage to Dr. Tobie Matthew, later to become Archbishop of York.

The manuscript is a particularly brief and spare example of women's life-writing. Yet the title, "The birthe of all my children," articulates a sense of selfhood in a woman who was twice widowed and survived all but two of her six children. That it is a genuine life document is also suggested by palaeographic evidence, which indicates that it was annotated and updated over time. The undated manuscript appears to have been composed in at least two stages, between 1583 and her death. The first version simply recorded the births and baptisms of her children. Later annotations, identified by a darker ink, a thinner nib, and the squeezing of additions into the available space, give details of the deaths of three of the children.

The meticulously recorded and varied locations of the children's births and deaths bear witness to key events in Frances's life. Widowed while pregnant with her first son, she stayed for a time with her sister Elizabeth Day, whose husband was provost of Eton College. Later locations trace the progress of her second husband through a series of promotions.

Notably, Frances gives the same careful information for her first unnamed still-born daughter as for her other children. She could not have been given a Christian name without baptism, but she was otherwise accorded the same attention as her siblings, both within this document and in her burial at Salisbury Cathedral, where Tobie held a prebend.

The names of the children's godparents indicate aristocratic and Puritan connections, further extending Frances's impressive array of connections with the church by birth and marriage. Her sister Anne is mentioned, who had married Herbert Westfailing, Dean of Christ Church, an ardent opponent of Catholicism. Both Laurence and Joan Humfrey were godparents, another close connection with Puritanism, since Humfrey was a leading protagonist in the Vestiarian Controversy of the mid-1560s.

The document also reveals the Matthew's connections with the aristocratic Sidney family. The writer Mary Sidney was a friend of the Matthews, and worshipped at Salisbury Cathedral. She became Mary Matthew's godmother; the child may well have been named after her. Philip Sidney was educated alongside Tobie at Christ Church, and later he and Henry Herbert, Mary's husband, sponsored Tobie's clerical career.

This understated and poignant document appears to hint at maternal partiality in Frances's moving remark "my most deerly-beloved sonne" on the death of her youngest child, Samuel. In her will she founded two scholarships at Peterhouse in his memory. She may recollect Samuel all the more fondly as she dwelt on the continued disappointments caused by her two remaining sons.

Borne at Eaton Colledge

Matthew parker my first sonn was borne in the year 1575. the 11.
of July being, saterday betwext .9. er.10 of the clocke at night, his
godmother, my Mother, his godfathers my Brother Daye, er my Brother
parker. he departed this Life in March next following. and was
buryed in Eaton church.
Borne at Salesbury

Toby Matthew was borne. 1577 the therde of october being. Thursday
a littell after thre of the clocke in the after noone, his godmother my
Mother inlawe, his godfathers Mr Estcourte er Mr weekes.

Borne at Salesbury

My first Daughter was still borne. 1579. the seconde of August
being, Tusdaye at 12. of the clocke at night, and buryed in the
Cathederall church. at Salesbury
Borne at oxforde in Christ church

John. Matthew was borne 1580 the sixt of December being: Tuseday
at fiue of the clocke in the morneing. his godmother, my Sister
westfailling, his godfathers, Docter Humfrie, er Docter Cullpepper.

Borne at Salesbury

Mary Matthew was borne 1582. the 24. of october being, wensday
at fiue of the clocke in the after noone, her godmothers the countice
of pembrok, er my Mother, her godfather Docter Rihyt, shee departed
this Lyfe the Easter next following er was buryed in the Cathederall.
church at Salesbury.
Borne at oxforde in Christ church

Samuell Matthew was borne 1583. the fift of Eebruary being
wensdaye at two of the cloke in the morneing his godmother Mris
Humfry, his godfathers, Docter Slithers, er Docter withington.

This Samuell Matthew, my most deerly-beloued somme, departed
this Life most Christianly the 15. of June 1561 and is buryed in
Peeter-House in Cambridg.   1601.

6.1: Frances Matthew, "The birthe of all my children" (1583-1629). By kind permission of the Dean and
Chapter of York.

Her apparently high standard of education and the Sidney family connection suggest Frances had a particular interest in literature and learning, and indeed this is supported by other evidence. Frances later had some connection with the diarist Lady Anne Clifford, who recorded spending time with "Mrs Matthews the Bishop's wife" when traveling through York. In addition to founding the scholarships at Peterhouse, she is best remembered for leaving her husband's library of 3,000 volumes to York Minster, forming the nucleus of the modern Minster Library's collection, an act described on her memorial as "A rare Example That so great Care To advance Learning Should Lodge In a woman's breast."

Transcription

Borne at Eaton Colledg

Matthew Parker my first sonn was borne in the year 1575–the-11–of-July being Saterday betwext-9–&-10 of the clocke at night, his godmother, my Mother, his godfathers, my Brother Daye, & my Brother Parker. He departed this Life in March next following, and was buryed in Eaton Church./

Borne at Salesbury

Toby Matthew was borne-1577–the therde of october being Thursday a littell after thre of the clocke in the after noone, his godmother my Mother inlawe, his godfathers, Mr. Estcourte & Mr. Weekes.

Borne at Salesbury

My first Daughter was still borne 1579 the seconde of August being Tusdaye at 12–of the clocke at night, and buryed in the Cathederall church at Salesbury

Borne at oxforde in Christ Church

John Matthew was borne 1580 the Sixt of December being Tuseday at five of the clocke in the morneing, his godmother, my sister westfailling, his godfathers, Docter Humfrie, & Docter Cullpepper.

Borne at Salesbury

Mary Matthew was borne 1582–the-24–of October being wensday at five of the clocke in the after noone, her godmothers the countice of Pembrok, & my Mother, her godfather Docter whyt, shee departed this Lyfe the Easter next following & was buryed in the Cathederall Church at Salesbury./

Borne at Oxforde in Christ Church

Samuell Matthew was borne 1583–the fift of February beinge wensdaye at two of the cloke in the morneing, his godmother Mistress Humfry, his godfathers, Docter Slithers, & Docter withington. This Samuell Matthew, my most deerly-beloved sonne, departed this Life most Christianly the 15–of June 1561./1601. and is buryed in Peeter-House in cambridge./.

JANE BIRD
INDEPENDENT

Frances Matthew. "The birthe of all my children" (1583–1629). York Minster Archives. Add Mss 322.

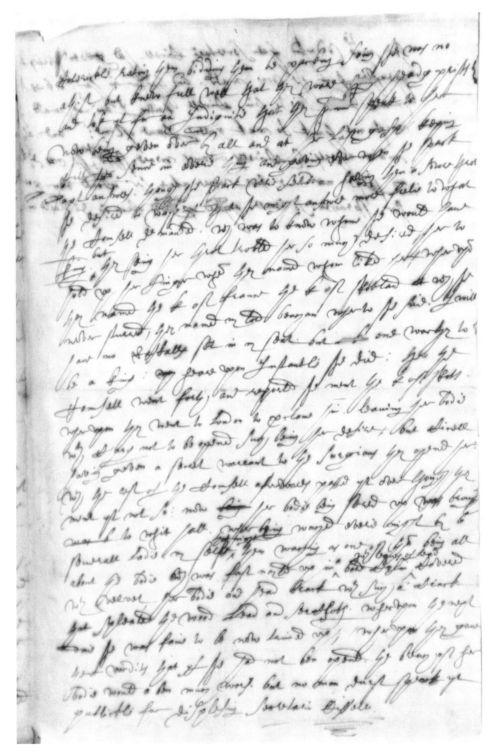

6.2: Elizabeth Southwell (Dudley), "A True Relation of what succeeded at the sickness and death of Queen Elizabeth" (1607). Courtesy of the Archives of the British Providence of the Society of Jesus.

Elizabeth Southwell (Dudley), "A True Relation of what succeeded at the sickness and death of Queen Elizabeth" (1607)

Transcription

cholericklie rating them bidding them be packing, saing she was no atheist, but knew full well that they were [illegible] hedg prists and tok yt for an yndignite that they should speak to her[.] Now being geven over by all and at her last gaspe keeping still her sence in everie thing and giving ever when she spack apt answers. though she spack verie seldom having then a sower throt she desired to wash yt that she might answer more freelie to what the Counsell demanded. which was to know whom she would have king. but they seing her throt trobled her so much desired her to hold up her finger when they named whom liked her whereupon they named the K of france the K of Scotland at which she never sturred, they named my lord beacham wherto she said. I will have no Raskalls son in my seat but [illegible] one worthy to be a king: Heareupon ynstantlie she died: Then the Counsell went forth and reported she meant the K of Scots. wherupon they went to London to proclame him. leaving her bodie with Charg not to be opend such being her desire, but Cicell having geven a secret warrant to the surgions they opened her: which the rest of the Counsell afterwards passed yt over though they meant yt not so: now her bodie being seared up was brought to whit hall. wher being wached everie night by 6 severall Ladies. my self that night ther waching as one of them being all about the bodie which was fast nayled up in a bord coffin with leaves of lead Covered with velvet, her bodie and head break with such a Crack that spleated the wood Lead and ser cloth. wherupon the next daie she was faine to be new trimmed up; wherupon they gave their verdits that yf she had not ben opened the breath of her bodie would a ben much wors. but no man durst speak yt publickli for displeasing *Secretarie Cissell.* //

Commentary

Elizabeth Southwell's manuscript "A True Relation of what succeeded at the sickness and death of Queen Elizabeth" is one of the few eyewitness accounts of Queen Elizabeth I's death, and the only surviving account written by a woman. Southwell, who was 16 or 17 at the time of the events she describes, was a maid of honor to the queen and a member of the powerful Howard family. At a time when fortunes were expected to change rapidly with the arrival of the queen's successor, Southwell would have been expected to advance her family's wealth and power through an arranged marriage. That she chose to do otherwise sets her apart from other aristocratic women of her generation and, unfortunately, has made her manuscript an object of suspicion to historians.

In 1605, after the events described in her manuscript but before the manuscript was written, Southwell disguised herself as a page and left England in the company of her married cousin, Robert Dudley, son of the Earl of Leicester, whose legitimacy was in dispute. Dudley had just lost a lawsuit in which he attempted to recover some of his father's property and was traveling until the scandal faded. Once they reached the Continent, Dudley and Southwell converted to Catholicism and married. In the first few years of her marriage, Southwell is reported to have had five miscarriages; she later bore 13 children. Social historians usually interpret this number of pregnancies as the sign of a happy marriage. Southwell died in 1631.

Southwell's account of the queen's death contains details about the queen's illness—descriptions of hallucinations, signs of witchcraft, rude remarks—that other accounts lack. But because of Southwell's personal history, and particularly because of her Catholicism, the manuscript is treated as an unreliable historical source. The chief problem comes near the end of the manuscript, the section reproduced here, in which Southwell reports that during the queen's wake, her corpse exploded, breaking through the coffin and its lead liner and necessitating that the body be "new trimmed up" the next day.

Elizabeth had ordered that her corpse not be "opened" or embalmed after her death, perhaps fearing that an examination of her uterus would lead to suspicions that she had borne children, thus throwing the succession to the throne into question. An unembalmed or hastily embalmed corpse could produce enough methane to cause an explosion, but Southwell's account can also be read as a Catholic fantasy, a fitting end to a monarch so corrupt that her flesh could not remain intact. It is because of this possibility, exploited by the Jesuit Robert Persons when he used Southwell's manuscript in diatribes against the Queen, that historians have dismissed Southwell's account as Jesuit propaganda.

But a more careful look at the manuscript reveals that Southwell had a sophisticated knowledge of court politics. She effectively discredits her family's enemy Robert Cecil, and she questions James VI's title to the English throne. The king's succession depended on the insistence of Elizabeth's councillors that the dying Queen had named him to succeed her. Southwell's is the only account of the Queen's final hours not to contain a scene in which Elizabeth says or somehow indicates James is to succeed her.

The Southwell manuscript was written or dictated on 1 April 1607. It is written in a clear secretary hand and covers four sides of two sheets. The ink has bled through the paper making two of the four sides difficult to read. The manuscript came into the possession of Father Robert Persons, a Jesuit priest whose opposition to the English monarchy took the form of words and actions dedicated to its overthrow; Southell's "True Relation" is currently held among a collection of Persons's papers at Stonyhurst College, Lancashire, but will eventually be transferred to the Jesuit archives in London.

Elizabeth Southwell's manuscript is worthy of further study because of its descriptions of the political maneuvering surrounding the death of Queen Elizabeth I; the transition to James's rule appears smooth because it was successful, but Southwell demonstrates that there were many points at which it might have gone wrong. Southwell's manuscript is also valuable because of its revealing account of the final days of a powerful woman; the efforts to transform Elizabeth from a living, breathing and often cantankerous monarch into the idealized Virgin Queen are in need of the type of correction Southwell provides. And finally, the manuscript is worth studying because of its author, a woman who forged a successful place for herself in an Italian court, who managed a large household, and who, without this evidence of her careful powers of observation and interpretation, would be known only as "the faire yong mistress Southwell" who got herself involved in a "great scandal" (Lotti 49; 177).

CATHERINE LOOMIS
UNIVERSITY OF NEW ORLEANS

Elizabeth Southwell. "A True Relation of what succeeded at the sickness and death of Queen Elizabeth" (1607). Archives of the British Providence of the Society of Jesus Shelfmark Stonyhurst ANG. iii 77.
Third page.

Grace (Sherrington) Lady Mildmay, "The Autobiography of Grace Lady Mildmay" (1617–20)

Lady Mildmay's autobiography was written for her family and general readers between the death of her husband in 1617 and her own death in 1620. Its eighty-five manuscript pages precede her much longer "Book of Meditations," a lifelong compilation of private thoughts on scriptural passages and themes. The page reproduced here derives from a prominent early section in which she warmly recalls her relationship with her governess, Mrs. Hamblyn. It is a personal account of educational experiences and daily activities common to many upper-class country gentlewomen.

As a woman of moderately strong Calvinist views, Lady Mildmay takes pride in having been raised to lead a morally scrupulous life, in which she continually analyzes her own motives and—as she mentions at the bottom of this page—scrutinizes the falsely ingratiating behavior of family acquaintances, several of whom are singled out for criticism. Her demonstration of integrity serves a conscious rhetorical purpose, since Lady Mildmay writes to offer her readers moral and spiritual advice, and to defend her actions in a violent inheritance dispute with her sister. In the preceding pages she lists her secular and religious reading—the Bible, chronicle histories, legal texts, Foxe's *Book of Martyrs*, moral treatises and the like—and here indicates some of the imaginative and practical uses to which she puts these works. Literacy and numeracy are central: Mrs Hamblyn encourages her to express herself either by "ciphering" (in various signs or characters) or by composing fictional letters to real or invented people. She practices complex arithmetical calculations in preparation for managing the finances of her future extended household (described in a later section of the autobiography). She also studies books of herbal remedies ("Dr Turners Herball") and surgery ("Bartholomew Vigoe") that will enable her to provide healthcare for her family and the local community, just as Mrs. Hamblyn and her mother have done. Like other Protestants, she reads and sings the Psalms for profit and pleasure (perhaps in the versions composed by Mary [Sidney] Herbert, Countess of Pembroke, as other women such as Aemilia Lanyer attest during this period), and she plies her needle to create intricate embroidery, with Mrs. Hamblyn's own patterns and skill as models. In all these instances, Lady Mildmay celebrates the importance of her familial, and especially female, heritage, and its legacy to her children through her writing and material bequests.

which we haue not, & thereby discouer our folly, &
giue occasion to be laughed att /

J delighted so much in her company that J would
sitt with her all the daye in her chamber, & by my
good will, would neuer goe from her, embraceing
alwayes her rebukes & reproofes /

And when shee did see me ydly disposed, shee would
sett me to cipher with my peïm, & to cast vp and
prooue great sumes & accomptes, & sometymes set
me to wryte some supposed lettir to this or that
body concerning such & such things, & other
tymes set me to reade in Dr Turners Herball, & in
Bartholomew Vigoe, & other tymes set me to sing
psalmes & somtymes set me to some curious worke
for she was an excellent workewoman in all kyndes
of needle worke, & most curyously she would pforme
it .

And when J was not wth her she would be sure to
be with me at my heeles to see where & wth whome
J was, & what J did or spake, such was her honest
& faithfull care to performe the trust wth my
Mother reposed in her .

She gaue me warning of a gentlewoman who frequented my fathers house, to take heed of her, for
that she was of a subtill spirit full of wordes and
questions, & of an vndermyning disposition, a
busy body

6.3: Grace (Sherrington), Lady Mildmay, "The Autobiography of Grace Lady Mildmay" (1617–20).
Reproduced with permission of Northamptonshire Libraries and Information Services.

Transcription

Which we have not, & thereby to discover our folly, &
give occasion to be laughed att.

I delighted so much in her company that I would
sitt with her all the daye in her chamber, & by my
good will, would never goe from her, embraceing
alwayes her rebukes & reproofes.

And when shee did see me idly disposed, shee would
sett me to cipher with my penn, & to cast up and
proove great summes & accomptes, & sometymes set
me to wryte a supposed letter to this or that
body concerning such & such things, & other
tymes set me to reade in Doctor Turners Herball, & in
Bartholomew Vigoe, & other tymes set me to sing
psalmes & somtymes set me to some curious worke
for she was an excellent workewoman in all kynds
of needle worke, & most curyously shee would performe
it.

And when I was not with her she would be sure to
be with mee at my Heeles to see where & with whome
I was, & what I did or spake, such was her honest
& faithfull care to performe the trust which my
Mother reposed in her.

She gave me warning of a gentlewoman who frequented my fathers house, to take heed of her, for
that she was of a subtill spirit, full of wordes and
questions, & of an undermynning disposition, a

busy body

RANDALL MARTIN
UNIVERSITY OF NEW BRUNSWICK

Grace (Sherrington), Lady Mildmay. "The Autobiography of Grace Lady Mildmay" (1617–20), sometimes misleadingly referred to as Lady Mildmay's journal. Northampton Central Library Number 10,
accession number 7839. Page 11.

THE

HISTORY

OF

The LIFE, REIGN, and DEATH

OF

EDWARD II.

King of England,

AND

LORD of IRELAND.

WITH

The Rise and Fall of his great Favourites,

GAVESTON and the *SPENCERS.*

Written by *E. F.* in the year 1627.
And Printed verbatim from the Original.

Qui nescit Dissimulare, nequit vivere, perire melius.

LONDON:

Printed by *J. C.* for *Charles Harper*, at the Flower-de-luce in
Fleet-street ; *Samuel Crouch*, at the Princes Arms in
Popes-head-Alley in *Cornhil* ; and *Thomas Fox* , at
the Angel in *Westminster*-hall. 1 6 8 o.

6.4: Elizabeth (Tanfield) Cary, Viscountess Falkland, *The History of Edward II* (written 1627–28; pub. 1680).
By permission of the Folger Shakespeare Library.

Elizabeth (Tanfield) Cary, Viscountess Falkland, *The History of the Life, Reign, and Death of Edward II* (written 1627–28; pub. 1680)

The History of Edward II (Wing 313, reel 93) is written in strongly rhythmic prose sometimes scannable as blank verse and is interspersed with verse orations printed as prose. Just as its narrative mingles literary forms, hybridity distinguishes Cary's approach to historiography and characterization, creating complexities and paradoxes anticipated by several elements of her title page.

By focusing on the life of a king, Cary's work seems to hearken back to Tudor chronicle history, which tended to uphold traditional political order. Edward II provided a notorious example of disordered rule because his indulgence of two favorites, Piers Gaveston and Hugh de Spencer, and political incompetence had plunged the country into civil war. By mentioning the ultimate destruction of all three, the title page advertises Cary's work as moral history, in which Edward's public and personal behavior will be judged against traditional values of kingship.

On the other hand, the Latin motto *Qui . . . melius* (He who does not know how to dissimulate cannot live, but must perish) alludes to James I's motto, "He who does not know how to dissimulate cannot rule," which is indebted to Machiavelli's new philosophy approving expediency in the pursuit of power and disjoining ethical principles from politics. Machiavelli also exemplified a new approach to writing history, which was less concerned with detecting a divine will in human affairs or expounding moral truths than with investigating secular causes of events in rigorous narratives enlivened by vividly drawn characters and first-person speeches. Cary's *History of Edward II* shares many features of this artistically and ideologically revisionist "practical" history, which was also designed to allude to contemporary figures and events. As overreaching Machiavels, Gaveston and Spencer parallel James I's controversial favorites, George Villiers, Duke of Buckingham, and Robert Carr, Earl of Somerset.

Yet despite the *History*'s emphasis on shrewd analysis and historical reenactment, the title page omits any mention of Cary's most psychologically complex and sympathetic character, Queen Isabel. This absence corresponds to an ambiguous status in Cary's narrative. On the one hand, her agency becomes crucial to mobilizing national opposition to Edward and Spencer, but on the other she remains "marginal," as Cary states, to England's wider story of its (mostly male) monarchs.

This situation parallels the erasure of Cary's authorship of her own work by an erroneous attribution in a related volume. Although she can be indisputably identified with the "E.F." (Elizabeth Falkland) of this title page and the ensuing preface to the reader, a revised abridgement of her *History* published in 1680, probably meant to comment on the 1679–81 Exclusion Crisis, was attributed to her husband (Viscount Falkland and sometime deputy lord lieutenant of Ireland, which probably explains Cary's additional title for Edward, "Lord of *Ireland*"). Although this attribution is impossible, since Falkland died in 1633, certain scholars have projected it back to challenge Cary's authorship of the original *History* written early in 1628 (old style dating, 1627). Ironically, this reprises the traditional view that history could or should be written only by men, an assumption eloquently refuted by Cary's revisionist interpretation of Isabel's activist role and her trenchant historical interrogation—both moral and practical—of Machiavellian patriarchy.

RANDALL MARTIN
UNIVERSITY OF NEW BRUNSWICK

Elizabeth Cary. *History of Edward II* (1680). Wing F313. Folger Shakespeare Library. Title page F313.

Nouember the 10th 1632

The Memorandum of Martha Moulsworth
widdowe

The tenth day of the winter month, Nouember
A day which I must onely still remember
did open first these eies, and shewed the light
Now on that day vpon that daie I write

[margin: Nouember 10th 1632]

This season fitly willinglie combines
the birth day of my selfe, & of these lynes
The tyme the clock the yearly stroke is one
that clocke by striking fiue whorehand gone
Stowe hsews, how many hannings it will giue
He onely knowes in whome we are, & liue

[margin: my muse is a tell clocke enstrikd euery stroke wth a coupled rymd so many tymes viz 55 Acts 17.28.9]

In carnall state of sin originall
I did not stay one whole day naturall
The seale of grace in Sacramentall water
So soone had I, so soone become the daughter
of earthly parents, & of heauenlie father
Some christen late for state, the wiser rather

My Name was Martha, Martha tooke much payne
our Sauiour christ his guesse to entertaine
God gyue me grace my Inward house to dight
that he wth me may suppe, & stay all night

[margin: Luke 10.14]
[margin: Revela: 3.20: Luke 24.29]

My father was a Man of spotles fame
of gentle Birth, & Dorsett was his name
He had, & left lands of his owne possession
he was of Senick trade by his profession
His Mother oxford knowenge wth his worth
arayd in scarlett Robe did send him forth
By him I was brought vpp in godlie pietie
In modest chearefullnes, & sad sobrietie
Nor onlie so, Beyond my sex & kind
he did wth learninge Lattin deck the mind
And why nott so? the muses ffemalls are
and therfore of vs ffemalls take some care
Two vniuersities we haue of Men
o that we had but one of women then

6.5: Martha Moulsworth, "The Memorandum" (1632). The James Marshall and Marie-Louise Osborne Collection, Beinecke Rare Book and Manuscript Library, Yale University.

Martha Moulsworth, "The Memorandum of Martha Moulsworth, Widdowe" (1632)

Transcription

                     November the 10th *1632*
                     The Memorandum of Martha Moulsworth
                            Widdowe
                     The tenth day of the winter month November
                     A day which I must duely still remember
                     did open first theis eis, and shewed this light

November 10th 1632   Now on thatt day* uppon thatt daie I write
                     This season fitly willinglie combines

my muse is a tell   the birth day of my selfe, & of theis lynes
clocke, & ecchoeth   The tyme the clocke, the yearly stroke is one
everie stroke with   thatt clocke by Fiftie five retourns hath gonn
a coupled ryme   How Few, how many warnings itt will give
so many tymes   he only knowe s in whome we are, & live
viz 55
Acts 17.28 v   In carnall state of sin originall
                     I did nott stay one whole day naturall
                     The seale of grace in Sacramentall water
                     so soone had I, so soone become the daughter
                     of earthly parents, & of heavenlie Father
                     Some christen late for state, the wiser rather

Luke 10. 14   My Name was Martha, Martha tooke much payne
                     our Saviour christ hir guesse to entertayne
                     God gyve me grace my Inward house to dight
Revelations 3. 20:   thatt he with me may supp, & stay all night
Luke 24. 29

                     My Father was a Man of spottles Fame
                     of gentle Birth & Dorsett was his name
                     He had, & left Lands of his owne possession
                     he was of Levies tribe by his proffession
                     his Mother oxford knowenge well his worth
                     arayd in scarlett Robe did send him Forth
                     By him I was brought upp in godlie pietie
                     In modest chearefullnes, & sad sobrietie
                     Nor onlie so, Beyond my sex & kind
                     he did with learninge Lattin decke [my] mind
                     And whie nott so? the muses Femalls are
                     and therfore of us Females take some care
                     Two universities we have of men
                     o thatt we had but one of women then

Commentary

Although one can readily interpret Martha Moulsworth's 1632 poem, "The Memorandum of Martha Moulsworth Widdowe," by reading it meticulously, one may also discern a great deal about the poem by carefully scrutinizing the original physical document itself.

The poem begins unlike many others written during the Renaissance in that Moulsworth provides the date—"November the 10th *1632*"; in fact, the year is the only part of Moulsworth's poem that is underlined, manifesting its importance to her. Barbara Lewalski confirms that the poem is "carefully dated" (Introd. 1. 1552). The appearance of the date on the document is important simply by its very presence because most poets of the era did not consider the date on which a poem was composed to be worthy of inclusion; very few Renaissance poems supply such a date. In addition, the poet even writes down the date again shortly thereafter in a marginal note to the left of line 4. Moulsworth's "Memorandum" demonstrates that the poet underwent many significant changes in her life, such as marrying and burying three husbands. Her decision to provide a date for the manuscript suggests that she is writing about her present emotions, how she feels about her life at this moment of her existence. 10 November 1632, is an important date to her; she calls it "the birth day of my selfe, & of theis lynes" (l. 6), indicating that she correlates her birth(day) with the birth of this autobiographical poem. It is clear that Moulsworth intermingles her life story with the poem, for she has lived fifty-five years and her poem consists of fifty-five couplets.

The next two lines beneath the date serve as her title. Many lines of the poem—such as lines 43, 44, 51, and 53—are longer than both lines of the title combined, and on the first page of Moulsworth's handwritten manuscript, line 17 is considerably longer than the title. These facts suggest that the writer purposefully chose to place the word "Widdowe" on a separate line from the rest of the title. Although Moulsworth possesses sufficient room on the first line to include her entire title, she decides to put the last word— "Widdowe"—on the following line, thus setting it apart and emphasizing it. Although she lauds her three deceased husbands, she is proud to have survived them and wears the label "Widdowe" as a badge of honor. Despite her love for her three husbands, in her patriarchal culture she has most probably not enjoyed much autonomy but is now enjoying, at age fifty-five, her freedom—hence, again, "the birth day of my selfe." Matthew Steggle claims that Moulsworth's use of tricolons, which she employs judiciously at the poem's climaxes (such as line 95), indicates her desire for freedom: "thematically, it can be said that three is the number of conclusion in this poem: it is a rhetorical reflection of the declaration to stop at three husbands" (30). The text also manifests that her freedom is new, which is perhaps another reason for writing the poem; to Moulsworth, her widowhood symbolizes a rebirth of herself, for she has been married for practically her entire adult life. Moulsworth notes that she first married at age twenty-one, for a period of five years and eight months, with a subsequent one-year mourning period (lines 49–54). Her second marriage lasted ten years and nine months, with a subsequent three-year, eight-month mourning period (lines 55–56). Moulsworth's third marriage survived for eleven years and eight months (line 63). Therefore, Moulsworth was married for twenty-eight years and one month, with four years and eight months of mourning. These figures indicate that she has been a widow for approximately one year, perhaps less if she rounds off the age at which she married for the first time. Evidently, she has been married or in a period of mourning for a deceased husband during practically all of her adult life. As Mary Ellen Lamb observes, the design of the poem indicates that "Moulsworth structured her life in terms of her marriages; in fact, page breaks in the manuscript coincide with its division into thirds (or almost thirds) corresponding to the three periods of Moulsworth's life; before her marriages, during her marriages, and after her marriages" ("The Poem" 92). And prior to her marriages, she lived under the authority of her father (who died when she was three years old) and her stepfather, Ralph Johnson. After the first funerals of her first two husbands, she initiated periods of mourning, for a part of her had died along with her husbands. After the death of the third husband, she mourned initially, but she now experiences a feeling of rebirth and autonomy—a freedom she refuses to relinquish. And she celebrates this rebirth and liberty by writing her "Memorandum."

In her "Memorandum," Moulsworth stresses her education and her faith in God. Although the reader can discern these strong interests in the poem itself, they are also apparent in the poet's notes that appear in the left margin of the work. By appending these marginal notes, Moulsworth guides, to some extent her readers' interpretations, encouraging them to focus on certain lines that she considers to be of primary importance. Her allusions to the Bible, for example, manifest to readers her excellent command of Scripture and her intellect. These allusions support her argument that women, like men, deserve formal educations. In his discussion of the vicar Thomas Hassall's sermon on the death of Martha Moulsworth, Robert Evans notes that the poet "must have had an active hand in tutoring many of the grown children who now sat among her mourners, including her executrix, Elizabeth Thorowgood Rawdon. Perhaps she even helped educate her numerous step-grandchildren. In any case, Hassall's words suggest that Moulsworth's remarks in the 'Memorandum' about the need for a women's university reflect her own experience as an educator who had herself taught girls but who could teach them only to a limited extent" ("The Life" 70). Furthermore, Moulsworth must have been proud that her father had been a tutor of the prominent Sir Philip Sidney. John Shawcross observes, contrariwise, that women in Moulsworth's era almost never published because any female who did was considered a ridiculous person, a hermaphrodite, or a monster—three descriptions that derive from Dorothy Osborne's description of Margaret Cavendish in a letter to Sir William Temple (166); the fact that this is a female's description of another woman, and that it is addressed to a man, is even more telling. If a woman's perception of female poets publishing is male chauvinistic, one can only guess how men of the era felt. This attitude probably had the most negative impact on women who aspired to have formal education. Perhaps, then, Moulsworth's marginal notes are her way of demonstrating that women are indeed capable of erudition, intelligence, and mastery of Scripture, and that they therefore deserve the opportunity to acquire formal educations in a university.

ERIC STERLING
AUBURN UNIVERSITY MONTGOMERY

Martha Moulsworth. "The Memorandum of Martha Moulsworth / Widdowe." Yale University Beinecke Library Osborn MS fb 150. Page dated November 10th 1632.

so great and violent a trouble, that casting himself on the
ground he would not rise nor eate from morning till night,
weeping even to roaring; using for arguments (to make her
returne) the disgrace of their company, and that she would
hurt others making them afraid of them, and that every
one would say this was the end of those that receaved their
opinions, but seeing he noway prevailed wth her (but only to
sitt fasting wth him all day) he went his way, coming no more
to her, none of her former acquaintance of that kind, yet
she vsed allwayes, those that were deserving of them, more respectfully then ordinary, and had her house after frequented by
some others, who being morall and of good parts, were very welcome thither, and indeed out of her loue and esteeme of learning,
she had a most particular devotion and desire to their conversions, having principally (as she professeth in the Epistle to
the reader) for the sakes of the scholers of Oxford and Cambridge (who doe not generally vnderstand french) translated
Cardinall Perones workes.

Her Lords Agent in England, wthout staying to expect order from his lord (who yet as soone as he knew wt had past
was exceedingly angry wth her) immeadiatly stops her allowance,
so as she (who never was much aforehand) was in a little while
brought to some extreamity, being constrained to send her children (for her eldest daughter was gone from
her before, to court, being one of the first English mardes
that had the honer to serue her Majesty) and those that
waited on them, abroad to diners and suppers, not being
willing to part wth them altogether, till they should be taken from her, wch they were very soone by her Lords command to her chiefe servant, who together wth them tooke
away all her old servants (but only one young maide, whom

6.6: Anne or Lucy Cary, "Lady Falkland: Her Life" (c. 1645). Courtesy of the Archives Départmentales du Nord, Lille. Photo: Jean-Luc Thierry.

Anne or Lucy Cary, "Lady Falkland: Her Life" (c. 1645)

Transcription

so great and violent a trowble, that casting himself on the ground he would not rise nor eate from morning till night, weeping even to roaring; using for arguments (to make her returne) the disgrace of thier company, and that she would hurt others making them afraid of them, and that every one would say this was the end of those that receaved their opinions, but seeing he no way prevailed with her (but only to sitt fasting with him all day) he went his way, coming no more to her, no more did none of her former acquaintance of that kind, yet she used allwayes, those that were deserving of them, more respectfully then ordinary, and had her house after frequented by some others, who being morall and of good parts, were very wellcome thither, and indeed out of her love and esteeme of learning, she had a most particular devotion and desire to their conversions, having principally (as she professeth in the Epistle to the reader) for the sakes of the scholers of Oxford and Cambridge (who doe not generally understand french) translated Cardinall Perones workes.

Her Lords Agent in England, without staying to expect order from his lord (who yet as soone as he knew what had past was exeedingly angry with her) immediately stops her allowance, so as she (who never was much aforehand) was in a little while brought to some extreamity, being constrained to send her children (for her eldest daughter was gone from her before, to court, being one of the first English maides that had the honer to serve her Majesty) and those that waited on them, abroad to thier frinds to dinners and suppers, not being willing to part with them alltogether, till they should be taken from her, which they were very soone by her Lords command to her chiefe servant [marginal note: Mr Hitchcock.], who together with them tooke away all her old servants (but only one young maide [marginal note: Besse Poulter.], whom

---

Commentary

Lady Falkland: Her Life, held in the Archives Départmentales du Nord, Lille, France, is a rich and highly crafted account of the contentious life of the author Elizabeth Cary (c.1585–1639). Four of Cary's daughters were nuns in the Benedictine Convent at Cambrai, and the unsigned manuscript biography, written in a legible italic hand, was composed by one of them. Though the identity of the biographer is uncertain, Lucy Cary is the most probable candidate for authorship (see Latz, and Wolfe "Scribal"); an argument has also been made for Anne Cary (Foster). The biographer notes that it was "through reading, [that Cary] grew into much doubt of her religion," (Wolfe, *Life* 110), and after over twenty years of spiritual turmoil Elizabeth Cary had, by December 1626, converted to Roman Catholicism. Phrases such as "after she was a Catholic" resonate throughout the biography, reminding the reader that Cary's conversion, referred to as her "reconciliation," is the determining moment in the narrative of *Life*.

Queen Henrietta Maria, wife of King Charles I, was Roman Catholic, and there was widespread concern (and undoubtedly some anticipation) that she would offer encouragement to English Catholics, especially to those who, like Cary herself, were of high enough rank to be associated with the court. Though Cary's eminent patrons provided assistance, she nonetheless experienced personal and public ramifications of her religious dissent. As this selection suggests, spirituality was not separable from day-to-day existence, and Elizabeth Cary's break from the Church of England was also a break from familial and social order. Her husband ceased financial support, which greatly depleted Cary's household and placed her in relative poverty. At times near starvation, she sent her children to dine with friends: here and elsewhere, lack of food foregrounds the ongoing tension between religious conviction and maternal obligation. Soon after, her husband removed their children from her care. Cary's fantastic struggle to gain back custody was driven by both parental and spiritual interests, and her goal was eventually realized, in part through the bold kidnapping of her two youngest sons. It was not uncommon for English Catholic gentry to defy the law and covertly send their children overseas to receive an education, as did Cary. That six of her offspring converted to Catholicism—four daughters were nuns; two sons, however, eventually left the Catholic Church—speaks to the significant role women played in the education, religious and otherwise, of their children.

In the midst of detailing marital rejection and familial isolation, *Life* briefly returns to Cary's love of learning and proficiency with languages. By introducing her translation of the work of the Counter-Reformation controversialist Jacques Davy du Perron (1556–1618), the biographer invokes Cary's intellect, offsetting domestic loss by placing her within a broader Catholic community. Her translation, entitled *The Reply of the Most Illustrious Cardinall of Perron* and published in 1630 in Douai, was dedicated to Henrietta Maria, at whose court Anne served, and who would later become a benefactor of the Paris Convent, founded in part by Anne (Latz 79). Like much sectarian writing that would have been subject to censorship in England, it was printed abroad. In what is certainly a narrative flourish, *The Reply* is associated not only with Elizabeth Cary's religious belief, but with that of her husband as well. Presenting the religion that initially fractured the family as the influence that may ultimately bring them together, *Life* subsequently reports that on his deathbed Henry Cary refused to affirm his Protestantism. The biographer optimistically suggests that Cary's translation of *The Reply*, which was "found in [Henry Cary's] clossett after his death, all noated [i.e., annotated] by him," may have "inclined him to haue a desire of being a Catholike" (Wolfe, *Life* 151).

Kristin Lucas
McGill University

Anne or Lucy Cary. "Lady Falkland: Her Life." Archives Départementales du Nord 20H9, fol.14r.

Joyce Jefferies, spinster, Financial Diary (1638–49)

Commentary

It was not unusual in early modern England for spinsters and widows to lend money as a means of earning a living. The financial diary of Joyce Jefferies, a spinster living in and around the city of Hereford until her death in 1650, is almost certainly the most detailed account of such activities by an unmarried woman up to that time. Jefferies inherited legacies from her father, Henry Jefferies; her mother, Anne, née Barnaby; her stepbrother Humphrey Coningsby; and her cousin Thomas Coningsby. In addition to some investments in agricultural activities, she lent money at current interest rates to borrowers scattered over several counties. Although the total of her wealth cannot accurately be estimated, these sources yielded up to £650 a year in income during the period covered by the diary (1638–49). This allowed Jefferies to play an active and genteel role in the social and financial circles of the West Midlands and even extending to London.

The document itself remains in manuscript form as British Library, Egerton MS. 3054. It is almost entirely written by Jefferies herself and is divided into two parts. The opening twenty-three folios, entitled "A New Booke of Receights of Rents Anueties and Interest moneys," provide a detailed record of her income from moneylending and other sources. Plate 1 shows returns from her loans, with name of borrower, principal and term, and income received. Following 17 blank folios, a second section of 48 folios entitled "A Booke of New Disbursements" records both professional and (especially) personal and household expenditures of all sorts. Its wealth of detail and breadth of subject matter allow an extensive reconstruction of the circumstances and major events of the last decade of Jefferies's life. It shows her full engagement in the social and cultural life of her milieu, and especially her ties and relations with other women. Plate 2 shows her total expenditures.

The diary has been known since the mid–nineteenth century by antiquarians, who have found it informative but have not placed it into any particular interpretive context. More recent scholarship has found it useful for its insights into both contemporary moneylending practices and the social world of spinsters of that time. It shows us that a spinster of gentle but certainly not aristocratic status, given a nest egg on which to build, could sustain herself quite comfortably in mid-seventeenth century provincial society. Although she was compelled to abandon her house in the City of Hereford during the civil wars (she describes for us its destruction as a defensive measure against approaching parliamentary troops), and despite the consequent necessity of frequent moves from the residence of one friend or relative to another during these years, she engaged freely in the material culture of the day. We know that she kept a coach and coachman as well as one or two household servants at all times. We know that she entertained and enjoyed invitations to entertainments elsewhere. We know, too, that she regularly contributed to her preferred parish church; bought jewelery, clothes, a pet caged bird, and a pair of spectacles; and gave both frequent and even lavish benefactions on a considerable number of friends, relatives, and servants. Finally, the accounts of her expenditures are sufficiently ample to afford one other impression that is particularly germane to this volume: a strikingly large proportion of her domestic purchases was

6.7(1): Joyce Jeffries, spinster, Financial Diary (1638–49).
By permission of The British Library.

Transcription

Plate 1.[1] A New Booke of Receights of Rents Anueties [fol.] 1
and Interest moneys begining at St mary day 1638
written at Heryford, at John fletchers howse[2]

Rece of Thomas Caswalle seriton[3] of Leominster
6: months usse, for £20 due february 17–1638_____16s
Rece of Mr william Moris of Hampton court[4]_____50s
9: yeares & halfs usse for £7 10s Stock due January 19:1637
the Rest I forgave his father & him
Rece of mr James Newton of bodenham :6:months_____40s
usse for £80 upon morgage of land due January 26 1637
Rece of John Wimmes 6: months Rent for the free towne
farme, & my free hould I heve. due at St mary day 1638_____£47 5s
Rece from my cosin brabazon of Eaton:[5] by Mr cales moore
6 months usse for £150 due Aprill 18:1638_____£6
Rece of Mr John Walle of Kingsland: 2: yeares usse
for £40 Stock due January 26 1637_____£6 8s
Rece of him in full disscharge of the charge in
Law of the Above written £40_____£4 14s
Rece from my Cosin Thomas Barneby of bromyerd :12:
months usse for £60 due february 13: 1637: by Mr Evet_____£4 16s
Rece of Daniell Powle of Leinterdine[6] & Mr Richard
Acton of Ivington :6: months usse for £20_____16s
due Aprill the 7: 1638 first tyme.
Rece of James Bithell of New church :2: yeares
usse for £10 due 7: 1638_____32s
my cosin browne had 6s for law charges of mr betsell
Rece of Mr Isack Weaver of the broome in pembruge
parish[7] 6: months usse for £50 due May:3: 1638_____40s
Rece of Edmund Steade[8] of leominster :6: months
usse for £10 due Aprill.11.1638_____8s
Rece of Thomas badnidge glover 6:months usse
for £10 due may-8–1638_____8s
Rece of John Wanklin: from his father William
wanklin of leominster one yeares usse for
£15 due Aprill-4–1638_____24s
Rece of James seaburn & francis caradine mercer[9]
6: months usse for £20 due march 15–1637_____16s
Rece of William Brainch for afatt wether_____13s 6d
Rece of mr John weaver of wiggmor 6:months
usse for £50 due Aprill 24:1638_____40s
Rece of James Dudson of Sutton: one years
usse for £20 due January-5:1637_____32s

6.7(2): Joyce Jeffries, spinster, Financial Diary (1638–49).
By permission of The British Library.

Rece of worthy Mr fitzwilliam Conyngesby[10] my
half yeares Anuety: due at St mary day 1638_____ £33 6s
out of the lordship of Nene Sollers: & cutston[11]
Rece the same tyme of Mr Conyngesby my half
yeares Anuety given me by Sir Thomas Coningesby[12]_____ £5
Rece of mr Thomas Hackluit of Kintley: 6:months
usse for £200 upon a stattute due June 9:1638_____ 1s

£140 6s tru cast

Transcription

Plate 2. 1639 Aprill	Heryford Dissbursments	[fol.] 32
13	gave the clarcks wyfe of all saints in heriford	
	for dressing up my seate at church_____	4d
19	gave my cosin Cosin John	
	Hackluit: som tyme of Eaton_____	5s
	for half adaies hedging and fencing abowte	
	the corn in weggnoll. 2: men_____	8d
	more for diching & fencing the same corn_____	4d
	paid powell the walker & dier for cullering	
	& pressing 7: yeardes: of musk culler cloth_____	8s 2d
Elyza Acton	for Elyza: Actons[13] winter gowne	
gowne	for cullering 8: yeards of bastard skarlet	
	for her Riding Shute & the pressing_____	8s 8d
	for scowring 8: yeardes of greene carpeting	
	& pressing the same carpit & cobert cloth_____	2s 8d
Rent	paid the widdow beedlston:[14] 6: months _____	20s
24	Rent for the howse next myne: due at St mary day 1639.	
	paid mr John Haggley: vicker of alsaints in	
	heryford: for my offerings at Ester and for_____	10s
30	teith of my gardins	
poore of	paid half a years usse for the mainteinance	
Nene	of the poore of Nene Solers: due at holirooday 1639_____	8s
	gave my ould cosin blunts wyfe_____	6d
	for 2: trisells for the end of the spitt_____	6d
May	Inke—1d gave my cosin Harbert Jeffreys__10s_____	10s 1d
1	gave my cosin Phillips maid brought chikins_____	6d
4	gave Joane Halle brought chickins from kintley_____	1s
mellin	gave Elyza: Acton-5s & mr maiors porter-4d_____	5s 4d
at the law	Sent to mr Henry mellin: maiore of herifford_____	10s
day	gave the waites: at the maiors feast_____	1s
	To John Bache for helpping with my coults to herifford___	8d
coache	gave francis Stock mr Church his carter for	
mares	teachinge my 2:yong: bay coache mares to draw_____	3s 4d

12	gave mrs mary wallwin:1s & mrs Rogers-1s_____	2s
starche	for 12: pownd of white starch_____	4s
usse	paid Anne Davies 6:months usse for	
	£20 that I owe her due Aprill 28:1639_____	16s
	paid mr mellins the maiers for charidge of	
18	one Loade of the ellme that I bought at ailston_____	20d
John	paide John heane for helpping to pille	
heane	up powles & drawes in my new wood pile	
	6: daies: and 2: half daies in all_____	4s 06
Smith	Hugh Watkins bill paid for shiring	
	and Removinge my 3: mares_____	3s 4d
	to Harry meredith smith for mending the	
	Iron of my Coach boote: & pinnes_____	10d
22	for 2: paps of blak pines_____	6d
the charge of	Imprimus for 3 red skinnes: & nailes of brass_____	8s
my 4: new	for cotten & 300: of tacks_____	14d
cheiers vide	for 500: of bushell nails-10d-square tacks-200 3d_____	13d
[2]: of Stanill	blue & [y]elow Statute Lace that lacked 2:yerd quarter____	5d
[&] 2:green	for 8: oz of crule to make up the fringe_____	2s 6d
[c]loth	for 8: [y]elow ship: skinnes at 8d apeece_____	5s 4d
	For a yeard of powle davy[15] to line the armes of	
	The 2: Stamill cheiers[16]_____	1s
	Paid Rowland Androse for making up those	
	4: cheiers: 2: stamill, & 2: greene_____	5s

£7–13s–5d–06– tru cast

Notes

1. Marginalia on this page have not been transcribed because the tightness of the manuscript's binding makes it impossible to see anything more than is shown in the left margin here.

2. Jefferies lived in a house in Widmarsh (now Widemarsh) Street, Hereford, owned by John Fletcher, for which she paid three pounds twice a year. She continued to live there even after Fletcher's death in March 1642, paying rent to his widow instead.

3. I.e., "servitor," meaning "servant."

4. This is not a reference to the royal palace but rather a Herefordshire village and manor of the same name.

5. Probably Wallace Brabazon, a prominent gentleman and former sheriff of Herefordshire, whose seat at Eaton was a mile from Leominster. Moore was his servant.

6. I.e., Leinwardine, Herefordshire, northwest of Hereford.

7. "The Broom" appears to be an inn, of which Weaver is the keeper.

8. Steade served as bailiff of the town of Leominster in 1638–39.

9. Both were mercers, Caradine of Withington, Herefordshire and Seaborn of Worcester.

10. Joyce Jefferies's cousin, who lived ca. 1593–1666, and who sometimes served as sheriff of Herefordshire.

11. A Shropshire parish and manor, the lordship of the latter having been held by Jefferies's mother, Anne, and inherited by the Conyngsbys.

12. Father of Fitzwilliam and prominent member of the shire gentry, d. 1626.

13. Eliza Acton was Jefferies's god-daughter, distant cousin, and companion until her marriage in 1643. Jefferies supported her until that time and gave her a dowry of £800.

14. Jefferies rented a house from Beedleston for the use of her indigent cousin Jane Gorton.

15. "Poldavy" a canvas-like cloth woven especially in Brittany.

16. "Stammel chairs," stammel being a coarse red-dyed woollen cloth or a cloth dyed red so as to look like stammel.

from female rather than male retailers and craftspeople. It suggests that Jefferies was not only a self-reliant and independent woman herself, but also that she consciously and continually supported the similarly independent activities of numerous other women in the three-county region of her activities.

Robert Tittler
Concordia University

Joyce Jefferies, spinster, Financial Diary (1638–49). British Library Egerton MS. 3054. fol. 1r and fol. 32r.

6.8: Mary Penington, "An account . . . of her Exercises from her Childhood till her convincement," transcribed by her son John Penington (1655-1710). Courtesy of the Library Committee of Britain Yearly Meeting, Library of the Religious Society of Friends, London.

Mary Penington, "An account left by my dear mother Mary Penington of her Exercises from her Childhood till her convincement," transcribed by her son John Penington (1655–1710)

Transcription

to be banished. This thing struck deep into me & strong cryes were in me for them, & for the innocent people in the nation, & it wrought strongly in me, that I could not sit at my work; but was strongly inclined to go into a private room, & shutting the door kneeled down & poured out my soul to the Lord in a very vehement manner for a pretty time, & I was wonderfully melted & eased & felt peace in the thing, & acceptation with the Lord, & that this was prayer which I was never acquainted before, either in my selfe or from any one. Not long after this, word was brought to the house, that a Neighbouring Minister, that had been suspended by the Bishops for not being subject to their Canons, was returned to his people again, & that he was to preach at the place where he did formerly 3. years before, being suspended so long. I hearing of it desired to go, but was reproved by those that had the education of me, as being not fit to leave my parish Church; but I could not comply with their mind in it, but I must go, & when I came the Minister was one called a Puritan, & he prayed fervently & in much sense, & then I felt this is that is prayer: & that my mind pressed after but could not come at it, in my own will, only had tasted of it that time I mentioned before. Now I knew this was prayer, but here I mourned sorely, for that I kneeled down morning after morning & night after night, & had not a word to say, & the trouble of this was so great that I thought it was just I perish in the night, because I had not prayed, & in the day that my food might not prosper with me, because I could not pray. I was exercised with this a great time; then I could not come to the common Prayer that was read in the Family at nights. Also I could not kneel down when I came into their worsship house (as was the custom & I had been taught) but this Scripture was in my mind, Be more ready to hear, than offer the sacrifice of fools: & I could not but read the Bible or some book whilest the Priest read common Prayer at their worship house, & at last I could neither kneel nor stand up to join with the Priest in his Prayer before the Sermon, neither did I care to hear them preach, but my mind ran after hearing the Non-conformist called a Puritan aforementioned, but I by constraint went in the morning with those of the family where I was, but could not be kept from the Puritan Preacher in the Afternoon: I went through much suffering for this thing, being forced to go on foot 2. or 3. miles, & none permitted to go with me; but as a servant in compassion would sometimes run after me, lest I should be frighted going alone. I was very young but so zealous in this, that all their threatnings & reasonings could not keep me back, & in short time I would not hear the Priest where we dwelt at all, but went wet or dry, to the other place, & in the family I would go in to hear Scripture read, & if I did happen to go in before they had done their prayers, I would sit when they kneeled. These things wrought me much trouble in the family, & there was none to take my part; but 2 of the maidservants were inclined to mind what I said against their prayers, & so refused to join with them, at which the Governors of the family were much disturbed, & made me the subject of their discourse in Company, as that I would pray with the spirit, & rejected godly mens prayers, & I was Proud & a Schismatick, & that I went to those places to meet young men & such like. In this time I suffered not only from these persons to whom I was by my Parents committed (who both died when I was not above 3. years of age) but also suffered much from my Companions & Kindred; notwithstanding in this zeal I grew much, & was sequestred from my vain Company, & refused carding & such like things, & was a zealous keeper of the Sabbath, not daring to eat or be cloathed with such things as occasioned trouble, or spent time on that day. I was given up to hearing & praying. I minded not those Marriages propounded to me of vain persons, but having desired of the Lord that I might have one that feared him, I had a belief, that though then I knew none of my outward rank that was such a one, yet that the Lord would provide one for me; & in this belief I went, not regarding their reproaches, that would say to me, no Gentleman (but mean persons) was of this way, & that I would have some mean one or other; but they were dissappointed, for the Lord toucht the heart of him that was afterwards my husband, & my heart cleaved to him for the Lords sake. He was of a good understanding & cast off those dead superstitions that were manifest to him in that day, beyond any that I then knew of his rank & years, which were but small, for that stature he was of in the things of God, being but about 20. years of Age. He pressed much after the knowledg of the Lord & walked in his fear. We being both very young were joined together in the Lord, & refused a ring & such like things then used, & not denied by any that we knew of. We lived together about 2. years & a month. We were zealously affected, daily exercised in that we judged to be the service & worship of God. We scrupled many things

---

Commentary

Mary (Springett) Pening ton's autobiographical manuscripts, which no longer exist in autograph, were preserved by her two eldest sons from her second marriage to Isaac Pening ton, Quaker mystic and writer. John's copy ends with Mary's prophetic dream about her Quaker conversion. Edward's version includes his mother's later, unusual additions to her spiritual autobiography: the newly converted family's economic and social degradation; the renovation of a new home after their expulsion from Isaac's estate; and her epistolary biography of her first husband, William Springett, addressed to her grandson, Springett Penn, a suspenseful, lively narrative, particularly in its account of Mary's hazardous journey to attend her first husband's deathbed.

Mary Pening ton's manuscripts illuminate the obstacles facing seventeenth-century women who sought a different spiritual life than that offered by England's national church (the Anglican, or Established, Church) and enforced by the gentried, conforming family. Orphaned at age three, Mary lived in the Anglican household of Sir Edward Partridge until her marriage at eighteen. Mary fully experiences her inability to pray with spiritual openness after a moment of "true prayer," triggered by one of the autobiography's rare intersections between the political upheavals of the 1630s and Mary's on-going spiritual crisis. Told that "Prynne, Bastwick, & Burton, were sentenced to have their ears cut, and to be banished" (125), Mary finds herself moved to extemporaneous and emotionally fervent prayer of the kind Puritans aspired to. John Bastwick, doctor and Presbyterian, William Prynne, lawyer, and Dr. Henry Burton, dissenting minister, were charged with seditious libel, tried by the Star Chamber and condemned to public mutilation and lifelong confinement for their books and sermons, all vitriolic attacks on the Church and its bishops. Like these Puritan icons of resistance, Mary defies authority in the name of her developing religious convictions. After this moment of "true prayer," Mary seeks an intimate relationship with God, rejecting Anglicanism in favor of a nonconformist preacher's ministry. Resisting her insertion into the community structures of the Established Church, Mary uses the space of Anglican worship as a forum within which to oppose publicly this religion's ritual and "dead superstitions"(such as kneeling or standing while the priest reads from the Book of Common Prayer), which have replaced a passionate, individualized faith.

Mary's spiritual radicalism disrupts both public and private spheres, as she pairs her resistance to the Established Church with her resistance to the patriarchal family. Her refusal to participate in family prayer constitutes a rejection of the authority of "those who had the education of [her]" to fashion her life. Moreover, in persuading two of the family's maidservants that formalized prayer was not "true prayer," Mary encourages an insurrection against the authorities of the family that violates gender and class hierarchy. When the two servants refuse to attend family common prayer, "the Governors of the family" launch a formidable attack against Mary's character, one that relies on seventeenth-century constructions of femininity. By making Mary "the subject of their discourse in Company," family authorities hope to shame her into obedient silence and conformity, since such public and contemptuous speech damaged a woman's reputation. In short, they punish her publicly for her own public rejection of their authority and that of the Established Church, by accusing her of being driven by licentious rather than spiritual desires, and of attending these nonconformist services "to meet young men & such like." The linkage of independence with sexual incontinence was a common tactic to control unruly women.

Friends and family reiterate Mary's bleak marriage prospects, indicating the mutually reinforcing relationship between Anglicanism and class. Threatened with marriage outside the gentry, since "no Gentleman (but mean persons) was of this way," Mary stands firm in her beliefs, finally marrying William Springett, Puritan gentleman and Partridge's nephew. With her husband's support, Mary rejects public and private Anglican worship: "We married without a ring: and, by his desire, many of the usual, dark, formal words were left out of the ceremony" (127). They "edit" their Anglican bibles, tearing out those parts that nonconformists generally perceived as unsanctioned additions to God's word; they reject the two sacraments of the Anglican Church—Communion ("Bread and Wine") and Baptism. Although Mary does not explain why she and William decide against Independency, the Independents's relative emphasis on the role of the intellect in the believer's spiritual life may have repulsed two young people who sought a religion that would answer "the cry of [their] hearts." Mary's refusal to baptize her daughter functions as the final public rejection of community, familial, and church authority.

Mary's further trials reveal a spiritual autobiography that both conforms to and deviates from generic conventions. Deciding that "the Lord and his truth was, but that it was made known to none upon the earth," Mary turns from ascetic religious devotions to "recreations," such as "carding, dancing, singing and frequenting Musick meetings" (127). While the alternation of hope and despair is typical of many spiritual autobiographies, Mary's is atypical in reversing "the received wisdom about the interplay of worldliness and religion," where it is expected that "churchgoing or other forms of religious devotion lead one away from the follies and vanities of the world" (Burns 71); that is, Mary later "declares that she [has] taken up vain and carnal activities *because* she [has] tried so hard to seek the Lord" and found "emptiness in all the available ways of Christian worship"

Burns (72). In rejecting baptism and formal prayers for spontaneous private devotions, Mary realizes that she has simply traded one set of formal duties for another.

Like many seventeenth-century spiritual autobiographies, Penington's is structured through "a constant movement of conviction of sinfulness followed by the experience of forgiveness, not just once in a lifetime, but continually" (Hinds 152). The sectarian manuscript culture within which her autobiography was written, reproduced, and circulated, however, allows for interesting generic innovations. Female spiritual autobiographers intent on the print market found themselves in a double bind; the emphasis on the spiritual and the exclusion of the material was typical of the genre, yet to suppress the details of "homes, families, and selves" was to suggest that "women's proper areas of concern . . . were of secondary or even peripheral importance," a threatening stance to contemporary male readers and critics. To include such details, however, would be to court charges of "vainglory and immodesty," since they would imply "the singularity and inherent interest of [the autobiographers's] own circumstances" (172). Sectarian women writers often responded by suppressing details of family life, but Penington's introspective autobiography does not slight the concerns of family. The family as obstacle to Penington's spiritual journey is clearly delineated, as is the new type of family that she and her first husband attempt to create. Like Agnes Beaumont's spiritual autobiography, Mary Penington's suggests that the female spiritual autobiographer's double bind and the silences it creates are largely a function of female authorship in seventeenth-century print culture.

MARIE LOUGHLIN
OKANAGAN UNIVERSITY COLLEGE

Mary Penington. "An account left by my dear mother Mary Penington of her Exercises from her Childhood till her convincement." Transcribed by John Penington. Library of the Religious Society of Friends (London) Penington MSS, Vol. iv.; MS Vol 344. Page 126.

Elizabeth With of Woodbridge, *Elizabeth Fools Warning* (1659)

Elizabeth Fools Warning, a collection of six poems printed in London in 1659, claims to offer "a true and most perfect relation of all that has happened to her since her marriage" and "a Caveat for all young women to marry with old men." The author is identified as "*Elizabeth With* of Woodbridge," and much evidence confirms this identification. With's poems provide what is apparently one of the few extensive depictions of the breakdown of a seventeenth-century middle-class marriage, especially as recounted by a wife. Although historians agree about the potential value of such evidence, With's case seems to have gone virtually unnoticed.

With claims to have lived in Woodbridge, Suffolk, during the 1650s. While still young and relatively poor, she was courted by an older, wealthy widower whose first wife had allegedly hanged herself. The widower, however, promised Elizabeth happiness, prosperity, and fine clothes, and she confesses that one of her motives in marrying was a desire to live and dress well. She says that her "dame" (presumably an employer) advised her to wed, and that she married without consulting her family. Within weeks, however, her marriage began to crumble, partly thanks to the widower's malicious sister, who encouraged him to strip Elizabeth of her rich clothes and to give the finery to his daughter. Shortly after marrying, With claims, her husband dowsed her with water after she merely picked a cherry from one of his trees.

Their relations soon went from bad to worse. She claims that he often attacked her both verbally and physically, and that her stepchildren and sister-in-law joined in the psychological abuse. Nevertheless, she eventually did bear him a son and daughter, but she alleges that these births so enraged her miserly, alcoholic husband that he thereafter locked her out of their bedroom. After enduring this life for nearly a decade, With left their home, her husband agreeing to pay a small yearly stipend for her lodging. She nursed a poor woman and then kept house, sleeping on a floor mat (after refusing her sister-in-law's offer of a tawdry mattress). She claims to have suffered severe poverty, surviving only thanks to the assistance of a "son" (perhaps a stepson) named Thomas. Matters became even more desperate when her husband refused the promised stipend. At this point she decided she must move to London, but even this event was not uncomplicated. After she paid a male horse owner to transport her belongings, her husband and his allies accused her of having absconded with a married man—a charge she bitterly denies. As she writes, she fluctuates between a desire to make her husband literally pay (in court) and a hope that they might eventually reconcile.

How much of this is true? Surviving records indicate that much is, and nothing turned up so far undermines the basic accuracy of the story. Obviously With presents only her version of events, but many of her assertions can be easily corroborated. Her poems, moreover, elaborately confirm scores of claims made in recent studies of the status of women and the breakdowns of marriages in seventeenth-century England. The poems particularly illustrate the especially precarious positions wives faced when marriages failed. When the poems are seen in this larger context, one can only admire With's strength and resourcefulness. She seems to have been enormously patient and forbearing—a woman who endured nearly ten years of pain but who seems to have been determined not only to survive physically and psychologically but also to assert and preserve her social (and self-) respect. Many persons might easily have been broken by the suffering she endured, and

(3)

But Grace, Vertue, Goodnesse
  above all I desire:
Let husband, sister, daughter all
  against me conspire,
God turn their hearts, and keep them
  from hells tormenting fire.

Elizabeth Fools Warning.

ALl you young women that live here in
                      (health
Marry not with old men, hoping to get wealth.
For riches have wings, and flie like the wind,
I married for riches, but none could I find.
Were I now to marry, learn would I more
For now I am forced my living to get. (wit,
I married in youth, a man struck in age,
Who vowed fond love, but fell into rage:
Instead of a kisse, I oft got a Ban,
And many a curs'd blow from my old man:
Oh, foolish, simple, Eve, hadst thou been wise,
Thou mights have liv'd on earthly Paradise;
But now thou mayest repent, alas, too late,
Yet be contented with this thy mean estate.
When I in Woodbridge liv'd a maid,
All my good fortunes were betraid,
By an ancient widower living nigh,
Who cast on me a deceitful eye;
He said, if I would be his wife,
That I should live a happy life;
My Dame her councel did me give,
And said how bravely I might live;
And if now young, I let my Fortune flip,
I never should at such a brave match tip:
For then he told me flat and plain,
         A 3   That

6.9: Elizabeth With of Woodbridge, *Elizabeth Fools Warning* (1659). By permission of The British Library.

we can only wonder what ultimately happened to With herself. However, the fact that she did not collapse but instead used her pain as raw material for her self-assertive poems, and that she also had the temerity to publish her testimony, makes her seem both a remarkable woman and a fascinating historical figure.

ROBERT C. EVANS
AUBURN UNIVERSITY MONTGOMERY

Elizabeth With. *Elizabeth Fools Warning, being a true and most perfect relation of all that has happened to her since her marriage. Being a caveat for all young women to marry with old men. [In verse.]* London, 1659. 8o. British Library E.2122.(1.) Page A3.

164.

Anne C[oun]t[es]s Dowag[er] of Dorsett, Pembroke
And Montgomery

with her Mo[the]r it being not a Yeare old, & it was y[e] 1[st] time, y[t] ever this Lady Dungarvan came into Ireland, or went beyond the Seas, & her Sister Mary is now beyond Seas in Turky at Constantinople: And they came into England again, in y[e] Yeare 1663, & so to their House in White fryers, where & in other places in England they continued till their 2[d] Daughter Ele[anor] came to be Married y[e] 11th of Aprill in y[t] Yeare to my eldest Grandson Nicholas L[or]d Tufton, who by y[e] death of his father y[e] 7th of May following came to be Earle of Thanett, & a little after this Marriage, in July following, they all came downe into y[e] North to their house at Lonsborrow in Yorkshire, from whence, after a while my L[or]d of Cork & his Lady w[th] Most of their Children came to Bolton Abby in Craven to lye there for a time, & in y[t] time they went also into my Castle of Skypton & Tower of Barden for a while to see them & about y[t] time did their s[ai]d 2[d] Daughter, & her Lord My Grandchild & y[e] Earle of Thanett come hither into this Apple by Castle in Westmorland to me, for a few Nights.

1663.

In the Yeare of our Lord God 1663, as y[e] Yeare begins on New Yeares day, The 2[d] day of Aprill in this Yeare, did My Grand Child M[r] John Tufton come from his journey from London, hither into y[e] Barden Tower to me, where I then kissed him with much Joy, a little before supper, & he now told me how he set forwards on his journey from London, hitherwards from his Mo[the]r & 2 of his Sisters, Lady Frances, & Lady Cicely y[e] 26 day of March last, for he & they came up hither from Hothfield in Kent, & on my L[or]d of Thanett y[e] 18[th] of y[t] same Month whither his Mother & 2 Sisters returned back again on y[e] 27[th] day, & when he now came hither home, he began to lye in y[e] best room in this Barden Tower, at y[e] bend of y[e] great Chamber, where My Daughter of Northampton lay, when She was last here, & his Man Jo: Frodsley who is Newly come to him, in y[t] room within it, & I had not seen any Grand child of Mine, since y[e] death of my daughter of Nor thampton & 3 of her Children, till now y[t] I saw this Jo: Tufton, & this was y[e] 1st time y[t] any of my Daughter of Thanetts children ever lay in y[t] Barden Tower, & this Grandchild of mine was the More welcome to me, in regard he had escaped death very Nar rowly, by a dangerous Sicknes he had in France, y[e] last yeare, w[ch] caused me to have in a thankfull remembrance Gods great Mer cies to me & Mine: Ps. 23. v. 4. 5. Ps. 116. v. 12. 13.

And y[e] 6[th] day of May in y[t] Yeare, being Wednesday, did I & o[ur] my Grand Child M[r] Jo: Tufton & my whole family remove from Barden Tower in Craven, after I had now layn in it, ever since y[e] 26 of Sept[embe]r last till now, & came y[e] Nearest way through y[e] New Park to Skypton Ca[s]: into y[e] New repaired Old buildings there, to lye now for a time in y[e] Chamber there, wherein my self was borne, for tho' y[e] y[e] chief parts of y[e] Castle, were pulled downe by y[e] command of Cromwell, ab[t] y[e] end of December 1648. yet did I cause it to be re builded in y[e] yeares, 1657. 1658, & 1659, & I was not in this Skypton Ca[s]: since y[e] 9[th] of Dec[embe]r 1639, when I went out of it last, to lye first of all in Barden Tower, till y[t] time y[t] I now came to lye in it again, & tho I was near y[e] s[ai]d Castle of Skypton & y[e] Walls of it, with My Blessed Mother about
the

6.10: Lady Anne Clifford, Countess Dowager of Dorset, Pembroke, and Montagmery, "Lives of the Lady Anne Clifford . . . (1590-1676) and of her parents summarized by herself." By permission of The British Library.

Lady Anne Clifford, Countess Dowager of Dorset, Pembroke and Montgomery, "Lives of the Lady Anne Clifford, Countess of Dorset, Pembroke and Montgomery (1590–1676) and of her parents, summarized by herself" (1663)

Transcription

In the Year of our Lord God 1663, as the Year begins on New Years day, the 2nd day of Aprill in this Year, did My Grand Child Master John Tufton come from his Journey from London hither into this Barden Tower to me, where I now kissed him with much Joy, a little before Supper, & he now told me how he set forwards on his Journey from London, hitherwards from his Mother & 2 of his sisters, Lady Frances, & Lady Cicely the 26 day of March last, for he & they came up thither from Hothfield in Kent, from my Lord of Thanett the 16th of the same Month whither his Mother & 2 sisters returned back again the 27th day, & when he now came hither to me, he begun to lye in the best room in this Barden Tower, at the end of the great Chamber, where My Daughter of Northampton lay, when she was last here, & his Man John Geatley, who is Newly come to him, in the room within it, & I had not seen any Grandchild of Mine, since the death of my daughter of Northampton & 3 of her Children, till now that I saw this John Tufton, & this was the first time that any of my Daughter of Thanetts children ever lay in this Barden Tower, & this Grandchild of mine was the More wellcome to me, in regard he had escaped death very Narrowly, by a dangerous sickness he had in France, the last year, which caused me to have in a thankfull remembrance Gods great Mercies to me & Mine: Psalm 23.v.4.5. Psalm 116.v.12.13.

And the 6th day of May in this Year, being Wednesday, did I with my Grand Child Master John Tufton & my whole family remove from Barden Tower in Craven, after I had now layn in it, ever since the 26 of September last till now, & came the Nearest way through the Haw Park to Skypton Castle into the New repaired Old buildings there, to lye now for a time in the Chamber there, wherein myself was borne, for though that and the chief parts of the Castle, were pulled down by the command of Cromwell, about the end of December 1648, yet did I cause it to be rebuilt in the Years 1657, 1658, & 1659, & I was not in this Skypton Castle since the 9th of December 1659, when I went out of it last, to lye first of all in Barden Tower, till this time that I now came to lye in it again, & though I was near the said Castle of Skypton and the walls of it, with My blessed Mother about the [12 October 1607]

Commentary

Lady Anne Clifford was not a poet, a dramatist, or prose fiction writer, but she must be understood nonetheless as an "author" whose extensive autobiographical texts were self-consciously created and re-created for others' benefit and edification. The most significant part of Clifford's record were her written accounts of her life, which appear in three distinct forms: as informal daily diaries; as annual summaries, or "chronicles"; and as a formal autobiography that documents her life from conception to 1650. Clifford scholar Katherine Acheson has suggested that this wide range of materials represents different steps in Clifford's deliberate process of representing her life as she intended to be remembered, with chronicles prepared from diaries and her autobiography growing out of chron-

icles. This understanding complicates the already complex issue of how to read autobiographical writing; the "truth-value" traditionally accorded apparently unmediated texts
such as diaries is clearly challenged by the deliberate editorial work of Anne Clifford. An
additional challenge posed by her writings is in the light they shed on theories of representation and subjecthood for women of her era. What can we newly understand about
early modern women's subjectivity by studying Anne Clifford's acts of and interest in representation?

The text reproduced here is from the annual summaries, 1650–75, which survive in
several manuscripts and at least one print edition. This particular version is from the
Harley manuscript owned by the British Library (Harley 6177); the hand seen here is not
Clifford's own. Pictured here is the first page of the entry for 1663, chronicling selected
events in April and May of that year.

Several elements in the particular text reproduced are worth noting. First, throughout these pages Clifford characteristically preoccupies herself with time and with the
ordering of time. The heading "In the Year of our Lord God 1663, as the Year begins on
New Years Day" appears with the corresponding year for every year for which we have a
chronicle, and imposes uniformity on the years past, some of which are many years apart.
The cumulative effect of such regularity is a kind of telescoping of time and events that
erases the untidy and haphazard reality of living life forward. Also worthy of note is
Clifford's description of returning to her birth chamber in Skipton Castle in 1663, sev-
enty-three years later. Her careful marking of days and years past is significant, as is her
overall sense of an order to things: "it is to be accounted a . . . providence of God that now
in the 73rd year of my age, I should come to be again in that chamber" (MS Harl. 6177,
page 165 not photographed). The order to these years is in fact her own ordering; our
sense of their unfolding is hers.

Second, there is the inclusion of psalm references. Such invocations depicting
Clifford's great piety were not only an important part of her self-image, but also of her
self-presentation to others. This is not unique to her; chaste religious practice and piety
were important qualities for women in particular to emphasize in themselves, and were the
qualities for which others recognized them. Even more important, the only realm within
which it was faultless for women to have a "public voice" was that of religion. For an otherwise bold woman like Clifford, a reputation as pious and devout was ameliorative. Her
inclusion of psalm verses, while genuine, is probably self-conscious.

HEATHER EASTERLING
UNIVERSITY OF WASHINGTON

Lady Anne Clifford. *Diary of Anne Clifford, countess of Pembroke.*
British Library MS Harl. 6177. Page 164.

Lucy (Apsley) Hutchinson, "The Memoirs of the Life of Colonel Hutchinson" (c. 1664)

Commentary

Lucy Hutchinson's "The Memoirs of the Life of Colonel Hutchison" were not published until 1806, when Julius Hutchinson, a descendant, edited the notebook and gave it the title Memoirs (by which it is still known); the manuscript is in the Nottinghamshire County archives (DDHU 4). The first unpaginated verso page of the notebook identifies the scope of the work "Written by Lucy the Wife of Col Hutchinson, being a History of his life, particularly of his conduct in the Great Rebellion." Lucy Hutchinson's preferred title for the work, it seems, would have been "The Life of John Hutchinson of Owthorpe in the County of Nottingham Esquire." This is the title at the top of page 30 of the notebook, where Hutchinson begins her chronological account of her husband's life.

The manuscript was completed after John Hutchinson's death in 1664, but parts of it were written nearly twenty years before, "transcrib'd out of a more particular collection," a notebook now in the British Library (B.M. Add. MS. 25,901), and evidently written between October 1642 and February 1645. The notebook of the memoirs, now in Nottingham, omits some details from the B.M. manuscript and rewrites some passages. The Nottingham manuscript is in Hutchinson's own hand; this notebook was originally accompanied by a fragment of Hutchinson's (unfinished) autobiography. That manuscript has disappeared; most editions of the memoirs include a reprint of the version of her life Julius Hutchinson published in 1806.

Page 55 of the memoirs memorably shows a key facet of the Hutchinsons' relationship and the main reason why there is a resurgence of interest in Hutchinson's writing. John Hutchinson was dissuaded from marrying Lucy because of her learning, which led her to "the negligence of her dresse, and habitt, and all womanish ornaments, giving herselfe wholly up to studie and writing." Rather than being deterred, John Hutchinson instead "prosecuted his love with so much discretion, duty and honour" that they married. Lucy's commitments to scholarship fueled the marriage from the beginning. She portrays her husband and herself in the third person. This writing strategy is found frequently in seventeenth-century autobiographies and is a mark of earlier women's writing, such as *The Life of Margery Kempe* (though Hutchinson's "Life of Herself" is written in the first person). The effect here is that both Lucy and John Hutchinson are seen with great clarity, the vivacity of these portraits lies at the heart of the *Memoirs*, as do Hutchinson's own suppressed emotions in the face of the tumultuous events, for her main purpose in writing the *Memoirs* was to preserve her husband's memory for her children.

Hutchinson was strongly influenced by classical historians such as Tacitus and Plutarch. From them she takes the strategies of using eyewitness accounts to describe events, to draw characters and from these to announce a clear moral code. Thus on page fifty-five we learn not only how Hutchinson shunned "all womanish ornaments," while, having chosen Mr. Hutchinson as a "happie relief," "how civilly she entertained him." She notes also Mr. Hutchinson as a "person of vertue and honor" whose love for her was "constant & honorable." John and Lucy Hutchinson are placed as vital and virtuous characters, their marital romance surviving the great trauma of the English Civil Wars, which is Hutchinson's larger subject, and on which historians have frequently cited Hutchinson as a memorably eloquent eyewitness.

55

of others, and being a little disturbd with these things,
and melancholly, m.r Hutchinson appearing, as he was,
a person of vertue and honor, who might be advantagi-
ably and safely converst with, she thought god had
sent her a happie reliefe. M.r Hutchinson on the
other side, having bene told, and sieing how she shund
all other men, and how civilly she entertaind him,
beleiud that a secret power had wrought a mutuall
inclination betweene them and dayly frequented her mothers
house, and had the oportunitie of conuersing with her,
in those pleasant walkes, which, at that sweete season
of the spring, invited all the neighbouring inhabitants
to seeke their ioyes, where though they were neuer alone,
yet they had euery day oportunity for converse with
each other, which the rest shard not in, while euery
one minded their owne delights. they had not six
weekes enioyd this peace, but the young men and
weomen, who saw them allow each other that kindnesse
which they did not comonly afford to others, first began
to grow iealous, & at envious at it, and after to vse all
the mallitious practises they could invent to breake
the friendship. among the rest, that gentleman who
at the first had so highly commended her to m.r Hutchinson,
now began to caution him against her, and to disparidge
her, with such subtile insinuations, as would haue ruind
any loue lesse constant & honorable then his, the women
with wittie spite represented all her faults to him,
which chiefely terminated in the negligence of her
dresse, and habitt, and all womanish ornaments, giving
hirselfe wholly vp to studie and writing. m.r Hutchinson,
who had a very pleasant and sharpe witt, retorted
all their mallice, with such iust reproofes of their idlenesse and vanity, as made them hate her, who without
affecting it, had so engagd such a person in her protection,
as they with all their arts could not catch. he in the
meane time prosecuted his loue, with so much discretion,
duty and honor, that at the length, through many

6.11: Lucy (Apsley) Hutchinson, "The Memoirs of the Life of Colonel Hutchinson" (c.1664).
Reproduced by permission of the Principal Archivist and of Nottingham City Council.

Transcription

of others, and being a little disturbd with these things, and melancholly, mr Hutchinson appearing, as he was, a person of vertue and honor, who might be advantageably and safely converst with, she thought god had sent her a happie reliefe. Mr Hutchinson on the other side, having bene told, and seing how she shund all other men, and how civilly she entertaind him, believd that a secret power had wrought a mutuall inclination betweene them and dayly frequented her mothers house, and had the opertunitie of conversing with her, in those pleasant walkes, which, at that sweete season of the spring, invited all the neighbouring inhabitants to seeke their joyes, where though they were never alone, yet they had every day opertunity for converse with each other, which the rest shard not in, while every one minded their owne delights. they had not six weekes enjoyd this peace, but the young men and weomen, who saw them allow each other that kindnesse which they did not commonly afford to others, first began to grow jealous, & envious at it, and after to use all the mallitious practises they could invent to breake the friendship; among the rest, that gentleman who at the first had so highly commended her to mr Hutchinson, now began to caution him against her, and to disparedge her, with such subtile insinuations, as would have ruind any love lesse constant & honorable then his, the weomen with wittie spite represented all her faults to him, which chiefly terminated in the negligence of her dresse, and habitt, and all womanish ornaments, giving herselfe wholly up to studie and writing. mr Hutchinson, who had a very pleasant and sharpe witt, retorted all their mallice, with such just reproofes of their idlenesse and vanity, as made them hate her, who without affecting it, had so engagd such a person in her protection, as they with all their arts could not catch; he in the meane time, prosecuted his love, with so much discretion, duty and honor, that at the length, through many

Mark Houlahan
University of Waikato

Lucy Hutchinson. "The Memoirs of the Life of Colonel Hutchinson." Nottingham County Archives DDHU 4. Page 55.

6.12: Agnes Beaumont, "Divine Appearances. Or A very Wonderfull Account of the Dealings of God with Mrs. Agnes Beamount . . . written by her self" (c.1674). By permission of The British Library.

Agnes Beaumont, "Divine Appearances. Or A very Wonderfull Account of the Dealings of God with Mrs. Agnes Beamount . . . written by her self" (c. 1674)

Agnes Beaumont's tale of escalating risk began in 1674, when she and her brother convinced a reluctant John Bunyan to give her a ride on his horse to a church meeting that he was to lead. Slanderous gossip quickly spread in her small town. Beaumont returned home to find her widowed father had locked the door on her. She spent a freezing night in the barn and the rest of the weekend pleading with her father for the right to continue to attend the church meetings of her choice. Eventually, she was allowed back into the house. Her conscience was uneasy, though, as she worried that by obeying her mortal father she had offended her heavenly father and bargained away her immortal soul. Two nights later, her father died suddenly, and a neighbor reported to the coroner his suspicions that she had killed her father. If she were found guilty, she would be hanged.

Beaumont's narrative of these "persecutions" is vivid, and the brief story has great focus and rhetorical momentum. Because her accuser was a rejected suitor pressing for a monetary settlement, her tale also illustrates an argument that nonconformist leaders were making at the time, that religious persecution was likely to be economically motivated and often had economic consequences. The freedom of religion, they were arguing, ought not to be assumed to pose a threat to civil authorities. As useful as the narrative might have been to that case, Beaumont's story was not published, no doubt because it raised the inflammatory specter of a sexually charged spirituality. But lack of print publication is not the same as lack of circulation or readership. There are two closely related manuscripts preserved in the British Library, confirming that Beaumont had a circle of readers and that the manuscripts passed through various hands.

Both manuscripts are undated. Both may be fair copies. Egerton 2414 is the source of 2128. Egerton 2414 has none of the conventional finishing touches of publication, not even a title or author. Even so, it is a carefully and clearly written document. Egerton 2128 is more conventionally presented; its title page is shown here. Still, it is a close textual copy of the first, with the addition at the end of several concluding paragraphs that describe further eruptions of scandalous reports about Beaumont's relationship with Bunyan and her supposed danger to the community.

Each manuscript contains marginal and endnotes by readers. One note at the end of 2414 reads "her name Agnes." Another note in a different hand at the beginning reads "Written by one Agnes ——— of Edworth, Beds. intimately acquainted with John Bunyan." In yet another ink, another hand has inserted a caret below the line drawn blank by an earlier reader for the surname and written "(Beaumont)" above the line. Three separate hands have contributed to the preservation of Beaumont's identity. As a communal affirmation, the naming is a signal confirmation of Beaumont's truthfulness. Beaumont may offer her narrative to God's judgment, but her readers have also given witness to her credibility.

Kathleen Lynch
Folger Institute

Agnes Beaumont. "Divine Appearances. Or A very Wonderfull Account of the Dealings of God with Mrs. Agnes Beamount . . . written by her self" (c. 1674). British Library Manuscripts Egerton 2128. Title page.

6.13(1): Elizabeth Freke, "Elizabeth Frek Her Book" (1705). By permission of The British Library.

Elizabeth Freke, "Elizabeth Frek Her Book" (1705)

Transcription
Plate 1

[1704/5 January] 1705. January the first, I beged of Mr Frek to give my deerst son fiffty pounds & A years Intrest For A New years Guift, Which he Gave him, And I Gave him Ten pounds for a New years Guiftt. EF.

 The Nextt day Mr Frek & I in my Chamber speaking of itt by our selves; only my Maide, Who had lived a greatt While With mee; my daughter in her own Chamber stood harkning att the doore, Flew into the Chamber to us; & told Mr Freke, her father In Law, hee might be asshamed, to speake of such A Triffell as thatt Guift before my servantt, & she said she had a good mind to kick her downe staires; & said she would begone Iff I did nott Turne her outt of doors Soe affter I were forced to discharge her, & take A stranger aboutt my selfe affter she had Lived three Tims With me & the Last time Two years want on Month.

 my daughter was neer to month [at Bilney] and Never said to her Father or me Good Night or Good Morrow.

[1705 May the 7] Monday the 7 of May My deer son, his Wife & my Two deer Grand Chilldren Left me allone att Billney & wentt a Way for London, Mr Frek Carring [*sic*] them all up att his Charge, as he did Eight of Neer half A yeare; in Which Time I offten beged of my daughter the youngst Children her son John: finding him noe Favourite & I loved him to my soule because he was the pictture of my deerst son, butt she as Cruelly deneyed him to me & Caryed him A Way from me, Which Turned me to a violentt sickness for Above six week. I though[t] [it] would have binn my last.

[May 10] Nott with standing this, & severall other Cruelltys to me, I sent my daughter up to London, (paid on sight by my Cosin John Frek) A hundred pounds, to ease ther expences In London; for Which And ther half year being With me att Billney eight of them servants & horses and all maner of bills

6.13(2): Elizabeth Freke, "Elizabeth Frek Her Book" (1705). By permission of The British Library.

Transcription
Plate 2

of bills, pothecarys, Letters, Smiths, neer Twenty pound In Corde, &c. 5 Asses, & A horse to drive them to Bristoll, all which Never deserved thanks from them.

[May 27]   While Munday the 27 of May I writt to this my said daughter, for God sake to Carry my Two deer Grandchildren outt of London for elce there I should Loose them; since she would nott be soe kind to trust me with either of them (soe longe as till she went for Ireland;) butt weer never thought fitt to be Answered by Letter or otherways Itt being neer to month since—[*sic*].

[June 10]   June the Tenth Sunday, aboutt two A Clock, my deerest Grandchild I had soe often beged for Being like my own deer son, neer Fowre years old, (& in my eyes the Lovelyest Child was ever seen, (by mee) by Name Mr John Frek, he with his Brother Mr Percy Frek, and Mr Molson ther Landlord to sons Wher they Lodged, Wher Thom Molson found my sons pockett pistolls Charged And primed, & soe Left by his Man Perryman Which Pistoll the Lad took, & discharged by accident In the head of my deerst, & Best Bloved Grandchild Mr John Frek; The Bullett wentt yn Att the eye, and tho' all the Means of London was used yett noe help soe thatt on Wensday the thirteenth of June aboutt 5 A Clock in the Morning, my deer babe Gave up his soule to my God, Who Would nott have taken Roott & Branch from me had itt bin Left by my Cruell daughter [apparently overwritten by "Children"]. butt, God forgive them & I shall ever Lamentt ytt for I had sett my whole hartt on ytt. Which itt has brok thatt & me for any Comfortt in this life: E Frek.

[June 18]   Munday June the eighteenth my deerst Grandchild Mr John Frek was Brought downe from London In A herse to me to be heer Intered In Billney Chancell wher he Lyes att the uper end & Where God willing I will Lye by him as fast as I Can gett to him, I Lost my Child to show their undutifullness & Cruellty to me Which God forgive them. E Frek

Commentary

"Some Few remembrances of my misfortuns which have attended me in my unhappy life since I were married": so Elizabeth Freke lightheartedly entitled her reminiscences. These writings consist of two manuscripts: a diary commencing in Elizabeth's middle age and a memoir composed near the end of her life, in which she cements her perception of herself, while still continuing the more impromptu daily entries in her diary. While the later memoir, read in conjunction with the diary, reveals much of the processes of construction involved in life-writing, the earlier manuscript, from which the entries are drawn, allows us access to a more spontaneous—less constructed—version of Elizabeth Freke's life. The sequence of recollections, diary entries, letters, recipes, news items, and inventories contained in this earlier diary span forty-three years of Elizabeth's life, through marriage, motherhood, and widowhood. Together, these materials tell a remarkable story of a woman determined to establish some measure of security in a world marked by frustrating unpredictability.

As their title implies, Elizabeth Freke's writings focus mainly on her impressions of the personal and practical difficulties that beset her. She wrote for herself, not for an imagined audience, her diary offering her a means to purge her anger, frustration, and sorrow not otherwise available in her rather lonely existence. Elizabeth's personal engagement with her text is notable in a period when women's diaries more often consist of spiritual musings or lessons for posterity, which reveal little about the writers' personal feelings. If Elizabeth's frankness, by contrast, sometimes makes her seem avaricious, argumentative, and self-absorbed, it equally helps us to sympathize with her vision of a world in which years of industry, determination, and practicality are time and again vitiated by contingency and misfortune, keeping happiness perpetually at bay.

Elizabeth's early goals seemed within reach for the daughter of a wealthy gentleman. Marrying for love, at the age of thirty-one, she imagined a future with a protective husband, attentive children, economic success, and a well-furnished home. These expectations become clear only as we read of her anger and despair over their failure to materialize. Her husband, Percy ("Mr. Freke"), proved an early disappointment, spending much time and money building up an estate in his native Ireland. Mr. Freke's lengthy absences upset Elizabeth, who noted that in the first three years of her marriage she had had "Very Little of my husbands Company, which was Noe small Griefe to mee I Being Governed In this my Marriag wholly by my affections." Later in her life, she focused on the social and economic (rather than emotional) consequences of having "my husband allwais Living from mee, & I all A Lone," resenting being forced to "shifft for [her] selfe and Familly." Elizabeth was equally dissatisfied by the failure of her only child, her son Ralph, to "wantt or vallue the kindness of [his] poor distracted mother." Ralph even went so far as to marry, without Elizabeth's "Blessing or Consentt," a woman who not only treated her "Rudely," but also set up house in Ireland, distancing Elizabeth from her son and grandchildren. In addition to this familial discord, Elizabeth worried throughout her married life about being left with "nott a place to put my unhappy head in," seven times having had to face "bare walls and a naked house," when her husband, often without her knowledge, appropriated her wealth and property for his Irish estate building. Time and time again Elizabeth managed to get her "Little house . . . Well Furnished," only to have this small security vanish. Elizabeth believed that a concentration of wealth and material goods was not only a means to reinforce her own identity in an unstable environment, but would also enable her to obtain the love and loyalty of her family and friends; she deeply resented these losses.

Nevertheless, by the time she turned 64 (in January 1705, the entries reproduced here), Elizabeth Freke seemed to have acquired some measure of happiness. Her long-absent husband, though aged and unwell, now lived with her permanently. Her son, Ralph, was visiting for the first time since his marriage, and better still had brought two of his children with him. Elizabeth especially delighted in her youngest grandson, John, who reminded her of her own child. As a grandmother, she was hoping to achieve some of the emotional satisfaction that she missed as a mother. To top it off, Elizabeth was the owner of the now well-furnished Bilney manor in Norwich, complete with reliable servants, and ready money to spend on her "Young Family." As the diary entries indicate, however, the events of 1705 did not go smoothly at all. Elizabeth's imperious daughter-in-law forced her to dismiss a valued servant, and her son remained undutiful, failing to thank her for her generosity and refusing to allow her to care for her favorite grandchild, John, even for the duration of their visit to England. Tragedy struck when three-year-old John was accidentally shot in the head and died three days later. Described by Elizabeth as "the most fattallest thing that ever Hapned to mee," this accident temporarily conquered her tenacity, resulted in an uncharacteristic desire for her own demise, and reinforced her perception that she lived in a world tossed by fortune, in which "we were all like to be Lost by most Tempestyous Wynds and Raine," and neither "frinds [nor] children" could be relied upon.

Despite stubborn industry and the best intentions, Elizabeth Freke, a woman often "A lone," regarded herself throughout her remembrances as a long-suffering victim of unreliable family, brutish tenants, chance fires and rains, and accidental gunshots. She died a wealthy widow at age 73, but claimed to have faced "enough to distract any poor Mortall." She reiterated that "not one friend or Relation had ever Appeered to my Assistance In any or all my Troubles; but my dependance is Wholly on God." Besides God, however, she also depended on a fiercely guarded security in the form of material wealth, an obsession that occupies many of her diary entries in later life. By placing her eventual material success against a background of adversity, Elizabeth Freke invites us to regard her as a strong woman prevailing through faith, industry and determination. We must also consider, though, whether her final economic security, so jealously inventoried in her old age, was an adequate replacement for the emotional attachments that she clearly desired when she embarked on her marriage for love.

Aki Beam
McMaster University
and
Daniel Woolf
University of Alberta

Elizabeth Freke. "Elizabeth Frek Her Book" (1705). Part of the Freke Papers, spanning approximately 1677–1714. British Library Additional MS 45718. Pages 120 and 121.

The
Countesse
of Mountgomeries
URANIA.

Written by the right honorable the Lady
MARY WROATH.
Daughter to the right Noble Robert
Earle of Leicester.
And Neece to the ever famous, and re-
nowned S.t Phillip Sidney knight. And to
y.e most exalt Lady Mary Countesse of
Pembroke late deceased.

LONDON
Printed for IOH MARRIOTT
and IOHN GRISMAND. And
are to bee sould at theire shop-
pes in St Dunstons Church-
yard in Fleetstreete and in
Poules Alley at y.e signe of
the Gunn.

6.14: Lady Mary (Sidney) Wroth, *Urania* (1621). Milner Library Special Collections,
Illinois State University.

Lady Mary (Sidney) Wroth, Title page, *Urania* (1621)

Lady Mary Wroth's romance *The Countesse of Mountgomeries Urania* was entered in the Stationers' Register on 13 July 1621. A roman à clef with thinly veiled characters and events, the *Urania* was strongly protested by noblemen who saw the book as a personal attack upon their reputations. Perhaps the most famous protest lodged was that of Edward Denny, Baron of Waltham, who sought King James's help to stop sale of the romance upon recognizing himself in the story of Sirelius's father-in-law in Book IIII. Josephine Roberts points out that although much controversy ensued, including Wroth's defensive statement in a letter to George Villiers, Duke of Buckingham, that the books "were solde against my minde I never purposing to have had them published," there is no record of a warrant issued for their recall (cv–cvi). Whether or not Wroth personally complied with Marriott and Grismand or an intermediary provided them with the manuscript, the information offered by the elaborately engraved title page suggests that careful consideration went into preparation of the book for publication.

Simon van de Passe, a Dutch artist "who was known for his portraits of the royal family as well as of the leading members of the Sidney-Herbert circle," engraved the title page (cvi). The cartouche centered at the top reveals Wroth's familial and literary connections with her father, Robert Sidney, Earl of Leicester; her uncle, Sir Philip Sidney (author of *The Countess of Pembroke's Arcadia*, which provides both inspiration and a model for Wroth's romance); and her aunt, Mary Sidney Herbert, Countess of Pembroke and a well-known literary figure in her own right. It seems that the strongholds of family reputation and literary circle association are boldly invoked for the reader in an attempt to protect Wroth from the stigma attached to a woman publishing her writing during this period.

The illustration on the title page depicts the Throne of Love, the scene of a central episode in Book I, in which a small band of travelers, including Urania, Selarina, Parselius, and Leandrus, disembark on a strange island where they see "a rare and admirable Pallace" that is "scituated on a Hill, but that Hill formed, as if the world would needs raise one place of purpose to build Loves throne upon." Wroth writes, "The Hill whereon this Pallace stood was just as big as to hold the House: three sides of the Hill made into delicate Gardens and Orchards: the further side was a fine and stately Wood." She continues,

> At the foote of this Hill ranne a pleasant and sweetly passing river, over which was a Bridge, on which were three Towres: Upon the first was the Image of Cupid, curiously carv'd with his Bow bent, and Quiver at his backe, but with his right hand pointing to the next Towre; on which was a statue of white Marble, representing Venus, but so richly adorn'd, as it might for rareness, and exquisitenesse have beene taken for the Goddesse her selfe, and have causd as strange an affection as the Image did to her maker, when he fell in love with his owne worke. Shee was crowned with Mirtle, and Pansies, in her left hand holding a flaming Heart, her right, directing to the third Towre, before which, in all dainty riches, and rich delicacy, was the figure of Constancy, holding in her hand the Keyes of the Pallace: which shewed, that place was not to be open to all, but to few possessed with that virtue. (48)

The detailed way in which the title-page illustration matches Wroth's description of the scene suggests that the engraver was given specific directions and made thoroughly acquainted with the passage in question. Roberts opines that Wroth herself might have provided him instructions, noting that "other aristocratic authors offered explicit guidance to the engraver concerning the choice of illustrations for their works" (cvi). On the whole, Wroth's title page provides an excellent example of an image-conscious public presentation of the work by a woman writer and raises fascinating questions about the depths of the writer's involvement in the publication process.

JULIE D. CAMPBELL
EASTERN ILLINOIS UNIVERSITY

Lady Mary Wroth. *The First Part of the Countesss of Mountgomeries Urania.* London: John Marriott and John Grismand, 1621. Illinois State University, Milner Library PR 2399 .W7 U7 1621. Title page.

Lady Mary (Sidney) Wroth, Last page of Part 1 *Urania* (1621)

The First Part of the Countesse of Mountgomeries Urania ends abruptly, mid-sentence:

> Amphilanthus must goe, but intreates Pamphilia to goe as far as Italy with him, to visit the matchles Queene his mother, she consents, for what can she denye him? all things are prepared for the journey, all now merry, contented, nothing amisse; greife forsaken, sadnes cast off, Pamphilia is the Queene of all content; Amphilanthus joying worthily in her; And

The abrupt stop may be an imitation of the ending of Sir Philip Sidney's *The Countess of Pembroke's Arcadia,* which also ends midsentence. The *Arcadia* ended in this fashion because of Sidney's untimely death, and the printer used an ornament to provide a visual closure for the work. Regarding the conclusion of Wroth's romance, there seems to have been confusion on the printer's part as to how the page should end. Roberts notes that he "left the rest blank possibly in the expectation that he would receive some concluding matter" (cx). The volume ends with the appendage of the sonnet sequence, *Pamphilia to Amphilanthus.* The continuation of the romance, however, is to be found in *The Second Part of the Countesse of Mountgomeries Urania,* which also stops midsentence.

The *Second Part* remained in a holograph manuscript in two volumes at the Newberry Library until it was edited by Josephine Roberts, Suzanne Gossett, and Janel Mueller and published in 1999 by Medieval and Renaissance Texts and Studies. It takes up where the *First Part* leaves off, beginning, "And thus they with Joyes plenty like the richest harvest after a longe time of dearthe." In the *Second Part,* Wroth continues the adventures of the characters from the *First Part* and follows the developments of their lives.

In her introduction to the *First Part,* Roberts suggests that the fair copy of the *First Part* (no longer extant) may have ended with "And" as the catchword and that the printer "may have simply printed the word without knowing that it belonged to the second part of *Urania*" (cxi). Support for this view may be gleaned from the copy of the *Urania* owned by Dr. Charlotte Kohler, which contains Wroth's handwritten corrections. In this volume, Wroth or someone scratched through "And." Unfortunately, it is impossible to say whether or not this particular change is authorial, because "it does not involve the use of ink (as in the case of Wroth's other corrections), and it could have easily been made by any of the successive owners of the volume" (cxvi). Roberts points out that other copies "show the ingenuity of unknown owners who sought to remedy the incomplete sentence by supplying either poetry or prose of their own composition" (cxvi).

The *First Part* was most likely printed by Augustine Mathewes and possibly in part by his partner John White. Mathewes's name does not appear on the title page, but the editors of the revised *Short Title Catalogue* suggest that he was the printer, judging by the type and the printer's ornaments (Roberts cvii–cviii). There are twenty-nine surviving copies of the *First Part,* and Roberts's collation of them reveals approximately 1,050 stop-press variants in the 1621 volume. Care was clearly taken in the publication of the *First*

returned, he leading her, or rather imbracing her with his cōquering armes, and protesting the water he dranke being mixed with her teares, had so infu-sed constancy and perfect truth of loue in it, as in him it had wrought the like effect, then were they the best bestowed teares that euer my eyes shed, though till now hardly haue they bin dry said she; speake not said hee of so sad a busines, we are now againe together, and neuer, so againe, I hope, to part, to her traine thus they arriued, but when knowne by them, they neuer staid to be called to kisse his hands, but ranne all at once, euery one striuing to be first, and all casting themselues at his feete, he tooke them vp, and with much noble kindnes receiued them; then they returned to the Cittie, and the next day to the wood againe to see the hell of deceit, but now no more to be abused, thence they brought with them the most loyall seruant, and the brauest friend that euer man had, the noble *Polarchos* ; *Amphilanthus* now recouered his Sword, and brought home his Armour, resoluing nothing should remaine as witnesses of his former sicklenes, or the property of that place, destroying the monument, the Charmes hauing conclusion with his recouering; but none but himselfe could haue gayned the Sword, because belonging to him, millions had tryed in the meane space, and all lamentably perplext; now all is finished, *Pamphilia* blessed as her thoughts, heart, and soule wished : *Amphilanthus* expresslesly contented, *Polarchos* truly happy, and ioyfull againe; this still continuing all liuing in pleasure, speech is of the Germans iourney, *Amphilanthus* must goe, but intreates *Pamphilia* to goe as far as *Italy* with him, to visit the matchles Queene his mother, she consents, for what can she denye him? all things are prepared for the iourney, all now merry, contented, nothing amisse ; greife forsaken, sadnes cast off, *Pamphilia* is the Queene of all content; *Amphilanthus* ioying worthily in her ; And

6.15: Lady Mary (Sidney) Wroth, *Urania* (1621). Milner Library Special Collections, Illinois State University.

Part; unfortunately, its controversial reception may have stopped Wroth from seeking publication of the "Second Part."

JULIE D. CAMPBELL
EASTERN ILLINOIS UNIVERSITY

But as the soules delights,
   So blesse my then blest eyes,
   Which vnto you their true affection tyes.

Then shall the Sunne giue place,
   As to your greater might,
   Yeelding that you doe show more perfect light.
O then but grant this grace,
   Vnto your Loue-tide slaue,
   To shine on me, who to you all faith gaue.

And when you please to frowne,
   Vse your most killing eyes
On them, who in vntruth and falshood lies,
But (Deare) on me cast downe
   Sweet lookes, for true desire;
   That banish doe all thoughts of faigned fire.

37.

NIght, welcome art thou to my minde distrest,
  Darke, heauy, sad, yet not more sad then I :
Neuer could'st thou finde fitter company
For thine owne humour, then I thus opprest.

If thou beest darke, my wrongs still vnredrest
  Saw neuer light, nor smallest blisse can spye :
  If heauy ioy from mee to fast doth hie,
And care out-goes my hope of quiet rest.

Then now in friendship ioyne with haplesse me,
  Who am as sad and darke as thou canst be,
  Hating all pleasure or delight of life,
Silence and griefe, with thee I best doe loue.

And from you three I know I cannot moue,
Then let vs liue companions without strife.

38.

WHat pleasure can a banish'd creature haue
  In all the pastimes that inuented are
By wit or learning ? Absence making warre
Against all peace that may a biding craue.

Can wee delight but in a welcome graue,
  Where we may bury paines? and so be farre
  From loathed company, who alwaies iarre
Vpon the string of mirth that pastime gaue.

                                    The

6.16: Lady Mary (Sidney) Wroth, *Pamphilia to Amphilanthus*, appended to *Urania* (1621).
By permission of the Folger Shakespeare Library.

Lady Mary (Sidney) Wroth, *Pamphilia to Amphilanthus*, appended to *Urania* (1621)

Lady Mary Wroth's *Pamphilia to Amphilanthus* can be regarded as the first complete sonnet sequence in English by a woman writer. Appended to the 1621 *Urania*, the sequence offers an original perspective on the female voice as lyric subject that at once draws upon and transforms the precedents offered by such earlier European women poets as Pernette du Guillet (*Les Rhymes*, 1545), Louise Labe (*Sonnets*, 1555), and Veronica Franco (*Terze rime*, 1575). Throughout her sonnet sequence, Wroth counterpoises speech and silence, absence and presence, in such a way as to decenter the authority of the male beloved, so that it is the woman, as speaking subject, who commands the balance of the discourse.

Revising the Petrarchan tradition of the sonnet sequence, Wroth structures her poems to evoke strong female ties to personified figures ranging from "Night" and "Fortune" to the mythic "Philomeale," whose roles as an imagined community of female friends for the speaker, Pamphilia, counteract the absence of the male Petrarchan lover, Amphilanthus. Instead of simply relying upon traditional Petrarchan alternations of day and night, Wroth moves beyond the dichotomy so favored by her male predecessors to represent "Night" in particular as a female companion in time of grief. The sustained lack of reference either to the male lover himself—named only in the title—or to his absence shifts the focus of the speaker's discourse from the masculine subject to her own construction of communal bonds with personified figures of female companionship and authority.

In Sonnet 37, "Night, welcome art thou to my minde distrest," Wroth's speaker embraces the triple companionship of "silence," "grief," and "Night" in personal terms that underscore her awareness of a shared female bond of suffering. Whereas Philip Sidney compares "night" and "thought," both figured as masculine in *Astrophil and Stella* 96, on the basis of their aesthetic similarities, Wroth references the explicitly feminized "Night" to decenter the role of the absent male beloved, relegating him in Sonnet 37 to the margins of Pamphilia's "freindship" with other female "companions." Rather than focusing upon the exclusivity of her pain in love, as do so many of her male contemporaries in the sonnet tradition, Wroth's speaker identifies herself throughout her sequence as part of a larger community of oppressed lovers, and embraces Night as a female friend in a shared time of trouble.

Wroth concludes *Pamphilia to Amphilanthus* with an affirmation of Pamphilia's discursive bond with her muse, the last figure of female authority, apart from the speaker herself, in the sonnet that closes the sequence. The collaboration between Wroth's female speaker and her female muse, recalling Aemilia Lanyer's representation of the bond between herself and her sacred sisters in *Salve Deus Rex Judaeorum* (1611), represents a final manifestation of her celebration of a community of personified female figures such as Night and Fortune. Pamphilia's commemoration of her poems to Night, as well as her injunction of her muse to silence in the final sonnet of the sequence, reveal at once the centrality of bonds between women to female discourse and the potential for a female-authored lyric protagonist finally to choose, unlike Ovid's Philomela, the point of closure for her own song.

NAOMI J. MILLER
UNIVERSITY OF ARIZONA

Lady Mary Wroth. *The Countesse of Mountgomeries Urania* (1621). Folger Shakespeare Library STC 26051. Page 22 of appendix.

selves) to some deformed slave. what is yor priviledg in being King:
if you must be bound in yor desires. never stand supplicateing to
them, whom by yᵉ law of yᵉ creation you may command: had I been as
neer, for yᵗ scornfull slutt. but now I thank my starrs I can dispise
her as much as shee disdained mee, and to say yᵉ truth, shee is too beautifull and witty for meanto a wife. for hee was noe foolish King yᵗ said
if a woman had but wit inough to know her husbands doublet from
his breeches, shee was wise inough. But for a Mistris! thᵉ Circle of
yᵉ Sun views not lovlier lass. this speech was needless to yᵉ King, for hee
was already but too much inflamed wth her love, but, continued hᵉ
if yor Majᵗie will have my poor advice flatter her awhile, and then
if shee yields not force her; for why should you loos yᵗ power wch is
given you from above: and have yor affeition trampled on (in dispet
of you) by an inconsiderable Trull. but oh said yᵉ King what will my
Zelbra say to have a Rivall in her love: yor Highnes said hᵉ habe
don her honor inough, in making her (of a Captive) a Queen: and it
were a high presumption in her to think to confine thᵉ thoughts of
so great a King, to her single embrace. Then yᵉ King embraceing him
in his arms said, now I know thou loves mee, & all yᵉ World shall know I love thee
so, they came into presence, thᵉ Queen rose up, and smileing, told yᵉ
King wt earnest contest had been between them, and how admirably
yᵉ Lady fidelia had set forth yᵉ felicity of a vertuous Maried Couple:
and how rarely Castabella had set forth yᵉ Excellency of her Sex in yᵉ
prais of Virginity. O said the King how unhappy was I to be absent:
why said Alphonso what can bee said of yᵗ despicable Sex: but yᵗ they
are Ambitious, Proud, Scornfull, Cowardly, Cruell, Wanton, Simple
and inconstant. But my Lord said yᵉ lovly fidelia can you make good
all those perticulars yᵗ you hold forth: if their Majᵗies will give mᵉ
leave I doubt not, but I shall vindicate my injured Sex and give
a true Character of yᵗ Animall called Man; and if you please to
the hearing, let him begin. In earnest said yᵉ King, I doe hugely
desire to hear wt you both can say; Come my dear love said hᵉ to yᵉ
Queen, let us sit and give ear to this admireable discourse, for so
it must needs bee, seing Don Alphonso is both learned and eloquent;
and yᵉ Lady fidelia (considering her Sex) is so too: Therefore Don Alphonzo do you (seing shee gives you that advantage) begin. Sanford
Don Alphonzo wth all my heart, first then yor highnes may be pleased
to know, yᵗ women were created only to bee Subservants to men, for
in all those numberless nations wch are guided by yᵉ unerring light
of nature, yᵉ women are absolute slaves; and among Jews, & Mahometans they are littᵉ or nothing better. ffor it is their faith that

                                                                        women

Lady Hester Pulter, "The Unfortunate Florinda" (c. 1660)

Transcription

selves) to some deformed slave. what is your priviledg in being King; if you must be bound in your desires; never stand supplicateing to them, whom by the law of the creation you may comand: had I been as you are, above the reach of humane law, I had not lost one minutes rest, for that scornfull Flurt. but now I thank my starrs I can dispise her as much as shee disdained me; and to say the truth, shee is too beautifull and witty for a wife: For hee was noe Foolish King that said if a woman had but wit inough to know her husbands doublet from his breeches, shee was wife inough. But for a Mistres! the Circle of the sun views not lovlier lass: this speech was needless to the King, for hee was already but too much inflamed with her love, but, continued he if your Majestie will have my poor advice flatter her awhile, and then if shee Yields not, force her; for why should you loos that power which is given you from above? and have your affection trampled on (in respct of you) by an inconsiderable Trull. but oh said the King what will my Zabra say, to have a rivall in her love? your Highnes (said he) have don her, honour inough, in making her (of a Captive) a Queen: and it were a high presumption in her to think to confine the thoughts of so great a King, to her single embrace. Then the King embraceing him in his, Arms said, now I know thou loves me, & all the World shall know I love thee[.] So they came into presence, the Queen rose up, and smileing, told the King what earnest contest had been between them, and how admirably the Lady Fidelia had set forth the felicity of A vertuous Maried Couple and how rarely Castabella had set forth the Excellency of her sex in the praise of Virginety. O said the King how unhappy was I to be absent? why said Don Alphonso? what can be said of that despicable sex? but that they are Ambitious, Prowd, Scornfull, Cowardly, Cruell, Wanton, simple and inconstant. But my Lord said the lovly Fidelia, can you make good all those perticulars that you hold forth? if their Majesties will give me leave I doubt not, but I shall vindicate my injured sex and give A true Character of that Animall called Man; and if you please to the hearing, let him begin. In earnest said the King, I doe hugely desire, to hear what you both can say; Come my dear love said he to the Queen; let us sit and give ear to this admireable discourse, For so it must needs be, seing Don Alphonso is both learned and Eloquent, and the Lady Fidelia (considering her sex) is so too: Therefore Don Alphonso do you (seing shee gives you that advantage) begin. I answerd Don Alphonso with all my heart, First then your highnes may be pleased to know, that weomen were created only to be subservants to men, for in all those numberless Nations which are guided by the unerring light of nature, the woemen are absolute slaves; and Among Jews, & Mahometans they are little or nothing better: For it is their faith that

Commentary

Lady Hester Pulter's "The Unfortunate Florinda" is a prose romance in two parts, dating in all likelihood from the late 1650s or early 1660s. Florinda, a young woman of marriageable age at the Spanish court, undergoes threats to—and ultimately the violation of—her chastity; meanwhile, a second female character, Fidelia, experiences shipwrecks, dresses as a boy, serves as a slave in England, and achieves happy union with her lover, Amandus, the prince of Naples.

"The Unfortuate Florinda's" eponymous heroine is "superlative in all vertues, especially Chastity" (f. 3ʳ) but is at fault in being too certain of her virtue's inviolability. Florinda rebuffs the marriage proposal of Don Alphonso, the favorite of the licentious and usurping Spanish monarch, King Roderigo. King Roderigo agrees to act as Don Alphonso's spokesman in love, but this scenario only inflames the king's own passion for Florinda, and Don Alphonso soon pledges to assist the king in convincing Florinda to "Yield in a dishonourable way" (f. 8ʳ). Don Alphonso declares to the king on the facing page that Florinda "is too beautifull and witty for a wife" but is the perfect mistress, and that the king should in any case force her; these are sentiments bred out of Don Alphonso's own humiliation and excessive pride.

Don Alphonso's misogyny is challenged on the facing page by Fidelia, whose mother dedicated her life to "thee vertuous Erudition of you, that you might not only bee vertuous by customary education, but out of choice and reason" (f. 9ʳ). Fidelia learns Latin and Spanish with her brother, despite the fact that "knowledg by most men [is] esteem'd noe ornament for a Woeman," because she wants to "read many Excellent books written in those Languages" (f. 12ᵛ); she also possesses "a naturall Eligance in her delivery" (f. 8ᵛ). Throughout the romance she is the voice of female reason, in conversation with Florinda and her friend Castabella, and in the passage in question she is an able spokeswoman for her sex.

Don Alphonso and Fidelia here begin a set-piece disputation that draws on the conventional terms of the "women controversy" (see chapter 2). Don Alphonso's accusations that women are "Ambitious, Prowd, Scornfull, Cowardly, Cruell, Wanton, simple and inconstant" are those thrown at women in tracts such as Joseph Swetnam's *The Araignment of Lewde, idle, froward and unconstant women* (1616), to which Rachel Speght and others replied. Fidelia defends women as being "the last and choicest of the works of Nature" and "of A more Unctious Nature Ayrey or Æthereall Nature then Man" (f. 26ʳ); these are defenses that, like Speght's and others', derive from Henricus Cornelius Agrippa's *Declamation on the Nobility and Preeminence of the Female Sex* (translated into English in 1542). Linda Woodbridge, Constance Jordan, and others have regarded the "women controversy" as a rhetorical game as opposed to serious engagements with misogyny, but in this set piece, Pulter utilizes conventional tropes to articulate her romance's moral core.

Fidelia's learnedness and her rhetorical skill set her apart from the other women in the romance, and her sense and success in love and life are grounded in her education and independent capacity for reason. Fidelia, nonetheless, marries happily and upholds the importance of wedded—rather than unattached and virginal—chastity. Pulter's verse encourages women to write religious "Rimes," but Fidelia's intellectual achievements are more wide-ranging and radical, perhaps because she occupies the imaginary world of romance. Fidelia is the central character of the first part of *The Unfortunate Florinda*; it is notable that the second part, which descends into a voyeuristic description of Florinda's rape and her planned revenge, is incomplete.

SARAH ROSS
MASSEY UNIVERSITY

Lady Hester Pulter. *The Unfortunate Florinda*. University of Leeds Library, Brotherton Collection MS Lt q 32, f. 25r (from rear of manuscript, inverted).

Mary Carleton, *The case of Madam Mary Carleton, lately stiled the German Princess* (1663)

The images discussed here were commissioned by Mary Carleton and used as a frontispiece to the pamphlet *The case of Madam Mary Carleton, lately stiled the German Princess*, published in 1663. This pamphlet, attributed to Mary Carleton, presents her defense against charges of bigamy. In the pamphlet, Carleton carefully positions herself, seeking to confirm her identity as a German princess. She includes letters to Prince Rupert of Germany and to the "Noble Ladies and Gentlewomen of England" as prefaces to her pamphlet in hopes of convincing her readers that she will gain recognition from Prince Rupert as well as to gain the sympathy of the noblewomen of England. Carleton maintains her claims of German nobility throughout "The case," even as she faces death on the scaffold in 1673. The prefatory portraits demonstrate the way in which Carleton uses language and visual representation together to create and present an identity.

The two portraits are particularly interesting in that they demonstrate Mary Carleton's self-conscious management of her image as she attempts to create her identity with the help of the public eye. The images of Mary in the two portraits are nearly identical, with the exception of her face, which is younger and rounder in the first, and more mature in the second. But the portraits also differ in their details; the accessories worn by Carleton and the shading used in each of the portraits are different. In the second portrait, everything is simplified and lightened, perhaps suggesting a freedom found through Mary's transgression of the boundaries of class, nation, and sex: transgressions not yet committed and a freedom not yet achieved in the first portrait, as indicated by Carleton's more intricate accessories and hair and the use of slightly darker cross-hatching. These portraits also represent a very classical-style body. Mary conveys herself in an orderly, regal, and almost statuesque manner that supports her claims to royalty and womanly propriety.

The text accompanying each portrait is also significant. A short verse underlines the first portrait:

> Behold my innocence after such disgrace
> Dares show an honest and noble Face
> Henceforth there needs no mark of me be known
> For the right Counterfeit is herein shown.

This verse emphasizes Mary's belief in her innocence and provides the reader with the "correct" interpretation of the portrait and of Carleton's character. In describing the portrait as the "right Counterfeit," Carleton "effectively demystifies essentialist notions of identity by calling attention to the fact that representation and self-representation can never be other than a 'counterfeit'" (Suzuki 69). A shorter, more ambiguous text literally frames the second portrait. Above the portrait appear the words "Mary Carleton Cald" and below are the words "the German Princess." The positioning of the text allows for at least two interpretations. The lines, read individually, emphasize Mary's identities as separate entities; first, one who is "cald" Mary Carleton and second, the German Princess. Read together, we see "Mary Carleton Cald the German Princess." In either case, the multiplicity and fluidity of Mary Carleton's identities is emphasized. Language and image col-

6.18: Mary Carleton, *The case of . . . the German Princess* (1663). Reproduced by kind permission of The Newberry Library, Chicago, Illinois.

laborate in these portraits, at once clarifying and complicating our interpretation of the text and the images, and demonstrating Mary Carleton's adeptness at fashioning her identity by making the observer complicit in the act.

BROOKE STAFFORD
UNIVERSITY OF WASHINGTON

Mary Carleton. *The case of Madam Mary Carleton, lately stiled the German Princess, truely stated: with an historical relation of her birth, education, and fortunes; in an appeal to his illustrious Highness Prince Rupert* (1663). Newberry Library Case E 5C 19414 FMP Record 1925. Frontispieces(s)

[4]

oh much more in vain to urge the nearness of our Relation. What Kin my charming *Silvia* are you to me? No tyes of blood forbid my Passion; and what's a Ceremony impos'd on man by custome? what is it to my Divine *Silvia*, that the Priest took my hand and gave it to your Sister? what Alliance can that create? why shou'd a trick devis'd by the wary old, only to make provision for posterity, tye me to an eternal slavery. No, no my charming Maid, tis nonsense all; let us (born for mightier joys) scorn the dull, *beaten road*, but let us love like the

Love-Letters

Between a

NOBLE-MAN

And his

SISTER.

LONDON,
Printed, and are to be sold by
Randal Taylor, near *Stationer's*
Hall. MDCLXXXIV.

6.19: Aphra Behn, *Love-Letters Between a Nobleman and His Sister* (1684). Bodleian Library, University of Oxford.

Aphra Behn, *Love-Letters Between a Nobleman and His Sister* (1684)

In November 1682, London's two theaters merged and the demand for new plays plummeted. Aphra Behn had made a good living writing a series of successful plays, but this development constrained her to look around for other work. A scandal had just broken out that provided her with the subject matter for her first novel, *Love-Letters Between a Nobleman and His Sister;* the title page capitalizes "noble-man" and "sister" to highlight its sensationalist theme of passionate incest among the nobility. In August, Henrietta Berkeley, the daughter of a prominent Tory, had eloped in the middle of the night from her parents' country estate to be with her lover, the Whig rebel Lord Grey. Her sister, Lord Grey's wife, was in turn engaged in an affair with the Duke of Monmouth, King Charles II's firstborn but illegitimate son. The duke was the Whig's highly popular candidate for the royal succession (see Behn's "Young Jemmy," item 8.18); he remained Lord Grey's close friend and political collaborator throughout the affair. These dramatic intersecting romantic and political triangles gave Behn the material she needed.

Over the following months, while her real-life hero secretly plotted with Monmouth to start a popular insurrection, Behn composed a series of fictional letters between Henrietta and her lover, lightly disguised as Silvia and Philander. This epistolary format was modeled on the *Lettres Portugaises* translated from French in 1678 by the Tory's chief propagandist, Roger L'Estrange. An account of intensely personal emotions, the *Lettres* created a genre that suited Behn. In spite of the dramatic events in which the lovers participate, her emphasis remains the tumultuous inner psychology of love.

In the eyes of the law, the affair was incestuous; Lord Grey was married to Henrietta's sister Mary and thus her brother-in-law, a nomination that carried a considerable weight. The brash hero of the *Letters,* however, adoitly counters with the rebellious thrust of the Restoration libertine: "what's a Ceremony impos'd on man by custome? . . . tis nonsense all." As rakish as the royalist Wilmore in Behn's popular play *The Rover,* Philander appeals seductively to nature to license his—and vicariously, the readers'—"mightier joys."

While she was composing the *Love-Letters* in June 1683, her dubious hero, Lord Grey, became a prime suspect in a suspected plot to kill the king and his brother. He was arrested and taken to the Tower, but his guard fell asleep and Grey walked down to the bank of the river Thames, thus making his escape. Henrietta joined him in the woods at his country estate, Up Park in Sussex, and together they set sail for France, at which point the novel ends. Only four months later, in October 1683, it was entered in the Stationers Register, indicating that the manuscript was ready and likely already printed. Its mix of politics and sexual intrigue proved so successful that Behn wrote two sequels over the coming years, loosely tracking her protagonists' fortunes from their flight to their return during the Monmouth Rebellion of 1685.

If Grey had not escaped, he may have suffered the laws' gruesome revenge for high treason: to be hanged, drawn, quartered, exposed in pieces on stakes around the city, and left there for years. Behn's political sympathies lay wholly with the King, yet in this love story, it is hard not to cheer for the hero and the heroine as they make their escape.

Francis Steen
University of California Santa Barbara

Aphra Behn. *Love-Letters Between a Nobleman and His Sister* (1684). Bodleian Library Vet. A3. f 494.
Title Page and page 4.

The Epistle Dedicatory.

true Story, of a Man Gallant enough to merit your Protection; and, had he always been so Fortunate, he had not made so Inglorious an end: The Royal Slave I had the Honour to know in my Travels to the other World; and though I had none above me in that Country, yet I wanted power to preserve this Great Man. If there be any thing that seems Romantick, I beseech your Lordship to consider, these Countries do, in all things, so far differ from ours, that they produce unconceivable Wonders; at least, they appear so to us, because New and Strange. What I have mention'd I have taken-care shou'd be

The Epistle Dedicatory.

be Truth, let the Critical Reader judge as he pleases. 'Twill be no Commendation to the Book, to assure your Lordship I writ it in a few Hours, though it may serve to Excuse some of its Faults of Connexion; for I never rested my Pen a Moment for Thought: 'Tis purely the Merit of my Slave that must render it worthy of the Honour it begs; and the Author of that Subscribing herself,

My Lord,

Your Lordship's most oblig'd

and obedient Servant,

A. BEHN.

THE

6.20: Aphra Behn, Dedication, *Oroonoko* (1688). Reproduced by permission of The Huntington Library, San Marino, California.

Aphra Behn, Dedication, *Oroonoko* (1688)

In her epistle dedicatory to Richard Lord Maitland, the fourth Earl of Lauderdale, Aphra Behn emphasizes the verity of the subsequent story of *Oroonoko*. Although it is likely, as Janet Todd has argued, that Behn did spend time in the novel's locale of Surinam, few critics read the work as an autobiographical account, despite Behn's titular promise that the work is "A True History." By explaining that she knew the royal slave Oroonoko, Behn lends authority to her narrative, but she qualifies this claim and puts herself in a secondary role as a transcriber merely telling the story to "preserve this Great Man." She continues to create this guise of humility both in the dedication, in which she explains the reason for some of the work's "Faults of Connexion," and in the novel itself, when her narrator bemoans the fate of Mr. Trefry, who died before he was able to write his version of the events and thus left only "a female pen" to celebrate the fame of Oroonoko.

Such humility is commonplace in early modern prefatory material, and Behn's modesty, like that of so many other writers, seems disingenuous. Earlier in the dedication, Behn compares the roles of the poet and painter, arguing that the work of poets (a group she includes herself in with the use of the pronoun "we") is superior to that of artists because of the longevity of literature. Also, in describing her writing process at the conclusion of this dedication, Behn creates an implicit competition between herself as narrator/author and her royal subject. If a poet can draw "the Soul and Mind" for perpetuity, then Behn herself may achieve greatness through her translation of Oroonoko's stories into a written form accessible to a European audience. Her discussion of those things that seem "Romantick" in her narrative underscores not only the strangeness of the new world and its inhabitants but also the process of imperial translation in which Behn writes of an African king/slave within the conventions of European romance and tragedy.

As an introduction to an imaginary autobiography or novella, her preface demonstrates the singularity of Behn's project by participating in the fictitious story that follows. When she describes herself as an "Eye-Witness to a great part, of what you will find here set down," Behn offers a first glimpse of the narrative persona who tells Oroonoko's story, but there are also important differences between the narrator of the preface and that of the novella. While the prefatory speaker allies herself with poets and writers of Romances, the speaker in *Oroonoko* portrays herself as an accidental author until the conclusion of the novella, when she writes, "I hope the Reputation of my Pen is considerable enough to make his Glorious Name survive to all ages." By referring to her reputation, Behn's narrator reminds us both of the prefatory narrator and of Behn herself, and she highlights the power of the female pen even as she pretends to dismiss it.

DEBORAH UMAN
EASTERN CONNECTICUT STATE UNIVERSITY

Aphra Behn. *Oroonoko: Or, the Royal Slave* (1688). Huntington Library RB 102830. Last two pages of
The Epistle Dedicatory.

Bibliography

Acheson, Katherine, ed. *The Diary of Anne Clifford, 1616–1619, A Critical Edition.* New York and London: Garland, 1995.

Agrippa, Henricus Cornelius. *Declamation on the Nobility and Preeminence of the Female Sex.* Albert Rabil Jr, Chicago and London: University of Chicago Press, 1996.

Amussen, Susan Dwyer. "'Being Stirred to Much Unquietness': Violence and Domestic Violence in Early Modern England." *Journal of Women's History* 6.2 (Summer 1994): 70–89.

Anselment, Raymond. "'The Wantt of Health:' An Early Eighteenth-Century Self-Portrait of Sickness." *Literature and Medicine* 15.2 (1996): 225–43.

———. "Elizabeth Freke's Remembrances: Reconstructing a Self." *Tulsa Studies in Women's Literature* 16.1 (1997): 57–75.

———, ed. *The Remembrances of Elizabeth Freke 1671–1714.* Camden Fifth Series, Vol 18. London: Cambridge University Press, 2001.

Athey, Stephanie, and Daniel Cooper Alarcón. "*Oroonoko*'s Gendered Economies of Honor/Horror: Reframing Colonial Discourse Studies in the Americas." *American Literature* 65 (1993): 415–43.

Barbour, Reid. "Lucy Hutchinson, Atomism and the Atheist Dog." *Women, Science and Medicine 1500–1700: Mothers and Sisters of the Royal Society.* Ed. Lynette Hunter and Sarah Hutton. Phoenix Mill, Gloucestershire: Sutton, 1997. 122–37.

Bernbaum, Ernest. *The Mary Carleton Narratives.* Cambridge, Mass: Harvard University Press, 1914.

Blecki, Catherine La Courreye. "Alice Hayes and Mary Penington: Personal Identity Within the Tradition of Quaker Spiritual Autobiography." *Quaker History* 65.1 (1976): 19–31.

Brant, Clare, and Diane Purkiss, eds. *Women, Texts and Histories, 1575–1760.* New York: Routledge, 1992. 164–94.

Brown, Laura. "The Romance of Empire: *Oroonoko* and the Trade in Slaves." *The New Eighteenth Century: Theory, Politics, English Literature.* Ed. Felicity Nussbaum and Laura Brown. New York: Methuen, 1987. 4–61.

Burns, Norman T. "From Seeker to Finder: The Singular Experiences of Mary Penington." *The Emergence of Quaker Writing: Dissenting Literature in Seventeenth-Century England.* Ed. Thomas N. Corns and David Loewenstein. London: Frank Cass, 1995. 70–87.

Camden, Vera J. *The Narrative of the Persecutions of Agnes Beaumont.* East Lansing, Mich.: Colleagues Press, 1992.

Campbell, Julie. "'Foolish Sport,' 'Delightful Games,' and 'Sweet Discourse': Intertextuality and the Inscription of Literary Circle Ritual in Sidney's *Arcadia*, Wroth's *Urania*, and Weamys's *Continuation of the Arcadia*." *Critical Approaches to English Prose Fiction 1520–1640.* Ed. Donald Beecher. Barnabe Riche Society Publications 9 Ottawa: Dovehouse, 1998. 63–84.

Carbery, Mary, ed. "Mrs Elizabeth Freke, her Diary 1671–1714." *Journal of the Cork Historical and Archaeological Society* 16–19 (1910–11).

———, ed. *Mrs Elizabeth Freke, her Diary 1671–1714.* Cork, Ireland: Guy and Company, 1913.

Clifford, Anne. *The Diary of Lady Anne Clifford.* Ed. Vita Sackville-West, London: Heinemann, 1923.

Coleman, Linda. "Gender, Sect, and Circumstance: Quaker Mary Penington's Many Voices." *Women's Life-Writing: Finding Voice, Building Community.* Ed. Linda S. Coleman, Bowling Green, Ohio: Bowling Green State University Popular Press, 1997. 93–107.

Depas-Orange, Ann, and Robert C. Evans, eds. "The Birthday of My Self": Martha Moulsworth, Renaissance Poet. *Critical Matrix: The Princeton Journal of Women, Gender, and Culture* (1996): 23–25.

De Quehen, Hugo. *Lucy Hutchinson's Translation of Lucretius' De rerum Natura.* Ann Arbor: University of Michigan Press, 1996.

Dolan, Frances E. "'Gentlemen, I have one more thing to say': Women on Scaffolds in England, 1563–1680." *Modern Philology* 92 (1994–95): 157–78.

Evans, Robert C. "'New' Poems by Early Modern Women: 'A Maid Under 14,' Elizabeth With, Elizabeth Collett, and 'A Lady of Honour.'" *Ben Jonson Journal* 7 (2000): 447–515.

———. "The Life and Times of Martha Moulsworth." *"The Muses Female Are": Martha Moulsworth and Other Women Writers of the English Renaissance.* Ed. Robert C. Evans and Anne C. Little. West Cornwall, Conn.: Locust Hill Press, 1995. 17–73.

——— and Anne C. Little, eds. *"The Muses Female Are": Martha Moulsworth and Other Women Writers of the English Renaissance.* West Cornwall, Conn.: Locust Hill Press, 1995.

Ferguson, Margaret W. "Juggling the Categories of Race, Class and Gender: Aphra Behn's *Oroonoko*." *Women's Studies: An Interdisciplinary Journal* 19 (1991): 159–80.

———. "The Authorial Ciphers of Aphra Behn." *The Cambridge Companion to English Literature, 1650–1740.* Ed. Steven N. Zwicker. Cambridge: Cambridge University Press, 1998. 225–49.

Foster, Donald W. "Resurrecting the Author: Elizabeth Tanfield Cary." *Privileging Gender in Early Modern England.* Ed. Jean R. Brink. Sixteenth Century Essays & Studies 23. Ann Arbor: Edwards Brothers, 1993.141–73.

Fraser, Antonia. *The Weaker Vessel: Women's Lot in Seventeenth-Century England.* New York: Vintage Books, 1985.

George, Margaret. "The Education of Elizabeth Freke." *Women in the First Capitalist Society.* Urbana: University of Illinois Press, 1988.

Gowing, Laura. *Domestic Dangers: Women, Words and Sex in Early Modern London.* Oxford: Clarendon Press, 1996.

Graham, Elspeth, Hilary Hinds, Elaine Hobby, and Helen Wilcox. eds. *Her Own Life: Autobiographical Writings by Seventeenth Century Englishwomen.* London and New York: Routledge, 1989.

Griffiths, R. G. "Joyce Jefferies of Ham Castle." *Transactions of the Worcestershire Archaeological Society.* n. s., 10 (1933): 1–32; (1934): 1–13.

Grundy, Isobel. "Women's History? Writings by English Nuns." *Women, Writing, History 1640–1740.* Ed. Isobel Grundy and Susan Wiseman. Athens: University of Georgia Press, 1992. 125–138.

Hackett, Helen. "The Torture of Limena: Sex and Violence in Lady Mary Wroth's Urania." *Voicing Women: Gender and Sexuality in Early Modern Writing.* Ed. Kate Chedgzoy et al. Pittsburgh: Duquesne University Press, 1997. 93–110.

———. *Women and Romance Fiction in the English Renaissance.* Cambridge: Cambridge University Press, 2000.

Hall, Kim F. "'I Rather Would Wish to Be A Black-Moor': Beauty, Race, and Rank in Lady Mary Wroth's *Urania*." *Women, "Race," and Writing in the Early Modern Period.* Ed. Margo Hendricks and Patricia Parker. London: Routledge, 1994. 178–94.

Hannay, Margaret Patterson. "Lady Wroth, Mary Sidney." *Women Writers of the Renaissance and Reformation.* Katharina M. Wilson. Athens: University of Georgia Press, 1987. 548–65.

———. *Philip's Phoenix: Mary Sidney, Countess of Pembroke.* Oxford: Oxford University Press, 1990.

Harding, Christopher, et al. *Imprisonment in England and Wales: A Concise History.* London: Croom Helm, 1985.

Harrison, G. B. *The Narrative of the Persecution of Agnes Beaumont in 1674.* New York: Richard R. Smith, 1929.

Hinds, Hilary. *God's Englishwomen: Seventeenth-century Radical Sectarian Writing and Feminist Criticism.* Manchester: Manchester University Press, 1996.

James, F. R. "The Diary of Joyce Jefferies." *Woolhope Naturalists' Field Club* (unnumbered volume for 1921–23): xlix–lx.

Jordan, Constance. *Renaissance Feminism: Literary Texts and Political Models.* Ithaca, N.Y., and London: Cornell University Press, 1990.

Kane, Stuart. "Wives with Knives: Early Modern Murder Ballads and the Transgressive Commodity." *Criticism* 38 (1996): 219–37.

Keeble, N. H. "'The Colonel's Shadow:' Lucy Hutchinson, Women's Writing and the Civil War." *Literature and the English Civil War.* Eds. Thomas Healy and Jonathan Sawday. Cambridge: Cambridge University Press, 1990.

Lamb, Mary Ellen. "Singing with the (Tongue) of a Nightingale." *Gender and Authorship in the Sidney Circle.* Madison: University of Wisconsin Press, 1990. 194–228.

———. "The Agency of the Split-Subject: Lady Anne Clifford and the Uses of Reading." *ELR* 22:3 (Fall 1992): 347–68.

———. "The Poem as a Clock: Martha Moulsworth Tells Time Three Ways." *"The Muses Female Are": Martha Moulsworth and Other Women Writers of the English Renaissance.* Ed. Robert C. Evans and Anne C. Little. West Cornwall, Conn.: Locust Hill Press, 1995. 91–99.

Latz, Dorothy. *"Glow-Worm Light": Writings of Seventeenth-Century Century English Recusant Women from Original Manuscripts.* Salzburg Studies in English Literature. Salzburg: Institut für Anglistik und Amerikanistik, Universität Salzburg, 1989.

Lewalski, Barbara. "Re-writing Patriarchy and Patronage: Margaret Clifford, Anne Clifford, and Aemilia Lanyer." *Yearbook of English Studies* 21 (1991): 87–106.

———. *Writing Women in Jacobean England.* Cambridge, Mass.: Harvard University Press, 1993.

———, ed. *The Poems and Polemics of Rachel Speght.* New York: Oxford University Press, 1996.

———. Introduction to 'The Memorandum of Martha Moulsworth, Widow.' *The Norton Anthology of English Literature.* 2 vols. 7th ed. New York: W.W. Norton, 1999. I, 1552–53.

Loomis, Catherine. "Elizabeth Southwell's Manuscript Account of the Death of Queen Elizabeth I." *ELR* 26.3 (Autumn 1996): 482–509.

Lotti, Ottaviano. *The Life of Sir Robert Dudley.* Trans. J. T. Leader. Florence, 1895; rpt Amsterdam, 1977.

Loughlin, Marie H. "Mary (Springett) Penington (c.1623–1682)." *The New Dictionary of National Biography.* Gen. Ed. Colin Matthew. Oxford: Oxford University Press, forthcoming (2004).

Lucas, Caroline. *Writing for Women: The Example of Woman as Reader in Elizabethan Romance.* Milton Keynes, U.K.: Open University Press, 1989.

Lynch, Kathleen. "Her name Agnes": The Verifications of Agnes Beaumont's Narrative Ventures." *ELH* 67 (2000): 71–98.

Martin, Randall. "The Autobiography of Grace, Lady Mildmay." *Renaissance and Reformation* 18.1 (1994): 33–82.

McDowell, Paula. *The Women of Grub Street: Press, Politics and Gender in the London Literary Marketplace 1678–1730.* Oxford: Clarendon Press, 1998.

Mendelson, Sara. "Stuart Women's Diaries and Occasional Memoirs." In *Women in English Society 1500–1800.* Ed. Mary Prior. London: Methuen, 1985.

———. *The Mental World of Stuart Women: Three Studies.* Brighton: Harvester, 1987.

Miller, Naomi J. "Rewriting Lyric Fictions: The Role of the Lady in Lady Mary Wroth's Pamphilia to Amphilanthus." *The Renaissance Englishwoman in Print: Counterbalancing the Canon.* Ed. Anne Haselkorn and Betty Travitsky. Amherst: University of Massachusetts Press, 1990. 295–310.

———. *Changing the Subject: Mary Wroth and Figurations of Gender in Early Modern England.* Lexington: University Press of Kentucky, 1996.

———— and Gary Waller, eds. *Reading Mary Wroth: Representing Alternatives in Early Modern England*. Knoxville: University of Tennessee Press, 1991.

Neale, J. E. "The Sayings of Queen Elizabeth." *History* 10 (October 1925): 212–33.

Norbrook, David. "Lucy Hutchinson's 'Elegies' and the Situation of the Republican Woman Writer (with text)." *ELR* 27.3 (1997): 469–521.

————. "A Devine Originall: Lucy Hutchinson and the 'Woman's Version.'" *TLS* (March 19, 1999): 13–15.

Oldham, James C. "On Pleading the Belly: A History of The Jury of Matrons." *Criminal Justice History* 6 (1985): 1–64.

Otten, Charlotte, ed. "Mrs. Elizabeth Freke." *English Women's Voices, 1540–1700*. Miami: Florida International University Press, 1992.

Parks, Joan. "Elizabeth Cary's Domestic History." *Other Voices, Other Views: Expanding the Canon in English Renaissance Studies*. Ed. Helen Ostovich, Mary V. Silcox, and Graham Roebuck. Newark: University of Delaware Press, 1999. 176–92.

Parry, Graham. "Lady Mary Wroth's *Urania*." *Proceedings of the Leeds Philosophical and Literary Society* 16 (1975): 51–60.

Penington, Mary. *Experiences in the Life of Mary Penington (written by herself), c. 1625–1682*. Ed. Norman Penney. London: Headley Bros., 1911. Preface by Gil Skidmore. London: Friends Historical Society, 1992.

Pollock, Linda. *With Faith and Physic*. London: Collins & Brown, 1993.

Quilligan, Maureen. "The Constant Subject: Instability and Female Authority in Wroth's Urania Poems." *Soliciting Interpretation: Literary Theory and Seventeenth-Century Poetry*. Ed. Elizabeth D. Harvey and Katherine Eisaman Maus. Chicago: University of Chicago Press, 1990. 307–35.

Roberts, Josephine A. "An Unpublished Literary Quarrel Concerning the Suppression of Mary Wroth's *Urania* (1621)." *Notes and Queries* 24 (1977): 532–35.

————. "Radigund Revisited: Perspectives on Women Rulers in Lady Mary Wroth's *Urania*." *The Renaissance Englishwoman in Print: Counterbalancing the Canon*. Ed. Anne M. Haselkorn and Betty S. Travitsky. Amherst: University of Massachusetts Press, 1990. 187–207.

————, ed. Introduction. *The First Part of the Countess of Montgomery's Urania. By Lady Mary Wroth*. Medieval and Renaissance Texts and Studies 140: Renaissance English Text Society Seventh Series 17. Binghamton: Medieval and Renaissance Texts and Studies, 1995.

Rose, Mary Beth. "Gender, Genre, and History: Seventeenth-Century English Women and the Art of Autobiography." *Women in the Middle Ages and the Renaissance: Literary and Historical Perspectives*. Ed. Mary Beth Rose. Syracuse, N.Y.: Syracuse University Press, 1985. 245–78.

Salzman, Paul. "Contemporary References in Mary Wroth's *Urania*." *Review of English Studies* 29 (1978): 178–81.

Sandy, Amelia Zurcher. "Pastoral, Temperance, and the Unitary Self in Wroth's *Urania*." *SEL* 42.1 (2002): 103–20.

Sharpe, J. A. "Domestic Homicide in Early Modern England." *Historical Journal* 24 (1981): 29–48.

————. "'Last Dying Speeches': Religion, Ideology and Public Execution in Seventeenth-Century England." *Past and Present* 107 (May 1985): 144–67.

Shawcross, John T. "'The Muses Female Are': Renaissance Women and Education." *"The Muses Female Are": Martha Moulsworth and Other Women Writers of the English Renaissance*. Ed. Robert C. Evans and Anne C. Little. West Cornwall, Conn.: Locust Hill Press, 1995. 163–72.

Shepherd, Simon. *The Women's Sharp Revenge: Five Women's Pamphlets from the Renaissance*. London: Fourth Estate, 1985.

Smith, Catherine. "Jane Lead: Mysticism and the Woman Cloathed with the Sun. " *Shakespeare's Sisters*. Ed. Sandra Gilbert and Susan Gubar. Bloomington: Indiana University Press, 1979. 3–18.

————. "Jane Lead: The Feminist Mind and Art of a Seventeenth-Century Protestant Mystic." *Women of Spirit: Female Leadership in the Jewish and Christian Traditions*. Ed. Rosemary Ruether and Eleanor McLaughlin. New York: Simon and Schuster, 1979. 55–63.

————. "Jane Lead's Wisdom: Women and Prophecy in Seventeenth-Century England." *Poetic Prophecy in Western Literature*. Ed. Jan Wojcik and Raymond-Jean Frontain. London, Ontario: Associated University Presses, 1984.

Spargo, Tamsin. "Contra-dictions: Women as Figures of Exclusion and Resistance in John Bunyan and Agnes Beaumont's Narratives." *Voicing Women: Gender and Sexuality in Early Modern Writing*. Ed. Kate Chedgzoy, Melanie Hansen, and Suzanne Trill. Renaissance Texts and Studies. Keele, Staffordshire: Keele University Press, 1996. 173–84.

Sperle, Joanne Magnani. *God's Healing Angel: A Biography of Jane Ward Lead*. DAI. Vol. 46, no. 5, 1985.

Steggle, Matthew. "Rhetorical Ordering in Moulsworth's 'Memorandum.'" *Central Matrix: The Princeton Journal of Women, Gender, and Culture* 10 (1996): 27–31. Also issued as *The birthday of my self: Martha Moulsworth, Renaissance Poet*, Ed. Ann Depas-Orange and Robert C. Evans. Princeton, N.J.: Critical Matrix, 1996.

Sutherland, James, ed. *Memoirs of the Life of Colonel Hutchinson with the Fragment of an Autobiography of Mrs. Hutchinson*. London: Oxford University Press, 1994.

Suzuki, Mihoko. "'The Case of Mary Carleton': Representing the Female Subject." *Tulsa Studies in Women's Literature* 12.1 (1993): 61–83.

Swan, Jesse. "Contextual Materials for the 1680 folio and octavo histories of Edward II by Elizabeth Cary, Viscountess Falkland." *Renaissance Women Online* http://www.wwp.brown.edu/texts/rwoentry.html.

Swift, Carolyn Ruth. "Feminine Identity in Lady Mary Wroth's Romance *Urania.*" Rpt. in *Women in the Renaissance: Selections from English Literary Renaissance.* Ed. Kirby Farrell, Elizabeth Hageman, and Arthur F. Kinney. Amherst: University of Massachusetts Press, 1988, 154–74.

Thomas, J. E. *House of Care: Prisons and Prisoners in England 1500–1800.* Nottingham: University of Nottingham Department of Adult Education, 1988.

Tittler, Robert. "Money-Lending in the West Midlands: The Activities of Joyce Jefferies, 1638–1649." *Historical Research* 67.164 (October 1994): 249–63.

———. "Joyce Jefferies and the Possibilities of Spinsterhood in Hereford." *Townspeople and Nation: English Urban Experiences, 1540–1640.* Ed. Robert Tittler. Stanford: Stanford University Press, 2001.

Todd, Janet. "Marketing the Self: Mary Carleton, Miss F and Susannah Gunning." *Studies on Voltaire and the Eighteenth Century* (1983): 95–106.

———, ed. *The Complete Works of Aphra Behn.* 6 vols. Columbus: Ohio State University Press, 1992.

———. *The Secret Life of Aphra Behn.* London: André Deutsch Limited, 1996.

———, and Elizabeth Spearing, eds. Counterfeit Ladies. New York: New York University Press, 1994.

Waller, Gary. *The Sidney Family Romance: Mary Wroth, William Herbert, and the Early Modern Construction of Gender.* Detroit, Mich.: Wayne State University Press, 1993.

Warnicke, Retha M. "Lady Mildmay's Journal: A Study in Autobiography and Meditation in Reformation England." *Sixteenth Century Journal* 20 (1989): 55–68.

Webb, John. "Some Passages in the Life and Character of a Lady Resident in the West Country." *Archaeologia* 37. pt. 1 (1857): 189–223.

Weller, Barry, and Margaret Ferguson, eds. *The Tragedy of Mariam with The Lady Falkland: Her Life.* Berkeley: University of California Press, 1994.

Wendorf, Richard. *The Elements of Life: Biography and Portrait-Painting in Stuart and Georgian England.* Oxford: Clarendon Press, 1990.

Wilcox, Helen. "Private Writing and Public Function: Autobiographical Texts by Renaissance Englishwomen." *Gloriana's Face: Women, Public and Private, in the English Renaissance.* Ed. S. P. Cerasano and Marion Wynne-Davies. Detroit, Mich.: Wayne State University Press, 1992. 97–62.

Williamson, George C. *Lady Anne Clifford, Countess of Dorset, Pembroke and Montgomery 1590–1676, Her Life, Letters, and Work.* Kendal: Titus Wilson and Son, 1923.

Witten-Hannah, Margaret A. "Lady Mary Wroth's *Urania*: The Work and the Tradition." Ph.D. diss., University of Auckland, 1978.

Wolfe, Heather, "The Scribal Hands and Dating of *Lady Falkland: Her Life.*" *English Manuscript Studies* 9 (2000): 187–217.

———, ed. *Elizabeth Cary, Lady Falkland: Life and Letters.* Tempe, Ariz., and Cambridge: MRTS and RTM, 2001.

Woodbridge, Linda. *Women and the English Renaissance: Literature and the Nature of Womankind, 1540–1620.* Brighton: Harvester Press, 1984.

CHAPTER 7

Translations/Alterations

The English language only very gradually became an acceptable medium for the cultured. During the Renaissance, educated males owned and read texts in their original (often classical) language. John Dee's catalogue, for example, lists primarily Latin texts, and the books in Lord Lumley's library were likewise almost all written in classical languages. But women readers, even those from the upper class, had little knowledge of the classics and thus were largely shut out of the world of higher learning along with the uneducated; or their reading was restricted to vernacular texts.[1] Translations, which could help bridge the two worlds, did increase in popularity as the decades went by, though the percentage of translated books printed in Elizabethan England was relatively small. Frances Egerton, Countess of Bridgewater (1585–1636), for example, owned no Latin or Greek texts, Heidi Brayman Hackel observes in a recent study of Egerton's library. Except for 18 French books, everything in her collection was in English. Still roughly 15 percent of the countess's books were translations, giving her access to texts she could otherwise not have read: Plutarch's *Lives*, Tacitus's *Annales*, Boethius's *Books of Philosophicall Comfort*, Tasso's *Godfrey of Bulloigne*, Cervantes's *Don Quixote*, and Boccaccio's *Decameron*, among others.[2]

Despite the paucity of classically educated women readers, however, women writers, in the face of many constraints, managed to produce translations and alterations—literary modes often neglected in present-day anthologies. The arts of translation and alteration are represented by several genres in this chapter, including plays, poetry, religious texts, philosophical treatises, and perhaps, most unexpectedly, entries from a manuscript jest book. Many of the authors featured here are better known to us not for their translations but for their other contributions to literature. For example, Katherine Philips is usually regarded as a poet, Aphra Behn as a playwright; yet both, in addition to a number of their contemporaries like Lucy Hutchinson, were recognized translators in their time.[3] In fact, in the Restoration period, translation work became a significant component of the livelihood of women writers.

The art of translation has traditionally been undervalued in our day. While this exercise was seen as less threatening than the production of original texts even in the early modern period because it "could be used to force them out of original discourse," the majority of female translators nevertheless felt compelled to justify their incursion into the literary world.[4] The translators, therefore, frequently negotiated between self-denial and self-assertion; on the one hand, they invoked the "humility topos"; on the other, they rewrote the original text even though their right to produce translations—an "acceptable" activity for women—did not "carry with it a licence to cross the boundaries of gender and subject matter to translate."[5] It is the nature of translations to take on a life of their own; in commenting on the alchemical nature of the translation, Walter Benjamin observes: "A translation touches the original lightly and only at the infinitely small point of the sense, thereupon pursuing its own course according to the laws of fidelity in the freedom of lin- guistic flux"; and Stephen Greenblatt recognizes: "there is no translation that is not at the same time an interpretation."[6] Still, translations and alterations produced by women raise questions about the choice of their particular source texts and their motives for translating or altering them. What is the purpose and effect of the rewriting? To what extent are devi- ations from the original text attributable to the limitations of the translator? What liberties might a translator take? What kind of reading or interpretive communities were imagined and created through the circulation of translated or altered texts that would otherwise have remained in the possession of a more selective readership? What claims to ownership or authorship does a translator have on the translated text and on the source text?

One of the early English translations featured in this chapter is by Anne (Cooke), Lady Bacon, daughter of Sir Anthony Cooke, a tutor to the young King Edward. Bacon's classical learning is evidenced in her translation of Bishop John Jewel's antipapal *An apolo- gie or answere in defence of the Churche of Englande* (1564), originally published in Latin, and used by Reformers to justify the secession from Catholicism in historical terms. Bacon's work in turn contributed to public political/religious discourse, including church politics. The achievement of *An apologie* was recognized by Theodore Beza, who dedicated his *Meditations* to Bacon. Bacon's translation of Jewel also invites comparison with the equally accomplished 1605 translation of John Ponet in *A Way of Reconciliation of a good and learned man* by her sister, Elizabeth Russell (chapter 4).

Plays constitute a significant number of the translations by early modern women writers, like Jane, Lady Lumley, who translated Euripides' verse play, *Iphigenia at Aulis* (1554), as *The Tragedie of Euripides called Iphigeneia translated out of Greake into Englisshe*. Lumley was criticized for her tendency to paraphrase rather than translate Euripides' text and to rely on Erasmus's Latin translation of the play in producing *The Tragedie of Euripides*. Though trained in the classics, Lumley possessed a limited knowledge of Greek, and Greek grammars and dictionaries at this time were few and crude. But as the achieve- ment of an adolescent woman, the translation has much to recommend it and, at moments, even rises above its many defects. Through the representation of the heroine Iphigenia, it questions the disposability of a women's life and teases the reader with oblique parallels to Lumley's own family, including her cousin, Lady Jane Grey Dudley, the nine-days' queen.[7]

Like Lumley, Mary Sidney Herbert was attracted to the genre of closet drama, which foregrounds states of mind rather than stage performance, while exhibiting its dialogic nature by also engaging political topics. Included in this chapter is her version of Robert Garnier's tragedy *Antoine*, printed twice during her lifetime. The translation, a prototype for the classical drama celebrated in Sir Philip Sidney's *Apology for Poetry*, experiments with Garnier's verse; in changing the style of the text, she alternates between rhyme and blank verse, reserving the latter for the monologues.

While *The Tragedie of Euripides* was the first English translation of a Greek drama, and the first produced by a woman, Margaret Tyler's *The Mirrour of Princely Deedes and Knighthood* (1578) was the first complete translation of a Spanish prose romance into English. Even more significantly, the latter was the first translation of the strictly secular romance genre by a woman, who may also have been a recusant Catholic.[8] Tyler's translation would require two justifications on her part: as a female writer, she would need to defend not only her entry into the world of literature but also her choice of romance, a genre frequently discredited for corrupting women readers. She addresses these concerns in "M.T. to the Reader"—a "kind of feminist manifesto that marks its author as a distinct voice among her female contemporaries" (Krontiris 45)—and in her dedication to Lord Thomas Howard that precedes it and is featured in this chapter. The text of *The Mirrour* is not radical though it offers a critique of dominant ideologies; while characterizing sexual modesty as a distinctly feminine trait, the play does at certain moments point to double standards in sexual conduct.

The first rhymed English translation of a French tragedy and the first heroic drama performed in English was produced by a woman who in our own day is commonly associated with a private circle of female friends, Katherine Philips. In her own time, however, Philips was best known for a work associated with the public, political sphere. *Pompey*, her translation of Pierre Corneille's *La Mort de Pompée* (1644), was available in manuscript in late 1662 or early 1663, and then printed with no indication of authorship, and finally performed on the Restoration stage in 1663. The translation reveals Philips's anxiety about presenting her text to the public, while exposing her interest in engaging political and intellectual issues of her day.[9] Her play initially met with success and made an impact in literary circles.[10] But just before her death in 1664, Philips's fears about public exposure seem to have been realized when she acknowledged the disgrace that covered the unauthorized publication of her collection, *Poems by the incomparable Mrs. K. P.*, printed by Richard Mariott.

Just as translation leads to alteration, so does the alteration of texts involve a certain amount of translation, though various women writers altered existing texts without translating them from another language. Some examples of poetry illustrate this point. The Devonshire Manuscript (c. 1530–45), a 124–page poetry miscellany, contains courtly verse and transcriptions, including transcribed extracts of medieval verses. The three women of the Tudor court known to have contributed to the manuscript and whose work represents some of the earliest evidence of women's literary efforts and achievements of this time are Lady Margaret Douglas, Mary Shelton, and Mary Howard. Among the verses on folio 90[r] and adjacent folios are stanzas adapted from William Thynne's 1532 edition of Chaucer's *Workes*, some of which convert misogynist attacks into defenses of women that denounce male infidelity. According to Elizabeth Heale, the women who used the manuscript seem particularly to have relished verse that "turned a similar rhetoric back against men," which they then used to serve a feminist end.[11]

Another, though different, example of a poem copied by female hands into manuscripts is Sir Walter Ralegh's popular "The Lie," which circulated widely in the early seventeenth century in manuscript form. The poem was emended by Anne Southwell after an amanuensis transcribed it. Lady Southwell is in fact one of many writers who personalized, rewrote, even "improved" existing poems. The transcribed and altered version of "The Lie" appears in one of two manuscripts associated with Southwell, whose self-attribution suggests that she laid claim to it. Ann Bowyer's commonplace book also includes a transcribed version of Ralegh's "The Lie" and offers further evidence of the circulation of literary texts in manuscript form.[12]

In the Restoration period, Aphra Behn asserted more boldly her desire for recognition as a poet and a translator through her translations of male-authored works, including Bernard de Fontenelle's *Entretiens sur las pluralité des mondes* and Abraham Cowley's *Plantarum*. That the act of translation rises above mere imitation is apparent in Behn's claim in "The Translatress in her own person speaks" that she merits inclusion in elite literary circles.

Though he remarked favorably on Behn's translation of Cowley, John Dryden, the English Restoration poet laureate, insisted on identifying the translator with the masculinist neoclassical tradition. In his commendatory verses, "To the Earl of Roscomon, on His Excellent Essay," prefaced to the earl's *Essay on Translated Verse* (1684), Dryden traces this tradition from the ancients through to the Italians, the French, and finally "*Brittain, last, / In Manly sweetness all the rest surpass'd.*"[13] The communion achieved between the "nobly born" translator and the author of his source text ultimately ensures that translation remains a male preserve. In the preface to his collection of translations from *Ovid, Boccaccio and others, Fables, Ancient and Modern* (1700), Dryden also emphasizes the translator's public, masculine function as a servant of the state who civilizes the nation.

Yet starting in the Restoration, women writers increasingly relied on translation work for their livelihood. This was the case with Behn, who devoted her final years largely to translating French texts. In her essay on the art of translating, attached to her translation of Bernard le Bovier de Fontenelle's *Entretiens sur la Pluralité des Mondes*, Behn speaks self-consciously yet assertively about her art of translation. In her preface to Fontenelle's *Discovery of New Worlds*, Behn negotiates between acknowledging the limitations of her ability and demonstrating her abilities as an active participant in male-dominated philosophical debates of the day.

An examination of early modern translations and alterations by women and of the circumstances in which they were produced (and justified) exposes, perhaps better than a study of any other genre, the kinds of networks and literary communities—imagined and actual—that writers developed at this time. As every entry in this chapter suggests, these networks crossed gender barriers, though all the source texts were predictably male-authored. The matter becomes more complicated in the final entry in this chapter featuring a translated translation of another philosophical treatise, Anne Finch, Viscountess Conway's *The Principles of the most Ancient and Modern Philosophy* (cited in chapter 5). Inspired by her association with the Cambridge Platonist Henry More (1614–87), Conway composed *The Principles of the most Ancient and Modern Philosophy*, which was translated into Latin by Francis Mercury Van Helmont in 1690. *Principia philosophiae antiquissimae et recentissimae* was then translated back into English two years later without reference to the English source text. One wonders to what extent the original author's gender was translated into her twice-translated text.

Notes

We gratefully acknowledge the assistance of Elizabeth Heale and Marguerite Corporaal.

1. Eve Rachele Sanders, *Gender and Literacy on Stage in Early Modern England* (Cambridge: Cambridge University Press, 1998), 104.
2. Heidi Brayman Hackel, "The Countess of Bridgewater's London Library," *Books and Readers in Early Modern*

England: Material Studies, ed. Jennifer Andersen and Elizabeth Sauer (Philadelphia: University of Pennsylvania Press, 2002), 145.

3. Lucy Hutchinson is featured in chapter 6 of this book. She was also a translator of Latin works like Lucretius's *De rerum natura* (1675). See *Lucy Hutchinson's Translation of Lucretius: "De rerum natura,"* ed. Hugh de Quehen (Ann Arbor: University of Michigan Press, 1996). On her English-language writings, see Lucy Hutchinson's *Order and Disorder*, ed. David Norbrook (Oxford: Blackwell, 2001).

4. Margaret P. Hannay, "Introduction," *Silent But for the Word: Tudor Women as Patrons, Translators, and Writers of Religious Works*, ed. Margaret Patterson Hannay (Kent, Ohio: Kent State University Press, 1985), 9.

5. Tina Krontiris, *Oppositional Voices: Women as Writers and Translators of Literature in the English Renaissance* (New York: Routledge, 1992), 17.

6. Walter Benjamin, "The Task of the Translator," *Illuminations*, ed. Hannah Arendt, trans. Harry Zohn (New York: Schocken Books, 1969), 80; Stephen Greenblatt, *Renaissance Self-Fashioning: From More to Shakespeare* (Chicago: University of Chicago Press, 1980), 115.

7. Patricia Demers, "On First Looking into Lumley's *Euripides*," *Renaissance and Reformation* 23.2 (1999): 35.

8. See Louise Schleiner, "Margaret Tyler, Translator and Waiting Woman," *English Language Notes* 29.3 (1992): 101–8.

9. Andrew Shifflett, "'How Many Virtues Must I Hate': Katherine Philips and the Poetics of Clemency," *Studies in Philology* 94.1 (1997): 107.

10. See Catherine Cole Mambretti, "Orinda on the Restoration Stage," *Comparative Literature* 37.3 (1985): 244–45.

11. Elizabeth Heale, "Women and the Courtly Love Lyric: The Devonshire MS (BL Additional 17492)," *Modern Language Review* 90 (1995): 313.

12. Victoria Burke, "Women and Early Seventeenth-century Manuscript Culture: Four Miscellanies," *The Seventeenth Century* 12.2 (1997): 135–50.

13. John Dryden, "To the Earl of Roscomon, on his Excellent Essay on Translated Verse," *The Works of John Dryden*, ed. H.T. Swedenborg et al. (Berkeley: University of California Press, 1972), 2: 172, l. 24–25.

Stanzas from Thynne's 1532 edition of Chaucer's *Workes* belonging to the debate about women, copied into the Devonshire Manuscript (c. 1530–1545)

Commentary

The Devonshire Manuscript (British Library Additional 17492) is an album belonging to the 1530s and early 1540s, containing a large number of short courtly verses, many of them by Sir Thomas Wyatt. By 1546 at latest, the manuscript is likely to have been in the possession of Lady Margaret Douglas, niece of Henry VIII, who was resident at the English court. While most of the fashionable verse copied into the manuscript is in scribal hands, a large number of verses are copied in personal hands, including those of Lady Margaret and Mary Shelton. Both women were in attendance on Queen Anne Boleyn in 1536, and both were close acquaintances of Mary Howard Fitzroy, Duchess of Richmond, who copied into the manuscript a poem by her brother the poet Earl of Surrey. Verses copied by Lady Margaret Douglas and Mary Shelton bear witness to their participation in the social enjoyment of, and perhaps their composition of, courtly verse. The two women copy alternate stanzas on some folios, alter "balets" for their own purposes, comment on the verses of others, and annotate verses for singing or copying.

The verses on folio 90ʳ are among a number copied on the final folios of the manuscript that were clearly collected to provide ammunition for the defense of women, very probably as part of a popular game of blame and defense. The stanzas are copied and, in the case of the first, adapted from a printed source, Thynne's 1532 edition of Chaucer's *Workes*. Thynne's edition gathered under Chaucer's name a number of poems, not all of them by him. The first stanza is adapted from a medieval translation of Ovid's *Remedia Amoris*. The original is a thoroughly misogynist attack on women. The penultimate line reads, in Thynne's version: "The cursydnesse yet and disceyte of women." The copyist of the Devonshire Manuscript has adapted this line to transform the stanza into praise of women. Almost all the stanzas copied onto these folios are in women's voices and defend or praise women. The two other stanzas copied on folio 90ʳ are from "La belle dame sans merci" by Sir Richard Roos, but were also printed in the 1532 Chaucer. The first, originally in a male voice, could be used by either a woman or a man, and the other is the only stanza on these folios in a man's voice. Both stanzas voice sentiments used elsewhere in the manuscript by both male and female speakers.

The hand that copied these stanzas has not been identified, although the stanzas were clearly selected primarily to voice a pro-woman point of view. The same hand also copied a group of verses (fols. 26ʳ-30ʳ) that relate to an illicit betrothal, contracted in 1536, between Lady Margaret Douglas and the poet Earl of Surrey's uncle, Lord Thomas Howard. The king had both the culprits confined in the Tower, where Howard died. One of these poems appears to be from Lady Margaret to her lover. Among the "balets" relating to this betrothal are two that also adapt stanzas from Thynne's Chaucer.

yff all the erthe were parchment scrybable
spedy for the hande / and all maner wode
were hewed and proporcyoned to pennes able
al water ynke / in damme or in flode
enery man beyng a parfyte scribe or goode
the faythfulnes yet and prayse of women
cowde not be shewyd by the meane off penne

O marble herte / and yet more harde perde
wych mercy may not perce for no labor
more stronge to bowe than ys a myghty tree.
What avayleth yow to shewe so great rygor
pleasyth yow more to se me dye thys houz
before yowr eyen for yowr dysporte and play
than for to shewe some comforte and socour
to respyte death / wych chaseth me alway,

Alas what shuld yt be to yow preiudyce
yff that a man do loue yow faythfully,
to yowr worshyp eschewyng euery vyce
so am J yowrs and wylbe veryly,
J chalenge nowght of ryght / and reason why,
for J am hole submyt vnto yowr serbyce
ryght as ye lyst yt be ryght so wyll J
to bynd myself were J was at lyberty,

7.1: Stanzas from Thynne's 1532 edition of Chaucer's *Workes*, copied into the Devonshire Manuscript (c.1530-1545). By permission of The British Library.

Transcription

yff all the erthe were parchment scrybable
spedy for the hande / and all maner wode
were hewed and proporcyoned to pennes able
al water ynke / in damme or in flode
every man beyng a parfyte scribe or goode
the faythfulnes yet and prayse of women
cowde not be shewyd by the meane off penne

O marble herte / and yet more harde perde
wych mercy may not perce for no labor
more stronge to bowe than ys a myghty tree
what avayleth yow to shewe so great rygor
pleasyth yt yow more to se me dye thys hour
before yowr eyen for yowr dysporte and play
than for to shewe some comforte and socour
to respyte death / wych chaseth me alway

Alas what shuld yt be to yow prejudyce
yff that a man do love you faythfully
to yowr worshyp eschewyng every vyce
so am I yowrs and wylbe veryly
I chalenge nowght of ryght / and reason why
for I am hole submyt unto yowr servyce
ryght as ye lyst yt be ryght so wyll I
to bynd myself were I was at lyberty

Elizabeth Heale
University of Reading

The Devonshire Manuscript. British Library Additional 17492. Folio 90ᵣ.

Iphigeneya.

Cho. / An dede by this meanes you shall get your
selfe a perpetuall renowne for ever.

Iphi. / Alas then Ione, which art to comforte to
mans sight, O thou light which doeste
make ioyfull al creatures, I shalbe
compelled by and by to forsake you all,
and to change my life.

Cho. / Beholde yonder goeth the virgine to be
sacrificed with a grete companye of
souldiers after hir, whos bewtifull face
and faire pace anone shalbe defiled
withe hir owne blude. Yet happneth
then O Iphigeneya, that withe thy den-
tion thou shalte purchase vnto the grecians a quiet passage which, I praye god
may not only happen fortunatelie vnto
them, but also that they may returne
againe prosperously witho a glorious
victorie.

Nun. / Come hether, O Clitemnestra, for I
muste speke withe you.

Clit. / Tell me I praie you what wolde you
withe me, that you call so hastely, is ther
any more mischefe in hande that I
muste heare of.
Nun.

Iphigeneya.

Clit. / And will you go awaye O daughter, leuinge
me your mother here.

Iphi. / Yea I muste mother, I muste go from you
vnto suche a place from whence I shall never
come againe, althoughe I have not deserued
it.

Clit. / I praie you daughter tarrie, and do not forsake your mother.

Iphi. / Suerlye I will goo hence, wherfore, if I
did tarrie, I shulde move you to more lamentation. Wherfore I shall desire all you women
to singe some songe of my deathe, and to
prophecie gud lucke vnto the grecians: for
withe my deathe I shall purchase vnto
them a glorious victorie, bringe me
therfore vnto the aultor of the temple
of the goddes Diana, that withe my
blude I maye pacifie the wrathe of the
goddes againste you.

Cho. / O a mene Clitemnestra of muste honor,
after what fasshion shall we lament, seinge
we may not greue any token of sadnes
at the sacrifice.

Iphi. / I wolde not have you to mourne for my
cause, for I will not refuse to die.
Cho.

7.2: Jane, Lady Lumley, Euripides' *Iphigeia at Aulis* (c. 1554). By permission of the British Library.

Jane, Lady Lumley, Euripides' *Iphigenia at Aulis* (c. 1554)

Transcription

Iphigeneya. /

Clit./ And will you go awaye, O daughter, levinge me, your mother, heare?

Iphi./ Yeae suerlye mother, I muste goo from you unto suche a place, from whence I shall never come ageine, althoughe I have not deserved it.

Clit./ I pray you daughter tarie, and do not forsake me nowe.

Iphi./ Suerlye I will goo hence Mother, for if I did tarie, I shulde move you to more lamentation. Wherfore I shall desier all you women to singe some songe of my deathe, and to prophecie good lucke unto the grecians: for withe my deathe I shall purchase unto them a glorious victorie; bringe me therfore unto the aultor of the temple of the goddes Diana, that withe my blode I maye pacifie the wrathe of the goddes againste you.

Cho./ O Quene Clitemnestra of moste honor, after what fassion shall we lament, seinge we may not shewe any token of sadnes at the sacrafice?

Iphi./ I wolde not have you to mourne for my cause, for I will not refuse to die.

Cho./

fol. 95r

Iphigeneya. /

Cho. / In dede by this meanes you shall get your selfe a perpetuall renowne for ever.

Iphi. / Alas thou sone, whiche arte comforte to mans life, O thou light whiche doeste make joyfull all creatures, I shalbe compelled by and by to forsake you all and to chaunge my life.

Cho. / Beholde yonder goeth the virgine to be sacraficed, withe a grete companye of souldiers after hir, whos bewtifull face and faire bodi anone shalbe defiled withe hir owne blode. Yet happie arte thou, O Iphigeneya, that with thy deathe thou shalte purchase unto the grecians a quiet passage, whiche I pray god may not only happen fortunatelie unto them, but also that they may returne againe prosperously withe a glorious victorie.

Nun. / Come hether, O Clitemnestra for I muste speke withe you.

Clit. / Tell me I praie you, what woulde you withe me, that you call so hastely, is ther any more mischefe in hande that I muste heare of?

Nun./

Commentary

Jane, Lady Lumley's translation of Euripides' tragedy *Iphigenia at Aulis*, probably written around 1554, is both the earliest extant piece of drama in English by a woman and the earliest known English translation of a play by Euripides. Jane Lumley received an excellent classical education in the household of her father, Henry Fitzalan, 12th Earl of Arundel, who was a great patron of learning and the arts. Although the earl's household could well have accommodated a performance of the play, no conclusive proof of a performance has yet been discovered. Nevertheless, the play is perfectly suited to representation upon the stage, and a successful production took place in the United Kingdom in 1997. This is hardly surprising when one considers that Euripides' play took first prize in the Athenian drama competition of 408 B.C., for which it was originally written.

The play opens with the Greek army becalmed at the port of Aulis. Led by Agamemnon, the army has set out to recover Helen (wife of Menelaus, Agamemnon's brother), from Troy. Calchas, the high priest, has prophesied that the army cannot leave Aulis until Agamemnon's daughter, Iphigenia, is sacrificed to the goddess Diana. Agamemnon has sent for his daughter and her mother, Clytemnestra, pretending that Iphigenia is to be married to Achilles. The first scene sees the repentant Agamemnon sending another message revoking the first, but the message is intercepted by Menelaus. During the ensuing confrontation, Clytemnestra and Iphigenia's arrival is announced. The charade of the impending nuptials is maintained until Clytemnestra encounters Achilles and discovers that he knows nothing about it. Agamemnon's servant, Senex, reveals the whole truth and Clytemnestra demands aid from Achilles. After breaking the news to Iphigenia, both women, together with the female Chorus, turn on Agamemnon and beg him to save his daughter. He refuses and leaves them, whereupon Achilles returns, with a company of his soldiers, to protect Iphigenia. Faced with internecine warfare among the Greeks and the rebellion of her mother against her father, Iphigenia agrees to die. This is the turning point of the play: Iphigenia chooses to die at the moment when she could be saved. She is therefore taken to the altar as a full subject of the state, giving her life for its good, rather than as a chattel slain by her father's will. Moments later, a messenger enters to tell Clytemnestra that Diana has miraculously removed Iphigenia from the altar, leaving a white deer in her place. Clytemnestra is sceptical, and her silent reception of the now triumphant Agamemnon suggests that her scepticism is never fully allayed.

Although recent feminist critics have been quick to see the value of Lumley's play both as an historical artifact and as a piece of dramatic literature, earlier scholars were more ambivalent, noting that her translation is incomplete, not particularly literal, and betrays some reliance upon Erasmus's Latin translation. The latter feature is most apparent in the use of Latin, rather than Greek, names throughout the text, that is, Ulysses rather than Odysseus, and the presence of Lumley's translation of Erasmus's prefatory "Argument." The "omissions" result from Lumley's rendering of the text in stark yet pithy prose, excising the elaborate rhetoric of the original and thereby reducing the role of the Chorus particularly. Read positively, these features constitute evidence that Lumley's interest lay in creating her own dramatic version of the story. Stripping away the rhetoric has two striking effects. First, the play becomes less rooted in Greek mythology and more open to allegorical interpretation; second, the simplicity of the prose disallows a sophisticated glossing over the appalling choice upon which the play turns. The translation facilitates the drawing of parallels with the deposition, incarceration and eventual execution of Lady Jane (Grey) Dudley, the nine-days' queen. Significantly, as well as sharing a Christian name, Jane Lumley and Jane Dudley were first cousins, they were born in the same year, and they were both highly educated in the classics. The volume containing the Greek and Latin texts of *Iphigenia at Aulis* came into Lumley's hands when the newly instated Mary I gave the library of the disgraced Archbishop Thomas Cranmer to her father as a reward for his loyal service. That service entailed the betrayal of his niece, who resembled his daughter in name, age, and scholarly nature. It is possible, even probable, that Lumley saw contemporary resonances in the story of *Iphigenia at Aulis* and created a play designed to draw upon them.

Any allusion to contemporary politics was of necessity subtly nuanced, especially as Jane Lumley belonged to a Catholic dynasty that actively supported Mary I. For example, Lumley's translation does not direct the audience to view Iphigenia's prospective death per se either as just or unjust. Rather, the play invites the audience to consider a situation in which legitimate female authority is compromised by ambitious men. Though this is most obviously seen in Agamemnon's deception of Clytemnestra and Iphigenia, the goddess Diana is also compromised to some extent. Until Iphigenia makes her decision to die, the voices calling for her death are exclusively male, including the high priest Calchas, who is the source of the prophecy that Diana requires Iphigenia's death. With the exception of Achilles, the voices calling for Iphigenia to be saved are female, i.e., Clytemnestra, the Chorus, and Iphgenia herself. However, the events at the sacrificial altar show that Calchas's interpretation of Diana's wishes, and therefore the position of Agamemnon, Ulysses, et al., is completely wrong. Diana manifestly does not require the sacrifice of Iphigenia, placing her sympathies unequivocally with the women of the play. Given the reluctance of Mary I to order Jane Dudley's execution (a decision eventually forced upon her by Wyatt's rebellion), it is possible to detect a double protest in Lumley's translation: against the death of her cousin and the otherwise male-dominated political context that obliged Mary to consent to it.

STEPHANIE HODGSON-WRIGHT
UNIVERSITY OF GLOUCESTERSHIRE

Jane, Lady Lumley. Euripides' *Iphigenia at Aulis* (c. 1554) British Library MS Royal 15 A ix. 94v-95r.

Churche of Englande.

Church of God. Jwys it is not so hard a matter to finde out Goddes Churche, yf a manne will seeke it earnestlye and diligentlye. For the Churche of Godde is sette vpon a highe and glistering place in the toppe of an hill, and buylte vpon the foundacion of the Apostles and prophettes: There saith Augustine, lette vs seeke the Churche; there lette vs trye oure matter. And as he saith againe in an other place, The Churche must be shewed out of the holy and canonicall scriptures: and that whiche can not bee shewed out of them, is not the Churche. Yet for all this J wote not howe, whether it be for feare or for conscience, or despearing of victory, these mē alway abhor and flie the woorde of God, euen as the theefe fleeth the gallowes. And no wonder truely, for lyke as men saye the Cantharus by and by perissheth and dyeth, assone as it is laide in balme, notwithstandinge balme be otherwise a most sweete smellynge ointment: euen so these men

August, de Vnitate Eccle. cap. 3.

Idem.ca.4o

J.iii.   well

7.3: Anne (Cooke), Lady Bacon, John Jewel's *An apologie or answere in defence of the Churche of Englande* (1564). By permission of the Folger Shakespeare Library.

Anne (Cooke), Lady Bacon, John Jewel's *An apologie or answere in defence of the Churche of Englande* (1564)

With her four sisters and four brothers, Anne Cooke benefited from a classical education in their family home, Gidea Hall, Essex. Her parents, Sir Anthony Cooke and Lady Anne Fitzwilliam Cooke, both contributed to Bacon's intellectual and spiritual development. As she attests in the dedication to her translation of *Fouretene Sermons of Barnardine Ochyne* (1551?), Bacon owes much to her mother: "the Orygynal of whatsoever is, or may be converted to ani good use in me, hath frelye proceded (thoughe as the minister of GOD) of youre Ladyshyppes mere carefull, and Motherly goodness." This translation of Italian sermons by Bernardino Ochino, a Protestant exile and protégé of Archbishop Cranmer, indicates Bacon's early and active commitment to the dissemination of Reformation doctrine. Like her sister, Mildred, who married the preeminent Elizabethan Privy Councillor, William Cecil, in 1556 Anne Cooke also married an influential government official, Sir Nicholas Bacon, Privy Councillor, Lord Keeper of the Great Seal, and head of the Chancery court. She was mother to six children by his first marriage and gave birth to two sons, Anthony and Francis. Francis became one of the most influential statesmen, scholars, and authors of his time.

Anne Bacon's most important work was a brilliantly executed translation of Bishop John Jewel's treatise, *An Apologie or answere in defence of the Churche of Englande, with a briefe and plaine declaration of the true Religion professed and used in the same* (1564). In 1561, in the face of European and papal overtures urging Protestant England to submit to the Council of Trent, Elizabeth I's new administration determined instead to continue opposing papal supremacy and ceremonies associated with Roman Catholicism and to develop an English reformed church founded on Scripture and adhering to the doctrine and practices of the primitive church. As the Queen's Council perceived, this English church clearly needed a manifesto to answer its foreign critics and to articulate its doctrines, and the *Apologia Ecclesiae Anglicanae* (1562) by John Jewel, Bishop of Salisbury, provided that text. Perhaps taking advantage of her husband's acquaintance with Bishop Jewel, Bacon translated his text and sent it to Jewel and to the Archbishop of Canterbury for endorsement.

Bacon's printed work is introduced by Matthew Parker, Archbishop of Canterbury, who claims that Bacon's "studious labour of translation" has "singularly pleased my judgement, and delighted my mind." His praise clarifies that Bacon's translation is at the center of the church's efforts to disseminate its doctrines, as he refers to "this publike worke" that has made Jewel's "good woorke more publikely beneficiall." And since translation into English is crucial for the spread of Reformation doctrine, he commends Bacon because she has "honourablie defended the good fame and estimation of your owne native tongue, shewing it so able to contend with a worke originally written in the most praised speache." The page selected here indicates clearly how Bacon turned Jewel's impassioned defense of the scripturally based "true church" into lucid, vivid English.

Elaine Beilin
Framingham State College

Anne (Cooke), Lady Bacon. Translation of John Jewel, *An apologie or answere in defence of the Churche of Englande* (1564). Folger Shakespeare Library STC 14591, sig. Liiiv.

To the right honourable the Lord Thomas Haward.

NOT being greatly forwarde of myne own inclination, (right honourable) but forced by the importunity of my friends to make some triall of my selfe in this exercise of traslation, I haue aduentured vpon a peece of worke not in deede the most profitablest, as entreting of arms, nor yet altogether fruitlesse, if example may serue, as being historicall, but the while, either to be born withal for the delight, or not to be refused for the straengenes farther I mean not to make boaste of my trauaile, for the matter was offred not made choice off, as ther appeared lykewise little lybertie in my first yelding. The earnestnesse of my friends perswaded me that it was conuenient to lay forth my talent for encrease, or to fette my candle on a candlestticke, and the consideration of my insufficiency droue me to thinke it better for my ease, eyther quite to bury my talent, there by to auoyde the breaking of thriftlesse debtes, or rather to put my candle cleane out, then that it should bewray euery vnswept corner in my house: but the opinion of my friendes iudgement preuailed aboue mine owne reason, So vpon hope to please them I first vndertooke this labour, & I haue gone thorow withall, the rather to acquaint my selfe with mine olde reading: wherto since the dispatch ther off, I haue made my friends priuie, & vpon their good liking with request thereto, I haue passed my graunt vnto the for the publicatio, referring to my selfe the order for the dedication, so as I should thinke best either for the defence of my worke, or for some perticuler merite towards me. And heerein I tooke no long leysure to finde out a sufficient personage. For the manifolde benefits receyued from your honourable parents my good Lord

A.iii.

The Epistle Dedicatorie.

Lord and Lady, quickly caste me of that doute, and presented your honour vnto my viewe: whome by good right I ought to loue and honour in especiall, as being of them begotten, at whose handes I haue reaped especiall benefit. The which benefit if I should not so gladly professe openly, as I willingly receiued being offred, I might well be challenged of vnkindenesse: But were I as able to make good my part, as I am not ignorant what may be required at my hands, I would hope not to be founde vngraceful. In the meane time this my trauaile I comend vnto your Lordshippe, beseeching the same, so to accept thereof, as a simple testimony of that good will which I beere to your parets while they liued the being their serua, & now do owe vnto their ofspring after their decease, for their demerits, Vnder your honours protectio I shal lesse fere the assault of the enuious, & of your honours good acceptatio I haue some hope in the mildenes of your Lord.ships nature, not doubting but that as your Lordshippe hath giuen no smal signification in this your noble youth of wisedome and courage to so many as knowe you, it being the only support of your auncestours lyne: so the same, lykewise will maynteine your auncestours glorye & the hope of your owne vertues with affabilitie & gentlenesse, which was the proper commendation of your parents. The almightie encrease this hope with the other vertues before named, to the good hope of your countries peace, your Princesse safetie, and your owne honour, with the ioy of your kinred & friends, whom not a few your parents good deseruing hath assured vnto you, and of whose ernest prayers you shal not faile, to further your weldoing. Amongst them though last in worthinesse, yet with the formost in well wishing and desire of well deseruing your honour shall finde me,

Your honours humbly most assured,

Margaret Tyler.

7.4: Margaret Tyler, Dedication, *The Mirrour of Princely Deeds and Knighthood* (1578). Reproduced by permission of *The Huntington Library, San Marino, California.*

Margaret Tyler, Dedication, *The Mirrour of Princely Deeds and Knighthood* (1578)

Margaret Tyler's dedication, "To the right honourable the Lord Thomas Howard," follows immediately after the title page to the first quarto edition of her translation of *The Mirrour of Princely Deedes and Knighthood* (London: Thomas East, 1578), sig. A2r-A2v.

The Mirrour was the first complete translation of a Spanish prose romance into English and, even more significant, the first translation of the strictly secular romance genre by a woman. The genre of romance was deemed inferior and morally suspect at the time, and Tyler, especially as a woman, felt the need to defend her choice of text and its publication. Although her address "To the Reader" is better known, her dedication to Howard that precedes it is an important site for constructing her persona and defense.

Her opening words in the dedication to Howard deliberately suggest that her translation and its publication were a response to the demands of her friends and not due to any desire on her part for fame. The placing of the word "not," with its decorated capital, at the very beginning of her dedication strongly indicates, both verbally and visually, her lack of unwomanly forwardness in this enterprise. As well, the use of the word "forced" emphasizes pointedly the almost involuntary nature of her translating and publishing activities. Throughout the dedication, Tyler is careful to choose images (candle, candlestick, coin, and unswept floor) from biblical parables (Matthew 5:15, Matthew 25:14–30) that allude to common domestic activities that would be suitable for a respectable and pious woman to use. Many male authors take a similar stance of humility, of unwillingness, in their dedications, but for women, whose right and ability to write and publish was open to serious question, it was an absolute necessity to safeguard their personal reputation from any suggestion of immodesty and pride.

Like all dedications, Tyler's contains the typical praise of the dedicatee's wisdom and nobility and the usual request for protection from critics. Unlike many dedications, however, this one is addressed to someone whom the author knows personally. Tyler makes it clear that while she may have been pushed into publication, she carefully chose her dedicatee herself. She reveals her connection to the Howard household, especially to Lord Howard's late parents, from whom she had received many benefits. In her request for Howard's protection from the "assalt of the envious" (A2v) and for his acceptance of her work, she appeals to his filial love and family pride. Such a personal connection makes the typical flattery of the dedicatee seem more sincere and less tiresome. Perhaps by stressing this former tie of service to the patron's parents, Tyler hopes not only to move the son to a like benevolence, but also to make the appeal seem less presumptuous and public, and thus more suitable for her as a woman.

Because of its firm assertion of the author's proper modesty, Tyler's dedication allows her to make a lengthier and much bolder justification of her translation and of prose romances in general in the address "To the Reader" that follows it.

JANE FARNSWORTH
UNIVERSITY COLLEGE OF CAPE BRETON

Margaret Tyler. *The Mirrour of Princely Deedes and Knighthood* (1578). Huntington Library RB 62809.
A2r-A2v.

Antonius:

Soone as he saw from ranke wherein he stoode
In battell fight, my Gallies making saile:
Forgetfull of his charge (as if his soule
Vnto his Ladies soule had bene enchain'd)
He left his men, who so couragiouslie
Didleaue their liues to gaine him victorie.
And carelesse both of fame and armies losse
My oared Gallies follow'd with his Shipp.
Companion of my flight, by this base parte
Blasting his former flourishing renowne.
Eras. Are you therefore cause of his ouerthrowe?
Cl. I am sole cause: I did it, only I.
Er. Feare of a woman troubled so his sprite?
Cl. Fire of his loue was by my feare enflam'd.
Er. And should he then to warre haue ledd a Queene?
Cl. Alas! this was not his offence, but mine.
Antony (ay me! who else) obtaine a chiefe!)
Would not I should haue taken Seas with him:
But would haue left me fearfull woman farre
From common hazard of the doubtfull warre.
O that I had beleu'd! now, now of Rome
All the great Empire at our beck should bende.
All should obey, the vagabonding Scythes,
The feared Germains, back-shooting Parthians,
Wandring Numidians, Brittons farre remoou'd,
And towry nations (scorched with the Sunne.
But I car'd not: so was my soule possest,
(To my great harme) with burning iealousie:
Fearing least in my absence Antony
Should leauing me retake Octauia.
Char. Such was the rigour of your destinie.

Cl. Such

Antonius.

Cl. Such was my errour and obstinacie.
Ch. But since Gods would not, could you doe withall?
Cl. Alwaies from Gods good happ, not harms, do fall.
Ch. And sdaue they not all power on mens affaires?
Cl. They neuer bow so lowe, as worldly cares.
But leaue to mortall men to be dispos'd
Free'ie on earth what euer mortall is.
If we then be sometimes some faultes commit,
We may them not to their high maiesties,
But to our selues impute; whose passions
Plunge vs each day in all afflictions.
Wherewith when we our soules do thorned feele,
Flatt'ring our selues we say they deft vs are:
That Gods would haue it so, and that our care
Could not empeach but that it must be so.
Char. Things here belowe are in the heau'ns begot,
Before they be in this our worlde borne:
And neuer can our weaknes turne awry
The fickle course of powerfull destinie.
Nought here force, reason, humaine prouidence,
Holie deuotion, noble bloud preuailes:
And Ioue himselfe (whose hand doth heauens rule,
Who both to Gods and men as King commaunds,
Moues aire and sea (with twinckling of his eie,
Who earth (our firme support) with plenty stores,
Who all can doe, yet neuer can vndoe
What once hath been by their hard lawes decreed.
When Troian walles, great Neptunes workmanship,
Emiron'd were with Greekes, and Fortunes whele
Doubtfull ten yeares now to the campe did turne,
And now againe towards the towne return'd:

H 2

Hou

7.5: Mary (Sidney) Herbert, Countess of Pembroke, *Antonius* (1592). By permission of The British Library.

Mary (Sidney) Herbert, Countess of Pembroke, *Antonius* (1592)

Mary Sidney Herbert, one of the most renowned patrons of the arts in Elizabethan liter-ature, was also a renowned translator, responsible for a widely read English version of the Psalms (initially started by her brother Philip), a translation of Petrarch's *Trionfo della Morte*, and a version of Robert Garnier's tragedy *Antonie*, which was printed twice in her lifetime (in 1592, under the title *Antonius*, and in 1595, as *The Tragedie of Antonie*). The title page of the 1592 edition specified clearly that the tragedy had been "done in English by the Countesse of Pembroke," an unusual declaration of authorial control, a control also apparent in her stylistic alterations of Garnier's drama.

Sidney's choice of this specific text for translation reveals a strong interest in individ-ualism and the assumption of personal responsibility. Garnier's play could be taken as a key example of Senecan tragedy, a genre based on the confrontation between the individual and the adverse forces of circumstance: the stoic renunciation to material pleasure and the recognition of worldly vanity are the moral bases of Senecan ethics, leading the heroes to an ascetic cultivation of virtue. The play delineates the evolution of the two main charac-ters, Anthony and Cleopatra; from an initial belief in a deterministic Fortune, they come to acknowledge their personal responsibility over their destiny; in contrast to this evolution, the chorus offers a steady counterpoint that places all its emphasis on Fortune's power.

The most distinctive characteristic of Mary Sidney's translation is the stylistic alter-ation between the rigid sentences used by the Chorus and in some of the dialogues, and the supple, richly flowing language which is used in the characters' monologues. The fac-simile showcases this major innovation introduced by Sidney: Garnier's text was entirely written in decasyllabic couplets; Sidney keeps the couplet form for some dialogues and for the Chorus, but the monologues are entirely in blank verse. The contrast between both forms, subtly controlled by the translator, produces some of the most memorable moments of the play. The text was not meant to be staged; it was meant, like most closet drama, to be read in private, or perhaps read aloud in a group; the nuances of the poetic voice were, therefore, of the utmost importance for the overall effect. In this particular example from Act II, Cleopatra laments that she has abandoned Antony just before his battle against the Romans, indirectly causing his defeat. In her blank-verse enumeration of the empires that Antony intended to conquer and the evocation of her "burning jeal-ousie," the speaker is carried away by her remembrance. However, in her brief conversa-tion with Charmian, the style shifts to sententious couplets, reasserting the speaker's per-sonal determination ("such was my errour and my obstinacie"), but also, in stark contrast to Charmian's fatalism, Cleopatra's unambiguous assumption of personal responsibility and her denial of any desire to blame forces external to herself (*Char:* "And have they not all power on mens affaires?", *Cleo.* "They never bow so low, as worldly cares.") Form and content subtly reinforce each other, the *sententiae* of the couplets opposed by the freely flowing blank verse of Cleopatra's speech so as to highlight the contrast between imper-sonal fate and personal will.

Joan Curbet
Universitat Autònoma de Barcelona

Antonius, a Tragedie, written also in French by R. Garnier . . . done in English by the Countesse of Pembroke (1592). British Library C.57.d.16. H1v–H2.

7.6: Lady Anne Southwell, Commonplace book entry on Ralegh's "The Lie" (after 1592). By permission of the Folger Shakespeare Library.

Lady Anne Southwell, Commonplace book entry on Ralegh's "The Lie" (after 1592)

Transcription

Goe sole the bodies guest	Tell those that braveth most
Upon a thankeles arrand	They begg for more by spendinge
feare not to touch the best	And in their greatest Cost
The truth shalbe thy warrand	Seeke nothinge but Commendinge
And yf they dare reply	And yf they doe deny
boldlie give them the lye	Then give them all the lye
Goe tell the Court yt gloze	Tell schooles ar not sounde profounde
And shines lyke rotten wood	And onelie live by seeminge
Goe tell the Church it shewes	Tell artes they want true grounde
Whats good but doth noe good	And thrive but by esteeminge
Yf Court or Church reply	Yf schooles or artes reply
Give Court and Church the lye	Give schooles and artes the lye
Tell potentates they live	Tell phisicke of her boldenes
Actinge but others actions	Tell nature of decay
Not loved unles they give	Tell Charitie of coldenes
Not strong but by their factions	Tell justice of delay
Yf potentates reply	And yf they doe deny
Give potentates the lye	Then give them all the lye
Tell men of high Condition	Tell beautie it is a flourish
That rules affayres of state	Tell tyme it steales a way
Their purpose is ambition	Tell thoughts they all must perish
Their practise onlie hate,	And fortune doth betray
And yf they doe deny	And yf they this deny
Then give them all the lie	Then give them all the lye

Now when thou hast as I	—	Commaunded thee done blabbinge
Allthough to give the lye	—	Deserves noe les then stabbinge
Stabb at thee he that will	—	Noe stabb the sole Can kill

Anne Southwell

Commentary

"The Lie," a poem usually attributed to Sir Walter Ralegh, was one of the most popular poems circulating in manuscript during the late sixteenth and early seventeenth centuries. Even though the printing press had been established in England since 1476, writers such as Sir Philip Sidney, John Donne, Thomas Carew, and Ralegh preferred their works to circulate in handwritten copies, often to ensure a select readership of their verse. Anne, Lady Southwell, is one of many people who personalized, rewrote, even "improved" existing poems, since when texts entered the realm of manuscript transmission, contemporaries often interacted with this material as they recorded it in their own volumes.

This page comes from one of two manuscripts associated with Southwell, consisting of mainly original verse. It contains digressive poetry on the Decalogue, elegies, and shorter religious and secular lyrics, like the humorous, "All maried men desire to have good wifes:/ but few give good example by thir lives." Southwell knew leading figures of the period and was, according to her epitaph, "Publiquely honoured by her soveraigne." Compiled by several secretaries, her second husband, and Southwell herself, sometimes in a collaborative role, the volume constructs Southwell as an accomplished poet, and poems written by other writers are not attributed to them, most strikingly on this page in which Southwell's distinctive signature at the bottom attributes Ralegh's poem to herself. Her hand is evident at several places on this page, indicating that though an amanuensis transcribed the poem she imprinted her own stamp on it. She changed the first line of the second stanza in the right-hand column from "Tell schooles they want profoundenes" to "Tell schooles ar not sounde profounde," so that it rhymes with the third line, "Tell artes they want true grounde," and she has intensified the fourth line from "live" to "thrive."

Using the 1611 printed version (see Appendix, "The Lie," at the end of this entry) as a benchmark, we can see that Southwell's scribe has copied stanzas one through five, eleven, a combination of stanzas nine and ten, an invented one of her own (the fourth stanza in the right-hand column), and stanza thirteen, the final stanza of the printed version. She has eliminated the other stanzas. This in itself is not unheard of in the thirty-one extant manuscript versions of the poem listed in Peter Beal's *Index of Literary Manuscripts*, but some of her emendations appear to be unique. For example, besides inventing her own stanza and combining lines from two stanzas into one, she uses the word "deny" (in lieu of the more common "reply" and "lie") three times in the poem. In spite of this creativity her version is identical to many extant versions of this poem in that most of them have "that rules affaires of state" (or a very slight variation on this) in line two of stanza four, instead of the printed version's "that manage the estate." Manuscript transmission was distinct from print, leading compilers to copy certain variants, but also allowing them to creatively rewrite the words of poets as they adapted them to their own purposes.

VICTORIA BURKE
UNIVERSITY OF OTTAWA

Lady Anne Southwell. Commonplace book. Folger Shakespeare Library MS V.b.198, f. 2r.

Appendix

The Lie
by Sir Walter Ralegh

Go, soul, the body's guest,
Upon a thankless arrant;
Fear not to touch the best;
The truth shall be thy warrant.
Go, since I needs must die,
And give the world the lie.
Say to the court, it glows
And shines like rotten wood;

Say to the church, it shows
What's good, and doth no good:
If church and court reply,
Then give them both the lie.

Tell potentates, they live
Acting by others' action,
Not loved unless they give,

Not strong but by affection.
If potentates reply,
Give potentates the lie.

Tell men of high condition
That manage the estate,
Their purpose is ambition,
Their practice only hate:
And if they once reply,
Then give them all the lie.

Tell them that brave it most,
They beg for more by spending,
Who, in their greatest cost,
Seek nothing but commending:
And if they make reply,
Then give them all the lie.

Tell zeal it wants devotion;
Tell love it is but lust;
Tell time it metes but motion;
Tell flesh it is but dust:
And wish them not reply,
For thou must give the lie.

Tell age it daily wasteth;
Tell honour how it alters;
Tell beauty how she blasteth;
Tell favour how it falters:
And as they shall reply,
Give every one the lie.

Tell wit how much it wrangles
In tickle points of niceness;
Tell wisdom she entangles
Herself in over-wiseness:
And when they do reply,
Straight give them both the lie.

Tell physic of her boldness;
Tell skill it is prevention;
Tell charity of coldness;
Tell law it is contention:
And as they do reply,
So give them still the lie.

Tell fortune of her blindness;
Tell nature of decay;
Tell friendship of unkindness;
Tell justice of delay:
And if they will reply,
Then give them all the lie.

Tell arts they have no soundness,
But vary by esteeming;
Tell schools they want profoundness,
And stand too much on seeming:
If arts and school reply,
Give arts and school the lie.

Tell faith it's fled the city;
Tell how the country erreth;
Tell, manhood shakes off pity;
Tell, virtue least preferreth:
And if they do reply,
Spare not to give the lie.

So when thou hast, as I
Commanded thee, done blabbing,
Although to give the lie
Deserves no less than stabbing,
Stab at thee he that will,
No stab thy soul can kill.

7.7: Ann Bowyer, Commonplace book entry on Ralegh's "The Lie" (after 1592). Bodleian Library, University of Oxford

Ann Bowyer, Commonplace book entry on Ralegh's "The Lie" (after 1592)

Transcription

goe soule the bodies guest upon a thankelesse errante
spare not to touche the beste the truth shalbe thy warante

Goe sines I needes must die & give theme all the Lie
Say to the courte it glowes & shines like rotten wood

Say to the chirche it shewes whats good but dothe noe good
yf court or church reply then give them bothe the Lye

Tell men of hie condition that rules affaires of state
Their purpouse is ambition their practise onelie hate

& as ye dooe replie still give them all the Lye
Tell those that brave it moust that begge for more by spendinge

whoo in ther greateste coste seeke nothinge but commending
& when thow haste as I commanded thee doon blabbinge allthough to give the

Ly deserve noe lesse then stabbinge stabe at the he that will noe stabb the seule can kill

Happie is he that standethe free Frome everie kinde of toyle
save from the foulde that was of oulde & tillge of the soile
& hathe noe trayne in usures gaine of marchandise noe warr
& flyes the gates of hie estates & pleadinges at the barr
Noe day soo cleere but bringes at lengthe darke nighte
fare flowres dooe fade as faste as the doo growe
noe torche nor lampe but burnes away there light
sunne shines awhile then under cloude dothe goe
the life of man is heere compared soe it lastes a space
Till borrowed breathe be payd & then could corse in tombe
or grave is layd noe honner wealthe force nor wisdome for
nor worldly praise prolonges our days whe[n] death drawes neere
& man may live noe more the greateste kings ar onlye borne to die
Like poreste men ther passage home the take & nobel hartes
that sitt in honors hie & all estates an ende of liffe must make

[written sideways]
your grace did promise one a time to grante me reason for my rym
but from that time unto this season I neither hard of rime nor reason

---

Commentary

This page contains four poems (or fragments of poems) that all run together and are not clearly differentiated from one another. The top half of the page consists of a heavily altered version of "The Lie" (see Appendix to previous entry on Anne Southwell); four lines in the middle are from a different poem on the happy life of the farmer; the bottom part of the page is the first half of an elegy by Thomas Churchyard; two lines written sideways are also by Churchyard.

Ann Bowyer transcribed the popular Ralegh poem in her commonplace book. In this manuscript she and two others have written out sententious and proverbial material (mainly by Drayton, Spenser, and Chaucer), a description of the miraculous preservation of the body of Thomas Grey, handwriting exercises, a list of ink and colors, and several poems. Bowyer was the daughter of an urban craftsman, and thus firmly in the "middling classes" of early modern society, and her manuscript gives us insight into the range of material available to her, and the use to which she put poetry written by others.

Bowyer appears to have valued poems for the pithy commonplaces contained within them. She shaped a version of "The Lie" into a series of couplets, and has not separated it from the poems that follow it. In fact, her fondness for couplets goes against the logic of the content and rhyme scheme of the poem. What are typically six-line stanzas in printed versions and other manuscript versions are condensed into three-line stanzas by Bowyer, but she left space between every two lines. Bowyer has omitted over half of most versions of the poem and compressed the final stanza into two lines, suggesting a space restriction. As with Southwell, Bowyer's variants indicate that she was transcribing from a strand of manuscript transmission, writing "that rules affaires of state" in the same line Southwell has. Like Southwell, Bowyer has also made some independent choices in her transcription. At line nine Bowyer wrote "& as ye dooe replie" instead of the printed and manuscript tradition, which read "and if they once reply," or a slight variation on the same. Bowyer omitted eight stanzas; compared with the 1611 published version of the poem, Bowyer includes the first two stanzas of the printed version, lacks the third, includes the fourth and two-thirds of the fifth, lacks stanzas six through twelve, and includes the thirteenth.

"The Lie" inspired answer poems. On this page, the poem is immediately followed by an excerpt on the happy life of a farmer, who avoids war, high position, and courts of law (beginning, "Happie is he that standethe free"), which is in turn followed by the first fifteen lines of Thomas Churchyard's epitaph on William Somerset, Earl of Worcester (beginning, "Noe day soo cleere"). Significantly, Bowyer copied the introductory section before Churchyard speaks specifically about Worcester, and she altered her penultimate line to "& nobel hartes" from Churchyard's "And noble Earles." She turned an elegy on a specific person into a poem commenting on man's short life, which no amount of honors will prolong. A final couplet on this page in the manuscript, written sideways, has been attributed to Thomas Churchyard in a Folger Shakespeare Library manuscript (X.d.177). It is a complaint about not getting any patronage for his poetry. This scepticism about courtly privilege fits well in a manuscript of moralistic extracts, a manuscript that gives valuable insight into how an early modern woman read and responded to popular works in her culture.

Victoria Burke
University of Ottawa

Ann Bowyer. Commonplace book. Bodleian Library MS Ashmole 51. Fol. 6r.

Dame Alice L'Estrange and Lady Hobart in "Merry Passages and Jeasts," collected by Sir Nicholas Le Strange (c. 1650)

Commentary

From the 1630s to the 1650s Sir Nicholas LeStrange (or L'Estrange) wrote down jests told by family and friends at Hunstanton, his family's estate in Norfolk. Sir Nicholas took pains with his collection, giving it a title, "Merry Passages and Jeasts," neatly numbering each jest, and making revisions throughout. What is most unusual, and most useful to a scholar, is that he provided his readers with an index to his sources, identifying who told him each joke. He credits women, including his mother, wife, sister, aunt, and cousin, with supplying him with 79 of the 551 jests that he attributes (60 more are called "anonymus"). In other words, more than 15 percent of the "authorized" jests come from women. Many jests are strikingly localized, identifying members of the Hunstanton social circle or local residents. This page was chosen because all of the jests on it are by women; but read straight through, the 93–page volume has a distinct tone of call-and-response (or tit for tat), because many "sources" are also characters in other jests, both as laugh getters and as butts. Like a play text or a musical score, his manuscript gestures outward toward a world of "playing" in the broadest sense, audible, social, vibrant—a world that acknowledged some women as laugh getters, satirists, and storytellers.

Sir Nicholas's main source was his mother, Dame Alice L'Estrange (1575–1656), whom he credits with 43 jests. In his index he identifies her variously as "My Moth:" or "My mother" and occasionally, "Ma Mere. " She seems to have enjoyed telling and hearing bawdy stories, such as the one about a jailer whose plight resembles that of Freud's Rat Man (jest 8). She also seems to have been proud of her education, judging from her many jests at the expense of the witless and the illiterate. Some quips mock lower-status women (jests 9 and 10) and quite a few level at pretentious men. Ignorant clergymen are a favorite satiric target, as they are for women represented in the printed jest books. She tells of a preacher turning to the wrong page while reading aloud from the Bible, getting flustered when "the congregation laughs in their sleeves," then suddenly bursting out: "I am not such an asse but I can find the right place!" (jest 460).

"Lady Hobart," the source for jest 7, is probably Dorothy Hobart, a second cousin to Sir Nicholas and wife of Sir Henry Hobart; but she may be Frances Egerton, who married Sir John Hobart, according to H. F. Lippincott, the editor of the only complete edition of "Merry Passages and Jeasts." Like many others in this book, her jest appears to record an actual bit of table talk, but it is unusual in that she serves as both source and narrator. Sir Nicholas's next most fruitful source after his mother (with 38 jests to her 43) was his father, Sir Hamon L'Estrange, sometime Sheriff of Norfolk and MP from Castle Rising. A determined Royalist, he led the defense of King's Lynn, which was besieged in 1643, capitulating the same year. The family suffered much for its Royalist intransigence in a strongly Parliamentarian region. Dame Alice showed great acumen and spirit in managing the family's large estate, filling her account book with "outspoken and indignant comments" about the Roundheads who punished, fined, and harassed them (Ketton-Cremer). She did not live to see the Restoration, but her youngest son, Roger, went on to become Licenser and Surveyor of the Press under Charles II. Sir Nicholas never achieved anything to rival Roger's fame, although many Shakespeare scholars know his name because "Merry

6

Sr Henry Sidny dranke one time to an old
woman that was exceeding deafe and satt at
the lower end of the Table, in a glasse of sacke,
but with the annexion of this Phrase, that Ioe
your bedfellow this night; She seeing the sacke,
(Her eyes being better then her eares) replyde,
I thanke your good worshipp, with all my Hart,
you know whats good for an old woman.

7

The Lady Hobart every one being sett at the
table, and no body blessing it, but gazing
one vpon an other, in expectation who should be
Chaplaine: well sayes my Lady, I thinke I must say
as one did in the like case, god be thanked,
No body will say grace.

8

An arrant Queane in Norwich (that they vsd to
call Cold=Rost) came once to Sr philipp woodhouse
(who loud to heare newes) and told him that she had
the heauiest newes to relate that euer he heard: I
prythe whats that, sayes he; O Sr Roore worsly the
Jaylor had such an Hole eaten in his Arse last
night with Ratts, that I warrant your worshipp
may turne your Nose in't.

9

A Traueller enquiring his way of a Northerne
lasse; whay Man, (says she) you must first
Raide me vp this way, then Raide me downe
that way, and then Raide me to the left hand.

10   daughter

A plaine Country wife, her, being rauisht, cam
to complaine to a Justice of Peace, that such an
one had newly Rauld her daughter, and she would
craue his worshipps warrant. and another complain
that one had refresht her Daughter.

7.8: Dame Alice L'Estrange and Lady Hobart in "Merry Passages and Jeasts" (c. 1650). By permission of the British Library.

Transcription

6

Sir Henry Sidny dranke one time to an old
woman that was exceeding deafe and satt at
the lower end of the Table, in a glasse of sacke,
but with the annexion of this Phrase, that I be
your bedfellow this night; she seeing the sacke
(her eyes being better then her eares) replyde,
I thanke your good worshipp, with all my Hart,
Sir you know whats good for an old woman.

7

The Lady Hobart every one being sett at the
table, and no body Blessing it, but gazing
one upon an other, in expectation who should be
Chaplaine: well, sayes my Lady, I thinke I must say
as one did in the like case, God be thanked,
No body will say Grace.

8

An arrant Queane in Norwich (that they usd to
call Cold=Rost) came once to Sir Philipp Woodhouse
(who lov'd to heare newes) and told him that she had
the heaviest newes to relate that ever he heard: I
Prythe whats that, sayes he; O Sir, poore Worsly the
Jaylor had such an Hole eaten in his Arse last night
with Ratts, that I warrant your worshipp
may turne your Nose in't.

9

A Traveller enquiring his way of a Northerne
Lasse; whay Man (says she), you must first
Raide me up this way, then Raide me downe
that way, and then Raide me to the left hand.

10

A plaine Country Wife, her daughter being ravisht, came
to complaine to a Justice of the Peace, that such an
one had newly Raveld her daughter, and she would
crave his worshipps warrant. and another complaind,
that one had Refresht her Daughter.

Passages" contains a rare contemporary jest about Shakespeare and Jonson: "Shakespeare was Godfather to one of Ben: Johnsons [*sic*] children, and after the christning, being in a deepe study, Johnson came to cheere him up, and askt why he was so Melancholy? no faith Ben: (sayes he) not I, but I have been considering a great while what should be the fittest gift for me to bestow upon my Godchild, and I have resolvd at last; I prithee what, sayes he? I faith Ben: I'le e'en give him a douzen good Lattin Spoones, and thou shalt translate them" (jest 11, "Mr Dunn"). In this jest, "Lattin" puns on "laten" and "Latin," the metal and the language.

Rendered memorable by their promise of momentary social triumph, these tales circulated through interpenetrating worlds of print, speech, writing, and gesture. Turning these miniature scripts into jest/gest entails more than voice. Surely anyone who would try to tell jest 9 "straight," without hand movements or any attempt at a Northern accent, would fail miserably in delivering its bawdy directions about how to "Raide me" this way and that. Are the women who told these jests their "authors," or perhaps their "publishers" in the early modern sense of making them known to a public? Are they transmitters of culture or creators of it? In putting their names to jokes, folklore, and gossip—just as male authors did in popular literature and in stage plays—the women arguably stake a claim to authorship, though of a transient sort. Transcribed by a male hand, the handwritten jest bears an insistent trace of orality greater than that of print; but this manuscript, by restricting itself to the genre of jests, insistently evokes the printed jest anthology as well. Its painstaking transcriptions possess a quality of "imprintedness," an exact wording worth repeating, transcribing, and even correcting: some of the emendations are in handwriting different from Sir Nicholas's, and these may have been inserted by the true "authors" of these jests.

PAMELA ALLEN BROWN
UNIVERSITY OF CONNECTICUT

Sir Nicholas Le Strange. "Merry Passages and Jeasts" (c. 1650) British Library Harley MS. 6395. Fol. 1v. The mid–17th century manuscript contains 660 jests with a list of sources.

Katherine (Fowler) Philips, *Pompey, a Tragedy* (1663)

Although in our century Katherine Fowler Philips is mainly remembered as the "match-less Orinda" who wrote poems on the subject of platonic female friendship, in her own lifetime it was her translation of Pierre Corneille's *Pompée* "more than any of Philips's other works" that "spread her fame" (Cotton 52). Visiting Dublin in June 1662 , Philips was taken up in the lively literary society gathered there and encouraged to work on an English translation of Corneille's tragedy under the patronage of the earl of Orrery. While Philips translated the play, Waller and a group of prestigious court wits were also under-taking a translation of *Pompée*. However, Philips's work was rapidly completed and became the first rhymed English translation of a French tragedy. Rendering Corneille's French alexandrines into English heroic couplets, Philips further added five songs that she had composed to serve as interacts.

In the dedication of her translation to the Countess of York, Philips refers to her translated play as "some untimely flower" whose "bashful head . . . With conscious blushes would have sought a shade" were it not for the Countess's protection of her text against "strict Eyes"(Dd). Although translation, as an art of reproduction, was regarded as one of the "acceptable literary areas"(Krontiris 17) for women, Philips's comment reveals her anx-iety about presenting her text to the public view and her fear that her translation was an inappropriate and shameful act for a woman in a society that commanded woman to "tip her tongue with silence" (Brathwaite 38–39) and that equated the "Poetess" with the "Punk" (Pearson 9). In spite of Philips's display of feminine reluctance and sexual shame at presenting her translation to the public and emerging from the feminine "shade" of anonymity and privacy, her *Pompey* was the first play translated or written by a woman to be staged. Impressed by Philips's accomplishment, the earl of Orrery arranged a public performance of the play in February 1663, which he financed and supported.

Considering the persona of the feminine bashful, modest woman who avoids public exposure that Philips set up in her dedication, her choice for a play to be translated can be considered remarkable. As becomes clear from this scene, the heroine, Cleopatra, does not correspond to the ideal of the silent and submissive woman that dominated society in Restoration England. Instead of observing modesty of utterance, and restricting the use of her voice to matters belonging to the feminine, private sphere, Cleopatra openly interferes with and intervenes in the public area of politics. Rather than meeting her brother's gov-ernment with feminine silence, Cleopatra asserts her voice to claim that Ptolomon should not be swayed by the false views expressed by his political advisers, since his execution of Pompey, committed through their advice, has already evoked Caesar's displeasure and thus endangered Ptolomon's power. In addition, Cleopatra refuses to assume the conventional female role of the object of exchange that is subjected to man's will. When Ptolomon pro-poses to marry her off to Caesar, Cleopatra indignantly replies: "Make your own Presents, I'le dispose of mine." In other words, Cleopatra insists upon her autonomy, her position as a subject who may dispose of and control her own fate. Moreover, Cleopatra displays an unwomanly "Ambition" to obtain her share of rule in the kingdom of which she has been unjustly deprived.

Ambitious, bold and outspoken, Cleopatra contrasts with the persona that Philips adopts in her dedication. One may therefore wonder why Philips chose to translate a drama that represented such a deviant woman from a social point of view. Did Cleopatra

(21)

CLEOPATRA.

I've much endur'd, and more may apprehend?
For such a Politician is not Nice,
And you are alwaies steer'd by his advice.

PTOLOMY.

If I believe him, I his prudence fee.

CLEOPATRA.

And I who fear him, know his cruelty.

PTOLOMY.

For a Crown's safety all things just appear.

CLEOPATRA.

That kind of equity creates my fear,
My share of Power hath been by it lost,
And now it has the head of *Pompey* cost.

PTOLOMY.

Never a game of State was more advis'd,
For else by *Cesar* we had been surpris'd:
You see his speed, and we had been subdu'd,
Before we could in our defence have stood.
But now I to a Conquerour so great,
Your Heart may offer, and my Royal feat.

CLEOPATRA.

Make your own Presents, I'le dispose of mine,
Nor others Interests with yours combine.

PTOLOMY.

Our Blood's the same, uniting me and you.

CLEOPATRA.

You might have said, our Rank unites us too,
We both are Sovereigns, yet 'twill be confest,
There is some difference in our interest.

PTOLOMY.

Yes, Sister, for my Heart is well content
Only with *Egypts* narrow Continent.
But now your Beauty, *Cesar's* heart does wound,
Tagus and *Ganges* must your Empire bound.

CLEOPATRA.

I have ambition, but it is confin'd,
It may surprize my Soul, but never blind.

T up-

---

94   LA MORT

CLEOPATRE.

Non, mais en liberté ie tis de son proiet.

PTOLOMEE.

Quel proiet faisoit-il dont vous peussiez vous plaindre?

CLEOPATRE.

I'en ay souffert beaucoup, & i'auois plus à craindre,
Vn si grand Politique est capable de tout,
Et vous donnez les mains à tout ce qu'il resout.

PTOLOMEE.

Si ie suy ses conseils, i'en cognoy la prudence.

CLEOPATRE.

Si i'en crain les effets, i'en voy la violence.

PTOLOMEE.

Pour le bien de l'Estat tout est iuste en vn Roy.

CLEOPATRE.

Ce genre de iustice est à craindre pour moy,
Apres ma part du sceptre à ce tiltre vsurpée,
Il en couste la vie, & la teste à Pompée.

PTOLOMEE.

Iamais vn coup d'Estat ne fut mieux entrepris,
Le voulant secourir Cesar nous eust surpris,
Vous voyez sa vitesse, & l'Egypte troublée
Auant qu'estre en defense en seroit accablée:
Mais ie puis maintenant à cét heureux vainqueur
Offrir en seureté mon Throsne & vostre cœur.

CLEOPATRE.

Ie feray mes presens, n'ayez soin que des vostres,
Et dans vos interests n'en confondez point d'autres.

PTOLOMEE.

Les vostres sont les miens estans de mesme sang

CLEOPATRE.

Vous pouuez dire encor estans de mesme rang
Estans Roys l'vn & l'autre, & toutefois ie pense

Que

7.9: Pierre Corneille, *La mort de Pompée: Tragédie* (1644), and Katherine Philips, *Pompey, a Tragedy* (1663). By permission of The British Library.

embody Philips's secret desires for autonomy, power, ambition, and publicity that she sought to cover up by the image of the socially acceptable bashful, uncomfortable female translator? Did Philips choose to work on a play with a defiant yet virtuous female character as the means to legitimise female autonomy and outspokenness while keeping up the appearances of femininity herself? A comparison of Philips's translation with Corneille's original shows, notably, that in rendering Cleopatra's speeches in English, Philips seems to have subdued Cleopatra's aggressive self-assertion a little at times, so that her English Cleopatra appears more modest and feminine than Corneille's original Egyptian princess. For example, Cleopatra's sentence "I have ambition, but it is confin'd" suggests a restriction of her ambition imposed from outside, beyond her complete control. By contrast, the same line in Corneille's French, "J'ai l'ambition, mais je la sais régler," creates the impression that Cleopatra is actively in charge of her character and existence. Likewise, Philips's Cleopatra refers to her royal power as having become "lost" to her, whereas Corneille's princess dares to use the expression "usurpée," a phrase that suggests the illegitimate appropriation of her queenly rights and her urge to stand up for herself. Thus, her contemporary admirer "Philo-Philippa"'s statement that Corneille's play was "polish'd by thy Pen" does not seem to apply to Philip's choice of words only but to her refinement of Cleopatra as well.

MARGUERITE CORPORAAL
UNIVERSITY OF GRONINGEN

Katherine Philips. *Pompey, a Tragedy* (1663). British Library 11737.d.8. Gg2., page 21.

Pierre Corneille. *La mort de Pompée: Tragédie* (Paris, 1644). British Library C.34.i.10. B5v, page 34.

A

DISCOVERY

O F ·

𝔑𝔢𝔴 𝔚𝔬𝔯𝔩𝔡𝔰.

From the *FRENCH.*

Made *ENGLISH*
By Mrs. *A. BEHN.*

To which is prefixed a PREFACE,
by way of ESSAY on Tranflated
PROSE: wherein the Arguments
of Father *Tacquet*, and others, againft
the Syftem of *Copernicus* (as to the
Motion of the Earth) are likewife
confidered, and anfwered: Wholly
new.

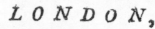

LONDON,
Printed for *William Canning,* at his Shop
in the *Temple-Cloyfters,* 1688.

7.10: Aphra Behn, Fontenelle's *A Discovery of New Worlds* (1688).
Courtesy of the William Ready Division of Archives & Research Collections, McMaster
University Library, Hamilton, Ontario.

Aphra Behn, Fontenelle's *A Discovery of New Worlds* (1688)

The title page from Aphra Behn's translation of Bernard le Bovier de Fontenelle's *Entretien sur la pluralité des mondes*, translated as *A Discovery of New Worlds,* appears on the facing page. Behn (1640?-89), best known for her relatively successful career as a playwright in 1670s London, was also an outspoken commentator on religion, science, and philosophy. Particularly at the end of her career, after the uproar over the Popish Plot had forced her and many others off the stage, Behn turned to prose, publishing her translation of Fontenelle in 1688. Though by the end of the seventeenth century translation was hardly a novel literary undertaking for a woman, Behn's translation of Fontenelle is notable for its avoidance of purely devotional subject matter. The title page refers to "a PREFACE, by way of ESSAY on Translated PROSE; wherein the Arguments of Father *Tacquet,* and others, against the System of *Copernicus* (as to the Motion of the Earth) are likewise considered, and answered." Behn's lengthy preface, in which she takes on one of the most heated philosophical debates of the late seventeenth century—the relationship between science and religion—establishes her as fully involved in an issue we have come to associate only with male voices. Behn is surely aware of this, apologizing early in the preface that she can take these philosophical arguments only "as far as a Woman's Reasoning can go" (A1). But this appeal to the familiar "humility topos" is typically, for Behn, disingenuous; the reader of the preface quickly discovers that a woman's reasoning can go a long way indeed, as Behn proceeds with an extended and complicated mathematical, geometrical, and finally theological rebuttal to an attack on Copernican astronomy by one Father Tacquet, a fundamentalist supporter of the Ptolemaic system.

An example of Behn's carefully reasoned, but also wonderfully tongue-in-cheek, response to Tacquet can be drawn from her exegesis of Joshua 10—a text Tacquet used to support his Ptolemaic astronomical bias—in which Joshua commands the sun and moon to stand still. After first baldly reminding her readers that "the Scripture was not designed to teach us Astronomy" (A3v), Behn goes on to say,

> If the Sun did move, according to the system of Ptolemy, where was the necessity of the Moon's standing still? For if the Moon had gone on her Course, where was the Loss or Disorder in Nature? . . . What is there in all this wonderful stop of Time, that is not as strong for the System of Copernicus, as for that of Ptolemy? And why does my belief of the Motion of the Earth, and the Rest of the Sun contradict the holy Scriptures? Am not I as much obliged to believe that the Sun lodges in a Tabernacle? (as in Psal.19) Are not all these Allegorical Sayings? (A5–A6).

Though all but ignored in Behn criticism, the preface and its accompanying translation establish Behn (and, by extension, other learned women) as fully participant in the philosophical foment of the late seventeenth century in England.

LISA SCHNELL
UNIVERSITY OF VERMONT

Aphra Behn. *A Discovery of New Worlds / from the French made English by Mrs. A. Behn; to which is prefixed a preface by way of essay on translated prose* (1688). McMaster University, Mills Memorial Library Research Collections: B 16886. Title page.

142   *Of* PLANTS.   BOOK VI.

By thee, the first new sparks of Life, not yet
Struck up to shining flame to mature heat,
Sprinkled by thy moist Poison fade and die,
Fatal *Sabina* Nymph of Infamy.
For this the *Cypress* thee Companion calls,
Who piously attends at Funerals:
But thou more barbarous, dost thy pow'r employ,
And even the unborn Innocent destroy.
Like Face destructive thou, without remorse,
While the the Death of even the Ag'd deplores.
   Such *Cyparissa* was, that baleful Boy,
Who was belov'd by the bright God of Day;
Of such a tender mind, so soft a Breast,
With so compassionate a Grief opprest.
For wounding his lov'd Dear, that down he lay
And wept, and pin'd his sighing Soul away.
Apollo pitying it, renew'd his fate
And to the *Cypress* did the Boy translate,
And gave his hapless life a longer Date.
Then thus decreed the God —— and thou oh Tree,
Chief Mourner at all Funerals shall be.
And since so small a cause such grief cou'd give,
Be't still thy Talent (pitying youth) to grieve.
Sacred be thou in *Pluto's* dark abodes,
For ever sacred to th' Infernal Gods!
This said, well skill'd in truth he did bequeath
Eternal life to the dire Tree of Death,
A substance that no Worm can e'r subdue
Whose never-dying Leaves each Day renew,
Whose Figures like aspiring flames still rise,
And with a noble Pride salute the Skies.
   Next the fair Nymph that *Phœbus* does adore,
But yet as nice and cold as heretofore:
She hates all fires, and with aversion still
She chides and crackles if the flame she feel.
Yet though she's chaff, the burning God no less
Adores, and makes his Love his Prophetess.
And even the Murmurs of her scorn do now
For joyful Sounds and happy Omens go.
Nor does the Humble, though the sacred Tree
Fear wounds from any Earthly Enemy;
For he beholds when loudest storms abound,
The flying thunder of the Gods around,
Let all the flaming Heav'ns threat as they will
Unmov'd th' undaunted Nymph out-braves it still.
   Oh thou!
Of all the woody Nations happiest made
Thou greatest Princess of the fragrant shade,
But shou'd the Goddess *Dryas* not allow
That Royal Title to thy Vertue due,

At

BOOK VI.   *Of* PLANTS.   143

At least her justice must this truth confess
If not a Princess, thou'rt a Prophetess,
And all the Glories of immortal Fame
Which conquering Monarchs so much strive to gain,
Is but at best from thy triumphing Boughs
To reach a Garland to adorn their Brows,
And after Monarchs, Poets claim a share
As the next worthy thy priz'd wreaths to wear.
Among that number, do not me disdain,
Me, the most humble of that glorious Train
I by a double right thy Bounties claim,
Both from my Sex, and in *Apollo's* Name:
Let me with *Sappho* and *Orinda* be
Oh ever sacred Nymph, adorn'd by thee;
And give my Verse Immortality.
   The tall *Elate* next, and *Pence* stood
The stateliest Sister-Nymphs of all the wood.
The flying Winds sport with their flowing Hair,
While to the dewy Clouds their lofty heads they rear.
As mighty Hills above the Valleys show,
And look with scorn on the descent below,
So do these vie ... their humbler Tops they rise.
So much a... , the Mountains where they grow.
So stood the Giants that besieg'd the Skies,
The terror of the Gods! they having thrown
Huge *Ossa* on the Leafy *Pelion*,
The *Firr* with the proud *Pine* thus threatning stands
Lifting to Heav'n two hundred warring hands,
In this vast prospect they with ease survey
The various figur'd Land and boundless Sea,
With joy behold the Ships their timber builds,
How they've with Cities stor'd once spacious Fields.
   This Grove of *English* Nymphs, this noble train
In a large Circle compass'd their Queen,
The Scepter bearing *Dryas* ——
Her Throne arising Hillock where she sat
With all the Charms of Majesty and State,
With awful Grace the numbers she survey'd,
Dealing around the favours of her shade.
If I the voice of the loud winds could take
Which the re-echoing Oaks do agitate,
'Twou'd not suffice to celebrate thy Name
Oh sacred *Dryas* of Immortal Fame.
If we a faith can give Antiquity
That sings of many Miracles, from thee
In the worlds Infant Age Mankind broke forth,
From thee the noble Race receiv'd their Birth;
Thou then in a green tender Bark were clad,
But in *Deucalion's* Age a rougher covert had,

The Trembling tree in her own Person speaks.

More

7.11: Aphra Behn, Cowley's *Of Plants*, Book VI, "Of trees" (1689). Courtesy of the William Ready Division of Archives & Research Collections, McMaster University Library, Hamilton, Ontario.

Aphra Behn, Cowley's *Of Plants*. Book VI. "Of trees" (1689)

Known today primarily as a playwright, novelist, and poet, Aphra Behn turned to translation toward the end of her career. Behn was a prolific translator, producing English versions of several French prose works, including La Rochefoucauld's *Réflexions ou Sentences et Maximes morales* and Bernard le Bovier de Fontenelle's *Entretiens sur la pluralité des mondes*. To the latter, she attached an essay on her translation practice that was influenced by the essays of Dryden and Roscommon but unique as a discussion of the practice of translating prose as opposed to verse. As a poet, Behn is also invested in the potential of translation, dedicating poems to the translator Thomas Creech and penning numerous imitations and translations of her own, such as "A Paraphrase on Oenone to Paris," which was included in Jacob Tonson's *Ovid's Epistles, Translated by several Hands* (1680) and "The Disappointment," a loose translation of Benech de Cantenac's "*L'occasion perduie recourverte.*"

One of several translators to render Abraham Cowley's *Plantarum* into English, Behn demosntrates a skill that is recognized in the collection's preface by Nahum Tate and later by John Dryden, who suggests that this translator "of the fair sex," who may not even know Latin, puts to shame those who do. Whether or not Behn actually knew Latin remains a subject of debate. As Janet Todd explains, Behn's knowledge of French may have given her enough understanding of Latin to follow the original with the help of a crib sheet or of someone versed in Latin. At the same time, however, an English translation of the poem was printed in 1680, and Todd concludes that it is unlikely that Behn relied on this version because her translation is closer to the original. In other works such as her preface to *The Dutch Lover* and her *Essay on Translated Prose*, Behn draws attention both to the fact that women were often denied a classical education and to her own limitations because she can translate only from a vulgar language such as French.

The interruption in which "the Translatress in her own person speaks" is a remarkable moment in which Behn draws attention to herself not just as a translator but as a female poet who desires the fame and praise so freely given to her male counterparts. Notably, the brief digression follows a passage devoted to the garland of Apollo. That a poem about trees would involve the story of Daphne and Apollo is expected, but Cowley's poem alludes to this myth several times, and in his paraphrase of Ovid's narrative, Cowley emphasizes Daphne's hatred of the pursing god and reveals how Apollo's violation and silencing of the nymph is transformed into the "joyful Sounds" of poetry. When Behn asks for fame as a poetess along with Sappho and Orinda (poet and playwright Katherine Philips), she appears not to disrupt the narrative tradition of Apollo and his laureates but rather asks that women be included in an overwhelmingly male line of poets. By choosing two women, however, known for poetry that celebrates the erotic attachments between women, Behn offers the possibility of a lineage of women writers who could earn glory independent of the tradition of male poet laureates.

DEBORAH UMAN
EASTERN CONNECTICUT STATE UNIVERSITY

Aphra Behn. *Of Plants*. Book VI. "Of trees." *The third part of the works of Mr. Abraham Cowley: being his Six books of plants, never before printed in English . . . Now make English by several hands.* (1689). McMaster University, Mills Memorial Library Research Collections D 1201. Pages 142–43.

THE
PRINCIPLES
Of the moſt Ancient and Modern
PHILOSOPHY,
CONCERNING

God, Chriſt, and the *Creatures,* viz.
of Spirit and Matter in general;
whereby may be reſolved all thoſe
Problems or Difficulties, which
neither by the School nor Common
Modern Philoſophy, nor by the
Carteſian, Hobbeſian, or *Spinoſian,*
could be diſcuſſed.

BEING

A little Treatiſe publiſhed ſince the Author's Death, tranſlated out of the *Engliſh* into *Latin,* with Annotations taken
from the Ancient Philoſophy of the *Hebrews;* and now again made *Engliſh.*

By *J. C. Medicinæ Profeſſor.*

Printed in *Latin* at *Amſterdam,* by *M.
Brown,* 1690. And Reprinted at *London,* 1692.

7.12: Anne (Finch), Viscountess Conway, *The Principles of the most Ancient and Modern
Philosophy* (translated back into English, 1692, by an unknown hand). The Thomas Fisher
Rare Book Library, University of Toronto.

Anne (Finch), Viscountess Conway, *The Principles of the most Ancient and Modern Philosophy* (Latin translation, 1690; translated back into English, 1692, by an unknown hand)

The uncredited author of this "little Treatise" was Anne, Viscountess Conway (1631–79), one of the most learned women of the seventeenth century. As a student and close friend of Cambridge Platonist Henry More (1614–87), Anne Conway had read a wide range of scientific, philosophical, and theological works written in Latin, Hebrew, and Greek. While Conway's original English treatise, *The Principles of the most Ancient and Modern Philosophy*, has been lost, a Latin translation was brought to Holland by her friend and physician, Francis Mercury van Helmont (1614–98), and published posthumously in 1690. In 1692, another unknown translator, "J. C. *Medicinæ Professor*," translated the work back into English, without reference to the original English version. The frontispiece displayed is from a copy held at the Thomas Fisher Rare Book Library of the University of Toronto; the Fisher catalogue speculates that the translator was Jodocus Crull, a physician who often published his works and translations either anonymously or with the initials J. C.

Anne Finch—not to be confused with Anne Finch, Countess of Winchilsea née Kingsmill (1661–1720)—was the daughter of Sir Heneage Finch and Elizabeth Cradock Bennet, and had all the benefits and distinctions of her class. Her father, a prominent political figure whose positions included Sergeant-at-Law, Recorder of London, and Speaker of the House of Commons, died shortly before she was born. Little is known of her childhood or early education. Conway's correspondence, compiled by Marjorie H. Nicolson in 1930, demonstrates the breadth of learning that she achieved later in life. On 11 February 1651, Anne Finch married Edward Conway (1623–83), who was later made the third viscount of Conway and Killultagh and, after her death, the first earl of Conway. A bout of fever at the age of twelve is thought to have brought on the headaches that Conway suffered from for the remainder of her life. The attention that Conway received from the seventeenth-century medical community and the extensive correspondence chronicling her illness make Conway an intriguing figure in the history of medicine. The exact nature of Conway's illness remains mysterious, but she underwent extensive treatments and subjected herself to a variety of dangerous procedures in an attempt to alleviate her pain. During her life, Conway was treated by a multitude of physicians, including William Harvey, F. M. van Helmont, and Theodore Mayherne; she also appears in a medical treatise of Thomas Willis, a well known seventeenth-century physician who specialized in neurological disorders. Toward the end of her life and much to the dismay of her friends and family, Conway converted to Quakerism.

Conway's philosophical treatise details a system of monistic vitalism that responds to the limitations of "*Cartesian, Hobbesian or Spinozian*" philosophies. Conway argues that the Cartesian dualism does not account for the ways in which body and spirit interact; instead, she insists that body and spirit are the same substance in different forms. In an attempt to avoid the materialist tendencies of Hobbesian philosophy, Conway insists that spirit is the primary substance of the universe. Unlike Spinozian monism, however, Conway makes a clear distinction between God and his creation. While Conway's refutation of her predecessors is limited, the importance she gives to Descartes, Hobbes, and Spinoza by placing them in her title situates her text within a contemporary philosophical context. The influence of Conway's friendships with More and van Helmont is also apparent in the text. Although the monism of Conway's system is a distinct departure from the dualism of the Cambridge Platonists, Conway's treatise addresses many of More's own criticisms of contemporary philosophy. Conway also incorporates elements of the Lurianic Cabbala, which her physician, van Helmont, introduced to her (Hutton 1996). Indeed, some elements of Conway's text bear such a striking resemblance to van Helmont's work that one nineteenth-century critic, Heinrich Ritter, erroneously attributed the text to its editor (Merchant 256).

Kristin Downey

McMaster University

Anne Conway. *The Principles of the most Ancient and Modern Philosophy concerning God, Christ, and the creatures, viz. of spirit and matter in general, whereby may be resolved all those problems or difficulties, which neither by the school nor common modern philosophy, nor by the Cartesian, Hobessian, nor Spinosian, could be discussed. Being a little treatise published since the author's death, translated out of the English into Latin, with annotations taken from the ancient philosophy of the Hebrews; and now again made English, by J.C.* (Printed in Latin, Amsterdam, 1690; in English, London, 1692). Thomas Fisher Rare Book Library at the University of Toronto, hob RBSC 1. Title page.

Bibliography

Anne Cooke Bacon. *The Early Modern Englishwoman: A Facsimile Library of Essential Works*. Series I, Part 2. Aldershot, Hants: Ashgate, 2000, Vol. 1.

Ballaster, Ros. "The first female dramatists." *Women and Literature in Britian 1500–1700*. Ed. Helen Wilcox. Cambridge: Cambridge University Press, 1996, 267–90.

Baron, Helen. "Mary (Howard) Fitzroy's Hand in the Devonshire Manuscript." *Review of English Studies* 45 (1994) 318–35.

Beal, Peter. "Notions in Garrison: The Seventeenth-Century Commonplace Book." *New Ways of Looking at Old Texts: Papers of the Renaissance English Text Society, 1985–1991*. Ed. W. Speed Hill. Binghamton, N.Y.: Medieval and Renaissance Texts and Studies, 1993. 131–47.

Beilin, Elaine. *Redeeming Eve: Women Writers of the English Renaissance*. Princeton: Princeton University Press, 1987.

Booty, J. E., ed. *An Apology of the Church of England by John Jewel*. Charlottesville: University Press of Virginia, 1963.

Brathwaite, Richard. "The English Gentlewoman." *The Whole Duty of a Woman: Female Writers in Seventeenth-Century England*. Ed. Angeline Goreau. New York: Dial Press, 1985. 38–40.

Brown, Stuart. "Leibniz and More's Cabbalistic circle." *Henry More (1614–1687) Tercentenary Studies*. Ed. Sarah Hutton. Boston: Kluwer Academic Publishers, 1990. 77–95.

Burke, Victoria E. "Ann Bowyer's Commonplace Book (Bodleian Library Ashmole MS 51): Reading and Writing Among the 'Middling Sort.'" *Early Modern Literary Studies* 6.3 (2001): <*http://purl.oclc.org/emls/06–3/burkbowy.htm*>.

Child, Harold H., ed. *Iphigenia at Aulis by Lady Lumley*. Oxford: Malone Society, 1909.

Conway, Anne. *The Principles of the Most Ancient and Modern Philosophy*. Ed. and trans. Allison Coudert. New York: Cambridge University Press, 1996.

Corneille, Pierre. "Pompée." *Théâtre Complet de Corneille*. Ed. Maurice Rat. Vol. 2. Paris: Editions Garnier Frères, 1977.

Cotton, Nancy. *Women Playwrights in England, c. 1363–1670*. London: Associated University Presses, 1980.

Crane, Frank D. "Euripides, Erasmus and Lady Lumley." *Classical Journal* 39 (1944): 223–28.

Findlay, Alison, Stephanie Hodgson-Wright, and Gweno Williams. *Women Dramatists 1550–1670: Plays in Performance*. Lancaster: Lancaster University Television, 1999.

———— and Stephanie Hodgson-Wright with Gweno Williams, *Women and Dramatic Production 1550–1700*. London: Longman, 2000.

Greene, David H. "Lady Lumley and Greek Tragedy." *Classical Journal* 36 (1941): 536–47.

Harrier, Richard C. "A Printed Source for 'The Devonshire Manuscript'." *Review of English Studies* 11 (1960): 54.

Heale, Elizabeth. "Women and the Courtly Love Lyric: The Devonshire MS (BL Additional 17492)." *Modern Language Review* 90 (1995): 96–313.

Hobbs, Mary. *Early Seventeenth Century Verse Miscellany Manuscripts*. Aldershot: Scolar Press, 1992.

Hodgson-Wright, Stephanie. "Jane Lumley's *Iphigenia at Aulis*: multum in parvo, or, less is more." *Readings in Renaissance Women's Drama: Criticism, History and Performance 1594–1998*. Ed. S. P. Cerasano and Marion Wynne-Davies. London: Routledge, 1998. 129–41.

Hutner, Heidi, ed. *Rereading Aphra Behn: History, Theory, and Criticism*. Charlottesville and London: University Press of Virginia, 1993.

Hutton, Sarah, and Majorie Hope Nicolson, eds. *The Conway Letters: The Correspondence of Anne, Viscountess Conway, Henry More, and their Friends 1642–1684*. Rev. ed. Oxford: Clarendon Press, 1992.

Hutton, Sarah. "Of Physic and Philosophy: Anne Conway, F.M. van Helmont and Seventeenth-Century Medicine." *Religio Medici: Medicine and Religion in Seventeenth-Century England*. Ed. Ole Peter Grell and Andrew Cunningham. Aldershot: Scholar Press, 1996. 228–246.

Ketton-Cremer, Robert W. *Norfolk in the Civil War: A Portrait of a Society in Conflict*. Hamden, Conn.: Archon Books, 1970.

Klene, Jean. "Recreating the Letters of Lady Anne Southwell." *New Ways of Looking at Old Texts: Papers of the Renaissance English Text Society, 1985–1991*. Ed. W. Speed Hill, ed. Binghamton, N.Y.: Medieval and Renaissance Texts and Studies, 1993. 239–52.

————, ed. *The Southwell-Sibthorpe Commonplace Book: Folger MS. V.b.198*. Tempe, Ariz.: Medieval and Renaissance Texts and Studies, 1997.

Krontiris, Tina. "Breaking Barriers of Genre and Gender in Margaret Tyler's Translation of The Mirrour of Knighthood." *English Literary Renaissance* 18 (Winter 1988): 19–39.

————. *Oppositional Voices: Women as Writers and Translators of Literature in the English Renaissance*. London: Routledge, 1992.

Lamb, Mary Ellen. "The Myth of the Countess of Pembroke: The Dramatic Circle." *Yearbook of English Studies* 11 (1981): 195–202.

Lippincott, H. F., ed. *Merry Passages and Jeasts—A Manuscript Jestbook of Sir Nicholas Le Strange (1603–1655)*. *Elizabethan & Renaissance Studies* 29. Salzburg: Institut für Englische Sprache und Literatur, 1974.

Love, Harold. *Scribal Publication in Seventeenth-Century England*. Oxford: Clarendon Press, 1993.

Mackerness, E. D. "Margaret Tyler: An Elizabethan Feminist." *Notes and Queries* 190 (1947): 112–13.

Marotti, Arthur F. *Manuscript, Print, and the English Renaissance Lyric*. Ithaca, N.Y.: Cornell University Press, 1995.

Merchant, Carolyn. "The Vitalism of Anne Conway: Its Impact on Leibniz's Concept of the Monad." *Journal of the History of Philosophy* 17 (1979): 255–69.

Nichols, J. G. "Notices of Sir Nicholas Lestrange, Bart, and His Family Connexions." *Anecdotes and Traditions*. Ed. William Thoms. London: Camden Society, 1839.

Pearson, Jaqueline. *The Prostituted Muse: Images of Women and Women Dramatists.* Brighton: Harvester, 1988.

Purkiss, Diane, ed. *Three Tragedies by Renaissance Women*. London: Penguin, 1998.

Remley, Paul G. "Mary Shelton and Her Tudor Literary Milieu." *Rethinking the Henrician Era. Essays on Early Tudor Texts and Contexts.* Ed. by Peter C. Herman. Urbana: University of Illinois Press, 1994. 40–77.

Roberts, Josephine. "Mary Sidney, countess of Pembroke." *English Literary Renaissance* 14.3 (1984): 426–37.

Schleiner, Louise. "Margaret Tyler, Translator and Waiting Woman." *English Language Notes* 29 (1992): 1–8.

———. *Tudor and Stuart Women Writers*. Indianapolis and Bloomington: Indiana University Press, 1994.

Schnell, Lisa J. "Parenthetical Disturbances: Aphra Behn and the Rhetoric of Relativity." *Semiotic Inquiry* 12 (1992): 95–113.

Smith, Bruce R. *The Acoustic World of Early Modern England: Attending to the O-Factor.* Chicago: University of Chicago Press, 1999.

Todd, Janet, ed. *The Complete Works of Aphra Behn.* 6 vols. Columbus: Ohio State University Press, 1992.

———. *The Secret Life of Aphra Behn.* London: André Deutsch Limited, 1996.

———. *The Critical Fortunes of Aphra Behn.* Columbia, S.C. : Camden House, 1998.

Waller, Gary. *Mary Sidney, Countess of Pembroke: A Critical Study of her Writings and Literary Milieu.* Salzburg: Institut fur Englische Sprache und Literatur, 1979.

———. "Introduction." Mary Sidney Herbert, *Translation of Philippe de Mornay, A discourse of Life and Death; Antonius, a Tragedie*. Aldershot: Ashgate Press, 1996.

Willetts, Pamela. "Sir Nicholas Le Strange and John Jenkins." *Music and Letters* 42 (1961): 30–43.

Woudhuysen, H.R. *Sir Philip Sidney and the Circulation of Manuscripts 1558–1640*. Oxford: Clarendon Press, 1996.

CHAPTER 8

Poetry

Edward Phillips's "Women Among the Moderns Eminent for Poetry," printed in 1675, listed the following noteworthy female English poets: "Anne Askew, Anne Bradstreet, Arabella, Astrea Behn, Lady Bacon, Catherine Philips, Lady Elizabeth Carew, Elizabetha Joanna Westonia, Lady Jane Grey, Margaret, Dutchess of New-Castle, Mary, Countesse of Pembroke, Lady Mary Wroth, Mildreda, Lady Russell."[1] Yet in the Restoration period the interest in recovering early modern female writers receded into the background as neoclassicism and emerging notions of canonicity established priorities for readers and writers alike.

The "Renaissance" for women, if it happened, occurred in the late twentieth century, largely through the archival and editorial work of feminist scholars and editors.[2] One of the major results has been the excavation of a tradition of women's verse produced during the age of Spenser, Sidney, Donne, Milton, and Dryden. The early modern female poets who make up this countercanon represent a range of backgrounds from the middle class (Lanyer, Whitney) to the aristocracy (Wroth, Cary, Herbert, Pulter).[3] Together the poets form a tradition insofar as "they respond in similar ways to a shared set of political and cultural problems: shifting configurations of monarchic, religious, and linguistic authority; and attention to the place of gender in debates about political and linguistic authority."[4] The entries featured in this chapter display the diversity and dialogic nature of early female poetry especially well. Included in this section are samples and analyses of frontispieces and front matter from poetry volumes, poetic translations, occasional poems, religious sonnets, love poems, eulogies, and satires, which provide evidence of the multifarious attempts at self-expression and literary achievement by the poets.

An examination of the early female poets, however, reveals as much about their exclusion from literary life as its does about their accomplishments within the narrow circuits to which they were confined. Early modern poetry with which most contemporary scholars and students are familiar was traditionally the province of male writers educated in the classics, and often having an upper-middle-class or ruling-class affiliation. But verse was also a medium for popular expression—particularly in such forms as sonnets and ballads—and was even a recognized mode of female expression. Yet the concept of a female poet was an aberration at best and a violation of the natural and social order at worst. In many cases, their works never survived, having been destroyed by the writers themselves in response to the stigma against women entering the public sphere. The restricted reproduction and circulation of verse during this time also gave poetry little chance of seeing the light of day after its conception. Among the few poets whose works were copied and distributed were Katherine Philips and Anne Wharton, the circulation of manuscripts being, as Elaine Hobby reminds us, "the normal way to make writing public before the widespread use of printed books."[5]

Even though the printing press had been established in England since 1476, many of the best-known writers of the early modern period, including Sir Philip Sidney, John Donne, Thomas Carew, and Sir Walter Ralegh, circulated their poems in manuscript form to restrict their circulation to "fit" audiences.[6] Margaret Ezell, Arthur Marotti, and Harold Love have demonstrated that female poets too were more active in circulating manuscript poetry rather than printed verse.[7] Lady Hester Pulter's religious verse, written in manuscript between the Civil War and Interregnum periods, was addressed to royalists, particularly female royalists. As poetry passed from hand to hand, women sometimes wrote poems in response to earlier ones. This is the case with Lady Anne Southwell and Ann Bowyer (chapter 7), who produced altered versions of Ralegh's manuscript poem, "The Lie." Southwell and Bowyer, like many other female poets and compilers (see chapter 7), were also involved in assembling manuscript miscellanies—handwritten collections of poetry either copied or contributed by family and friends—which became an important literary activity for literate English women generally. Miscellanies provide information about the various networks to which the compilers belonged. Later, printed collections of verse, like Aphra Behn's, would combine conventions of manuscript miscellanies with those of the newly evolving print miscellany.[8]

The development of a print culture turned out to be a mixed blessing for female writers, who were both liberated and stigmatized by print. In reading female verse, one must be conscious of the voices and imprints of the compositors, printers, and booksellers, who serve as the poets' midwives, while also speaking for the poets, after them, or in spite of them. Adopting a conventional rhetorical posture, Anne Bradstreet declares that her well-meaning brother-in-law, John Woodbridge, printed *The Tenth Muse* (London, 1650) "without [her] knowledge, and contrary to her expectation"; Woodbridge defends himself, however, by insisting that he was looking after Bradstreet's best interests since corrupt manuscript versions were being circulated and printed.[9] When copies of women's writings wound up in the hands of unscrupulous booksellers, the authors lost their rights over the publication and integrity of their works. A volume of Katherine Philips's poems, the title page of which bears her initials, appeared without her permission in 1664. The preface of Sarah Fyge Egerton's *The Female Advocate* (1686) states that Egerton had not intended the publication of her poem in its original form. The first printing, she maintained, relied on a manuscript for whose flaws Egerton held the (presumably male) compositors responsible. Yet she was nevertheless exiled by her father for the unauthorized production and printing of a second edition of her text (1687).

Literary women published for a variety of reasons. Margaret Cavendish sought fame through writing; Lady Mary Wroth published because of financial need. Patronage and profit are additional factors that need to be considered in any female literary history or study of early modern poetry. Among female patrons was the Lady Margaret, Countess Dowager of Cumberland and Countess of Bedford, who is best known for her patronage of John Donne.[10] Aemilia Lanyer, who benefited from her connection with the court of King James and Queen Anne of Denmark, was eager to attract patrons and thus names the Lady Cumberland and the Queen among the nine dedications to specific aristocratic women in the preface to her volume *Salve Deus Rex Judaeorum* (1611).[11] As the blatant appeals to her upper-class female dedicatees indicate, Lanyer, like Isabel Whitney, also turned to writing for economic reasons, though unlike Whitney, Lanyer could not rely on the popularity of her writings.

The writings of women who managed to compose verse in the face of restraint and resistance merit attention. Studies of the female poetic tradition reveal immediately that poetry, even occasional verse, tends to be self-conscious and dialogic on various levels. Many poems, for example, imitate, respond to (directly or discursively), engage, or even anticipate other texts, as various entries in this chapter demonstrate.[12] We thus provide suggestions for creative pairings of female and male poems, pairings that invite an examination of women's verse not as "a separate, homogeneous genre," but as contributions to a broad and diverse literary tradition in which, moreover, writers of both sexes participated, despite their different relations to centers of power.[13]

A Meditation of a Penitent Sinner (1560) by Anne Vaughan Locke should, for instance, be placed next to the religious sonnets composed in 1597 by her son, Henry Locke, in which he assumes the voices of scriptural figures like Jonah, David, and Judith. Isabella Whitney's verse epistles on the subject of love's constancy can be juxtaposed with the amorous songs in Thomas Campion's *Book of Airs* (1601) and, of course, with John Donne's poems on inconstancy. Mary Sidney Wroth's sonnet sequence, *Pamphilia to Amphilanthus* (1621), has commonly been compared to Philip Sidney's 1591 *Astrophil and Stella*, though it recuperates Petrarchism for women writers, lovers, and dreamers. In the epitaph, "To the Angell Spirit of the Most excellent, Sir Phillip Sidney" (1623)—one of only four "original" works by the Mary Sidney Herbert, the Countess of Pembroke celebrates her brother's achievements while also cautiously displaying her own. Comparisons between the different manuscript versions and the printed version of "To the Angell Spirit" in Samuel Daniel's *The Whole Workes of Samuel Daniel Esquire in Poetrie* (1623) reveal that the material context or placement of the poem affects its meaning.

Various other pairings enrich the study of both female- and male-authored poems of the period. "The Doleful Lay of Clorinda" by Mary Sidney Herbert might be juxtaposed with Henry Vaughan's "Silence, and Stealth of Days," which also mourns a brother's death (*Silex Scintillans*, 1650, 1655). Aemilia Lanyer's "The Description of Cooke-ham" (1611) might be paired with "So Cruel Prison" by Henry Howard, Earl of Surrey (first published in *Tottel's Miscellany*). Or Lanyer's country-house poem could be interpreted as a feminist complement to a poem it anticipates—Ben Jonson's "To Penshurt" (1616). Lanyer's *Salve Deus Rex Judaeorum* (1611) and Milton's *Paradise Lost* (1667, 1674) have also been productively paired.[14] Moreover, the representation of dreams and of Eve in both enable a useful comparison between these poems and Rachel Speght's *Mortalities Memorandum, with a Dreame Prefixed* (1621), and also with the contrasting condemnation of the first woman in Alice Sutcliffe's "Of our losse by Adam" (*Meditations of Man's Mortalitie*, 1634). Diana Primrose's celebration of Elizabeth I's virtues in *A chaine of pearle, or A memoriall of Queene Elizabeth* (1630) might enrich the reading of William Shakespeare's nostalgic dramatization of Elizabeth's future glory in Act 5, Scene 4 of the play *Henry VIII* (1613). The final poem in *Eliza's Babes*, "Wings my Doves you have now obtain'd" (1652) is produced in imitation of George Herbert's emblem poem, "Easter Wings" (1633) to which Hester Pulter's manuscript emblem poems can also be compared. As well, poems from An Collins's *Divine Songs and Meditacions* (1653) have been juxtaposed with Herbert's lyrics, a pairing that invites a rereading not only of Collins but also of Herbert, his literary heritage, and critical reception.[15] Katherine Philips's female friendship poems might be examined in relation to those of John Donne, George Turberville, and William Cartwright, as well as in terms of the Society of Friendship, the poems of Philo-Philippa, and the manuscript culture in which Philips—as one of the foremost writers of the seventeenth century—occupied a special place.[16]

The relationship between self-abnegation and self-promotion is central to female writing.[17] Occasional verse and political poetry, though highly stylized or conventional, renegotiated the boundaries of personal and public. Self-revelation paradoxically underlies poetry glorifying royalist power, as in Diana Primrose's *A chaine of pearle* (1630); Rachel Jevon's "Exultationis carmen" (1660), which commemorates Charles II's return; Ephelia's *A Poem as it was Presented to His Sacred Majesty On the Discovery of the Plott* (1679); and Aphra Behn's "A Congratulatory Poem To Her Sacred Majesty Queen Mary, Upon Her Arrival in England" (1688).

An examination of the front matter in female-authored poetry volumes further exposes the multiple levels of signification and also the contradictions inherent in the process of self-fashioning. The relationship between the self represented in poetry and the image or engraving of the poet that sometimes appears at the start of a volume is frequently elusive, both concealing and revealing the poet's identity. The title page of Anne Dowriche's magisterial verse-narrative *The French Historie* (1589), featuring an emblem of Truth, is noteworthy in this regard. It exposes the dominant concerns of the *Historie* and the ideological position of the poet, who otherwise presents the account of the French civil wars through the voice of a male narrator. The frontispiece portrait from Ephelia's *Female Poems on several Occasions* (1679, 1682), examined in chapter 10, is intriguing for a different reason, as the question of "Ephelia" authorship has been the subject of extensive scholarly debate, which has yielded intriguing results, if not a highly probable identification.[18] The prefatory materials in Anne Killigrew's posthumous *Poems* (1686) are equally provocative. The materials include Killigrew's engraved self-portrait, which exhibits her mastery of contemporary artistic conventions and her privileged social status. In the ode he wrote after her death to preface her *Poems*, John Dryden praises Killigrew's achievements in poetry and painting.

The dialogic nature of poetry extends to the conversations about class and culture. The poets all speak in the various languages of their cultures and social classes. The process of self-representation through poetry is enabled and prevented by historical conditions, cultural expectations, social position, and personal circumstances. Aristocratic women like Mary Wroth and Elizabeth Cary, who were required to adhere more stringently to traditional notions of female decorum, were eventually forced to withdraw their published books from circulation altogether. Like Cary, Mary Sidney Herbert is much more cautious about challenging cultural stereotypes of women. The strongest, most direct opposition comes mainly from women of the middle classes, like Isabel Whitney, Tina Krontiris observes.[19] The study of the early modern female poetic tradition, then, is enabled and enriched by locating the poets in relation to the various social networks and literary cultures of the period.

Notes

We are grateful for the assistance of Linda Vecchi and Robert C. Evans on this chapter introduction.

1. Edward Phillips, *Theatrum Poetarum, or a Compleat Collection of the Poets etc* (London 1675), 253ff.

2. *A Paradise of Women: Writings by English Women of the Renaissance*, ed. Betty Travitsky (Westport, Conn.: Greenwood Press, 1980); Elaine Beilin, *Redeeming Eve: Women Writers of the English Renaissance* (Princeton, N.J.: Princeton University Press, 1987); *Kissing the Rod: An Anthology of Seventeenth Century Women's Verse*, ed. Germaine Greer, Susan Hastings, Jeslyn Medoff, and Melinda Sansone (London: Virago, 1988; New York: Farrar Straus and Giroux, 1989); Barbara Kiefer Lewalski, *Writing Women in Jacobean England* (Cambridge, Mass.: Harvard University Press, 1993); Elizabeth H. Hageman, "Women's Poetry in Early Modern Britain," *Women and Literature in Britain, 1500–1700*, ed. Helen Wilcox (Cambridge: Cambridge University Press, 1996), 190–208.

3. *The Renaissance Englishwoman in Print: Counterbalancing the Canon*, ed. Anne M. Haselkorn and Betty S. Travitsky (Amherst: University of Massachusetts Press, 1990).

4. Carol Barash, *English Women's Poetry, 1649–1714* (Oxford: Clarendon Press, 1996), 2.

5. Elaine Hobby, *Virtue of Necessity: English Women's Writing 1649–88* (London: Virago, 1988), 129.

6. See Richard B. Wollman, "The 'Press and the Fire': Print and Manuscript Culture in Donne's circle," *Studies in English Literature* 33 (1993): 85–97.

7. Margaret M. J. Ezell, *The Patriarch's Wife: Literary Evidence and the History of the Family* (Chapel Hill: University of North Carolina Press, 1987); Harold Love, *Scribal Publication in Seventeenth-Century England* (Oxford: Clarendon Press, 1993); Arthur F. Marotti, *Manuscript, Print, and the English Renaissance Lyric* (Ithaca, N.Y.: Cornell University Press, 1995).

8. Anne Russell, "Aphra Behn's Miscellanies: The Politics and Poetics of Editing," *Philological Quarterly* 77.3 (1998): 319.

9. Elizabeth Wade White, *Anne Bradstreet: "The Tenth Muse"* (New York: Oxford University Press, 1971), 255; Margaret J. M. Ezell, "Literary Pirates and Reluctant Authors," *Social Authorship and the Advent of Print* (Baltimore: Johns Hopkins University Press, 1999), 45–60.

10. Barbara K. Lewalski, "Lucy, Countess of Bedford: Images of a Jacobean Courtier and Patroness," *Politics of Discourse: The Literature and History of Seventeenth-Century England*, ed. Kevin Sharpe and Steven Zwicker (Berkeley: University of California Press, 1987), 137–58.

11. On the dynamics of Lanyer's patronage poetry, see Kari Boyd McBride, "Sacred Celebration: The Patronage Poems," *Aemilia Lanyer: Gender, Genre and the Canon*, ed. Michael Grossman (Lexington: University Press of Kentucky, 1998), 60–82.

12. Some of these creative pairings are suggested in *Female and Male Voices in Early Modern England*, ed. Betty S. Travitsky and Anne Lake Prescott (New York: Columbia University Press, 2000).

13. Though her own rich and informative essay concentrates primarily on the tradition of women's verse, Bronwen Prince recommends examinations of the "common poetic conventions and poetic practices that men and women of this period share" ("Women's Poetry 1550–1700: 'Not Unfit to be Read,'" *A Companion to Early Modern Women's Writing*, ed. Anita Pacheco [Oxford: Blackwell, 2002], 286).

14. See Josephine A. Roberts, "Diabolic Dreamscape in Lanyer and Milton," *Teaching Tudor and Stuart Women Writers*, ed. Susanne Woods and Margaret P. Hannay (New York: Modern Language Association, 2000), 299–302.

15. Thomas Healy, *New Latitudes: Theory and English Renaissance Literature* (London: Arnold 1992), 49–52.

16. See Peter Beal, "'The virtuous Mrs Philips' and 'that whore Castlemaine': Orinda and her Apotheosis, 1644–1668," *In Praise of Scribes: Manuscripts and their Makers in Seventeenth-Century England* (Oxford: Clarendon Press, 1998), 147–91. Also see Claudia A. Limbert, "'The Unison of Well-Tun'd Hearts': Katherine Philips' friendships with male writers," *English Language Notes* 29.2 (1991): 25–38.

17. On the question of anonymity in female verse, see Jane Stevenson and Peter Davidson, "Introduction," *Early Modern Women Poets (1520–1700): An Anthology*, ed. Jane Stevenson and Peter Davidson (Oxford: Oxford University Press, 2001), xxxiv–xxxvii.

18. *Ephelia*, intro. and ed. Maureen E. Mulvihill (Burlington, Vt.: Scolar/Ashgate, 2003); "Thumbprints of Ephelia (Lady Mary Villiers): The End of an Enigma in Restoration Attribution. A Multimedia Archive—Text, Image, Sound," *(Re)Soundings* 2.3 (2001), 98 frames; "Sly Stuart Duchess: The Many Masks of Mary Villiers ('Ephelia')," *The Female Spectator* (Chawton House Library, Hampshire, U.K.: Summer, 2002, 1–6).

19. Tina Krontiris, *Oppositional Voices: Women as Writers and Translators of Literature in the English Renaissance* (New York: Routledge, 1992), 145.

8.1: Anne Locke, Preface, *A Meditation of a Penitent Sinner* (1560). By permission of the Folger Shakespeare Library.

Anne Locke, Preface, *A Meditation of a Penitent Sinner: Written in Maner of a Paraphrase upon the 51. Psalme of David* (1560)

A Meditation Of A Penitent Sinner: Written in Maner Of A Paraphrase upon the 51. Psalme of David appeared in 1560 appended to a translation of four sermons by John Calvin—*Sermons of John Calvin, upon the songe that Ezechias made after he had been sicke, and afflicted by the hand of God, conteyned in the 38. chapter of Esay / Translated out of Frenche into Englishe.* Its apparent author, Anne (Vaughan) Locke (the name is variously spelled Locke, Lock, or Lok; she is also known by her third husband's name, Anne Prowse), dedicated the work to the duchess of Suffolk. The *Meditation* presents twenty-one sonnets expanding upon the nineteen verses of this central Penitential Psalm; another five prefatory sonnets set the tone of penitential introspection. Amplifying the Psalm in a coherent and often skillful manner, *A Meditation* can be considered the first sonnet sequence in English.

The *Meditation* sonnets, appended to what is clearly Locke's own translation of Calvin's four sermons, pose difficult issues of authorship, most perplexingly the accompanying note attributing the work to a "frend." That last clause suggests the work is not actually Locke's, and, until recently, scholars speculatively assigned the sonnets to the Scottish Reformer John Knox, with whom Locke resided in Geneva in 1557–59. However, Knox's biographers do not claim the work as his and, given Anne Locke's other literary endeavors—including her translation *Of the Markes of the Children of God from Jean Taffin* (1590)—we have good reason to assume the work is hers. Moreover, the attribution to "my frend" strongly resembles other modesty formulas in the early modern period that distance women writers from the still-suspect activity of authorship. Locke's title page nicely illustrates the difficult issue of determining authorship in a period of fluid intertextuality and underlying hostility to women's writing.

The first two "Prefatory Sonnets" set a remarkable tone, as Locke adapts the penitence of David the Psalmist. In so doing, Locke not only establishes her own voice in relation to Psalm 51, but connects to previous literary appropriations, notably Thomas Wyatt's translations of the *Penitential Psalms* (1549). Like Wyatt's dramatic prologues, which interlink the Psalm translations, Locke's "Prefatory Sonnets" establish a sense of personal engagement and identification with David; as in Wyatt's sequence, the lines between the love sonnet and the spiritual sonnet—between secular and sacred—are blurred by this dramatic, personal narrative. Here and throughout the sequence Locke establishes an astonishing regularity in both English rhyme scheme and iambic pentameter, an achievement quite profound in light of the sonnet's very brief English history before 1560. In fact, Locke's proficiency as a sonnet writer accentuates the relative roughness of poets like Wyatt and his fellow writers published in the influential *Tottel's Miscellany* (a collection of lyric poetry published in 1557, also known as *Songs and Sonnets*).

Prefatory Sonnet 1 laments the speaker's "daseld sight"(4) and "dimmed and fordulled eyen" (9), and in so doing adopts an image that dominates much of the century's devotional verse. Here Locke shows some proficiency in developing the two-sided nature of that image. While those eyes may be "daseld" and full of the vision of "lothesome filthe," they are also "dimmed and fordulled" with "teares" of penance, "Sent from the fornace of a gretefull brest" (9, 10, 12). Locke expands the image into the next poem—loosely linking them, as she does all five sonnets—moving from the general complaint of missing the "comfort of the light" to the explicit characterization of the speaker as a "blinde wretch."

Locke also joins a growing tradition of Protestant exegesis that draws especially upon the emotional drama of David's Psalms, particularly Psalm 51. The translation of "maister Calvines worke" and the *Meditation* sonnets place her soundly in the realm of writing practices actually sanctioned for early modern women: translation, paraphrase, and personal meditation upon biblical texts. Locke effectively uses this freedom, establishing herself not only as an important voice in emerging Protestant discourses but as a strong poetic voice in the still nascent English sonnet form. In this sense, *A Meditation* participates in—and helps to found—a tradition extending through Mary Sidney, Aemilia Lanyer, and An Collins.

JOHN OTTENHOFF
ALMA COLLEGE

Anne Locke. Preface, *A Meditation of a Penitent Sinner: Written in Maner of a Paraphrase upon the 51. Psalme of David* (1560). Calvin, Jean, 1509–64. *Sermons de Jehan Calvin sur le cantique que feit le bon roy Ezéchias après qu'il eut été malade et affligé de la main de Dieu. English. Sermons of Iohn Caluin, vpon the songe that Ezechias made after he had bene sicke, and afflicted by the hand of God, conteyned in the 38. chapiter of Esay. Translated out of Frenche into Englishe* (1560). Folger Shakespeare Library STC 4450. Pages [Aa1r] and [Aa2r].

Isabella Whitney, *The Copy of a letter* (1567)

Recognized as England's first published female author of secular verses, Isabella Whitney might easily lay claim to the role of Virginia Woolf's "Judith Shakespeare." In an age when women were instructed to be "chaste, silent and obedient," Whitney's corpus of writings, including her lamentory love epistle, *The Copy of a letter, lately written in meeter, by a yonge Gentilwoman: to her unconstant Lover* (1567) and her poetic miscellany, *A Sweet Nosgay, or Pleasant Posye: Contayning a Hundred and Ten Phylosophicall Flowers* (1573), demonstrates that not all early modern women were intimidated by the patriarchal controls of sixteenth-century society.

Little biographical information exists about Whitney aside from that found in her writings. From the numerous verse epistles addressed to family members included in *A Sweet Nosgay* and a few slight personal documents, it is known that Whitney was born into a large, fairly well-established Cheshire family whose most recognizable member is Geoffrey Whitney, author of the popular *A Choice of Emblems* (1589). Although Whitney refers to herself as a "Gentilwoman," the Whitney family was probably of the lesser gentry. Whitney and her sisters (as suggested by her advice in her "A Modest Meane for Maides" see selection 3.1) maintained their existence as household servants in the employ of unidentified London homeowners. The fact that Whitney's publications are addressed to personal friends and family relations, and not to members of the court or city, indicates that she was not privileged in education or associations that might have "elevated" her condition and "explained" her literary activities.

Whitney's first publication, *The Copy of a letter*, contains four verse epistles on the subject of love's constancy. Two are presented from the female perspective: "To her unconstant Lover" and "An Admonition to al yong Gentilwomen, and to all other Mayds in general to beware of mennes flattery," and are the work of Whitney. The latter two verses, "A Love letter sent by a Bachelor, (a most faithfull Lover) to an unconstant and faithless Mayden" and "Against the wilfull Inconstancie of his deare," were most likely written by men. The printer, Richard Jones, may have procured these latter verse epistles to provide a "gender balance" to the poems written by Whitney. Jones published all of Whitney's poetry, including, perhaps, some lyrics found in such Tudor miscellanies as *A Gorgeous Gallery of Gallant Inventions* (1578) and *A Handful of Pleasant Delights* (1566?, 1584) and was known as a producer of inexpensively designed verse collections and ballads. Whitney is apparently the only female author whose works he printed.

The Copy of a letter, like all Whitney's verse, is written in the familiar "fourteeners" popularized by numerous sixteenth-century ballad writers. Her works reveal that her education included some study of Scripture, some classical literature (particularly the works of Ovid that had been recently translated into English, for example, George Tuberville's 1567 translation of *The heroycall epistles*) and some contemporary literature. While written on the subject of love, the verse epistles that make up *The Copy of a letter* are not love poems. Particularly, the letter "To her unconstant Lover" is a personal rebuke by a jilted woman whose lover has deserted her (and foresworn their betrothal) to marry another. Following in the style of the Ovidian *Heroides*, Whitney identifies various male classical figures (Aeneas, Theseus, Jason) who are noted for their inconstancy as negative exempla for her lover. Though the examples are commonplace, Whitney's mode of personal address and touches of humor (having drawn attention to Jason's "perpetuall fame," she quips,

GALESVS CYMON

And fretfull spight, had pearce his gall
on Seas by whyrlynge blasts,
And Enuies belching Falnes were stopde
by VENVS slowynge Wope:
And tracte of time, ware out of mynde,
all gnawyng cares anoye.
And LETHE guisse in drenchyng brink
the death of PASIMONDE:
And IPHIGENIA, now Lischargde
of former bowed honor.
Did pince at length with loftyng mynd,
to CYMONS gentel hearte:
And by the graunte of wished grace,
deuo2ce his fo2mer smarte.
And thus they passe their happy dayes,
in neuer dyenge blisse:
Of subiche, I craue of God, fo2 aye
god Ladies neuer misse.

FINIS.

Amore manco la libertà
Ben fu saggio colui, chi primo
amore gerzon dipinse.
Chiusa fiammaé piu ardente.
Il fuoco risfresto, molto piu
fieramente cnoce.
Che quello, il quale per ampio luogo,
manda le fiamme sue.

The Copy of a let-
ter, lately written in meeter,
by a yonge Gentilwoman; to
her vnconstant Louer.

With an Admonitio to al yong
Gentilwomen, and to all other
Mayds in general to beware
of mennes flattery.
By IS. VV.

Newly ioyned to a Loueletter
sent by a Batcheler, (a most faithfull Louer) to an vnconstant
and faithlesse Mayden.

Imprinted at London, by
Richarde Ihones: dwel-
ling in the vpper end of
Fleetlane; at the
Signe of the
spred Egle.

8.2: Isabella Whitney, *The Copy of a letter* (1567). Bodleian Library, University of Oxford.

"wherfore dyd I terme it so?/ I should have cald it shame" [A3v]) enliven the text and raise it above the common stuff (such as the male-authored poems appended to her own). In a show of remarkable generosity and "sisterly fellow-feeling" toward her rival, Whitney prays that her former lover's new wife will be blessed with the beauty of Helen, the patience of Penelope, and the constancy of Lucrece (A4v). Yet the subtlety of Whitney's attack is evident here. Helen's beauty led to her husband's death and the destruction of Troy; Penelope was besieged for ten years by one hundred greedy suitors, and Lucrece was raped and physically mutilated by her brother-in-law. The second of Whitney's poems, "An Admonition," transfers these particular laments to more general principles of good conduct and virtuous living for "all" young English maidens.

Appearing when it does in the early years of Elizabeth's reign, well before the first flowering of Elizabethan poetry, Whitney's *Copy of a letter* is a notable work of original versification. The additional fact that it was penned, published, and promoted by a *female* author should be sufficient cause to move this work from beyond its consideration as an interesting curiosity into the full light of liteary acclaim.

Linda Vecchi
Memorial University of Newfoundland

Isabella Whitney. *The Copy of a letter, lately written in meeter, by a yonge Gentilwoman: to her unconstant Lover* (1567). Bodleian Library: 8° H 44(6) Art. Seld. Sig. A1r.

208 OF ORNAMEMT. LIB. III.

The doubt of future foes,exiles my present ioy,
And wit me warnes to shun such snares as threaten mine annoy.
For falshood novv doth flow,and subiect faith doth ebbe,
Which would not be,if reason rul'd or wisdome weu'd the webbe.
But clowdes of tois vntried,do cloake aspiring mindes,
Which turne to raigne of late repent,by course of changed vvindes.
The toppe of hope supposed,the roote of ruth vvil be,
And frutelesse all their graffed guiles,as shortly ye shall see.
Then dazeld eyes vvith pride,vvhich great ambition blinds,
Shalbe vnseeld by vvorthy wights,vvhose foresight falshood finds.
The daughter of debate,that eke discord doth sovve
Shal reap no gaine where formor rule hath taught stil peace to growe.
No forreine banisht vvight shall ancre in this port,
Our realme it brookes no strangers force,let them elsvvhere resort.
Our rusty svvorde vvith rest shall first his edge employ,
To polle their toppes that seeke,such change and gape for ioy.

In a worke of ours entituled [*Philo Calia*]where we entreat of the loues betwene prince *Philo* and Lady *Calia*,in their mutual letters,messages,and speeches:we haue strained our muse to shew the vse and application of this figure,and of all others.

CHAP. XXI.

Of the vices or deformities in speach and vvriting
principally noted by auncient Poets.

IT hath bene said before how by ignorance of the maker a good figure may become a vice,and by his good discretion ,a vicious speach go for a vertue in the Poeticall science. This saying is to be explained and qualified , for some maner of speaches are alwayes intollerable and such as cannot be vsed with any decencie, but are euer vndecent namely barbarousnesse,incongruitie, ill disposition,fond affectation,rusticitie,and all extreme darknesse,such as it is not possible for a man to vnderstand the matter without an interpretour,all which partes are generally to be banished out of euery language,vnlesse it may appeare that the maker or Poet do it for the nonce,as it was reported by the Philosopher *Heraclitus* that he wrote in obscure and darke termes of purpose not to be vnderstood,whence he merited the nickname *Scotinus* , otherwise I see not but the rest of the common faultes may be borne with some-

8.3: Elizabeth I, "The doubt of future foes" (written c. 1570; pub. 1589). By permission of the
Folger Shakespeare Library.

Queen Elizabeth I, "The doubt of future foes" (written c. 1570; pub. 1589)

Queen Elizabeth I's "The doubt of future foes" is probably a response to the Northern Rebellion (1569), an attempt by northern Catholics to wed Mary, Queen of Scots to the Earl of Norfolk and reestablish Catholicism in England under a Catholic queen. The rebels were defeated and punished, and Mary continued living as a prisoner in England, a "daughter of debate, that eke discord doth sowe." The poem is a brooding meditation on false friends and treason, as well as a confident statement of Elizabeth's own power and authority.

The poem began circulating in manuscript around 1570, having apparently been copied from the queen's papers by Mary Willoughby, a gentlewoman of the Privy Chamber, whom Elizabeth reprimanded "for spreading evil bruit of her writing such toyes." At least eight manuscript copies have been found, as well as this version published in George Puttenham's *The Arte of English poesie* (1589), where the poem appears as an example of the rhetorical figure *exargasia*, or "gorgious," the "last and principall figure of our poeticall Ornaments." Puttenham says that he finds "none example in English meetre, so well maintayning this figure as that dittie of her Maiesties owne making passing sweete and harmonicall," and notes especially that such a gorgeous figure is best "deciphered by the arte of a Ladies penne, her selfe beyng the most bewtifull, or rather bewtie of Queenes." This is an extraordinary piece of literary criticism, rare in praising a woman as a writer. Interestingly, Puttenham does not reveal where he got the poem. The book was designed for "our Soueraigne Lady the Queene . . . for her recreation and service," and was published just one year after the defeat of the Spanish Armada and two years after Mary's execution, though much of it was probably written earlier. This timing adds extra interest to Puttenham's praise of the "wisdome and pacience" with which Elizabeth dealt with Mary.

Modern criticism has been divided about the queen's poem. C. S. Lewis dismisses Elizabeth as a "minor (or minimal) Drab poetess." Although he does not discuss her poetry specifically, he elsewhere complains that its form, *Poulter's Measure*, a couplet consisting of an Alexandrine followed by a Fourteener, is too stodgy. Steven W. May, by contrast, calls it a "most imaginative use of poetry," and further notes that, among the courtier poets of the time, she is unusual in using poetry "as an outlet for personal reflection." The poem is an impressive technical achievement. Note especially the sustained and almost medieval use of alliteration, as in "reason rul'd or wisdome weu'd the webbe" (line 4). Elizabeth also employs a number of compelling nature images, especially of infertility and barrenness, as in her claim that the discord "sowed" by Mary "Shal reap no gaine." Part of the poem's forcefulness also derives from Elizabeth's confident use of future-tense verbs in her forthright declaration of her own power. An excellent example of the queen's verse, the poem also demonstrates the roundabout ways even a woman as important as the queen might be published in the late sixteenth century.

NELY KEINANEN
UNIVERSITY OF HELSINKI

Elizabeth I, "The doubt of future foes," in George Puttenham's *The Arte of English Poesie* (1589). Folger Shakespeare Library STC 20519. Page 208.

THE
French Historie.

That is;

A lamentable Difcourfe of three of the chiefe, and moft famous bloodie broiles that haue happened in *France*
for the Gofpell of Iefus Chrift.

Namelie;

1 The outrage called *The winning of S. Iames his Streete*, 1557.
2 The conftant Martirdome of *Annas Burgæus* one of the K. Councell, 1559.
3 The bloodie Marriage of *Margaret* Sifter to *Charles* the 9. *Anno* 1572.

Publifhed by A.D.

*All that will liue godlie in Iefus Chrift, fhall fuffer perfe-
cution.* 1. Tim. 3.2.

Imprinted at London by *Thomas
Orwin* for *Thomas Man.*
1589.

8.4: Anne Dowriche, *The French Historie* (1589). By permission of the Folger Shakespeare Library.

Anne Dowriche, *The French Historie* (1589)

The French Historie relates three "famous" (i.e., notorious) episodes from the sixteenth-century wars of religion in France, in which Huguenots (French Protestants) are executed or murdered by Catholic partisans. Its title page reveals considerable verbal and visual information about Dowriche's programmatic structure, main themes, and ideological position.

In portraying the Huguenots as heroic pacifists and martyrs, Dowriche models her presentation on John Foxe's popular *Book of Martyrs* (1563). The Huguenots' political struggles against repressive policies are epitomized by Senator Annas Burgaeus (mentioned in the second section title) and anticipated by the biblical epigraph "All . . . persecution", correctly 2 Timothy 3:12, which invites the reader to interpret their calamities in relation to early Christian persecution. The Huguenots' defense of Reformation principles would have resonated strongly in the minds of contemporary Puritan readers, who commonly regarded England as Europe's divinely chosen nation struggling against continental Catholic powers and the forces of Satan (who first incites a raid on a prayer meeting in St. James Street in Paris and orders the execution of the congregation—the subject mentioned by the first section title—and later inspires the St. Bartholomew's Day massacre, which followed the royal marriage of the third section title).

These themes are also alluded to by the title-page emblem of a naked woman wearing a crown, with scourges at her back, and striding over what appear to be flames. She portrays Verity, bearing the motto VIRESCIT VULNERE VERITAS: Truth flourishes from a wound. Her imperviousness to injury anticipates the spiritual triumph over physical torment that will define Dowriche's martyr-heroes, and her vigor is suggested by the sprouting and strongly rooted plants beside her. Her nakedness symbolizes the unselfconscious moral integrity intrinsic to human nature before the fall into original sin. Or if the fig leaf she holds is not merely pictorial modesty, it is Truth after this event, when she is perpetually defamed. Verses that appear at the end of the volume identify her crown as a crown of peace. But this royal emblem also suggests nationalist sovereignty, as do the roses encircling the image, both of which anticipate the work's militant appeal to Queen Elizabeth to support English Protestantism and persecute Catholic conspirators. The elegant swirls and architectural details framing Truth's image anticipate Dowriche's artfully poetic reconstructions of history and prominent attention to female activism.

The volume was published once in London by T. Orwin for T. Man (*Short Title Catalogue* 7159, microfilm reel 289) and simultaneously for W. Russell "dwelling at Exeter" (*STC* 7159.3, reel 1751). This second location is explained by Dowriche's West Country connections. As Anne Edgcombe, she grew up in Cornwall and in 1582 married Hugh Dowriche, rector of Honiton, near Exeter, where she wrote *The French Historie* in 1589.

RANDALL MARTIN
UNIVERSITY OF NEW BRUNSWICK

Anne Dowriche. *The French Historie.* (1589). The Folger Shakespeare Library STC 7159. Title page.

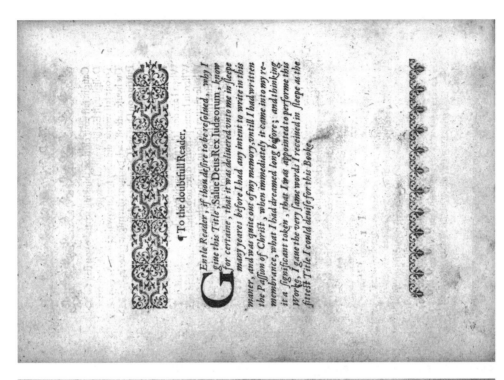

8.5: Aemilia Layner, *Salve Deus Rex Judaeorum* (1611). Reproduced by permission of The Huntington Library, San Marino, California.

Aemilia Lanyer, *Salve Deus Rex Judaeorum* (1611)

Aemilia Lanyer's title page and endnote to her *Salve Deus Rex Judaeorum* (London: Valentine Simmes, 1611) present an interesting contrast between opening formality and closing intimacy.

The title page to Lanyer's work sets a learned tone, with its Latin and biblical title (which translates as "Hail God King of the Jews"), suggesting a work of some authority and religious seriousness. Its listing of the book's contents, however, proposes something out of the ordinary: women, at least biblical women, will be a significant subject along with Christ's Passion, the central theme. Already in the title page we see the coming together of Lanyer's major concerns: the preeminence of Christ's sacrifice for the health of each soul and the important place virtuous women hold in establishing and maintaining Christianity. These linked concerns appear in every work in the book and are developed fully in *Salve Deus* proper. We are also informed on the title page that other unnamed pieces—they turn out to be nine dedications to specific aristocratic women, a dedication "To all vertuous Ladies in generall," a prose dedication "To the Vertuous Reader," and the country-house poem "The Description of Cooke-ham"—are included. (Not all dedications appear in all the extant copies of the book.) Eight of the dedications to specific women are in verse and only one, that to Margaret, Countess of Cumberland, Lanyer's chief patron, is in prose. The countess of Cumberland plays a major role in both *Salve Deus* itself and "The Description of Cooke-ham" as the model Christian woman and reader. The dedications link actual, living women to Christ, to virtue, and to Lanyer herself. Dedications were very rarely noted on title pages at the time, but the fact that Lanyer omits the name of the country-house poem may suggest she does not see it as very important in comparison with her major religious work, or perhaps that the printer did not feel it to be important. Title pages were set by the printer, and authors did not always plan or approve them. Lanyer is then carefully identified, and her status as a married woman with connections to the court is emphasized—she is thus respectable and potentially significant because of her connections.

The endnote, "To the doubtfull Reader," appears at the end of the entire volume and, with its explanation of how Lanyer came up with her title, *Salve Deus Rex Judaeorum*, harks back to the opening. By this point, the author has addressed her various readers often and we are now in a more intimate relationship with her. The fact that the title came to her in a dream suggests that Lanyer was inspired to write this work and, because the dream occurred long before she wrote her poem, the work almost seems predestined and by implication God's will. That Lanyer is doing God's will and work in her *Salve Deus Rex Judaeorum* is the strongest argument and justification she could make for writing it, and her most powerful defense for being a published woman writer.

Mary Silcox
McMaster University

Aemilia Lanyer. *Salve Deus Rex Judaeorum* (1611). Huntington Library RB 62139. Title page A1r, and "To the doubtfull Reader" I1v.

28 *Mortalities Memorandum.*

Those daily obiects man doth speculate,
Present vnto his thought, that he *must die*;
For all things in this world declare and shew,
That man is subiect to *Mortalitie*;
Those vegetiues, which bud and spring out most,
Doth *Hyems* kill, and cut away with frost.

1.Pet. 3:10.
The elements must be dissolu'd with heate,
The *Macrocosmus* it must passe away,
Luke 21:33.
And man the *Microcosmus* needs *must die*,
Both young and old *must* goe to *Golgotha*.
Faire buildings leuell with the ground must lye,
And strongest Cities come to nullitie.

Dan. 6:15.
The *Medes* and *Persians* did their lawes confirme
So strongly, that they could not altred bee,
And this appointment *all men once must die*,
Heb. 9:27.
Is as infallible, as their decree.
2.Sam. 14:14. We needs must die, to pay what God doth lend,
Life had beginning, and *must* haue an end.

From earth man came, to dust he *must* returne,
This is the descant of *Deaths* farall dittie,
All men are mortall, therefore *must* they die,
Heb. 13:14.
And *Paul* sayth, *Here is no abiding Cittie.*
Mans dayes consume like wax against the Sunne,
Iob 7:6.
And as a Weauers shittle swiftly runne.

That thing, which may bee, may be doubted off,
And as a thing vncertaine passe neglected;
But things that *must* be, greater heed require,
And of necessitie *must* bee expected.
Then thinke on *Death*, ere *Death*, for truth doth show,
That *Death must* come, but when we may not know.
The

Mortalities Memorandum. 29

The second motiue moouing thought of *Death*,
Is the impartialitie of it,
Respecting neither persons, age, or sexe,
By bribes sinister it doth none acquit;
Friends nor intreaties can no whit preuaile,
Where *Death* arrests it will admit no Bayle.

What is become of *Absolom* the faire?
Dauid the Victor, *Salomon* the wise?
Crœsus the worldly rich, *Draus* the wretch?
Sampson the strong, that was bereft of eyes?
From these, and more then these, with whetted knife,
Death hath cut off the siluer thread of life.

It is hereditarie vnto all,
Lazarus dead, *Diues* must also die,
Luke 16:20.
Passe from his downe-bed to his bed of dust,
And vntill doomes day in earths bowels lye.
Death scatters that, which life had carking got,
And casts on youthfull yeares old ages lot.

Like *Iehues* shaft it spares not *Iorams* heart,
2.King 9:24.
But makes Kings subiect to a weldesse power.
Dauid must yeeld to tread the beaten path,
2.King 2:5.
When *Death* with open mouth meanes to deuoure.
And hauing changed corps to dust, who then
Can well distinguish Kings from other men?

The greatest Monarch of earths Monarchie,
Whom God with worldly honours highly blest,
Deaths Besome from this life hath swept away,
Gen 5:5.
Their stories Epilogue is *Mortuus est*.
For *Death* to all men dissolution brings,
Yea, the *Catastrophe* it is of Kings.
E 2
Great

8.6: Rachel Speght, *Mortalities Memorandum, with a Dreame Prefixed* (1621). By permission of The British Library.

Rachel Speght, *Mortalities Memorandum, with a Dreame Prefixed, imaginarie in manner; reall in matter* (1621)

This poem of almost 800 lines is a lengthy meditation on the Christian topos of the vanity and transience of human life, weaving together scriptural and classical sources (probably from a personal commonplace book) to incite "oblivious persons . . . to premeditation of, and preparation against their last houre," according to Speght's professed aim in the dedication. After recalling her first published work as a heroic battle against "a full fed Beast," the misogynist Joseph Swetnam, Speght moves from the first-person narrative of the prefatory *Dreame* poem to a far more impersonal voice in *Mortalities Memorandum*. This new voice sheds the particularities of class and gender as it takes on Death, who, unlike Joseph Swetnam, devours all "Respecting neither persons, age, or sexe." Transcending gender allows the narrator to assume a virtually divine tone of authority, and her own cadences merge with those of Scripture: "*We needs must die.*" While here the first person plural appears to include all mortals, the implied readership of Speght's poem is actually the godly elect who alone need not fear death: "The godly onely comfort finde in *Death*, / They view the end, and not regard the way, / And with the eye of faith they see, that God / Intends more good to them, then earth can pay" (26). The Calvinist context for Speght's poem is essential to recovering its agenda.

Speght's direct appeal to Calvinist readers was a potentially dangerous gambit; the following year King James himself issued "Directions Concerning Preachers," in which all preaching about Calvinist doctrines such as "the deep points of predestination, election, reprobation" was forbidden, as was any discussion of "the power, prerogative, jurisdiction, authority, or duty of sovereign princes." This was in response to a political and religious crisis. Although James saw himself as a monarch of peace and religious toleration, many English Protestants were sharply critical of his failure to support his son-in-law Frederick's seizure of the throne of Bohemia for the Protestant cause. Thus many texts published in 1621 "concerned themselves with James's foreign policy, the crisis in Bohemia, and, by implication, the royal prerogative" (Salzman 32). While *Mortalities Memorandum* is not overtly political, it constantly alludes in an authoritative tone to the leveling power of Death and, with allusions to regicidal prophets such as Jehu, anointed by God to destroy King Joram, it hints daringly at the vulnerability of reprobate kings. Christopher Hill points out that, some thirty years later, "Milton used the fact that Jehu killed his rightful king at the bidding of a prophet to argue that 'it was not permissible and good to put a tyrant to death because God commanded it, but rather God commanded it because it was permissible and good'" (67). As Hill points out, "Men knew their Bible very well in the seventeenth century, and could convey messages through allusions to it which are lost on a godless age" (49).

It may be significant that the printer of *Mortalities Memorandum*, Edward Griffin, died the same year that it was printed; his business was taken over by his widow, Anne, who carried it on by herself for about two years (McKerrow 172). Apart from her gender, Anne Griffin was probably, like Speght, a Calvinist. In 1634, she reprinted Calvin's *Institution of Christian Religion,* and in 1637, she was reprimanded by Archbishop Laud for publishing Thomas Becon's *Displaying of the Popish Mass.* Anne Griffin may well have been interested in Rachel Speght both as a Calvinist and as a woman.

Christina Luckyj

Dalhousie University

Rachel Speght. *Mortalities Memorandum, with a Dreame Prefixed, imaginarie in manner; reall in matter* (1621). British Library 11626.d.70. Pages 28–29.

To the Angell Spirit of the most ex-
cellent, Sr. Phillip Sidney.

O the pure Spirit, to thee alone addrest
Is this ioynt worke, by double intrist thine,
Thine by his owne, and what is done of mine
Inspir'd by thee, thy secret powre imprest.
My Muse with thine, it selfe dar'd to combine
As mortall stuffe with that which is divine:
Let thy faire Beames giue lustre to the rest.

That Israels King may daygne his owne transform'd
In substance no, but superficiall tire:
And English guis'd in some sort may aspire
To better grace thee what the vulgar form'd.
His sacred Tones, age, after age admire
Nations grow great in pride, and pure desire
So to excell in holy rites perform'd.

O had that soule which honour brought to rest
To soone not leaft, and reaft the world of all.
What man could shew, which we perfection call,
This precious peece had sorted with the best.
But ah! wide festred wounds that neuer shall
Nor must be clos'd, vnto fresh bleeding fall,
Ah memory, what needs this new arrest.

Yet blessed griefe, that sweetnes can impart
Since thou art blest. Wrongly do I complaine,
What euer weighs my heauy thoughts sustaine
Deere feeles my soule for thee. I know my part

Nor be my weaknes to thy rites a staine
Rites to aright, life bloud would not refraine:
Assist me then, that life what thine did part.

Time may bring forth, what time hath yet supprest
In whom, thy losse hath layd to vtter wast
The wracke of time, vntimely all defac't,
Remayning as the tombe of life disceast:
VVhere, in my heart the highest roome thou hast,
There, truly there, thy earthly being is plac't
Triumph of death: in life how more then blest.

Behold, O that thou were now to behold,
This finisht long perfections part begun
The rest but peec'd, as leaft by thee vndone,
Pardon blest soule, presumption ouerbold:
If loue and zeale hath to this error run
Tis zealous loue, loue that hath neuer dum,
Nor can enough, though iustly here contrould.

But since it hath no other scope to go,
Nor other purpose but to honour thee,
That thine may shine, where all the graces be;
And that my thoughts, (like smallest streames that flow,
Pay to their sea, their tributary fee)
Do striue, yet haue no meanes to quit nor free,
That mighty debt of infinits I owe.

To thy great worth which time to times inroule
VVonder of men, sole borne, soule of thy kind
Compleat in all, but heauenly wast thy mind,
For wisdome, goodnes, sweetnes, fairest soule:
To good to wish, to faire for earth, refin'd
For Heauen, where all true glory rests confin'd.
And where but there no life without controule.

Nor

8.7: Mary (Sidney) Herbert, Countess of Pembroke, "To the Angell Spirit of the most excellent, Sir Phillip Sidney" (1623). Reproduced by permission of The Huntington Library, San Marino, California.

Mary (Sidney) Herbert, "To the Angell Spirit of the most excellent, Sir Phillip Sidney" (1623)

Mary Sidney's "To the Angell Spirit of the most excellent, Sir Phillip Sidney" was printed in Samuel Daniel's *The Whole Workes of Samuel Daniel Esquire in Poetrie* (1623) preceding Daniel's "A Letter written to a worthy Countesse." A more complete and possibly later variant of this poem is included in the "J" or Tixall manuscript, so called because it was once part of the Tixall library, originally formed in the early seventeenth century by Sir Walter Aston. In this manuscript, which has the date 1599 on the title page, "To the Angell Spirit" begins the completed translation of the *Psalms* and is placed immediately before a dedicatory poem to Queen Elizabeth.

This poem, which in the Tixall manuscript served as an introduction to Philip and Mary Sidney's metrical translation of the Psalms, is one of only four "original" works by the countess of Pembroke. Although Sidney primarily practiced the art of translation (an activity deemed suitable for virtuous women), here she establishes her poetic voice in an original work. Significantly, however, this poem is presented in the context of translation and thus demonstrates that for Sidney translation and originality were inextricably linked. For instance, while the Psalms may be considered "merely" translations, critics such as Margaret Hannay and Susanne Woods acknowledge both the originality of Sidney's poetics and the influence of her virtuosity on the development of English lyric poetry. At the same time, as an epitaph for her brother, "To the Angell Spirit" can be viewed, like translation, as a type of secondary creation that announces its dependence on a male origin and thus is appropriate as women's work. In her analysis of this poem, Beth Wynne Fisken argues that Sidney manipulates conventions of apology and humility that are socially acceptable for women in order to reveal and conceal her unprecedented ambitions and abilities as a poet independent of the brother whose praises she sings.

Like other translation prefaces, "To the Angell Spirit" addresses the practice of collaboration, but while a work such as the earl of Roscommon's "An Essay on Translated Verse" describes translation in terms of friendship and an implied competition between the translator and the original author, the process for Mary Sidney is far more complicated, involving the combined efforts of sister and brother to translate the word of David, who already served as a translator of the word of God. Within the first two stanzas Sidney details this elaborate interaction, alternating the possessive pronouns "thine" and mine" and suggesting the potential for rivalry involved in the creation of "this joynt worke." Although she expresses humility in contrasting her mortal verse to the divine writings of her brother, Mary highlights the daring nature of her enterprise when she claims ownership of her muse.

The second stanza of the printed copy of "To the Angell Spirit," unlike the manuscript version, draws attention to the Englishing of the Psalms and describes a translation competition between countries. Sidney's emphasis on the vernacular and the pride of nations hints at a patriotic spirit common to numerous English translations, and while a eulogistic preface to a sacred translation may seem a strange place to find nationalist sentiments, both of the Sidneys understood their work as an important contribution to an English aesthetic tradition. For Mary Sidney, her experiments with form, meter, and rhyme allow her to display her own skill as a poet and demonstrate the expressive capabilities of the English language.

DEBORAH UMAN
EASTERN CONNECTICUT STATE UNIVERSITY

Mary Sidney. "To the Angell Spirit of the Most excellent, Sir Philip Sidney." *The Whole Workes of Samuel Daniel Esquire in Poetrie* (1623). Huntington Library RB 60945.

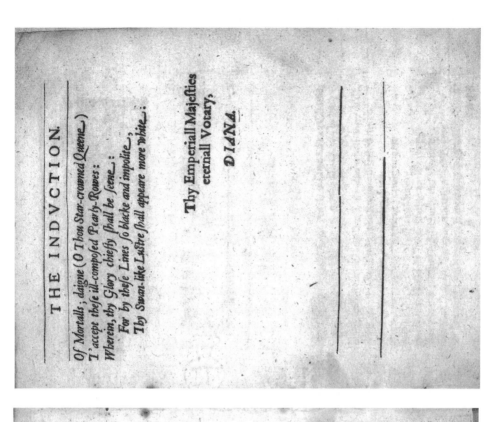

8.8: Diana Primrose, *A chaine of pearle* (1630). Reproduced by permission of The Huntington Library, San Marino, California.

Diana Primrose, *A chaine of pearle* (1630)

Diana Primrose's "The Induction" forms an introduction, both stylistically and thematically, to her poem *A chaine of pearle, Or A memoriall . . . of Queene Elizabeth* (London: Thomas Paine, 1630), sig. A3r-A4v.

The subject of Primrose's induction and her poem is Elizabeth I. She opens her induction with a comparison between Elizabeth and Phoebus, the sun god, often used to symbolize monarchs. Just as he is preeminent in the firmament, so is she in the world. The use of a male god emphasizes the queen's unusual position of power for a woman and appropriates his masculine strength and power for her. In addressing Elizabeth as a goddess who lives on in the hearts of her people, Primrose draws attention to the one element she and Elizabeth have in common—they are both women: Elizabeth is "Empresse of our Sex." The complex union of Elizabeth's masculine role and feminine nature, treated in the poem proper, is introduced here.

Because Elizabeth is beyond all compare, the poet faces a problem: "How shall I blazon thy most Royall parts?" As a woman, Primrose may feel her inability to do her subject justice even more sharply than a male poet. Although she admits that Elizabeth deserves "Apollo's Quill" to delineate her greatness, Primrose goes on to point out that even a humble worshipper can please the gods, and thus she is justified in praising this divine queen. Primrose's metaphor for her poem of praise, "Pearly-Rowes," uses Elizabeth's favorite gem, the pearl, with all its traditional associations of virginity and purity. Jewelery is closely connected to feminine beauty, the dressing of a mistress by her maid, and royal gifts, and is therefore very appropriate for a woman poet to use when offering her verses to a queen. The image is also strongly visual, as the queen was often portrayed with ropes of pearls around her neck and waist, and single pearls encrusted on her dresses. Primrose expands this image in the last lines of the induction with a clever play on the queen's favorite colors of black and white and the black ink and white paper of her verses. The black suggests the ill-favoredness of the verse in contrast with the white, lustrous beauty of its subject. Here Primrose renders the usual and somewhat tired modesty topos with subtlety and wit.

Throughout the induction, Primrose alludes to many of the mythic roles that Elizabeth played as queen. The word "blazon" conjures up the blazons of the sonneteers and Elizabeth's role as the desired lady of courtly love, a role she relished and used to great advantage politically. Elizabeth is also referred to as a star-crowned queen, a description that contains echoes of her role as a substitute for the Virgin Mary in Protestant English hearts. The closing salutation to the induction further emphasizes Elizabeth's incomparable and divine nature. Primrose calls herself an "eternall votary" (a nun vowed or devoted to the worship of a particular deity) of Elizabeth. The author's very name, with its reference to the goddess of chastity with whom Elizabeth was often associated, and to the primrose, one of the English flowers of the spring connected to Elizabeth as Flora or pastoral queen of shepherds, may, in fact, be a "nom de plume" devised to honor the queen. With this closing salutation, the reader is left with the image of Diana (the poet and, by implication, the Greek deity) pledging service to Elizabeth, a queen more glorious than a goddess and fully worthy of the praise of her ten virtues that follows in Primrose's *A chaine of pearle*.

Jane Farnsworth
University College of Cape Breton

Diana Primrose. *A chaine of pearle, Or A memorie of the peerles graces, and heroick vertues of Queen Elizabeth, of glorious memory. Composed by the noble lady, Diana Primrose* (1630). Huntington Library RB 16913. A3v-A4r.

They count not
of their reckoning at last day.
But time of Grace, once lost,
is without call,
So headlong to destruction,
they doe fall.

Pride, of all other
sembleth most the Divell:
'Twas Pride, threw Sathan
downe from Heaven to Hell:
'Twas Pride, that Author was
of all mans evill:
'Twas Pride, made Eve
desire still to excell;
When Sathan said,
as Gods, you then shall be;
Incontinent, she tasted
of that Tree.

This

This Lep'rous frame,
infecteth so the bloud,
That through her off-spring,
it hath wholly runne;
Before the child can know,
the bad from good;
Nature, this hurt hath done.
It straight is proud,
A female sinne,
it counted was to be,
But now Hermophrodite,
proved is shee.

Like Ivdas, Sathan
with each mortall deales,
His haile, is Hate,
his flattering kisse, is death,
Hee every where
still watching, creeping steales,

With

8.9: Alice Sutcliffe, "Of our losse by Adam," *Meditations of man's mortalitie* (1634). By permission of the Folger Shakespeare Library.

Alice Sutcliffe, "Of our losse by Adam," *Meditations of man's mortalitie* (1634)

In his commendatory poem prefacing Alice Sutcliffe's *Meditations of man's mortalitie, or, A way to true blessednesse,* Thomas May implores her readers not to "distaine to take that knowledge, Which a Womans skill can bring / All are not Syrens notes that women sing." Such knowledge, he suggests, is contained in what the table of contents describes as her "treatise," intended to instruct the reader, as the title of the volume suggests, toward "A way to true blessednesse," or eternal salvation. In instructing man on how to prepare for death, Sutcliffe's volume stems from the tradition of *ars moriandi* or "art of dying" literature. As Mary Catherine O'Connor has explained, while beginning in England as a Catholic tradition, such literature "crops out time and time again in a great body of Protestant writing" (195).

Sutcliffe begins both the six prose meditations and the accompanying long poem by illustrating humankind's inherent wickedness and the ephemerality of life before concentrating on the mercy of God for those who repent their sins and live righteously. In the prose mediations she caustically proclaims that "no dead carrion so lothsomly stinketh in the nostrils of an earthly man, as doth the wicked, abhominable unrepentant man in the presence of God" (17–18). Abounding in biblical imagery interspersed with exegetical deliberation, the meditations have a sermonlike quality characteristic of the Protestant tradition. As Barbara Lewalski explains, one of the characteristics that distinguishes Protestant discourses from Catholic tracts is "the near-identification of sermon and meditation in terms of methods and purpose" (83).

Sutcliffe opens the poem, "Of our losse by Adam," with the story of the Creation to illustrate how sin and death came into existence. The poem contains the longest development of a *compostio loci* in her book, in which she treats the Fall as though it were happening in the present, heightening the sense of immediacy in addressing the event. She employs the traditional view of Eve as the primary sinner and root cause of all humankind's woes, admonishing her as a "wicked woman to cause thy husband dye" (144). She refers to the oft-quoted line in Genesis that sublimates a wife to the power of her husband, commanding Eve that "Obedience to thy Husband yield thou must" (41). Sutcliffe argues that pride, traditionally regarded as the greatest of the seven deadly sins, was indeed the source of all evil and that it found its beginning in Eve. She claims, "Twas Pride, made Eve desire still to excell; / When Sathan said, as Gods, you then shall be; / Incontinent, she tasted of that Tree." Eve's "Lep'rous sinne" was thus passed on to all her offspring so that what was originally a "female sinne" became "Hermaphrodite" (160–61). As can be seen in the accompanying facsimile of the two stanzas on the sin of pride, each line of iambic pentameter in the poem was divided so that each stanza appeared in twelve lines, which results in the rhythm being somewhat disrupted. This was likely done because of the limited size of the duodecimo page.

Sutcliffe's traditional portrayal of Eve is similar to that found in Anna Trapnel's untitled book (Bod. 1. 42. Th., p. 211). Contrasting views may be found in the defenses of women, such as Rachel Speght's *A Mouzell for Melastomus* (1617) and Aemilia Lanyer's *Salve Deus Rex Judaeorum* (1611), 761–832. For a detailed listing of contrasting works, see Germaine Greer et al., *Kissing the Rod*, p. 92.

DARCY MAYNARD
MEMORIAL UNIVERSITY OF NEWFOUNDLAND

Alice Sutcliffe. *Meditations of man's mortalitie, or, A way to true blessednesse The second edition, enlarged* (1634). Folger Shakespeare Library STC 23447. Pages 160–61.

(103)

Wings my Doves you have now obtain'd
To flee to that Invincible Rock
Where you may hide you safe
In those Clifts of Security
From your Malignant Enemies,
Who may flee after you.
And think to graspe you,
And so to hurt you,
But they cannot.

But you may without any gaul tell them,
You are plac'd beyond their envies reach,
And with that blest Apostle may say
'Tis a small matter for me to be judg'd
By you, or of mans judgement
The Lord is Judge of all;
He judgeth me, and I
Am safe under
His powerfull Wings.

8.10: Anonymous, "Wings my Doves you have now obtain'd," *Eliza's Babes* (1652).
By permission of The British Library.

Anonymous, "Wings my Doves you have now obtain'd," *Eliza's Babes* (1652)

The printed text and watermarks of the two extant copies of *Eliza's Babes* (London: M.S. for Laurence Blaiklock, 1652)—University of Illinois Library, shelfmark, 821/EL48, and British Library, shelfmark, E 1289/1—are almost identical except for one major difference. Only the British Library copy retains the final page (103). This unique page is given over entirely to Eliza's remodeling of George Herbert's "Easter-wings" pattern poem from *The Temple* (1633), making Eliza one of the earliest female imitators of Herbert. Her poem "Questions and Answers" (55), also imitates Herbertian vocabulary and tone.

Throughout *Eliza's Babes* the author refers to her literary works not only as babes but also as doves. In "The Virgin's Offering" and "To my Doves" (5–6), she explains that her poems and meditations are like the two doves offered by the Virgin Mary when she presented Christ in the Temple (Luke 2:24). The referent is not always clear, and often the doves appear to represent Eliza's faith or her self in Christ. In "To my Doves" Eliza indicates that she initially intended to release her doves in print posthumously, but decided instead to release them as a thank offering while she yet lived.

The final poem, "Wings my Doves," concludes the issues of the text by asserting that Eliza has achieved her final, unassailable security in Christ. The Davidic desire for doves' wings to flee to refuge from his enemies (Psalm 55:6) is fulfilled by the security experienced by the sheltering dove of Canticles 2:14 and is overlain with the psalmist's idea of safety under the protective wings of God (Psalm 17:8; 36:7; 57:1; 91:4).

Eliza also boldly asserts in the second stanza, echoing Paul (1 Corinthians 4:3–4), that she is beyond the judgment of men and subject only to God. Both here and in the page from "The Royall Priest-hood" (as well as numerous other places in *Eliza's Babes*), Eliza authorizes her own practices and beliefs by citing Paul, while ignoring his stipulation that forbids women to speak in public congregations (1 Timothy 2:11–12). Anna Trapnel, likewise, repeatedly reads her own situations in terms of Pauline precedents in her *Report and Plea* (1654). In this poem Eliza ingeniously aligns herself with three male authority figures: Herbert, Paul, and God—all of unimpeachable orthodoxy.

It is of interest that Eliza refers to "Malignant Enemies" in line five. The word "malignant" was used during the 1640s by parliamentarian sympathizers as a term of reproach applied to "popish" royalists. Eliza's reformist position is affirmed by her choice of publisher, Laurence Blaiklock, who published a parliamentarian newssheet during the Civil Wars, and printer, Matthew Simmons, who was responsible for publication of Independent/Congregationalist, Particular Baptist, and Behmenist material. By the end of her book Eliza has achieved a threefold assurance of security: bodily safety during the Civil Wars; spiritual safety via the assurance of salvation in Christ; and a safety of identity whereby she debunks gender-biased critiques and affirms that women are "by election capable of as great a dignity as any mortall man" (100).

L. E. Semler
University of Sydney

Anonymous. "Wings my Doves you have now obtain'd," *Eliza's Babes* (1652).
British Library E 1289/1. Page 103.

(63)

A Song composed in time of the Civill Warr, when the wicked did much insult over the godly.

WIth *Sibells* I cannot Devine
Of future things to treat,
Nor with *Parnassus* Virgins neat
Compose in Poëms neat
Such mentall motions which are free
Conceptions of the mind,
Which notwithstanding will not be
To thoughts alone confind.

With *Deborah* t'were joy to sing
When that the Land hath Rest,
And when that Truth shall freshly spring,
Which seemeth now deceast,
But some may waiting for the same
Go on in expectacion
Till quick conceipt be out of frame,
Or till Lifes expiracion.

Therefore who can, and will not speak
Betimes in Truths defence,
Seeing her Foes their malice wreak,
And some with smooth pretence

And

(64)

And colours which although they glose
Yet being not ingraind,
In time they shall their luster lose
As cloth most foully staind.

See how the Foes of Truth devise
Her followers to defame,
First by Aspersions false and Lies
To kill them in good Name;
Yet here they will in no wise cease
But Sathan counse they take
To spoyl their Goods and Wealths increase,
And so at Life they make.

Such with the Devill further go
The Soule to circumvent
In that they seeds of Error sow
And to false Worships tempt,
And Scripture falsly they apply
Their Errors to maintain,
Opposing Truth implicitly
The greater side to gain.

And to bind Soul and Body both
To Sathans service sure
Therto they many ty by Oath,
Or cause them to endure
The Losse of lightsom Liberty
And suffer Confiscacion,
A multitude they force therby
To hazard their Salvation.

Another

8.11: An Collins, "A Song composed in time of the Civill Warr, when the wicked did much insult over the godly," *Divine Songs and Meditacions* (1653). Reproduced by permission of The Huntington Library, San Marino, California.

An Collins, "A Song composed in time of the Civill Warr, when the wicked did much insult over the godly," *Divine Songs and Meditacions* (1653)

Nothing more is known about An Collins other than what little autobiographical information her poems reveal in her only extant work, *Divine Songs and Meditacions*, printed in 1653 by Richard Bishop. Her name appears twice in the book: on the title page and at the end of the volume's preface, "To the Reader." Because "An" is an uncommon spelling, many readers have supposed it to signify "Ann" or "Anne," while others have proposed "Anthony" and even the generic "an," arguing that the author's identity could have been unknown to the printer.

An Collins's religious beliefs have been variously defined as anti-Puritanical, Calvinist, Catholic, anti-Calvinist, and Quaker; her politics have likewise been described in a number of ways: critical of sectaries and Independents, pro-Commonwealth, opposed to the radical wing of Parliament, anti-Commonwealth, and Royalist. There is agreement, however, upon at least one defining characteristic of *Divine Songs and Meditacions*: the central role of physical and spiritual affliction. In her poems An Collins intimates often that she endured chronic physical suffering, although she does not specify the cause or course of her illnesses. She also frequently expresses her spiritual anguish, which shapes her search for "free / Concepcions of the mind" (lines 5–6). Her poems record the transformation of bodily pain into internal peace and consolation; of her soul's distress into Truth [that] shall freshly spring" (line 11). *Divine Songs and Meditacions* thus constitutes a work of mourning through which Collins turns private losses into spiritual gain, revealing a sacred pattern for her secular life.

Collins fashions her own mourning as a model for her reader's spiritual conversion and social commitment to the ongoing work of Reformation. One poem in particular, "A Song composed in time of the Civill Warr, when the wicked did much insult over the godly," best exemplifies those motivations. This elegy (13 stanzas; 104 lines) has a three-part structure: an opening section in which Collins explores possible rhetorical contexts and poetic personae for the work's design and social critique (lines 1–24); second, a catalogue of the enemies of Reformation (lines 25–64); and last, an invocation of an impending apocalypse (lines 65–104). Published after the Civil Wars (1641–49), the poem responds to the continued political conflicts between Parliamentarians and Royalists, and opposes, in particular, the Engagement Oath of January 1650.

Throughout 1649 and 1650 propagandists for the parliamentary government encouraged the swearing of oaths of allegiance; such enforcement generated resistance, especially among Presbyterians and Church of England adherents. The Engagement Oath illustrates the culmination of this parliamentary movement, which has come to be called the "Engagement Controversy." In the elegy's sixth stanza, Collins levels a strong charge against that unpopular oath. Such pledges of allegiance were protested by many religious and political groups, including Levellers, Quakers, Independents, Millenarians, and both General and Particular Baptists. Opponents indeed faced "The Losse of lightsom Liberty" (line 45), as Collins asserts, by imprisonment and torture. Collins's apt use of the word "Confiscacion" (line 46) may refer to the Rump Parliament's segregation of Royalists' estates between 1649 and 1653.

Collins's poem appraises the corrupt politics of Parliament and the Council of State through a mournful renunciation of the "seeds of Error" (line 35) that yields an apocalyptic consolation: "Truth will spread and high appear, / As grain when weeds are gon, / Which may the Saints afflicted cheare / Oft thinking hereupon" (lines 97–100). She enumerates "the Foes of Truth" (line 25) in stanzas four through seven, then asserts paradoxically that some of those "Enimies / To Lady Verity" (line 49–50) will momentarily triumph: "Yet these are they, as some conceit, / Who must again reduce, / And all things set in order strait / Disjoynted by abuse" (line 57–60). In this and the majority of elegies in her volume, An Collins articulates both devotion and dissent, praise and protest through the conversion of physical and spiritual strife into redemptive knowledge.

W. SCOTT HOWARD
UNIVERSITY OF DENVER

An Collins. "A Song composed in time of the Civill Warr, when the wicked did much insult over the godly." *Divine Songs and Meditacions* (1653). Huntington Library RB 54047 (Wing C5355). Pages 63 and 64.

Lady Hester Pulter, "Then if your Husbands rant it high and Game" (1640–65)

Commentary

Lady Hester Pulter's verse is extant in the University of Leeds Library, Brotherton Collection MS Lt q 32, a bound manuscript in a scribal hand, with authorial alterations and additions in Pulter's autograph. Brotherton MS Lt q 32 contains two series of poems. The first comprises occasional and devotional lyrics, and the second is a series of 54 emblem poems. Pulter's poem series date between the early 1640s and about 1665; she was writing during these years in "royalist retirement" at her home of Broadfield, Hertfordshire, and her verse articulates her strongly royalist politics.

The poem on the facing page is the second half of her twentieth emblem, which opens with the image of the turtle dove. Pulter's emblem poems are unconventional in that they are not preceded by a picture or an epigrammatic verse; rather, Pulter presents the central image verbally in the first part of her verse and develops its significance in the second. The turtle dove in this emblem and other of Pulter's poems represents constant, devoted love; following the death of her mate, the turtle dove in this verse will "never Couple more." In the couplet immediately preceding the lines reproduced on the facing page, Pulter incites: "Then Ladyes immitate this Turtle Dove / And Constant bee unto one onely Love" (f. 103v).

Pulter goes on to contrast the turtle dove's chaste love to the dissolute morality of her times—the Protectorate of Oliver Cromwell. Pulter's verse as a whole associates the city and the Parliamentarian political center with unchastity, and here she advises women to keep away from social centers (Hyde Park, Mulberry Garden, and other spots), where countesses, duchesses and the Protector's daughter are to be found. Rather, the virtuous woman should follow Pulter's own example and her "Councell"; she should know these places by name only and dedicate herself to "writeing harmles Rimes."

Pulter's notion of female chastity is carefully nuanced. "Anchorites I would not have you turn / Nor Halcions, nor bee your Husbands Urn," she writes, indicating that the chaste and virtuous woman need not be entirely subservient to her husband. But religious writing is her most appropriate occupation: "spend your dayes / In setting Forth Your great Creators praise." God is "the fountain of all good" and is to be the focus of the virtuous woman's love but, in keeping with Pulter's other religious verses, the love of God is also the model for "subsolary" love, or the love of spouses, children, relatives, and others on earth—of those "atie'd by Mariage, Grace, and blood." Pulter returns at the conclusion of this poem to the image of the turtle dove: it is an emblem in this world of "Chast and vertuous love," and if one achieves a love of God and of one's human relations as pure as the turtle dove's, then death will bring no change in one's nature, but only a "chang [of] place."

Pulter's religious verses and her emblem series (which is essentially devotional) enact and uphold a chaste, female love of God against England's wider political context. Pulter's retreat into the writing of religious verse, and the retreat she advocates for other "Ladyes" in the twentieth emblem, is necessary because of, and defines itself against, the vice and iniquity of England after Charles I's fall. Brotherton MS Lt q 32 is addressed to royalists—and particularly female royalists—in the world at large. We have no evidence of the

Then if your Husbands rant it high and Game
Besure you double not their Guilt, and shame
Laws of Hide Park, Hanes, Luford Johns, and Kates
Spring, Mulbery Garden, let them have a Date
But not these follyes at soe dear a Rate
These Places I know onely by their names
But tis these places which doe blast your fames
Who would with their dear Reputation part
To eat a scurvey Cheescak or a Tart
For such poor follyes who abroad would Roame
Have wee not better every day at home
They say to plays and Taverns some doe goe
I say noe Modest Ladyes will doe soe
Though Countis, Dutchis, or Protectors Daughter,
Those Places haunt, their follyes Run not aftr
Bee Modest then and follow mine advice
You'l find that vertue's Pleasanter then vice
Yet Anchorites I would not have you turn
Nor Halcions, nor bee your Husbands Urn
But Chastly live and Rather spend yor dayes
In Setting fforth Your great Creators praise
And for diversion pass your Idle times
As I doe now in writing harmles Rimes
Then for your Honnours, and your fair Souls Sake
Both my example, and my Councell take,
In fine love God, the fountain of all good
Next those aded by Mariage, Grace, and blood,
Soe lets live here in Chast and vertuous love
As weele goe on Eternally above
Then o my God Assist mee with thy Grace
That when I die I may but chang my place.

8.12: Lady Hester Putler, "Then if your Husbands rant it high and Game" (1640-65).
Leeds University Library, Brotherton Collection.

manuscript's immediate circulation, but its topical concern and its explicit address to an audience illustrate that a mid-seventeenth century woman's religious verse in manuscript could engage conceptually and literally with its social and political contexts.

Transcription

Then if your Husbands rant it high and Game
Besure you Double not their Guilt and shame
Leave of Hide Park, Hanes, Oxford Johns, and Kates
Spring, Mulbery Garden, let them have a Date
Buy not these Follyes at soe dear A Rate
These Places I know onely by their names
But t'is these places which doe blast your Fames
Who would with their dear reputation part
To eat a scurvey Cheescak or A Tart
For such poor follyes who A broad would Roame
Have wee not better every day at home.
They say to plays and Taverns some doe goe
I say noe Modest Ladyes will doe soe
Though Countis, Dutchis, or Protectors Daughter,
Those Places haunt, their Follyes run not after
Bee Modest then and follow mine advice
You'l find that vertue's Pleasanter then vice
Yet Anchorites I would not have you turn
Nor Halcions, nor bee your Husbands Urn
But Chastly live and rather spend your dayes
In setting Forth Your great Creators praise
And for diversion pass your Idle times
As I doe now in writeing harmles Rimes
Then for your Honnours, and your fair souls sake,
Both my example, and my Councell take,
Infine love God, the fountain of all good
Next those atie'd by Mariage, Grace, and blood,
Toelets live here in Chast and vertuous love
As wee'le goe on Eternally above
Then o my God Assist mee with thy Grace
That when I die I may but chang my place.

Sarah Ross
Massey University

Lady Hester Pulter. "Then if your Husbands rant it high and Game" (1640–65). *Poems breathed forth by the nobel Hadassas, and The Unfortunate Florinda, by Lady Hester Pulter.* University of Leeds Library, Brotherton Collection MS Lt q 32. Fol. 104r.

(5)

With You to earth *Aſtræa* fair is come,
And Golden times in Iron ages room :
Much Honour hath both Church and State adorn'd,
Since You, our Faiths Defender, are return'd ;
For of the Church the Honour and Renown,
Are unto Kings the ſtrongeſt Towre and Crown :

Behold how *Thames* doth ſmooth her ſilver Waves!
How gladly ſhe, Your gilded Bark receives ;
Mark how the courteous Stream her Arms doth ſpread,
Proud to receive You to her watry Bed.
The old *Metropolis* by Tyrants torn,
Your preſence doth with beauteous youth adorn.
On You how doe the raviſh't people gaze ?
How do the thronging Troops all in a maze
Shout loud for joy, their King to entertain,
How do their Streets with Triumphs ring again.

GReat CHARLS, Terreſtrial God, Off-ſpring of Heaven,
You we adore, to us poor mortals given,
That You (*Our Life*) may quicken us again,
Who by our Royal MARTYRs death were ſlain ;
For we on earth as Corps inanimate lay,
Till You (*Our Breath*) repaired our decay :
Loe how old *Tellus* courts Your Sacred Feet,
Array'd with flowery Carpets peace to greet ;
As *Phœbus* when with glorious Lamp he views,
Earth after Winter, tender graſs renews ;
So through the world Your radiant Vertues Shine,
Enlightning all to bring forth Fruits Divine :
Or as the drops diſtil'd by *April* ſhowrs,
Produce from dryeſt earth impriſoned flowers ;

C   So

8.13: Rachel Jevon, *Exultationis carmen* (1660). Reproduced by permission of The Huntington Library, San Marino, California.

Rachel Jevon, *Exultationis carmen* (1660)

Rachel Jevon's name and life are witnesed by only four known documents: her Latin poem, published in 1660, congratulating Charles II on his restoration to the throne of England; her English version (also 1660) of the same congratulatory poem; a parish record of the baptism of Rachel Jevon in Broom, Worcestershire, 1627; and two (unpublished) petitions to the king in "May?" of 1662, one for "the place of one of the meanest servants about the Queen," and the other for "the place of Rocker to the Queen." The first petition gives bibliographical information that Rachel's father, "a loyal clergyman in the diocese of Worcester, though threatened and imprisoned, contrived to preserve his flock, so that not one took arms against His Majesty, but could only give his children education, without maintenance."

This petition features three qualities of the writer also developed in the congratulatory poems two years earlier: education, loyalty to the monarchy, and humility. The Latin and English "exultation" poems exhibit competency in Latin and extensive reference to classical mythology that are rare in a woman at the time. They gush loyalty to the monarchy and Charles. In the English poem, Jevon asserts that

> Though for my Sexes sake I should deny [to write],
> Yet Exultation makes the Verse, not I;
> And shouting cryes, *Live Ever* CHARLES, and *Be*
> *Most Dear unto thy people, They to Thee.* (ll. 9–12)

When Charles was being hunted in western England after the defeat of the Royalist army at Worcester, she among others (presumably her family and congregation), she explains, prayed unceasingly for his safety until he escaped overseas (ll.47–58). Jevon's writing exudes humility, from the preface, "The Unworthiest of His Majesties Hand-maids with all Humility offers this Congratulatory Poem," to these lines:

> Before Your Sacred Feet these Lines I lay,
> Humbly imploring, That with Gracious Ray,
> You'l daign these first unworthy Fruits to view,
> Of my dead Muse, which from her Urn You drew, (ll. 5–8)

to her reference to "my unlearned Quill" (1.24). The close fit between the poems and the petitions two years later led Elaine Hobby to conclude that the congratulatory poem (English) "was not the naïve outpouring [of joy] that it might at first appear." It seemed "a planned strategy of publicising her learning, loyalism and humility," in order to win a job (*Virtue of Necessity* 19).

The page reproduced here, the fifth of the seven pages to the poem (lines 107–36 of the 190 total lines), celebrates Charles' return to London. At the top of the page (ll. 107–8), the restoration of the monarch (Charles) is figured as a return of the goddess of justice, Astraea, in a new Golden Age. Lines 113–22 are a formal (indented) song of his triumphal welcome by the river, the city, and the people. In the lower half of the page, beginning with a large initial, the words "GReat CHARLS, Terrestrial God, Off-spring of Heaven, / You we adore, to us poor mortals given" (ll. 123–24) express Jevon's enthusiasm (in the classical sense of "filled with the god") for the king, as does "You (*Our Life*) may quicken us again" and "You (*Our Breath*) repaired our decay" (ll. 125, 128). The language is that used for God, the Creator and Spirit (= "breath"). Charles is compared to the spring sun, bringing forth new life, flowers, and fruit on the earth.

JOSEPH CROWLEY
AUBURN UNIVERSITY MONTGOMERY

Rachel Jevon. *Exultationis carmen: To the Kings most Excellent Majesty upon his most desired return and Carmen thriambeytikon Regiae Majestati Caroli II. Principum et Christianorum Optimi in Exoptatissimam ejus Restaurationem* (1660). Huntington Library RB 125990. Page 5.

Katherine (Fowler) Philips, Epitaph on her mother-in-law (1667)

Katherine Fowler Philips (1632–64) was widely known to her contemporaries as "the Matchless Orinda." "Orinda" was her self-chosen literary nom de plume, but the adjective "matchless" was meant to honor her incomparable poetic skill. The modifier, however, also suggests just how unusual her achievement was as a widely praised woman writer. Perhaps no other English female poet before her achieved greater respect from her peers, both male and female alike. For this reason alone, Philips's career marks an important turning point in the development of English literary history. Katherine Fowler was married to James Philips, a fifty-four-year-old Welshman, by the time she was sixteen. Although their relationship was apparently emotionally close, and although she bore him two children (including a boy who quickly died), Philips and her husband differed significantly not only in age but also in politics: she was a fervent Royalist, while he was a committed servant of Cromwell's republic. Her serious devotion to her writing, and his willingness both to tolerate and to encourage her literary ambitions, signal the kinds of changes in women's possibilities that Philips not only exemplified but inevitably helped promote.

Philips's own epitaph on the death of her mother-in-law, reprinted here, nicely implies the nature and extent of those changes. The poem depicts the standard trajectory of many a woman's life in seventeenth-century England. Philips describes (and celebrates) her mother-in-law's existence mainly as a series of committed, self-sacrificing relations with *others*: the mother-in-law is depicted first as the descendant of an "Honour'd Lin[e]age," then as the daughter of a respectable family, then as the young but (in a couplet missing from the present text) also "vertuous, prudent, humble Wife" of a husband to whom her early marriage was apparently arranged, then as a mother who experienced fifteen pregnancies during thirty-seven years of marriage, and then as an "honourable Widow" for another twenty-four years. Even after her husband's death, Mrs. Philips (whose first name and maiden name are never mentioned) is praised for a life spent in devotion to others, whether the "Crown, and Church," her friends or the poor, or the orphans whom she charitably fed. The main focus of her devotion, of course, was the patriarchal God who stood at the head of the vast hierarchy of complicated social obligations the poem describes. Katherine Philips extols her mother-in-law's life, and in some respects (her early arranged marriage, her loyalty to "Crown, and Church," her own commitment to Christian virtue) Philips obviously lived aspects of that life herself.

The poetess, however, also enjoyed, in many other ways, an existence quite unlike the one she praises. Katherine won fame primarily as a writer rather than as a wife; she gave mental birth to numerous poems, plays, and letters rather than undergoing fifteen physical pregnancies; and the relations for which she is often most remembered were not with her husband, children, wider families, or the deserving poor, but with the literary female friends who were members of her far-flung intellectual coterie. Katherine Philips' epitaph on "*Mrs.* Philips" thus praises the kind of feminine life that her own life had begun to help undermine or transform. In this and in other respects it is a work fraught with paradox.

For a good text of the poem, see *The Collected Works of Katherine Philips: The Matchless Orinda, Volume I: The Poems*, ed. Patrick Thomas (Stump Cross: Stump Cross Books, 1990), 198–99. The text printed here is from the 1667 edition of Philips' *Poems*—the first edition to include this particular poem. The final four lines of the poem do not appear in this photograph (since they are printed on the facing page), and the 1667 text also does

128   POEMS.

An Epitaph on my Honoured Mother-in-Law
Mrs. Phillips *of* Portheynon *in* Cardigan-ſhire,
who dyed Jan. 1. *Anno* 166⅔

READer ſtay, it is but juſt ;
    Thou doſt not tread on common duſt.
For underneath this ſtone does lye
One whoſe Name can never dye :
Who from an Honour'd Linage ſprung,
Was to another matched Young ;
Whoſe happineſs ſhe ever ſought ;
One bleſſing was, and many brought.
And to her ſpouſe her faith did prove
By fifteen pledges of their Love.
But when by Death of him depriv'd,
An honourable Widow liv'd
Full four and twenty years, wherein
Though ſhe had much afflicted been,
Saw many of her Children fall,
And publick Ruine threaten all.
Yet from above aſſiſted, ſhe
Both did and ſuffer'd worthily.
She to the Crown, and Church adher'd,
And in their Sorrows them rever'd,
With Piety which knew no ſtrife,
But was as ſober as her life.
A furniſh'd Table, open door,
That for her Friends, this for the Poor
She kept ; yet did her fortune find,
Too narrow for her nobler Mind ;
Which ſeeking objects ro relieve,
Did food to many Orphans give,
Who in her Life no want did know,
But all the Poor are Orphans now.
Yet hold, her Fame is much too ſafe,
To need a written Epitaph.

                                              Her

8.14: Katherine Philips, Epitaph on her mother-in-law (1667). Courtesy of the William Ready
Division of Archives and Research Collections, McMaster University Library, Hamilton, Ontario.

not include a couplet present in Thomas's text (which is based on manuscript MS 776 in the National Library of Wales). The 1667 text also differs in various small ways from the text Thomas prints and thus illustrates the significance of varied printed (and manuscript) versions of literary works.

ROBERT C. EVANS
AUBURN UNIVERSITY OF MONTGOMERY

Katherine Philips. "Epitaph on her mother-in-law" (1667). *Poems by the most deservedly admired Mrs. Katherine Philips, the matchless Orinda / to which is added, Monsieur Corneille's Pompey & Horace, tragedies. With several other translations out of French* (1667). Mills Memorial Library Research Collection, McMaster University D 1055. Page 128.

To the Excellent *Orinda*.

Et the male *Poets their male* Phœbus *chuſe*,
Thee I *invoke*, Orinda, *for my Muſe*;
He *could but force a Branch*, Daphne *her Tree*
Moſt freely offers to her Sex and thee,
And ſays to Verſe, ſo unconſtrain'd as yours,
Her Laurel freely comes, your fame ſecures:
And men no longer ſhall with raviſh'd Bays
Crown their forc'd Poems by as forc'd a praiſe.

    Thou glory of our Sex, envy of men,
Who are both pleas'd and vex'd with thy bright Pen:
Its luſtre doth intice their eyes to gaze,
But mens ſore eyes cannot endure its rayes;
It dazles and ſurprizes ſo with light,
To find a noon where they expected night:
A Woman Tranſlate Pompey! *which the fam'd*
Corneille *with ſuch art and labour fram'd*!
To whoſe ſcloſe *verſion the* Wits *club their ſence*,
And a new Lay poetick S M E C *ſprings thence*!
Yes, that bold work a Woman *dares* Tranſlate,
Not to provoke, nor yet to fear mens hate.
Nature doth find that ſhe hath err'd too long,
And now reſolves to recompence that wrong:
Phœbus *to* Cynthia *muſt his beams reſigne*,
The rule of Day and Wit's now Feminine.

    That Sex, which heretofore was not allow'd
To underſtand more than a beaſt, or crowd;
Of which Problems were made, whether or no
Women had Souls; *but to be damn'd, if ſo*;
Whoſe higheſt Contemplation could not paſs,
In mens eſteem, no higher than the Glaſs;
And all the painful labours of their Brain,
Was only how to Dreſs and Entertain:
Or, if they ventur'd to ſpeak ſenſe, the wiſe
Made that, and ſpeaking Oxe, like Prodigies.

                                                          From

8.15: Philo-Philippa, "To the Excellent Orinda" (1667). Courtesy of the William Ready Division of Archives & Research Collections, McMaster University Library, Hamilton, Ontario.

Philo-Philippa, "To the Excellent Orinda" (1667)

Katherine Philips (1632–64) was one of the most widely praised women of her time and is increasingly seen as an important figure in seventeenth-century English literature. Although she was born into a Puritan family and soon married a much older Parliamentarian, Philips herself was a Royalist, with many friends who shared her political views and literary inclinations. After the Restoration, her writings became even more widely appreciated, thanks partly to her friendship with Charles II's Master of Ceremonies, Sir Charles Cotterrell. In 1663 her translation of Corneille's play *Pompée* (see selection 7.9) was successfully performed, and she was undertaking a similar translation when she died in 1664. Her death unleashed even more praise from male authors, and several of these eulogies preface her 1667 *Poems*. Among the most interesting praises published there, however, is a long poem, apparently by a female, identified only as "Philo-Philippa." Philips herself had mentioned being commended by someone "who pretends to be a Woman, [and] writes very well," but the author's true identity remains obscure.

Philo-Philippa's eulogy, the opening lines of which are reproduced here, has been called "extraordinary, both in the violence of its conceits and the degree of radical feminism it expresses" (Greer et al.). It has also been dismissed, however, as a "poor" (if historically interesting) poem (Souers). Closer examination suggests that Philips was more accurate than Souers in assessing the work's poetic skill, and the poem also helps refute modern views of Philips as a "safe" writer whom men admired because she failed to threaten their cultural domination (Hilda L. Smith). Philo-Philippa, at least, seems to have disagreed.

The unknown writer displays many of the talents she praises in Philips, including education, wit, clarity, force, and structural sophistication. Note, for instance, how she juxtaposes "Thee" and "I" in line 2; or how she sustains the image of light throughout lines 9–14; or the clever alliteration of "noon" and "night" in line 14; or how often and effectively she uses balanced phrasing (as in lines 1 and 2, and in lines 6, 8, 9, 10, 14, 16, and 20). Such balance implies rational control and conscious art, as well as strength and self-assurance—qualities especially important for an angry (female) author to display in a highly emotional poem. She puns on the word "unconstrain'd" in line 5 (implying that Philips's verse is at once freely inspired, uncontrived, and unhampered in its subjects); she implicitly compares sexual and literary compulsion in lines 1–8 (see Greer et al.); and in the closing lines of the excerpt, she wittily shows how some men egotistically accuse women of egotism, thereby demonstrating the very vanity they associate with females. Like many works by women from this period (including those of Philips herself), this poem deserves much fuller appreciation as a piece of skillful writing.

ROBERT C. EVANS
AUBURN UNIVERSITY MONTGOMERY

Katherine Philips. "To the Excellent Orinda" (1667). *Poems by the most deservedly admired Mrs. Katherine Philips, the matchless Orinda / to which is added, Monsieur Corneille's Pompey & Horace, tragedies. With several other translations out of French* (1667). Mills Memorial Library Research Collection, McMaster University, D 1055.

236

The Author to her Book.

THou ill-form'd offspring of my feeble brain,
      Who after birth did'ft by my fide remain,
Till fnatcht from thence by friends, lefs wife then
Who thee abroad, expos'd to publick view, (true
Made thee in raggs, halting to th' prefs to trudg,
Where errors were not leffened (all may judg)
At thy return my blufhing was not fmall,
My rambling brat (in print) fhould mother call,
I caft thee by as one unfit for light,
Thy Vifage was fo irkfome in my fight ;
Yet being mine own, at length affection would
Thy blemifhes amend, if fo I could :
I wafh'd thy face, but more defects I faw,
And rubbing off a fpot, ftill made a flaw.
I ftretcht thy joynts to make thee even feet,
Yet ftill thou run'ft more hobling then is meet ;
In better drefs to trim thee was my mind,
But nought fave home-fpunCloth, i'th' houfe I find
In this array, 'mongft Vulgars mayft thou roam
In Criticks hands, beware thou doft not come ;
And take thy way where yet thou art not known,
If for thy Father askt, fay, thou hadft none :
And for thy Mother, fhe alas is poor,
Which caus'd her thus to fend thee out of door.

8.16: Anne Bradstreet, "The Author to her Book," *Several Poems* (1678).
Courtesy of Hamilton College Library.

Anne Bradstreet, "The Author to her Book," *Several Poems* (1678)

Several Poems presents the prefatory material and poems from *The Tenth Muse Lately Sprung Up in New England* (London, 1650) in the original order. "The Author to her Book" opens the section of new material, which includes personal poems and elegies on the deaths of grandchildren.

Anne Dudley was born in 1612 in Lincolnshire, England, into a family that highly valued literacy. Her father and her husband, Simon Bradstreet, served in the household of Bridget, Countess of Lincoln. Bridget is the woman to whom Elizabeth Clinton dedicates her work on breast-feeding, *The Countess of Lincolnes Nurserie* (1622). Bradstreet emigrated to Massachusetts Bay in 1630. Although *Several Poems* refers to its author as "A Gentlewoman of New England," Bradstreet participated in a wholly English literary world. She just happened to be, as Bathsua Makin remarks in her 1673 *Essay* on women's education, "now in America."

Bradstreet's original volume was published in London allegedly without her knowledge, as her brother-in-law John Woodbridge acknowledges in his prefatory epistle. But that admission itself reveals something about seventeenth-century literary culture. Woodbridge claims to have published it because "divers had gotten some scattered papers, affected them well, [and] were likely to have sent forth broken pieces." At this time, gentlepersons did not enter print until after their deaths, when friends might bring out a commemorative volume. During their lives, they circulated their writing in manuscript to select readers, called coterie circles, which could be quite large. "The Prologue" in *The Tenth Muse* suggests that Bradstreet envisioned her poems as a cohesive collection and that her literary activity was well known. She may not have intended her poems for publication, but they were circulating in manuscript, widely enough to get to "divers" persons, some of them in England.

"The Author to her Book" adopts the common topos of the book as offspring, adapted cleverly to the circumstances of her book's publication, to the crafts of writing and bookmaking, and to her sex. Bradstreet develops an image of herself "lying-in" with a new baby, who is "snatcht" from her side by misguided friends and "exposed" to public view. This "child" is brought to the press in "raggs," of which paper was made, with uneven "feet" (metrical units); all her motherly care fails to improve the "child's" appearance; she has only homespun in which to dress it. She sends the "child" forth again because she cannot provide for it at home. But for all its pose of modesty, this poem does assert Bradstreet's originality and authorship: "if for thy Father askt, say thou hadst none." This book is hers alone.

MARGARET THICKSTUN
HAMILTON COLLEGE

Anne Bradsteet. *Tenth Muse Lately Sprung Up in America. Several poems compiled with great variety of wit and learning, full of delight. . . .2nd ed., corrected by the author and enlarged by an addition* (Boston, 1678). Hamilton College Library PS 711 A1 1678. Page 236.

A POEM as it was PRESENTED
TO HIS
SACRED MAJESTY
On the Difcovery of the *PLOTT*,

Written by a Lady of Quality.

AILE Mighty Prince! whom Heaven has de-
To be the chief delight of human kind :   (fig'nd
So many Vertues croud your Breaft that we
Do alwaies queftion your Mortality :
    Sure all the Planets that o're Vertue raigns,
Shed their beft Influence in your *Royal* Veins :
You are the Glory of *Monarchial* Pow'rs,
In *Bounties* free as are defcending fhowr's ;
Fierce as a Tempeft when ingag'd in VVar,
In *Peace* more mild than tender Virgins are ;
In pitying *Mercy*, you not imitate
The Heavenly Pow'rs, but rather emulate.
None but your felf, your fuffrings could have born
With fo much *Greatnefs*, fuch Heroick fcorn,
When *Hated* Traytors do your *Life* purfue,
And all the *World* is fill'd with *Cares* for you ;
VVhen every *Loyal Heart* is funk with fear,
Your felf alone doth unconcern'd appear ;
Your *Soul* within, ftill keeps it's lawful ftate,
Contemns and dares the worft effects of *Fate,*
As the bright Majefty fhot from your Eye,
Aw'd your tame Fate, and rul'd your deftiny.
Though your *Undaunted foul* bare you thus high,
Your *follid Judgement* fees ther's danger nigh ;
Which with fuch care and Prudence you prevent
As if you fear'd not but t'would crofs th'event.

Your *Care* fo nobly looks, it doth Appear
Tis for your *Subjects*, not your *Self* you fear :
Heaven! make this Princes Life your neareft care,
That does fo many of your *Beft Vertues* fhare :
If *Monarchs* in their *Actions* copy you ,
This is the neareft *Piece* you ever drew :
Blaft every hand that dares to be fo bold,
An *Impious* VVeapon 'gainft his *Life* to hold :
Burft every *Heart* that dares but *Think* him ill ;
Their *Guilty* fouls with fo much *Terrout* fill ,
That of *themfelves* they may their Plott unfold ;
And *Live* no longer then the *Tale* is told.
Safe in your *Care*, all elfe will needlefs prove
Yet keep him *fafe* too in his *Subjects* Love.
Your Subjects *View* You with fuch *Loyal* Eyes
They know not how they may their *Treafure* prize.
Were *You* defencelefs, they would round you fall ,
And *Pile* their bodies to build up a wall.
VVere you diftre'ft , 'twould prove a gen'rous ftrife,
VVho firft fhould lofe his *Own*, to fave *Your* Life.
But fince kind *Heaven* thefe *Dangers* doth remove,
VVee'l find out other wayes t'exprefs our Love.

   Wee'l force the Traytors all, their fouls refign,
   To herd with him that taught them their defign.

             F I N I S.

Printed in the year 1679.

8.17: Ephelia, *A Poem . . . To His Sacred Majesty On the Discovery of the Plott* (1679).
Reproduced by permission of The Huntington Library, San Marino, California.

Ephelia, *A Poem as it was Presented To His Sacred Majesty, On the Discovery of the Popish Plott* **(1679)**

First published in a licensed, variant text in 1678, this single-sheet broadside poem is the work of "Ephelia," whom recent research has identified as possibly Mary Villiers, later Stuart, Duchess of Richmond & Lennox, a highly placed woman writer at the Restoration court. Her service as a Stuart courier-intelligencer during the Civil Wars is documented in the letters of Charles II. Her concealed authorship notwithstanding, Ephelia devised clever ways to inscribe her identity in her writings. Here, she imprints herself in the wood-cut device in the poem's incipit, in which we see a female figure, in her ducal coronet, hailing her poem's addressee, Charles II. A ducal image of Villiers with her coronet, signature hair-style, and jewelry is at Petworth House.

The emergency which precipitated this poem was the Popish Plot, a hoax which convulsed London and the Stuart monarchy. The Plot was orchestrated by the king's domestic and foreign enemies with a view to destabilize the Stuart administration. Its conduits, Titus Oates and Israel Tonge, convinced Parliament, the court, and most English citizens that English Catholics were conspiring to assassinate Charles II, put his Catholic brother on the throne, and recatholicize England. Twenty-four Catholic peers were executed. London writers, from Grub Street hacks to the poet-laureate, produced a flow of material—broadsheets, ballads, cartoons, newspapers—so profuse that Luttrell's Popish Plot catalogue (1680) saw several editions. Ephelia's contribution was privately printed and circulated to a select coterie. Notice the poem's incomplete imprint, dated but without publisher or place of publication. Strategically, she published her poem as a broadsheet (or broadside), a format that could be speedily produced and disseminated.

Generically, this is a declamatory poem of filial and political solidarity, addressed to a panicked monarch who fears the loss of his subjects' loyalty – and his own head. The opening section (ll. 1-28) is Tory propaganda, written in the style of royal panegyric. In elevated diction, the opening lines conflate Milton's heroic rhetoric with Dryden's cool legislative style; and characteristic of Ephelia's openings, this one is loud and energetic, calculated to rivet the attention of addressee and reader: "*HAILE* Mighty Prince!" The poet then justifies her claims by amplifying the king's style of governance and personal attributes. In the central section (ll. 29- 40), she introduces a spiritual digression, which moves the poem from secular to sacred. Turning to the divine prototype of all kings, the poet petitions paradise: "Heavens! Make this Princes Life your nearest care." This reflective moment is unique in the frenzied literature of 1678-9; it also discloses a special relationship between subject and king. But Ephelia then counterbalances this sentimental interval with strong, masculine lines, her diction harsh, her imagery violent: "Blast every hand, ….Burst every *Heart.*" In the concluding unit (ll. 41-50), she re-establishes the poem's opening ethos by reassuring her king of the fidelity he continues to inspire: "Were You defenceless, [your subjects] would round you fall, / And Pile their bodies to build a wall."

Written in allegiance by a Catholic court insider to a (crypto)-Catholic king, at a time when London Catholics feared for their lives, this poem is an achieved text of Stuart loyalty and an early model of women writers' civic duty to engage in state affairs.

Maureen E. Mulvihill
Princeton Research Forum

Ephelia. *A Poem as it was Presented to His Sacred Majesty on the Discovery of the Plott. Written by a Lady of Quality* (1679). Huntington Library RB 471489.

Young Jemmy:
OR,
The Princely Shepheard.

Being a most pleasant and delightful New Song.

In bless Arcadia where each Shepherd feeds, | For he with glances could enslave east he bears,
His numerous flocks, and tunes on tender reeds; | But fond Ambition made him to depart ;
His song of love, while the fair nimphs trip round, | The Fields to Court, led on by such as sought
The chief among st 'em was young Jemmy found : | To blast his Vertues, which much sorow brought.

To a pleasant New Play-house Tune. Or, In January last, Or, The Gowlin.

YOung Jemmy was a Lad,
of Royal Birth and Breeding :
With every Beauty clad,
and every Beauty exceeding.
A Face and shape so wondrous fine,
so charming every part :
That every Lass upon the Green,
for Jemmy had a heart.

But Jemmy's powerful Eyes
young Gods of Love are playing,
And on his face there lies
a thousand smiles betraying.

But Oh he dances with a grace,
none like him e're was seen :
Do God that ever fancied was,
had so become a man.

To Jemmy every Swain
obsiously doft his Bonnet :
And every Lass bid strait,
to gase him in her Sonnet :
The pride of all the Youths he was,
the glory of the Groves ;
The pleasure of each tender Lass,
and theam of all their Loves.

But My unlucky fate,
ah Curse upon Ambition:
The busie foes of State,
have ruin'd his condition :
For glittering hope he left his shade,
his glorious hours are gone ;
By flattering fools and Knaves betray'd,
poor Jemmy is undone.   (tray'd,

Then Jemmy none more kind,
and courteous had been ever :
Thinking the like to find,
but be as yet ne'er ne'er :
For the false Swains that lead him forth
to expectations high ;
Design'd but to Eclipse his worth,
have Jemmy to out-bye.

But Jemmy saw not this,
when in the Groves delighting :
Nor thought to tread amiss,
at such a fair inviting.
But Jemmy was mistaken there,
for he was led astray ;
Whilst each kind Swain and Nymph so
for Jemmy sigh'd all day.   (fair,

For Jemmy's, love the streams
ran hoarse as if with mourning :
The Birds forgat their Lemms
and Flowers to late adorning.
The pleasant Plains hung down their
as sweating part of his grief :   (heads,

And insisting he had longer staid,
but Jemmy'd no belief.

For Jemmy's strutting Rams,
with pouthful blood were flowing ;
Which made him raise his strains,
to his almost undoing.
Though each kind Stranger did pay
he would again return :
And tread still in the pleasant Way,
but Jemmy it did scorn.

For Jemmy in fierce Arms,
more then his Crook delighting :
Despis'd the Wood-Nymphs charms,
that were so much inviting.
And dreams of digging Trenches deep,
storming each For and Town ;
Ambition still disturb'd his sleep,
whilst Jemmy fought renown.

But Jemmy now may see,
that he was to to ruine,
By such as glad would be
of his utter undoing.
Yet that his Wandrings he'd retrieve,
the wishes of the Swains ;
And in Arcadia happy live,
where his great Father reigns.

FINIS.

Printed for P. Brooksby, at the Golden-ball
in West-smithfield.

8.18: Aphra Behn, "Young Jemmy" (1681). Bodleian Library, University of Oxford.

Aphra Behn, "Young Jemmy" (1681)

This illustrated blackletter ballad was hawked in the streets of London some time between April and October 1681. Like most ballads, it was anonymous; in this case, we can confidently attribute it to Aphra Behn, one of the most prominent playwrights of the Restoration and an ardent supporter of the Duke of York, the future James II. Four of the stanzas were shortly after published in Ephelia's *Female Poems on Several Occasions* (131–33; cf. this volume), in Playford's *Wit and Mirth* (98), and in Behn's own *Poems Upon Several Occasions*. Its ostensible theme is the declining fortunes of a pastoral charmer. A contemporary audience, however, would have recognized it as a clever piece of political propaganda. Designed to discredit the king's firstborn but illegitimate son, the duke of Monmouth, popularly known as Young Jemmy, and his Whig political allies, it was likely sponsored by Charles II's Tory administration.

Ballads were the sensationalist tabloids of the time, recounting stories of murder, betrayal, and love, of battles and coronations. Selling for a penny or less—the price of a beer—they were sung in the streets, in coffeehouses, and in company around the fire. Because they appealed directly to basic human interests, their potential audiences were much larger than that of closely reasoned political tracts. They represented an attractive tradition that allowed Behn to cast the complex political situation at the time into the appealing mold of a simple country life with transparent emotions and motivations.

"Young Jemmy" relates the story of a "Princely shepherd" who lives happily in a classical Arcadia. Like the real Young Jemmy, he is handsome, excellent at dancing, and adored by the "fair nymphs." His mien is as divine as any Greek god "that ever fancied was." When "expectations high" lure him from his idyllic rural pastimes, "the streams / ran hoarse, as if with mourning," as they did at the death of Orpheus, the mythical Greek poet and musician (cf. *Ovid's Metamorphoses*). It is his kind and courteous nature that exposes him to unscrupulous individuals; "By flattering Fools and Knaves betray'd," he is "led to ruin."

The archaic setting of the ballad world thinly veils the timeliness of the theme. In 1679, the aging Charles II fell ill, raising concerns about the succession. Since he had no legitimate children, his brother James, Duke of York, was next in line to the throne. A sizable majority in Parliament fretted that York, who had converted to Catholicism, would favor an absolutist form of government along the lines of Louis XIV's France and force the reintroduction of that ideological bogeyman, "Popery." Through a series of Parliamentary bills, the Whigs attempted to exclude the King's brother—inevitably dubbed Old Jemmy—from the royal line. Their leader, the Earl of Shaftesbury, proposed that the crown should instead pass to the Protestant duke of Monmouth, Young Jemmy. But the king refused; he responded by repeatedly dissolving Parliament, and in the spring of 1681, he moved decisively to crush the opposition (Clifton, 134–35). They could now be ridiculed as the "busie Fops of State"; their effort to make Monmouth king had ended in a humiliating defeat, as the ballad triumphantly observes.

The King's intransigence, however, radicalized the opposition. The venture that ended badly for Young Jemmy and the Whigs in 1681 led directly to the formulation of the principles behind the Bill of Rights (cf. Locke, *Two Treatises*) and not long after to the Revolution of 1688.

Francis F. Steen
University of California at Santa Barbara

Aphra Behn. "Young Jemmy" (1681). Bodleian Library Douce Ballads 2 Fol. 259 b.

(3)

The Devil's Strength weak Woman might deceive,
But *Adam* tempted only was by *Eve.*
Eve had the strongest Tempter, and least Charge ;
Man's knowing most, doth his Sin make most large.
But though Woman Man to Sin did lead ?
Yet since her Seed hath bruis'd the Serpent's Head :
Why should she be made a publick scorn,
Of whom the great Almighty God was born ?
Surely to speak one slighting Word, must be
A kind of murmuring Impiety :
But still their greatest haters do prove such
Who formerly have loved them too much :
And from the Proverb they are not exempt ;
Too much Familiarity has bred Contempt ;
For they associate themselves with none,
But such whose Virtues like their own, are gone ;
And with all those, and only those who be
Most boldly vers'd in their Debauchery :
And as in *Adam* all Mankind did die,
They make all base for ones Immodesty ;
Nay, make the Name a kind of Magick Spell,
As if 'twould censure married Men to Hell.

Woman, ye Powers ! the very Name's a Charm,
And will my Verse against all Criticks arm.
The *Muses* or *Apollo* doth inspire
Heroick Poets ; but your's is a Fire,
Pluto from Hell did send by *Incubus,*
Because we make their Hell less populous ;
Or else you ne'er had damn'd the Females thus :

But

8.19: Sarah Fyge (Egerton), *The female advocate* (1686). By permission of The British Library.

Sarah Fyge (Egerton), *The female advocate: or, An Answer to a late satryr against the pride, lust and inconstancy, & c. of woman* **(1686)**

Sarah Fyge Egerton's *The female advocate: or, An answer to a late satyr against the pride, lust and inconstancy of woman* (1686) is a remarkable poem, not only because of its force, passion, wit, and wisdom but also because Fyge was merely fourteen when she composed it. She replied to Robert Gould, her older opponent, with fierce self-confidence—but apparently without her father's knowledge or permission. He therefore eventually banished her to the country to live with relatives. This exile occurred, ironically, after she published a second edition (1687), often seen as an effort to soften her sometimes caustic tone. Its preface claims that she never intended her book to be printed in its original form. The first printing, she asserted, relied on an uncorrected, uninhibited manuscript, and she even suggested that the (presumably male) compositors had changed or inserted words where the manuscript was illegible. The result was a poem she considered both faulty as a work of art and occasionally too sharply satirical for public consumption. Her modifications tried to rectify such shortcomings, but the new preface should not be viewed (as it sometimes is) as a significant surrender, for it is not only longer than the first but often just as feisty. Thus Fyge emphasizes her commitment to artistic integrity, implying her clear intention to correct the aesthetic flaws found in (or introduced into) the original printing. She refuses to concede that critics have influenced her decision to revise, claiming that she had never intended to publish some passages included in the original version. She also indicates that her effort at moderation partly responds to Gould's own recent similar decision—a decision perhaps partly prompted by her effective counterattack.

Page three of the original (1686) edition of *The female advocate*, reproduced here, defends Eve against Gould's attacks. Various differences between this printing and the second (1687) edition help illustrate Fyge's revising process. Some corrections are minor; some are artistically important; while some affect the poem's larger tone and substance. A minor change occurs, for instance, in line 2, where "tempted only" becomes in 1687 "only tempted." Line five becomes clearer in punctuation, meaning, and meter by becoming "But tho' that Woman Man to Sin did lead." A similar change occurs two lines later with the addition of "thus" after "Why should she." The most interesting alteration, however, was Fyge's decision to drop the four lines immediately following the italicized "Proverb." Perhaps she (or her father) felt that an ad hominem attack on her opponent's alleged "Debauchery" went too far, especially coming from a fourteen-year-old young lady! All these alterations indicate the importance of knowing which edition of a text a reader (or scholar) is using.

Robert C. Evans
Auburn University Montgomery

Sarah Fyge Egerton. *The female advocate: or, An answer to a late satyr against the pride, lust and inconstancy, & c. of woman* (1686). British Library 840h.40a. Page 3.

8.20 Anne Killigrew, *Poems* (1686) Courtesy of the William Ready Division of Archives & Research Colelctions, McMaster University Library, Hamilton, Ontario.

Anne Killigrew, Frontispiece self-portrait, *Poems*, (1686)

Anne Killigrew (1660–85) is both well known and little studied. Much commentary on her was inspired by (and still often focuses on) the ode John Dryden wrote after her youthful death to preface her posthumous *Poems*. Dryden praises both her poetry and her painting—the "sister arts" in which she excelled while a maid of honor of the famously pious duchess of York. Killigrew's engraved self-portrait, which also prefaces the *Poems*, seems relevant to her writing in numerous ways. Both the poems and the painting indicate her self-confessed desire for fame; both imply a privileged education; both show a mastery of contemporary artistic conventions; both reflect an upper-class milieu; both indicate an interest in intellectual accomplishment rather than in mere aristocratic frivolity; both convey qualities of reason, restraint, modesty, and controlled emotion; both illustrate a growing interest in women as distinct personalities; and both display a woman praised by contemporaries as much for physical beauty and moral character as for strictly artistic talents. The woman who painted this sober, somber portrait of herself (well dressed and well coifed but displaying neither ostentatious jewelry nor obvious cleavage) also wrote poems on such themes as worldly vanity; male infidelity; male heroism; feminine virginity and faithfulness; the omnipresence of pain, death, grief, and woe; the opposition of reason and sensuality; the temptations of lust and the ideal of true love; the shallowness of many youth; and the ideal of a well-governed mind and body. Both the poems and the painting reflected credit on her prominent family (particularly her father, who arranged for their publication and requested Dryden's ode); both reflected her family's literary and artistic inclinations (her uncles William and Thomas wrote plays, and Thomas also staged dramas and operas in his own theater); and both show how the status of women had begun to change since the days of Killigrew's mother (of whom almost nothing is known). As an author, Killigrew consciously modeled herself on her great contemporary, Katherine Philips ("the matchless Orinda"), whose writings similarly extol Christian piety, rational conduct, and stoic self-restraint. Killigrew admired Philips for having been praised mostly for talent rather than beauty, but the works of neither have yet received much sustained attention as skillful *writing*—as works of art. Instead, both women still tend to be studied as representative personalities, although today they tend to be hailed as forerunners of feminism rather than as exemplars of beauty and virtue. Both women died young; both succumbed to smallpox; but both lived long enough to display genuine skills—skills that suggested enormous potential and that merit serious, attentive study.

Robert C. Evans
Auburn University Montgomery

Anne Killigrew. *Poems* (1686). Mills Memorial Library Research Collection, McMaster University C 2954. Frontispiece self-portrait.

Bibliography

Allibone, S. Austin. *A Critical Dictionary of English Literature and British and American Authors*. Philadelphia: J. B. Lippincott Co., 1899.

Aughterson, Kate, ed. *Renaissance Woman: Constructions of Femininity in England: A Sourcebook*. London: Routledge, 1995.

Barash, Carol. *English Women's Poetry, 1649–1714: Politics, Community, and Linguistic Authority*. Oxford: Oxford University Press, 1996.

Bath, Michael. *Speaking Pictures: English Emblem Books and Renaissance Culture*. London: Longman, 1994.

Behn, Aphra. *The Collected Works of Aphra Behn*. Ed. Janet Todd. 10 vols. Columbus: Ohio State University Press, 1993.

Beilin, Elaine V. *Redeeming Eve: Women Writers of the English Renaissance*. Princeton, N.J.: Princeton University Press, 1987.

———. "Writing Public Poetry: Humanism and the Woman Writer." *Modern Language Quarterly* 51 (1990): 249–71.

———. "'Some freely spake their minde': Resistance in Anne Dowriche's *French Historie*." *Women's Writings and the Reproduction of Culture in Tudor and Stuart Britain*. Ed. Mary Burke et al., Syracuse, N.Y.: Syracuse University Press, 1998. 119–40.

Bell, Maureen, George Parfitt, and Simon Shepherd. *A Biographical Dictionary of English Women Writers 1580–1720*. Boston: G. K. Hall, 1990.

Berry, Boyd M. "*Divine Songs and Meditations* (book review)." *Journal of English and Germanic Philology* 98.2 (1999): 260–4.

Blain, Virginia, Patricia Clements and Isobel Grundy. *The Feminist Companion to Literature in English*. New Haven, Conn.: Yale University Press, 1990.

Bose, Mishtooni. "Divine Songs and Meditations." *Review of English Studies* 49.196 (1998): 513–14.

Bradner, Leicester, ed. *The Poems of Queen Elizabeth I*. Providence, R.I.: Brown University Press, 1964.

Clifton, Robin. *The Last Popular Rebellion*. New York: St. Martin's Press, 1984.

Collins, An. *Divine Songs and Meditacions*. Ed. Stanley Stewart. Los Angeles: William Andrews Clark Memorial Library, 1961.

———. *Divine Songs and Meditacions*. Ed. Sidney Gottlieb. Tempe, Ariz.: Medieval & Renaissance Texts & Studies, 1996.

Davidson, Peter. "Green Thoughts. Marvell's Gardens: Clues to Two Curious Puzzles." *Times Literary Supplement* 5044 (December 3, 1999): 14–15.

——— and Jane Stevenson, eds. *Early Modern Women Poets (1520–1700): An Anthology*. Oxford: Oxford University Press, 2001.

Dyce, Alexander Rev. *Specimens of British Poetesses*. London: T. Rodd, 1825.

Ezell, Margaret. *Writing Women's Literary History*. Baltimore: Johns Hopkins University Press, 1993.

Felch, Susan M., ed. *The Collected Works of Anne Vaughan Lock*. Tempe, Ariz.: Medieval & Renaissance Texts & Studies, 1999.

Fisken, Beth Wynne. "'To the Angell spirit . . .' Mary Sidney's Entry into the World of Words." *The Renaissance Englishwoman in Print: Counterbalancing the Canon*. Ed. Anne M. Haselkorn and Betty Travitsky. Amherst: University of Massachusetts Press, 1990. 263–75.

Gim, Lisa. "'Faire Eliza's Chaine': Two Female Writers' Literary Links to Queen Elizabeth I." *Maids and Mistresses, Cousins and Queens: Women's Alliances in Early Modern England*. Ed. Susan Frye and Karen Robertson. New York: Oxford University Press, 1999. 183–98.

Gottlieb, Sidney. "An Collins and the Experience of Defeat." *Representing Women in Renaissance England*. Ed. Claude J. Summers and Ted-Larry Pebworth. Columbia: University of Missouri Press, 1997. 216–26.

Graham, Elspeth, Hilary Hinds, Elaine Hobby, and Helen Wilcox, eds. *Her Own Life: Autobiographical Writings by Seventeenth-Century Englishwomen*. London: Routledge, 1989.

Greene, Roland. "Anne Lock's *Meditation*: Invention Versus Dilation and the Founding of Puritan Poetics." *Form and Reform in Renaissance England: Essays in Honor of Barbara Kiefer Lewalski*. Ed. Amy Boesky and Mary Thomas Crane. Newark, N.J.: University of Delaware Press, 2000. 153–70.

Greer, Germaine, Susan Hastings, Jeslyn Medoff and Melinda Sansone, eds. *Kissing the Rod: An Anthology of Seventeenth-Century Women's Verse*. New York: Farrar, Straus and Giroux, 1988.

Griffith, A. F. *Bibliotheca Anglo-Poetica*. London: Thomas Davison, 1815.

Grossman, Michael, ed. *Aemilia Lanyer: Gender, Genre and the Canon*. Lexington: University Press of Kentucky, 1998.

Hannay, Margaret P., ed. *Silent But for the Word: Tudor Women as Patrons, Translators, and Writers of Religious Works*. Kent, Ohio: Kent State University Press, 1981.

———. "'This Moses and This Miriam': The Countess of Pembroke's Role in the Legend of Sir Philip Sidney." *Sir Philip Sidney's Achievements*. Ed. M.J.B. Allen, Dominic Boher-Smith, Arthur F. Kinney, and Margaret M. Sullivan. New York: AMS Press, 1990. 217–26.

———. "'Wisdome the wordes': Psalm Translation and Elizabethan Women's Spirituality." *Religion and Literature* 23.3 (Autumn 1991): 65–82.

———. "'Strengthning the walles of . . .Ierusalem': Anne Vaughan Lok's Dedication to the Countess of Warwick." *ANQ* 5.2–3 (April-June 1992): 71–75.

_____, Noel J. Kinnamon, and Michael G. Brennan, eds. *The Collected Works of Mary Sidney Herbert Countess of Pembroke*. 2 vols. Oxford: Clarendon Press, 1998.

Hazlitt, W. Carew. *Hand-Book to the Popular, Poetical, and Dramatic Literature of Great Britain*. London: John Russell Smith, 1867.

Hensley, Jeannine, ed. *The Works of Anne Bradstreet*. Cambridge, Mass.: Belknap Press of Harvard University, 1967.

Hill, Christopher. *The English Bible and the Seventeenth-Century Revolution*. Harmondsworth: Penguin, 1994.

Hind, Arthur M. *An Introduction to a History of the Woodcut*. 2 vols. London, 1935; rpt. New York: Dover, 1963.

Hobby, Elaine. *Virtue of Necessity: English Women's Writing 1649–88*. London: Virago, 1988.

_____. "'Discourse so unsavoury': Women's published writings of the 1650s." *Women, Writing, History*. Ed. Isobel Grundy and Susan Wiseman. Athens: University of Georgia Press, 1992. 16–32.

Howard, W. Scott. "Fantastic Surmise: Seventeenth-Century English Elegies, Elegiac Modes, and the Historical Imagination from Donne to Philips." Ph.D. Diss. University of Washington, 1998. UMT 9836188.

_____. "An Collins and the Politics of Mourning." *Speaking Grief in English Literary Culture, Shakespeare to Marvell*. Ed. David Kent and Margo Swiss. Pittsburgh: Duquesne University Press, 2002. 177–96.

Hughey, Ruth. "Forgotten Verses by Ben Jonson, George Wither, and Others, to Alice Sutcliffe." *Review of English Studies* 10 (1934): 156–64.

Kenyon, John. *The Popish Plot*. London: Heinemann, 1972.

Keohane, Catherine. "'That Blindest Weaknesse Be Not Over-Bold': Aemilia Lanyer's Radical Unfolding of the Passion." *English Literary History* 64 (1997): 359–90.

Lewalski, Barbara. *Donne's "Anniversaries" and the Poetry of Praise: The Creation of a Symbolic Mode*. Princeton: Princeton University Press, 1973.

Locke, John. *Two Treatises of Government*. [1690, *ESTC* R2930]. Ed. Peter Laslett. New York: Cambridge University Press, 1988.

Lowndes, William Thomas. *The Bibliographer's Manual of English Literature*. Rev. ed. London: Henry G. Bohn, 1862.

Martin, Randall. "Anne Dowriche's *The French History*, Christopher Marlowe, and Representations of Machiavellian Agency." *Studies in English Literature* 39.1 (Winter 1999): 69–87.

May, Steven W. *The Elizabethan Courtier Poets: The Poems and Their Contexts*. Columbia: University of Missouri Press, 1991.

McDowell, Paula. *Women of Grub Street: Press, Politics, and Gender in the London Literary Marketplace, 1678–1730*. Cambridge: Cambridge University Press, 1998.

McKerrow, R. B. *Printers' and Publishers' Devices in England and Scotland 1485–1640*. London: Bibliographical Society, 1913.

Morin-Parsons, Kel, ed. *"A Meditation of a Penitent Sinner" : Anne Locke's Sonnet Sequence with Locke's Epistle*. Waterloo, Ontario: North Waterloo Academic Press, 1997.

_____. "'Thus Crave I Mercy': The Preface of Anne Locke." *Other Voices, Other Views: Expanding the Canon in English Renaissance Studies*. Ed. Helen Ostovich, Mary V. Silcox, and Graham Roebuck. Newark, N.J.: University of Delaware Press, 1999. 271–89.

Morton, Richard, intro. *Poems (1686) by Anne Killigrew*. Gainesville, Fla.: Scholars' Facsimiles & Reprints, 1967.

Mulvihill, Maureen E. "Thumbprints of Ephelia: The End of an Enigma in Restoration Attribution, with a first annotated Key to *Female Poems by Ephelia* (1679). Text, Image, Sound." *(Re)Soundings* 3.1 (2000) *http://www.millersville.edu/~resound/ephelia/*.

_____, ed. *Ephelia*. Burlington, Vt.: Ashgate, 2003.

Norcliffe, Mary Eleanor. "An Collins: Mistress of Religious Verse." Ph. D. diss., University of Massachusetts, 1998.

O'Connor, Mary Catherine. *The Art of Dying: The Development of the Ars Moriendi*. New York: Columbia University Press, 1942.

Ottenhoff, John. "Mediating Anne Locke's Meditation Sonnets." *Other Voices, Other Views: Expanding the Canon in English Renaissance Studies*. Ed. Helen Ostovich, Mary V. Silcox, and Graham Roebuck. Newark, N.J.: University of Delaware Press, 1999. 290–310.

Person, James E., Jr., ed. *Literature Criticism from 1400 to 1800*. Vol. 12. Detroit: Gale, 1986.

Rathmell. J. C. A., ed. *The Psalms of Sir Philip Sidney and the Countess of Pembroke*. New York: New York University Press, 1963.

Robson, Mark. "Swansongs: Reading Voice in the Poetry of Lady Hester Pulter. *English Manuscript Studies* 9 (2000): 238–56.

_____. *Lady Hester Pulter, Poems Breathed Forth by the Noble Hadassas*. Leeds Texts and Monographs, forthcoming.

Rowton, Frederic. *The Female Poets of Great Britain*. Philadelphia: Henry Carey Baird, 1854.

Salzman, Paul. *Literary Culture in Jacobean England: Reading 1621*. Houndmills, Basingstoke: Palgrave Macmillan, 2002.

Scheick, William J. *Authority and Female Authorship in Colonial America*. Lexington: University Press of Kentucky, 1998.

Schlueter, Paul, and June Schlueter; eds. *An Encyclopedia of British Women Writers*. 2d ed., enl. New Brunswich, N.J.: Rutgers University Press, 1998.

Schweitzer, Ivy. *The Work of Self-Representation: Lyric Poetry in Colonial New England*. Chapel Hill: University of North Carolina Press, 1991.

Semler, L. E. "Who is the Mother of *Eliza's Babes* (1652)? 'Eliza,' George Wither and Elizabeth Emerson." *Journal of English and Germanic Philology* 99.4 (2000): 513–36.

———. *Eliza's Babes or The Virgin's Offering (1652): A Critical Edition.* Madison, N.J.: Fairleigh Dickinson University Press, 2001.

———. "The Creed of *Eliza's Babes* (1652): Nakedness, Adam and Divinity." *Albion* 33 (2001): 185–217.

Shattock, Joanne. *The Oxford Guide to British Women Writers.* London: Oxford University Press, 1993.

Sider, Sandra, and Barbara Obrist, eds. *Bibliography of Emblematic Manuscripts.* Montreal & Kingston: McGill-Queen's University Press, 1997.

Skwire, Sarah E. "Women, Writers, Sufferers: Anne Conway and An Collins." *Literature and Medicine* 18.1 (1999): 1–23.

Smith, Hilda L. *Reason's Disciples: Seventeenth-Century English Feminists.* Urbana: University of Illinois Press, 1982.

Smith, Rosalind. "'In a mirrour clere': Protestantism and Politics in Anne Lok's *Misere mei Deus.*" *This Double Voice: Gendered Writing in Early Modern England.* Ed. Danielle Clarke and Elizabeth Clarke. New York: St. Martin's Press, 2000. 41–60.

Souers, Philip Webster. *The Matchless Orinda.* Cambridge, Mass.: Harvard University Press, 1931.

Stewart, Stanley N. *The Enclosed Garden.* Madison: University of Wisconsin Press, 1966.

Sutcliffe, Alice. *Meditations of Man's Mortalities or, A Way to True Blessedness.* 2d ed. London: Alsop and Fawcett, 1634. Facsim ed. *The Early Modern Englishwoman: A Facsimile Library of Essential Works, Part 1: Printed Writings, 1500–1640.* Gen. ed. Betty S. Travitsky and Patrick Cullen, Vol. 7. Aldershot: Scholar, 1996.

Travitsky, Betty. *Paradise of Women: Writings by Englishwomen of the Renaissance.* Westport, Conn.: Greenwood Press, 1981.

Wilcox, Helen. "'Is This the End of This New Glorious World?': *Paradise Lost* and the Beginning of the End." *The Endings of Epochs.* Ed. Laurel Brake. Cambridge: D. S. Brewer, 1995. 1–15.

———. "Entering The Temple: Women, Reading, and Devotion in Seventeenth-Century England." *Religion, Literature, and Politics in Post-Reformation England, 1540–1688.* Ed. Donna B. Hamilton and Richard Strier. Cambridge: Cambridge University Press, 1996. 187–207.

———. "'My Soule in Silence'?: Devotional Representations of Renaissance Englishwomen." *Representing Women in Renaissance England.* Ed. Claude J. Summers and Ted-Larry Pebworth. Columbia: University of Missouri Press, 1997. 9–23.

Williams, I. A. "Bibliographical Notes & News." *London Mercury* 9 (November 1923–April 1924): 528–32.

Wilson, Katharina M., ed. *Women Writers of the Renaissance and Reformation.* Athens: University of Georgia Press, 1987.

Woods, Susanne. "Introduction" and "Textual Introduction." *The Poems of Aemilia Lanyer: Salve Deus Rex Judaeorum.* Ed. Suzanne Woods. New York: Oxford University Press, 1993. xv–li.

Zim, Rivkah. *English Metrical Psalms: Poetry as Praise and Prayer, 1535–1601.* Cambridge: Cambridge University Press, 1987.

Zwicker, Steven N., and Kevin Sharpe, eds. *Politics and Discourse: The Literature and History of Seventeenth-century England.* Berkeley: University of California Press, 1987.

CHAPTER 9

Plays

The early modern period was the golden age of drama in England as the plays of William Shakespeare, Christopher Marlowe, Ben Jonson, Thomas Dekker, Thomas Kyd, John Webster, Richard Brome, Thomas Heywood, and Thomas Middleton were produced for the stage and increasingly for the marketplace. As authorship more often than not was collaborative, many productions of the period represent combined achievements. (Contemporary scholarship in contrast tends to privilege the role and "inspiration" of individual authors, while characterizing collaborations as second-rate.) Dramatic genres of the early modern period included tragedies, comedies, tragicomedy, masques, speaking pageants, and processions. Located in the less reputable parts of the city, the Globe, Fortune, Curtain, and Red Bull theaters attracted audiences from all levels of society. Private performances were also popular, and those reserved largely for the gentry and the well-to-do were staged in family estates in the country, in universities, as well as at the Inns of Court, guildhalls, at Blackfriars, the royal court, and in other private theaters. A Puritan ban on stage plays closed the theaters in 1642; but drama, rather than dying, went underground and found expression in private performances, closet dramas, political dialogues, and in a host of other genres in which the dramatic form had been realigned, as demonstrated by Lois Potter, Dale Randall, Nigel Smith, and Susan Wiseman.[1] New editions of old plays also appeared, many of which would eventually be performed on the Restoration stage.

Following the reopening of the theaters in 1660, playwrights John Dryden, William Davenant, Roger Boyle, Robert Howard, George Etherege, William Congreve, and Aphra Behn struggled to meet the demands of playgoers hungry for entertainment. According to front and end matter in printed plays, Restoration theater audiences were comprised of royalty, the upper class, gallants, citizens, and prostitutes. In actuality, however, theater-goers represented a range of ancestral, commercial, and professional interests.[2] On the stage, heroic drama, popular in the 1660s, was intended to celebrate the values of a restored Augustan culture and politics, which, however, never materialized. In the 1670s, Restoration comedies shared the stage with heroic drama, which eventually found a more comfortable niche in opera. By the end of the century, satires on London life anticipated the early-eighteenth-century dramatist's concern for moral rectitude.

This account of stage history, does not, however, come full circle, particularly if we consider the changing roles of women in the theater and even behind the scenes between the 1590s and the close of the seventeenth century. Traditionally the contributions of early modern women to the stage have been undervalued in literary and dramatic criticism. In 1929 Virgina Woolf sought to address this oversight by casting Judith Shakespeare, William Shakespeare's sister, into a fictive role as a playwright, and presenting her with a salary and a room of her own where she could write.[3] While Woolf was mistaken in assuming that the Restoration dramatist, Aphra Behn, had no actual female precursor, she rightly recognized both the obstacles faced by early modern women playwrights and their omission from studies of the theater and from the English canon itself.

In an era when women's writing and women's public voices were frequently discredited, the production of play texts and their performances on the public stage was nothing less than scandalous. Though women did not make their entry into the professional theater until 1660, several did nevertheless manage to create rooms of their own for and by writing plays or through alternative performances.[4] Still, it is hardly surprising that the work of the earliest English women dramatists, including Elizabeth Cary, Mary Wroth, and Elizabeth Brackley and Jane Cavendish, first of all exhibits the dramatist's self-consciousness, and, second, that the issue of their plays' performability and performance history remains to this day a subject of critical debate. At the same time, the genre, the audience, or the readership for which the plays were intended and the conditions under which they were produced and then circulated differed considerably among these playwrights. Doing justice to the plays and the writers who composed them involves an examination of the circumstances in which each text was written, as well as of the significance of the plays in their manuscript or printed versions—that is, their status as texts rather than as performances alone. Moreover, while the roles of the female characters in each play are certainly noteworthy in the context of this book, equally so are the self-representations of the playwrights who develop personas, sometimes multiple or multifaceted ones, for themselves behind the scenes. The self-reflexive and meta-dramatic commentaries are typically found in the front and end matter of playtexts, and are directed at readers rather than audiences. The identity of the persona projected could be as elusive and complex as that of any of the characters and should not be reduced to a mirror image of the playwright herself. Alexandra G. Bennett recently observed, for example, that while Elizabeth Cary's marital struggles and unpopular religious convictions are frequently used as a gloss for interpreting *The Tragedie of Mariam*, the play is "not simply a tale of one woman's unshakable integrity in the face of oppression, but instead an exploration of duplicity, multiplicity, and their implications for women."[5]

The Tragedie of Mariam was the first original drama published by an Englishwoman. Elizabeth Cary's life and work in turn inspired her daughter to produce the first biography of an Englishwoman—*Lady Falkland: Her Life* (see chapter 6). The play was written a number of years before it was published in 1613, an extraordinary feat at a time when women's public voices were denounced as immodest and even subversive. As a closet drama and a tragedy that portrays a woman's subjectivity, *The Tragedie of Mariam* operates as print and performance. Like most plays by early modern women, it is a study in negotiation, balancing defiant, outspoken female characters Mariam, Salome, and Alexandra with the chorus's pronouncement on women's proper conduct. Cary self-consciously mediates between the ideal of female silence reinforced by conduct manuals and the possibilities afforded to women "as speaking and performing agents" (Bennett 298). Though only publicly circulated for a brief time, *Mariam* influenced future women writers who reworked Cary's themes in the changing scene of the Restoration and beyond.

One of the best-known female authors of the Jacobean era, Lady Mary (Sidney) Wroth used her literary background as a foundation to produce transgressive versions of literary heroes, as well as to interrogate gender politics and the positions of women writers, particularly in *The Countesse of Montgomeries Urania* (1621) (see chapter 6). Wroth deserves credit not only for being the first Englishwoman to write a prose romance and a secular sonnet sequence but also for composing the first original female-authored pastoral drama. About the same time that she produced *Urania*, Wroth was encouraged by her aunt, Mary Sidney Herbert, the Countess of Pembroke—to whose example Cary was also indebted—to write the play "Loves Victorie," likely intended for amateur performance at the Wroth estate.[6] The play does not address the kind of contentious issues raised in *Urania*, but its silences and omissions nonetheless expose the frustrations of courtly women and women writers of the time, and its punning references to Wroth's own dissatisfaction with her "rustic" husband especially mark the dangers of loveless marriage.[7] An incomplete, unsigned version in the Huntington Library, written in two different scripts, is one of two extant manuscript copies and provides the opportunity to see the process involved in the composition of the work.[8]

"Keeping the drama alive was a royalist preoccupation during the interregnum,"[9] and recent studies of literature and specifically of the dramatic texts produced during the mid–seventeenth century recognize the contribution of women dramatists to this undertaking.[10] The Cavendishes played the greatest part in ensuring the survival of the Royalist dramatic tradition. The manuscript version of Lady Jane Cavendish and Lady Elizabeth Brackley's "The concealed Fansyes"—a romantic comedy composed by the two women while imprisoned in Welbeck Abbey during the Civil War— raises the vexed issue of women's right to speak and write, an entitlement that the play itself defends. Though a "private" text, it acquired a social function through its circulation.[11] The play's performance may also have been envisioned, as it contains elements of the masque as well as conventions of stage plays, like dramatic dialogues rather than poetic monologues.[12]

Margaret Cavendish, the extraordinarily prolific stepmother of Jane Cavendish and Elizabeth Brackley, helped sustain the Royalist literary tradition during the Civil War and into the Restoration. As well as being the first Englishwoman to publish her husband's biography, her own autobiography, philosophical treatises (see chapter 2), scientific writings, science fiction, and literary criticism on Shakespeare and Jonson, Cavendish also became the first to publish her collected plays. She wrote the 19 plays in the earliest of her two folio collections of drama (1662) prior to her return to England in the Restoration. As such, they were not destined for the public stage, though they may have been performable.[13] On the one hand, a number of Cavendish's plays, including *Youths Glory and Deaths Banquet* and *The Convent of Pleasure* featured in this chapter, are, like the plays of Cary, Wroth, and Cavendish and Brackley, directed at audiences. On the other, Cavendish devoted considerable attention to their printing, suggesting that her dramatic works were intended for reading. Appropriately, the publication of Cavendish's dramatic works coincided with the revival of theatrical productions in the Restoration.

The Restoration of Drama

After being widely circulated in manuscript form, Katherine Philips's translation of Corneille's *Pompée*, titled *Pompey*, was the first female-authored play to appear on the Restoration stage (see chapter 7). Performances of plays translated from French sources, along with revivals of pre-Civil War plays, were popular in the theaters in the early years of the Restoration. The public's insatiable desire for courtly entertainment resulted in a demand even for plays produced by women, though female playwrights attracted no less scandal for their exposure than did their predecessors.

Still, Elizabeth Polwhele, Frances Boothby, Aphra Behn, Ariadne, Mary Delariviere Manley, Ephelia, Mary Pix, Catharine Trotter, and Susanna Centlivre joined their male counterparts in writing for the Restoration theater. Some of these playwrights also designed plays specifically for the marketplace, which gradually displaced the patronage system and became one of the social forces that transformed the literary sphere. Aphra Behn, who, unlike most male dramatists, did not enjoy the benefits of patronage at the beginning of her career, composed plays both for public entertainment and for financial reasons, a fact to be kept in mind when interpreting her work. While the lack of patronage may have afforded her a greater sense of independence, Behn also felt compelled to cater to her readers' interests. Her method of producing plays thus involved, Janet Todd observes, "study[ing] what the spectators desired and then giv[ing] them what they had shown by their patronage they wanted."[14] Behn's first plays, moreover, were all published by different, cheap publishing houses. Likewise deprived of patronage, Ariadne addresses her preface in *She Ventures and He Wins* (1696) to her readers and appeals for their support. As still another entry in this chapter demonstrates, Mary Pix, in the dedication to her play, *The Deceiver Deceived* (1698), discusses the commercial pressures on her as a playwright. And Susanna Centlivre, who follows Behn's lead, also earned an income by writing for the stage, having begun her career in the theater by working first as an actress. The interrelated roles of the female playwright and actress merit further examination in studies of women's contributions to theater culture.

Denied an education in the classical language and literatures, female dramatists, with the notable exception of playwrights like Trotter, Manley, and Pix, contributed less to the tradition of heroic drama than to the more popular repertoire of Restoration comedy, which focused on London society and issues of love, courtship, marriage, and adultery. Moreover, female-authored comedies tended to differ from those produced by their male counterparts through the interrogation of gender identities, sexuality, and women's inferior status. Female characters, now for the first time played by actresses, were cast as protagonists, flouting gender expectations and, like the female playwrights, finding themselves torn between the pressure to conform to socially determined requirements for female conduct and the imperative to subvert authority.

The playwright's own presentation of her multifaceted identity is characteristically part of her drama, Polwhele, Behn, Ariadne, Ephelia, Manley, and Centlivre being among the dramatists who developed and exhibited various self-portraits. A comparison of the melodramatic "The faythfull virgins" (c.1670) and the racy sex comedy "The Frolick's" (c.1671)—neither of which was published—reveals, for example, Elizabeth Polwhele's experimentation with different performances, representations of femininity, and self-constructions.[15] In general terms, Polwhele's "The faythfull virgins" celebrates female constancy while denouncing destructive male desire, thus anticipating the playwright Catharine Trotter's critique of Libertinism, a philosophy celebrating men's natural appetites and sexual escapades. In "The Frolick's," however, Polwhele indulges herself. After admitting her temerity in writing this kind of play: "I shall be taxed for writing a play so comicall, but those that have ever seene my faythfull virgins, and my Elysium will justifie me a little ffor writing this" (3r), Polwhele and her female characters produce their own scripts for the parts they perform in their respective worlds. Her dramas in turn influenced the sex comedies of Wycherley and Etherege in the mid-1670s.

The plays of Aphra Behn also demonstrated the female playwright's adeptness in producing sex comedies, of which *The Rover* (1677), then as now, is a famous example. *The Rover* would become one of Behn's two greatest successes on the Restoration stage, the other being her farce, *The Emperor of the Moon*. At the end of the printed version of *The Rover*, Behn defended herself against charges that she plagiarized Thomas Killigrew's closet drama *Thomaso, or the Wanderer* (1663), on which her play had nevertheless been modeled, thus challenging her audience to compare the two plays—in print as well as performance. Behn staged many of her plays at the Dorset Garden theater, which had been built for the Duke's company and was in operation by the end of 1671. As a theatrical innovator who took advantage of dramatic productions to add special effects to her dramas, she became a great asset to the Duke's Company. Like other Restoration theaters, the Dorset Garden was a proscenium stage, but the actors performed on the front of what essentially approximated a thrust stage, thus fostering a sense of intimacy between players and audiences. This theatrical intimacy, vivid in Behn's printed play texts, particularly in her addresses to readers, increasingly characterized dramatic texts at large.

Despite the repeated and even drastic efforts to undermine her public role and performances, Behn's influence was felt by many female playwrights of her day.[16] Ariadne, for example, identified Behn as her precursor in the preface to the reader in *She Ventures and He Wins* (1696). Produced in the same year as *She Ventures and He Wins*, Mary Delariviere Manley's *The Royal Mischief* (1696) complicates Behn's own experimentation with gender roles and unsettles conventional associations between women and social disorder, which Catharine Trotter also critiques her in plays.[17] Finally, Susanna Centlivre carried the tradition of the deceased Behn into the eighteenth century. Centlivre appropriated Behn's poetic name "Astraea," implying her identification with the late playwright, and underscoring Behn's continued influence on female artists of the period.[18] In 1700 Centlivre wrote her first play, *A Perjur'd Husband*, though her name did not appear regularly in the signatory position until she produced *The Busie Body* (1709), her ninth play.[19] By observing the conventions of Restoration drama while using her plays to denounce forced marriages and defend women's sexual, economic, and intellectual rights, Centlivre commented on the need to expand the realm of accepted conduct for women in general and women writers in particular.

In 1697 the anonymous play *The Female Wits; or The Triumvirate of Poets at Rehearsal* attacked female playwrights for their "scandalous" behavior. The targets included Catharine Trotter who was cast as Calista, a pretentiously learned lady, and Mary Pix, who had contributed some laudatory verses to the printed version of Manley's play, *The Royal Mischief*. The satire exposed the dramatist's uneasiness with his female rivals, whose wit posed a threat to "traditional perceptions of authorship as a masculine prerogative."[20] *The Female Wits* represents Manley, singled out for her libertine reputation, as the arrogant poetess Marsilia, who violates the conventions of the stage and thus deserves to have her rights as a dramatist revoked. Though a work of fiction, *The Female Wits* did betray the kinds of repressive attitudes that forced playwrights like Philips, Manley, Behn, and their sisters including the fictional Judith Shakespeare—to challenge patriarchal limitations and justify themselves as artists on and off the stage.

Notes

We gratefully acknowledge the assistance of Matthew Steggle, Jane Milling, Anne Kelley, and Susan Georgecink.

1. See Lois Potter, *Secret Rites and Secret Writing: Royalist Literature, 1641–1660* (Cambridge: Cambridge University Press, 1989); Dale B. J. Randall, *Winter Fruit: English Drama, 1642–1660* (Lexington: University Press of Kentucky, 1995); Nigel Smith, *Literature and Revolution in England 1640–1660* (New Haven, Conn.: Yale University Press, 1994); Susan Wiseman, *Drama and Politics in the English Civil War* (Cambridge: Cambridge University Press, 1998).

2. For Samuel Pepys's reading of Restoration audiences, see Helen McAfee, *Pepys on the Restoration Stage* (New York: Benjamin Blom, 1916), 277–85. Emmett L. Avery confirms that Restoration theater audiences represented a cross section of society and a wide range of interests in the plays ("The Restoration Audience," *Philological Quarterly* 45 [1966]: 54–61).

3. Virginia Woolf, *A Room of One's Own* (1929; St Albans: Triad Paperbacks, 1977).

4. The role of elite women in masquing has long been a topic of study, but scholars have begun to address performances by foreign actresses, professional dancers and musicians, and nonelite women in parish and guild drama, among other types of female performance. A forthcoming volume on this topic is *Women Players in Early Modern England 1550–1660: Beyond the All-Male Stage*, ed. Pamela Allen Brown and Peter Parolin (Aldershot: Ashgate). On women acting in places and ways that complicate the concept of the all-male stage, see Stephen Orgel, *Impersonations: The Performance of Gender in Shakespeare's England* (Cambridge: Cambridge University Press, 1997), esp. 1–30; and Ann Thompson, "Women/'women' and the Stage," *Women and Literature in Britain, 1500–1700*, ed. Helen Wilcox (Cambridge: Cambridge University Press, 1996), esp. 110.

5. Alexandra G. Bennett, "The Female Performativity in the *Tragedy of Mariam*," *Studies in English Literature* 40.2 (2000): 298.

6. See Margaret Ferguson, "Sidney, Cary, Wroth," *A Companion to Renaissance Drama*, ed. Arthur F. Kinney (Oxford: Blackwell, 2002), 482–506. See Sidney Herbert in chapter 7 of this book.

7. See G. F. Waller, *English Poetry of the Sixteenth Century* (London: Longman, 1986), 12; and Margaret Anne McLaren, "An Unknown Continent: Lady Mary Wroth's Forgotten Pastoral Drama, '*Loves Victorie*,'" *The Renaissance English Woman in Print: Counterbalancing the Canon*, ed. Anne M. Haselkorn and Betty S. Travitsky (Amherst: University of Massachusetts Press, 1990), 276–94; and Helen Ostovich, "Hell for Lovers: Shades of Adultery in *The Devil Is an Ass*," *Refashioning Ben Jonson: Gender, Politics and the Jonsonian Canon*, ed. Julie Sanders, Kate Chedgzoy, and Sue Wiseman (London: Macmillan, 1998), 155–82, esp. 163–64.

8. Josephine A. Roberts, "The Huntington Manuscript of Lady Mary Wroth's Play, *Loves Victorie*," *Huntington Library Quarterly* 46.2 (1983): 156–74.

9. Elaine Hobby, *Virtue of Necessity: English Women's Writing 1649–88* (London: Virago, 1988), 102.

10. See Randall, *Winter Fruit*, 321–36, and especially Susan Wiseman, "Gender and status in dramatic discourse: Margaret Cavendish, Duchess of Newcastle," *Drama and Politics*, 91–113.

11. On the social nature of Brackley and Cavendish's manuscript volume, see Margaret J. M. Ezell, *Social Authorship and the Advent of Print* (Baltimore: Johns Hopkins University Press, 1999), 43–44; Ezell, "'To Be Your Daughter in Your Pen': The Social Function of Literature in the Writings of Lady Elizabeth Brackley and Lady Jane Cavendish," *Huntington Library Quarterly* 51 (1988): 281–96; rpt in *Readings in Renaissance Women's Drama: Criticism, History, and Performance 1594–1998*, ed. S. P. Cerasano and Marion Wynne-Davies (London and New York: Routledge, 1998), 246–58.

12. The concealed Fansyes, which may have been performed in the mid-1640s, deals with the regrettable absence of courtly values. See Lisa Hopkins, "Play Houses: Drama at Bolsover and Welbeck," *Early Theatre* 2 (1999): 25–44.

13. See Alison Findlay, Gweno Williams, and Stephanie J. Hodgson-Wright, "The Play is ready to be Acted: Women and Dramatic production," *Women's Writing* 6.1 (1999): 129–48. On the synthesis of print and performance techniques in Cavendish's closet plays, see Marta Straznicky, "Reading the Stage: Margaret Cavendish and Commonwealth Closet Drama," *Criticism* 37.3 (1995): 355 -91. On closet drama as political discourse, see Karen Raber's *Dramatic Difference: Gender, Class and Genre in the Early Modern Closet Drama* (Newark, N.J.: University of Delaware Press, 2001).

14. Janet Todd, "Pursue that way of fooling, and be damn'd: Editing Aphra Behn," *Studies in the Novel* 27.3 (1995): 304–20.

15. Judith Milhous and Robert D. Hume, "Two plays by Elizabeth Polwhele: *The Faithfull Virgins* and the *Frolicks*," *Papers of the Bibliographical Society of America* 71.1 (1977): 8.

16. On the censorship or the interdiction of plays during the Restoration, see *The London Stage, Part I, 1660–1700*, ed. William Van Lennep (Carbondale: Southern Illinois University Press, 1965). For Behn's arrest, see p. 311. On Behn and the Restoration political climate, see Melinda Zook, "Contextualizing Aphra Behn: Plays, Politics, and Party," *Women Writers and the Early Modern British Political Tradition*, ed. Hilda L. Smith (Cambridge: Cambridge University Press, 1998), 75–93.

17. Cynthia Lowenthal, "Portraits and Spectators in the Late Restoration Playhouse: Delariviere Manley's *Royal Mischief*," *Eighteenth Century: Theory and Interpretation* 35.2 (1994): 123.

18. See Suzanne Kinny, "Confinement Sharpens the Invention: Aphra Behn's *The Rover* and Susanna Centlivre's *The Busie Body*," *Look Who's Laughing: Gender and Comedy*, ed. Gail Finney (Langhorne: Gordon and Breach, 1994), 82.

19. Richard C. Frushell, "Biographical Problems and Satisfactions in Susanna Centlivre," *Restoration and 18th Century Theatre Research* 7.2 (1992): 4.

20. Laurie A. Fink, "The Satire of Women Writers in *The Female Wits*," *Restoration: Studies in English Literary Culture, 1660–1700* 8.2 (1984): 64. Link observes that "the attack on, and the self-defence of, *The Female Wits* may help define more precisely some of the changes the drama as a whole underwent during the last decade or so of the century" (69).

THE TRAGEDIE

What then to doe directly contrarie?
Yet life I quite thee with a willing spirit,
And thinke thou could'st not better be imploi'd:
I forfeit thee for her that more doth merit,
Ten such were better dead then she destroi'd.
But fare thee well chaft Queene, well may I see
The darknes palpable, and riuers part:
The sunne stand still. Nay more retorted bee,
But neuer woman with so pure a heart.
Thine eyes graue, maiestie keepes all in awe,
And cuts the winges of euery loose desire:
Thy brow is table to the modest lawe,
Yet though we dare not loue, we may admire.
And if I die, it shall my soule content,
My breath in *Mariams* seruice shall be spent.

Chorus.

TIs not enough for one that is a wife
To keepe her spotles from an act of ill:
But from suspition she should free her life,
And bare her selfe of power as well as will.
Tis not so glorious for her to be free,
As by her proper selfe restrain'd to bee.

When she hath spatious ground to walke vpon,
Why on the ridge should she desire to goe?
It is no glory to forbeare alone,
Those things that may her honour ouerthrowe,
But tis thanke-worthy, if she will not take
All lawfull liberties for honours sake.

That wife her hand against her fame doth reare,
That more then to her Lord alone will giue
A priuate word to any second eare,
And though she may with reputation liue,
Yet though most chaft, she doth her glory blot,
And wounds her honour, though she killes it not.

When

OF MARIAM.

When to their Husbands they themselues doe bind,
Doe they not wholy giue themselues away?
Or giue they but their body not their mind,
Reseruing that though best, for others pray?
No sure, their thoughts no more can be their owne,
And therefore should to none but one be knowne.

Then she vsurpes vpon anothers right,
That seekes to be by publike language grac't:
And though her thoughts reflect with purest light,
Her mind if not peculiar is not chaft.
For in a wife it is no worse to finde,
A common body, then a common minde.

And euery mind though free from thought of ill,
That out of glory seekes a worth to show:
When any's eares but one therewith they fill,
Doth in a sort her purenes ouerthrow.
Now *Mariam* had, (but that to this she bent)
Beene free from feare, as well as innocent.

Actus quartus : Scena prima.

Enter Herod and his attendants.

Herod.
HAile happie citie, happie in thy store,
And happy that thy buildings such we see:
More happie in the Temple where w'adore,
But most of all that *Mariam* liues in thee.
Art thou return'd? how fares my *Mariam*? *Enter Nuntio.*
Nuntio. She's well my Lord, and will anon be here
As you commanded. *Her:* Muffle vp thy browe.
Thou daies darke taper. *Mariam* will appeare.
And where she shines, we need not thy dimme light,
Oh hast thy steps rare creature, speed thy pace:
And let thy presence make the day more bright,
And cheere the heart of *Herod* with thy face.

It

9.1: Elizabeth (Tanfield) Cary, Viscountess Falkland, *The Tragedie of Mariam* (1613). Reproduced by permission of The Huntington Library, San Marino, California.

Elizabeth (Tanfield) Cary, Viscountess Falkland, *The Tragedie of Mariam* (1613)

Elizabeth Cary is probably best known to modern readers for *The Tragedie of Mariam, the faire queen of Jewry,* which is now regularly read alongside other plays of the Elizabethan and Jacobean eras. Cary was an educated gentlewoman who, in addition to *Mariam,* wrote or translated several other works. Ironically—for the play's central conflict concerns the proper behavior of women at a time when their public voice was widely condemned as immodest and even dangerous—*Mariam* was published in 1613, apparently without Cary's permission, then quickly withdrawn from circulation. The Chorus's speech that closes Act III, scene iii throws into relief the question of women's role in marriage and society, explicitly in terms of female speech; speaking and having "public language" are distinctly foregrounded in this critical meditation on the behavior of a "proper wife." Here, Cary voices conventional discourse on the subject of women, public and private, via the words she gives to her Chorus, a contrast to different outspoken and transgressive women of the play, especially Mariam herself. The traditional role of the Chorus in classical drama was of an aloof third party, usually representing the collective or conventional wisdom of the society, and the Chorus in *Mariam* is no exception. That the "collective wisdom" of this Chorus is so rigidly at odds with the sympathetic figure of Mariam, and thus dramatically "off the mark," is a crucial aspect of Cary's rhetorical vision for her play and central to the power of its critique of such a voice's actual wisdom.

Note the different points at which female speech is elided with female chastity and sexual morality: "And though her thoughts reflect with purest light,/ Her mind if not peculiar is not chast./ For in a wife it is no worse to finde,/ A common body, then a common minde." In these lines the word "chast," which is unambiguously associated with sexual integrity and purity, describes the mind of the public-voiced woman whose thoughts are not "peculiar" (i.e., belonging exclusively) to her husband. Female desire, as expressed through writing or speech, is a dangerously unruly thing even after marriage.

In such lines as "When she hath spacious ground to walke upon,/ Why on the ridge should she desire to goe?" Cary deftly captures the particular dilemma of being thoughtful, ambitious, and female instead of male. There is apparently no room for this combination within the discursively delimited parameters of womanhood in the world of the Chorus (and of the play). That this was arguably true in the world that Cary inhabited and within which she wrote *Mariam* creates significant irony in the views expressed here, so at odds with her life and very publication. As a result, the temptation to read much of *Mariam* autobiographically—as Cary's personal meditation on the plight of women like her—is difficult to resist.

While such a reading enables us to reflect upon the problems confronting early modern writing women, to read women's texts as invariably autobiographical can be limiting. As Callaghan says, the autobiographical bias is problematic because it demands the reader "displace the critical focus from the text onto the elusive and perhaps inscrutable woman who lurks . . . behind it" (165). We need not read this play as purely autobiographical to appreciate it as Cary's investigation of the power and problems of speech, both for women and from authorized societal discourse.

HEATHER EASTERLING
UNIVERSITY OF WASHINGTON

Elizabeth (Tanfield) Cary, Viscountess Falkland. *The Tragedie of Mariam, the faire queene of Jewry. Written by that learned, vertuous, and truly noble ladie, E.C.* (1613). Huntington Library RB 80841. Act III, scene iii, ll. 215–50.

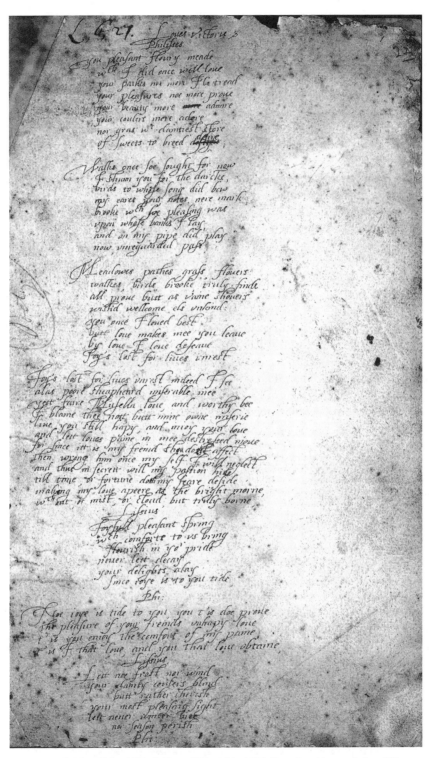

9.2.1: Lady Mary (Sidney) Wroth, "Loves Victorie" (c. 1622). Reproduced by permission of The
Huntington Library, San Marino, California.

Lady Mary (Sidney) Wroth, "Loves Victorie" (c. 1622)

Transcription

Loves Victorie[1]

Philisses[2]

You pleasant floury meade[3]
which I did once well love
your pathes noe more Ile tread
your pleasures noe more prove
your beauty more admire
your coulers mere adore
nor gras with daintiest store[4]
of sweets to breed desire.

Walks once soe sought for now
I shunn you for the darcke,
birds to whose song did bow
my eares your notes nere mark;
brooke which soe pleasing was
upon whose banks I lay,
and on my pipe did play
now, unreguarded pass,

Meadowes, pathes, grass, flouers
walkes, birds, brooke, truly finde
all prove butt as vaine shouers
wish'd wellcome els unkind:
you once I loved best
butt love makes mee you leave
by love I love deseave[5]
Joy's lost for lives unrest

Joy's lost for lives unrest indeed I see
alas poore sheapheard miserable mee
yett faire Musella love, and worthy bee
I blame thee nott, butt mine owne miserie

live you still hapy, and injoy your love,
and lett loves paine in mee destressed move
for since itt is my freind thou doest affect
then[6] wrong him once my self I will neglect,
and thus in secrett will my passion hide
till time, or fortune doth my feare deside
making my love apeere as the bright morne,
without, or mist, or cloud, but truly borne,

Lissius

Joyfull pleasant spring
which comforts to us bring
flourish in your pride
never lett decay
your delights alay
since joye is to you tide[7]

Phi:[8]
Noe joye is tide to you, you t'is doe prove[9]
The pleasure of your freinds unhapy love
t'is you enjoy the comfort of my paine,
t'is I that love, and you that love obtaine,

Lissius,

Lett noe frost nor wind
your dainty coulers blind[10]
butt rather cherish
your most pleasing sight
lett never winter bite
nor season perish.

Phi:

Notes

1. 1.2.1–52 in the complete version of the play.
2. Philisses enters alone.
3. meadow.
4. abundance.
5. deceive.
6. rather than.
7. tied.
8. Philisses speaks aside—Lissius cannot hear him.
9. taste.
10. obscure.

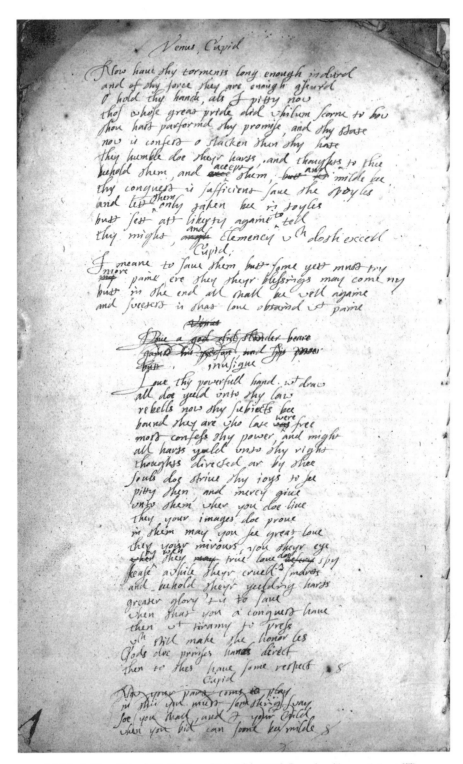

9.2.2: Lady Mary (Sidney) Wroth, "Loves Victorie" (c. 1622). Reproduced by permission of The Huntington Library, San Marino, California.

Transcription

Venus, Cupid[2]

Now have thy torments long enough indurd
and of thy force they are enough assur'd
O hold thy hande, als[3] I pitty now
thos whose great pride did whilum[4] scorne

    to bow
thou hast parformd thy promise, and thy
    state
now is confest[5] o slacken then thy hate
they humble doe theyr harts; and thoughts to
    thee
beehold them, and [exc] accept them, [butt

    kr] and milde bee
thy conquest is sufficient save the spoyles
and lett them only taken bee in toyles[6]
butt sett att liberty againe to tell
thy might [angh] and clemency which doth

    excell

Cupid:

I meane to save them, butt some yett must

    try
[my] more paine ere they theyr blessings
    may come ny
butt in the end all shall bee well againe
and sweetest is that love obtaind with paine

[Venus]

[Love a god did slander beare]
[gainst his parson, and his power]
[butt,]

Musique[7]

Love thy powerfull hand with draw
all doe yeeld unto thy law
rebells now thy subjects bee
bound they are who late [was] were free
most confess thy power, and might
all harts yeild unto thy right
thoughts directed ar by thee
souls doe strive thy joys to see
pitty then, and mercy give
unto them wher you doe live
they your images doe prove
in them may you see great love
they your mirours, you theyr eye
[wher] by which they [may] true love doe
    [descry][8] spy
[s][9] cease awhile theyr cruell smarts
and beehold theyr yeelding harts
greater glory 'tis to save
when that you a conquest have
then with tiranny to press[10]
which still make[11] the honor les
Gods doe prinses hands direct
then to thes have some respect,

Cupid
[Now your part coms to play]
[in this you must somthing sway]
[soe you shall, and I your child]
[when you bid can soone bee milde]

Notes

1. Because this text contains a great number of authorial revisions, deletions have been noted in square brackets—an alteration of normal transcription principles for this volume.

2. Act 2, sc. 4 in the complete version. Venus speaks the first speech.

3. alas.

4. once, in the past.

5. Your position is now acknowledged.

6. "toyles" may mean "nets," but perhaps "struggles" is more apt in light of the battle image conveyed by "spoiles" in the previous line.

7. As is the case at the top of the page, Wroth has not entered a speech heading. The Penshurst Manuscript has "song of the Priests" here. Perhaps Wroth meant to have Venus speak these lines in the initial version, since in the deleted final lines Cupid seems to respond to Venus rather than to a group of priests. Nevertheless, the lines have a song- and chorus-like feel to them.

8. "Descry" means perceive or discern, as does "spy." Notice that the rewritten line has the same rhythm as the first version.

9. Wroth has crossed out the letter *s*.

10. oppress.

11. makes.

Commentary

"Loves Victorie" is an important, early example of pastoral drama by a female author. It was probably composed in the early 1620s and remained unpublished in its own day. The play follows the conventions of pastoral and tragicomedy. Mary Wroth includes the usual scenes of pastoral "play" (in which characters pose riddles, confess their love, and have their fortune told) and combines near-tragedy, reminiscent of *Romeo and Juliet*, with low comedy and a miraculous ending typical of romance plays of the period. Some of the characters may stand for real figures like Wroth herself, her lover William Herbert, her husband Robert Wroth, and even her famous uncle Philip Sidney and his beloved Penelope Rich.

Within the conventions of the pastoral form, however, Wroth highlights concerns specific to women. The male characters represent different types of lovers, but the female characters are more complex. They all respond in their own way to the social expectations that restrain women even in this seemingly free pastoral world. The heroine, Musella, chooses suicide with her lover Philisses over disobedience to her mother, who wants her to marry an unappealing but wealthy clown named Rustic. She is contrasted with others, like the unsympathetic Climeana, who daringly takes the initiative in courtship, and the fickle yet friendly Dalina, who eventually concludes a bargain-marriage with Rustic.

The presence of stage directions in the text suggests that it was intended for private, amateur performance in a rich household, perhaps at the Wroth estate in Enfield. Two manuscripts survive: the complete Penshurst manuscript (published in a facsimile edition by Michael Brennan) and an incomplete version in the Huntington Library, from which two pages are reproduced here. In a 1983 article, Josephine Roberts has persuasively argued that the Huntington manuscript is an early draft of the play. There are two types of handwriting, both almost certainly Mary Wroth's own: a formal italic hand, used to copy finished pages, and an informal cursive hand, in the not yet finished sections. The Huntington manuscript, therefore, gives us the chance to see an early modern female dramatist at work.

The first page reproduced here is the opening of the manuscript, written in the formal hand. The only corrections that have been made are minor: "delight" has been changed to "desire," a repeated word has been deleted, and the spelling of "dost" has been corrected. The opening speeches by Venus and Cupid are missing. Wroth evidently wrote the frame to the play later and began with scenes that involve the shepherds and shepherdesses. This page shows two different male attitudes to love. Philisses pines for Musella but suspects she loves Lissius; Lissius refuses to fall in love and innocently celebrates the landscape. In light of the range of female characters in the play, it is significant that Wroth has chosen to offer male perspectives on women first—by the time the female characters enter the stage, the burden placed on them by suffering lover and confirmed bachelor alike directs our understanding of their behavior. This helps us appreciate the complexities that underlie the ways in which women position themselves in relation to love, even, or perhaps especially, in a pastoral setting.

The second page reproduced here is a draft version of the last scene of Act 4. Here, Wroth is working on the frame plot. She tinkers with individual words and lines and even deletes entire speeches toward the end. In Venus's second speech, she changes "where they may true love descry" into "by which they true love doe spy." In the first version, Cupid and mortals gaze at each other. Cupid sees a "mirror" of his own power in the lovers, and the lovers can see true love in his eye. The revision makes the relationship more interesting because it adds another possible interpretation. Now, the line can also be read as conveying the idea that the lovers use Cupid's eye, stepping out of their own positions to see what true love is with his eye. Note also the stage directions on this page: "Venus, Cupid" (who are to enter the stage) and "Musique." At the bottom, Wroth has put the slashed initial *S* that follows most of the passages in informal hand in the manuscript. The letter represents the Sidney monogram. Indeed, after Wroth decided to cancel the lines spoken by Cupid, she did not cancel the original monogram, but added another after "respect," to signal or endorse her changed text. Its presence suggests that Wroth felt it was important to establish her authority over the draft sections of the text and to claim her literary heritage as one of the Sidney family, with its famous authors Philip and Mary Sidney.

This particular scene must have been important to Wroth, because the tone of Venus and Cupid shifts from benign meddling in human affairs to stern control. Cupid strikes us as almost power hungry, while Venus has a hard time trying to stop him from victimizing the humans. The playfulness of the earlier exchanges between the two gods has made way for a politically charged battle of the wills. The scene highlights the ambiguous effect of love on the female characters in the play, who struggle less with love *per se*, as the men do, than with social constraints because of their gender. Venus uses the term "tyranny" to describe the rule of love, a break with the pastoral, comic mode. Silvesta, perhaps the most interesting of the female characters in the play, offers another perspective on the relationship of women to love. She has sworn chastity and maintains her independence in spite of the advances of Forester, a Platonic lover. Even after Forester has shown himself willing to die for her and she swears her love for him in gratitude, it remains unclear whether Venus and Cupid can ever rule this mortal. Silvesta's early exit prevents us from seeing her married along with Musella and the other "good" women in the play.

Because of the play's range of female positions on love, modern readers disagree on its gender politics. Wroth's ambivalent exploration of her subject allows her readers (and audiences) to think for themselves about the connections between gender and the pastoral form. Although it has taken students of the Renaissance a long time to discover "Loves Victorie," it is clearly worthy of our study today, as it offers a fascinating example of and perspective on pastoral drama by one of the earliest female playwrights in English.

MARTINE VAN ELK
CALIFORNIA STATE UNIVERSITY, LONG BEACH

Lady Mary (Sidney) Wroth. "Loves Victorie" (c. 1622, Huntington date 1630). Huntington Library HM 600. Pages 1r and 20v.

Lady Jane Cavendish and Lady Elizabeth (Cavendish) Brackley, "The concealed Fansyes" (c. 1645)

Commentary

Lady Jane Cavendish (1621–69) and Lady Elizabeth Brackley (1626–63) were the two elder daughters of William Cavendish, Earl (later Marquis and then ultimately Duke) of Newcastle, an amateur playwright and literary patron who commissioned Ben Jonson to write masques for the entertainment of Charles I at each of his two great houses, Welbeck Abbey and Bolsover Castle, on the borders of Nottinghamshire and Derbyshire. Newcastle, who was the governor of the young prince of Wales, was close to the court and was a prominent Royalist commander in the Civil War. After the defeat at Marston Moor and his subsequent exile (during which he married Margaret Lucas, later to be famous in her own right as the author Margaret Cavendish), Lady Jane and Lady Elizabeth defended Welbeck against the Parliamentarians. "The Concealed Fansyes," a sophisticated and highly allusive play, reflects their lives during this troubled and uncertain period. It examines women's roles in courtship and marriage (some have seen the play's Lady Tranquillity as a satirical portrait of their future stepmother), as well as bearing clear marks of their early exposure to a variety of theatrical forms.

The page reproduced here is the first and sets the tone for much of what is to come. It is written in an elegant, clear hand (it is not known which sister's). The use of abbreviated speech prefixes suggests familiarity with the conventions of theatrical manuscripts. The sisters also use the trick that even Shakespeare took time to learn, of starting their play with a lively, snappy exchange rather than with one or more long speeches. While use of the word "humour" in his opening speech points us straight to the humor comedies of Jonson, the name of Presumption further recalls Jonson's personified abstractions. The first character to speak is called Courtly, and the play is very much about the nature of courtly values and of what is to be done in a world where the court is no longer operating: Courtly and Presumption feel the loss of gentlemen ushers and pages, and of the imagery of Cupid and Hymen so much associated with the love cults fostered by Queen Henrietta Maria. One word is underlined: Sceane. This is a crucial word in the play, which is markedly metatheatrical; one of the women in it is able to conduct herself well before the Parliamentarians because she "practised Cleopatra," and all are very aware of the roles they play: as Presumption says here, they all know their "Sceane self." The page ends with Presumption's resonant question: "Doth shee speake much," which touches on the vexed issue of women's right to speak and write; the very existence of the rest of the play answers the question with a resounding and, for once, an unabashed affirmative.

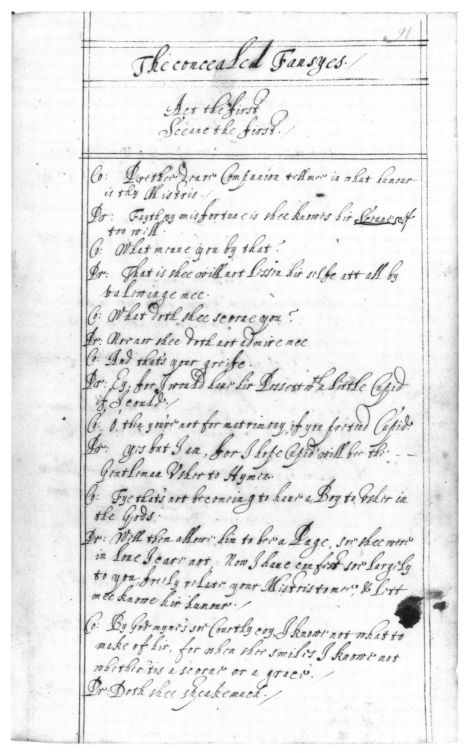

9.3: Lady Jane Cavendish and Lady Elizabeth (Cavendish) Brackley, "The concealed Fansyes" (c. 1645). Bodleian Library, University of Oxford.

Transcription

The concealed Fansyes.

Act the first
Sceane the first.

Co: Prethee deare Companion tell mee in what humour is thy Mistris.
Pr: Fayth my misfortune is shee knowes hir <u>Sceane</u>self too well.
Co: What meane you by that?
Pr: That is shee will not lessen hir selfe att all by valewinge mee.
Co: What doth shee scorne you?
Pr: Noe nor shee doth not admire mee
Co: And that's your greife.
Pr: Ey, for I would have hir Possest with a little Cupid if I could.
Co: O then you're not for matrimony, if you pretend Cupid.
Pr: yes but I am, for I hope Cupid will bee the Gentleman Usher to Hymen.
Co: Fye that's not becoming to have a Boy to usher in the Gods.
Pr: Well then allowe him to bee a Page, soe shee were in love I care not. Now I have
     confest soe largely to you; freely relate your Mistris to mee, & lett mee knowe hir
     humour.
Co: By God myne's soe Courtly coy, I knowe not what to make of hir, for when shee
     smiles I knowe not whether 'tis a scorne or a grace.
Pr: Doth shee speake much.

Lisa Hopkins
Sheffield Hallam University

Lady Jane Cavendish and Lady Elizabeth Brackley. "The concealed Fansyes." Bodleian Library MS
Rawl. Poet 16. 91r.

Scene 18.

Enter two Gentlemen.

1. G *Eentleman*. The Miracle is deceas'd, the Lady *Sanspareile* I hear is dead.

2. *Gent*. Yes, and it's reported her Statue fhall be fet up in every College, and in the moft publick places in the City, at the publick charge; and the Queen will build a Sumptuous and Glorious Tomb on her fleeping Afhes.

1. *Gent*. She deferves more than can be given her.

2. *Gent*. I hear her death hath made her Father mad.

1. *Gent*. Though her death hath not made every one mad like her Father, yet it hath made every one melancholy; for I never faw fo general a fadnefs in my life.

2. *Gent*. There is nothing moves the mind to fadneffe, more than when Death devours Youth, Beauty, Wit, and Virtue all at once.

Ex.

Scene 19.

There is a Hearfe placed upon the Stage, covered with black, a Garland of Ciprus at the head of the Herfe, and a Garland of Mirtle at one fide, and a Bafket of Flowers on the other.

Enter the Lady Innocence *alone, dreft in white, and her hair bound up in feveral coloured Ribbons; when fhe firft comes in fpeaks thus.*

L *Ady Innocence*. O Nature, thou haft created bodies and minds fubject to pains & torments, yet thou haft made death to releafe them! for though Death hath power over Life, yet Life can command Death when it will; for Death dares not ftay, when Life would paffe away; Death is the Ferry-man, and Life the Waftage. *She kneels down and prayeth*

But here great Nature, I do pray to thee,
Though I call Death, let him not cruel be :
Great |*ove I pray, when in cold earth I lye,*
Let it be known how innocent I die.

[Then fhe rifes and directs her felf to her Herfe.]

Thefe Verfes the Lord Marqueffe writ.

Here in the midft my fadder Hearfe I fee;
Covered with black, though my chief Mourners be,
Yet I am white, as innocent as day,
As pure as fpotleffe Lillies born in May;
My loofe and flowing hair with Ribbons ty'd,
To make Death Amorous of me, now his Bride;

X x   *watches*

9.4: Margaret Cavendish, Marchioness (later Duchess) of Newcastle, *Youths Glory and Deaths Banquet* (1662). By permission of the Leeds University Library, Brotherton Collection.

Margaret Cavendish, Marchioness (later Duchess) of Newcastle, *Youths Glory and Deaths Banquet* (1662)

Youths Glory and Deaths Banquet (in two parts) was published in Margaret Cavendish's first folio collection of drama: *Playes* (1662), which comprised 19 plays. Cavendish's most consistent dramatic themes are the bad bargain that marriage offers women, and individual female protagonists' creative but ultimately fruitless searches for feasible alternatives. The main plot of *Youths Glory and Deaths Banquet* represents the brilliant Lady Sanspareille's rejection of marriage in order to pursue her intellectual ambitions and effectively embody a female university in her own person; her plan is tragically compromised by her father's patriarchal control and latent incestuous feelings. Cavendish's depiction of the intensity of the father-daughter bond in the play recalls the passionate tone of manuscript writings addressed to her husband, William Cavendish, Duke of Newcastle, by his daughter by his first marriage, Jane Cavendish, an unpublished dramatist and poet. A dramatist and literary patron himself, Newcastle established a productive tutelary relationship with the various women in his life.

Cavendish's plays do not appear to have any contemporary recorded performance history, but productions by the *Margaret Cavendish Performance Project* since 1995 have established that her plays are eminently performable. In 2000 an abridged version of *Youths Glory and Deaths Banquet* (producer Gweno Williams) was filmed in York. This extract demonstrates the skillful way in which Cavendish juxtaposes and intercuts parallel dramatic plots in short cumulative scenes, to highlight her main themes. The use of visual staging devices, including symbolic costume, properties, and stylized action, is confident and effective.

The secondary plot of *Youths Glory and Deaths Banquet* deals with the fatal subversion of Lady Innocent's arranged marriage through the machinations of her husband's mistress. Lady Innocent's self-staged death ritual constitutes a highly charged meta-theatrical scene full of dramatic irony; it is secretly watched by her husband, who believes it to be only a self-indulgent performance: "What are you acting a melancholy Play by your self alone?" (174).

Cavendish's consistent reversals of the dramatic gender balance are amongst the most striking and appealing protofeminist features of her plays. Her admirable and heroic female protagonists are distinguished by aptronyms: Lady Sanspareille, Lady Innocent, Lady Victoria, Lady Happy. Their actions drive the plot and they speak the most lines; male characters are subsidiary and often, as here, reduced to anonymous gentlemen commentators on the main action. In most cases, however, Cavendish's female protagonists eventually disappear from the play in a conservative and compromised moment of closure achieved through death or marriage. Lady Sanspareille is the eponymous "Youths Glory" of the title; her tragic embodiment as "Deaths Banquet" foregrounds the eroticized gender politics of the play. The play's female protagonists are ultimately revealed as objects of the male gaze; Sanspareille's male audiences have been admiring her beautiful body (to be multiplied in replica as a public monument), as much as her intellect.

Cavendish was particularly vigilant about the printing of her works, perhaps seeing folio publication of her plays (following Jonson, Shakespeare, and Beaumont and Fletcher) as her only available alternative to public performance. She and Newcastle appear to have funded or subsidized her numerous publications; she presented copies to individuals and institutions.

Her two folio play collections constitute some of the earliest published evidence in English of literary collaboration between a wife and a husband. Cavendish provides scrupulous deferential textual credits for Newcastle's intermittent contributions. His usual additions are verses or songs, although in some plays he contributes bawdy sections of prose. His funeral epitaphs for Cavendish's tragic heroines are typically lyrical and stylized, as in this example.

The overt connection between death and marriage for women established here and in other 1662 plays recapitulates the tragic plots of earlier male public theater dramatists, particularly John Ford. The parallel funeral scenes that conclude both plots are sexualized in a manner recalling the tomb scene in *Romeo and Juliet* (Cavendish was the first published woman critic of Shakespeare).

GWENO WILLIAMS
YORK ST. JOHN UNIVERSITY COLLEGE

Margaret Cavendish, Duchess of Newcastle. *Playes written by the thrice noble, illustrious and excellent princess, the Lady Marchioness of Newcastle* (1662). Leeds University Library, Brotherton Collection Lt q NEW. Page 173.

Margaret Cavendish, Duchess of Newcastle, *The Convent of Pleasure* (1668), Ending revised by her husband, the Duke of Newcastle

Sophie Tomlinson has already noted of *The Convent of Pleasure* that "In some copies of the 1668 *Plays* the final two scenes after the revelation of the Princess as a man are headed with a pasted-in slip reading 'Written by my Lord Duke' (p. 47), but with no indication, as with similar instances elsewhere in Cavendish's texts, of where 'my Lord Duke's' ends" (157). The Fisher Library at the University of Toronto has one of these copies of *Plays, Never Before Printed* (see illustration). Tomlinson argues that "There are two ways of construing this textual anomaly: either Cavendish lost interest after the disclosure of the Princess as a man and left the writing of the rest of her play to her husband, or she did write the final two scenes, which poke fun at Puritan prurience and older women's sexual desires, but suspected they would be thought unseemly coming from a woman." Newcastle probably wrote the final two scenes, given that their bawdy humor and wordplay are more characteristic of him than of Cavendish. Cavendish's loss of interest may signify the marital dispossession of her own material interest in the text to Newcastle, rather than a lack of engagement in the ending of the work.

Cavendish's resignation of her own authorship into the hands of her husband has direct parallels with the main action of the play. Newcastle's takeover of the text resonates with the Prince's final relationship with Lady Happy. In the last two scenes Lady Happy speaks only a few lines. In marrying the Prince without property negotiations, she also abandons ownership of the Convent; the Prince will dispose of his "bounty in a Present" (V.iii., p. 52). In addition, Lady Happy loses her name; earlier a servant points out to his master that marriage would mean that she "must change her Name; for the Wife takes the Name of her Husband, and quits her own" (II.i., p. 9). The Lady Happy can be happy no longer. Her final question, addressed to the fool, Mimick—"What you Rogue, do you call me a Fool?" (V.iii, p. 51)—has an unfortunate answer for the feminist critic. The judgment following the anti-marriage theatricals that "*Marriage is a Curse we find,/ Especially to Women kind*" (III.x., p. 30) remains valid. As Williams points out, these horrific scenes are central to the play's structure and argument (102); instead of negating these plays-within, the "happy" ending reinforces their anti-marriage message. Newcastle's last words turn the Convent into a bawdy joke and firmly contain its previously wayward heroine within the bonds of matrimony. Like most of the text, the Duke's scenes suggest that marriage silences and disempowers women.

In the 1662 *Playes*, Cavendish represents her textual collaboration with Newcastle as a "*treble marriage*" of "*Souls, Bodies, and Brains*," where Newcastle is the masculine wit and she the feminine (A6r). This couple is "*united in one Love*" (A6r), with the obvious corollory that the one must be the husband. Here, Cavendish happily accepts the normative idea of marriage. But Cavendish's energetic critiques of marriage elsewhere in her work suggest that she does not totally approve of its effects on women (see Smith 84–85, Mendelson 32–34, and Williamson 51–52), and the ending of *Convent* points to a certain tension within her marriage. Similarly, Karen Raber examines some of Newcastle's other textual interventions and suggests that his choices sometimes "partially subvert his apparent sanction of Margaret Cavendish's plays" ("Our wits" 482). While Cavendish accepts the inevitability of the comic resolution of the plot—she did, after all, write act five scene

The Embassador kneels and kisses her Hand.

Princ. But since I am discover'd, go from me to the Councellors of this State, and inform them of my being here, as also the reason, and that I ask their leave I may marry this Lady; otherwise, tell them I will have her by force of Arms.   *Exit Embassador.*

M. *Mediat.* O the Lord! I hope you will not bring an Army, to take away all the Women; will you?

Princ. No, Madam *Mediator*, we will leave you behind us.   *Exeunt.*

SCENE II.

Enter Madam Mediator lamenting and crying with a Handkerchief in her hand.

VVritten by my Lord Duke.

O Gentlemen, that I never had been born, we're all undone and lost!

Advis. Why, what's the matter?

M. *Mediat.* Matter? nay, I doubt, there's too much Matter.

Advis. How?

M. *Mediat.* How, never such a Mistake; why we have taken a Man for a Woman.

Advis. Why, a Man is for a Woman.

N   M. *Mediat.*

9.5: Margaret Cavendish, Duchess of Newcastle, *The Convent of Pleasure* (1668). The Thomas Fisher Rare Book Library, University of Toronto.

one where the Prince violently demands Lady Happy's hand—the congruence of Cavendish's textual disappearance and Lady Happy's situation seems too apt to be coincidental. Cavendish was no fool; paradoxically, Newcastle's ending increases the potency of the antimarriage message of *Convent.*

TANYA WOOD
UNIVERSITY OF TORONTO

Margaret Cavendish, Duchess of Newcastle. *The Convent of Pleasure. Plays, Never Before Printed.* (1668). 1–54. The Thomas Fisher Rare Book Library, University of Toronto E-10 861 RBSC 1. Page 47.

the faythfull virgins.

Dutch. Enforme me sir, why y' haue brought mee here
daugh. that you shall gueß; by thoße w:ch now aprov.

— The Sceane Opens discovering,
rmira, mirantha; and Eregila like
a woman in white — with sparckling
wreaths or Coronetts vpon their heads
dead on a Couch: Statenor's head
plac't on Eragilas lap; at the
other side, the sceane Fragilius
and the duke are
Layde.

Cleop. J sayde you should be satisfied by mee
what Author'd this vnheard of Tragedy Lo the pros lo.
Dutch. what fattall objects do my sences surprise
shewing my soule strange horrours throw my Eyes
J death, never knew a tryumph like to this —
Cleop. this does Excell even all the victory's
he ever gain'd ore nature here to fore
and if his ill Succeß must still deplore,
yet there's not one; w:ch he did here subdue
But owes a ruin, leß to him then you.
you were the Cause of all the spoiles you see
for w:ch Lady; you should strangly punisht be
no punishment, indeed Can reach y:or Crime.
you would Confeß it if you knew your sinn
but ya're halfe Ignorant of what y'aue done,
although

9.6: Elizabeth Polwhele, "The faythfull virgins" (c. 1670). By permission of Cornell
University Library Rare Manuscript Collection, Kroch Library.

Elizabeth Polwhele, "The faythfull virgins" (c. 1670)

Transcription

[running head]   The faythfull virgins

Dutch. Enforme me Sir, why ye have brought mee here.

Cleop. that you shall guess; by these which now apear.

> The Sceun Opens discovering,
> Umira, Merantha; and Erasila like
> a woman in white—with sparckling
> wreaths or Coronetts upon their heads
> dead on a Couch: Statenor's head
> plac't on Erasila's lap; at the
> other side, the scen Trasilius
> and the duke are
> Layde

Cleop. I sayde you should be satisfied by mee
　　　　What Auther'd this unheard of Tragedy   [to the Lords]

Dutch. what fatall objects do my sence surprise
Showing my soule strange horrour's throw my Eye's
death, never knew a tryumph like to this —

Cleop. this does excell ev'en all the victory's
　　　　he Ever gain'd ore nature here'to fore
　　　　and I his ill success must still deplore
　　　　yet there's not one; which he did here subdue
　　　　but owe's a ruin, less to him then you.
　　　　you were the Cause of all the spoiles you see
　　　　for which Lady, you should strangly punisht be
　　　　no punishment, indeed can reach your Crime.
　　　　you would Confess it if you knew your sinn
　　　　but y'are halfe Ignorant of what y'ave done

Commentary

"The faythfull virgins" is one of three dramas by Elizabeth Polwhele, about whom we know nothing beyond what she reveals in the dedication of her comedy "The Frolick's" (c.1671) to Prince Rupert, where she declares: "I shall be taxed for writing a play so comicall, but those that have ever seene my faythfull virgins, and my Elysium will justifie me a little For writing this—I am younge no Scholer; and what I write I write by nature not by art" (3r). No record of the Elysium has been found so far, but a play called "The faythfull virgins" exists in manuscript, the hand matching that of "The Frolick's" and concluding with the intials E. P. Her modern editors, Milhous and Hume, propose an Elizabeth Polwhele born c.1651, daughter of the nonconformist vicar of Tiverton, Devonshire. This Elizabeth married another prominent clergyman, Stephen Lobb, sometime well before 1678 (when she bore him a son), her marriage perhaps accounting for the absence of any further dramatic writing after 1671.

It is immediately apparent that "The faythfull virgins" is a performance text. The manuscript reads, "This Tragedy apoynted to be acted by the dukes Company of Actors." The most likely date for the production is c.1670, before "The Frolick's" (and before Elysium too), when the Duke's Company was managed by Lady Davenant. The script's theater-conscious style shows in its combination of verbal exchanges with effects drawn from earlier Renaissance dramas such as dumb show, metatheater, and tableaux like the one featured on the facsimile page. In this scene from the end of the play, Polwhele uses an old-fashioned "discovery" to create an equally traditional stereotyping of woman as virgin and whore. The faithful virgins of the title, Umira, Merantha, and Erasila, appear "with sparckling wreaths or Coronetts upon their heads" as sacrificial victims of passive constancy. The Duchess is brought on to view the corpses of heroines, heroes, and villains and is told by Cleophon, "you were the Cause of all the spoiles you see," because of her jealousy, voluptuousness, and inconstancy.

At first glance, Polwhele seems to ignore the possibility of using the stage to advance feminist thinking. However, in the context of the rest of the play, her reproduction of old-fashioned stereotypes seems highly ironic, combined as it is with a sharp, critical perspective on male desire. The Duchess is in fact a scapegoat, a victim of the Duke's lust. The newly appointed Duchess finds that "he must have mistresses and often change" while she, "a scorn'd wife Must as a Cypher stand" (52v–53). The plot's immediate relevance to the English royal household, where Queen Catherine of Braganza had to endure the shame of Charles II's spectacularly public desire for mistresses, can hardly have been missed. The script (including the lines above) was censored by Henry Herbert, but the cuts were not full enough to expunge the critical commentary on Charles II's behavior. Behind the old-fashioned forms of Jacobean tragedy and Tudor morality play, Elizabeth Polwhele represents the king as a vicious villain and simultaneously mocks the crude stereotyping of woman as whore.

The treatment of the eponymous heroines also moves beyond the stereotyped images because Polwhele celebrates their passivity as a positive strength. Although they are relatively static figures, and rivals in love, Umira and Merantha develop a deep sisterly relationship. The vigil they keep by the hearse of their beloved Philamon unexpectedly offers a rare opportunity for women's love for each other to grow. Merantha kills herself out of love to the "dear virgin" Umira and in this final scene, they are discovered together, with the third faithful virgin of the title, Erasila. She offers another example of quiet female strength in adversity. Disguised as the page Floradine until the final scene, she suffers unrequited love for Statenor, whose head she cradles in a powerful pieta-like image of selfless care.

ALISON FINDLAY
LANCASTER UNIVERSITY

Elizabeth Polwhele. "The faythfull virgins" (c. 1670). Bodleian Library MS. Rawl. Poet. 195. Fol. 77r.

Elizabeth Polwhele, "The Frolick's: or The Lawyer Cheated" (c.1671)

Commentary

Polwhele's racy, fashionable comedy "The Frolick's" (c.1671) offers a completely different perspective on desire from "The faythfull virgins," as the dedication to Prince Rupert (quoted above) acknowledges. Perhaps as a result of her increased familiarity with the theater world, Polwhele wryly celebrates erotic exchange with a special focus on the actress's power to manipulate the scene. She admits that "encouraged much by Mrs Fame, I have for some minuets throwne my foolish modesty aside, and with a boldness that does not well become a virgin," dedicated the play to Prince Rupert. Given the play's interest in the relationship between erotic desire and performance, the dedication was highly appropriate, since his mistress, Margaret Hughes, had been an active member of the King's company from 1668 until late 1669 or early 1670 and from 1676 to 77. Margaret Hughes may have been associated with the fate of "The Frolick's" since the manuscript is labelled "Arthur Hewes 1681," the man in question possibly being Margaret's brother. Prince Rupert was a close friend of Killigrew, who ran the King's Company, so the dedication also implies a patronage that might lead to production, although no record survives of the play having been performed. Polwhele's apparent change of theater company for this play is perhaps explained by the fact that the Duke's had turned to producing tragedies, whereas the King's Company were celebrated for producing "gay couple" plays starring Charles Hart and Nell Gwyn. "The Frolick's," with its sharp-witted heroine Clarabell, could have been written for Nell Gwyn.

Polwhele's skill at using dramatic effects to interrogate the sexual dynamics of the fashionable theater-going world of Restoration London is evident in "The Frolick's." The female characters in both main plot and subplot have to function within a milieu apparently governed by the provocation and satisfaction of male sexual pleasure, but Polwhele shows how they use their acting skills to manipulate their status as eroticized objects and advance their interests as subjects. The facsimile page offers a snapshot of Clarabell's witty technique, or "frolique," as Rightwit calls it. She is cross-dressed as a young man, the "breeches role" (in which Nell Gwyn excelled), giving the character and the actress license to play. In the "frolick" of boy's clothing, Clarabell can escape her identity as her father's possession and the possibility of an arranged marriage, and can pursue her passion for the rakish hero Rightwit, by joining him in a tavern. At the same time, the disguise constructs her and the actress as a spectacle of pleasure. Rightwit finds her "preetily metamorphos'd" (42v), her legs and thighs a source of delight to him and to some spectators in the theater no doubt.

Polwhele's play takes the frolic of cross-dressing further, into the realm of farce, to interrogate the position of the actress as the object of desire and the assumptions that surround her. Having noted that the tune "the frolick" would be "an Admirable stirring dance," Clarabell laments the lack of female company and proposes that her suitors, Sir Gregory and Mr. Zany (neither of whom recognize her), "disguise and act" the parts of women. Once the tavern mistress furnishes them with clothes, they "strive which shall woman it best" (48r) and dance "the frolicks". The cross-dressed Clarabell dances the male part to the cross-dressed Sir Gregory's lady (48r). She deftly outwits her suitors, who are left with the tavern bill to pay, and are then arrested in their women's clothes as "lewd

Clar. you are perfict in it —
'tis an Admirable stirring dance
But we want women, let some
of us diggiuex and act them.
Righ.   'twould be a handsom frolique
and worth talking on.
Frq.   'tis alamoad to be talk'd on
I will be one that will
diggiuex: ile not be Bofled.
Rand. I have parsonated mayde
marrian in a Country morris
when I was a boy, and have
been held to doe it well.
pray let me act the
other. I am sure I can parform.
Clar. no quastion — mistris Can
you doe us the fauor to
furnish us with som Cloaths
Mrs.   yes Sir; if they will pleage
to walk allonge with me
                              Rand.

9.7: Elizabeth Polwhele, "The Frolick's: or The Lawyer Cheated" (c. 1671). Bodleian Library, University of Oxford.

best's in petticoats" considered "not worthy to be styl'd women" (52r). This is one of several means through which Polwhele explores the performative quality of gender and the power of women to "master" events.

Transcription

Clarb.	you are perfict in it—
	'tis an Admirable stirring dance
	but we want women; let some
	of us disguise and act them.
Right.	'twould be a handsom frolique
	and worth talking on.
Sr Gr.	'tis alamoad to be talk'd on
	I will be one that will
	disguise: ile not be bafled.
Zany.	I have personated mayde
	Marrian in a Country morris
	when I was a boy, and have
	been held to doe it well.
	Pray let me act the
	other I am sure I can perform it.
Clarb.	no question—mistris Can
	you doe us the favor to
	furnish us with som Cloaths
Mrs.	yes Sir; if they will please
	to walk allonge with me

ALISON FINDLAY
LANCASTER UNIVERSITY

Elizabeth Polwhele. "The Frolick's: or The Lawyer Cheated An new Comedey, the first Coppy written by Mrs. E. P." (1671). Cornell University Library Rare Manuscript Collection, Kroch Library 4600 Bd MS /43 MRC. Page 47r.

EPILOGUE.

THE Banisht Cavaliers! a Roving Blade!
A Popish Carnival! a Masquerade!
The Devel's in't if this will please the Nation,
In these our blessed times of Reformation,
When Conventickling is so much in fashion.
And yet——
That Mutinous Tribe less Factions do beget,
Than your continual differing in Wit;
Your Judgment's (as your Passion's) a disease:
Nor Muse nor Miss your Appetite can please;
You're grown as Nice as queasie Consciences,
Whose each Convulsion, when the Spirit moves,
Damns every thing that Maggot disapproves.
With Cunning Rule you won't the Stage refine,
And to Dull Method all our Sense confine.
With th' Insolence of Common-Wealths you rule,
Where each gay Fop, and politick grave Fool
On Monarch Wit impose, without controul.
As for the Last, who still seldom sees a Play,
Unless it be the old Black Fryer's way,
Shaking his empty Noddle o're Bamboo,
He Cry's——Good Faith, these Playes will never do.
——Ah, Sir, in my young days, what lofty Wit,
What high-strain'd Scenes of Fighting there were writ:
These are slight airy Toys. But tell me, pray,
What has the House of Commons done to day?
Then shews his Politicks, to let you see,
Of State Affairs he'll judge as notably,
As he can do of Wit's and Poetry.
The younger Sparks, who hither do resort,
Cry,——
Pox o' your gentile things, give us more Sport;
——Damn me, I'm sure 'twill never please the Court.
Such Fops are never pleas'd, unless the Play
Be stuff't with Fools, as brisk and dull as they:

Such might the Half-Crown spare, and in a Glass
At home, behold a more Accomplisht Ass,
Where they may set their Cravats, Wigs and Faces,
And Practise all their Buffoonry Grimasses:
See how this——Huff becomes,——this Damny,——stare,——
Which they at home may act, because they dare,
But——must with prudent caution do elsewhere.
Oh that our Nokes, or Tony Lee cou'd show
A Fop but half so much to th' life as you.

Post-script.

THis Play had been sooner in Print, but for a Report about the Town (made by some either very Malitious or very Ignorant) that 'twas Thomaso alter'd; which made the Bookseller's fear some trouble from the Proprietor of that Admirable Play, which indeed has Wit enough to stock a Poet, and is not to be piec't or mended by any but the Excellent Author himself; That I have stoln some hints from it, may be a proof that I valu'd it more than to pretend to alter it; bad I had the Dexterity of some Poets, who are not more Expert in stealing, than in the Art of Concealing, and who even that way out-do the Spartan-Boyes. I might have appropriated all to my self, but I, vainly proud of my Judgment, hang out the Sign of Angellica, (the only stoln Object) to give Notice where a great part of the Wit dwelt; tho if the Play of the Novella were as well worth remembring as Thomaso, they might (baring the Name) have as well said, I took it from thence: I will only say the Plot and Bus'ness (not to boast on't) is my own: as for the Words and Characters, I leave the Reader to judge and compare 'em with Thomaso, to whom I recommend the great Entertainment of reading it, tho bad this succeeded ill, I shou'd have had no need of imploring that Justice from the Criticks, who are naturally so kind to any that pretend to usurp their Dominion, they won'd doubtless have given me the whole Honour on't. Therefore I will only say in English what the famous Virgil does in Latin; I make Verses, and others have the Fame.

FINIS.

Such

9.8: Aphra Behn, *The Rover* (1677). Beinecke Rare Book and Manuscript Library, Yale University.

Aphra Behn, *The Rover* (1677)

At the end of the printed version of *The Rover*, Aphra Behn attached this postscript in which she denies charges that she plagiarized Thomas Killigrew's *Thomaso, Or the Wanderer: A Comedy*. Despite this statement, Behn's play is an adaptation of Killigrew's work, maintaining the basic plot and characters. As several scholars have argued, Behn's disingenuous claim that the sign of Angellica is "the only stoln Object" from *Thomaso* serves as a challenge to her audience to compare and contrast the two plays and as a subtle suggestion that the revision is superior to the original. Furthermore, critics such as Heidi Hutner and Laura Rosenthal find that *The Rover* offers an important but veiled critique of Killigrew's presentation of gender and the marketplace.

The heading of "Post-Script" for this concluding paragraph reminds the reader that these words are written and would not be included in a performance of *The Rover*. Unlike the epilogue, the postscript is not heard by the play's audience. Although Behn's adaptation of Killigrew's work transformed the ten-act original into a play that could actually be staged, her inclusion of the postscript in the second and third issues of the play suggests that she is constructing herself not just as a writer of frivolous entertainment but also as an author whose works should be read and taken seriously.

At the same time, by mentioning that she has indeed stolen not only the character of Angellica Bianca but also the scenes involving Angellica's purloined portrait, Behn highlights the shared initials of playwright and courtesan and considers the place of a female writer in a literary marketplace. This equation is part of Behn's ongoing project of fashioning herself as an author, a project inextricably linked to her role as a thieving imitator. For her final words of the postscript Behn chooses a translated quotation that refers to a lesser poet who tried to pass off Virgil's words as his own. With this reference, Behn shows her interest in translation—a practice she turns to later in her career—but she is careful not to identify with the supposed plagiarist. Instead she is eager to compare herself with not just a member of a privileged class but the archetypical poet of empire. While attempting to deflect charges of being like the plagiarizing lesser poet, Behn simultaneously assumes that she and Virgil have faced similar slanders, and she furthermore appropriates a piece of Virgil's reputation to strengthen her own claim to fame as an author who deserves praise and not derision.

Deborah Uman
Eastern Connecticut State University

Aphra Behn, *The Rover. Or, The Banish't Cavaliers* (Second edition, 1677). Beinicke Library, Yale University 1971 574. Epilogue and Post-script.

On several Occasions. 21

Epilogue.

The Play is damn'd; well, That we look'd to hear,
Yet Gentlemen, pray be not too severe,
Though now the Poet at your Mercy lies,
Fates wheel may turn, and she may chance to rise.
Though she's an humble Suppliant now to you,
Yet time may come, that you to her may Sue.
Pardon small Errors, be not too unkind,
For if you be, she'l keep it in her mind;
The self same usage that you give her Play,
She'l copy back to you another day.
If you her Wit, or Plot, or Fancy blame,
VVhen you Addresses make, She'l do the same;
But if you'l Clap the Play, and Praise the Rime,
She'l do as much for you another time.

C 3 Welcome

9.9: Ephelia, Epilogue, *The Pair-Royal of Coxcombs, Performed at a Dancing-School* (1679). With kind permission of Maureen E. Mulvihill, Princeton Research Forum, Princeton. Photo: Daniel R. Harris.

Ephelia, Epilogue, *The Pair-Royal of Coxcombs, Performed at a Dancing-School* (1679)

Epilogues to new plays by women writers were keenly anticipated in the Restoration play-house. Approaching stage center—chin up, arms akimbo, sometimes clad in men's "breeches"—celebrity actresses (e.g., Nell Gwyn) confronted the audience with saucy lines, hoping to influence the play's reception. These epilogues often focused on gender issues; hence, the popular "she-epilogue," which we have here. The actress would charm, wheedle, and petition the audience—especially (male) critics—for support ("Clap the Play . . . Praise the Rime"). Light raillery was also in her arsenal ("Gentlemen, be not too severe"). Most predictably, the "she-epilogue" tendered rational arguments for the play's success and equal treatment of women's work. This page, by "Ephelia" (see 8.17 and 10.9 for speculation on the Mary Villiers attribution), presents an epilogue with all these features, but also gestures to an important subject in feminist scholarship: censorship.

We know little about this Epilogue's play, *The Pair-Royal of Coxcombs*, evidently Ephelia's only (recorded) venture in playwriting. Yet we can reconstruct something of its contours by examining all the play's four excerpts in *Female Poems . . . by Ephelia* (1679, 1682): its prologue, its two pathetic songs for female voice, and its epilogue. The play was doubtless staged in the early years of the Restoration, before the furor of the Popish Plot (1678) would have preempted a play such as this. Its amusing title suggests that, generically, the play was a pastiche, conflating old and new vogues: the satiric humors comedies of Jonson, the tragicomedies of Beaumont and Fletcher (whose *Coxcombe* was revived, 1668–69 Season), and the libertine sex comedies of the early Restoration. Other models for the play's epilogue emanate from the "she-epilogues" of Behn's plays prior to 1678 (cf. *The Forced Marriage*, 1670; *The Dutch Lover*, 1673; *Abdelazar*, 1677). The play's male principals, represented under the cover of fictitious, silly names, must have been the two most recognizable of royal coxcombs at the Restoration court: Charles II and his brother, James, Duke of York. Though a rollicking good romp, the play evidently carried sensitive overtones, putting every man out of his humor.

Why was the play "damn'd"? In this pivotal first line of the Epilogue, "Ephelia" tells us that her play did not fail but was officially silenced by the court. Supporting this deduction is the fact that it never saw a second production after its premiere (see Van Lennep, Milhous and Hume, and Danchin). What went wrong? The Lord Chamberlain could prohibit a play if it were seditious, obscene, libelous, plagiarized, or offensive to the monarchy (*The London Stage* I: xxi–clxxv). Only two plays by Restoration women writers were silenced on the latter ground: the anonymous *Romulus and Hersilia* (1682), whose epilogue by Behn was a harsh rebuke of Monmouth, the King's favorite son; and Ephelia's play. The key to the play's suppression may be in one of the two women's songs. She reveals that her inconstant "Swain" is actually her adulterous husband, a "breaker of Sacred Vows." Now if this play is a public exposé of the degenerate moral character of Stuart leadership, then the play's two songs for female voice were sung by actresses representing the abused wives of these paired royals: Queen Catherine and Anne Hyde. Little wonder the play was damned, and not acted on the London stage, but at a dancing school (possibly Hicksford's, *The London Stage* I: xv). Clearly, *The Pair-Royal* was an unlicensed play. And clearly its published Epilogue is not the stage epilogue, but one prepared *after* the curtain fell, prepared not for the playhouse that cried down the play, but for readers of *Female Poems . . . by Ephelia*, in 1679, and thereafter.

The fate of Ephelia's play is an object lesson in cultural constraints against women writers. Even Mary Villiers, a de facto Stuart, could go too far. The larger subject behind this core text is censorship: the stilling of a bold female pen.

MAUREEN E. MULVIHILL
PRINCETON RESEARCH FORUM

Ephelia. Epilogue. *The Pair-Royal of Coxcombs, Acted at a Dancing-School* [c. 1660s-1677]. *Female Poems On several Occasions*. (1679). From the author's copy, purchased in 1986 from James Cummins, Bookseller, New York. Page 21.

Ariadne, *She Ventures and He Wins* (1696)

She Ventures and He Wins opened the season of the newly formed company at Lincoln's Inn Fields in September 1695. On the title-page of the printed version, which appeared the following year, the author is identified only as "a Young Lady." The preface is signed "Ariadne," a pseudonym presumably designed to distinguish the writer from the other playwriting young ladies who litter this period of theatrical history. It has not been possible to identify Ariadne. Greer et al suggest she was a man, and Kendall thinks this was the first work from Mary Pix. The play is clearly by someone who knew the actors well and may even have been written by an actress, perhaps Elizabeth Currer, who had played Ariadne in Behn's *The Rover Part II.* The play was "brought in by Mrs. Barry," the *Post Boy* records, and recommended to the new company. Mrs. Barry, who was to play the ingenious yet virtuous Urania, was a shareholder in the actor-run company at Lincoln's Inn Fields, which was in desperate need of a repertoire and offered a fresh market for new playwrights. Ariadne identifies herself as a first-time writer in the preface, explaining that this was "first I ever made Publick by appearing on the Stage."

   This rather underwritten city comedy was not a success despite containing a number of popular audience-pleasing elements: breeches roles, a rake tested, numerous disguises, and the farcical antics of Squire Wou'dbe, whose cross-dressing was yet another failed attempt to bed the desirable Urania, and who ends the play ignominiously duped in a bed trick. Unfortunately for the author and the actors' company, the poor audience for the play caused the theater to close briefly (Novak 51). The preface to *She Ventures and He Wins* was written after the debacle and might account in part for its apologetic tone. As a newcomer, Ariadne did not seek, or could not find, either a dedicatee or commendatory poems to support the printed text. This was often the case with novice playwrights of either sex. Thomas Scott, whose *The Mock Marriage* had run at Theatre Royal against *She Ventures,* had his play printed without a dedication by Ariadne's booksellers, Henry Rhodes, Harris and Briscoe. In the absence of a patron to appeal to in a dedication, Ariadne addresses the preface to the reader. Preface and prologue are reproduced here so that the variety of self-constructions of the author can be observed and the apparent demureness of the preface can be counterbalanced by the prologue's knowing coquetry.

   The preface is a series of carefully positioned justifications for printing that begins with conventional apologies for the inadequacies of the dramatist's "Self and Play." Although the play was boldly sent "bare-fac'd" into the public domain without a dedication, the author, likening herself to many women in the theater audience, chose to remain masked behind the pseudonym. The play's employment of crowd-pleasing elements gives the lie to the claim that the author was "unacquainted" with the stage. Her apology for her lack of learning, and thus the "naked Simplicity" of her language, is one frequently used by commercial writers, both male and female, notably Behn. The preface centers strategically on the figure of Aphra Behn as a precursor for Ariadne's work. Behn was still a significant force, whose collected novels and a first biography were printed in 1696, seven years after her death. Yet Ariadne chooses to date her own "scribling" from her childhood, by implication prior to inspiration by Behn. Indeed, deferral to the incomparable Behn apparently inhibited Ariadne's writing. Yet the choice of pseudonym, genre of play, and the explicit references to Behn here and in the prologue indicate that she was a useful figure for Ariadne. The preface goes on to imply that the play was an adaptation, a fashionable claim

SHE VENTURES,

AND

HE WINS.

A COMEDY,

Acted at the

New Theatre,

IN

Little Lincoln's-Inn Fields,

By His Majesty's Servants.

Writen by a Young Lady.

LONDON.

Printed for *Hen. Rhodes*, at the Corner of *Bride-Lane*,
in *Fleet-street*; *J. Harris*, at the *Harrow* in the *Poultry*;
and *Sam. Briscoe*, at the Corner of *Charles-street*, in
Russel-street, near *Covent-Garden*, 1696.

☞ A New Comedy, call'd, *The Mock-Marriage.* Written by Mr. *Scot.*

THE
PREFACE.

I Dare not venture to send this Play bare-fac'd
into the World, without saying something in
its Defence: I am very sensible of the many
nice Judgments I expose my self to, who may justly
find an infinite Number of Faults in it; which, I
profess ingenuously, I am not able to mend; for,
indeed, I am altogether unacquainted with the Stage
and those Dramatick Rules, which others have with
so much Art and Success observed. It was the
first I ever made Publick by appearing on the Stage,
which, (with the Advantage it met with, of admirable Acting) is all the Recommendations I have for
exposing it, in its own naked Simplicity, without any
Ornaments of Language or Wit; therefore, I believe, the best Apology I can make for my Self and
Play, is, that 'tis the Error of a weak Woman's Pen,
one altogether unlearn'd, ignorant of any, but her
Mother-Tongue, and very far from being a perfect
Mistress of that too; and confess I have but just Wit
enough to discern I want it infinitely; yet these Rea-

A 2   sons

The Preface.

sons which should have disswaded me, could not conquer the Inclinations I had for Scribling from my
Childhood. And when our Island enjoyed the Blessing of the Incomparable Mrs *Behn*, even then I had
much ado to keep my Muse from shewing her Imper-
tinence; but, since her death, has claim'd a kind of
Privilege; and, in spite of me, broke from her
Confinement.

The Plot was taken from a small Novel; which, I
must needs own, had Design and Scope enough to
have made an excellent Play, had it met with the
good Fortune to have fall'n into better Hands; but,
as it is, I venture to send it abroad, where, if it finds
but a favourable Reception from my own Sex, and
some little Incouragement from the other, I will
study in my next to deserve it: Which then, perhaps,
may make me ambitious enough to be known; but,
in the mean time, I humbly beg the Favour to bor-
row the Name of

ARIADNE.

PRO-

PROLOGUE.

Spoken by Mrs. *BOWMAN*, in
Man's Cloaths.

This is a Woman's Treat yare like to find;
  Ladies, for Pity; Men, for Love be kind;
Else here I come, her Champion, to oppose
The two broad-sides of dreadful Wits and Beaux:
'Tis odds indeed; but if my Sword won't do,
I can produce another Weapon too.———
But to my Task,——— Our Author hopes indeed,
You will not think, though charming Aphra's dead,
All Wit with her, and with Orinda's fled.
We promis'd boldly we wou'd do her Right,
Not like the other House, who, out of Spite,
Trump'd up a Play upon us in a Night.
And it was scarcely thought on at the most,
But Hey-Boys, Presto! conjur'd on the Post.
These Champions bragg'd they first appear'd in Field,
Then bid us tamely article and yield;
So did the French, and thought themselves secure;
But, to their cost, have fairly lost Namur.
And so much, Gentlemen, by way of Satyr,
Now I am come t'examine your good Nature:
Since 'tis a Lady hopes to please to Night,
I'm sure you Beau's will do the Ladies Right.
Clap ev'ry Scene; and do your selves the honour,
Loudly to boast the Favours you have done her.
So may the Play-House, Park, and Mall befriend you,
And no more Temple-Garden Broils attend you.

EPI-

9.10: Ariadne, *She Ventures and He Wins* (1696). By permission of The British Library.

to make, although the "small Novel" it was allegedly drawn from has not been identified. Novellas or short fiction had provided a rich seam for playwrights to mine, and adaptations abounded during the autumn season of 1695, including Southerne's adaptation of Behn's *Oroonoko* and Trotter's version of her *Agnes de Castro*, both staged by the Theatre Royal.

The demure reticence of "a weak Woman's Pen" in the preface is not quite so evident in the prologue. Mrs. Bowman, dressed as a man in preparation for her role as the disguised Juliana, was given the prologue to speak. Ariadne created through her a champion for her writing who, with mock bravado, threatened to produce both her sword and "another weapon" if the house proved unfriendly. The prologue also offered an attempt to place the new work in the admittedly recent female tradition of stage writing: "You will not think, though charming Aphra's dead,/ All Wit with her, and with Orinda's fled." This image wryly summons reference to the parlous state of English theater since Charles II had died and James II had fled into exile. William III hardly visited the theater, partly because he spoke little English and partly because he was always abroad fighting the fiendishly complex war against the French. The prologue to *She Ventures* is one of the first to pick up the topical military reference and apply it to the battle between the two theaters. The other house, the Theatre Royal, who had indeed "first appeared in the field," managing an early opening in the spring before the breakaway group of actors could muster their forces, are cast as the French. The battle of the theaters is paralleled with the recent reports from the Continent concerning the French defeat at Namur. Ariadne terms this topicality of commentary "satire." She denigrates the unseemly haste of the other house's staging of, probably, *The Mock Marriage*. Powell's prologue to *Bonduca; or, The British Worthy*, the play that was staged at the rival house immediately after *She Ventures*'s demise, was a direct reply to the accusations of Ariadne's prologue. The Theatre Royal's speed in mounting a new show was positively weighted by being likened to the military triumph of Hensier, who, "by swift Marches, gain'd his Work;/ And Cut off the Provision of the Turk." Ariadne's prologue ends by sexualizing the relationship of the audience to the author, but only through mockery of the conventional images of the "Beau's" from the mouth a of a cross-dressed actress.

JANE MILLING
UNIVERSITY OF EXETER

TO THE
READER.

I Shou'd not have given my self and the Town the trouble of a Preface, if the aspersions of my Enemies had not made it necessary. I am sorry those of my own Sex are influenced by them, and receive any Character of a Play upon trust, without distinguishing Ill nature, Envy and Detraction in the Representor.

The principal Objection made against this Tragedy is the warmth of it, as they are pleas'd to call it; in all Writings of this kind, some particular Passion is describ'd, as a Woman I thought it Policy to begin with the softest, and which is easiest to our Sex. Ambition, &c. were too bold for the first flight; all wou'd have condemn'd me if venturing on another I had fail'd, when gentle love stood ready to afford an easy Victory, I did not believe it possible to pursue him too far, or that my Lawrel shou'd seem less graceful for having made an entire Conquest.

Leonora in the double discovery, and part of Aurenge-Zebe, have touches as full of natural fire as possible. I am amaz'd to know the Boxes can be crowded, and the Ladies sit attentively, and unconcern'd, at the Widow Lackitt, and her Son Daniel's Dialect, yet pretend to be shock'd at the meaning of blank Verse, for the words can give no offence; the shutting of the Scene I judged Modester (as being done by a Creature of the Princess,) than in any terms to have had both the Lovers agree before the Audience, and then retire, as resolving to perform Articles; the Pen shou'd know no distinction. I shou'd think it but an indifferent Commendation to have it said she writes like a Woman: I am sorry to say there was a Princess more wicked than Homais. Sir John Chardin's Travels into Persia, whence I took the story, can inform the Reader, that I have done her no Injustice, unless it were in punishing her at the last; which the Historian is silent in. Bassima's severer Vertue shou'd incline my Audience to bestow the same Commendation which they refuse me, for her Rivals contrary Character.

I do not doubt when the Ladies have given themselves the trouble of reading, and comparing it with others, they'll find the prejudice against our Sex, and not refuse me the satisfaction of entertaining them, nor themselves the pleasure of Mrs. Barry, who by all that saw her, is concluded to have exceeded that perfection which before she was justly thought to have arrived at; my Obligations to her were the greater, since against her own approbation, she excell'd and made the part of an ill Woman, not only entertaining, but admirable.

To

9.11: Mary (Delariviere) Manley, *The Royal Mischief* (1696). By permission of The British Library.

Mary (Delarivière) Manley, *The Royal Mischief* (1696)

Like Catherine Trotter and Mary Pix, Delarivière Manley found an opening for her work in the London theaters once the United Company at the Theatre Royal had their monopoly overturned. In 1696 she was at the beginning of her literary career and had only an epistolary satire to her name. Always a prolific writer, rather than one play she produced a comedy and a tragedy, the former in a week according to her preface to *The Lost Lover*. Some theater historians have suggested that after a dismal run of her comedy at the Theatre Royal, Manley took the tragedy to the other playhouse. This incident is depicted in *The Female Wits* (performed 1697), Powell's biting satire on the three newly arrived female dramatists. Marsilia, a personation of Manley, flings down her book and storms off to the other house when the actors are uncooperative. Rushing to the other theater is a rehearsal play convention; Bayes does exactly the same in *The Rehearsal*. Interestingly the portrayal of Marsilia in *The Female Wits* owes much to Manley's own self-portrait in her preface and letters, and to her creation of the crazed female poetess, Orinda, in *The Lost Lover*. Manley was very alert to the demands, pitfalls, and potential of public writing by women and during her life re-created her public image to suit the genre, mode, or moment of her publication.

The prefatory material to *The Royal Mischief* is no less careful in its construction of her authorial persona. Her name appears on the title page as well as at every available opportunity within the text. The bold and direct address "To the Reader" was primarily used to counter the accusation of obscenity in the play. She refutes the charges on three counts, first through comparison with Dryden's *The Spanish Friar* and *Aureng-Zebe* and Southerne's adaptation of Behn's *Oroonoko*, all of which, she argues, contain passionate scenes and language. Manley asserts that "words can give no offence," particularly since her play was composed in the culturally élite blank verse. For her, the force of a performance lies in its physical representation, and on these grounds she defends her decision to have the eunuch Acmat discretely close the scene leaving Homais and her lover, Levan Dadian, behind it. There is some justice in her complaint that this presentation is less suggestive than showing them exiting in lusty haste, since in Act III, Scene i of *The Royal Mischief* the scene closes on the already wilted pair, who have fainted after their first almost chaste kiss.

Second, Manley defends the presentation because it was historical, that is, not of her own creation. She directs the reader to the source text and adds that she has reformed historical fact by providing dramatic justice and punishing the ambitious Homais. However, she also illustrates why the play's morality was questioned, since she adds a paean to Mrs. Barry's playing of Homais, who "made the part of an ill Woman, not only entertaining, but admirable." Finally she suggests that the real issue troubling the critics is "prejudice against our Sex," although this defense is voiced only in the context of a plea to female readers and audience members not to boycott her work. It is a moot point as to whether the satiric portrayal of herself and this heroic tragedy in *The Female Wits* kept Manley off the stage, or whether she found the market for journalism and short novellas more lucrative.

JANE MILLING
UNIVERSITY OF EXETER

Mary Delarivière Manley. *The Royal Mischief. A tragedy [in five acts and in verse]* (1696) British Library 841.c.5.(8.). To the Reader, A3.

PROLOGUE, spoken by Mr. *Bowen*

Deceiv'd Deceiver, and Impostor cheated!
An Audience and the Devil too defeated!
All trick and cheat! Pshaw, 'tis the Devil and all,
I'll warr'nt ye we shall now have Cups and Ball;
No, Gallants, we those tricks don't understand;
'Tis t'other House best shows the slight of hand:
Hey Jingo, Sirs, what's this! their Comedy?
Presto be gone, 'tis now our Farce you see.
By neat conveyance you have seen and know it
They can transform an Actor to a Poet.
With empty Dishes they'll set out a Treat,
Whole Seas of Broth, but a small Isle of Meat:
With Powder le-Pimp of Dance, Machine and Song,
They'll spin ye out short Nonsense four hours long:
With Fountains, Groves, Bombast and airy Fancies
Larded with Cynthias, little Loves and Dances:
Which put together, makes it hard to say,
If Poet, Painter, or Fidler made the Play.
But hold, my business lies another way.
Not to bespeak your praise by kind perswasions,
But to desire the favour of your patience.

      Our Case is thus:
Our Authoress, like true Women, shew'd her Play
To some, who, like true Wits, stole't half away.
We've Fee'd no Councel yet, tho some advise us
T' indite the Plagiaries at Apollo's Sizes?
But ah, how they'd out face a Damsel civil:
Who've impudence enough to out face the Devil:
Besides, shou'd they be cast by prosecution,
'Tis now too late to think of restitution;
And faith, I hear, that some do shrewdly opine
They Trade with other Muses than the nine.

      I name no names, but you may easily guess,
They that can cheat the Devil can cheat the Flesh.
Therefore to you kind Sirs, as to the Laws
Of Justice she submits her self and Cause,
For to whom else shou'd a wrong'd Poet sue,
There's no appeal to any Court but you.

EPI-

9.12: Mary Pix, *The Deceiver Deceived* (1698). By permission of The British Library.

Mary Pix, Prologue, *The Deceiver Deceived* **(1698)**

Mary Pix (1666–1709) was one of the most prolific female playwrights of the Stuart period. *The Deceiver Deceived*, her fourth play, was rejected by the company at the Theatre Royal, Drury Lane, although they had staged Pix's first tragedy and comedy during the previous season in 1696. She was forced to take the comedy to the rival company at Lincoln's Inn Fields. However, George Powell, a leading actor and writer at the Theatre Royal, almost immediately plagiarized large sections from the rejected play and had it staged as *The Imposture Defeated; or, A Trick to Cheat the Devil*. In the dedication of *The Deceiver Deceived*, Pix makes a restrained reference to the "little Malice of my Foe." However, she was far more outspoken in the prologue, which had prefaced the play in performance, reproduced here, and which was included in her printed text as convention demanded.

Pix shows herself to be a consummate professional in her prologue writing. She identifies the plagiarism of her work as part of the rivalry between the two houses. Although nowhere named, the audience would have recognized the thinly veiled and scathing picture of Powell's transformation from "an Actor to a Poet." Her prologue is written in casual verse and allows Bowen, who took the role of Machiavellian steward Gervatio in the play, to establish a conspiratorial relationship with the audience. The antics of the other house are likened to the magic tricks of street con men, and the better technical resources of the Theatre Royal are dismissed as "Bombast and airy Fancies." Pix carefully presents herself, through the mouth of Bowen, as "a Damsel civil," although she is far more concerned to highlight her status as "a wrong'd Poet" than her gender. Accusations of plagiarism or borrowing follow many playwrights during this period of theater history, but Pix's prologue offers an intriguing twist when it throws up the suggestion of legal action. To have sought actual redress through the courts would have been a most unusual move, because there were no effective copyright laws for dramatists at this time. Her prologue is accurate in concluding that the only source of redress was audience support, but her robust defense shows how equipped she was to survive the cut and thrust of commercial theater writing.

In fact *The Imposture Defeated* was relatively distinct in tone and form since Powell had adapted sections of Pix's plot, notably "Bondi the pretended blind man," as a musical drama. However, Pix's accusation in the theater and in print, coupled with a paper bullet in her defense from Congreve, put Powell on the defensive. In the preface to his play he claims he "never read" her work, although it is difficult to see how he could maintain his ignorance of the play's content as he admits he was "a Solicitor to the Company to get it Acted." Pix garnered much from the fiasco, including the public support of leading actors, especially Mrs. Barry, as well as literary friends Peter Motteux and William Congreve. This play was more successful in print than on the stage, and Richard Basset, who printed and sold many of Pix's twelve plays, kept it in stock for several years.

JANE MILLING
UNIVERSITY OF EXETER

Mary Pix. *The Deceiver Deceived: a comedy [in five acts and in prose]* (1698). British Library 83.b.9. (4).
Prologue.

TO HER
Royal Highneſs
THE
PRINCESS.

MADAM,

MY happy ſucceſs in one bold Attempt, not only encourages but forces me to a much greater, aſpiring to lay this Triffle at your Royal Highneſs's Feet ; when a Woman appears in the World under any diſtinguiſhing Character, ſhe muſt expect to be the mark of ill Nature, but moſt one who ſeems deſirous to recommend her ſelf by what the other Sex think their peculiar Prerogative. This, Madam, makes me fly to the Protection of ſo great a Princeſs, though I am ſenſible ſo high an Honour muſt raiſe me many more Enemies, making me indeed worthy of Envy, which I am but too well ſecur'd from in my ſelf (though an undertaking ſo few of my Sex, have ventur'd at, may draw ſome Malice on me) but 'tis my happineſs that the thing which will moſt reaſonably make me the object of Enmity, will be my ſafety againſt the effects of it. What inſolence dare injure one they find in your Royal Preſence, and under your Illuſtrious Patronage ?

A 2   Nor

The Epiſtle Dedicatory.

Nor need your Highneſs diſdain to look Favourably down upon this humble Preſent ; though I have hitherto ſeem'd to offer it only for my own ſecurity, I may ſay it in ſome meaſure merits your regard, though the performance much unworthy of it, its End is the moſt noble, to diſcourage Vice, and recommend a firm unſhaken Virtue ; that muſt receive your Royal Highneſſes Approbation, ſince 'tis the ſame Great deſign as that of your own Admirable Life, but with what diſadvantage imitated ! how muſt I Bluſh for the Copy when I caſt my Eyes upon ſuch an Excellent Original !

But here permit me, Madam, to decline attempting your Encomium, as a mark both of the moſt profound reſpect, and higheſt Admiration, beſt expreſs'd by an awful ſilence, which confeſſes you above all Praiſe ; but were it poſſible for ſome Nobler Pen to reach the height of your Perfections, the Work wou'd be Superfluous, ſince they need not ev'n the Luſtre of your Rank to make 'em conſpicuous to the World, or to engage Mankind in your Service ; nor be offended, moſt Illuſtrious Princeſs, if I ſay, 'tis they more even than your Royal Birth, make me Ambitious with all Submiſſive Duty, to be allowed the Title of

Your Royal Highneſs's

Moſt humbly devoted,

Moſt Obedient Servant.

Catharine Trotter (Cockburn), Dedication, *Fatal Friendship* (1698)

Catharine Trotter (1674– or 1679–1749) wrote five plays that were performed on the London stage between 1695 and 1706. *Fatal Friendship*, her second play, was the most popular with her contemporaries. It demonstrates the tragic consequences of allowing expediency to override moral considerations. When the principal male protagonist, Gramont, needs to raise money to pay a ransom for the release of his friend Castalio, he chooses to enter into a bigamous marriage with a rich widow rather than trusting to Providence to provide a solution. His action eventually results in his death and that of Castalio, hence the fatal nature of his friendship. The Dedication is to Her Royal Highness, the Princess Anne of Denmark, who succeeded to the throne in 1702. In her opening sentence, Trotter makes reference to the success of her previous play, *Agnes de Castro*, which had been performed in circa December 1695. She then pointedly draws attention to her sex with the remark that women who participate in public endeavors attract unfavorable notice, "ill Nature," to themselves. This remark is particularly telling if it is read within the contemporary context of the constraints placed on women to remain chaste, silent, and obedient. Furthermore, as Trotter remarks, a hostile reaction is particularly likely when women encroach on territory that has been traditionally male, that is, that "the other Sex think their peculiar Prerogative," as she has in this case by writing for the stage. Until the second half of the seventeenth century, plays for public performance had been penned exclusively by male writers. The encroachment of women into this sphere drew down on them considerable hostility, especially from the professional male "hack" writers like Robert Gould and Thomas Brown. The choice of Princess Anne as a dedicatee is not in itself necessarily a feminist gesture, as many writers, both male and female, dedicated works to her at this time. Trotter makes this choice more significant, however, in that she converts it to an implicit plea for female solidarity by flying "to the Protection of so great a Princess" when faced with male hostility. An unusually high proportion—three out of five—of her plays are dedicated to women.

On the second page of her Dedication, Trotter emphasizes that the purpose of her play is to discourage vice and recommend a "firm unshaken Virtue." In this insistence on the necessity for fixed moral principles, Trotter is opposing the kind of moral and political expediency associated with the philosophy of Thomas Hobbes, for example, in his *Leviathan* (1651). This concern with ethical practice is a feature of both her literary and her philosophical writing. In 1702 she published her first philosophical essay, in defense of John Locke's *Essay of Human Understanding* (1690), which she prefaced with an address to Locke, the first page of which is reproduced in this volume (see chapter 2). The extravagant praise of the Princess which concludes the Dedication was the conventional form of rhetoric applied to dedicatees in this period. The fact that Trotter signed her name to the Dedication to *Fatal Friendship* indicates that she was prepared to take a stand as a female writer rather than hiding behind anonymity.

ANNE KELLEY
INDEPENDENT

Catharine Trotter (Cockburn). "To Her Royal Highness The Princess" (unpaginated). *Fatal Friendship*. (1698). Wing C4802. Mills Memorial Library Research Collections, McMaster University C 2517.

(55)

Lef. You muſt teach 'em the Art then—— But prithee ſhoul'd I, out of a fooliſh ſcruple, tie my ſelf to *Beau.* when we are weary of one another ;

Mir. Or lay the Yoke upon a freſh Lover, that will hold out longer.

Lef. And bear it eaſier ; how ſhall I reſolve ? I think they had beſt throw Dice for me.

Mir. E'en put it to the Vote.

Lef. With all my heart.

Mir. What ſay you, Gentlemen? *Lesbia* is ſo unwilling to diſoblige either of you, ſhe's reſolv'd to be his, that has moſt Voices for him.

Beau. What ſhe pleaſes.

Cr. I ſhall never diſpute her will.

Cl. This is extreamly new ; but I don't know why it ſhou'd not be brought into a Cuſtom to Marry, as well as to Divorce by Vote ; unleſs indeed, that getting rid of our Wives, will be more for the general good.

Mir. Well, Sir, which are you for ?

Cl. Since there is ſo good a Relief, for him that will ſooneſt be weary of her.

Gr. That I grant, is on *Beaumine*'s ſide.

Mir. What ſay you, *Conſtant* ?

Con. I am for him that loves her beſt.

Gr. That favours me.

Bon. I am for him that won't quarrel with her.

Beau. That's likely to be me, for I ſhall be leaſt with her.

Lu. I am for him that can plead moſt right in her.

Beau. Ah the Devil ! that's me again.

Ph. I am for him that ſhe loves beſt.

Mir. And I for him that ſhe loves leaſt.

Beau. That has undone me ; 'twas pure Malice, *Miranda.*

Lef. The odds are on *Beaumine*'s ſide, whether I declare I love him leaſt, or beſt, there's a Vote for him ; his right is indiſputable, he ſays he ſhan't quarrel with me, and he's weary of me already ; ſo there can be but two againſt him.

Beau. You'll find hereafter there were more ; my late ſuſpicion of you gave me ſuch diſquiets, as ſhew'd me how dear you are to me ; and the proofs of your innocence confirm my Love, with my Eſteem.

Lef. Which to preſerve, and for all our quiets, I propoſe that for the future, *Grandfoy*, be a Stranger to us.

Bon. Oh ! that's cruel—— Sir, my Couſin has a great kindneſs for you, and your Lady, I'll engage he'll do her no harm.

Beau. Oh, no Sir.

Gr,

9.14: Catharine Trotter (Cockburn), *Love at a Loss* (1701). Courtesy of the William Ready Division of Archives & Research Collections, McMaster University Library, Hamilton, Ontario.

Catharine Trotter (Cockburn), *Love at a Loss* (1701)

Love at a Loss, or, Most Votes Carry It was performed in November 1700 and printed in London in 1701 for William Turner at the Angel, near Lincoln's Inn Fields. It is reprinted in facsimile in Edna Steeves, ed., *The Plays of Mary Pix and Catharine Trotter*, 2 vols (New York: Garland, 1982), vol. 2: *Catharine Trotter*.

Love at a Loss is Catharine Trotter's only comedy. It concerns the misunderstandings and misadventures of three sets of lovers. This play has several unusual features. The women are clever, strong, manipulative, and firmly in control of events, which is unusual even in comedy of this period. It is also unusual to come across a comedy that overtly debates a serious philosophical issue as this does. One of the central themes of the play is a critique of Libertinism, a philosophy that celebrated man's natural appetites, especially the freedom to indulge in sexual adventure without social constraints such as marriage. Comedies of this period frequently feature a male "rake" figure who embodies many libertine qualities and is singularly successful at seducing women, only to discard them, the libertine philosophy apparently having more to offer men than women. In *Love at a Loss*, the rake figure, Beaumine, is not the usual powerful Lothario but is exposed as vain, self-deluding, and easily duped by women. Having seduced Lesbia with promises of marriage and a contract signed in blood, he has repeatedly made excuses to delay the official formalities. He eventually repents his vaunted antimarriage stance when it becomes clear to him that his neglect of Lesbia and pursuit of other women has driven her away.

The scene reproduced here is from the closing minutes of the play, the penultimate page of the printed play text. Lesbia, now undecided whether to honor her previous contract and marry Beaumine, or whether to choose another suitor, Grandfoy, whom she really prefers, allows the other characters to decide on this ethical dilemma. This maneuvre can be read as a demonstration that contractual obligation is an important issue for the stability of society as a whole. The involvement of the other characters in this unusual vote scene extends the debate beyond the personal preference of Lesbia. The characters vote one by one for Grandfoy or Beaumine, often giving witty reasons for their choice. Beaumine's ultimate victory can be read as a qualified endorsement of the marriage contract. As this is the choice of the assembled characters, we can infer that this is the best decision for society in general. For this contract to be viable in practice, however, Beaumine has to repent of his former louche behavior. This is important within the context of the play, which has demonstrated that to treat women with disrespect is ultimately destructive of the happiness of both partners. The play closes, then, with a reformed rake, vowing to honor his wife, as to dishonor her is to reflect dishonor on himself. Overall, *Love at a Loss* enacts the argument that both men and women benefit from mutual respect springing from a sense of moral responsibility, and that libertinism, by contrast, is a shortsighted and socially destructive philosophy. This concern with the social consequences of ethical practice is typical of all Trotter's writing.

ANNE KELLEY
INDEPENDENT

TO THE
RIGHT HONOURABLE
JOHN Lord *SOMMERS*,
Lord-President of Her MAJESTY's most Honourable Privy-Council.

May it please Your Lordship,

AS it's an Establish'd Custom in these latter Ages, for all Writers, particularly the Poetical, to shelter their Productions under the Protection of the most Distinguish'd, whose Approbation produces a kind of Inspiration, much superior to that which the *Heathenish* Poets pretended to derive from their Fictions *Apollo*: So it was my Ambition to Address one of my weak Performances to Your Lordship, who, by Universal Consent, are justly allow'd to be the best Judge of all kinds of Writing.

I was indeed at first deterr'd from my Design, by a Thought that it might be accounted unpardonable Rudeness to obtrude a Trifle of this Nature to a Person, whose sublime Wisdom moderates that Council, which at this Critical Juncture, over-rules the Fate of all *Europe*. But then I was encourag'd by Reflecting, that *Lelius* and *Scipio*, the two greatest Men in their Time,

Epistle Dedicatory.

Time, among the *Romans*, both for Political and Military Virtues, in the height of their important Affairs, thought the Perusal and Improving of *Terence's* Comedies the noblest way of Unbinding their Minds. I own I were guilty of the highest Vanity, should I presume to put my Compositions in Parallel with those of that Celebrated *Dramatist*. But then again, I hope that Your Lordship's native Goodness and Generosity, in Condescension to the Taste of the Best and Fairest part of the Town, who have been pleas'd to be diverted by the following SCENES, will excuse and overlook such Faults as your nicer Judgment might discern.

And here, my Lord, the Occasion seems fair for me to engage in a Panegyrick upon those Natural and Acquired Abilities, which so brightly Adorn your Person: But I shall resist that Temptation, being conscious of the Inequality of a Female Pen to so Masculine an Attempt; and having no other Ambition, than to Subscribe my self,

My Lord,

Your Lordship's

Most Humble and

Most Obedient Servant,

SUSANNA CENTLIVRE.

9.15: Susanna (Freeman) Centlivre, *The Busie Body* (1709). Beinecke Rare Book and Manuscript Library, Yale University.

Susanna (Freeman) Centlivre, Dedication, *The Busie Body* (1709)

The Busie Body, the ninth of Susanna's nineteen plays, was a great hit—a rare treat for play-wrights at this time. It opened on 12 May 1709, at the Theatre Royal, Drury Lane and had a thirteen-night run. It was so popular that the following season it was revived in the Theatre Royal's two houses for six nights apiece. *The Busie Body* was the first play that Susanna published under her new married name, having tied the knot with Joseph Centlivre, Queen Anne's yeoman of the mouth, in 1707. It also marked her triumphant return to London after the difficult years since 1706, when she was forced to take her writing to a touring troupe.

Centlivre's dedication contains all the conventional elements of this kind of writing. She figures herself as "weak" and in need of "Protection," submitting her performance to Lord Somers's judgment. She concludes the paean with what had become a commonplace of female dedication writers, the "Inequality of a Female Pen to so Masculine an Attempt" as describing the full glory of the dedicatee. While this response is clearly gendered, it only echoes the kind of position adopted by most male dedication writers, who find their pens, for a variety of reasons, unequal to the task of adequately praising their patrons. Centlivre's dedication is noteworthy on two counts. First, she employs the classical model of Terentian comedy as a defense not only for her own work and her dedication but for theater itself. Reading comedy could be construed as "improving" and a way of "unbending" the noble mind. Through this reference she implies a level of self-education that was only recently fashionable for women. Indeed, earlier female dramatists had bewailed their lack of learn-ing. The second surprising element is her pointed reference to the political significance of her patron and the political context of the original production and publication in 1709. The Whigs, who had until this time been in the ascendant under Queen Anne, were to lose their grip on royal favor through their tireless prosecution of the war against the French and Spanish. Lord Somers had been a moderate spokesman for the party and attempted to curb Marlborough's excessive demands, save the party's fortunes, and broker some kind of peace with the French. Somers's involvement in these peace negotiations and the ongoing hostil-ities inspire her to cast him as concerned with "the Fate of all Europe." Yet her choice of martial image demonstrates her unstinting support for the war against the French and Spanish. The political flavor of her writing naturally inflects the very plot of the play. *The Busie Body* is a witty, involved story that follows the fortunes of Isabinda, who evades the Spanish rule of her father and a Spanish match, to marry Whiggish Charles Gripe.

The play was a financial success for Centlivre. Mottley, one of her eighteenth-century biographers, reports that this dedication of the play to lord Somers netted her forty guineas, and he adds that she "could shew (which I believe few other Poets could, who depended chiefly on their Pen) a great many Jewels and Pieces of Plate, which were the Produce of her own Labour, either purchased by the Money brought in by her Copies, her Benefit-Plays, or were Presents from Patrons" (Mottley 188). Centlivre also received her author's benefits on the third, sixth, and possibly even ninth and twelfth night and later made more from two benefit performances commanded by George I and the future George II. Centlivre even made money from the printing—Bernard Lintot paid her ten pounds for the printing rights—as well as receiving income from the sales of the printed text.

Jane Milling
University of Exeter

Susanna Centlivre. *The Busie Body : a comedy : as acted at the Theatre-Royal in Drury-Lane by Her Majesty's servants* [1709] Beinecke Library, Yale University (Non-Circulating) 1977 2816. Dedication pages: To the Right Honourable John, Lord Sommers.

Bibliography

Backscheider, Paula, ed. *Restoration and Eighteenth-Century Dramatists. Dictionary of Literary Biography.* Vol. 84. Michigan: Gale Research, Bruccoli Clark Layman, 1989.

Battigelli, Anna. *Margaret Cavendish and the Exiles of the Mind.* Lexington: University Press of Kentucky, 1998.

Beilin, Elaine. *Redeeming Eve: Women Writers of the English Renaissance.* Princeton, N.J.: Princeton University Press, 1987.

Bennett, Alexandra G. "Female Performativity in the *Tragedy of Mariam.*" *Studies in English Literature* 40.2 (2000): 2293–309.

Blaydes, Sophia. "Catharine Trotter." *Restoration and Eighteenth-Century Dramatists.* Ed. Paula Backscheider. *Dictionary of Literary Biography* 84. Michigan: Gale Research, Broccoli Clark Layman, 1989. 317–33.

Bowerbank, Sylvia, and Sara Mendelson, eds. *Paper Bodies: A Margaret Cavendish Reader.* Peterborough: Broadview Press, 2000.

Bowyer, J. *The Celebrated Mrs Centlivre.* Durham, N.C.: Duke University Press, 1952.

Brennan, Michael G., ed. *Lady Mary Wroth's Love's Victory: The Penshurst Manuscript.* London: Roxburghe Club, 1988.

Burroughs, Catherine. "Hymen's Monkey Love: *The Concealed Fancies* and Female Sexual Initiation." *Theatre Journal* 51.1 (1991): 21–31.

Callaghan, Dympna. "Re-reading Elizabeth Cary's *The Tragedie of Mariam, Faire Queen of Jewry.*" *Women, "Race," and Writing in the Early Modern Period.* Ed. Margo Hendricks and Patricia Parker. London: Routledge, 1994. 163–77.

Cerasano, S.P., and Marion Wynne-Davies, eds. *Renaissance Drama by Women: Texts and Documents.* London: Routledge, 1996.

———, eds. *Readings in Renaissance Women's Drama.* London: Routledge, 1998.

Clark, Constance. *Three Augustan Women Playwrights.* New York: Peter Lang, 1986.

Cotton, N. *Women Playwrights in England.* Lewisburg, Pa.: Bucknell University Press, 1980.

Danchin, Pierre, compiler. *Prologues and Epilogues of the Restoration, 1660–1700: A Tentative Check-List.* Nancy, France: Université de Nancy, 1978.

DeRitter, Jones. "The Gypsy, the Rover, and the Wanderer: Aphra Behn's Revision of Thomas Killigrew." *Restoration* 16 (1992): 82–92.

Ezell, Margaret. "'To be your daughter in your Pen': The social functions of literature in the writings of Lady Elizabeth Brackley and Lady Jane Cavendish." *Readings in Renaissance Women's Drama: Text, Criticism, Performance 1550–1998.* Ed. S. P. Cerasano and Marion Wynne-Davies. London: Routledge, 1998. 246–58.

Ferguson, Margaret W. "The Spectre of Resistance: *The Tragedie of Mariam* (1613)." *Staging the Renaissance: Reinterpretations of Elizabethan and Jacobean Drama.* Ed. David Scott Kastan and Peter Stallybrass. London: Routledge, 1991. 235–50.

———, and Barry Weller, eds. *The Tragedy of Mariam, the Fair Queen of Jewry (with The Lady Falkland, Her Life) by Elizabeth Cary.* Berkeley: University of California Press, 1994.

Findlay, Alison. "Playing the scene self : Jane Cavendish and Elizabeth Brackley's *The Concealed Fancies.*" *Enacting Gender on the English Renaissance Stage.* Ed. Viviana Comensoli and Anne Russell. Urbana: University of Illinois Press, 1998. 154–76.

———, Gweno Williams, and Stephanie Wright. "'The Play is ready to be Acted': Women and Dramatic Production 1550–1670." *Women's Writing* 6. 1 (1999): 129–48.

———, Stephanie Hodgson-Wright, and Gweno Williams. *Women Dramatists 1550–1670: Plays in Performance.* Video. Lancaster: Women and Dramatic Production with Lancaster University Television, 1999.

———. "(En)Gendering Performance: Staging Plays by Early Modern Women." *Crossing Boundaries: Attending to Early Modern Women.* Ed. Jane Donawerth and Adele Seeff. London: Associated University Presses, 2000. 289–308.

———, and Stephanie Hodgson-Wright, with Gweno Williams, *Women and Dramatic Production 1550–1700.* Longman's Medieval and Renaissance Library. Harlow: Pearson Education, December 2000.

Finney, Gail, ed. *Look Who's Laughing: Gender and Comedy.* Langhorne: Gordon and Breach, 1994.

Fitzmaurice, James, Josephine A. Roberts, Carol L. Barash, Eugene R Cunnar, and Nancy A. Gutierrez, eds. *The Tragedie of Mariam, Faire Queen of Jewry. Major Women Writers of Seventeenth Century England.* Ann Arbor: University of Michigan Press, 1997.

Foxton, R. "Delarivière Manley and 'Astrea's Vacant Throne'." *Notes and Queries,* n.s.33 (1986): 41–42.

Frushell, R. "Biographical Problems and Satisfactions in Susanna Centlivre." *Restoration and Eighteenth Century Theatre Research* 7.2 (1992): 1–17.

Gallagher, Catherine. *Nobody's Story: The Vanishing Acts of Women Writers in the Marketplace, 1670–1820.* Berkeley: University of California Press, 1994.

Gutierrez, Nancy. "Valuing Mariam: Genre Study and Feminist Analysis." *Tulsa Studies in Women's Literature* 10 (Fall 1991): 233–51.

Hamlin, William M. "Elizabeth Cary's *Mariam* and the Critique of Pure Reason." *Early Modern Literary Studies* 9.1 (May 2003); <*http://www.shu.ac.uk/emls/emlshome.html*>.

Haselkorn, Anne M., and Betty S. Travitsky, eds. *The Renaissance Englishwoman in Print: Counterbalancing the Canon.* Amherst: University of Massachusetts Press, 1990.

Hopkins, Lisa. Review of *The Tragedy of Mariam* and *The Concealed Fancies*. *Bulletin of the Society for Renaissance Studies* 12 (1995): 7–8.

———. "Judith Shakespeare's Reading: Teaching *The Concealed Fancies*." *Shakespeare Quarterly* 47 (1996): 396–406.

———. "Play Houses: Drama at Bolsover and Welbeck." *Early Theatre* 2 (1999): 25–44.

———. *The Female Hero in English Renaissance Drama*. Basingstoke: Palgrave, 2002.

Howe, Elizabeth. *The First English Actresses: Women and Drama 1660–1700*. Cambridge: Cambridge University Press, 1992.

Hume, Robert D.. *The Development of English Drama in the late Seventeenth Century*. Oxford: Oxford University Press, 1976.

Hutner, Heidi. "Revisioning the Female Body: Aphra Behn's *The Rover*, Parts I and II." *Rereading Aphra Behn: History, Theory, and Criticism*. Ed. Heidi Hutner. Charlottesville: University Press of Virginia, 1993. 102–20.

Kelley, Anne. *Catharine Trotter: An Early Modern Writer in the Vanguard of Feminism*. Aldershot: Ashgate Publishing, 2002.

Kendall, K., ed. *Love and Thunder: Plays by Women in the Age of Queen Anne*. London: Methuen, 1988.

Lewalski, Barbara. "Mary Wroth's *Love's Victory* and Pastoral Tragicomedy." *Reading Mary Wroth: Representing Alternatives in Early Modern England*. Ed. Naomi J. Miller and Gary Waller. Knoxville: University of Tennessee Press, 1991. 88–108. Revised in *Writing Women in Jacobean England*. Cambridge, Mass.: Harvard University Press, 1993, esp. 296–307.

———. *Writing Women in Jacobean England*. Cambridge, Mass.: Harvard University Press, 1993.

Lock, F. *Susanna Centlivre*. Boston: G.K.Hall, 1979.

McClaren, Margaret Anne. "An Unknown Continent: Lady Mary Wroth's Forgotten Pastoral Drama, 'Loves Victorie.'" *The Renaissance Englishwoman in Print: Counterbalancing the Canon*. Ed. Anne M. Haselkorn and Betty S. Travitsky. Amherst: University of Massachusetts Press, 1990. 276–94.

Mendelson, Sara Heller. *The Mental World of Stuart Women: Three Studies*. Brighton: Harvester, 1987.

Milhous, Judith, and Robert D. Hume. "'Lost' Plays of the Restoration." *Harvard Library Bulletin* 25 (1977): 5–33.

Miller, Naomi J. *Changing the Subject: Mary Wroth and Figurations of Gender in Early Modern England*. Lexington: University Press of Kentucky, 1996.

———. "Domestic Politics in Elizabeth Cary's *The Tragedie of Mariam*." *SEL* 37 (1997): 353–69.

Mottley, J. "A list of all the Dramatic Authors, with some Account of their Lives." *Scanderbeg: or Love of Liberty*. Ed. Thomas Whincop. London, 1747.

Mulvihill, Maureen E. "A Feminist Link in the Old Boys' Network: The Cosseting of Katherine Philips." *Curtain Calls: British and American Women and the Theater, 1660–1820*. Ed. M. A. Schofield and C. M. Macheski. Athens: Ohio University Press, 1991. 71–104.

———. "Thumbprints of Ephelia: The End of an Enigma in Restoration Attribution, with a first annotated Key to *Female Poems by Ephelia* (1679). Text, Image, Sound." *(Re)Soundings* 3.1 (2000) http://www.millersville.edu/~resound/ephelia/.

———, ed. *Ephelia*. Burlington: Ashgate, 2003.

Novak, M. "The Closing of the Lincoln's Inn Fields Theatre in 1695." *Restoration and Eighteenth-Century Theatre Research* 14.1 (1975): 52–2.

Pearson, Jaqueline. *The Prostituted Muse: Images of Women and Women Dramatists 1642–1737*. Hemel Hempstead: Harvester Wheatsheaf, 1988.

Polwhele, Elizabeth. *The Frolicks*. Ed. Judith Milhous and Robert D. Hume. Ithaca, N.Y., and London: Cornell University Press, 1977.

Quinsey, Katherine, ed. *Broken Boundaries: Women & Feminism in Restoration Drama*. Lexington: University Press of Kentucky, 1996.

Raber, Karen. "'Our wits joined as in Matrimony': Margaret Cavendish's *Playes* and the Drama of Authority." *English Literary Renaissance* 28 (1998): 464–93.

———. *Dramatic Difference: Gender, Class and Genre in the Early Modern Closet Drama*. Newark, N.J.: University of Delaware Press, 2001.

Randall, Dale B.J. *Winter Fruit: English Drama 1642–1660*. Lexington: University Press of Kentucky, 1995.

Roberts, David. *The Ladies: Female Patronage of Restoration Drama*. Oxford: Clarendon Press, 1989.

Roberts, Josephine A. "The Huntington Manuscript of Lady Mary Wroth's Play, *Loves Victorie*." *Huntington Library Quarterly* 46.2 (1983): 156–74.

———. "Deciphering Women's Pastoral: Coded Language in Wroth's *Love's Victory*." *Representing Women in Renaissance England*. Ed. Claude J. Summers and Ted-Larry Pebworth. Columbia: University of Missouri Press, 1997. 163–74.

Roh, Seung-Hee. "Seduction of Masquerading Signs: Aphra Behn's Authorship and *The Rover*." *English Language and Literature* 41 (1995): 1099–1122.

Rosenthal, Laura J. *Playwrights and Plagiarists in Early Modern England: Gender, Authorship, Literary Property*. Ithaca, N.Y.: Cornell University Press, 1996.

Rubik, M. *Early Women Dramatists 1550–1800*. London: Macmillan, 1998.

Schofield, Mary Anne, and Cecilia Macheski. *Curtain Calls: British and American Women and the Theatre, 1660–1820*. Columbus: Ohio University Press, 1991.

Scouten, Arthur H., and Robert B. Hume. "Restoration Comedy and its Audiences, 1660–1776." *Yearbook of English Studies* 10 (1980): 1–69.

Smith, Hilda L. *Reason's Disciples: Seventeenth-Century English Feminists*. Urbana: University of Illinois Press, 1982.

Steeves, Edna, ed. *The Plays of Mary Pix and Catharine Trotter*. 2 vols. New York: Garland, 1982.

Summers, Montague. *The Playhouse of Pepys*. London: Kegan Paul, Trench, Trubner and Co. Ltd, 1935.

Swift, Carolyn Ruth. "Feminine Self-Definition in Lady Mary Wroth's *Love's Victorie* (c. 1621)." *English Literary Renaissance* 19.2 (1989): 171–88.

Todd, Janet, ed. *The Collected Works of Aphra Behn*. 10 vols. Columbus: Ohio State University Press, 1992.

Tomlinson, Sophie. "'My Brain the Stage': Margaret Cavendish and the Fantasy of Female Performance." *Women, Texts and Histories 1575–1760*. Ed. Clare Brant and Diane Purkiss. London: Routledge, 1992. 134–63.

Trease, Geoffrey. *Portrait of a Cavalier: William Cavendish, First Duke of Newcastle*. London: Macmillan, 1979.

Van Lennep, William, Emmett L. Avery, and Arthur H. Scouten, eds. *The London Stage*. 11 vols. Carbondale: Southern Illinois University Press, 1962–68.

Waller, Gary. *The Sidney Family Romance: Mary Wroth, William Herbert, and the Early Modern Construction of Gender*. Detroit: Wayne State University Press, 1993, esp. 237–45.

Wiley, Audrey Nell, ed. *Rare Prologues & Epilogues, 1642–1700*. London: Allen & Unwin., 1940.

Williams, Gweno. "'Why may not a Lady write a good Play?': Plays by Early Modern Women Reassessed as Performance Texts." *Readings in Renaissance Women's Drama: Criticism, History, and Performance 1594–1998*. Ed. S. P. Cerasano and Marion Wynne-Davies. London: Routledge, 1998. 95–107.

———. *Margaret Cavendish: Plays in Performance* Video. Lancaster: Women and Dramatic Production with Lancaster University Television, 2001.

Williamson, Marilyn L. *Raising Their Voices: British Women Writers, 1650–1750*. Detroit: Wayne State University Press, 1990.

Wynne-Davies, Marion. "'Here Is a Sport Will Well Befit This Time and Place': Allusion and Delusion in Mary Wroth's *Love's Victory*." *Women's Writing* 6.1 (1999): 47–63.

Chapter 10

Applied Arts and Music

This concluding chapter features visual arts and music but also highlights the interrelationship of different artistic mediums of writing, needlework, painting, calligraphy, and musical composition. These artistic forms of expression engage different interpretive practices. Examinations of the various arts of the early modern period also challenge contemporary assumptions about women's involvement in the world of art. Ultimately, this chapter invites a reconsideration of the primacy given to writing and to print in our investigations of women's contributions to culture in the early modern age and even in our own day.

Most kinds of artistic expression by women in the early modern age were designated as "domestic." This characterization applied particularly to needlework, which in turn was judged a sanctioned form of expression and creativity for women (like the composition of translations in chapter 7). Still, feminist critics remain divided about whether stitching and sewing were liberating or self-abnegating activities for women; while Rozsika Parker maintains that "the embroiderer's silence, her concentration . . . suggests a self-containment, a kind of autonomy," Lena Cowen Orlin identifies these forms of creativity with the invisibility of the artists. [1] The feminine needle is thus the antithesis of the masculine sword and the pen that Renaissance writers associated with manliness and heroism.[2]

Like poetry, however, needlework could make public statements, and as material objects, artworks by women did perform cultural and even political work. Themes woven into embroidery became more secularized after the long tradition of religious embroidery in England came to an end, particularly when the Reformation rejected ornamental art objects displaying sacred subjects. The secularization of themes in embroidery can also be attributed to the development of a more prosperous society, represented in part by the construction and furnishing of new houses.[3] Ann Jones and Peter Stallybrass have recently argued that embroidery and sewing, especially in an aristocratic setting, were means for artistic display, and, moreover, that the needle did serve as a kind of pen that even enabled women to access the public world: "Whatever repressive and isolating effects sewing as a disciplinary apparatus might have been intended to produce, women used it both to connect to one another within domestic settings and to articulate public roles for themselves in the outer world, as well."[4]

This redirection of needlework as public statement appears in some of the works associated with Elizabeth I, whose personal and political history is partly conveyed in art form. In her childhood, Elizabeth I embroidered a cover for a work she translated as "The glasse of the synnefull soule" (1544). The embroidery bears the initials of Katherine Parr, for whom the gift was intended.[5] In its social and political milieu, Elizabeth's work, then, acquired added significance; as a material object and gift, it makes a statement about the desire of the yet-illegitimate Elizabeth for integration into her father's family. As a translation of *Le miroir de l'âme pécheresse* by Marguerite d'Angouleme, Queen of Navarre, who was at heart a Reformer,[6] "The glasse of the synnefull soule" is a vehicle for the promotion of the Protestant tradition, to which Elizabeth, at the behest of her father and stepmother, now began to establish her lifelong allegiance.[7]

Art is a carrier of traditions, identities, relationships, and alliances. Elizabeth's translation of *Le miroir*, which Marguerite may have presented to Anne Boleyn, ritualizes the advancement of Protestantism and the establishment of Elizabeth's family ties. Other kinds of art of the same period, though seemingly unsophisticated, perform similar kinds of work. Lady Elizabeth Tyrwhit's *Morning and evening praiers* (1574), which may have belonged to Elizabeth I, professes its Protestantism in its symbolic cover design, its contents, and as a material object bound with copy of the Litany and Katherine Parr's *Prayers and Meditations* (c. 1574). The final entry with a connection to Elizabeth I is "A short and sweet sonnet made by one of the maides of honor upon the death of Queene Elizabeth, which she sowed uppon a sampler in red silke" (1603). "A short and sweet sonnet," though commemorating Elizabeth, appeared in the reign of James in a 1612 collection by Richard Johnson, thus acquiring an added political significance as a critique of the king's reign.

Artworks offer spaces and places for identity formation. While the poems in an entry below, Esther Inglis's *Octonaries* (c. 1600), bear the signature of Inglis's husband, who may have been responsible for their translation, Inglis's own identity is represented by her calligraphy, and in many of her other extant manuscripts by the self-portraits that appear in the spaces of the pages. Rooms too can bear signatures, and here we might recall the semantic connection between "room" and "stanza." The textiles of Hardwick Hall, particularly those of Bess of Hardwick (1518–1608), an important patroness of architecture who commissioned the construction of Hardwick Hall and two other houses, remain one of the most important collections of original sixteenth-century furnishings in England. The Hardwick Hangings alone—the result of a remarkable, unusual collaboration between the Protestant Bess of Hardwick and the staunchly Catholic Mary, Queen of Scots—exhibit a rich and virtually inexhaustible "iconographic programme."[8]

A more contained and private space displaying the work of a female is Lady Anne Drury's oratory at Hawstead Place near Bury St. Edmunds, England. This place of prayer is transformed into a fantasy world with symbolic and enigmatic emblematic panels, suggesting that the tiny room was conceived as "a live-in book."[9] The images portray the mysteries of spirituality and the human condition but do not readily lend themselves to interpretation, certainly not in any linear fashion. Still, they provide glimpses into an interior world of a woman whose art helped convey her sense of melancholy. In the later seventeenth century, the identification of textile furnishings (and of embroidery) in aristocratic houses with a form of signature or intellectual pursuit is extended by Hannah Wolley to the adornment of middle-class homes in her *Supplement to the Queen-like Closet; or, a little of Every Thing* (1674–75). Wolley includes such instructions in the *Supplement* for such practices as dyeing cloth, covering soft furniture, and making artificial flowers and wax-works, and she also explains how properly to depict classical gods and goddesses as well as figures from Bible stories (see chapter 3).

Women of the period used other art forms, including music, to express their states of mind. Before female voices were regularly heard in early modern professional perform-ances, women's involvement with music was largely restricted to private performances and to the transcription of music books.[10] Lady Margaret Wemyss's manuscript music book, which contains pieces for instrumental music, provides some information about the train-ing this Scottish woman received in the art of music during the 1640s. More than that, the manuscript also reveals Wemyss's active engagement with the music scripts insofar as it contains her transcriptions and even her signature. Lady Mary (Harvey) Dering like-wise received an education in music, having been the student of the composer Henry Lawes, who included some of her songs in his 1655 and 1659 music books. One of her later songs, which is represented here, offers a setting for love lyrics composed by her hus-band, "A false designe to be cruel." There is another context—or political climate—in which to situate the song. As in the case of the elegiac "A short and sweet sonnet," Dering's song, composed during the Interregnum, has political implications in its repre-sentation of a resistance to the Puritan ban on art and Royalist ideals of love. Katherine Philips also wrote songs, and in particular a poem about Henry Lawes. In her case, too, this artistic work exposes a continuing Royalist culture during the Interregnum.

In the Restoration period, when classical values and tastes were reintroduced, the number of recognized artistic venues for personal and emotional expression declined. Ann Finch resists this tradition through the composition of song lyrics in which music serves as a metaphor. The verses and corresponding notes convey the poet's melancholy in *The Spleen: A Pindarique Ode*, which was written c. 1694 and published in 1701. Melancholy had a wealth of associations, ranging from a serious affliction to a fashionable one. Finch's theme takes us back to the age of melancholy, though Finch reworks the music-melan-choly relationship discussed earlier in the seventeenth century by Robert Burton in his famous, gargantuan *Anatomy of Melancholy*.[11] To recognize Finch's experimentation with the lyrical tradition is to add another level of complexity to her poems and to invite a reconsideration of how they were circulated, received, and even performed.

Another Restoration work, an extant nineteenth-century engraving of a seventeenth-century portrait allegedly of Aphra Behn (late 1670s–early 1680s), attributed by tradition to Mary Beale, provides a unique "interface" between a professional woman painter and England's first professional woman writer. The juxtaposition of the Behn portrait by a contemporary female painter ("Mistress Mary Beale") with the engraving by a nineteenth-century male engraver, James Fittler, yields fascinating insights into the complex repre-sentations of Behn. The portrait of Behn might also be compared with the frontispiece portrait of Ephelia produced at the same time for her volume *Female Poems on several Occasions* (1679, 1682) (see chapter 8).[12]

By investigating the development of early, largely nonverbal forms of artistic expres-sion by women, we learn, finally, to appreciate the relationship among female artists, like Beale and Behn, as well as among female artists and male writers or editors. Although some of the women represented in this chapter designed their own circles through the cre-ation or circulation of their art, others inverted the entrenched male-female hierarchy, which designated the male as creator and the female as a muse or simply as the object of representation. Here Anne Drury is no longer just John Donne's patron but has a room of her own; Esther Inglis emerges as a creator while her husband serves as translator; the music book of Lady Margaret Wemyss, containing songs transcribed from books of airs by Thomas Morley and Thomas Campion, exhibits a young woman's authoritative tastes in music. The interaction between Mary Dering and Henry Lawes registers in works by each of them, while, at the end of the Restoration period, lyrics by Ann Finch inspired the music of Henry Purcell.

Notes

We gratefully acknowledge the assistance of Pamela Brown, Susan Frye, and Lena Orlin.

1. Lena Cowen Orlin, "Three Ways to be Invisible in the Renaissance: Sex, Reputation, and Stitchery," *Renaissance Culture and the Everyday*, ed. Patricia Fumerton and Simon Hunt (Philadelphia: University of Pennsylvania Press, 1999). Rozsika Parker, *The Subversive Stitch: Embroidery and the Making of the Feminine* (New York: Routledge, 1984), 10.

2. Interestingly, however, Robert Matz has recently observed that Sir Philip Sidney's efforts at maintaining this distinction fail, and that he in fact aligns writing with the feminization of aristocratic culture. The conditions of writing are leisure, solitude, and private concentration, thus connecting the poet's work with the ornamental needlework of court ladies rather than to actions in the public sphere and battlefield. See Robert Matz, *Defending Literature in Early Modern England: Renaissance Literary Theory in Social Context* (Cambridge: Cambridge University Press, 2000).

3. Donald King and Santina Levey, *The Victorian & Albert Museum's Textile Collection: Embroidery in Britain from 1200 to 1750* (London: Victoria & Albert Museum, 1993), 15.

4. Ann Rosalind Jones and Peter Stallybrass, "The Needle and the Pen: Needlework and the Appropriation of Printed Texts," *Renaissance Clothing and the Materials of Memory* (Cambridge: Cambridge University Press, 2000), 148.

5. On the surrounding culture of gift giving, see Lisa M. Klein, "Your Humble Handmaid: Elizabethan Gifts of Needlework," *Renaissance Quarterly* 50.2 (1997): 459–93.

6. Anne Lake Prescott, "The Pearl of the Valois and Elizabeth I: Marguerite de Navarre's *Miroir* and Tudor England," *Silent But for the Word: Tudor Women as Patrons, Translators, and Writers of Religious Works*, ed. Margaret Patterson Hannay (Kent, Ohio: Kent State University Press, 1985), 62. Also see Maureen Quilligan, "Elizabeth's Embroidery," *Shakespeare Studies* 28 (2000): 208.

7. David Starkey, *Elizabeth: The Struggle for the Throne* (New York: HarperCollins, 2001), 47–49. For the full text of Elizabeth's translation, see *Elizabeth's Glass*, ed. Marc Shell (Lincoln: University of Nebraska Press, 1993).

8. Margaret Ellis, "The Hardwick Wall Hangings: An Unusual Collaboration in English Sixteenth-Century Embroidery," *Renaissance Studies* 10.2 (1996): 280–300; Susan Frye, "Sewing Connections: Elizabeth Tudor, Mary Stuart, Elizabeth Talbot, and Seventeenth-Century Anonymous Needleworkers," *Maids and Mistresses, Cousins and Queens: Women's Alliances in Early Modern England*, ed. Susan Frye and Karen Robertson (New York: Oxford University Press, 1999), 169–74. On Bess of Harwick, also see chapter 5 of this book for Bess of Hardwick's letter to her workman (1590).

9. Jane Hill, "Lady Drury's Closet," *World of Interiors* 20.11 (2000): 148, illustration caption.

10. On musical performances in the early modern period, see Edward Huws Jones, *The Performance of English Song 1610–1670, Outstanding Dissertations in Music from British Universities*, ed. John Caldwell (New York & London: Garland, 1989). For professional women singers in sixteenth-century England, see James Stokes, "Women and Mimesis in Medieval and Renaissance Somerset (and Beyond)," *Comparative Drama* 27 (1993): esp. 180–81; and Hyder Rollins, who mentions that a "gypsy balladsinger" named Alyce Boyce performed for Elizabeth ("The Black-Letter Broadside Ballad," *PMLA* 27 [1919]: 319).

11. Katharine M. Rogers, "Finch's 'Candid Account' vs. Eighteenth-Century Theories of the Spleen," *Mosaic* 22.1 (1989): 17–19.

12. See Maureen Mulvihill's attribution of Ephelia's work to Lady Mary Villiers, Duchess of Richmond and Lennox in the on-line journal *[Re]Soundings* 2.3 [2001]).

10.1: A Girdle-book (c. 1540) containing Elizabeth Tyrwhit's *Morning and evening praiers* (1574) and Queen Katherine (Parr)'s *Prayers and Meditations* (c. 1574). By permission of the British Library.

A Girdle-book (c.1540) containing Lady Elizabeth Tyrwhit's *Morning and evening praiers* (1574), and Queen Katherine (Parr)'s *Prayers and Meditations* (c. 1574).

This eighteenth-century etching is of a tiny gold-and-enamel girdle prayer-book housed in the British Museum. Bound in it are a unique copy of Lady Elizabeth Tyrwhit's *Morning and evening praiers* (printed by Christopher Barker, 1574) and incomplete copies of Katherine Parr's *Prayers and Meditations* (c. 1574), known popularly as "The Queen's Prayers," and a Kalendar. This scale drawing of the covers appeared in *The Gentleman's Magazine* in April 1791 and the discussion in issues from August 1790 through April 1791 of the book's provenance gestures toward the particularly female and domestic world in which it resided. The tiny book re-creates a female family circle, in that it appears to have belonged to Elizabeth I (*GM* 1791 28) and contains works by both her stepmother, Parr, and her temporary governess, Tyrwhit. The texts, inscriptions, and illustrations on the covers and the type of book itself indicate their affiliation with Protestantism.

Girdle prayer books served both religious and decorative purposes by having bindings made of wood or metal, often silver or gold, with a loop at the top so that they could be worn on a chain around the waist or the neck. Typically, they contained works of private devotion and reached a peak of popularity from 1530 to 1560 (Tait, "Girdle" 30), following the first wave of Protestantism in England. This particular binding was made by Hans of Antwerp, a Dutch goldsmith residing in London, around 1540 (Tait, "Goldsmiths" 113). On the front cover, in relief with white, black and green enamel, is an illustration of Moses raising the Brazen Serpent (Numbers 21:8), while the back, in white and black, depicts the Judgment of Solomon (1 Kings 3:27), an especially domestic theme. The accompanying inscriptions read, respectively, "Make The a fyre serpent an[*sic*] sett it up for a sygne that as many as are bytte maye loke upon it an[*sic*] lyve" and "Then the kyng answered an[*sic*] sayd gyve her the lyvyng child an[*sic*] slayet not for she is the mother thereoe[*sic*]." The spine has an intricate pattern worked in relief with black enamel. That it is a very personal book is indicated by the fact that all the texts were printed well after the production of the binding and have been cut down to fit into it.

Tyrwhit was connected to both the other women associated with the book, as friend and lady-in-waiting to Katherine Parr and, briefly, governess to the young Princess Elizabeth. In 1546, before Henry VIII's death, Tyrwhit and two other ladies-in-waiting were ordered arrested for heresy because of their involvement in the queen's Protestant circle. Tyrwhit's relationship to Elizabeth was forged during a scandal in 1547–48, in which Princess Elizabeth apparently carried on an affair with Thomas Seymour, who was married to Parr. Because Elizabeth's governess, Katherine Ashley, was implicated in the engineering of the relationship, she was replaced for some months in 1549 by Tyrwhit, whose husband was charged with investigation of the affair (Plowden 110–13; Weir 560). Tyrwhit was also present when Parr died of puerperal fever after the birth of her first child in 1548 (Weir 559). Tyrwhit appears not to have held further offices and died in London in March 1578.

PATRICIA BRACE
LAURENTIAN UNIVERSITY

The Gentleman's Magazine and Historical Chronicle. For the Year MDCCXCI. Volume XLI. Part the First. By Sylvanus Urban, Gent. (1791). British Library RAR052. Plate 2.

10.2: Elizabeth Tudor, Embroidered cover of "The glasse of the synnefull soule" (1544). Bodleian Library, University of Oxford.

Elizabeth Tudor, Embroidered cover of "The glasse of the synnefull soule" (1544)

In December 1544, the then eleven-year-old Elizabeth presented to her stepmother, Queen Katherine Parr (sixth wife of Henry VIII), a prose translation of Marguerite of Navarre's French religious poem *Le miroir de l'âme pécheresse*. Marguerite supported ecclesiastical reform and so the text would have appealed to Katherine; Elizabeth may have had a more personal reason for selecting this text, as Marguerite may have presented Anne Boleyn with a copy of her work in 1534–35. Elizabeth probably embroidered the cover of this little book herself and the text is neatly written in her own handwriting. Both activities, translation (especially of devotional works) and embroidery, were considered appropriate for women. Elizabeth possibly turned to them to prove to her step-mother that she had not been idle at a time when Elizabeth had quarreled with her father, been removed from court, but then had been returned through Parr's intervention. "Pusilanimity and ydlenes," she writes in an accompanying letter to the queen, "are most repugnante unto a reasonable creature" and "the witte of a man, or woman, [will] waxe dull, and [be] unapte to do, or understand any thing perfittely onles it be always occupied upon some manner of study." Therefore, she says, she has translated the poem, "joining the sentences together as well as the capacity of my simple wit and small learning could extend themselves."

Marguerite's poem is a long, and some say dull, analysis of her relationship with God, beginning with dejection at her own sinfulness, but moving finally to her joy at realizing that, no matter what she does, God always takes her back. Elizabeth's translation errors offer "a tantalizing glimpse" into Elizabeth's childhood feelings about her mother's (and one of her stepmother's) beheadings, as well as her anger at her father (Prescott 68). For example, Marguerite says that, unlike God, no husband will forgive his wife's adultery. Elizabeth translates that "Therebe inoughe of them, wiche for to avenge their wronge, did cause the judges to condemne hym to dye," substituting a masculine pronoun "hym" for "her." She then crosses out the "hym" and writes "them" above it.

The embroidered cover is worked in chain stitch, one of the most common stitches used in the early modern period, in gold and silver wire on blue corded silk. At the center are the initials KP, for Katherine Parr. Surrounding these initials is a complex "knot" design that mimics the lovers' knot patterns often used in Tudor formal gardens. Lisa M. Klein suggests that the outline refers to Henry VIII's name and titles, with a cross and shield signifying Henry's role as defender of the faith. The garden theme continues in the four corners, with four pansies embroidered in purple and yellow thread twisted with gold—possibly a pun on the French word *pensée*, "thought" or "idea," drawing attention "to the thoughtful work of translation and the prayerful act of meditation" (Klein 477–78). Moreover, Klein notes, pansies were also called "love-in-idleness," so in choosing the pansy Elizabeth could be contrasting her own industry with her needle to the "idleness" suggested by the flower, or perhaps contrasting the vain love of the flower to the sacred love described in the poem.

Gifts of needlework, an especially important social phenomenon, validated the time women spent plying their needles in a sanctioned form of activity and personal expression.

Nely Keinanen
University of Helsinki

Elizabeth Tudor, Embroidered cover of "The glasse of the synnefull soule." Bodleian Library MS Cherry 36.

10.3: Elizabeth Talbot, Countess of Shrewsbury (Bess of Hardwick), "Diana and Actaeon" (1597). National Trust Photo Library. Photo: John Hammond.

Elizabeth Talbot, Countess of Shrewsbury (Bess of Hardwick), Embroidered panel "Diana and Actaeon" (1597)

New Hardwick Hall, completed in 1597 by Elizabeth Talbot following the death of her third and final husband, George Talbot, Earl of Shrewsbury, is a treasure house of needle-work pieces produced under her direction from the 1570s. Talbot was, after Queen Elizabeth, the wealthiest woman in England; she had made a series of marriages that brought her from impoverished member of the gentry to lady in waiting to countess; she was now free of her contentious husband and resolved to build and furnish her final home, which itself may be considered her greatest work. Like many powerful women of the period, Talbot's choice of subjects demonstrates imaginative connections with assertive women from myth and history, including Penelope, Lucrece, and Diana. Diana appears in particular in one of three similar pieces clearly produced in Talbot's household, most likely drawn out by one of the professional embroiderers whom she kept in her employ, and displaying her ini-tials, ES, prominently intertwined in the far right corner—the same initials that appear on the roof of New Hardwick Hall at intervals and over the fireplace in her Great Hall.

This needlework panel of Diana and Actaeon, though mentioned in discussions of Talbot's embroidery, has been unreproduced and undiscussed, perhaps because the power of the central female figure is so conspicuous and because it does not seem to be an embroidered copy of a print. Although the Diana and Actaeon design was doubtless drawn by a professional and the needlework accomplished with the aid of several mem-bers of her household, Elizabeth Talbot's choice of design resonates in this panel, which captures two parts of the encounter between goddess and mortal male. First, there is the moment in which Actaeon stands confidently, hand on hip, observing Diana, seated bathing with her ladies, legs decorously together, mirror in her hand. Actaeon's arrogance is represented not only by his masterful stance but by the ribbon floating above his head announcing in large letters "*Actæon ego sum*": the dominant male, so sure of his masculine identity, unblinkingly observes the goddess bathing. Second, there is the moment in which Diana, having caught Actaeon in the process of watching her bathe, is turning him into a stag; although only his head, like Bottom's, is translated, his dogs have already turned on him and begun to devour him.

This second moment depicts Diana's power during Actaeon's transition from man to beast; her action is her triumph. As in the first moment, Diana is naked, but now she is an indecorous female figure slightly bent over and with legs apart, ignoring the towel her attendant holds ready for her. Rainbows of power arc from Diana's upturned hands across the first, confident body of Actaeon to reach and transform the body of the second Actaeon, in the act of falling to the ground, powerless to prevent his metamorphosis. In emphasizing Diana's strength rather than her shame, the needlework panel claims the per-spective of an active, powerful female figure over the confident pleasures of the male voyeur, and in that sense represents Talbot's own disdain toward the male gaze as well as a sense of the transformations she wrought by building and furnishing New Hardwick Hall.

SUSAN FRYE
UNIVERSITY OF WYOMING

Elizabeth Talbot. Embroidered panel, "Diana and Actaeon" (1597). The National Trust
Photographic Library.

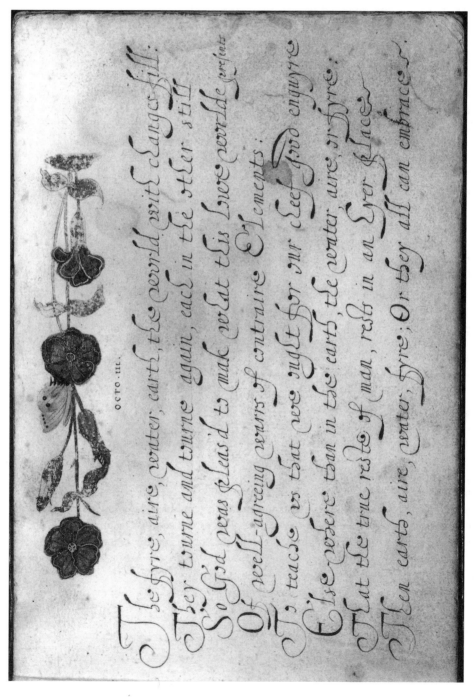

10.4: Esther Inglis, Calligraphy of "Octonaries" (c. 1600). By permission of the Folger Shakespeare Library.

Esther Inglis, Calligraphy of "Octonaries" (c. 1600)

Esther Inglis (1571-1624) was a woman of multiple names and multiple talents. Born Esther Langlois, she fled from France to England with her family (c. 1569) to avoid persecution of Protestants. Her father taught French in Scotland while her mother, Marie Presot, probably first taught Esther the calligraphy at which she soon exceled. Although Esther married Bartholomew Kello c. 1596, she signed her work with her maiden name, which she later anglicized. Over fifty of her beautifully composed manuscripts survive, often colorfully illuminated and containing small self-portraits. One volume includes more than forty styles of script, and several works are amazingly tiny. Inglis presented her texts (usually based on the Bible or moralistic poems) to the wealthy or well-born, from whom she received sufficient payments to earn a decent income.

Among her most intriguing works are the "Octonaries"—fifty poems of eight lines each. Modern studies sometimes imply that she may have composed either the original poems or their translations from French. Recently, however, their author has been identified as Antoine de la Roche Chandieu (1534-1591). Inglis herself probably did not prepare the translations, since her own English was awkward. Perhaps they were translated by her husband, who did the same with other works. In any case the "Octonaries" deserve attention, both as poems and as rich examples of Renaissance calligraphy.

The illustration shows the third "Octonarie" from a manuscript (V.a. 91) held by the Folger Library. The French original appears on the left, the translation on the right as follows:

> The fyre, aire, water, earth, the world with changes fill:
> They tourne and tourne again, each in the other still
> So God was pleas'd to mak what this lowe worlde presents
> Of well-agreeing warrs of contraire Elements:
> To teache us that we ought for our cheef good enquyre
> Else-where than in the earth, the water, aire, or fyre:
> That the true reste of man, rests in an hyer place
> Then earth, aire, water, fyre; Or they all can embrace.

By heavily accenting the four elements, the poem implies both their importance and substantiality. Yet the continually quick succession of these monosyllables, as well their constantly varied order, already suggests mutability (a central theme). Their very repetition implies both change and stasis, as does the phrase "turn and turn again," just as "still" can mean both "even now" and "always." Similarly, "world" in line one can function as both subject and direct object, while line seven plays with "rest" as both a noun and verb. The poem's fundamental paradox of constant change within a larger harmonious unity, meanwhile, is epitomized by the reference to "well-agreeing warrs." Such analysis, however, only scratches the verbal surface and doesn't begin to address either the complex contributions of Inglis's drawings and varied letterings or the place of them all within the unique larger manuscript.

Robert C. Evans
Auburn University Montgomery

Esther Inglis. Calligraphy of "Octonaries" (c. 1600). Folger Shakespeare Library V.a.91. Octo III.

A Crowne-Garland,

She our kind Mistris was,
full foure and forty yeare,
England she gouernd well
not to be blamed:
Flanders she suceerd still,
and Ireland tamed.
France she befrended,
Spaine she hath foiled:
Papists reiected,
and the Pope spoyled.
To Princes powerfull,
to the world vertuous
To her foes mercifull,
to subiects gracious.
Her soule is in heauen,
the world keepes her glory:
Subiects her good deeds,
and so ends my story.

The

of Golden Roses,

and then obeyed Gods command,
And left his Crowne to Mary heere,
whose fiue years raigne cost England deare
Oh mourne, mourne, mourne faire Ladies,
Iane your Quéen the flower of Englands dead.

Elizabeth raigned next to her,
Europes pride and Englands starre:
A fairer world, for such a Quéene,
vnder heauen was neuer séene.
A mayd, a Saint, an Angell bright,
in whom all princes tooke delight:
Oh mourne, mourne, mourne faire Ladies,
Elizabeth the flower of Englands dead.

A short and sweet sonnet made by one of the
maides of honor vpon the death of Queene
Elizabeth, which she sowed vppon a sampler
in red silke.

To a new tune or to Phillida flouts me.

G One is Elizabeth,
whom we haue lou'd so deare:
Sh

10.5: "A short and sweet sonnet made by one of the maides of honor upon the death of Queene Elizabeth, which she sowed upon a sampler in red silke" (1603). Bodleian Library, University of Oxford.

"A short and sweet sonnet made by one of the maides of honor upon the death of Queene Elizabeth, which she sowed uppon a sampler in red silke" (1603)

This poem is included in Richard Johnson's 1612 collection *A Crowne-Garland of Goulden Roses. Gathered out of Englands royall garden*, a work advertising itself as "Being the lives and strange fortunes of many great personages of this Land." Johnson's collection contains a number of sensational ballads, some of them centered on female figures. "The wofull death of Queene Iane Wife to King Henry the eight. and how King Edward was cut out of his mothers belly" is typical of Johnson's taste.

The "short and sweet" sonnet on Queen Elizabeth illustrates many of the frustrations we face when studying early modern women's literature. The poem is difficult to find; it is one of dozens of poems in a neglected early modern collection that has been reprinted once, in 1842. The poem is competent, but its blunt and unornamented style, desirable qualities in verse one must embroider on a sampler, make it unlikely to be the object of conventional literary analysis. Still, the sonnet is of historical interest. Unlike most of the other elegies to the dead queen, it does not focus on her prolonged virginity but instead attends to her political accomplishments, emphasizing her good government and her maintenance of peace and Protestantism. It is the only contemporary elegy with even a remote claim to female authorship. But the sonnet is presented anonymously, and its worth as a historical source is limited by this.

The poem's value is also limited by its medium. The sampler on which it was embroidered in red silk may be no more than Johnson's attempt to lend the poem an air of authenticy to increase sales. No such sampler survives. Very little seventeenth-century fabric, embroidered or otherwise, does (see Nely Keinanen's entry on Queen Elizabeth's embroidery, 10.2). Women, regardless of social class, were frequently enjoined to keep their hands busy with embroidery; rather than the books necessary for "toylsome studies," the anonymous author of *A Booke of Curious and strange Inventions, called the first part of Needleworkes* (1596) asserts of women, "Their milke white hands the needle finer fits." It is certainly possible that what Johnson printed had made its first public appearance in thread. Yet this detracts from the poem's literary value. We continue to give priority to published or manuscript texts, and have yet to see the publication of the collected works of embroiderers.

Given the efforts King James made to redirect the court and country's attention away from Elizabeth and toward himself, the sampler could represent something a bit more subversive than a *memento mori* or remembrance of the queen. James was not "lov'd so deare" as Elizabeth had been, nor was he out foiling Spain or actively rejecting Papists. He was not widely noted for being gracious to his subjects. For the poet-embroiderer to contend that "the world keepes [Elizabeth's] glory" and to claim that the late queen's "Subjects [keep] her good deeds" in effect diminishes James's accomplishments. If this particular maid of honor kept the sampler nearby, she demonstrates what *A Booke of Curious and strange Inventions* argues: "In needle works there doth great knowledge rest."

CATHERINE LOOMIS
UNIVERSITY OF NEW ORLEANS

Anonymous sampler text printed in Richard Johnson. *A Crowne-Garland of Goulden Roses*.
Bodleian Library 8 C 93 Art (4).

10.6: Lady Anne (Bacon) Drury, Photograph of her closet (c. 1612). By Permission of Ipswich
Borough Council Museums and Galleries.

Lady Anne (Bacon) Drury, Photograph of her closet (c. 1612)

The panels pictured opposite are part of a room owned and very possibly created by Lady Anne Drury (1572–1624), now known only as patroness of the poet John Donne. The wainscoted walls consist of panels of painted pictures and Latin mottoes, grouped under Latin sentences taken from classical and biblical texts. Some panels have been borrowed from popular emblem books, common proverbs, and works like Aesop's Fables. The sources of other panels are more recondite, while still others are perhaps original compositions of the room's creator. Below the "emblems" are panels of various herbs and plants seemingly chosen for their symbolic significance rather than being what we would call "merely" decorative. The room has been designed as a kind of three-dimensional emblem book (Farmer 105), but the order in which the panels are to be read, if there is one, is not clear. There are no signatures on the paintings, but one Latin sentence (see picture) points to a female owner/designer. Instead of exactly quoting Cicero's Latin proverb "*Nunquam minus solus, quam cum solum,*" or "Never less alone than when alone" (an expression of the joys of solitude with a well-stocked mind and/or library), the creator has modified the adjective "alone" (*solus, -a, -um*) to reflect a feminine rather than a masculine subject: the original *solus* has become *sola*. Other elements pointing to the closet's creation by or for Lady Anne are the early Jacobean clothing worn by some of the painted figures and a letter from her manservant who asks "what writtings [she] would have brought out the Closset" (University of Chicago Library; Bacon Collection 4221). The room's neglect by scholars in any discipline (one article in four hundred years; see Farmer) is perhaps a reflection of the difficulty of establishing "authorship," but also the result of the low value placed on women's "texts," whether literary or extraliterary (see Seeff and Travitsky 22) and the difficulty of imposing our own categories of meaning on an age that did not distinguish in the same way between the printed text and, for example, domestic decoration (Freeman 92).

Rather than putting pen to paper, Lady Drury has put paint to panel to create a "theatre" or "garden" (metaphors used by emblem book writers) of some sophistication into which she can, literally, enter and read, mentally strolling among the flowers of moral wisdom and acting out, in her own private theater, her spiritual regeneration. When read together, the panels exhibit a *contemptus mundi* theme and reflect a struggle with ambition, pride, and even despair in the face of overwhelming disappointments, such as Lady Anne faced in the deaths of both her children and in the frustrations of her husband's career at court.

Such tiny rooms (seven feet square) were new to early modern architecture and allowed their owners, male and female, complete privacy from other family members and/or servants for reading, writing, or praying. This paradoxical freedom within the domestic sphere was celebrated in the diaries and other writings of many seventeenth-century women, such as Lady Anne Clifford, but regarded suspiciously by male authors of conduct books such as Richard Brathwait. A woman alone, even within the domestic sphere, Brathwait worries, can still transgress the boundaries established for virtuous behavior, for with her books in her study she can be, as the Latin sentence suggests, "Alone, and yet not alone."

HEATHER MEAKIN
CASE WESTERN RESERVE UNIVERSITY

Photograph of Lady Anne Drury's closet. By permission of Ipswich Borough Council Museums and Galleries.

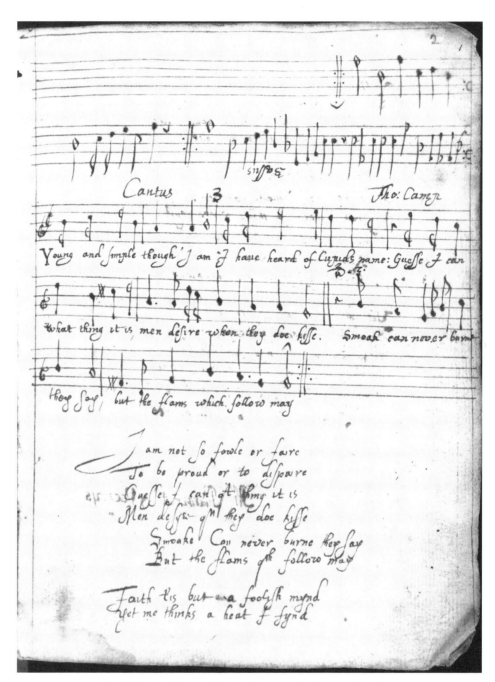

10.7: Lady Margaret Wemyss, Music book (c. 1643-49). Courtesy of the National
Library of Scotland. Reproduced by permission of Lord Strathnaver.

Lady Margaret Wemyss, Music book (c. 1643–49)

Transcription

Bassus [written upside down]

Cantus   Thomas Campion

Young and simple though I am I have heard of Cupids name: Guesse I can
what thing it is, men desire when they doe kisse. Smoak can never burne
they say, but the flams which follow may

I am not so fowle or faire
To be proud or to dispaire
Guesse I can what thing it is
Men desyre when they doe kisse
     Smoake Can never burne they say
     But the flams which follow may

Faith t'is but a foolish mynd
Yet me thinks a heat I fynd

Commentary

Music was often part of an early modern girl's education. Girls from the upper, and
increasingly middling, classes were given lessons for lute, voice, viols, and virginals, and
they were key participants in domestic music making of this period. Robert Burton in his
Anatomy of Melancholy suggests that musical skills were not practiced after marriage: "our
young women and wives, they that being maids took so much pains to sing, play, and
dance, with such cost and charge to their parents to get these graceful qualities, now being
married will scarce touch an instrument, they care not for it." One manuscript source, the
music book of Lady Margaret Wemyss, gives us insight into how music was taught to one
young woman in Scotland during the 1640s.

This manuscript contains 17 songs for voice and bass viol, 27 poems, and 91 pieces
or fragments of pieces for lute. Wemyss, the daughter of a Scottish earl, wrote her name
at several points and transcribed many of the poems and some of the solo lute music. The
manuscript, begun when Wemyss was aged about 12 and finished sometime before her
death at age 18 or 19, retains its original parchment binding. The first part of the volume,
headed "A Booke Containing some pleasant aires of Two, Three, or fowre voices Collected
out of diverse Authors Begunne june 5 1643," consists of songs transcribed from books of
airs by Thomas Morley and Thomas Campion, probably by a music teacher. This teacher
was probably a Scot, given his tendency to use q instead of w to abbreviate such words as
what (q^t) in line three of the first verse below the staves, and when (q^n) in line four. These
songs all contain a line or two of music for bass viol, headed "Bassus," and several lines for
treble voice, headed "Cantus," under which is the first verse of the song. Subsequent verses
tend to be written below the staves. The bass viol part has been written at the top of the
page and upside down, obviously so that the singer and instrumentalist could use the same

copy of music when playing, indicating that this volume was used in performance of some type. The layout of the pages in the printed volumes of Morley and Campion differs somewhat from the transcription in Wemyss's music book. The main omission in Wemyss's is of lute tablature below the cantus line to accompany the songs. Wemyss's teacher has omitted the additional lute part, likely because by this time, the 1640s, it was becoming more fashionable for a singer to be accompanied by the bass viol than by the lute. This song, "Young and simple though I am I have heard of Cupids name" (from Campion's fourth book of airs, c. 1618), is the one song of the seventeen in this section of the manuscript that is spoken in a female voice. It is also the only song at the end of which Wemyss has signed her name (visible in the bleedthrough three lines below the staves).

Victoria Burke
University of Ottawa

The music book of Lady Margaret Wemyss. National Library of Scotland Dep. 314/23, fol. 2r.

Lady Mary (Harvey) Dering, Musical setting for "A false designe to be cruel," as printed in Henry Lawes, *Select Ayres and Dialogues* (1659)

Mary Dering's setting of her husband Edward's poem, "A false designe to be cruel," is a work that can generate several distinct—yet equally valid—texts. The song commands its performers to interpret and ornament according to contemporary performance practices invisibly embedded in the musical structure. According to Royalist composer-publisher John Playford (1623–86), trills should be added at "Closes, Cadences, and other places, where by a long Note an Exclamation or Passion is expressed" (53). Likewise, lyrics should govern vocal dynamics: "those that well understand the conceit and the meaning of the Words . . . can distinguish where the Passion is more or less required" (41). The best way to encounter this liberating performative indeterminacy is to sing Dering's song.

The song is arranged for a vocalist accompanied by theorbo (a large lute with two sets of strings), or bass viol (also known as the viola da gamba), a four-stringed bowed instrument similar to a cello. The musical notation appears quite modern, with a few exceptions. The marks in bass and treble at each line's end are "Directs," or cues to prepare the performer for the next note. Small *x*'s indicate sharps. The mark in the treble in the first measure is a quarter rest; the mark on beat one, measure seven, an eighth rest. Dots, then termed "Pricks of Perfection," increase the note they follow by one half its value, regardless of interceding barlines (see measure eight, treble, beat one).

Charges of notational inaccuracy plagued Playford, as his preface indicates. More importantly, manually copied music, distributed in a select circle of patrons, connoted status; printed music, destined for wider circulation and calculable profits, did not: "I resolve to meet with those Mistakers, who have taken up a new (but very fond) opinion, That Musick can-not as truely be Printed as Prick'd, (and which is more ridiculous) that no Choice Ayres or Songs are permitted by Authors to come in print." This second point contextualizes Mary Dering's contribution to the *Select Ayres.*

Mary Harvey, daughter of a Levant merchant, may have begun her music lessons at Mrs. Salmon's school in Hackney, where she met Katherine Philips ("the matchless Orinda") and Mary Aubrey. At 16, Mary secretly married her cousin William Hauke, but her father annulled the marriage in the Ecclesiastical Courts to enable a more advantageous match with Sir Edward Dering of Surrenden-Dering in 1648. Her three-thousand-pound marriage portion undoubtedly benefited Dering's Civil War–ravaged estate.

After marriage, Dering's lessons continued with composer Henry Lawes (1596–1662). Lawes's 1655 *Second Book of Select Ayres and Dialogues* contains three songs by Dering and is dedicated to her. He writes: "some which I esteem the best of these Ayres, were of your own Composition . . . you are not only excellent for the time you spent in the practis of what I Set, but are yourself so good a Composer, that few of any sex have arriv'd to such perfection." Lawes's compliment betrays his reliance upon aristocratic patrons following the collapse of Charles I's court, where he had served as a musician.

Thus, the inclusion of this song in Lawes's 1655 and 1659 collections, printed by Playford, may be interpreted cynically as a blatant casting after patronage. It might also be read as a Royalist act of resistance to the stark aesthetic of the Cromwellian regime, since the song reflects earlier Cavalier ideals of love. The lyrics, which criticize the dissembling behavior of a coquette, offer an interesting contrast to Mary Harvey Dering's own love history. Ornaments, it seems, are not the only unseen subtext to Dering's song.

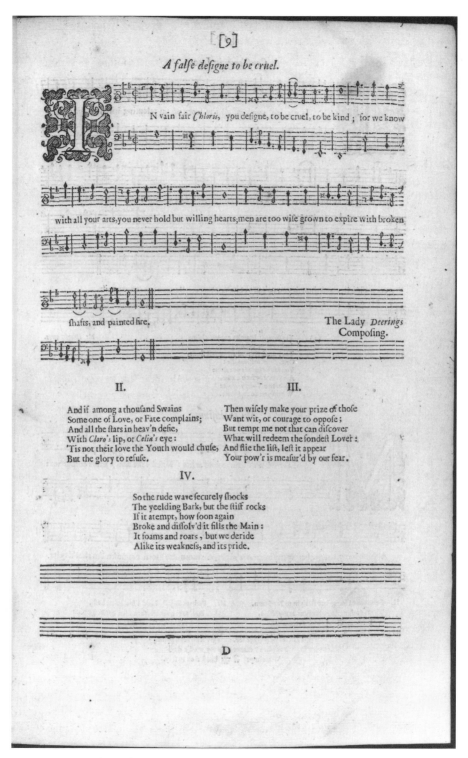

10.8: Lady Mary (Harvey) Dering, Musical setting for "A false designe to be cruel," as printed in Henry Lawes, *Select Ayres and Dialogues* (1659). By permission of The British Library.

Lawes's *Second Book of Select Ayres and Dialogues* (1655) contains two further songs by Mary Dering: "When First I saw fair Doris' eyes," and "And is this all? What one poor Kisse" (24). A recording of Mary Harvey's "A false design to be cruel" is available on a CD entitled "Non Tacete! (I'll Not be Silent): Music Written by Women Before 1800," ARS FEMINA, Linda De Rungs, soprano; violins and continuo. NRARS 002.

LESLIE RITCHIE
QUEEN'S UNIVERSITY

Henry Lawes. *Select Ayres and Dialogues For One, Two, and Three Voyces; to the Theorbo-Lute or Basse-Viol. Composed by John Wilson, Charles Colman (Doctors in Musick) Henry Lawes, William Lawes, Nicholas Lanear, William Webb (Gentlemen and Servants to his late Majesty in his Publick and Private Musick. And other Excellent Masters of Musick* (1659). British Library K.7.i.19.(1.) Page 9.

10.9: Ephelia, *Female Poems on several Occasions* (1679). By permission of the
Folger Shakespeare Library.

Ephelia, Frontispiece, *Female Poems on several Occasions* (1679)

The frontispiece portrait from Ephelia's *Female Poems on several Occasions* (1679, 1682) has presented a tantalizing puzzle for feminist literary scholars. The woman pictured here cannot be identified by her looks as any known restoration-era person, and the fictitious name, "Ephelia," was designed to effectively disguise the real identity of the book's author. Our contemporary interest in recovering and understanding texts by early modern women has made the identity of Ephelia an important and hotly contested issue.

Although the identity of Ephelia has been lost (and may never have been widely known), some scholars (see Chernaik, Greer) speculate that the works appearing behind this page were written by a man or a group of men and women who chose to represent the collection as "by Ephelia." The portrait would thus represent not any real woman but a parody of a particular type of restoration aristocrat whose sentiments and concerns are established within the text. The pieces within this collection include several different kinds of poetry, written in various voices, or different persona, ranging from romantic lament to political commentary. We do know that other published collections of seventeenth-century "occasional poetry" were pulled together from various places and from more than one poet. If a group of restoration wits created *Female Poems*, then its interest to contemporary readers remains largely historical, as a record of questionably serious perspectives on (and by?) aristocratic women in the era of Charles II.

We also know, however, that early modern writers often created poetic personae with Greco-Roman derived names, like "Ephelia," which conveyed to readers the poet's participation in the classical literary heritage. Creating a classical pseudonym would allow a woman writer to deflect the ridicule almost certain to accompany the act of publishing one's work (and Ephelia was later mocked as a "ragged Jilt"). Remaining anonymous would hold further appeal for a woman who intended the text to be an entertaining puzzle for friends and acquaintances to enjoy. Such a woman would be traceable through the allusions she makes to real persons and events in her poetry; she may also have left clues to her identity in the frontispiece portrait.

Engraved frontispiece portraits such as this one were regularly employed to communicate meaningful messages to readers. Many details here are available for interpretation: the possibly fabricated coat-of-arms at the top of the portrait; the woman's brooch with another figure inside; a knotted piece of ribbon resting on the pedestal; the figure's provocative dress; her facial expression and hairstyle. The composition of the portrait may reflect features used in other engravings of the period to suggest a relationship to other writers. We have no record of the success or print run of *Female Poems*, and its scarcity suggests that it was published with the intention of reaching only a small audience of friends and admirers capable of properly decoding its clues.

The image here, as well as the text of *Female Poems*, contains interesting signs to suggest that Ephelia may have been Lady Mary Villiers. Since Lady Mary would have been almost sixty years old at the time her book was published, part of her trickery would have involved including a portrait of a much younger woman; this conjecture also posits that she cleverly dedicated the book to "the Excellent Princess MARY, Duchess of Richmond & Lenox"—herself! The evidence suggesting that Lady Mary is Ephelia (see Mulvihill) involves many detailed connections among her life experiences and personal relationships and the content of *Female Poems*. If she is in fact the author of the collection, then the book becomes of great interest to feminist literary critics and historians as the work of the most highly placed woman writer at the second Caroline court.

Susan Hrach Georgecink
Columbus State University

Ephelia. *Female Poems on several Occasions. Written by Ephelia* (1679). Early English books, 1641–1700; 645:16. Wing P2030. Folger Shakespeare Library P2030. Frontispiece.

Mary Beale, Portrait of Aphra Behn (c. 1682)

Portraits of Englishwomen in the seventeenth century, from the elegant mannequins of Van Dyck to the languorous courtesans of Lely, were seldom realistic. This page presents a seventeenth-century portrait allegedly of Aphra Behn, attributed by tradition to Mary Beale (image 10a), and its familiar nineteenth-century engraving (image 10b) by James Fittler, A.R.A., after a drawing by Thomas Uwins, R.A., keeper of the Royal Galleries and the National Gallery librarian of the Royal Academy. The Beale portrait is remarkable for its realism and its genius in fixing character. The engraving holds our interest for its representation of the woman writer in the nineteenth century.

Two Englishwomen achieved career fame during the closing years of the seventeenth century: the writer Aphra Behn (*c.* 1640–89) and the painter Mary Beale (1632–99). Commoners from the educated middle class, their rise to glory was unprecedented at a time when the literary and art markets were strong male preserves. Behn is now a familiar, if not protean, figure to students of early feminist history; but Mary Beale has only lately come into view, thanks to the energetic work of Richard Jeffree (1930–91). Traditionally judged but a talented protégée and copyist of Sir Peter Lely, "the Excellent Mistress Beale, Paintress" has undergone a reassessment by the art establishment in three recent exhibitions. Sir Oliver Millar judges her "the most prolific woman painter [in England] before Angelica Kauffmann." Other specialists praise her diversified subject matter, varied styles, and use of extraordinary colors. Mary Beale is now judged the most successful—indeed, the only—professional Englishwoman painter at work in Restoration London. Her husband's detailed notebooks (Bodleian Library, Oxford) valuably document Beale's rise to fame, happy society of friends, and the rapidly expanding clientele that visited her studio in Pall Mall, London. At the height of her fame, in 1677, Mary Beale received commissions for eighty portraits, bringing into her bustling household over four hundred pounds—an astonishing fact of her biography. In addition to her busy career in portraiture, which included paintings by several other notable women of her day (the lampoonist-courtesan Katherine Sedley; the memoirist Lady Anne Fanshaw), Beale was attracted to emerging feminist issues. For example, her "Discourse on Friendship" (c. 1666; BL Harl. MS. 6828, f 510) considers female friendship, marriage, and gender equality (see Barber).

The common link between Beale and Behn was Lely, who may have suggested Behn to Beale as a challenging subject, one to be captured far differently on canvas from his own "official," formal portrait. Plausibly, the two women may have met at Lely's studio in Covent Garden, where Beale, a frequent visitor, was permitted to observe her Dutch master's methods. Other possibilities are the poet-miniaturist Thomas Flatman and the portraitist John Greenhill, both mutual acquaintances of Beale and Behn. Or perhaps Beale's fine eye closely observed this large, public woman at a distance, only to put down on canvas a bit later her own "Behn," caught in an unguarded moment.

To date, four images of Behn are recorded by art historians: (1) John Riley's *Behn*, an unremarkable head-and-shoulders of a sweet-faced naïf, or at least such is the case in the extant engraving of the portrait by Robert Wise, which serves as the frontispiece portrait to Behn's *Poems* (1684), *Plays* (1716), and other works; (2) Sir Peter Lely's very fine, but dark and somber oval of Behn, with cartouche (c. 1670s), in the private collection of Arthur D. Schlechter; (3) Mary Beale's head-and-bust of Behn, which we see here (9" x 12"; unsigned, undated; c. late 1670s to early 1680s). And (4) a sketch of Behn (21 May 1873), from a portrait now presumed lost, by Sir George Scharf, first director of the National Portrait Gallery, London. In view of what we know of Behn's character and appearance, Beale's portrait and

10.10b: Engraving by James Fittler (1822) courtesy of the National Portrait Gallery, London.

Mary Beale's most effective and loving advocate.

10.10a: Mary Beale, Portrait of Aphra Behn (c.1682). By permission of St. Hilda's College, Oxford, UK / Bridgeman Art Library.

This page is dedicated to the memory of Richard Jeffree (1930-1991),

Scharf's sketch appear to depict the same woman. One sees this in the sitter's mouth, chin, and overall demeanor. The Beale *Behn* was attributed to Mary Beale and identified as a portrait of Behn in 1822, evidently, when the portrait received prestigious attention through Fittler's engraving. While Lely's *Behn* is predictably the finest image, and though art historians remain skeptical of the authenticity of the Beale *Behn*, it is the Beale that continues to find favor among Behn scholars, drama bibliographers, and their publishers.

Little wonder today's feminists often select the Beale *Behn* as a pictorial complement to their scholarship. The image articulates much of the sitter's character and frank sexual dualism. Beale's canvas does not depict a genteel, fashionable lady, but rather a bare-knuckled careerist, up from the mean streets of London, burning to make her mark. It is all there—the strength, the ambition—in the eyes and in the attitude of the chin and the mouth, a mouth that all but smirks and eyes that lock the viewer in a bold, ironic gaze. And then the hair. Behn's lush chestnut locks are not fashionably dressed, but cascade in unruly curls over her neck, shoulders, and chest. But most remarkable is her physical presence on the canvas: she is large and robust. This is a woman whom contemporaries—even the sitter herself—regarded as a curious admixture of male and female impulses. Dryden called her a "wond'rous Amazon"; Robert Gould called her "Sappho," the classical prototype of the bisexual woman poet. And Behn sexes her own creative gifts in the masculine gender: "All I ask is the privilege for my masculine part, the poet in me" (Preface, *The Lucky Chance* [1686]). Lesbian feminists rejoice to find in Behn's canon tender sapphic verse to women friends, in which she adopts the persona of a wooing beau ("To the fair Clarinda, who made Love to me, Imagin'd more than Woman"). The "Ephelia" poet celebrates Behn's sexual dualism in a poem of uncommon sorority: "You write so sweetly, that at once you move, / The Ladies Jealousies, and Gallants Love; / Passions so gentle, and so well exprest, / As needs much be the same fill your own Breast; / Then Rough again, as your Inchanting Quill / Commanded Love, or Anger at your Will: / As in your Self, so in your Verses meet, / A rare connextion of Strong and Sweet" ("To Madam Behn," *Female Poems on several Occasions* [1679, 1682], 72–73). Behn's seductive complexity lives on the canvas of Beale's picture. And how interesting, too, that the draughtsmanship of the sitter's mouth, hair, and bosom resemble that in some of Beale's self-portraits, suggesting perhaps the painter's special identification with her subject, something not uncommon in the intimate dynamics of the portraiture medium. Today's readers can observe readily enough that the nineteenth-century engraving of the Beale *Behn* by Fittler softens (even prettifies and "feminizes") the Beale image by stripping it of its rich androgynous complexity.

Archival images of early women writers, be they portraits or frontispieces, are valuable physical evidence of the writers' self-representation. Such images also shed light on the writers' contemporary status and how they were viewed by their culture. If the images are truly drawn "from the life," something of the sitters' temperament also may be transmitted. But these early images, as seductive as they are to us today, can be misleading and misread since most of them have yet to receive a full and dedicated assessment by art specialists.

Maureen E. Mulvihill
Princeton Research Forum

Mary Beale (1632–99). Portrait of Aphra Behn (1640–89) (oil on panel). Bridgeman Art Library, St. Hilda's College, Oxford SHC 188290. James Fittler. Portrait of Aphra Behn (engraving). National Portrait Gallery, London NPG D6859.

THE

SPLEEN,

A Pindarique

O D E.

By a *LADY.*

Together with

A Profpect of DEATH:

A Pindarique E S S A Y.

——*Sed Omnes una manet Nox,
Et Calcanda femel via Lethi.*

. Hor.

L O N D O N:

Printed and Sold by *H. Hills,* in *Black-fryars,* near
• the Water-fide. 1709.

(8)
Now Harmony in vain we bring,
Infpire the Flute, and touch the String;
From Harmony no help is had :
Mufick but fooths thee, if too fweetly fad ;
And if too light, but turns thee gladly mad.
Not skilful *Lower* thy Source cou'd find,
Or through the well-diffected Body trace
The fecret and myfterious ways,
By which thou doft deftroy and prey upon the Mind ;
Tho' in the Search, too deep for Humane Thought,
With unfuccefsful Toil he wrought,
Till in purfuit of thee himfelf was by thee caught;
Retain'd thy Prifoner, thy acknowledg Slave,
And funk beneath thy Weight to a lamented Grave.

10.11: Anne (Kingsmill) Finch, Countess of Winchilsea, *The Spleen* (1709). Courtesy of the William Ready Division
of Archives & Research Collections, McMaster University Library, Hamilton, Ontario

Anne (Kingsmill) Finch, Countess of Winchilsea, *The Spleen, A Pindarique Ode* (1701; 1709)

Spleen, in Anne Kingsmill Finch's day, was a complex term that referred not only to a bodily organ but to mental and physical symptoms of melancholy. The debt her poem, *The Spleen: A Pindarique Ode*, owes to Robert Burton's 1621 *The Anatomy of Melancholy* in this regard has been well noted. Yet the final section of Finch's irregular ode rejects Burton's emphatic assertion that music is a cure for melancholy. Why might Anne Finch resist this notion?

Finch suffered from disabling attacks of spleen all her life. Orphaned at age three, she grew up in the homes of her grandmother, Bridget, Lady Kingsmill, and her uncle, William Haslewood, where she probably overheard news of the many familial lawsuits concerning her inheritance. Her father's will specifically provides for her education, but no details concerning her lessons survive. At age 21, she went to serve Mary of Modena at court, where she met educated women such as Anne Killigrew and Lady Susan Bellasyse. She married fellow courtier Heneage Finch in 1684, when she was twenty-two, although the marriage license gives her age as "ab. 18 years." Her poems to him, often written under the pen name "Ardelia," portray a loving marriage. However, following James II's deposition in 1689, the Finches were forced to retire to the country. They never regained their former social prominence, owing to their refusal to abandon their allegiance to James II; they also inherited huge debts with the unexpected titles of earl and countess of Winchilsea when Heneage's nephew Charles died in 1712. Causes for melancholy—including criticism of her writing—were not wanting, as Finch's apostrophe to the spleen indicates:

> In me alas! thou dost too much prevail,
> I feel thy force, while I against thee rail;
> I feel my Verse decay, and my crampt Numbers fail.
> Through thy black Jaundies I all Objects see,
> As dark and terrible as thee;
> My Lines decry'd, and my Imployment thought
> An useless Folly, or presumptuous Fault. (ll. 74–80)

Despite trips to Tunbridge Wells in 1685 and 1706 in search of a physical cure, Anne Finch's melancholy persisted. In her poem "Ardelia to Melancholy," she tells of other methods she has adopted to banish spleen:

> . . . I confesse, I have apply'd
> Sweet mirth, and musick, and have try'd
> A thousand other arts beside,
> To drive thee from my darken'd breast. (ll.6–9)

An abundance of references to music and performance in poems such as "To the Nightingale," "A Song on Greife," and, most important, *The Spleen* suggest that music was an important source of metaphor and even formal poetic structure for Finch. In this poem, music fails Ardelia and even "augment[s]" her melancholy (l. 13); she concedes victory to "her dusky, sullen foe" (l. 23).

Finch's assessment of music as a short, but ultimately ineffective, "reprieve" (l.11) from spleen is directly countered by Burton's *Anatomy*. While Burton acknowledges that music may cause "a pleasing melancholy," for those who are "discontent, in woe, fear, sorrow, or dejected," he writes, "it is a most present remedy: it expels cares, alters their grieved minds, and easeth in an instant" (II: 118). Like the melancholic state it cures, music acts on body and mind, and restores harmony in both: "In a word, it is so powerful a thing that it ravisheth the soul, *regina sensuum*, the queen of the senses, by sweet pleasure (which is a happy cure), and corporal tunes pacify our incorporeal soul; *sine ore loquens, dominatum in animam exercet* [speaking without a mouth, it exercises domination over the soul], and carries it beyond itself, helps, elevates, extends it" (II: 116).

In *The Spleen: A Pindarique Ode*, written around 1694 and first published in Charles Gildon's 1701 *A New Miscellany of Original Poems on Several Occasions* (Reynolds lii), Finch admits music's power over the senses. However, she stresses the act of performance over that of audition, as the text shows. Music, a flawed human art form performed with the body, cannot transcend the physical, and thus only exacerbates one's original symptoms and mental tendencies. Far from representing a fixed system of signs that may combine to "ravish" or "elevate" the soul of the receptor by producing a determinate meaning, music, as Finch evidently experiences it, is ruled by the interpretive disposition of performer and auditor.

This, then, is the context for noting that Finch's first published works were songs. Circulation of Finch's poetry in musical form rarely enters into discussions of her reputation, but this distribution of her work was undoubtedly encouraging to her as a writer and influential on her peers. "'Tis strange this Heart" was set by R. Courteville and published in a music book entitled *Vinculum Societatis* ("A Song on Greife" was set by Mr. Estwick Rogers, *Selected Poems* 25). "Love thou art best of Human Joys" appeared in Thomas Wright's *The Female Vertuoso's, A Comedy* (1693) and in the *Lady's Journal* that year (McGovern 70). Her works were published anonymously; this anonymity may or may not have been preserved during performances.

Henry Purcell (1659–95) also set "Love thou art best of Humane joys" in 1694; it was republished by Purcell's widow in *Orpheus Britannicus* (1698; 1706). A reprint of the 1698 edition is now readily available to performers. The song is set in a minor key, as a dialogue between two voices with bass accompaniment. The voices engage in intimate, imitative gestures that eventually cadence on a perfect unison—on the word "dispute." At the declaration that without love, music "is but Noise," both voices enter into a prolonged melisma at the distance of a third, momentarily obliterating the sense of the words in sheer virtuosic "Noise." In short, Purcell's music comments ironically on Finch's verse. It does so by using a technical brilliance similar to Finch's narrative shifts in *The Spleen*, where the poet veers from sympathizing with the real sufferer of severe melancholy to satirize the coquette who "Assumes a soft and melancholy Air" (l. 103) to entice her lover.

At a time when the poet John Dryden declaimed, "What Passion cannot MUSICK raise and quell!" (l.16, "A Song for St. Cecilia's Day," 1687), when musician-publisher John Playford noted, "It [Music] abateth Spleen and Hatred" (*Of Musick in General, And of its*

Divine and Civil Uses, A7), Anne Finch's resistance to Burton's opinion that music "is a sovereign remedy against despair and melancholy" (II:117) in *The Spleen* and other poems represents a surprising affirmation of her own experience with attacks of melancholy, and of her personal experience of making and listening to music.

Leslie Ritchie
Queen's University

A Lady [Anne Finch, Countess of Winchilsea]. *The Spleen, A Pindarique Ode. Together with A Prospect of Death: A Pindarique Essay* (1709). McMaster University, Mills Research Collection. Disbound. Title page and page 8.

Bibliography

Bald, R.C. *Donne and the Drurys*. Cambridge: Cambridge University Press, 1959; rpt. Westport, Conn.: Greenwood Press, 1986.

Barber, Tabitha. "The Art of Friendship." *Mary Beale: Portrait of a Seventeenth-Century Painter, her Family and her Studio*. Catalogue, Geffrye Museum, 21 September 1999 to 30 January 2000. Ed. David Dewing. London: Geffrye Museum Trust Ltd., 1999. 23–42.

Brathwait, N. *A Closet for Ladies and Gentle Women*. London, 1608.

———. *The English Gentlewoman*. London, 1631.

Burton, Robert. *The Anatomy of Melancholy: What it is, with all the Kinds, Causes, Symptomes, Prognostickes, & Severall Cures of it*. Ed. Holbrook Jackson. London: Dent, 1932; rpt. New York: Vintage Books, 1977.

Campion, Thomas. *The Third and Fourth Booke of Ayres [ca. 1618]*. Ed. David Greer. Menston: Scolar, 1969. Vol. 2 of F. W. Sternfeld, ed., *English Lute Songs 1597–1632. A Collection of Facsimile Reprints*.

Cato, Nancy. *The Lady Lost In Time*. Sydney: Collins, 1986.

Chernaik, Warren. "Ephelia's Voice: The Authorship of Female Poems (1679)." *Philological Quarterly* 74.2 (Spring 1995): 151–67.

Corbett, Margery, and Ronald Lightbown. *The Comely Frontispiece: The Emblematic Title-Page in England, 1550–1660*. Boston: Routledge and Kegan Paul, 1979.

Craig-McFeely, Julia. "English Lute Manuscripts and Scribes 1530–1630." 3 vols. Ph. D. diss. University of Oxford, 1994.

Daly, Peter M., ed. *The English Emblem and the Continental Tradition*. New York: AMS Press, 1988.

———, and Mary V. Silcox. *The Modern Critical Reception of the English Emblem*. Munich; London; New York; Paris: K. G. Saur, 1991.

Doughtie, Edward. *English Renaissance Song*. Boston: Twayne, 1986.

Durant, David. *Bess of Hardwick: Portrait of an Elizabethan Dynasty*. New York: Atheneum, 1978.

Ellis, Margaret. "The Hardwick Hall Hangings: An Unusual Collaboration in English Sixteenth-century Embroidery." *Renaissance Studies* 10 (June 1996): 280–300.

Farmer, Norman K., Jr. "Lady Drury's Oratory: The Painted Closet from Hawstead Hall." *Poets and the Visual Arts in Renaissance England*. Austin: University of Texas Press, 1984. 77–105.

Freeman, Rosemary. *English Emblem Books*. London: Chatto & Windus, 1948.

Frye, Susan. "Sewing Connections: Elizabeth Tudor, Mary Stuart, Elizabeth Talbot, and Seventeenth-Century Anonymous Needleworkers." *Maids and Mistresses, Cousins and Queens: Women's Alliances in Early Modern England*. Ed. Susan Frye and Karen Robertson. New York: Oxford University Press 1999. 165–82.

Gent, Lucy, ed. *Picture and Poetry, 1560–1620: Relations Between Literature and the Visual Arts in the English Renaissance*. Leamington Spa: James Hall, 1981.

———, ed. *Albion's Classicism: The Visual Arts in Britain,1550–1660*. New Haven, Conn.: Yale University Press, 1995.

Greer, Germaine. "How to Invent a Poet." *Times Literary Supplement*, no. 4708 (25 June, 1993): 7.

Hobby, Elaine. *Virtue of Necessity: Englishwomen's Writing, 1649–88*. Ann Arbor: University of Michigan Press, 1989.

Jeffree, Richard. "Mary Beale." *Dictionary of Art*. Ed. Jane Turner. 34 vols. London: Macmillan, 1996. 3.444.

———, and Elizabeth Walsh. *The Excellent Mrs Mary Beale*. Exhibition catalogue. Introd. Sir Oliver Millar, KCVO. Geffrye Museum, London, 13 October–21 December 1975; Towner Art Gallery, Eastbourne, 10 January–21 February 1976. London: Inner London Education Authority, 1975.

Jones, Ann Rosalind. "Dematerializations: Textile and Textual Properties in Ovid, Sandys, and Spenser." *Subject and Object in Renaissance Culture*. Ed. Margaret de Grazia, Maureen Quilligan, and Peter Stallybrass. Cambridge: Cambridge University Press, 1996. 189–212.

———, and Peter Stallybrass. *Renaissance Clothing and the Materials of Memory*. Cambridge: Cambridge University Press, 2000.

Jones, Edward Huws. *The Performance of English Song 1610–1670*. New York: Garland, 1989.

Jorgens, Elise Bickford, ed. *English Song 1600–1675. Facsimiles of Twenty-Six Manuscripts and an Edition of the Texts*. 12 vols. New York: Garland, 1986–89.

Kerr, Jessica M. "Mary Harvey—The Lady Dering." *Music & Letters*. 25 (1944): 23–33.

King, Donald, and Santina Levey. *The Victoria & Albert's Museum's Textile Collection: Embroidery in Britain from 1200 to 1750*. London. Victoria & Albert Museum, 1993.

Klein, Lisa M. "Your Humble Handmaid: Elizabethan Gifts of Needlework." *Renaissance Quarterly* 50 (1997): 459–93.

Levey, Santina M. *Elizabethan Treasures: The Hardwick Hall Textiles*. London: National Trust, 1998.

McDowell, Joan Allgrove. "The Textiles at Hardwick Hall." *Hali Magazine*, nos. 39 and 40, 1988.

McGovern, Barbara. *Anne Finch and Her Poetry: A Critical Biography*. Athens: University of Georgia Press, 1992.

McMullan, Gordon, ed. *Renaissance Configurations: voices/bodies/spaces, 1580–1690*. New York: St. Martin's Press, 1998.

Mulvihill, Maureen E., ed. *Ephelia*. Burlington, Vt.: Ashgate, 2003.

———. "'Butterfly' of the Restoration Court: A preview of Lady Mary Villiers, the New 'Ephelia' Candidate." *ANQ* 9.4 (1996): 25–39.

———. "The Eureka! Piece in the 'Ephelia' Puzzle: Book Ornaments in Attribution Research and a New Location for Rahir Fleuron 203 (Elsevier, 1896)." *ANQ* 12.3 (1999): 23–34.

Nevinson, J. L. "Embroidered by Queen and Countess." *Country Life*. January 22, 1976.

Orlin, Lena Cowen. "Three Ways to be Invisible in the Renaissance: Sex, Reputation, and Stitchery." *Renaissance Culture and the Everyday*. Ed. Patricia Fumerton and Simon Hunt. Philadelphia: University of Pennsylvania Press, 1999. 183–203.

Parker, Rozsika.. *The Subversive Stitch: Embroidery and the Making of the Feminine*. New York: Routledge, 1984.

Playford, John. *An Introduction to the Skill of Musick. In Two Books*. 7th ed., corrected and enlarged. London: Printed by W. Godbid, for J. Playford at his Shop in the Temple near the Church 1674. Reprinted by the Gregg Press, 1966.

Plowden, Alison. *The Young Elizabeth*. London: Macmillan, 1971.

Prescott, Anne Lake. "The Pearl of Valois and Elizabeth I: Marguerite de Navarre's Miroir and Tudor England." *Silent But for the Word: Tudor Women as Patrons, Translators, and Writers of Religious Works*. Ed. Margaret P. Hannay. Kent, Ohio: Kent State University Press, 1985. 61–76.

Purcell, Henry. *Orpheus Britannicus: A Collection of the Choicest Songs for One, Two, or Three Voices*. London, 1698; rpt. Ridgewood, New Jersey: The Gregg Press, 1965.

Reynolds, Myra. *The Poems of Anne Countess of Winchilsea*. Chicago: Universtiy of Chicago Press, 1903.

Rogers, Katharine M., ed. *Selected Poems of Anne Finch Countess of Winchilsea*. New York: Frederick Ungar, 1979.

———. "Finch's 'Candid Account' vs. Eighteenth-Century Theories of the Spleen." *Mosaic: A Journal for the Interdisciplinary Study of Literature* 22 (Winter 1989): 17–27

Seeff, Adele F., and Betty S. Travitsky, eds. *Attending to Women in Early Modern England*. London: Associated University Press, 1994.

Shell, Marc. *Elizabeth's Glass*. Lincoln: University of Nebraska Press, 1993.

Spring, Matthew. "The Lady Margaret Wemyss Manuscript." *The Lute: Journal of the Lute Society* 27 (1987): 5–29.

Stowe. *The Stowe Catalogue: Priced & Annotated by Henry R. Forster*. London, 1848.

Summers, Montague. "A Portrait of Mrs Behn." *TLS*. November 26, 1914, 523.

———, ed. "The Portraits of Mrs Behn." *Works of Aphra Behn*. 6 vols. London, 1915. Vol. 1.

Swain, Margaret. *The Needlework of Mary Queen of Scots*. London: Van Nostrand Reinhold, 1973.

———. *Figures on Fabric: Embroidery Design Sources and Their Application*. London: Adam & Charles Black, 1980.

Tait, Hugh. "The Girdle-prayerbook or 'Tablett': An Important Class of Jewellery at the Court of Henry VIII." *Jewellery Studies* 2 (1985): 29–58.

———. "Goldsmiths and Their Work at the Court of Henry VIII." *Henry VIII: A European Court in England*. London: Collins and Brown, 1991.

Uwins, Mrs. Thomas. *A Memoir of Thomas Uwins, R.A.* 2 vols. London, 1858.

Vieth, David M. "A 'Lost' Lampoon by Katherine Sedley." *Manuscripts* 6 (1954): 160–65.

Vinculum Societatis, or, The Tie of Good Company: Being a choice collection of the newest songs now in use; with a thorow bass to each song for the harpsicord, theorbo, or bass-viol: the first book of this character. London, 1687.

Weir, Alison. *The Six Wives of Henry VIII*. London: The Bodley Head, 1991.

Williamson, Marilyn L. *Raising their Voices: Englishwomen's Writing, 1649–88*. Ann Arbor: University of Michigan Press, 1989.

CONTRIBUTORS'
BIOGRAPHIES

Jennifer Andersen, Associate Professor of English at California State University, San Bernardino, has published on various aspects of early modern English print culture. Her coedition (with Elizabeth Sauer) *Books and Readers in Early Modern England: Material Studies* was published by the University of Pennsylvania Press in 2002. She is currently editing a collection of essays on pamphlet genres and writing a book about Andrew Marvell's critique of commercial and partisan print.

Aki Beam is a doctoral candidate in History at McMaster University. She has presented papers on beauty and the elderly body, and aged identity construction in seventeenth-century courts, and written on old age for the *Reader's Guide to British History* (forthcoming). She is currently completing her dissertation on women and aging in early modern England.

Elaine Beilin is Professor of English at Framingham State College and the author of *Redeeming Eve: Women Writers of the English Renaissance* (Princeton, 1990) and numerous articles on early modern women writers. She edited *The Examinations of Anne Askew* (Oxford, 1996) and is currently writing a cultural history of Askew.

Jane Bird read English and Philosophy (B.A. Hons.) at the University of York, United Kingdom, graduating in 2001. She now works for De Montfort University and Learn MK, the lifelong learning project of the Open University and De Montfort University, Milton Keynes.

Mary Blackstone is Professor in the Department of Theatre at the University of Regina. Her published research focuses on the patronage of the performing arts and the politics of culture in early England and includes a book chapter in *Shakespeare and Theatrical Patronage in Early Modern England* (Cambridge University Press, 2002). She recently served as a member of the Social Sciences and Humanities Research Council of Canada.

Caroline Bowden is Associate Research Fellow at St Mary's College, Strawberry Hill, Twickenham, England, where she is developing a prosopographical project on English and Irish convents in the seventeenth and eighteenth centuries. She has published papers on female education in early modern England and has contributed a chapter on Rachael Fane to *Early Modern Women's Manuscript Writing* (Ashgate, forthcoming).

Sylvia Bowerbank is Professor of English at McMaster University, Hamilton, Ontario. Her publications include numerous articles; five entries in the *New Dictionary of National Biography*: Jane Taylor, Anna Seward, Joanna Southcott, Anne Bathurst, and Jane Lead; and a forthcoming book, *Speaking for Nature: Women and Ecologies in Early Modern England* (Johns Hopkins, 2004). She has coedited (with the historian Sara Mendelson) *Paper Bodies: A Margaret Cavendish Reader* (Broadview, 2000).

Patricia Brace, Assistant Professor of English at Laurentian University, has published essays on Isabella Whitney and Abraham Fleming. Her facsimile edition of Elizabeth Tyrwhit's *Morning and Euening Praiers* was published by Ashgate in spring 2002.

Pamela Allen Brown is Assistant Professor of English at the University of Connecticut, Stamford. Her articles have appeared in *The Ben Jonson Journal, ELR*, and *Shakespeare Yearbook*. Her book, *Better a Shrew Than a Sheep: Jesting Women in the Dramas of Early Modern Culture*, was published by Cornell University Press, 2002, and she is presently coediting (with Peter Parolin) *Women Players in England 1500–1660: Beyond the All-Male Stage* (Ashgate).

Victoria Burke is Assistant Professor of English and Associate Dean, Faculty of Arts, at the University of Ottawa. She works on the Perdita Project, which is producing a comprehensive guide to women's manuscript compilations, 1500–1700. She has coedited *The 'Centuries' of Julia Palmer* (2001), and has had articles published in journals such as *The Seventeenth Century, English Manuscript Studies*, and *The Library*.

Heather Campbell is Associate Professor of English and Associate Dean, Faculty of Arts, at York University, Toronto, Canada. She has published articles on Shakespeare and Marvell, and is currently preparing a collection of the writings of seventeenth-century English and American women, and a study of autobiographical writing by women in early modern England and New England.

Julie Campbell, Assistant Professor of English at Eastern Illinois University, has published on Mary Wroth, the Sidney Circle, Anna Weamys, Shakespeare, and Isabella Andreini in *Comparative Critical Approaches to English Prose Fiction, 1520–1640, Women's Writing*, and *Shakespeare Yearbook*. An essay on Andreini is forthcoming in *Beyond the All-Male Stage, 1500–1660* (Ashgate). Her translation of Andreini's *La Mirtilla* is forthcoming from MRTS, and her book *Subject to Debate: Renaissance Women Writers and the Influence of Literary Circle Ritual* is under consideration at another press.

Philip Collington is Assistant Professor of English at Niagara University in New York State. He has articles on sexual anxiety and imprisonment in Renaissance drama published in *Shakespeare Yearbook, English Literary Renaissance*, and forthcoming in *Shakespeare*

Quarterly, *Comparative Drama*, and *Medieval and Renaissance Drama in England*. He is currently completing a book-length study of Shakespearean cuckoldry anxiety.

Marguarite Corporaal is Lecturer in English at the University of Groningen, the Netherlands. She has published on Elizabeth Cary, Katherine Philips, and Margaret Cavendish in such journals as *Historica* and *In-Between*, and is contributor to the bibliographical projects *Annotated Bibliography of English Studies* and *Annual Bibliography of English Language and Literature*.

Joseph Crowley, Associate Professor of English at Auburn University Montgomery, Alabama, has published on old English dialects and glosses and on Ane Lawraunce's 1610 letter to Thomas Sutton. He has written on Rachel Jevon for the *New Dictionary of National Biography* and for *Early English Women's Writings, 1660–1700* (Ashgate), both forthcoming.

Joan Curbet is Associate Professor in the department of Filologia Anglesa i Germanistica, Universitat Autonoma de Barcelona.

James Daybell, formerly Research Fellow in History at the University of Reading, England, is now Assistant Professor of History at Central Michigan University. He is editor of *Early Modern Women's Letter-Writing, 1450–1700* (Palgrave, 2001) and *Women and Politics in Early Modern England* (Ashgate, 2003). He published numerous articles on early modern women, and recently completed a monograph *Pricy and Powerful Communications: Women Letter Writers in Tudor England* (Oxford University Press, forthcoming).

Kristin Downey is a PhD candidate in the English Department at McMaster University. Her dissertation examines the consolidation of sexual identity in contemporary mass-market romance fiction.

Heather C. Easterling, a doctoral candidate in English at the University of Washington, Seattle, has written on Elizabeth Cary, Mary Wroth, and Anne Clifford, and her dissertation focuses on language as a topos for other cultural anxieties, many concerned with women, in early-seventeenth-century drama. Currently, she is also coediting a volume of essays addressing pedagogy in literature courses.

Robert C. Evans, Professor of English at Auburn University Montgomery, Alabama, has published on a variety of early modern authors, including Martha Moulsworth and Ben Jonson (*Ben Jonson and the Poetics of Patronage*, 1989, and *Jonson and the Contexts of His Time*, 1995). His editions of four relatively unknown texts by early modern women appear in volume 7 of the *Ben Jonson Journal*.

Doreen Evenden, Associate Professor of History, retired from Mount Saint Vincent University, Halifax, is now a research associate of the Department of History, McMaster University. Her study, *The Midwives of Seventeenth-century London*, was published by Cambridge University Press in 2000. She has also published on early modern English female surgeons and seventeenth-century popular medicine; entries on Elizabeth Blackwell and Margaret Stephen appear in the *New Dictionary of National Biography*.

Margaret J. M. Ezell, John Paul Abbott Professor of Liberal Arts, English, Texas A&M University, is the author of many articles and books on early women writers, including *The Patriarch's Wife: Literary Evidence and the History of the Family* (Chapel Hill, 1987), *Writing Women's Literary History* (Baltimore, 1993), *Cultural Artifacts and the Production of Meaning: The Page, the Image, and the Body*, edited with Katherine O'Brien O'Keeffe (Ann Arbor, 1994), and *Social Authorship and the Advent of Print* (Baltimore, 1999).

Jane Farnsworth, Assistant Professor of English at the University College of Cape Breton, Sydney, Nova Scotia has published on English emblem writers, Caroline drama, and women's relationships in such journals as *SEL: Studies in English Literature 1500–1900* and *Emblematica*. She is currently editing and contributing to an anthology of new articles on George Wither's emblems for Brepols Press.

Alison Findlay is Senior Lecturer in English at Lancaster University, England. Her publications include *Illegitimate Power: Bastards in Renaissance Drama* (Manchester University Press, 1994) and *A Feminist Perspective on Renaissance Drama* (Blackwell, 1998). She is codirector of an interdisciplinary research project on early modern women's drama, coauthor of *Women and Dramatic Production 1550–1700* (Pearson, 2000), and recently became a general editor for *Revels Plays* (Manchester University Press).

Susan Frye is Professor of English and Women's Studies at the University of Wyoming. She is author of *Elizabeth I: The Competition for Representation* (Oxford University Press, 1993, 1997) and coeditor with Karen Robertson of *Maids and Mistresses, Cousins and Queens: Women's Alliances in Early Modern England* (Oxford University Press, 1999), and her current manuscript, *Women's Work and Women's Writing*, explores women's textuality.

Susan H. Georgecink, Assistant Professor of English at Columbus State University, Georgia, has written a dissertation on English literacy practices in the early seventeenth century. She has received a grant from the James F. and Mary Loudermilk Fund to pursue work on early modern mothers' legacies in print and in manuscript.

Loreen L. Giese, Associate Professor of English at Ohio University, Athens, Ohio, works primarily on early modern English drama and London Consistory Court Depositions. In addition to publishing articles on Shakespeare's plays and on courtship and marriage practices evidenced in the London Consistory Court records, she edited *London Consistory Court Depositions* (1997) and has finished a book entitled *Courting the Law: Shakespearean and Legal Practices of Wooing and Wedding* (Palgrave, 2004).

Laura Gowing, Lecturer in Early Modern History, King's College London, works on early modern women and the law. Her books include *Domestic Dangers: Women, Words and Sex in Early Modern London* (Oxford University Press, 1996) and *Women's Worlds in*

Seventeenth Century England, edited with Patricia Crawford (Routledge, 2000). Her most recent book is *Common Bodies: Women, Touch and Power in Seventeenth-century England* (Yale, 2003).

Roxanne Harde is a Lecturer in English at Queen's University, Kingston, Ontario, and has begun a postdoctoral fellowship at Cornell University, funded by the Social Science and Humanities Research Council of Canada. Her article on the mother's legacy books appeared in *The Journal of the Association for Research on Mothering*. Her work has also appeared in the journals *Legacy* and *Critique*, and in the collections *Things of the Spirit*, *Catching a Wave*, and *Essays in American Sports Literature*.

Elizabeth Heale is Senior Lecturer of English at the University of Reading, England. She has published *The Faerie Queene. A Reader's Guide* (2d ed., 1999), *Wyatt, Surrey and Early Tudor Poetry* (1998), and *Autobiography and Authorship in Renaissance Verse* (Palgrave, 2003). She has also published articles on the Devonshire MS and on sixteenth-century miscellanies.

Carrie Hintz is Assistant Professor of English at Queens College/CUNY and is currently completing a book about Dorothy Osborne. She has published on Osborne, Margaret Cavendish, utopian writing, and pedagogy. Her coedited collection (with Elaine Ostry) entitled *Utopian and Dystopian Writing for Children and Young Adults* is forthcoming from Routledge in 2003.

Elaine Hobby, Professor of Seventeeenth-Century Studies, Department of English and Drama, Loughborough University, England, is the author of *Virtue of Necessity : English Women's Writing,1649–88* (University of Michigan Press, 1988) and coeditor of *Her Own Life: Autobiographical Writings by Seventeenth-Century Englishwomen* (Routledge, 1989). Her recent edition of *Jane Sharp, The Midwives Book* (Oxford, 1999), is related to her current research on the history of the early modern midwifery manual in English, a project supported by the Wellcome Institute for the History of Medicine.

Stephanie Hodgson-Wright, formerly Senior Lecturer in English Studies, University of Gloucestershire, England, moves to the University of Huddersfield in January 2004. She has edited *The Tragedy of Mariam* and contributed volumes to the *Early Modern Englishwoman* series. With Alison Findlay and Gweno Williams she published *Women and Dramatic Production 1550–1700* and *Women Dramatists 1550–1670: Plays in Performance* (Lancaster University TV), winner of the EMW award for best collaborative project 1999. Her anthology of women's writing 1588–1688 is forthcoming (Edinburgh University Press, 2002).

Lisa Hopkins, Professor of English at Sheffield Hallam University, England, has published books on John Ford, Shakespeare, and Marlowe. She has two recent books: *The Female Hero in English Renaissance Tragedy* (Palgrave, 2002) and *Writing Renaissance Queens: Texts By and About Elizabeth I and Mary Queen of Scots* (University of Delaware Press, 2002).

Mark Houlahan, Lecturer in English at the University of Waikato, New Zealand, has published essays and notes on prophecies and politics in the English Civil War in the works of Hobbes and Milton, and on the uses of John Bunyan, Daniel Defoe, and the works of Shakespeare in settler colonies like his own.

W. Scott Howard, Assistant Professor of English at University of Denver, has essays in *Speaking Grief in English Literary Culture: Shakespeare to Milton* (Duquesne University Press, 2002); and forthcoming in *Grief and Gender, 700–1700* (St. Martin's Press); and *The World in Time and Space* (Talisman House).

Sarah Hutton, Reader in Renaissance and Seventeenth-Century Studies, Middlesex University, England, has published *New Perspectives on Renaissance Thought* (with John Henry, 1990); *Henry More (1614–1687), Tercentenary Studies* (1992); a revised edition of Marjorie Nicolson's *Conway Letters* (1992); an edition of Cudworth, *Treatise Concerning Eternal and Immutable Morality* (1996); and *Women, Science and Medicine, 1500–1700* (with Lynette Hunter, 1997).

Martin Ingram is a Fellow, Tutor, and University Lecturer in Modern History at Brasenose College, Oxford. His publications include *Church Courts, Sex and Marriage in England, 1570–1640* (Cambridge, 1987), and numerous articles on crime and the law, sex and marriage, and religion and popular customs. He has also published on the history of climate.

Nely Keinanen, Senior Lecturer in English at the University of Helsinki, has published a textbook, *Reading Our World: A Guide to Practical and Theoretical Criticism*, and has contributed a chapter to *The Cultural Politics of Early Modern Friendship* (Palgrave) on Queen Elizabeth's relationships with her women (forthcoming).

Anne Kelley, independent scholar, has published on Catharine Trotter in *Women's Writing* and *Notes and Queries*, and contributed biographies of Trotter and Mary Pix for the *New Dictionary of National Biography*. Her edition of plays by Pix and Trotter was volume 2 of the series *Eighteenth-Century Women Playwrights* published by Pickering & Chatto (London, 2001). Her monograph, *Catharine Trotter: An Early Modern Writer in the Vanguard of Feminism*, was published by Ashgate in May 2002.

Catherine Loomis, Assistant Professor of English at the University of New Orleans, has published an essay about and transcript of Elizabeth Southwell's eyewitness account of the death of Queen Elizabeth. She compiled and edited *The Dictionary of Literary Biography Documentary Series* volume on William Shakespeare.

Marie H. Loughlin, Associate Professor of English at Okanagan University College, British Columbia, has written articles on Aemilia Lanyer and Ben Jonson for *ELH* and *Renaissance Quarterly*, and biographies of seventeenth-century Quakers Mary Penington and Elizabeth Stirredge for the *New DNB*. Author of *Hymeneutics: Interpreting Virginity on the Early Modern Stage* (Bucknell University Press, 1997), she is now completing a monograph, *Virginity in Early Modern Women's Writing*.

Kristin Lucas is a doctoral candidate in English, McGill University, Montreal. She is completing a dissertation entitled "In Print and Play: Protestant Articulations of Community," which examines narratives of social and moral obligation in a range of popular material, including drama and religious writing.

Christina Luckyj, Associate Professor of English at Dalhousie University, Halifax, is the author of *A Winter's Snake: Dramatic Form in the Tragedies of John Webster* (1989) and *"A Moving Rhetoricke:" Gender and Silence in Early Modern England* (Palgrave, 2002), as well as essays on Webster, Shakespeare, and Mary Wroth in *Renaissance Drama*, *SEL*, and *English Studies in Canada*. She also edited Webster's *The White Devil* for New Mermaids (1995).

Kathleen Lynch is Executive Director of the Folger Institute, Washington D.C. She has published essays on the ecclesiastical politics of *The Temple* and the dramatic festivity of *Bartholomew Fair*. Her article on "The Narrative Ventures of Agnes Beaumont" appeared in *ELH*.

Randall Martin, Associate Professor of English at the University of New Brunswick, Frederickton, has written articles on Isabella Whitney, Grace Mildmay, and Anne Dowriche. His scholarly anthology *Women Writers in Renaissance England* was published by Longmans in 1997, and Ashgate will issue his volume *Great and Bloody News: Women and Murderers in News Pamphlets and Broadside Ballads, 1577–1697* in Series III of *The Early Modern Englishwoman*.

Darcy Maynard graduated with a B.A. (Hons.) in 1999 and an M.A. in 2000 from Memorial University of Newfoundland, St. John's. She edited part of Alice Sutcliffe's *Meditations on Man's Mortalitie* for her honor's thesis. She plans to continue to pursue her interest in the English Renaissance and early modern women writers in graduate work.

Heather L. Meakin, Assistant Professor of English at Case Western Reserve University, Cleveland, has a book with Oxford University Press: *John Donne's Articulations of the Feminine*. Her current work includes a book-length project on Lady Drury's painted closet, as well as articles on funeral elegies of early modern women, and early modern representations of Mary Magdalene.

Sara Mendelson is Associate Professor in the Arts and Science Programme at McMaster University, Hamilton, Ontario, and a Fellow of the Royal Historical Society. She is the author of *The Mental World of Stuart Women: Three Studies* (University of Massachusetts, 1987), *Women in Early Modern England 1550–1720* (Oxford, 1998) (with Patricia Crawford), and *Paper Bodies: A Margaret Cavendish Reader* (Broadview, 2000) (with Sylvia Bowerbank), as well as articles on Stuart women's diaries, early modern sexual identities, women's working lives, and women's civility in seventeenth-century England.

Jean LeDrew Metcalfe has edited a critical edition of Elizabeth Joscelin's *The Mothers Legacy to her Vnborn Childe* (University of Toronto Press, 2000). She has also published articles on Ben Jonson, Edmund Waller, and John Dryden.

Naomi J. Miller, Associate Professor of English and Women's Studies at the University of Arizona, writes on early women writers and gender. Her *Changing the Subject: Mary Wroth and Figurations of Gender in Early Modern England* (University Press of Kentucky, 1996) received a 1997 Honorable Mention for Best Scholarly Book in Early Modern Women's Studies from the Society for the Study of Early Modern Women. She also edited *Reading Mary Wroth* (University of Tennessee Press, 1991) with Gary Waller; and *Maternal Measures: Figuring Caregiving in the Early Modern Period* (Ashgate, 2000) with Naomi Yavneh, which won the 2001 Best Collaborative Project Award, also from EMW.

Jane Milling, Lecturer in Drama at Exeter University, United Kingdom, has published on early modern women dramatists and performers. She published *Modern Theories of Performance: From Stanislavski to Boal*, with Graham Ley (Palgrave, 2001), is currently coediting the *Cambridge History of British Theatre*, and is working on a study of Susanna Centlivre.

Linda C. Mitchell, Associate Professor of English at San Jose State University, California, has published several articles on grammar, lexicography, and pedagogy in such publications as *European Association of Lexicography* and *Studies in Early Modern Philosophy*. She is the author of *Grammar Wars: Language as Cultural Battlefield in 17th- and 18th-century England* (Ashgate 2001) and with Carol Poster the forthcoming *Letter-Writing Instruction Manuals from Antiquity to the Present* (University of South Carolina Press).

Gerald Morton, Professor of English at Auburn University Montgomery, Alabama, has written on Jacobean and Edwardian subjects as well as American popular culture and has also published on business and professional writing. His *A Biography of Mildmay Fane, Second Earl of Westmorland, 1601–1666: The Unknown Cavalier* appeared in 1990; he is the author or editor of four other books.

Maureen E. Mulvihill, a researcher with the Princeton Research Forum, has published broadly on women writers. Her *Poems by Ephelia* (1992) was nominated for the MLA First Book Prize. She has been an NEH Fellow (1990) and a Frances Hutner Awardee (Princeton, 1997). Her updated edition of *Ephelia* has been published by Ashgate in 2003. She is at work on a book about Mary Tighe.

Minna Nevala is a researcher in the Research Unit for Variation and Change in English at the Department of English, University of Helsinki. She is currently working on her doctoral dissertation on forms of address in early English correspondence. In addition to her doctoral work, she has also edited a collection of women's letters from seventeenth-century Norfolk, tentatively called *The Gawdy Women*.

Lena Cowen Orlin, Professor of English at the University of Maryland Baltimore County and Executive Director of the Shakespeare Association of America, is the author of *Private Matters and Public Culture in Post-Reformation England* (1994) and *Elizabethan Households* (1995). She is the editor of *Material London, ca. 1600* (2000) and coeditor, with Stanley Wells, of *Shakespeare: An Oxford Guide* (2003).

Helen Ostovich, Professor of English at McMaster University, Hamilton, Ontario, is the author of several articles on Jonson and Shakespeare, and has produced several modern critical editions of plays including *Jonson: Four Comedies* (Longman, 1997) and *Every Man Out of his Humour by Ben Jonson* (Revels Plays, Manchester University Press, 2001). Her edition of *The Magnetic Lady* will be part of the new *Cambridge Complete Works of Ben Jonson* (forthcoming 2005). She also edits *Early Theatre: A Journal Associated with the Records of Early English Drama*, is series editor for Studies in Performance and Early Modern Drama at Ashgate, and recently became a general editor for Revels Plays.

John Ottenhoff, Professor of English at Alma College, Alma, Michigan, teaches courses in Shakespeare, linguistics, and humanities computing. His publications include articles about Anne Locke's and George Herbert's sonnets, typology, and sacred parody; he is currently working on a book about the sixteenth-century devotional lyric.

Minna Pallander-Collin is a Senior Researcher at the English Department of the University of Helsinki. She is the author of *Grammaticalization and Social Embedding* (Helsinki: Modern Language Society, 1999) and has published several articles on grammaticalization, historical sociolinguistics, and male and female language in Renaissance English. She is currently working on patterns of interaction in early English correspondence.

Leslie Ritchie, Assistant Professor of English at Queen's University, is currently revising a book concerning eighteenth-century British women's writing about music. She has edited Canadian poet Duncan Campbell Scott's collected prose, published in *Eighteenth-Century Life*, and received a Governor-General's Academic Gold Medal for her graduate work at McMaster University.

Sarah Ross, formerly Associate Fellow of the Centre for the Study of the Renaissance, University of Warwick, is now Lecturer in English at Massey University, New Zealand. She has published on seventeenth-century women and manuscript culture and on Katherine Austen's religious manuscripts and miscellany.

Marjorie Rubright is a doctoral candidate in the Department of English Literature at the University of Michigan–Ann Arbor. Her research interests include constructions of motherhood in early modern England, the writing of Elizabeth I, visual culture, feminist theory, and the development of racialized identities in early modern England.

Elizabeth Sauer is Professor of early modern English literature and holds a Chancellor's Chair for Research Excellence at Brock University, St. Catharines, Ontario. Author of *Barbarous Dissonance and Images of Voice in Milton's Epics* (McGill-Queen's, 1996), she has recently completed *Textual Communities in England, 1640–1675*. Her coeditions include *Imperialisms: Historical and Literary Investigations 1500–1900* (Palgrave-Macmillan, 2004); *Books and Readers in Early Modern England* (Pennsylvania, 2002); *Milton and the Imperial Vision* (Duquesne, 1999), winner of the 2000 Irene Samuel Memorial Award from the Milton Society of America; and *Agonistics: Arenas of Creative Contest* (SUNY, 1997).

Lisa J. Schnell is Associate Professor and Director of Graduate Studies in English at the University of Vermont. In the field of early modern studies she has published articles on Aphra Behn, Aemilia Lanyer, and Rachel Speght. She is also the coauthor, with Andrew Barnaby, of *Literate Experience: The Work of Knowing in Seventeenth-Century English Literature* (Palgrave, 2002).

Liam E. Semler, Australian Research Fellow in English, University of Sydney, Australia, is author of *The English Mannerist Poets and the Visual Arts* (FDU, 1998) and editor of the critical (FDU, 2001) and facsimile editions of *Eliza's Babes* (Ashgate, 2002). His most recent articles on seventeenth-century verse and prose appeared in *Journal of English and Germanic Philology*, *English Literary Renaissance*, and *Albion*.

Brandie R. Siegfried is Associate Professor of English at Brigham Young University. She has published on Shakespeare, Herbert, Lanyer, Crashaw, Cavendish, Elizabeth I, and others in such journals as *Shakespeare Yearbook*, *George Herbert Journal*, and *Early Modern Literary Studies*. She has finished her first book, *The Women's Line: Literary Conquest in the Wake of Elizabeth Tudor* and is now on her second, *The Literary History of Gráinne Ni Mháille*.

Mary V. Silcox, Associate Professor of English at McMaster University, Hamilton, Ontario, has published widely on early modern emblem literature in journals such as *English Literary Renaissance* and *Emblematica*. Articles on Samuel Daniel's works are forthcoming, as is a book on the construction of death in the English emblem entitled *Spectacular Death*.

Elizabeth Skerpan-Wheeler, Professor of English at Texas State University–San Marcos, has published extensively on Milton and seventeenth-century verbal and visual rhetoric, beginning with her book *The Rhetoric of Politics in the English Revolution, 1642–1660* (1992). Her most recent work includes a two-volume edition of *Life Writings* in the Ashgate Early Modern Englishwoman series.

Melissa Smith is a Social Sciences and Humanities Research Council of Canada doctoral candidate in English at McMaster University, Hamilton, Ontario, working on a dissertation entitled Infected Texts: Epidemic Plots on the Early Modern Stage. She has had considerable professionable experience as a copyeditor with Broadview Press and Internet Shakespeare Editions <http://www.uvic.ca/shakespeare>, and as a typesetter and indexer. Her article, "The Playhouse as Plaguehouse in Early Modern Revenge Tragedy," is forthcoming in *The Journal of the Washington Academy of Sciences*.

Brooke Stafford is a Ph.D. candidate in English at the University of Washington in Seattle. Her primary research interests are early modern travel literature, representations of the New World in sixteenth- and seventeenth-century English and American literature, and representations ofcross-cultural contact in the period.

Francis Steen is Assistant Professor of Communication Studies at UCLA. He has published articles in journals such as *Style*, *Philosophy and Literature*, and *Auto/Biography Studies*. He is the coeditor of (and a contributor to) a forthcoming issue of *Poetics Today*.

Matthew Steggle, Lecturer in English at Sheffield Hallam University, England, has written about the Swetnam controversy in his book *Wars of the Theatres* (Victoria, 1998). His other publications on early modern women's writings include three articles on Martha Moulsworth and lives of early modern women writers for the *New Dictionary of National Biography*.

Eric Sterling, Distinguished Research Professor at Auburn University Montgomery, Alabama, has written extensively on dramatic literature. He published *The Movement Towards Subversion: The English History Play from Skelton to Shakespeare* in 1996. He won the College English Association's Scholar-Teacher Award (1996) and two awards from the Association of College English Teachers of Alabama (1997, 2001).

Margaret Thickstun, Professor of English at Hamilton College, Clinton, New York, has published *Fictions of the Feminine: Puritan Doctrine and the Representation of Women* (Cornell University Press, 1988) on the Puritan literary tradition, and articles on Milton, Bunyan, Swift, dissenting women writers, and sermons addressed to pregnant women. She is currently preparing a manuscript on moral education in *Paradise Lost*.

Robert Tittler, Professor of History at Concordia University, Montreal, works in early modern English political, urban, and cultural history. His most recent books are *Architecture and Power: the Town Hall in the English Urban Community* (Oxford University Press, 1991); *The Reformation and the Towns in England: Politics and Political Culture, 1540–1640* (Oxford University Press, 1998); and *Townspeople and Nation, English Urban Experiences, 1540–1640* (Stanford University Press, 2001).

Deborah Uman, Assistant Professor at Eastern Connecticut State University, has forthcoming articles on translation and ravishment in *A Midsummer Night's Dream* in *Allegorica* and on teaching close reading in the college classroom in *It Really Works!: A Sourcebook of Ideas from Award-Winning University English Teachers*. She is currently working on a book on early modern women translators.

Martine van Elk, Assistant Professor of English at California State University, Long Beach, has publications out and forthcoming on Renaissance literature, Shakespeare, and Hrotsvitha in a collection published by Ashgate, and journals *SEL* and *Philological Quarterly*. With Lloyd Edward Kermode she is currently coediting an early drama anthology, *English Drama from the Middle Ages to the Restoration*, which includes four plays by early modern women.

Linda Vecchi, Associate Professor of English at Memorial University of Newfoundland, has published and presented papers on Edmund Spenser, Shakespeare, Rachel Speght, and Elizabeth Whitney. Her article, "'Lawfull Avarice': Rachel Speght's *Mortalities Memorandum* and the Necessity of Women's Education," appeared in *Women's Writing*.

Her current research is for a study of early modern women's writings in education and critical theory.

Rachel Warburton, formerly Lecturer in English at the University of Toronto, is now Assistant Professor of English at Lakehead University, Thunder Bay, Ontario. In addition to two entries in the Brown Women Writers Project, *Renaissance Women On-line*, she has forthcoming articles on early modern female friendship in *The Cultural Politics of Early Modern Friendship* (Palgrave/St. Martin's) and medieval rape law in *Henry Street*.

Alan S. Weber is Managing Editor of the history of science journal *Isis* and Visiting Research Scholar in the Science and Technologies Department at Cornell University. His research interests include cultural and intellectual history. He has edited a volume of Renaissance women medical almanac writers for *The Early Modern Englishwoman* series (Ashgate), and his article on early modern women's medicine recently appeared in *ELR* (September 2002).

Gweno Williams, National Teaching Fellow and Reader in Early Modern Drama at York St. John University College, United Kingdom, has published in a variety of media on Margaret Cavendish's plays and performance. Her coauthored video *Women Dramatists 1550–1670–Plays in Performance* (with Alison Findlay and Stephanie Hodgson-Wright) won the Society for the Study of Early Modern Women's Outstanding Collaborative Project of 1999 Award. A video of selected Cavendish plays in performance is forthcoming.

Heather Wolfe, Curator of Manuscripts at the Folger Shakespeare Library, Washington, D.C., has published an edition of *The Life and Letters of Lady Falkland* (Cambridge, 2001) with 150 letters from and to her, her husband, her children, and various privy councilors. She has also written the catalogue for the Folger exhibition, "The Pen's Excellencie: Treasures from the Manuscript Collection," and articles on Cary, the writing and reading practices of English nuns, and editorial theory.

Tanya Caroline Wood has taught at the University of Auckland and the University of Toronto. She has published on J. R. R. Tolkien and Sir Philip Sidney, William Newcastle and Sir Walter Raleigh, and Margaret Cavendish. Her current project studies the adventures of Katherine Evans and Sarah Chevers in Malta.

Daniel Woolf, former Professor of History and Dean of Humanities at McMaster University, Hamilton, Ontario, is now Dean of Arts at the University of Alberta, Edmonton. He is the author of several books and articles on early modern cultural history including *The Rhetorics of Life-writing in Early Modern Europe: Forms of Biography from Cassandra Fedele to Louis XIV* (Michigan University Press, 1995), edited with Thomas F. Mayer; *A Global Encyclopedia of Historical Writing* (Garland Publishing, 1998); and *Reading History in Early Modern England* (Cambridge, 2000).

Index of Names and Titles